GIVE THE

SECOND EDITION

GIVE THEM WINGS

THE EXPERIENCE OF CHILDREN'S LITERATURE

SECOND EDITION

Edited by

Maurice Saxby, BA, MEd, ALAA

and

Gordon Winch, MA, MEd, PhD

Former Heads of the Department of English
Kuring-gai College of Advanced Education
(The University of Technology, Sydney)

M

Collection copyright © Maurice Saxby and Gordon Winch 1987
The chapters are copyright © 1987 by the individual authors

All rights reserved.
Except under the conditions described in the
Copyright Act 1968 of Australia and subsequent amendments,
no part of this publication may be reproduced,
stored in a retrieval system, or transmitted in any form or by any means,
electronic, mechanical, photocopying, recording or otherwise,
without the prior written permission of the copyright owner.

First published 1987, reprinted 1988, 1989
Second edition published 1991 by
MACMILLAN EDUCATION AUSTRALIA PTY LTD
107 Moray Street, South Melbourne 3205
Reprinted 1991, 1992, 1994

Associated companies and representatives
throughout the world

National Library of Australia
cataloguing in publication data

Give them wings.

> 2nd ed.
> Includes index.
> ISBN 0 7329 0565 6.
> ISBN 0 7329 0564 8 (pbk.).
>
> 1. Children's literature – History and criticism. 2.
> Children's literature – Study and teaching. 3. Children
> – Books and reading. I. Saxby, H.M. (Henry Maurice),
> 1924-   . II. Winch, Gordon, 1930-   . III. Title.

809.89282

Printed in Hong Kong

CONTENTS

PREFACE — vii

NOTES ON CONTRIBUTORS — ix

ACKNOWLEDGEMENTS — xiv

PART I   CHILDREN AND THEIR BOOKS

1   The Gift of Wings: The Value of Literature to Children
    MAURICE SAXBY — 3

2   The Light in the Eye: On Good Books for Children
    GORDON WINCH — 19

3   Children and Their Books: The Right Book for the Right Child
    1: LAURIE BRADY — 26
    2: ROBYN MORROW — 39

PART II   THE NATURE OF CHILDREN'S LITERATURE

4   First Flight: For the Very Young
    PATRICIA SCOTT — 61

5   Further Flight: The Picture Book
    CLARE SCOTT-MITCHELL — 75

6   Archetypal Literature: Folk and Fairy Stories
    MAURICE SAXBY — 91

7   The Wonder of Myth and Legend
    MAURICE SAXBY — 115

8   The Supreme Fiction: On Poetry and Children
    GORDON WINCH — 125

9   Tales of Adventure
    LOUIS LODGE — 151

10 Versions of the Past: The Historical Novel in Children's Literature
    MARGERY HOURIHAN — 163

11 The Family Story: A Context for Care
    LES INGRAM — 177

12 1: The Rise, Fall and Remarkable Revival of the School Story — 196
    2: Will Five Run Away with Biggles? — A Series Question
    KEN WATSON — 209

v

13	Feet on the Ground: The Problem Novel STELLA LEES	217
14	Shared Spaces: The Human and Animal Worlds JOYCE KIRK	229
15	Wings of Fact: Non-fiction for Children ELEANOR STODART	247
16	Inner Reality: The Nature of Fantasy GLENYS SMITH	259
17	Humour in Children's Literature MOIRA ROBINSON	277
18	Rites of Passage: Adolescent Literature BELLE ALDERMAN	290

PART III   THE INTERNATIONAL WORLD OF CHILDREN'S BOOKS

19	The International World of Children's Books MARLENE NORST	311
20	The Key to the Kingdom: Access to Children's Books in Australia ROSEMARY MOON	327
21	From Manuscript to Marketplace ANNE BOWER INGRAM	339

PART IV   LITERATURE AND RESPONSE

22	Space to Play: The Use of Analyses of Narrative Structure in Classroom Work with Children's Literature GEOFF WILLIAMS	355
23	Language and Literature: The Classroom Experience VIVIENNE NICOLL	369
24	Storytelling: A Shared Experience BARBARA POSTON-ANDERSON	405

APPENDIX

Australian Children's Books of the Year	419
Picture Books of the Year	421
Junior Books of the Year	422
INDEX	423

PREFACE

The growth of interest in the study of children's literature has been dramatic and widespread. As Humphrey Carpenter and Mari Prichard wrote in the preface to *The Oxford Companion to Children's Literature* (1984) when referring to this change

> ... the status of children's literature as a subject changed dramatically. From being the concern of a few brave individuals, who were often on the defensive against charges of triviality and were as likely to be collectors as critics, children's books became the focus of countless courses, conferences, centres of study, and works of scholarship. It might be said that the subject reached maturity.

The growth of interest referred to has stemmed, no doubt, from the recognition of the literary merit of the books themselves; it has stemmed no less from the belief that good books are of fundamental importance to the healthy development of children.

Give Them Wings: The Experience of Children's Literature is a response to the need for books that will serve the expansion of knowledge in the field and, as the first of its kind in Australia, breaks new ground in a number of ways. First, it provides a suitable text for students of children's literature; secondly, it covers a wide area of theory and practice in Australia; thirdly, it draws together a large amount of information to interest parents, teachers, librarians or scholars in the field who wish to learn more about children's books. Fourthly, it gives teachers practical guidelines for using good literature in the classroom when teaching reading, as well as for sheer enjoyment.

The book has a special design, set up by the editors, which could best be described as an integrated series of chapters on the nature and value of children's literature and the practice of sharing it. Part I of the book, *Children and their Books*, deals with the value of literature to children, what constitutes a good book and what should be considered when selecting the right book for a child. Part II, *The Nature of Children's Literature*, consists of fifteen chapters which focus on the various types of literature and some critical aspects of them. Part III, *The International World of Children's Books*, deals with the importance of books in international perspective, how access is provided to books and how a book comes to be. Part IV, *Literature and Response*, focuses on the practical issues and teaching applications of sharing books with children.

A list of children's books referred to in the text is added at the end of each chapter and a list of Australian Children's Books of the Year book award winners is provided in an appendix.

The contributors to this volume, who are described in the following section, are pre-eminent in their particular area of expertise. They come from various parts of Australia and from different professional areas.

It is hoped that this book will be used in a variety of ways, depending on the practice of the institution which selects it for its students. Because of its flexibility, its unique Australian emphasis and its range, it should prove to be a valuable resource in the study of children's literature. In the long run the benefit will come to children. Give them books; give them wings.

Maurice Saxby
Gordon Winch

NOTES ON CONTRIBUTORS

Maurice Saxby BA MEd ALAA was formerly Head of the Department of English at Kuring-gai College of Advanced Education and continues to lecture there in the children's literature courses which he did much to pioneer. He was the first national president of the Children's Book Council of Australia and the first Australian to be elected to the International Jury of the Hans Christian Andersen awards in children's literature. His writings include the two volumes of *A History of Australian Children's Literature*, a seminal work in the field. In 1983 he was awarded the Dromkeen Medal and in 1989 the Lady Cutler Award 'for services to children's literature' and in 1986 the Rotary Award for Vocational Excellence for 'raising consciousness of children's literature in Australia and overseas'.

Gordon Winch MA MEd Phd was the Head of the Department of English at Kuring-gai College of Advanced Education until his retirement in 1990. He continues to lecture in the literature and literacy courses offered by the College, now the University of Technology, Sydney. He has contributed widely to academic journals and has written a number of books for children, including a collection of verse. His *Teaching Reading: A Language Experience,* which he edited with Valerie Hoogstad, was published by Macmillan in 1985. He was the first president and one of the founders of the Primary English Teaching Association of New South Wales (PETA).

Belle Alderman BA MLn DLS is a Senior Lecturer in Librarianship at the Canberra College of Advanced Education and prior to that was a primary teacher librarian. She has been a judge for the Children's Book Council Awards, is the Australian Editor for *Phaedrus* and reviews for *The Canberra Times, Reading Time* and radio ABC-2CN. Her publications include *The Imagineers: Writing and Illustrating Children's Books* which she edited with Lauren Harman and *Resources for Young People: A Guide to National and Local Collections in the ACT*.

Barbara Poston-Anderson BA MA PhD ALAA is an Associate Professor in the Department of Information Studies at the University of Technology, Sydney. Previously she served as media specialist at the Hills Grammar School in Sydney where she promoted literature with children and young adults. Her major publications are in the areas of children's literature, storytelling, and readers' theatre. She is co-author of the book, *Readers' Theatre: A Practical Guide*.

Anne Bower Ingram OAM, children's book Editor, began her work in the retail trade and later took the position of the children's book reviewer for *The Sydney Morning Herald*. In 1971 she was invited by the late Sir William Collins to create an Australian Children's list.

Anne is still the editor of this list; however, since 1980 she has also worked as a freelance editor of children's books. She was one of the original members of the Children's Book Council in Queensland and has been an active member of the CBC in New South Wales, occupying the position of voluntary editor of *Reading Time* from 1970-7. In 1984 she received the Lady Cutler Award from the CBC of NSW, in 1985, the Dromkeen Medal and in 1986 an OAM for her services to children's literature in the Australia Day honours list.

Laurie Brady MA MEd PhD DipEd FTCL MACE is Associate Professor of Education at the Lindfield Campus of the University of Technology, Sydney. He has researched curriculum development, moral development and theories of teaching and is the author of *Curriculum Development in Australia, Models and Methods of Teaching,* and several books in the area of values development. Formerly an English Master in secondary schools, Laurie retains an active interest in literature and writing.

Margery Hourihan BA(Hons) MLitt is Head of the Department of English and Social Science at the Lindfield campus of the University of Technology, Sydney. She specialises in English and children's literature. Her thesis for her Master's degree was a study of the linguistic patterns of Rosemary Sutcliff's novels. At the University she teaches in the postgraduate diploma in Children's Literature and the MA in Reading and Children's Literature. Her special interests include the issues surrounding the depiction of male and female roles; fantasy and symbolism; and the linguistic dimensions of books written for children.

Les Ingram BA MLitt MEd MA MACE lectures in English at the University of Technology, Sydney. He specialises in literature and children's literature and is currently researching 'Planes of Narration' in children's books. He has lectured overseas and has a continuing interest in the inter-relationship of writing, drama and literature.

Joyce Kirk BA MLitt MA DipEd AALIA is currently Head of the School of Information Studies, University of Technology, Sydney. She has had extensive experience lecturing in children's literature in colleges and universities and providing in-service courses and continuing education workshops for teachers, librarians and parents involved in developing literature programs. She was the New South Wales judge for the Children's Book of the Year Awards, 1984-5.

Stella Lees BA (Hons) BEd ARMIT ALAA was formerly a Senior Lecturer in literature for children and young adults in the Department of Librarianship at Melbourne College of Advanced Education. She is editor of *A Track to Unknown Water,* the proceedings of the Second Pacific Rim Conference on Children's Literature, author of a number of critical articles on books for children and is currently involved in research on literature of the 1950s.

Louis Lodge MA has held the position of Lecturer in English at Kuring-gai College of Advanced Education since 1971. He has taught many courses in children's literature at the undergraduate and postgraduate levels and has had wide experience in schools as a teacher and as a principal with considerable opportunities for bringing literature to children. He has travelled to Britain and USA to observe and to participate in literature programs for children and is particularly interested in the relationship between literature and children's writing. He has contributed to a number of scholarly journals and books on the teaching of English.

Rosemary Moon BA(Hons) DipLib DipCommunic. Formerly library consultant for the State Library of New South Wales, Rosemary has recently taken up the position of Senior Librarian at the State Film Library. She is particularly interested in young adult literature and has carried out research in media and children. She organised the first State Children's Film Festival in 1985, has been a judge for the Premier's Literary Award, reviews for the ABC and is involved in the children's section of the Library Association of Australia.

Robyn Morrow BA DipChildLit is the proprietor of The Children's Bookshop, Beecroft, Sydney, of which she was a co-founder in 1971. Her work includes the selection of new titles for the bookshop and addressing groups of librarians, teachers and parents about children's books.

Vivienne Nicoll BA (Hons) was a primary teacher and teacher librarian before taking up a position as a Lecturer in the School of Education and Language Studies at Macarthur Institute in New South Wales. She is co-ordinator of the Graduate Diploma course in Reading and Language at that institution and is interested in literature-based programmes in schools. She publishes regularly in educational journals and is the current president of the Primary English Teaching Association of New South Wales (PETA).

Marlene J. Norst MA DipEd PhD was formerly Associate Professor in Modern Languages, Macquarie University, Sydney, where she taught in the areas of Children's Literature, German Language and Literature and Migration Studies. She has served on numerous statutory bodies including The Australian Commonwealth Schools Commission, Australian Ethnic Affairs Council, State Library Council of New South Wales and Macquarie University Council. She is a founding member and co-ordinator of *Languages Galore*, which promotes the writing, translation and dissemination of books in all languages for a multi-lingual Australia, and is a founding member of the Children's Literature Research Circle. Her publications include 'Story Traditions in the Multicultural Society' in Saxby, editor, *Through Folklore to Literature*, 'Kinder und Jugendliteratur' in Herd and Obermayer, editors, *A Glossary of German Literary Terms*, 'Bücher für das bilinguale Immigrantenkind in Australien' in Becker, editor, *Bücher für auslandische Kinder*, Frankfurt: Borsenverein des Deutschen Bucchandels and *The Australian National Survey of Ethnic Schools*.

Moira Robinson MA(Cantab). With her husband, Phillip, Moira owns a bookshop in Frankston on the Mornington Peninsula, a project they began twenty-one years ago. She is noted for her knowledge of children's literature and for her lecturing in the field. She works part-time as an academic and in 1984 was one of the main speakers at the Australian Reading Conference in Melbourne. She is well known for her publication *Puffins For Parents* and, among other writings, has contributed chapters on children's literature to Winch and Hoogstad, editors, *Reading: A Language Experience* (Macmillan) and McVitty, editor, *Word Magic: Poetry As A Shared Adventure* (PETA).

Patricia Scott BA(Hons) is a storyteller, lecturer and consultant in children's literature. She lives at Oatlands, Tasmania and works throughout Australia in schools, colleges and universities in areas relating to storytelling, literature and language development. She is the author of several conference papers and *Storytelling: a Guide to the Art* and author/collator of *I Had a Little Hen* and *Pigs Everywhere*, collections for young children.

Clare Scott-Mitchell BA DipSKTC teaches children's literature at Sydney College of Advanced Education, Institute of Early Childhood Studies. Her published works include two anthologies of verse for children *When a Goose Meets a Moose*, and *Apples from Hurricane Street*. She is currently working on a picture book.

Glenys Smith MA(Hons) DipTeach DipLib is a former lecturer in English, children's literature and school librarianship at Kuring-gai CAE and founding editor of *Scan*, review journal of the New South Wales Department of Education. She is joint author with Maurice Saxby of *Dimensions* (Methuen), a children's literature program for primary schools.

Eleanor Stodart BSc(Hons) is a part-time demonstrator in zoology at the Australian National University. She is author of a children's novel, *When the Mountains Change their Tune* and *Snails, Ants, The Bee, Grass, Trees, Alive and Aware* and *Alive and Active*, natural science books for children. She was editor of *Reading Time*, 1977–81 and has written articles on children's literature, mainly on non-fiction. She is also reviewer for *Reading Time* and *The Canberra Times*.

Ken Watson BA MEd(Hons) DipEd is Senior Lecturer in Language in Education, University of Sydney. He has had extensive teaching experience in secondary schools in New South Wales, the ACT and Britain. He is the author of *English Teaching in Perspective* and editor or co-editor of several books for English teachers, including *English Teaching from A to Z*, *Reading Is Response*, *English in Secondary Schools: Today and Tomorrow* and *Aspects of Children's Literature*.

Geoff Williams BA MA(Hons) lectures in courses in literacy and children's literature in the School of Teaching and Curriculum Studies, University of Sydney. He was awarded the University Medal for his research into children's small-group discussion of novels and is currently studying ways language constructs ideology in children's fiction.

ACKNOWLEDGEMENTS

The authors and publishers are grateful to the following for permission to reproduce copyright material:

Collins Publishers for the illustration from *The Tenth Good Thing About Barney* by Judith Viorst, © illustrations by Erik Blegvad 1971; Jonathan Cape Ltd for the illustration from *Mr Grumpy's Outing* by John Burningham and for the poem 'The Pasture' by Robert Frost from *The Poetry of Robert Frost*; Hodder & Stoughton Australia for the illustration from *Popcorn and Porcupines* by Gordon Winch, illustrated by Katrina Van Gendt; Spike Milligan Productions for the poem 'The Lion'; Michael Joseph Ltd for the poem 'The Tide in the River' by Eleanor Farjeon from *Silver Sand and Snow*; Atheneum Publishers for the poem 'Teevee' by Eve Merriam from *Catch a Little Rhyme*; Angus and Robertson publishers for the poem 'The Looking Glass' by C. J. Dennis from *A Book for Kids*; Oxford University Press for the poem 'Mick' by James Reeves from *The Blackbird in the Lilac*; Andre Deutsch for the poems 'I've Had This Shirt' and 'My Dad's Thumb' by Michael Rosen from *Mind Your Own Business*; Kestrel Books for the poem 'Not in Bed Yet!' by Max Fatchen from *Songs for My Dog and Other People*.

While every care has been taken to trace and acknowledge copyright, the publishers tender their apologies for any accidental infringement where they have been unable to do so. They would be pleased to come to a suitable arrangement with the rightful owner in each case.

PART I
CHILDREN AND THEIR BOOKS

1 THE GIFT OF WINGS: THE VALUE OF LITERATURE TO CHILDREN

MAURICE SAXBY

> He ate and drank the precious words,
> His spirit grew robust,
> He knew no more that he was poor,
> Or that his frame was dust.
> He danced along the dingy ways,
> And this bequest of wings
> Was but a book. What liberty
> A loosened spirit brings!
>
> Emily Dickinson

THE NATURE OF LITERATURE

The raw material of literature is experience of life. When ancient man began imaginatively to explore, shape and control his environment through dance, chant, song, painting and story seeking to bring under control the inexplicable and seemingly chaotic forces about and within him, he was creating a literature. Literature is man's attempt to record, explain and control experience, for as the folk tale of Rumpelstiltskin (Tom-Tit-Tot, or any other version) indicates — to verbalise and to name is to gain power over that which is named, be it person, place, event or phobia.

LANGUAGE AND LITERATURE

The earliest literature was verbal, and was transmitted orally through story. Once man became literate he was able self-consciously to use a love of language to shape experience; to order, pattern and craft his observations and ideas, selectively and rhythmically; to develop literary structures and narrative techniques, the recognisable patterns of story.

THE CRAFT OF LITERATURE

Over long years the technical skills of the craft of literature have been refined: shaping plot, creating character, establishing setting, developing theme. The author (no longer an anonymous voice) crafts these elements according to his writing skills and aesthetic sense into the form which best suits his subject and purpose: a poem, a play, a short story or a novel, be it for adults or children.

In recent times the writer-artist, or collaborating writer and artist have explored a common experience through print and picture. This form of literature — the picture book or illustrated book — is subject to double standards: verbal and artistic.

AN IMAGE OF LIFE

If literature has integrity — that is, if it explores, orders, evaluates and illuminates the human experience, its heights and depths, its pain and pleasure aesthetically and according to the creator's genuinely felt response — the end product becomes an image of life, and potentially a metaphor for living. The range of such images is as vast as human society and culture.

CHLDREN'S LITERATURE

When the image or metaphor is within a child's range of sensory, emotional, cognitive and moral experience and is expressed in linguistic terms that can be apprehended and comprehended by young readers, a book becomes classed as a children's one. Whilst there are those who write down to children, who condescend and trivialise, the best writers for children have consciously (or sometimes unconsciously) chosen the form of literary expression which best suits what they have to say about their explorations of life. Writers from Lewis Carroll, Kenneth Grahame, R. L. Stevenson, A. A. Milne and Beatrix Potter to Norman Lindsay, Ivan Southall, Philippa Pearce, Jenny Wagner, Maurice Sendak and Mitsumasa Anno (to name a few) have chosen the children's novel or picture book to express their personal insights into life's experiences.

Whilst children's books are usually shorter than those for adults (a matter of expectation and economics as well as attention span and concentration) they are not necessarily less complex. The linguistic pattern of a picture book like *Where the Wild Things Are* or *John Brown, Rose and the Midnight Cat* is a feat of selectivity equal to the crafting of a well-made sonnet. The techniques of Southall's *Josh* or Cormier's *I Am the Cheese* and the subtle narrative structure (discourse) of Chambers' *The Present Takers*, Pearce's *The Way to Sattin Shore* or Cynthia Voigt's *A Solitary Blue* imply and also determine their readership. Some children, sometimes, need help and unobtrusive guidance if they are to match the skills of the reader implied by the author and successfully to fill the 'telling gaps' within the structure.

RESPONSE

Reading, which is more than mere 'barking at print', requires a transaction with the author's text. The reader takes from the text in proportion to what he brings to it in terms of experience, insight, reading skill and a sensitive perception of life. Reading is thus an act of re-creation. It also operates as a spiral: the more one brings to the text the more one takes away to give to successive reading experiences.

LITERATURE AND EDUCATION

Literature thus becomes central to education in that it contributes to the reader's growing experience — and education is essentially the leading forth, the growth, of an individual through structured experience. As the compilers of the Plowden Report expressed it:

> We are convinced of the value of stories for children, stories told to them, stories read to them and stories they read for themselves. It is through story as well as through drama and other forms of creative work that children grope for the meaning of the experiences that have already overtaken them, savour again their pleasures and reconcile themselves to their own inconsistencies and those of others. As they 'TRY ON' first one story book character, then another, imagination and sympathy, the power to enter into another personality and situation, which is a characteristic of childhood and a fundamental condition for good social relationships, is preserved and nurtured. It is also through literature that children feel forward to the experiences, the hopes and fears that await them in adult life. It is almost certainly in childhood that children are most susceptible, both to living examples and to the examples they find in books. As children listen to stories, as they take down the books from library shelves, they may, as Graham Greene suggests in *The Lost Childhood*, be choosing their future and the values that will dominate it.
>
> (Plowden Report 1967: Sec. 595)

Paul Hazard put it metaphorically: 'Give us books', say the children, 'give us wings'. (Hazard 1947: 4) This bequest of wings should be the obsessive aim of anyone who claims to be an educator.

WHAT LITERATURE BEQUEATHS TO THE EXPLORING READER

The appeal of story is irresistible. It is essentially the ability to use language to shape story that is the hallmark of humanity. So the listener, or the reader — one who has given himself utterly to print — is bequeathed access to the accumulated experience and wisdom of the ages. But access does not mean immediate appropriation. The process is a leisurely one and develops as reading experiences proliferate and the spiral extends outward and upward.

EXPLORATION AND DISCOVERY

In the first instance the entrance to story (told or read) provides for exploration. Children can wander around inside the story as it were, trying on roles, predicting outcomes, even retreating when necessary. It is the same process that is at work when children play spontaneously and engage in their own unstructured drama. It is a discovery process that helps the child gradually order his environment as relationships become clearer, human motivation is made manifest (*John Brown, Rose and the Midnight Cat*), and the reader's role in a social matrix emerges (*The Bunyip of Berkeley's Creek*).

Whether the story be that of Peter Rabbit, Rosie the hen, Max, king of the Wild Things, Storm Boy, Julie of the Wolves, the Boy who was Afraid or Atreyu of *The Neverending Story* the listener or reader can join in, leaving the safety of home and hearth to go 'adventuring'. And when at last the tests and trials are over there is security and sanctuary at the journey's end. Even Mr Gumpy's outing culminates in a right royal feast. Max's supper will always be waiting for him — hot!

THE RANGE OF EXPERIENCE

Thus is vicarious experience gained. For experience — an element essential for personal growth — can be direct, indirect or imaginative. Literature provides a potent source of vicarious experience and so fires the imagination with sensory and emotive images to provoke imagined experience.

1. The Senses

From a child's earliest acquaintance with nursery rhymes, poetry, folk and fairy tales and picture books the senses of sight, sound, touch, taste and smell are aroused and stimulated:

> The Queen of Hearts
>   She made some tarts,
> All on a summer's day;
>   The Knave of Hearts
> He stole those tarts,
>   And took them clean away.

Charlotte's Web is redolent of manure and the farmyard, and follows the sensuous cycle of the seasons. *The Wind in the Willows* exudes sap and woodland textures; the *Book of Wirrun* soars upwards with tumbling wind waves, whilst below the slopes are dusted with purple' and the forest rises 'gold-edged against the setting sun'.

2. The Emotions

Latent emotion is aroused in the old rhymes like the troubling of the waters — 'Curly locks, Curly locks, Wilt thou be mine?' — and undoubtedly the immediate appeal of fairy tales is in the potency of their contained fear and wonder. In *Treasure Island* the bony clutch of Blind Pew is an experience to send shudders down the spine. Grief and loss can almost overwhelm the reader of *Storm Boy* or

Bridge to Terabithia; righteous indignation is one of the emotional gear-shifts in *Goodnight Mr Tom*; and acceptance born of suffering emerges in the reading of *Mama's Going to Buy You a Mockingbird*. Raymond Briggs' *Gentleman Jim* is as ominously threatening, in its own way, as his *When the Wind Blows*. Often emotional response comes after a sensory reaction, which is the great strength of Roald Dahl's writing, as evidenced in his personal story *Boy*, as well as in his riotously, wickedly and warmly funny extravagances *The BFG* and *The Witches*.

3. Language

And all the while the reader's language is being fed and enriched. Not just with the inventive vocabulary of Dahl's 'snozzcumbers' and 'whiz poppers' or White's contextual 'salutations', or the tongue-tapping phrases of Ogden Nash's *Custard the Dragon* who has 'realio, trulio daggers on his toes', but with continual exposure to the carefully-chosen word, the crafted sentence and the lyric prose of competent storytellers and novelists. A new word can shock: MacIntyre's 'paraphernalia' in *Katherine*, or the apprehension of an incongruous image such as Deborah Niland's 'Gobbling Grandmas', or the rhythmic delight of Pender's Barnaby in *Barnaby and the Horses*:

> What a strong, snorting, tossing sort of word it was,
> What a belonging sort of word!

Consider also the terse economy of telling in Wagner's *John Brown, Rose and the Midnight Cat*:

> Rose's husband died a long time ago.
> Now she lived with her dog.
> His name was John Brown.

All these add to a child's store of vocabulary, sharpen his sense of sentence and syntax, and help develop a harmony of utterance. For language is inextricably linked with experience; there can be no language growth when experience is stultified. Conversely, the wider a child's range of experience, the greater will be his store of language, to think with, to dream with, to grow and to fly with.

'Literature', says Aidan Chambers, 'offers us images to live with'. He elaborates:

> What we can do with ourselves is limited by what one can do with language. What a society does with literary language is the limit of what that society does for its people as a whole.
>
> Language is a condition of being human. Literature is a birthright. Entering into that birthright requires that every child be born into an environment that makes its birthright available, a gift to be desired.
>
> (Chambers 1985: 10)

PERSONAL GROWTH

In essence, growth in language is an index of personal growth. So literature, which is both life and language, offers unlimited potential. At times some children have to be led to appreciate their birthright, but once they enter into its fullness growth will be multifaceted.

1. Cognitive

Not only does literature provide images to live with, it provides knowledge to strengthen: the 'hard' knowledge of fact and data, and the 'soft' knowledge of the human heart — facts about human behaviour that cannot be isolated in a laboratory but which can be experienced.

When as a nine-year-old boy living in Broken Hill in the Australia of the Great Depression I read *Treasure Island*, I came to know exactly what a 'coracle' was; I also came to recognise that villainy can wear an attractive black patch. After reading *The Children of the New Forest*, I not only learned something of the geography and history of England, but became a confirmed and ardent Royalist, inwardly refuting my teacher's attempts to instil an admiration of Cromwell and his Roundheads. To this day I would prefer a dapper Cavalier dandy to a Puritan zealot. But later literature presented me with options of human belief and behaviour from which to choose.

It was not only *The Children of the New Forest*, but a host of reading experiences of good, bad and indifferent literature which provided a means of weighing my own life against a wider social context.

2. Social

It is through literature that an awareness of social values can grow. One's family is extended by hundreds of fictional families; one's school becomes no longer a one-teacher demountable; the school bully is not an isolated phenomenon. Above all, one leaves the cell of one's aloneness and becomes part of a society which is both past and present, white and coloured, and which crosses all barriers of class and creed, provided the reading experiences are wide and varied enough, and the response a genuine one.

Peter Rabbit breaks his mother's (society's) taboo and must pay for it; Josh, the universal poet, learns the hard way the price of being a Plowman. *A Candle for St Antony* is not only a study of two opposing milieux. Justin and Rudi are painfully forced to recognise the lowest common denominator in society. The children's novel of today encompasses the problems of the world. It is by facing these dilemmas — those of society and those of the inner self — that ethical and moral insights develop.

3. Ethical

If much traditional literature is fundamentally concerned with the battle between good and evil, contemporary literature, like the epics of old, is also concerned with the dark side of the hero figure (Ged in *A Wizard of Earthsea*), the grey areas of human behaviour (*People Might Hear You*, *The Shrinking of Treehorn*, *The Way to Sattin Shore*), and even intimates that it might be possible for the rats to inherit the earth (*The Chocolate War*). Novels such as *A Wrinkle in Time*, *Roll of Thunder Hear My Cry* and those of Cynthia Voigt present dynamic dilemmas that are far more real and soul-searching than those manufactured for a social science curriculum.

4. Spiritual

The great dilemmas are those of the human spirit. Ged's choices are as a refining fire, a cleansing of the spirit, a catharsis. It is Rudi's spirit that is tested in *A Candle for St Antony*, and it is Jess in *Bridge to Terabithia* who must learn to look beyond the here and now for reassurance. David in Anne Holm's *I am David* essentially grows in spiritual insight. His is a spiritual journey, and so it needs must be for the reader who accompanies him.

THE JOURNEY TO JOY

As the reader travels through the text he is being entertained if that text contains any potency for him at all. Even when he is not being challenged intellectually and contents himself with the roughage of mass-market fare he can be enjoying the familiar, the predictable. He may even enjoy a sense of superiority as he sits on the shoulder of the omniscient author.

In spite of the frequent charge that reading is a passive occupation, it is far from it. Even a hackneyed plot invites involvement. Mystery and suspense keep the reader guessing, and even the tritest Choose-Your-Own-Adventure or the most banal Fighting Fantasy require collaboration and a learning of the rules of the game.

But beyond the down-market and mass-market books there is Literature — with its more abiding satisfactions and rewards commensurate with the application, stamina and linguistic maturity that the reader brings to it.

James Joyce in *A Portrait of the Artist as a Young Man* defined artistic worth as wholeness, harmony and radiance. To radiance he implied his own term — epiphany: a revelation, an illumination. This is the supreme test of literary merit, and it is also the supreme gift of literature.

By this we can measure the great poetry, plays and novels of the ages. By this, too, we can measure seemingly simple stories such as *Where the Wild Things Are*, *The Bunyip of Berkeley's Creek*, *John Brown, Rose and the Midnight Cat*. And *The Secret Garden*, *Charlotte's Web*, *I am David*, *The Nargun and the Stars* are, by this standard, enduring books. For they are images, metaphors for living, from writers who have glimpsed something of the fullness and wholeness of life, and who have crafted their statements with harmony.

They are statements which allow space for reflective insight, and which yield their richness layer by layer. They emit radiance. With the radiance — the epiphany — comes Joy.

In C. S. Lewis' *The Lion, the Witch and the Wardrobe*, the White Witch offers Edmund Turkish Delight, a confection that once savoured creates a craving for more and yet more. So it is with Joy — Lewis' own term for the effects of radiance. Its quality is that

> ... of an unsatisfied desire which is itself more desirable than any other satisfaction ... anyone who has experienced it will want it again ... I doubt that anyone who has ever tasted it would ever ... exchange it for all the pleasures in the world. But then Joy is never in our power and pleasure often is.
>
> (Lewis 1955: 20)

It would seem to me that there is no higher point to be reached either in literature or in education.

WHAT, THEN, MAKES A GOOD BOOK FOR CHILDREN?

The answer to this frequent question would seem to be, 'one which provides space for exploration; which enlarges experience; and brings Joy'. A good book will make the reader hear, feel and see. In Rosenblatt's words, it will provide an 'aesthetic experience'. Paul Hazard answered his own question, 'What are Good Books?' with resounding surety:

> I like books that remain faithful to the very essence of art; namely, those that offer to children an intuitive and direct way of knowledge, a simple beauty capable of being perceived immediately, arousing in their souls a vibration which will endure all their lives.
>
> (Hazard 1947: 48)

And he adds:
- Books containing 'enchanting pictures that bring release and joy'.
- Books 'that awaken in them not maudlin sentimentality, but sensibility; that enable them to share the great human emotions; that give them respect for universal life — that of animals, of plants; that teach them not to despise everything that is mysterious in creation and in men'.
- Books 'that respect the valor and eminent dignity of play'.
- 'I like books of knowledge; not those that want to encroach upon recreation, upon leisure, pretending to teach anything without drudgery. There is no truth in that ... I like them especially when they distil from all the different kinds of knowledge the most difficult and the most necessary — that of the human heart'.

— Finally 'I like books that contain a profound morality.' Not books that preach or teach, but books 'that set in action truths worthy of lasting forever ... In short, I like books that have the integrity to perpetuate their own faith in truth and justice'.

(Hazard 1947: 43–5)

I doubt that any wiser or more encompassing statement on the subject has ever been made. But it is for the teacher, the librarian, the editor and the publisher to recognise the 'essence of art'. That recognition will only come when the reader himself can hear his own heartbeat, along with that of others.

Because this is essentially an aesthetic recognition and therefore difficult to define, most texts on children's literature provide criteria for book selection based on considerations of writing technique, setting up a rhetoric of fiction and isolating the technical skills of the novelist.

Children are indiscriminate readers, it is argued, and the avalanche of published mediocrity makes it possible for children to have a steady diet of indifferent books, and such a diet will produce emotional and aesthetic acne.

It is true that children, once they are 'hooked on books' are voracious readers but I have faith that provided their reading experiences are wide enough they will grow in discrimination. Like Holden Caulfield they will recognise those writers like Thomas Hardy who speak to the human heart, and they will experience that urge to give such writers a 'buzz' — to consolidate a transaction between writer and reader (Salinger: 1966).

It is also true that childhood and youth is a time of growing, of rapidly shifting interests and preoccupations; that there is indeed a right book for the right child at the right time. That trusted booklover in a child's life must be able to match the book to the child, not force the child to the book.

Therefore it is worth reiterating those factors that help craft fiction, but it is also worth considering questions of child appeal if we are indeed to become the catalyst which brings Joy to the heart of a child.

TECHNICAL CONSIDERATIONS

1. Idea or Theme

There should always be an inter-connecting thread which brings all the elements of a novel together in wholeness and harmony. A well-defined theme gives unity. *Charlotte's Web* follows the cycle of life and death — continuity of life — which is paralleled in the cycle of the seasons. Death is as necessary as procreation in that they are both part of the cycle. Every event and every character in *Charlotte's Web* supports the theme.

The theme of Joan Phipson's later books is that of a tide flowing, implying that we must flow with the tide if we are to become worthwhile people. To flow with the tide means to be in harmony with our environment, the land. Indeed the land must be recognised as a Force, that can work for us, or against us if we are hostile to it, or unworthy.

2. Plot or Story

To children, story (narrative) is of paramount importance and the story should have the power to absorb the reader totally. 'The will to tell a story that will rivet the audience, rather than the award panel, is the first gleam the critic needs to look for in a book'. (Leeson 1985: 148)

Most good children's novels (whether the structure be episodic as in *Wind in the Willows* or dramatic as in *Treasure Island*) are like good theatre in that they contain a central conflict situation. Many children's books are based on the conflict of man with his environment, of man with his fellow man, of man with society, or of man with himself — his fears, inadequacies, his perceived shortcomings. The Australian novels of Thiele, Southall, Norman embody all these conflicts. In *Blue Fin* they are all present in the one book.

A strongly-realised conflict (even in inward-looking journals and diaries like *Dear Mr Henshaw*, *Adrian Mole*, *Penny Pollard* or *Breaking Up*) provides both suspense and continuity, a strong forward movement which is necessary to capture and maintain interest until higher-level reading skills have developed.

3. Characters

Children should meet characters who are universal yet individual. Charlotte's faithfulness unto death is as recognisable as Mr Percival's, or Judy Woolcot's — or St Joan's. Whether characters are static and not fully rounded as are Charlie and Edie in *The Nargun and the Stars*, or kinetic (growing) and rounded as are Southall's children in, say, *Hills End*, they can be representative humans yet unique individuals. Increasingly, too, writers are recognising that youth frequently relates to the aged (*Wilfrid Gordon McDonald Partridge*). The fallacy that children's books must be about children of the same age as the implied reader has been exploded for all time by Patricia Wrightson's *A Little Fear* which is essentially about a remarkably doughty old lady, her dog and an Aboriginal imp.

4. Setting

A book's setting or environment can operate in a multiplicity of ways. It can determine the life-style of the characters, even who they are and what they are (*The Wind in the Willows*), thus motivating plot development and character growth. Lilith Norman's unnamed boy in *A Dream of Seas* is as obsessed by the sea as he is with his father's death by drowning. The setting — Bondi beach and the sea — becomes a metaphor, as do the seals who enter the currents of the boy's consciousness. The sea in Norman's book, like the river in *The Wind in the Willows* and the many islands in fiction, is archetypal: part of the universal myth, and of ageing life. Suburban, middle-class or working-class settings in writers like Betsy Byars, Eleanor Spence and Christine Nostlinger carry their own weight of implication.

5. Point of View

The tremendous popularity of writers like Beverly Cleary, Judy Blume, Betsy Byars, Roald Dahl and Paul Zindel is that they align themselves directly and unequivocally with their implied reader, and write from that reader's life perspective. American writers for children, particularly, have developed this democratic technique. Many of them, like Blume and Konigsburg, use not just the first person narrative (as Stevenson used Jim Hawkins in *Treasure Island*) and the intimately confidential letter or journal form (Cleary and Zindel), but also the traditional third person narrative. But whether it be through the intensely personal soliloquy of *Are You There, God? It's Me, Margaret*, or the omniscient author's stance of equality as in Dahl, Cynthia Voigt, Jean Little or Robin Klein, say, many other good contemporary writers can subtly align themselves with the imputed reader. Dahl does this by introducing lots of food and scatological, verbal and black humour, but also by outrageously taking sides with youth against adult authority. (At the same time Dahl is finely tuned to the injustices perpetrated against both young and old). Jean Little achieves intimacy by writing 'stage directions' from the point of view of the young protagonist and dropping unnecessary pronouns:

> When they were eating lunch, Jeremy looked at his father. Dad was sitting by the window and gazing far away over the lake. He seemed so remote that he was almost not there with them. His sandwich lay untasted on the plate. Jeremy reached out for a jar of mustard pickles. 'Dad', he said, touching his father's limp hand with the side of the jar and hearing his voice sounding out too loudly, 'would you care for some pickle?'

(Little 1984: 35)

Much about Jeremy and his relationship with his father is implied in this almost spare, direct narration.

Southall's multiple points of view and his use of mental monologue; Wrightson's composite voice (Charlie and Edie plus Simon in *The Nargun and the Stars*); the internalised narrative of Mayne or Garner (especially in *The Stone Book Quartet*); the time and tense shifts of Jill Paton Walsh, and similar techniques, all make great demands on the reader, but also allow for a greater range of response. The diversity of life must be reflected in literature.

6. Tone

Allied with the point of view taken is the author's tone. Blume always uses a sharing tone of voice, taking the reader into her confidence. Dahl nudges his readers in the ribs, an adult sharing an outrageous joke with the young. C.S. Lewis adopts an avancular, confidential tone (a sharing of insights and wonder); Stevenson has an urgent voice; Wrightson is detached, almost musing aloud at times. What children detect and reject is a condescending tone — the 'come now, little people' syndrome, to be avoided by teachers and writers alike.

7. Pace

The pace of the most popular writers today is fast and lively. Gene Kemp writes at the pace of a Secondary Modern playground at breaktime, but she is never breathless. In enduring books the pace is deliberate and regulated. *Charlotte's Web* moves with the coming and going of the seasons; *The Wind in the Willows* flows with the river. When the physical action in Southall or Pearce or Mayne slows down, the pace is pushed along by internal or reflective action. Cynthia Voigt's *Homecoming* drags its feet physically as the children lag on their self-imposed journey, but the tension is never lost, only slackened until it is taken up again. Wirrun's journey keeps pace with life itself, sometimes faltering or resting, sometimes hurrying with a sense of urgency. But it is never static.

8. Style

Ultimately it is the author's use of language that determines not only readership but the lasting quality of a book. Beatrix Potter proved once and for all that a storyteller need never write down to children. Her language is original and economical, yet measured. Her vocabulary is impeccable, and generations of children have enjoyed the sound and feel of words that most writers would deny them. Grahame's style, like that of all superior writers for children, has great ear as well as eye appeal. Good books for children are easy to read aloud.

Wrightson adapts her style to the stance and plane of storytelling. In the 'realistic' scenes of *The Nargun and the Stars* her prose is factual narration; in the 'fantasy' sections it is deeply lyrical and increasingly rhythmic. Always, every word is tactfully chosen so as not to draw attention to the imagery. Only in the Wirrun trilogy, where the implied reader is far more experienced, does the imagery leap from the page.

9. Levels of Meaning

Perhaps the supreme test of any book is that it allows the reader to take from it as little or as much as he needs or is ready for. It is multi-layered and reveals itself fully only to the explorative reader. Jeff Brown's *Flat Stanley* can be a humorous story based on impossibility and incongruity, a study of family relationships, what it means to be different, a sly pun on words, a satire on human disaffection or a timely example of dramatic irony. The layers of *The Shrinking of Treehorn* can similarly be peeled back.

John Brown, Rose and the Midnight Cat is at once the story of a widow's affection for her dog and a commentary on jealousy and the games people play. The midnight cat is an ambiguous image. But whatever the level of interpretation the reader chooses it sets up reverberations that can be conscious or unconscious. So too with Sendak's *Outside Over There*, a book of visual as well as verbal images that lead the reader far beyond the actual words of the text. *Rosie's Walk* (Hutchins), *A Walk in the Park* (Browne), *The Stone Book* (Garner), *A Wizard of Earthsea* (Le Guin), *Tom's Midnight Garden* (Pearce) and *Playing Beatie Bow* (Park) are other examples.

10. Narrative Discourse

To unravel the levels of meaning and to penetrate the layers of a book requires work on the part of the reader, and sometimes for the young reader guidance from a more experienced one is necessary. But if the book or story is to be accessible and not just an image so dense that all luminosity is dimmed, the author must provide clues in the act of narration, through his mode of 'discourse'. Narrative 'structure' or 'discourse' is a relatively new term in the criticism of children's literature, one borrowed from the so-called structuralists (e.g. Genette 1980, Chatman 1978). Simply put, once the author has taken the reader into his confidence, has 'forged an alliance and a point of view that engages a child, he can manipulate that alliance as a device to guide the reader towards the meaning he wishes to negotiate' (Chambers 1985: 41, 42)

Pat Hutchins does it by creating an irony between text and illustrations in *Rosie's Walk*; Sendak by using pictorial motifs in *Outside Over There*; Anthony Browne always through his illustrations (especially in *Hansel and Gretel*) and by obvious incongruities and apparent incompleteness of text; Garner by being both objective and subjective in his manner of narrative (*The Stone Book*); Jill Paton Walsh by using different sets of characters to indicate time shift in *Unleaving*.

Whilst an awareness of narrative discourse is becoming increasingly important in the criticism of children's literature, it might be helpful in evaluating children's books at this stage simply to look for narrative clues — the techniques of discourse that lead the reader deeper into the story and which will allow the story to work its own transformation in the heart and mind of the reader.

POPULARITY, CHILD APPEAL AND LITERARY QUALITY

Books like *Flat Stanley*, *Where the Wild Things Are*, *John Brown, Rose and the Midnight Cat*, *The Secret Garden*, *Charlotte's Web* and *Playing Beatie Bow* have the rare merit of receiving critical acclaim and possessing almost immediate and universal child appeal.

A complaint frequently raised by teachers and librarians is that award-winning books are not necessarily popular with children. Conversely, immediately popular books often fail to please the critics.

But the same is true of adult literature, music, painting and the arts generally. Perhaps it would be more helpful if adults concerned with what children read looked more closely at the implied reader in the book, and the clues provided by the narrative discourse and then weighed the *suitability* of any given text for any given reader. Because children are in a rapidly developing period, and because of their diverse environments and their great differences in genetic inheritance, what is suitable for one child is not necessarily suited to his opposite neighbour.

Given the nature of reading, a knowledge of the potential reader is as important in reading guidance as a knowledge of the text. Rosenblatt goes further:

> Understanding the transactional nature of reading would correct the tendency of adults to look only at the text and the author's presumed intention, and to ignore as irrelevant what the child actually does make of it.
>
> (Rosenblatt 1978: 272)

It is even more than that. It is, as Geoff Williams implies in Chapter 22, that concerned adults should ensure that children are not only given more demanding texts, with instant appeal, but that they should be introduced to texts that leave space for exploration from their earliest listening/reading experiences. Such texts need to be presented at regular intervals along the reading highway, and time should be set aside to help the young reader explore and discover. The books of Dorothy Neal White, Annis Duff and Dorothy Butler have been inspired by the mutual joy of child and adult journeying through literature together.

Books such as *The Very Hungry Caterpillar, The Bunyip of Berkeley's Creek, Outside Over There, Flat Stanley, The Shrinking of Treehorn, Josh, The Present Takers, The Way to Sattin Shore, Homecoming, The House that Was Eureka* are stepping stones, leading the reader further into Joy.

If the range of literature available today is opened to children who themselves are explorative, and who have a trusted and concerned adult to share in their discoveries, questions of censorship will not arise. If some books are felt to be too pessimistic (i.e. if the potential reader is not yet experienced enough to see that the rats' inheritance is only temporary), the concerned adult will see to it that there are books available that do link back to a reader's past experience yet will lead him forward in it.

It is for the authors to write — with integrity — from the fullness of their own experience. It is for the reader to dip one foot in, wade, or plunge in as the water is ready. It is for the librarian, the teacher, the parent, the caring adult to know the swimmer, to test the water, and, if necessary, to throw the swimmer in, but with a supportive hand if the shallows too quickly become depths.

As they share stories together both child and adult will be enlarged — transformed sometimes — in knowledge, perception and understanding of the world, of others, and of themselves: the many dimensions of the experience of being human.

REFERENCES

Butler, Dorothy, *Babies Need Books*. London: Bodley Head, 1980.
——————, *Cushla and Her Books*. London: Hodder & Stoughton, 1979.
Chambers, Aidan, *Booktalk*. London: Bodley Head, 1985.
Chatman, S., *Story Discourse: Narrative Structure in Fiction and Film*. London: Cornell University Press, 1978.
Duff, Annis, *Bequest of Wings*. New York: Viking, 1950.
——————, *Longer Flight*. New York: Viking, 1955.
Genette, G., *Narrative Discourse*. Oxford: Basil Blackwood, 1980.
Hazard, Paul, *Books, Children and Men*. Boston: The Horn Book, 1947.
Joyce, James, *A Portrait of the Artist as a Young Man*. London: Penguin, 1966.
Leeson, Robert, *Reading and Righting*. London: Collins, 1985.
Lewis, C.S., *Surprised by Joy*. London: Collins, 1959.
Little, Jean, *Mama's Going to Buy You a Mockingbird*. London: Kestrel, 1984.
Plowden, Bridget Lady, *Children and Their Primary Schools: A Report of the Central Advisory Council for Education*. London: HMSO, 1969.
Rosenblatt, Louise, 'The Literary Transaction: Evocation and Response' in *Theory Into Practice* Vol. xxi, No. 4, Autumn 1982.
Salinger, J.D., *The Catcher in the Rye*. London: Penguin, 1966.
White, Dorothy Neale, *Books Before Five*. Wellington, New Zealand: NZ Council for Educational Research, 1956.

BOOKS REFERRED TO IN THE CHAPTER

Blume, Judy, *Are You There, God? It's Me, Margaret*. Gollancz/Piccolo.
Briggs, Raymond, *Gentleman Jim*. Hamish Hamilton.
——————, *When the Wind Blows*. Hamish Hamilton.
Brown, Jeff, *Flat Stanley*. Methuen/Magnet.
Browne, Anthony, *A Walk in the Park*. Hamish Hamilton.
Burnett, Frances Hodgson, *The Secret Garden*. Puffin.
Carle, Eric, *The Very Hungry Caterpillar*. Hamish Hamilton/Puffin.
Cleary, Beverly, *Dear Mr Henshaw*. Julia MacRae/Puffin.
Cormier, Robert, *The Chocolate War*. Gollancz/Lions.
Dahl, Roald, *The BFG*. Cape/Puffin.
——————, *Boy*. Cape.
——————, *The Witches*. Cape/Puffin.
Ende, Michael, *The Neverending Story*. Puffin.
Fox, Mem, illustrator, Julie Vivas, *Wilfrid Gordon McDonald Partridge*. Omnibus.
Garner, Alan, *The Stone Book Quartet*. Collins.
Grimm, Jacob and Wilhelm, illustrator, Anthony Browne, *Hansel and Gretel*.
Grimm, Jacob and Wilhelm, illustrator, *Hansel and Gretel*. Anthony Browne, Julia MacRae.
Heide, Florence Parry, *The Shrinking of Treehorn*. Kestrel/Puffin.

Holm, Anne, *I am David*. Magnet.
Hutchins, Pat, *Rosie's Walk*. Puffin.
Klein, Robin, *Penny Pollard's Diary*. Oxford.
————, *People Might Hear You*. Puffin.
Le Guin, Ursula, *A Wizard of Earthsea*. Puffin.
L'Engle, Madeline, *A Wrinkle in Time*. Puffin.
Lewis, C.S., *The Lion, the Witch and the Wardrobe*. Bles.
Little, Jean, *Mama's Going to Buy You a Mockingbird*. Kestrel.
MacIntyre, Elisabeth, *Katherine*. Angus & Robertson.
Magorian, Michelle, *Goodnight Mr Tom*. Kestrel/Puffin.
Marryat, Captain, *Children of the New Forest*. Puffin.
Nash, Ogden, *Custard the Dragon*. Dent.
Niland, Deborah, *ABC of Monsters*. Hodder & Stoughton.
Norman, Lilith, *A Dream of Seas*. Collins.
Park, Ruth, *Playing Beatie Bow*. Nelson/Puffin.
Paterson, Katherine, *Bridge to Terabithia*. Puffin.
Pearce, Philippa, *Tom's Midnight Garden*. Puffin.
————, *The Way to Sattin Shore*. Kestrel/Puffin.
Pender, Lydia, illustrator, Inga Moore. *Barnaby and the Horses*. Oxford.
Potter, Beatrix, *The Tale of Peter Rabbit*. Warne.
Sendak, Maurice, *Outside Over There*. Bodley Head/Puffin.
————, *Where the Wild Things Are*. Puffin.
Southall, Ivan, *Hills End*. Puffin.
————, *Josh*. Angus and Robertson.
Spence, Eleanor, *A Candle for St Antony*. Oxford.
Stevenson, Robert Louis, *Treasure Island*. Puffin.
Taylor, Mildred D., *Roll of Thunder, Hear My Cry*. Puffin.
Thiele, Colin, *Blue Fin*. Rigby.
————, *Storm Boy*. Rigby.
Townsend, Sue, *The Secret Diary of Adrian Mole Aged 13¾*. Methuen.
Voigt, Cynthia, *Homecoming*. Collins.
Wagner, Jenny, *The Bunyip of Berkeley's Creek*. Puffin.
————, *John Brown, Rose and the Midnight Cat*. Puffin.
Walsh, Jill Paton, *Unleaving*. Avon/Bodley Head.
Wheatley, Nadia, *The House that Was Eureka*. Kestrel.
White, E.B., *Charlotte's Web*. Puffin.
Willmott, Frank, *Breaking Up*. Fontana Lions.
Wrightson, Patricia, *The Book of Wirrun: Trilogy: The Ice is Coming, The Dark Bright Water, Behind the Wind*. Hutchinson/Puffin.
————, *A Little Fear*. Hutchinson/Puffin.
————, *The Nargun and the Stars*. Hutchinson/Puffin.

FURTHER READING

Cairney, Trevor H. (ed.), *Children's Literature: A World of Dreams For Curious Castaways*.
Carpenter, Humphrey, *Secret Gardens: A Study of The Golden Age of Children's Literature*. Allen & Unwin.
Huck, Charlotte, *Children's Literature in the Elementary School* (3rd ed. updated). Holt, Rinehart and Winston.
Inglis, Fred, *The Promise of Happiness: Value and Meaning in Children's Fiction*. Cambridge University Press.
Meek, Margaret, *How Texts Teach What Readers Learn*. Thimble Press.

2 THE LIGHT IN THE EYE: ON GOOD BOOKS FOR CHILDREN

GORDON WINCH

> For a book by itself is nothing — a film shown in an empty cinema: one can only assess its value by the light it brings to a child's eye.
>
> Elaine Moss

The story of Peppermint, a frail white kitten, told in undistinguished flat American prose and illustrated with pictures that are totally without distinction, is beloved by a small girl and read to pieces. Why? Alison, the small girl, is an adopted child who, like Peppermint, has been taken home and treasured. The identification between the child and the story has produced in that young reader a rich and abiding delight which is at the root of every worthwhile response to literature. Because of its emotional content the book holds a message of supreme significance for Alison 'more important to that child's development than all the Kate Greenaway Medal-winning books put together' (Moss 1977: 142).

This reported incident raises a fundamental issue: a good children's book, whatever else its attributes, must bring light to a child's eye. That is, it must provide enjoyment and satisfaction for the young reader who is in the long run the final arbiter of worth. It is extremely important that children *want* to read the books that we as adults have written for them. We are, after all, intruders into the land of childhood, a domain most of us have long vacated, and into which we can regain entry only on the most temporary and intangible of visas. It could well be that our judgement of books, even if based on the most worthy of criteria, could be seriously awry in terms of the responses of real, live, flesh-and-blood children. It is a common complaint that prestigious awards in children's literature do not give sufficient weighting to the child as reader. Children themselves are often surprised and disappointed that their choices never win awards or, in many cases, never make the short list.

This argument does not mean that we should cast aside our responsibility for choosing children's books which we consider of real and enduring worth. If we did we would be renouncing our other responsibility of educating taste, and the child's reading world could become flooded with the most mediocre of series literature. It is a truism that the most popular children's books are not always the best. On the other hand it can be argued that the child needs to read everything; true judgement is only developed by exposure. As Judith Armstrong (1982: 118) puts it, 'those who were hooked young on the Famous Five are now more likely to be reading Booker Prize winners or modern poetry'. The main point is that a book which children do not enjoy is not a good children's book; what constitutes enjoyment is another matter.

John Rowe Townsend (1980: 196) takes up the issue in his answer to the question: What does literature offer? It offers, he says:

> ... above all, enjoyment: enjoyment not only in the shallow sense of easy pleasure, but enjoyment in the shaping by art of the raw material of life and enjoyment, too, of the skill with which that shaping is performed; enjoyment in the stretching of one's imagination, the deepening of one's awareness; an enjoyment which may be intense even if the literary work is sad or painful.

A good book reflects life and remakes it in a new form. A reader experiences through involvement in the story, and by interaction with the characters in it, a vicarious experience, an involvement, which stretches the imagination and takes the reader to realms not yet visited; it adds to and deepens his or her understanding of the world across the whole spectrum of pleasure and pain.

This extended view of enjoyment gives a new and valuable perspective as to what constitutes a good book for children. It will be useful to explore some aspects of the view in terms of a number of books children are known to enjoy.

SHAPING THE RAW MATERIAL OF LIFE

In *The Tenth Good Thing About Barney* (1971) Judith Viorst deals with the emotional impact caused by the loss of a pet. She tells the story of a child's reaction to it and shows his growing comprehension of the wider meaning of death. To begin, it is something that must be faced squarely and with true grief:

> My cat, Barney died last Friday.
> I was very sad.
> I cried, and I didn't watch television.
> I cried, and I didn't eat my chicken or even the chocolate pudding.
> I went to bed, and I cried.

The sense of loss and the recreation of it in the mind of the reader is heightened by Erik Blegvad's art which is in black and white, subdued and sensitive. The illustration on page 4 of the child being comforted by the mother is, I think, beautiful — and sad.

After the funeral, during which Barney is suitably interred, there is an argument between the little boy and his friend, Annie, from next door. Annie has a romanticised view of death: 'Annie said Barney was in heaven with lots of cats and angels, drinking cream and eating tins of tuna'. But not so the small boy: 'I said Barney was in the ground'. The discussion is devoid of sentimentality, but touching nevertheless. Dad, who is approached to solve the problem, and stop the ensuing fight, is suitably equivocal: 'Maybe Barney's in heaven, my father began ... And maybe, said my father, Barney isn't ... We don't know too much about heaven ... ' There is a return to stability in the comfort and strength of the family, as father and son work together in the garden. The gentle introduction to the fact of the cycle of birth, growth, decay, death and rebirth is effective and fitting:

> My father had a packet of little brown seeds.
> ... soon they'll grow a stem and some leaves
> and flowers. Things change in the ground, said
> my father.

And finally, the child's acceptance of all this and of the realisation that Barney was, not only part of the eternal scheme of things, but he was what he was:

> ... brave, I said.
> And smart and funny and clean.
> Also cuddly and handsome, and he only once
> ate a bird.
> It was sweet, I said, to hear him purr in my ear.
> And sometimes he slept on my tummy and kept
> it warm.
> Those are all good things, said my mother,
> but I still just count nine.
> Yes, I said, but now I have another.
> Barney is in the ground and he's helping to
> grow flowers.
> You know, I said, that's a pretty nice job for
> a cat.

It is no surprise to see that the cycle of nature is recreated in the story itself. The little boy has taken on the truth through his father's understanding; he has echoed his father's own words and has grown like the leaves and flowers in the garden.

The raw material of life (and death) is shaped in this book as it is with an older child, Jesse, in Katherine Paterson's *Bridge to Terabithia* (1978). Here the response is more sophisticated, befitting the child's age and the tragedy of the occasion. Leslie's death produces a range of reactions in Jesse: incredulity, grief, guilt, anger and, finally, acceptance and realisation of what Leslie has meant to him and what she has done for his life. It is a moving book which enriches any reader, as good literature always does.

ENJOYING THE SKILL OF SHAPING

The skill of writing is the skill of using words. Sometimes the words are acerbic, sharp as a scalpel, as in Leon Garfield's description of Jackson the street urchin in *Fair's Fair* (1981):

> Jackson was thin, small and ugly, and
> stank like a drain.

Or sometimes they are lilting and mellifluous as in Kenneth Grahame's description of Mole's walk beside the river in *The Wind in the Willows* (1908):

> The Mole was bewitched, entranced, fascinated. By the side of the river he trotted as one trots, when very small, by the side of a man, who holds one spellbound by exciting stories; and when tired at last, he sat on the bank, while the river, still chattered on to him, a babbling procession of the best stories in the world, sent from the heart of the earth to be told at last to the insatiable sea.

Or they may be riotous and inventive as in Roald Dahl's description of the 'awesome snozzcumber' in *The BFG* (1982):

> 'It's disgusterous!' the BFG gurgled.
> 'It's sickable! It's rotsome! It's maggotwise!
> Try it yourself, this foulsome snozzcumber!

They could also be busy and filled with sound and movement as in Colin Thiele's description of the birds of the South Australian Coorong in *Storm Boy* (1963):

> And so the water and the shores rippled and flapped with wings. In the early morning the tall birds stood up and clapped and cheered the rising sun. Everywhere there was the sound of bathing — a happy splashing and sousing and swishing. It sounded as if the water had been turned into a bathroom five miles long, with thousands of busy fellows gargling and gurgling and blowing bubbles together. Some were above the water, some were on it, and some were under it; a few were half on it and half under. Some were just diving into it and some just climbing out of it.

Whatever words do in a good book, they come together to tell a story: of Bilbo Baggins in *The Hobbit*; of Drem in *Warrior Scarlet*; of Mary in *The Secret Garden*; of Benjie in *The Eighteenth Emergency*; of Simon (and the Nargun) in *The Nargun and the Stars*. It is the skill of the writer that welds the words together so that they may work a special magic of their own.

STRETCHING THE IMAGINATION

Some books have qualities which widen the mind's eye: they take the reader far beyond the ordinary to a new and exciting experience. This experience can be of a sensory kind in which one sees or hears new things; it can be of an intellectual kind in which one thinks new things; it can be of an emotional or moral kind in which one feels and understands new things.

Pamela Allen's prize-winning picture book, *Bertie and the Bear* (1983), is a book of this kind. It is, as Pamela says, a noisy book: our senses soon tell us that, and our imagination is stretched to think of the IN-CRED-IBLE noise made by the Queen shoo shooing, the Admiral bong bonging, the Captain ooh oohing, the General toot tooting, the Sergeant bom bomming and the little dog yip yipping. They are certainly dramatic (and beautiful) noises. Likewise, the pages are full of shapes, colours and movement (Who could dance as beautifully as the bear?). Next, our minds are stimulated to think of the incongruity of the situation and the comedy of it all (all this for me?). If comedy is the laughter of the mind it appears in these pages. And then there is emotional appeal: fear and tension (Will the bear catch Bertie? What will happen if he does?) . . . and surprise . . . and relief!

Another book which shares many special qualities is John Burningham's *Mr Gumpy's Outing* (1970). There should be no surprise that children love it so. In it they find simple and flexible language filled with echoes of their own voices and of those around them: 'May we come with you?' said the children. 'Yes', said Mr Gumpy, 'if you don't squabble'. They find delightful wit: 'May I come, please, Mr Gumpy?' said the pig. 'Very well, but don't muck about'; they find original, appealing art which supports and amplifies the text (see over).

They find sensory pleasure in the rhythmical movement of the words; they find intellectual pleasure in the richness of the vocabulary and the linguistic variations within the text ('May we come with you? Can I come along, Mr Gumpy? I'd like a ride, will you take me with you? Have you a place for me . . .'); they find a moral side to the story (if you don't do what you're told . . .; after default, forgiveness; people and animals are what they are).

The book is so absorbing in its overall quality that the reader is drawn to the imaginative world it creates with no problem of suspension of disbelief. The tea party at the end, a perfect (and very

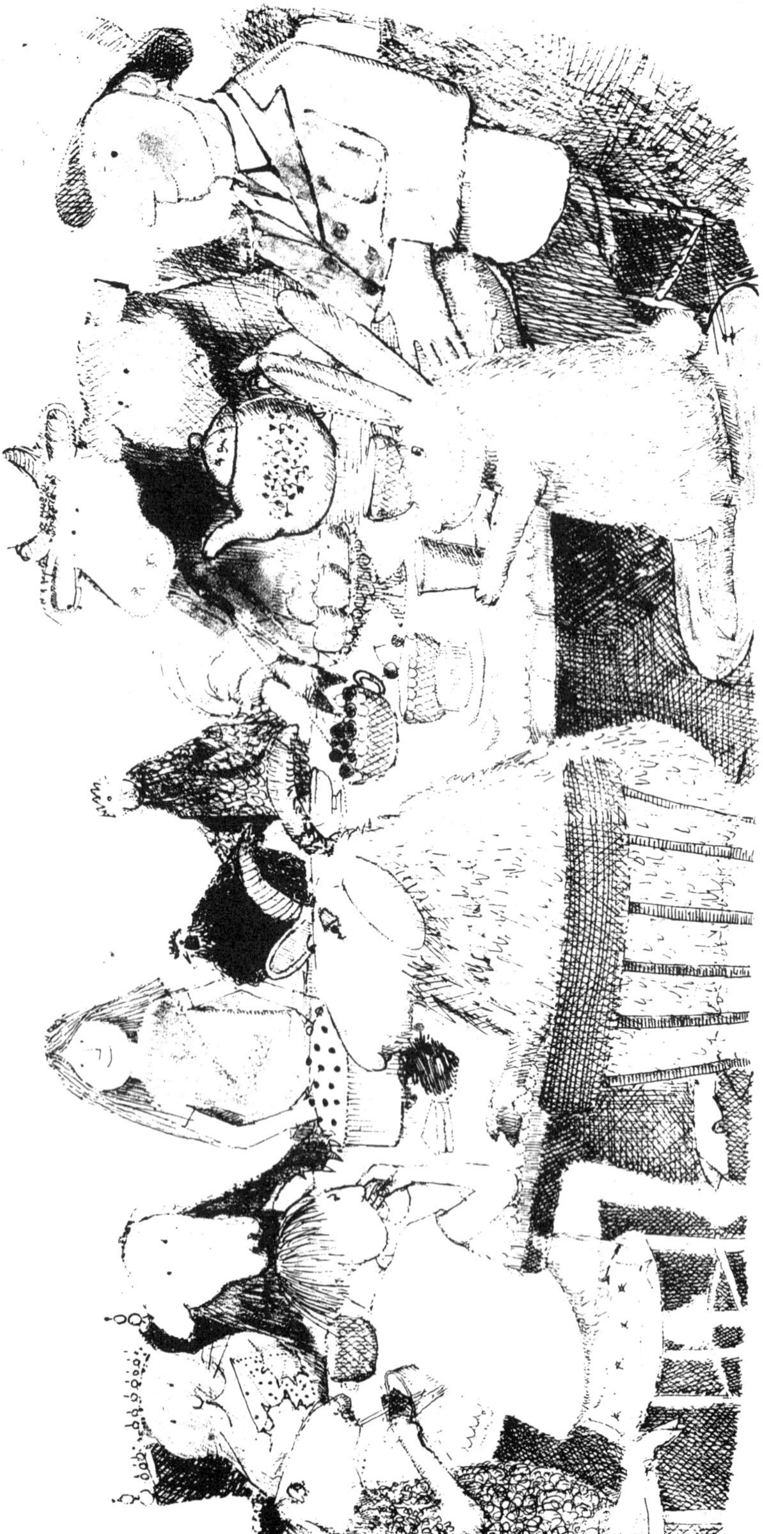

English) culmination to such an adventure, presents no problem in its anthropomorphism: the calf and the pig sit quietly next to Mr Gumpy and take their tea in one of the great double page spreads of picture book art. There is no mucking about.

When we come to books for the older child, who can read Katherine Paterson's *Bridge to Terabithia* without being moved or lifted to a higher level of understanding of what it means to lose someone you love? Who can read Ivan Southall's *Let the Balloon Go* (1968) without being transported to the topmost branches of that fearsome tree? The reader can feel the frustration and inner turmoil of John Clement Sumner as he struggles to find his identity. Who can read J.R.R. Tolkien's, *The Lord of the Rings* (1954) without having one's mind painted with the people of Middle Earth on a mighty imagined canvas?

Finally, children take what they want from books and their responses are not always searching or comprehensive. If a book is a good one it will be able to create enjoyment at many levels, in many ways and at many times. It will always bring light to a child's eye.

REFERENCES

Armstrong, Judith, 'In Defense of Adventure Stories' in *Children's Literature in Education* Vol. 13, No. 3, Autumn 1982.

Moss, Elaine, 'The "Peppermint" Lesson' in Meek, Margaret *et al.*, *The Cool Web*. London: Bodley Head, 1977.

Townsend, John Rowe, 'Standards of Criticism for Children's Literature' in Chambers, Nancy, editor, *The Signal Approach to Children's Books*. Harmondsworth: Kestrel, 1980.

BOOKS REFERRED TO IN THE CHAPTER

Allen, Pamela, *Bertie and the Bear*. Nelson.
Burnett, Frances Hodgson, *The Secret Garden*. Heinemann/Puffin.
Burningham, John, *Mr Gumpy's Outing*. Jonathan Cape/Puffin.
Byars, Betsy, *The Eighteenth Emergency*. Bodley Head/Puffin.
Dahl, Roald, illustrator, Quentin Blake, *The BFG*. Jonathan Cape.
Garfield, Leon, illustrator, Margaret Chamberlain, *Fair's Fair*. Macdonald.
Grahame, Kenneth, illustrator, E.H. Shepherd, *The Wind in the Willows*. Methuen/Magnet.
Paterson, Katherine, *Bridge to Terabithia*. Gollancz/Puffin.
Southall, Ivan, *Let the Balloon Go*. Methuen/Puffin.
Sutcliff, Rosemary, *Warrior Scarlet*. OUP/Puffin.
Thiele, Colin, *Storm Boy*. Rigby.
Tolkien, J.R.R., *The Hobbit*. Allen & Unwin/Ballantine.
———, *The Lord of the Rings*. Allen & Unwin.
Viorst, Judith, illustrator, Erik Blegvad, *The Tenth Good Thing About Barney*. Collins.
Wrightson, Patricia, *The Nargun and the Stars*. Hutchinson/Puffin.

3 CHILDREN AND THEIR BOOKS: THE RIGHT BOOK FOR THE RIGHT CHILD 1

LAURIE BRADY

> Books that reflect the child's perception of the world are the books children clamor for. Those books whose main characters reflect the complex psychological and emotional aspects of the reader gain wide readership, while those books which fail to reflect this viewpoint have a very low readership, no matter how beautifully written the book may be.
>
> Norma Schlager

The purpose of this chapter is to examine the developmental stages in the growth of children, and to discuss the implications of such stages for the selection of children's literature. Researchers have identified stages in the development of children's thinking, language, personality and morality, and the pertinent question is whether the characteristics of a particular stage and age can provide sufficiently clear guidelines for the selection of literature. If, for instance, it could be demonstrated that all children within a particular age range think and feel in substantially the same way about substantially the same subject matter, then such information would provide a valuable blueprint for selecting literature.

Schlager (1978: 142) acknowledges the indisputable contribution of the discipline of child development. She claims that 'the magic which lures children relates directly to child development, and by working not only at the quality of books produced for children, but at the children themselves, we as adults can begin to play our tune on the Pied Piper's flute'. But acknowledging the importance of understanding child development need not involve an unconditional acceptance of the validity of matching books to the characteristics of developmental stages.

The following premises are adopted for the examination of developmental stages to follow:

1. The declared or expressed interest of the child (whether for a particular book, format or subject), is a more important criterion for selection than any 'match' of literature to stage by an adult. However, such a premise does not necessarily negate the value of developmental stages as a predictor of interest. For instance, Schlager (1978) suggests that the interest of the child is not conscious, and that the key to such interest is child development.

2. A knowledge of child development in general, and developmental stages in particular, may provide valuable information for the selection of literature.
3. A knowledge of the developmental stages provides a guide for selection, and not a rigid blueprint. The concept of stages does have value in prediction, in that the stages remain constant across cultures. This means that while the 'content' of cultures changes (for example what we might think about euthanasia or sexual behaviour), the 'structure' (or how thought develops) remains the same for all people. Thus a developmental stage provides a source of information that does not vary significantly through time or geography, and which may therefore be refined through research.

   However, there is also a need to acknowledge the limitations of developmental stages as predictors of preference. The greatest area for caution is the variability of the stages. The existence and invariant sequence of the intellectual and moral stages has been impressively demonstrated, but there has been dispute as to the age span of such stages. For example, it is argued that a great many students in Australian schools do not acquire full formal operational thought (the final intellectual stage) until the age of fifteen, whereas for Piaget's sample, it was twelve. Donaldson (1978) refutes the stage ages of Piaget, claiming that given a meaningful language and setting, very young children can perform tasks which might be considered to be beyond them. In the area of moral development, it is virtually impossible to relate stages to age. In fact, Kohlberg (1975) claims that while a person may achieve moral autonomy (the final two stages) by mid-adolescence, the great majority of the adult population never reach it.

   There is also a problem of validity if the developmental stages are used as infallible guides for determining literary preference. The stages may give fruitful information on why children select certain literature, but the author is loath to concede that the stages explain all the reasons. For instance, a child may read for reasons quite apart from absolute literal comprehension. A preference for noble sentiment (even if not understood), or the colour and 'feel' of words may determine a child's preference at different ages.
4. The simple notion of matching the selection of literature to a child's developmental stage needs to be broadened to include the contribution of stages other than the child's own dominant or 'modal' stage. According to many stage theories, the child, at any point in time, experiences a stage 'mixture'; that is, he does not function exclusively according to a particular stage. Research on the universally accepted stages of moral development formulated by Kohlberg, has demonstrated that when people are exposed to moral reasoning one stage above their

own dominant stage, they are more influenced by it, and prefer it as moral advice. Such a knowledge suggests a matching of literature to a moral stage one above the child's own.

Following is an examination of the stages in intellectual (cognitive) development, moral development, personal and emotional development and language development. This examination is confined to an analysis of the characteristics of the stages, rather than the mechanisms of growth. The stages of physical development are not considered relevant in the examination, except in so far as they correspond with or contribute to development in other areas.

INTELLECTUAL DEVELOPMENT

The major theory of intellectual development is that of Piaget, who considers development in terms of progression through four fixed and age-related stages. Several points must be understood:
1. The ages given for particular stages are guides only.
2. All people pass through the same stages (though not all people may reason fully at the final stage level).
3. The stages are cumulative in that they incorporate thinking from the preceding stages.
4. Children who reason at a particular stage level for one subject may not function at this stage level in another subject.

The basic characteristics of the stages, and the approximate ages that apply, follow.

The Sensorimotor Stage (0–2 Years)

This stage is so called because development is based on information from the senses (*sensori*) and from the body (*motor*). There are two main characteristics:
— Children develop an understanding of *causality*, that is, they understand that events can be caused, and that they can therefore achieve personal goals.
— Children develop *object permanence*. Until about the age of one, babies believe that objects exist only if they can see them, so acquiring this concept is the beginning of understanding the world, because the child knows that objects have an independent reality.

The Preoperational Stage (2–6 Years)

This stage is so called because the child is beginning to master 'operations' (actions that are carried out mentally rather than physically). The main characteristics include the following:
— Children are egocentric because they find it difficult to put themselves in another's position, or take another's view.
— Children use symbols in a rudimentary way. Initially they use action symbols (miming a behaviour), and later they use verbal symbols in talking.

— Children do not understand the concept of *reversibility*. This refers to the ability to reverse thinking, or to see things 'the other way around'. For example, the preoperational child, when asked to place a row of objects 'the other way around', may begin correctly, but is likely to become confused.
— Children are not able to *conserve*. This refers to the ability to recognise that the attributes of an object, for example length and volume, remain the same, even if the appearance is changed. A preoperational child can watch an experimenter take one of two identical containers of water, and pour it into a taller and narrower container. The child, who agreed that both containers held the same amount, will then insist that the container in which the water reaches the greatest height, now holds more.

Possible implications for selecting literature include:
— Provision of a variety of visual material to illustrate.
— Provision of opportunities for children to manipulate (e.g. pop-up books).
— Provision of subject matter which discloses the multiple attributes of an object or situation.
— Selection of subject matter from the child's own experience, and avoidance of treating content which is too far removed from the child's limited horizons.

The Concrete Operational Stage (7–11 Years)

At this stage, children begin to understand the logical stability of the world. The main characteristics include the following:
— Children are able to conserve and reverse.
— Children are able to classify. This means that they can group objects according to common characteristics. For example, if they are given an assortment of leaves that differ according to shape and colour, they are able to classify subsets (brown serrated leaves, green smooth leaves, and so on).
— Children can seriate. This means that they can place things in logical order ($A<B<C$).
— Children are not able to consider hypotheses about abstract ideas, because their reasoning is limited to concrete situations.

Possible implications for selecting literature include:
— Provision of narrations or explanations that are logically ordered from simple to complex.
— Provision of subject matter that is not too complex in terms of the number of factors involved, the number of steps in a process, or the number of characters in a story.
— Provision of a variety of visual material, possibly including diagrams and models.
— Provision of subject matter that involves a narrator telling his own story, and subject matter that involves children projecting themselves into another time or location.

The Formal Operational Stage (12 Onward)

At this stage, the person is capable of abstract thinking. Main characteristics include the following:
— Children can reason 'scientifically' by mentally testing hypotheses.
— Children can solve problems by systematically exploring all the combinations.

Possible implications for selecting literature include:
— Provision of subject matter that allows children to explore causes and implications of behaviour.
— Provision of subject matter that enables children to see the inter-relationship of subplots.

MORAL DEVELOPMENT

The major theory of moral development is that of Kohlberg, who identifies six stages of development. Several points in relation to the stages must be understood:

1. The moral stages are 'structures' of moral reasoning. One of Kohlberg's greatest contributions was to distinguish 'structure' from 'content'. The choice a person makes in a given situation (to cheat or not to cheat) is the content of moral reasoning, but a person's reasoning about the choice determines the structure of the reasoning. Two people may have completely opposite views on a moral issue (different intent), and yet still be reasoning at the same stage level.
2. The stages form a fixed sequence, applying to all people irrespective of language or culture.
3. Each successive stage consists of a more complex way of experiencing the moral-social world.
4. Although an individual may be assigned a dominant (modal) stage, that individual may operate at different stages on different occasions.
5. It is very difficult to relate the stages to ages. As previously indicated, Kohlberg (1975) claims that only a small percentage of adults reason at the stage 5 or 6 level.

The stages of moral development are defined as follows:

Stage 1
Unquestioning deference to superior power. 'Goodness' or 'badness' is determined by the physical consequences of action.

Stage 2
Relationships are viewed in terms of those of the marketplace, rather than in terms of loyalty, justice or gratitude. The child believes that if 'you scratch my back, I'll scratch yours'.

Stage 3
'Good boy' or 'good girl' orientation. The child conforms to stereotypical images of majority behaviour. Good behaviour is viewed as that which earns approval.

Stage 4
Orientation towards authority, fixed rules and the maintenance of the social order. 'Right' behaviour involves doing one's duty, respecting authority and maintaining the social order.
Stage 5
Right action is defined in terms of general rights and standards which have been agreed upon by society.
Stage 6
Individual decisions are based upon principles of conscience and ethics which apply consistently and universally.

Possible implications for selecting literature include:
— Examination by the selector of the definition of each stage. For example, a child at stage 3 could be given literature depicting children earning parental approval for good behaviour; and a child at stage 4 could be given literature which focuses on children exercising responsibility, and doing their duty according to the established social order. However, in the absence of any age norms for the stages, such an examination presupposes a close knowledge of the children for whom the selection is made.
— Provision of subject matter which exposes the child to moral reasoning one stage above his own (given a knowledge of the child in question), as Turiel (1966) found that people prefer this as moral advice.

It may be helpful to note that there is a relationship between the intellectual stages of Piaget and the moral stages of Kohlberg. Moral reasoning depends on logical reasoning, and the intellectual stage sets a limit to the moral stage that can be attained. Kohlberg (1975) claims that a child whose stage is only concrete operational is limited to his moral stages 1 and 2; a child whose intellectual stage is only partially formal operational is limited to moral stages 3 and 4. The morally autonomous person (stages 5 or 6) must be formal operational.

EMOTIONAL AND PERSONAL DEVELOPMENT

Two theories of personality and emotional development are popular in the educational literature. The first is that of Maslow (1970) who claims that a person develops through a hierarchy of needs from basic survival necessities to the higher and more uniquely human needs. The needs in ascending order are physiological ones, safety needs, belongingness ones (love and affection), needs for esteem, self-actualisation, to know and understand, and aesthetic needs.

The process of 'becoming' involves the child's basic needs being met. The child needs to feel safe, secure and loved, and also feel that he is achieving before further needs can be fulfilled. The search for 'actualisation' may be lifelong, and may never be achieved. It is impossible to relate the stages to ages, because the movement through the stages is not always complete, and often variable. The selector can derive few implications from such a stage system, as literature is not instrumental in satisfying the basic needs.

The major theory of personality and emotional development is that of Erikson (1963), who identifies eight stages of development. Several points in relation to the stages must be understood:

1. The stages are descriptive (Erikson's own beliefs) rather than empirical (scientifically determined).
2. The stages are based on recurring themes in the emotional and social development of people studied in numerous societies.
3. The stages are interdependent; that is, achieving at later stages depends upon how earlier stages have been reached.
4. Each stage poses a developmental crisis that a person must satisfactorily resolve. The resolution may have a permanent effect on the child's self-image and perception of society.

The definitions of the eight stages, and the approximate ages that apply, follow:

Basic Trust versus Basic Mistrust (First Year)
Autonomy versus Shame and Doubt (Second Year)
Initiative versus Guilt (Preschool Years)
Industry versus Inferiority (Middle Childhood)
Identity versus Role Confusion (Adolescence)
Intimacy versus Isolation (Young Adulthood)
Generativity versus Stagnation (Prime of Life)
Ego Integrity versus Despair (Old Age)

Amplification of the first five stages follows. The latter three were considered beyond the scope of this book.

Trust versus Mistrust

Erikson claims that the child develops trust if the needs for food and care are met. The child is just beginning to realise its separateness from other people and objects, and this realisation makes trust very important. This stage corresponds with Piaget's sensorimotor stage.

Autonomy versus Doubt

The child can either exercise autonomy by behaving with some independence, or experience doubt when it senses an inability to manage the world. This stage also corresponds to Piaget's sensorimotor stage.

Initiative versus Guilt

The child can either display initiative in exploring the world on its own, or, if not allowed to do this, develop a sense of guilt. This stage corresponds with Piaget's preoperational one.

Industry versus Inferiority

The child can either develop pleasure from a completed task, or experience inferiority if a task is not completed. This stage corresponds with Piaget's concrete operational stage.

Identity versus Role Confusion

The child either develops a sense of personal identity, or feels ambivalent about his identity. This stage corresponds with Piaget's formal operational stage.

The possible implication for selecting literature is the provision of books which present subject matter showing children satisfactorily resolving the crisis applicable to the relevant stage and age. For example, a preschool child may respond to literature depicting children resolving the initiative versus guilt crisis by exploring the world with relative autonomy, pleasure and success. An adolescent may respond to literature relating the successful quest of peers for meaning and identity in a pluralistic society. Schlager (1978) analyses the popularity of Scott O'Dell's *Island of the Blue Dolphins* by relating its appeal to the theories of Piaget and Erikson. An Indian girl, Karana, is forced to live a solitary life and to cope with problems that threaten her survival. Her ability to deal effectively with these illustrates her resourcefulness and independence. Children at the industry versus inferiority stage respond to her ability to cope, her desire to test the limits of reality, and her growth as a result of these experiences.

LANGUAGE DEVELOPMENT

There are different views as to how children acquire language. One is the behavioural, which suggests that children learn by repeating sounds that produce a positive outcome. Thus a parent may reinforce a child by showing approval when the child makes a sound which approximates that denoting a particular object, like 'milk' or 'dad'. This view of language development emphasises the behaviour of the child.

Another view, stemming from the work of Chomsky (1957, 1965) emphasises thinking in the language learning process. Chomsky believes that children are born with an innate capacity for language which explains why they can say and understand sentences they have not learned before. Language for Chomsky operates on two levels: a 'deep structure' level of thought, and a 'surface structure' level of words and sentences. Children transform the ideas of the first level (deep structure) into words and sentences.

There are, however, a number of generally-accepted observations concerning the acquisition of language. A child's first words are likely to be repeated syllables comprising a vowel and consonant which are eventually shaped into established words. By the age of two years, the child can combine several words to express an impressive range of concepts embracing both objects and actions. At the end of the two word stage, the child uses a rudimentary grammar which involves intonation, word order and inflection. Even within the first two years, the child has discovered the structural principles of language. There continues to be a close interplay between cognitive understanding and linguistic ability, as the child uses language as a means of organising and explaining the world.

There are a variety of documented stages in the acquisition of language, but these are not detailed because they tend to be confined to the first six years of life (the years during which language skills are acquired), and this period represents a small section only of the years under consideration. There are developmental stages in the understanding of language in the first year of life, and stages relating to the development of meaningful speech utterances. Studies relate in detail the volume of vocabulary understood and spoken, consonant and vowel production, and average sentence length at particular ages.

A more recent area of research is the analysis of 'cohesive ties'. Halliday and Hasan (1976) indicate that 'cohesion' in books is achieved by a series of linguistic linking mechanisms or 'cohesive ties' (reference, substitution, ellipsis, conjunction, lexical cohesion). So comprehension is determined by the degree or quality of interactive 'cohesive chains' in a book.

The obvious implication in selecting literature for the young child is the provision of material that can be read and understood, or that can be used to extend the child's learning.

As foreshadowed, it must be understood that comprehension and appreciation involve both the cognitive and linguistic ability of the reader, and the structural organisation of the material selected. All three of these factors should be considered. In so far as the factors can be separated, the obvious questions to be considered by the selector are:

— Is the child intellectually capable of understanding the material?
— Is the child linguistically capable of interpreting the material?
— Is the structure of the material sufficiently coherent?

For example, John Burningham's *Mr Gumpy's Outing* (1970), is structured to extend the young child's language sophistication through both vocabulary, syntax and story pattern. The story relates how different animals ask Mr Gumpy if they can ride in his boat, and the questions posed by the animals present a variety of structures ('May we come with you? Can I come along? Will you take me with you? Can I come? Have you a place for me? Can we come? May I join you?'). Ruth Park's *Playing Beatie Bow* (1980) requires the language sophistication of older children, and provides extension in vocabulary (more difficult words and historical reference like boiling sugar, treacle, aniseed, mothballs, lavender and bodice); syntax, including differences in dialect; and story pattern involving flashbacks to the past.

A list of the relevant and major characteristics of selected age groups follows. As indicated in the introduction of this chapter, caution must be exercised in suggesting literature for stages according to definite age ranges. However, the list may be a fruitful guide for selection. Due to the problems of variability and validity previously outlined, no attempt is made to relate the comprehensive list of titles to specific characteristics within age groupings. Instead, the list of titles follows the list of characteristics.

THREE TO FIVE YEARS

— Functions at the preoperational stage of Piaget.
— Experiences the initiative versus guilt crisis of Erikson.
— Interprets good and bad in terms of both physical consequences and reward and punishment.
— Develops language rapidly (by five, is speaking in complex sentences).
— Develops perceptual skills (ability to discriminate colours, shapes; recognises distinctive attributes of similar objects).
— Possesses a very short attention span.
— Displays egocentric thinking and behaviour.
— Learns through first-hand experiences.
— Begins to assert independence.
— Seeks affection, help and attention to achieve.
— Displays curiosity about the world (asks countless questions).
— Learns through imaginative play.
— Needs adult approval.
— Possesses little sense of time.
— Develops interest in group activity (later in the period).

SIX AND SEVEN YEARS

— Moves toward the concrete operational thought of Piaget (begins to decentre, conserve and reverse thought).
— Experiences the industry versus inferiority crisis of Erikson.
— Perceives good as that which earns praise or approval.
— Continues to expand the scope of language.
— Develops attention span.
— Separates fantasy from reality more effectively.
— Bases learning on immediate perception and direct experience.
— Shows the beginning of abstract thinking, but learns best in concrete terms.
— Possesses a strong need for praise and approval.
— Displays sensitivity to the feelings and attitudes of other children and adults.
— Participates in a group as a group member.
— Has a growing sense of justice.
— Continues to seek independence from adults.
— Likes responsibility, but is insistent in the ability to cope with it.
— Displays egocentric behaviour and is often demanding.

EIGHT AND NINE YEARS

— Functions at the concrete operational level of Piaget (thought is now more flexible and reversible).
— Experiences the industry versus inferiority crisis of Erikson.
— Perceives rightness as keeping the rules.
— Regards peer group acceptance as increasingly important.
— Sees the viewpoints of others (is less egocentric).
— Develops concepts and spatial relationships.
— Appreciates imaginary adventure.
— Displays the ability to project self completely into dramatic situations.
— May possess interests and abilities markedly different from those of peers.
— Has varied interests in hobbies and collections.
— Displays an increasing ability to put ideas into words.
— Identifies self increasingly with group responsibility.
— Forms 'special' friendships.

TEN TO TWELVE YEARS

— Functions at the concrete operational level of Piaget, and is able to see more abstract relationships.
— Experiences the industry versus inferiority crisis of Erikson.
— Views rightness in terms of fairness.
— Possesses a strong interest in social activities (and establishing status within the sex group).
— Possesses an increased interest in the club or group (seeking the friendship of peers).
— Begins to adopt models other than parents (may even challenge parental authority).
— Displays an intense, sustained interest in specific activities.
— Develops a sense of his place in time.
— Seeks approval and wants to impress.
— Displays a skill and willingness to see the viewpoint of others.
— Searches for values.
— Displays a wide range of individual differences.
— Possesses a highly-developed sense of justice and concern for others.
— Displays a deeper understanding and acceptance of sex role.

THIRTEEN YEARS AND ADOLESCENCE

— Functions at the formal operational level of Piaget (the ability to predict, infer, hythothesise without reference to a concrete model).

— Experiences the identity versus role confusion crisis of Erikson.
— May be moving towards moral autonomy (Kohlberg's stages 5 and 6).
— Asserts independence from the family as a step towards adulthood.
— May identify with an admired adult.
— Displays interest in philosophical, ethical and religious issues.
— Searches for ideals.

REFERENCES

Ambron, S.R., *Child Development*. New York: Holt Rinehart & Winston, 1978.
Brady, L., *Models and Methods of Teaching*. Sydney: Prentice-Hall, 1985.
Chomsky N. *Syntactic Structures*. The Hague: Manton, 1957.
——————, *Aspects of a Theory of Syntax*. Cambridge, Mass.: MIT Press, 1965.
Donaldson, M., *Children's Minds*. London: Collins, 1978.
Erikson, E., *Childhood and Society*. New York: Norton, 1963.
Furth, H.G., *Piaget For Teachers*. Englewood Cliffs, New Jersey: Prentice-Hall, 1970.
——————, *Piaget and Knowledge, Theoretical Foundations*. Chicago: University of Chicago Press, 1981.
Halliday, M.A.K. and Hasan, R., *Cohesion in English*. London: Longman, 1976.
Huck, C.S., *Children's Literature in the Elementary School*. New York: Holt Rinehart & Winston, 1976.
Kohlberg, L., 'The Development of Children's Orientation Toward a Moral Order. 1. Sequence in The Development of Thought' in *Vita Humana*, 1963.
——————, 'Moral Education in the Schools: A Developmental View' in *The School Review* No. 74, 1966.
——————, 'The Child as a Moral Philosopher' in *Psychology Today* September 1968.
——————, 'Moral Education For a Society in Moral Transition' *Educational Leadership*, October 1975.
Maslow, A.H., *Motivation and Personality*. New York: Harper & Row, 1970.
Piaget, J., translator, M. Cook, *The Origins of Intelligence in the Child*. New York: International University Press, 1966.
—————— and Inhelder, B., translator, *The Psychology of the Child*. H. Weaver, New York: Basic, 1969.
Schell, R.E. and Hall, E., *Developmental Psychology Today*. New York: Random House, 1979.
Schlager, N. 'Predicting Children's choices in Literature: A Developmental Approach' in *Children's Literature in Education* Vol. 9, No. 3, 1978.
Turiel, E. 'An Experimental Test of the Sequentiality of Developmental Stages in the Child's Moral Judgments' in *Journal of Personality and Social Psychology* Vol. 3, No. 6, 1966.
Woolfolk, A.E. and Nicolich, L.M., *Educational Psychology For Teachers*. Englewood Cliffs, New Jersey: Prentice-Hall, 1980.

BOOKS REFERRED TO IN THE CHAPTER

Burningham, John, *Mr Gumpy's Outing*. Jonathan Cape/Puffin.
O'Dell, Scott, *Island of the Blue Dolphins*. Houghton Mifflin.
Park, Ruth, *Playing Beatie Bow*. Nelson/Puffin.

FURTHER READING

Dworetzky, J.P., *Introduction to Child Development* (2nd ed.). West Publishing Company, 1984.
Lefrancois, G.R., *Of Children: An Introduction to Child Development* (5th ed.). Wadsworth Publishing Company, 1986.
Rathus, S.A., *Understanding Child Development*. Holt Rinehart and Winston, 1988.
Santrock, J.W., *Life-Span Development* (2nd ed.). W.C. Brown Publishers, 1986.
Shaffer, D.R., *Developmental Psychology: Childhood and Adolescence* (2nd ed.). Brooks/Cole Publishing Company, 1989.
──────, *Social and Personality Development* (2nd ed.). Brooks/Cole Publishing Company, 1988.
Vander Zanden, J.W., *Human Development* (3rd ed.). Alfred A. Knopf, 1985.

CHILDREN AND THEIR BOOKS: THE RIGHT BOOK FOR THE RIGHT CHILD 2

ROBYN MORROW

> We have to know the books and the child to match them in terms of the complicated individuality of both.
>
> Margaret Meek

The most common question asked by parents who wish to provide the best book experience for their children is, 'What is a good book for a ... year-old?' The answer to this question is certainly difficult, if not impossible, to answer, as Laurie Brady has pointed out in the first part of this chapter. Studies of the intellectual, moral, emotional and linguistic growth of children give us guidelines but not absolute directions, as children differ enormously in their interests, needs and capacities. What is good for one is not necessarily good for another; what one child enjoys or understands does not give us a comforting universal to apply to the whole world of children.

In spite of these multiple and often confusing variations there are some things we can say about selecting books for children, and there are some things we must say. First, a child's own delight in a book is one of the best of all criteria: countless three to five-year-olds have loved Eric Carle's *Very Hungry Caterpillar* (1970) and Pat Hutchins' *Rosie's Walk* (1968). Their judgement tells us that these *are* books for them. Secondly, our knowledge of the development of children helps us in deciding that these are *indeed* books for them. Carle's book, for example, is simple and direct. Its uncomplicated story in perfect sequence is pitched at the intellectual level of the child, focusing on one matter, the tiny egg that becomes a small (and very hungry) caterpillar, and then a beautiful butterfly. This caterpillar grows because he eats and eats, and changes as caterpillars do. The book provides, through its tactile dimensions (the holes through every item the caterpillar eats) the most immediate of first-hand experiences, supported by the clear and dramatic colours which children of this age appreciate and understand. And the language! A simple narrative packed with new words: lollipops, watermelon, cocoon, and words that sound like the action itself (and — pop! — out of the egg ...). As to the rightness of it all, the caterpillar suffers directly for his behaviour: junk food produces stomach aches (when he ate through one green leaf he felt much better). Finally, the book is itself a work of art: its unity, its originality and its beauty make it a suitable book for a young child.

If we tie this information to what we know about children, it is clear that the book operates effectively at the preoperational stage of development, concerning itself with the egocentric nature of children, their ability to use simple rudimentary symbols, their need for material directly related to experience, their understanding of the physical consequences of action and their need for simple effective language.

Such analyses, however unfinished, do indicate that we can make an intelligent judgment about books, which *might* be right for children at different ages and stages. If we keep in mind the fact that our judgments are fallible and that essentially we are not fitting a book to a child but a child to a book, great value can be obtained by looking at the qualities of books and placing them, however tentatively, within children's developmental stages. John Burningham's *Mr Gumpy's Outing* (1970), after all, must cater to a different audience from that of Ruth Park's *Playing Beatie Bow* (1980).

In essence, then, there are two factors which must be considered in making the happy conjunction of child and book. One is the child: all we know about child development and one child in particular. The other is the book: all we know about the range or continuum of books for children. The first section of this chapter has given us considerable information about the nature of the child; this section will concentrate on the nature of the book.

HOW THE CHILDREN'S BOOKSELLER ANSWERS THE QUESTION: WHICH BOOK WILL I CHOOSE?

'I am looking for a book for an eight-year-old boy'. 'What book would you suggest to read to a three-year-old?' 'What would be a good book for a ten-year-old girl who loves horses?' 'I want a book for my nephew, who is five'. 'Could you recommend a book for a teenager who doesn't like reading?'

These comments and questions are everyday utterances to the ears of a children's bookseller and they all add up to much the same thing: Help me to make the correct choice or, in some cases, tell me which book to buy. What a responsibility!

My approach to the problem is first to collect data by asking questions:

1. Collecting Information about the Child
    — What is the chronological age of the reader?
    This information will narrow down the range of books which might be suitable, although it will only be a guide.
    — Is the child a keen reader? Is reading enjoyable? Does he or she read well?
    If the child is a slow reader and has problems with print, the type of book must not be too difficult in language and, possibly, thought content. Very competent, keen readers are usually easy to choose for in this regard.

— What is the child's experience with books?
  If the child is young, has he or she been exposed to books (bought and borrowed)? Is the child read to frequently?
  If the child is older are books available in the house? Does he or she visit the school or local library? Is reading part of the child's usual day?
— What are the child's interests?
  The child's life experience is important. If children's horizons have been widened through talk and involvement in many different activities they are usually interested in many more things and are more mature and sophisticated in their reading. A particular interest may be important also.

2. Showing a Range of Books

A range of books is then made available to the purchaser. My new knowledge about the reader helps me to decide; my knowledge of the books themselves adds the other important factor on which the remainder of this chapter will focus.

APPLYING THIS TECHNIQUE TO CLASSROOM AND LIBRARY

The above technique can be applied to the selection of books for children in classrooms and libraries. Very often the situation is similar and the solution can be obtained in much the same way. Teachers and librarians usually have one big advantage: the child is always present at the moment of choice. As stated above, the reader is, after all, the person who matters, the one to whom the book must appeal. Teachers, in particular, usually have a first-hand knowledge of children they teach, and this information is of great value when making judgements.

In a bookstore I come into contact with parents who respect the value of books, and children who want to read. Neither the parents nor the children are necessarily affluent; often the purchase of a book means doing without something else or is the result of careful saving. The argument that books are expensive is often refuted by the relative cheapness of the paperback market. Compare the price of a paperback book with some of the other items with which we entertain ourselves: a trip to the movies, the cost of a video tape — even a box of chocolates!

SOME COMMENTS ON COMMENTS ABOUT BOOKS AND CHILDREN

'I'll buy him a book when he's old enough to appreciate it'

Those of us who enjoy books ourselves will naturally want to hand on this enthusiasm to the young children with whom we are involved. Teachers and librarians can work wonders but there is no substitute for learning to love books at a very early age within the warmth of a family. Many parents today owe a debt to Dorothy Butler, whose publication *Babies Need Books* (1980) has helped build their confidence to start reading to the very young. Dorothy Butler and other enthusiasts for books for babies have also influenced the publishing world, resulting in the production of more and better books designed especially for the preschooler.

There are many glossy, laminated books with strong cardboard pages which are 'catalogues' of objects familiar to young children. The new flowering in publication has occurred, however, at a more sophisticated level. Two books which have more subtlety than first meets the eye are *Across the Stream* (1983) and *How Do I Put It On?* (1982). The first of these has beautifully designed pages with simple pictures of a duck family. A close reading of it reveals the use of irony: we are told that the hen and three chicks had a bad dream but nowhere do the words spell out exactly what this was. An observant reader, even a very young one, will notice what the bad dream is. In fact, this book resembles *Rosie's Walk* and *The Tale of Jemima Puddle Duck* (1908) in implying that a fox is to be dreaded to a degree almost beyond naming by a feathered creature. Similarly there is more than at first meets the eye in *How Do I Put It On?* in which the small bear character makes ridiculous mistakes in getting dressed (see later in this chapter).

I have mentioned these books as examples but there are many others of similar sophistication. Ron Maris' *Are You There, Bear?* (1984) contains references to his previous publication *My Book* (1983). *Each Peach Pear Plum* (1978) is full of literary allusions, referring to *The Three Bears*, and characters such as Tom Thumb, Mother Hubbard and Robin Hood. So the world of books for the preschooler is both very new and very old. Those stalwarts, *The Three Bears*, *The Three Little Pigs* and *The Three Billy Goats Gruff* are still among the favourite stories for three and four-year-olds, containing as they do the magical elements of repetition and tension. At least one collection of such stories is essential in a young family's library.

Some parents and teachers forget the importance of poetry in books for the very young. It is hard to choose from among the talented illustrators who have turned their hands to depicting the 'old favourite' nursery rhymes. The strong colours of Brian Wildsmith (1964), the muted tones of Harold Jones (1954), the delicate miniatures of Nicola Bayley (1975), or the outrageous humour of Raymond Briggs — how to choose among them? The next stage of enjoyment of verse is now catered for in *When a Goose Meets a Moose* compiled by Clare Scott-Mitchell (1980). Many of the favourite picture books are really illustrated poems which young children learn to chant. Some have strong rhyme and rhythm, such as *Mr Magnolia* (1980) and *The Winter Bear* (1974). Others are poetic in a gentler way. Consider the text in *John Brown, Rose and the Midnight Cat* (1977):

> But that night, when Rose was safe in bed,
> John Brown went outside.
> He drew a line around the house
> and told the midnight cat to stay away.
> 'We don't need you, cat,' he said.
> 'We are all right, Rose and I'.

A child whose imagination has been fed with such language and the beauty of its illustration will bring a very different attitude to the task of learning to read from that of someone who has not had such advantages.

'Thank goodness Little Johnny has learnt to read. I don't have to read aloud to him any more'

Schools in Australia are experiencing the influence of Margaret Meek, Jill Bennett and others who advocate learning to read with *real* books rather than specially-devised reading schemes. Young children who have been introduced to books at home have often gone on to master the technique of reading remarkably early. To a reading family, the distinction between a book to enjoy having read aloud and an 'early reader' is an artificial one.

Books like the *Meg and Mog* series by Nicoll and Pienkowski invite the child to participate in reading. The words 'catch that cat' in enormous red type just cry out to be read for oneself while the adult reading aloud continues with the narrative in *Mog at the Zoo* (1982). A great debt is owed by books such as these to the cartoon strip tradition.

Some of the simplest books, earlier referred to as books for babies, can serve as beginning readers also. Books by Watanabe, for example, have very large print and the simplest of texts.

Mouse Tales (1973) by Arnold Lobel and other books in the 'I Can Read' series are such delightful stories in themselves that they are equally successful as read-alouds and for the five or six-year-old beginning reader.

The early reading years (from approximately six to eight years) are a time when fairy tales can be shared by adult and child — such haunting stories as *Beauty and the Beast* and *Hansel and Gretel*. This is a time for sharing humour too: the *Worst Witch* (1974) series by Jill Murphy and *Flat Stanley* (1968) by Jeff Brown are examples which the infant school reader can often read aloud. But what of that Australian classic *The Magic Pudding* (1918)? I suspect that many copies have been given to children who have left them on the shelf unread because of the far-from-simple language. This book is, however, a feast to enjoy together in sessions of reading aloud.

'She's far too old for picture books'

It is foolish to assume that children living in such a visual world grow beyond pictures as their reading competence matures. As secondary school teachers can attest, the books of Anno and Anthony

Browne offer new insights even to that most sophisticated of creatures, the teenager. Sometimes an illustrator can help us to look again at a well-known story — a recent example is *Hiawatha's Childhood* (1984) illustrated by Errol Le Cain, which revitalises for child and adult alike the haunting words of Henry Wadsworth Longfellow. Sometimes the contemporary picture book has very few words, or none at all, like those of John F. Goodall and some books by Peter Spier. These wordless picture books are often among the most demanding books available for child and adult alike. A skilful author/illustrator like Graham Oakley can intersperse text and pictures to tell a story with amusing detail, as in his Church Mouse series.

The picture book now ranges from the simplest publication for a child in his first year of life to intricate collage works such as those by Jeannie Baker, very grown-up subject matter as in the *Hiroshima Story* (1983) by Toshi Maruki, to the short novel illustrated on every page such as *Thing* by Robin Klein and Alison Lester. To put age barriers on books such as these is to close doors to children and adults alike.

'She'll only read books about horses'

The most popular authors for competent readers of primary school age deal with the subjects closest to the readers' own lives — social relationships in the classroom and among the peer group. Such books as *Hating Alison Ashley* (1984) and *Cannily Cannily* (1981) and many books by Judy Blume deal with the problems of growing up. In encouraging children to read we are surely also trying to enlarge their world — 'giving them wings' should result in some flying to distant places and times as well as to those closer at hand. Once again an early start is very helpful. Two books within the range of most eight or nine-year-olds — *The Big Brass Key* (1983) by Ruth Park and *Something Special* (1985) by Emily Rodda, extend the imagination through time-travel. Both are short books, simple in structure and local in setting, but satisfying little stories which prepare the reader for longer journeys such as *Eleanor Elizabeth* (1985) or *Playing Beatie Bow* (1980).

Similarly, *Sadako and the Thousand Paper Cranes* (1981) takes us into another country (Japan) and confronts us with that most enormous of human problems, the consequences of a nuclear explosion.

The fantasy world in children's literature depends for its acceptance on a number of conventions. There is the one of entry into the other land (by falling, as in *Alice's Adventures in Wonderland* (1865) or by going through the back of the wardrobe in *The Lion, the Witch and the Wardrobe* (1950)).

The convention of the quest as in *The Hobbit* (1937) is one of the most universal in literature. But some of these ideas are strange to children who have no literary background. It is much easier to read about the here-and-now, the possible or the 'daydream' possible. The experience of the picture story books once again can help establish expectations to be carried forward into longer reading. Books such as John Burningham's *Come Away from the Water, Shirley* (1977) with its two levels of narrative, and Jill Murphy's *On the Way Home* (1982) in which events happen in reality and other events happen in Claire's imagination, are ideal preparation for the world of fantasy in literature. Teachers of 'remedial reading' could do well to introduce such a crash course in the use of the imagination.

Children of primary school age do *want* to use their imaginations. Favourite games and books at this age often involve pitting oneself against obstacles to survival. Many of the 'realistic' books favoured by the ten to thirteen-year-olds encourage the question 'what if I had to cope with this situation?' So the detailed realities of Laura's childhood in pioneer America, the struggles of the Pinballs — and their Australian counterparts the Leftovers — inspire flights of imagination although they could be described baldly as realistic fiction.

The task for the librarian, teacher and the informed bookseller is to become skilled in suggesting further books in chains of subject matter and theme. A young enthusiast for *Master of the Grove* (1982) may enjoy the books of Ursula Le Guin. A reader fascinated by the plight of the orphans in *Thursday's Child* (1970) must meet Will in *Goodnight Mr Tom* (1981).

'He's well past children's books now. He read *The Godfather* last week'

Like all the other age groups mentioned, the teenage stage is characterised by an erratic darting from one age level to another. The most skilful and experienced reader of secondary school age will have times of revisiting early favourites, reading strip format books such as the Asterix and Tintin series, and sampling hair-raising adult novels.

Some of the gems of children's literature demand the experience of a thirteen or fourteen-year-old. Unfortunately, there are still some professionals in teaching and libraries who consider 'children's literature' not relevant to high schools. A closer look at what this literature has to offer should convince them that it is a great shame for any reader, no matter how competent, to miss the satisfaction to be gained from such authors as Robert Westall, Joan Phipson and Cynthia Voigt.

A LOOK INTO SOME BOOKS

A Wordless Picture Book — A Narrative Without Words: *Sunshine* by Jan Ormerod (1981)

This book is about the early morning hours of a small girl's day. She wakes to the first rays of sunshine that enter her room, yawns, sits up, opens a book, takes it and her dolly to the room of her sleeping parents, and a sensitive treatment of the minutiae of a family morning begins. A story without visible words, but a story nevertheless, eloquent in every detail.

What is it about this book that a small child of two to five might enjoy? First, it is directly within a modern child's experience. Her family is a nuclear one but it is mother who goes out to work. The child can see herself in the pages. Next, the detail is simple, logical and real, tangible and satisfying: the trip to the toilet; the burning of the toast; the detail of dressing oneself, slowly and awkwardly, but successfully; also the moral consequence of sleeping in: lateness is a bad thing and must be paid for by fearful haste.

The social milieu of the book also rings true for that age: safety, security and love are all there.

The book elicits language and would stimulate the child to talk, to provide a special and personal story to run parallel to the narrative told in the pictures. Like all good books, *Sunshine* has other dimensions revealed as the book is read and reread: the child's growing sense of independence, the fallibility of adults, the touches of humour and drama. These features lift the book to a high level and extend its charm and its audience. It is a right book for many children.

A Simple Picture Book: *How Do I Put It On?* by Shigeo Watanabe (1982) illustrator, Yasuo Ohtomo

> This is my shirt.
> Do I put it on like this?
> No!
> I put my shirt over my head.

A simple text, accompanied by very clear pictures — against a plain white background a bear cub struggles to get dressed — comprise one of a very popular series of picture story books for preschoolers.

What is the secret of this book's success? It is not just a catalogue of items of clothing — shirt, pants, cap, shoes — but a carefully-patterned narrative. The bear puts his legs through his shirt sleeves and then corrects himself, putting the shirt over his head. Next he takes his pants and treats them similarly, putting them over his head, — then corrects this error, and so on. The actions form a pattern, as does the language — of statement, question, answer and correction. The reliability of the pattern appeals to the young child who is beginning to perceive books as part of the permanent world.

The author invites the young reader to identify with the bear cub by the use of the first person ('I', 'my'), but the humour also owes much to a feeling of slight superiority on the part of the child. 'Silly bear, how could he make such a mistake?' is the young reader's reaction, often only a few days after making the same one himself. Watanabe has selected subject matter from the child's own experience, and shaped it into a satisfying whole.

A Picture Book that is a Fantasy: *There's a Hippopotamus on Our Roof Eating Cake* by Hazel Edwards (1980) illustrator, Deborah Niland

The Australian writer Hazel Edwards has created a fantasy world which young children find very easy to enter. Like Watanabe in *How Do I Put It On?* she has used the first person ('I know, my Daddy' . . .) to establish the child in the family as the central character. But the book moves from domestic reality to fantasy very quickly and naturally:

> My Daddy says there's a hole in our roof.
> I know why there's a hole.
> There's a hippopotamus on our roof eating cake.

The pattern of the story is like that of a poem with a refrain, each page ending with a longer line including the word 'hippopotamus'. This pattern is echoed in the illustrations, colourful full-page depictions of the 'imaginary friend' hippopotamus at almost every opening.

This hippopotamus leads a life in some ways similar to that of the young child narrator — 'He's got a sore knee too' — but in other ways gloriously unlike: 'He can do what he likes'. So the story is full of wish-fulfilment for the reader, who would love to be able to watch television, draw with crayons and ride bikes without restriction.

The real world and the fantasy world are kept separate in this book. The child in the story says 'he told me' but the illustrator has nowhere depicted the imaginary animal and the child together. He is safely outside the house, on the roof, while she continues her secure domestic life below. In this respect the book can be contrasted with fantasy for older children (such as C.S. Lewis' *The Lion, the Witch and the Wardrobe*) in which the human and imaginary characters interact.

A More Complex Picture Story Book: *John Brown, Rose and The Midnight Cat* by Jenny Wagner (1977) illustrator, Ron Brooks

This picture story book fuses both picture and story into a whole: the illustrations both illustrate and extend the meanings of the words. It is a highly visual book and pitched well within the reader's immediate experience, in that it deals with pets. Much of its richness comes from the fact that it is not just a pet story: the meanings extend to issues of jealousy, trust, love, moral choice, old age and (perhaps) death.

For children who read it, the concrete situation relating to the three protagonists is on the surface a simple story. But on it, deeper meanings are painted. At this age, the simplicity of the plot and the carefully-wrought nature of the story line told in the third person is an ideal canvas.

The moral and social issues of John Brown's jealousy and fear, and of Rose's simple and uncomplicated emotional responses are well within the understanding of a young child. Likewise, the dog's change of heart, possibly as a result of a sense of guilt or fear can be readily understood, as can the physical consequences of Rose's unhappiness over the dog's attitude to the cat.

There is room, too, for an exploration of the need for love and affection, well understood by the young child as well as sensitivity to the justice of the cat's inclusion within the 'family'. The language flows like poetry and the story is beautifully structured, with a sense of cohesion of its elements at the levels of basic literal understanding and in the broader areas discussed above.

It is not difficult to see that *John Brown, Rose and The Midnight Cat* would enrich the reading experience of a six or seven-year-old. Like all good books it would appeal below that age, also, and certainly beyond it.

A Junior Novel: *Flat Stanley* by Jeff Brown (1968) illustrator, Tomi Ungerer

Flat Stanley is a junior masterpiece, providing a complete story for a young independent reader who might be placed in Piaget's concrete operational stage. The book is based on the impossible and hilarious fact that Stanley has been squashed flat by an enormous bulletin board and is half an inch thick; but entire in every other way. The incidents which follow stem from Stanley's state of flatness: he goes in and out of rooms by lying down and sliding through the crack at the bottom of a closed door; he descends through a grating to rescue Mrs Lambchop's favourite ring; he is posted in an enormous brown paper envelope to California for a holiday; he alerts the authorities to thieves who are intent on stealing valuable paintings while our hero is disguised as a shepherdess in a picture on a wall.

Once children enter the imaginative world of *Flat Stanley*, as they are able effectively to do at this age, they can enjoy the humorous incongruity of the situations, the matter-of-fact acceptance of Stanley's flatness by everyone in the story and the sheer originality of the plot.

The social order of the family and society generally is maintained in the book. Stanley uses his flat state to help right conquer, to assist others and to make the most of his new condition. Mr and Mrs Lambchop are also eminently respectable, 'in favour of politeness and careful speech', veritable pillars of society.

Although he does his duty in the context of the family, respects authority and maintains right, Stanley is no slavish conformist; he is resourceful (it is his idea to trap the robbers) and independent in thought ('Lower me', he said, 'and I will look for the ring'). Although underneath all this he wants to belong to a group — even after his achievement of fame at the capture of the thieves, Stanley senses the loneliness which being different can produce. He is very much a little boy of that age level in which being accepted by one's peers is so very important. It is fitting, maybe, that his brother Arthur, who has been jealous of Stanley's new and arresting quality is the one who has the final bright idea of bringing Stanley back to normal: he blows him up to his proper shape with a bicycle pump.

In terms of language, *Flat Stanley* is a narrative, simply told and with a logical rounded plot. It is a complete story with no end left untied. The short sentences and the simple concepts make it readily accessible to the junior reader. Its presentation and physical format alone would suggest it as a suitable book for young children. They will not be disappointed.

A More Complex Junior Novel: *The Eighteenth Emergency* by Betsy Byars (1973)

Betsy Byars' short novel is very popular with children. They read it with interest, responding to the humour, the tension, the credible working out of the plot. What is it that lifts the book to an elevated place in the estimation of children? Other books have humour, tension and a credible plot.

Possibly an important element of its appeal is the book's ability to recreate with accuracy a very recognisable problem in the lives of children: dealing with a bully who has you clearly in his sights. Mouse, like Karana in *Island of the Blue Dolphins* (1960), shows his ability to cope. Like her, he solves his problem with resourcefulness and independence and grows to a new level of maturity as a result. He is, again like Karana, at the period of middle childhood — Erikson's stage of Industry versus Inferiority — and emerges as a changed Benjie Fawley: Mouse no longer.

Mouse is a well-drawn character. He has a delightful sense of humour, true compassion for others, canine or human, and a courageous inner quality which emerges — almost unexpectedly — at the end of the novel.

It would be labouring the point to say that the language of *The Eighteenth Emergency* is perfectly aligned to the speech and experience of children. Every young reader will find him or herself there.

A Novel to Stir the Imagination: *Ronia, the Robber's Daughter* by Astrid Lindgren (1983)

This novel is by the celebrated Swedish author whose books about Pippi Longstocking have been favourites for many years. Like Pippi, Ronia is a very spirited heroine, capable of physical feats and with great strength of character. The setting, however, is different, for Ronia inhabits a fairy tale landscape of wild mountains and rivers, inhabited by harpies and dwarfs. Ronia's father, Matt, is a proud and fierce robber chief with a loathing and rivalry for Borka, the neighbouring chief.

A secret friendship develops between Ronia and Birk, the son of Borka. As well as following their adventures in overcoming the challenges of nature and of such creatures as harpies, the reader becomes involved in the moral dilemma of their defying their parents' wishes.

A reader of approximately ten to thirteen years will find much to absorb him or her in this book. There are the details of survival in the forest and the struggles of Ronia and Birk to establish themselves as individuals as well as members of their families. And the growth of their friendship and love for each other is not without humorous incidents.

A Novel for the Older Primary School Child: *Little Brother* by Allan Baillie (1985)

The story of Vithy's fight for survival in present-day Kampuchea certainly requires of the young Australian reader a 'skill and willingness to see the viewpoint of others'. Much is strange: the jungles and foodstuffs, the fear of strangers in this war-torn country. But the underlying themes of search for his brother and for the border engage the reader in issues of justice. And the practical methods used by Vithy are of great interest, including his resourcefulness in building a bike from a collection of bolts, rubber and old metal.

And Allan Baillie is certainly encouraging his readers in their search for true values when he describes Vithy's arrival at the deserted city of Phnom Penh, formerly so rich and vital:

> He walked slowly towards the centre of the city, feeling colder with each step. He passed many cars left by the side of the road, smashed, dented, sometimes burnt. A touch of wind whirled paper out of the gutter. Vithy was watching more paper money than he'd ever seen in his life littering the street ...

The author has succeeded in demonstrating the futility of money in such circumstances. In the book as a whole he has also succeeded, one would hope, in making the secure Australian child of upper primary school age more understanding of those who have experienced life as refugees.

A Young Adult Novel: *Playing Beatie Bow* by Ruth Park (1980)

Playing Beatie Bow adds many new dimensions to the young adult novel. It is a fantasy, an historical novel, a social one and an adventure story, all in one. At its centre is Abigail Kirk aged fourteen, 'a hot-headed rag of a child' who comes to physical and emotional maturity as a result of her journey back in time to Victorian Sydney.

Abigail establishes her identity by the end of the novel: she has struggled and emerged strengthened. The story is complex and requires the intellectual ability of formal operational thought to deal with its abstractions and subtle interplay of personalities and issues which abound in the work. The novel allows the reader to explore the lives of a different family from Abigail's own in a different historical period. Her experiences with them allow her to transpose a new and developed set of values to her modern family, to which she returns in the latter part of the book. Her early challenge to her mother's beliefs is softened by exposure, struggle and suffering: her movement to mature moral autonomy is fully realised.

The novel is strikingly mature and frank in its exploration of Abigail's path to maturity. It explores the questions of awakening love and loyalty and provides an effective picture of emotional growth. It also tells a good story. Its action is fast and gripping and its language rich and varied. The appeal of this book is not hard to fathom. It would be difficult for any young adult reader to put down.

A Novel for the Senior Reader: *The True Story of Lilli Stubeck* by James Aldridge (1985)

The reader is called upon to exercise mature intellectual skill in reading this novel. The analysis of complex characters and character relationships in a tightly-controlled plot is in itself a task for a reader who is capable of what Piaget calls formal operational thought.

The novel likewise appeals to the reader's sense of moral autonomy. The book is essentially about Lilli, a person of strong moral character, and her ability to preserve her integrity. She is only bowed by illness and remains a person who establishes and firms her personal identity. A reader is caught by the force of the interaction between Lilli Stubeck and Miss Dalgleish and suffers vicariously as the battle of wills is waged between them.

This is a powerful book in other ways: it recreates a period in Australia's past and reconstructs an imaginative locality which is as clear to the reader as a photograph; it delineates and pinpoints the social issues of wealth, poverty and prejudice in a little country town and holds the reader firmly in the grip of the narrative. The suspense is maintained to the end, as the narrator in the best use of this technique brings the story to a close.

The novel stretches the reader: in its language, its emotional power, its ability to produce a fictional world which both extends and enriches the reader's mind: certainly the right book for many young adult or adult readers.

All the books referred to in this chapter have literary qualities which transcend appeal to a narrow age range. In fact, almost all of them have something of value to offer to the adult reader. Books which are written specifically to meet the needs of a particular age group are usually, at best, undistinguished.

REFERENCES

Bennett, Jill, *Learning to Read with Picture Books*. Stroud: Thimble Press, 1979.
Butler, Dorothy, *Babies Need Books*. London: Bodley Head, 1980.
Meek, Margaret, *Learning to Read*. London: Bodley Head, 1982.

BOOKS REFERRED TO IN THE CHAPTER

Ahlberg, Janet and Allan, *Each Peach Pear Plum*. Kestrel/Picture Books.
Aldridge, James, *The True Story of Lilli Stubeck*. Hyland House.
Baillie, Allan, *Little Brother*. Nelson.
Bayley, Nicola, *Nursery Rhymes*. Cape/Puffin.
Blake, Quentin, *Mister Magnolia*. Cape/Picture Lions.
Briggs, Raymond, *The Mother Goose Treasury*. Hamish Hamilton/Puffin.
Burningham, John, *Come Away from the Water, Shirley*. Cape/Picture Lions.
——————, *Mr Gumpy's Outing*. Cape/Puffin.
Brown, Jeff, *Flat Stanley*. Methuen.
Byars, Betsy, *The Eighteenth Emergency*. Bodley Head/Puffin.
Carle, Eric, *The Very Hungry Caterpillar*. Hamish Hamilton/Puffin.
Carroll, Lewis, *Alice's Adventures in Wonderland*. Macmillan.
Coerr, Eleanor, *Sadako and the Thousand Paper Cranes*. Hodder & Stoughton.
Craft, Ruth, *The Winter Bear*. Collins/Picture Lions.
Edwards, Hazel, *There's a Hippopotamus on Our Roof Eating Cake*. Hodder & Stoughton.
French, Simon, *Cannily, Cannily*. Angus & Robertson.
Ginsburg, Mirra, *Across the Stream*. Julia MacRae/Puffin.
Gleeson, Libby, *Eleanor Elizabeth*. Angus & Robertson.
Hutchins, Pat, *Rosie's Walk*. Bodley Head/Puffin.
Jones, Harold, illustrator, compiler, Kathleen Lines, *Lavender's Blue*. Oxford University Press.
Kelleher, Victor, *Master of the Grove*. Kestrel/Puffin.
Kipling, Rudyard, *The Just So Stories*. Macmillan.
Klein, Robin, *Hating Alison Ashley*. Puffin.
——————, *Thing*. Oxford University Press.
Le Cain, Errol, *Hiawatha's Childhood*. Faber.
Lewis, C.S., *The Lion, the Witch and the Wardrobe*. Bles/Lions.
Lindgren, Astrid, *Ronia, The Robber's Daughter*. Viking/Puffin.
Lindsay, Norman, *The Magic Pudding*. Angus & Robertson.
Lobel, Arnold, *Mouse Tales*. World's Work/Puffin.
Magorian, Michelle, *Goodnight Mister Tom*. Puffin.
Maris, Ron *Are You There, Bear?* Julia MacRae.
——————, *My Book*. Julia MacRae.
Maruki, Toshi, *The Hiroshima Story*. Black.
Murphy, Jill, *On the Way Home*. Macmillan.
——————, *The Worst Witch*. Allison & Busby/Puffin.
Nicoll, Helen, *Mog at the Zoo*. Heinemann.
O'Dell, Scott, *Island of the Blue Dolphins*. Puffin.
Ormerod, Jan, *Sunshine*. Kestrel/Puffin.
Park, Ruth, *The Big Brass Key*. Hodder & Stoughton.
——————, *Playing Beatie Bow*. Nelson/Puffin.
Potter, Beatrix, *The Tale of Jemima Puddle Duck*. Frederick Warne.

Rodda, Emily, *Something Special.* Angus & Robertson.
Scott-Mitchell, Clare, *When a Goose Meets a Moose.* Methuen.
Streatfeild, Noel, *Thursday's Child.* Collins/Lions.
Tolkien, J.R.R., *The Hobbit.* Allen & Unwin.
Wagner, Jenny, *John Brown, Rose and the Midnight Cat.* Kestrel/Puffin.
Watanabe, Shigeo, *How Do I Put It On?* Bodley Head/Puffin.
Wildsmith, Brian, *Mother Goose.* Oxford University Press.

SOME RECENT PUBLICATIONS

PICTURE BOOKS

Adams, Jeanie, *Pigs and Honey.* Omnibus, 1990.
Ahlberg, Janet and Allan, *The Jolly Postman or Other People's Letters.* Heinemann, 1986.
Baillie, Allan and Tanner, Jane, *Drac and the Gremlin.* Viking/Kestrel, 1988.
Baker, Jeannie, *Where the Forest Meets the Sea.* Julia McCrae, 1987.
Base, Graeme, *Animalia.* Viking/Kestrel, 1987.
Burningham, John, *Oi! Get Off Our Train.* Jonathan Cape, 1989.
Dodd, Lynley, *Hairy Maclary from Donaldson's Dairy.* Mallinson Rendel/Era 1983.
Graham, Bob, *Crusher is Coming!* Viking, 1988.
——————, *Grandad's Magic.* Puffin, 1989.
Hunt, Nan and Niland, Deborah, *Families Are Funny.* Collins/Ann Ingram, 1990.
Lester, Alison, *Imagine.* Allen and Unwin, 1989.
——————, *The Journey Home.* OUP, 1989.
Mahy, Margaret and Allen, Jonathan, *The Great White Man-Eating Shark.* Dent, 1989.
Murphy, Jill, *Five Minutes Peace.* Walker, 1986.
Rosen, Michael and Oxenbury, Helen, *We're Going on a Bear Hunt.* Walker, 1989.
Waddell, Martin and Dale, Penny, *Once There Were Giants.* Walker, 1989.
——————, *Rosie's Babies.* Walker, 1990.
Wild, Margaret and Vivas, Julie, *The Very Best of Friends.* Margaret Hamilton, 1989.

BOOKS FOR THE OLDER READER

Baillie, Allan, *Hero.* Penguin, 1990.
——————, *Mates and Other Stories.* Omnibus, 1989.
Banks, Lynne Reid, *The Indian in the Cupboard.* Dent, 1981; Lions, 1988.
Caswell, Brian, *Merryl of the Stones.* UQP, 1989.
Duder, Tessa, *Alex.* OUP, 1987.
Gleeson, Libby, *I Am Susannah.* Angus and Robertson, 1987.
Hathorn, Libby, *Thunderwith.* Heinemann, 1989.
Jennings, Paul, *Unreal! Eight Surprising Stories.* Puffin, 1985.
Klein, Robin, *Came Back to Show You I Could Fly.* Viking/Kestrel, 1989.
Lowry, Lois, *Number the Stars.* Collins, 1989.
——————, *Rabble Starkey.* Houghton Mifflin, 1987.
Marsden, John, *So Much to Tell You.* McVitty, 1987.
Paterson, Katherine, *Park's Quest.* Gollancz, 1988.
Rubinstein, Gillian, *Skymaze.* Omnibus/Puffin, 1989.
——————, *Space Demons.* Omnibus/Puffin, 1986.

AN IDEAL READING PROGRESS

APPROXIMATE AGE

1   **Catalogues**

    b is for bear — Bruna (Methuen)

    Rhymes

    Mother Goose — Wildsmith (Oxford)
    This Little Puffin — Matterson (Puffin)

2   **Simple Picture Story Books**

    — introducing the experience of narrative progress as the page is turned:

3   — multi-sensory: *The Blanket* — Burningham (Cape)
    Rosie's Walk — Hutchins (Puffin)
    Where's Spot? — Hill (Puffin)
    The Very Hungry Caterpillar — Carle (Puffin)

    — with repetition: *Each Peach Pear Plum* — Ahlberg (Lion)
    Goodnight Owl — Hutchins (Puffin)
    The Three Billy Goats Gruff — Galdone (World's Work)

4   — with a central character the child can identify with:

    Harry the Dirty Dog — Zion (Puffin)
    Where the Wild Things Are — Sendak (Puffin)
    The Tale of Peter Rabbit — Potter (Warne)

    Books the Young Reader can Read Alone

    Meg and Mog — Nicoll (Puffin)

    Books to Look at and Read Together

5   — poetry: *When We Were Very Young* —

CHILDREN AND THEIR BOOKS: THE RIGHT BOOK FOR THE RIGHT CHILD   55

Roger was a Razor Fish — Bennett (Hippo)
The Owl who was Afraid of the Dark — Tomlinson (Puffin)
Flat Stanley — Brown (Magnet)
Tintin in America — Hergé (Magnet)
The Iron Man — Hughes (Faber)
The Worst Witch — Murphy (Puffin)
Fantastic Mr Fox — Dahl (Puffin)

The Worst Witch — Murphy (Puffin)
Fantastic Mr Fox — Dahl (Puffin)

Apples from Hurricane Street — Scott-Mitchell (Methuen)

— wordless books:
The Snowman — Briggs (Puffin)
Naughty Nancy — Goodall (Macmillan)

— stories from folk tale traditions:
The Giant Devil-Dingo — Roughsey (Collins)
The Tomten — Lindgren (Kestrel)
The Fairy Tale Treasury — Haviland (Puffin)

6

— more involved picture story books:
The Church Mouse — Oakley (Macmillan)
Jim and the Beanstalk — Briggs (Puffin)

7   — 'chapter' books to be read as serials:
Winnie the Pooh — Milne (Magnet)
Ramona the Pest — Cleary (Puffin)
Charlotte's Web — White (Puffin)
Finn Family Moomintroll — Jansson (Puffin)
The Lion, the Witch and the Wardrobe — Lewis (Lion)
The Little House in the Big Woods

8 — picture book format with mature themes:
   Feelings — Aliki (Bodley Head)
   The Angel with a Mouth-organ — Mattingley (Hodder)

9 ## Myths, Legends and Fairy tales

   Gods, Men and Monsters — Gibson (Hodder)
   King Arthur and his Knights of the Round Table — Lancelyn Green (Puffin)

10 ## Funny Books

   The Twenty-Seventh Annual African Hippopotamus Race — Lurie (Puffin)
   The Great Piratical Rumbustification — Mahy (Puffin)
   Asterix the Gaul — Goscinny (Hodder)
   The Eighteenth Emergency — Byars (Puffin)
   Midnite — Stow (Puffin)

11 ## Fantasy Stories it would be a Pity to Miss

   The Wind in the Willows — Grahame (Magnet)
   The Hobbit — Tolkien (Allen & Unwin)
   The Nargun and the Stars — Wrightson (Puffin)

12 ## Novels Dealing with the Survival of Young Characters

   The Present Takers — Chambers (Magnet)
   Julie of the Wolves — George (Puffin)
   Climb a Lonely Hill — Norman (Lion)
   Little Brother — Baillie (Nelson)
   Slake's Limbo — Holman (Lion)
   I am David — Holm (Magnet)

CHILDREN AND THEIR BOOKS: THE RIGHT BOOK FOR THE RIGHT CHILD   57

13 Exploration of Relationships

   The Secret Garden — Burnett (Puffin)
   The October Child — Spence (Oxford)
   Goodnight Mr Tom — Magorian (Puffin)
   Homecoming — Voigt (Lion)

14 Teenage Novels

   — dealing with troubling themes:
   I am the Cheese — Cormier (Lion)
   Children of the Dust — Lawrence (Bodley Head)

15 — developing the world of fantasy:
   The Wizard of Earthsea — Le Guin (Penguin)

Note: The paperback publisher has been quoted wherever possible but most of the books are also available in hardcover

PART II
THE NATURE OF CHILDREN'S LITERATURE

4 FIRST FLIGHT: FOR THE VERY YOUNG

PATRICIA SCOTT

> ... children who are not told stories and who are not read to will have few reasons for wanting to learn to read.
>
> Haley

THE NEED FOR STORIES

Babies Need Books — so runs the title of a book that has enriched our understanding of the responses of even very young children. Most educationists now accept this idea; perhaps not so many recognise, or actually state, that what babies really need is the *contents* of books: stories, with or without pictures, in prose and verse, and of many different kinds.

Books are the storehouse. Babies require a genie to unlock the store and share its riches. They are dependent upon others to select, buy, borrow and give them books and to share the contents.

A child in a house without books may be lucky enough to hear a wealth of traditional stories, rhymes and ballads told and sung throughout the day, but such opportunities are today rare. However, it is arguable that such a child will develop a better sense of story than the one who has lots of picture books but few or no fairy tales. As Tate (1984: 10) points out, 'modern stories are often very different in design from the traditional ones'.

The child who experiences songs, rhymes and stories in abundance, with and without books, is truly fortunate. A sense of story comes from hearing lots of stories, particularly fairy tales with their strong patterns and use of repetition. But family stories centring around the child or some other family member, and book stories, both those from picture books such as Pamela Allen's *Who Sank the Boat?* (1982) and those from collections such as Jean Chapman's *Tell Us Tales* (1978) are also important.

BOOKS AND THE PRESCHOOL CHILD

Because we have moved away from oral traditions, books rather than stories are seen as central by many, and book-related experiences are important for the preschool child. From listening and looking while he hears stories read, the child learns, without effort, the relationship between printed and spoken words:

> The child from a book-oriented home has normally developed high expectations of print, knowing that books bring him a special range of pleasures which he can obtain in no other way.
> He has built a set of language models for the written dialect and practised these models across his own tongue to the point where they have become part of his native language.
>
> (Holdaway 1980: 6)

The child has also learnt how to hold a book; how it is arranged and how the pages are turned; how print is usually sequenced in our books; quite often when he reaches school, he has learnt painlessly how to read and is ready to leap away. And, as shown in Clark's (1976) survey, he is likely to go on and do well throughout his schooling.

Perhaps, most importantly, the child from such a background knows that sounds, rhymes, rhythms and ideas, that catch and hold his imagination, can be caught and held in a thing called a book. Caught and held and reproduced again and again by those who share books with him.

If the stories read to him come from all kinds of books, story collections and longer stories as well as picture stories, he is more likely to realise the key role of *print*. And — an important consideration — he is likely to develop his own visual imagination. Many children come to our schools, and even pass through them, without learning to picture things for themselves. We have embraced pictorial symbols and audio-visual media without considering that they almost certainly limit a child's imagination in some ways while extending it in others.

There is a splendidly rich range of picture stories and illustrated books but few children meet even a small part of the riches and rarely is there an aware and pictorially literate 'other' to help them explore this material and develop its creative potential.

Concerning the media, Haley (1971) made an observation that should receive careful consideration: 'The audio-visual assault on our children's senses interferes with their *spontaneous play with words, ideas, images and objects*'.

BEGINNINGS

Ideally, stories begin from birth with nursery and play rhymes. (In American texts, you will find them referred to as Mother Goose rhymes). And, ideally, this will be a natural part of life rather than something that has to be done with a book close by to help with the words. It is sharing in loving, playful intimacy, while bathing, dressing and changing, that brings delighted response.

Another good introduction to the world of story is *peepo* — the reference is to the game rather than to the Ahlbergs' picture book. This first of baby games introduces him or her to the pleasure of safe surprise. Babies learn to anticipate, to expect that something will be repeated for their pleasure, and to know the satisfaction of repetition with variation, the underlying pattern for most of the favourite nursery tales that they will meet later.

PATTERNS

Pattern recognition is at the heart of all learning. Whether the patterns are formed by sounds — rhymes, music, a ticking clock — colours, shapes, pictorial symbols or facial features, early recognition of their existence gives a child an important start on the road to learning about all things.

Pattern with variation is also important and accounts for the fascination of some tunes, of wind on water, flickering fires and a dancing mobile hanging above a cot. Brian Wildsmith is one artist who has shared his own delight in colour and shape patterns in books a younger child can enjoy.

SOUNDS

Watch infants as they meet new sounds or variations of familiar ones. Try making popping noises, rolling your r's, or clicking tongue against palate. Attention is usually instant, particularly if you produce a range of such noises.

This pleasure in sounds can be exploited through books such as Pat Hutchins' *Goodnight, Owl!* (1973), Peter Spier's *Gobble, Growl, Grunt* (1971) and Pamela Allan's *Bertie and the Bear* (1983).

WORDS

A word on its own can be mouth-filling and satisfying. 'Yak' and 'iguana' are creatures outside the world of the average infant but they may be intrigued by the word sound. These are naming words that appear in Brian Wildsmith's *ABC* (1962). Children trying them for the first time often seem to be tasting and feeling them as they might some strange food.

New words that are not naming ones may need to be heard several times in context, and sometimes in several contexts, before their meaning develops. This is not a reason for avoiding them, but rather for using them whenever appropriate. Their meaning can be extended by an aware adult: 'Let's put on our gum-boots, then we can squelch through the mud, just like in *Mr Gumpy's Motor Car*' (1973).

When a child asks the meaning of a word, it is usually possible to answer briefly and to tie it back to the original context: 'Frugal? Well, we haven't much money at present, so we have to be careful with what we have; we have to be frugal. Hunca Munca didn't waste anything' (referring to Beatrix Potter's *The Tale of Two Bad Mice* (1904)).

If you do not know the meaning, then look it up in front of the child: 'I'll look in this big book that is all about words. It will tell us'. But only do this if the child wants to know and asks the meaning.

Berg (1977: 23) seems to suggest that *yak* and *queen* are inappropriate word/image combinations for an alphabet book. But Butler (1979) records several examples of Cushla's responses to Dick Bruna's *b is for bear* (1967), which contained images well outside her limited experience. And, in *Babies Need Books*, she tells of a grandson's visit to the zoo and his rediscovery of Zebra, Giraffe, Lion, until then known only through his books (1980: 24).

In general, it is adults, not children who are disturbed by unfamiliar words and images. We nearly always underestimate children's potential ability to cope with ideas. Or else we fail to facilitate understanding.

LANGUAGE

Words may exist in isolation or be strung together without meaning. Language implies words that take meaning from, and give it to, each other. 'Language is a social act' (Mackay 1976: 59) and one best acquired in the home in lively family discussion and through stories. In some homes there may be few or no books but a rich on-going dialogue and lots of stories. The Irish writer, Edna O'Brien, came from such a background.

But any family, even one where language is imaginatively used, can add to a child's pleasure in it through books. Most small children are unlikely, on their own initiative, to use phrases such as 'a big, roaring, yellow, whiskery lion' but once they have heard Margaret Mahy's *A Lion in the Meadow* (1969), the words might well become part of family lore. Margaret Mahy loves the colour and rhythm of language and this makes her stories and poems a delight to share with all ages. Many of them are in picture books but also appear in collections.

In another picture book, *Rosie's Walk* (1968), the author/artist Pat Hutchins uses very few words — only thirty-two of them — but the story is rhythmically phrased and satisfying to share. It is a perfect picture story for the two to six-year-old. Language and pictures are more closely integrated than we usually find and the text carries only half the story. But that half is complete in itself; try it aloud and see.

It is also a story that lends itself well to use as a play sequence when feeding or playing with an infant at the spoon-feeding stage. Used in this way, Rosie's personal story can be familiar even before the infant meets her in the wider context. It also lends itself well to group play: learn the words and use them in Hutchins' own phrases.

Stories like John Burningham's *Mr Gumpy's Outing* (1970),

Maurice Sendak's *Where the Wild Things Are* (1963), and Jenny Wagner's *John Brown, Rose and the Midnight Cat* (1977) are enjoyed by all ages, not just because they have good plots, themes to which we can relate, and attractive illustrations, but also, most importantly, because they are a pleasure to read aloud; their authors use language well. Get someone to read them out while you look away or close your eyes.

They use language with feeling, language which involves us emotionally. And this involvement is essential if language is to *live* and *work* for a child. Too often we approach language and language-related skills as though intellectual understanding were the sole key to them.

Berg (1977:9) gives an example of a baby 'concentrating ... on the *emotional feel* of communication which is exactly what children a little older do when they come to writing and reading, in natural loving conditions'. (Emphasis in the original but note the last phrase which also needs emphasis for our purposes).

THE PRINTED BOOK

While book design is important at all levels, it is particularly so in books intended for sharing with the younger child. Pictures and text should relate to each other not only in terms of the story but aesthetically and this includes their relationship to the page, and the use of space.

Look at *Where the Wild Things Are, The Tale of Peter Rabbit* (1905) and Quentin Blake's *Mister Magnolia* (1980) and notice how their author/artists have set out each double page spread. Sendak's use of space is fascinating to study — notice how, as the fantasy takes over, the illustrations use more and more space and then contract again as Max 'returns'. The realistic comment at the end, 'and it was still hot', has no accompanying picture.

PRINTED TEXT

Some common faults in printed text include:
— Print that is too small or too large in relation to page or illustrations.
— Poorly-spaced letters. Often it is the spacing rather than the size of the print that is at fault.
— Words that cannot be easily read because they are overlaid by the illustrations, something that happens in otherwise attractive books such as Leo Lionni's *Swimmy* (1973).
— Failure to observe the phrasing when setting out the text. Sometimes a phrase, or even a word, will be broken at the page turn.
— Lines of text that are too long for easy reading. This matters less when there are only one or two lines to a page.

These things may seem unimportant at a level where it is not a child who will be reading the story. But try reading aloud to a preschool or play group, or to just one child, from a poorly-designed book, and you will see *why* it matters.

Remember, too, that many of those whom we hope will share these books with children may not be expert at reading and may have little experience of reading aloud. And, an important point: the same books will also be tried by beginning readers.

ILLUSTRATIONS

Contrary to some statements which you will read, children tolerate and enjoy a wide range of illustrations. And, at least from twelve months onward, they prefer to have some variety.

At a certain stage they may show preference for a particular kind of illustration or a particular artist. I have vivid memories of a three-year-old boy who, when visiting the library, would take all the Wildsmith books from the display shelves, arrange them on a low bench, and spend long periods solemnly exploring each one, often returning to an earlier one to make some comparison.

Most writers suggest that the young child needs uncomplicated images, such as Bruna presents, but overall pattern, rather than complexity of detail, may be the important factor. Also, much probably depends on how pictures are shared and by whom. Many mothers believe it has to be a careful testing of the baby's ability to recognise objects and recall their names but this may be too limiting.

The pleasure and rewards for child and sharer are increased if the latter weaves simple stories around pictures; stories which name the objects depicted and bring them together in a narrative that refers back to the child.

There are many little stories now available in books specifically designed for use with infants. John Burningham, Helen Oxenbury and Brian Wildsmith have written and illustrated stories which allow for the limited concentration of the under-two's, or the older infant with little experience of story. The bear stories of Susanna Gretz, with their bright, clear colours and those of Shigeo Watanabe which are quieter but relate closely to the experiences of a small child, are particularly appealing.

SENSORY RESPONSES

In the early years, especially, story and book sharing should involve the child physically as well as emotionally: being cuddled during a simple, flowing story; tickled, dandled, bounced, danced or tossed into the air while a rhyme is sung or chanted. Most parents do these things instinctively.

It is important to recognise that the enjoyment of books may include a sensory response to the book as object. Many adults who read for pleasure will speak of loving the smell and feel of some books, possibly because such sensations are associated with memories of losing oneself in stories. This kind of sensory response has nothing to do with 'smellies' and 'feelies' and with books that have tags to pull and levers to push. Such books have their uses but rarely offer the total imaginative involvement of a good story.

However, at least two books have made creative use of holes, employing them as an integral part of the narrative. Eric Carle's *The Very Hungry Caterpillar* (1970) is one of the most widely-known and loved of picture stories for the preschool child and repays study to see the many things it includes: it is a counting book, an object recognition book, a day-naming book; it is phrased well and it is a good story with attractive illustrations. *Peepo!* by Janet and Allan Ahlberg (1981) is less of a story than a ramble through a world that, while superficially different, is very familiar to the infant. And, as happens when you take a small child rambling you must expect him to linger, side-track and double back as you go through the book.

IMAGES AND OBJECTS

A child actively involved with his family and surroundings shows a complex range of responses long before he walks and talks. The observant parent or carer will learn much about a child (and about children generally) from just watching and thinking about the child's expressions and actions.

If we make the most of images and objects in the house and environment, picture books are less important in the first couple of years. As already emphasised, the vital thing is to share stories told in lively language. This is not meant to suggest that picture books should not be used, but rather that their use is not of prime importance.

LOST FOR WORDS

To put it another way, most people today, other than those with severe sight handicaps, live in a world that is full of things to see, however dreary some of these may be. But many are *starved for words*. They lack the words to describe what they see or how they feel or, having some words, they lack the skill to pattern them into an interesting anecdote or to string them together into a story sequence. Their experiences with conversation and listening to stories have never involved them in an emotional response. They have never talked and argued in word-extended give-and-take with family and peers. They have never been enthralled by story in a way that returns them refreshed and with new awareness to the everyday world. They have never been involved in the basic communication game of playing with words: '... the efficient learning of a language depends upon our playing with it, savouring it, messing around with it' (Creber 1972: 68–9)

NONSENSE

Nonsense is a special kind of playing with words which has tremendous appeal for young children and which 'strengthens in the child's mind a sense of the real', (Chukovsky 1968: 90):

> The Owl and the Pussy-cat went to sea
> In a beautiful pea-green boat,
> They took some honey and plenty of money
> Wrapped up in a five-pound note.

At eight to nine months, Cushla was responding to the 'rhythmic rhyming text' of Lear's poem (Butler 1979: 28), and it continued to give pleasure as she grew older. For it is rhythmic, rhyming *and* nonsensical, like most of the best-loved poems for children. Poets who are enjoyed by young (and old) children, all share the ability to play with words and ideas as well as sounds and rhythms. Look at the poems of Eleanor Farjeon, Walter de la Mare, David McCord, Ogden Nash, Margaret Mahy, C.J. Dennis and Doug MacLeod; look at the poetry chosen by children for *I Like This Poem* edited by Kaye Webb (1979); look again at nursery rhymes. The playful possibilities of language are celebrated with joy in all these instances.

Nonsense is also plainly a part of favourite stories. Whoever met a whole lot of animals going for a ride in a boat or a car, as they do in *Mr Gumpy's Outing, Who Sank the Boat?* and *Mr Gumpy's Motor Car?* Children of all ages recognise the absurdity and love it. Chukovsky (1968) suggests in his fourth chapter that enjoyment of nonsense is a sign of developing maturity and is dependent upon the child knowing that it *is* nonsense; in other words, he must have a sense of the real before he can laugh at the idea of turning it inside out and upside down.

FINGER OR PLAY RHYMES

These belong to all cultures and have an important role in helping a child understand his physical self and his identity as an individual. They are usually his first introduction to play and play is the basis of much that is important in life. Lieberman (1977) sees playfulness as lying at the heart of such things as a sense of humour, spontaneity, joy in life, imagination and creativity.

Some of these rhymes, such as 'Pat-a-cake, Pat-a-cake', are likely to be found in any comprehensive collection of nursery rhymes such as Raymond Briggs' *The Mother Goose Treasury* (1966) and Kathleen Lines' *Lavender's Blue* (1954); or in song books such as Timothy John's *The Great Song Book* (1978) which is superbly illustrated by Tomi Ungerer. Others may appear only in collections such as *This Little Puffin* ... (1982) by Elizabeth Matterson and *Merrily, Merrily*. These include simple tunes when appropriate and indicate how to share the rhymes. A short, attractively-presented collection is Sarah Williams' *Round and Round the Garden* (1983).

The Ladybird series Learning with Traditional Rhymes offers moderately-priced little books that include photographic and other illustrations. Dorothy and John Taylor's *Finger Rhymes* (1976), for example, has photographs that show the absorbed and delighted interplay of mother and child.

NURSERY RHYMES

> The English nursery rhymes are often only music, singing vowels, repetition of sound, simple cadences stressed, full and sonorous rhymes. They are not unconscious of the fact that by placing rhythm at the beginning of life they are conforming to the general order of the universe. They have a harmony all of their own that is strange, mocking and tender. The sense is of less importance than the sound.
>
> (Hazard 1947: 81)

Hazard was a French Academician, who saw nursery rhymes as belonging more to the peoples of northern Europe and, in particular, the English. While children's rhymes and songs are found everywhere, no other culture seems to have invented, or taken from other areas of its heritage, such a rich and varied store of rhymes to share with its young. Something of their history can be learnt from Opie (1951) and Baring-Gould (1967). But you do not need to know their history to make the best use of them. Unselfconscious delight in their sounds and rhythms is the best approach to their use.

The Opies are recognised as the outstanding authorities in this area and their collections include some specifically intended for family sharing. The lively and attractive collection illustrated by Raymond Briggs, *The Mother Goose Treasury* (1966), has been based on the Opie selections. Nursery rhymes have always attracted illustrators and any listing includes some of the outstanding artists in the field of children's books: Kate Greenaway, Beatrix Potter, L. Leslie Brooke, Arthur Rackham, Feodor Rojankovsky and Brian Wildsmith are just a few.

In Australia, neither publishers nor artists seem to be interested in this area, although we have excellent poetry collections for children. *When a Goose Meets a Moose* by Clare Scott-Mitchell (1980) is a selection of verse which includes some nursery favourites. Two collections of rhymes and stories, specifically planned for this age group by Patricia Scott, include the appropriate nursery rhymes, *I Had a Little Hen* (1981) and *Pigs Everywhere* (1982).

A natural part of family sharing can involve rhymes chanted or sung almost any time through the day, in response to various situations. Recommended collections for family sharing include *The Mother Goose Treasury, Lavender's Blue, The Puffin Book of Nursery Rhymes* and *The Mother Goose Book*. They are best shared with one or two children at a time if you want them to enjoy the illustrations.

Smaller selections, such as David Mackay's *Sally Go Round the Sun* (1974) and Nicholas Tucker's *Mother Goose Lost* (1971), allow a child to have his own rhyme book and love it to pieces without causing too many traumas. Exploring a book often includes licking, chewing, crumpling and tearing it in the early stages, but most children quickly learn to take care of books.

ALPHABET AND COUNTING BOOKS

These may or may not be in story form; and any story may be quite brief, like Maurice Sendak's *One Was Johnny* (1962) or more extended, as John Yeoman's *Sixes and Sevens* (1976). The latter has strong appeal for seven or eight-year-olds. As with all books for the pre-school child, the emphasis should be on enjoyment when selecting and sharing this material. A child's pleasure will come from delight in rhyme or story (often only half-understood) as much as from pictures. The baby giggling and squirming while someone gently chants 'One, Two, Buckle My Shoe' while drying him, knows nothing about buckles and shoes but a lot about what gives him sensual pleasure. When he gets to the one-word stage, he is likely to cry 'more' as soon as you finish. Many of the counting rhymes, in particular, lend themselves to play, and the alphabet rhymes and stories can often be gleefully chanted as in the case of Maurice Sendak's *Alligators All Around* (1962).

Other books in these categories lend themselves more to exploring together when the child is beginning to enjoy this activity. Simple alphabet books such as *b is for bear*, Robert Broomfield's *The Baby Animal ABC (1968)* and Brian Wildsmith's *ABC* (1962) can be shared from an early age. And the adult who is not intimidated by Mitsumasa Anno's intellectual approach to illustrations may be surprised at how much an infant of two will enjoy looking for things once he has learnt that *Anno's Counting Book* (1975), for example, allows him to really *explore*.

John Burningham has recently produced a Number Play series which lives up to its name and is fun to use with a pictorially alert infant. His *Just Cats* (1983), for example, can be used as a wordless picture story to be expanded by the sharer, or as a gentle introduction to numbers up to five.

Brian Wildsmith's superbly-illustrated *ABC* marked a turning point in the use of colour in picture books and is still one of the most rewarding of pictorial alphabet books.

The Nilands have produced both a counting and an alphabet book: *Birds on a Bough* (1975) and *The ABC of Monsters* (1976). Peter Pavey's highly-imaginative *One Dragon's Dream* (1978) can be returned to again and again for new discoveries.

If a child shows no interest in it, put the book aside until a later date. Notice which books and pictures appeal to him and extend his interests through similar material. Certain animals may have a great appeal: for example, the hippopotamus seems particularly to attract children. There are often picture stories you can use, in this case:

There's a Hippopotamus on the Roof Eating Cake (1980) by Hazel Edwards might be well received.

WORDLESS PICTURE STORIES

Many illustrators have tried to do away with words and compose stories that are told through pictures alone. Some most delightful and imaginative stories are included amongst these: Raymond Briggs' *The Snowman* (1979), Shirley Hughes' *Up and Up* (1979), Mitsumasa Anno's *Anno's Journey* (1977), and Pamela Allen's *Watch Me* (1985), are some.

These are books to grow with. While they are enjoyed by all ages, they can be explored with pleasure by younger children either in association with an adult, or alone. The story a child tells from such a book may differ from the one you would tell but you might be surprised by the details he observes and by the way he interprets the pictures. It is important to realise that he can explore such books in his own way and at his own pace and return to them at will for further understanding, *just as we do.*

Not all books of this kind are successful as stories and some are difficult even for a mature picture reader. Two Australian books particularly suitable for the preschool child are Jan Ormerod's *Sunshine* (1981) and *Moonlight* (1982); the former won the Picture Book of the Year Award in 1982.

CONCEPT BOOKS

In addition to those books which look at numbers and the alphabet, or which name a variety of objects, there are many small books which look at particular concepts. These can be used to stimulate awareness of more abstract concepts in ways which are fun for a small child. Jan Pienkowski's *Homes* (1983), *Time* (1983), *Weather* (1983) and other titles are colourful examples of little books that a three or four-year-old enjoys, and that can feed into his own drawings and paintings.

John Burningham, Helen Oxenbury and Dick Bruna are among artists who look at ideas from the level of small children and each has produced several small books in this area. In many cases, such books have a simple story line but others rely on parents or some 'other' to discuss and expand upon what the pictures show.

AGE LEVELS

While you cannot expect a tiny baby to want to look at pictures and respond to a picture story, he may well gurgle happily while you recite 'Three Little Kittens' or read *The Tale of Peter Rabbit*. He does *not* need to understand the words — it could just as easily be told in Latin or Swedish. His response to picture stories will depend on his having learnt to look at pictures as things that help to tell stories and, at that stage, he will also have some understanding of the story sequence. It is wise to remember that a child understands far more than he can express in words: indeed, this is true of most of us.

While age levels may have to be stated, they are *always arbitrary* and take little account of individual experiences and development. No adult should be afraid to share with a child a book that she believes will appeal to him. At best, he will enjoy it and, if he does not, then the sharer will have learnt something from the experience.

GUIDES TO AGE APPEAL

Many of the people who compile lists or write texts about using books with children may have had few opportunities to try the books with one child, let alone several. Even when they have done so, the books they select will not appeal to all children.

Two outstanding writers with a passionate but reasoned interest in this area are Leila Berg and Dorothy Butler. Their books are inspiring and should be read by all who wish to learn more. *Babies Need Books* is the best available guide not only to the books, but to the *kind* of books, that children enjoy at various ages and stages up to the age of six. Few people have had the range of opportunities to study this area and none has used the opportunity to such good purpose as Dorothy Butler.

Following the publication of *Books Before Five* (White 1954), several people have kept records of their child's reading responses, noting their likes and dislikes. These have added to our understanding of the area but must be seen as individual responses which may have wider application.

Just as what we get from our own reading is in accordance with what we bring to it (Holland 1975), so will the mutual experience of book sharing be coloured by the parent's previous experiences and ideas.

DEVELOPMENTAL STAGES

These, like age levels, should not be interpreted too literally. Some see the idea of an infant's egocentric nature as meaning he will only accept stories about himself, or that he needs lots of stories about a child of the same age, living in the same sort of surroundings and doing the same sorts of things.

Look at some of the favourite stories and this is seen to be quite incorrect. To take a few at random: *The Very Hungry Caterpillar, Rosie's Walk, Mr Gumpy's Outing,* Marjorie Flack's *The Story about Ping* (1935), Wanda Gag's *Millions of Cats* (1928) — some old people, lots of animals and scarcely a child in sight.

It is story and the imaginative use of language which are the most notable features of the universally-loved picture books.

KNOWING THE MATERIAL

Each of us who studies this area starts from the same position and, while it takes time to build up knowledge of the books and experience in their use, there is no substitute for the personal approach. 'There is no "crash course" in children's literature which will make up for deficiencies in the [student's] own reading or his love of literature' (Saxby 1974: 272).

REFERENCES

Baring-Gould, W., *The Annotated Mother Goose*. Cleveland: The World Publishing Company, 1967.
Berg, D., *Reading and Loving*. London: Routledge & Kegan Paul, 1977.
Butler, D., *Babies Need Books*. London: Bodley Head, 1980.
——————, *Cushla and Her Books*. Auckland: Hodder & Stoughton, 1979.
Chukovsky, K., *From Two to Five*. Berkeley: University of California Press, 1968.
Clark, M., *Young Fluent Readers*. London: Heinemann, 1976.
Creber, J., *Lost for Words*. Harmondsworth: Penguin, 1972.
Haley, G., 'Caldecott Acceptance Speech' *Horn Book Magazine*. August 1971.
Hazard, P., *Books Children & Men*. Boston: The Horn Book, 1947.
Holdaway, D., 'Oral Foundations of Literacy' in *Reading Around* Vol. 8, No. 1, April 1980.
Holland, N., *5 Readers Reading*. New Haven: Yale University Press, 1975.
Lieberman, J., *Playfulness: Its Relation to Imagination and Creativity*. London: Academic Press, 1977.
Mackay, D., *Help Your Child to Read and Write and More*. Harmondsworth: Penguin, 1976.
Opie, I., *The Oxford Dictionary of Nursery Rhymes*. London: Oxford University Press, 1951.
Saxby, M., *Teaching the New English in Primary School*. Sydney: Novak, 1974.
Tate, A., 'Storying in Early Language Development' in *Australian Journal of Reading* Vol. 7, No. 1,
White, D., *Books Before Five*. London: Oxford University Press, 1954.

BOOKS REFERRED TO IN THE CHAPTER

Ahlberg, Janet and Allan, *Peepo*. Bodley Head.
Allen, Pamela, *Bertie and the Bear*. Nelson.
——————, *Watch Me*. Nelson.
——————, *Who Sank the Boat?* Nelson.
Anno, Mitsumasa, *Anno's Counting Book*. Bodley Head.
——————, *Anno's Journey*. Bodley Head.
Blake, Quentin, *Mister Magnolia*. Cape.
Briggs, Raymond, *The Mother Goose Treasury*. Puffin.
——————, *The Snowman*. Hamish Hamilton.
Broomfield, Robert, *The Baby Animal ABC*. Puffin.
Bruna, Dick, *b is for bear*. Methuen.
Burningham, John, *Just Cats*. Viking.
——————, *Mr Gumpy's Motor Car*. Cape/Puffin.

——————, *Mr Gumpy's Outing*. Cape/Puffin.
Carle, Eric, *The Very Hungry Caterpillar*. Hamish Hamilton/Puffin.
Chapman, Jean, *Tell Us Tales*. Hodder & Stoughton.
Edwards, Hazel, *There's a Hippopotamus on the Roof Eating Cake*. Hodder & Stoughton.
Flack, Marjorie, *The Story About Ping*. Puffin.
Gag, Wanda, *Millions of Cats*. Puffin.
Hughes, Shirley, *Up and Up*. Puffin.
Hutchins, Pat, *Goodnight Owl!* Puffin.
——————, *Rosie's Walk*. Puffin.
Lines, Kathleen *Lavender's Blue*. Oxford.
Lionni, Leo, *Swimmy*. Random House.
Mackay, David, *Sally Go Round the Sun*. Longmans.
Matterson, Elizabeth, *This Little Puffin . . .* Young Puffin.
Mahy, Margaret, *A Lion in The Meadow*. Puffin.
——————, *A Lion in the Meadow and 5 Other Favourites*. Dent.
Niland, Deborah, *The ABC of Monsters*. Hodder & Stoughton.
——————, and Kilmeny, *Birds on a Bough*. Hodder & Stoughton.
Nursing Mothers Association of Australia, *Merrily Merrily*.
Opie, Iona and Peter, *The Puffin Book of Nursery Rhymes*. Puffin.
Ormerod, Jan, *Moonlight*. Kestrel/Puffin.
——————, *Sunshine*. Kestrel/Puffin.
Pavey, Peter, *One Dragon's Dream*. Nelson/Puffin.
Pienkowski, Jan, *Homes*. Puffin.
——————, *Time*. Puffin.
——————, *Weather*. Puffin.
Potter, Beatrix, *The Tale of Peter Rabbit*. Warne.
——————, *The Tale of Two Bad Mice*. Warne.
Provensen, Alice and Martin, *The Mother Goose Book*. Julia MacRae.
Scott, Patricia, *I Had a Little Hen*. Storytellers' Press.
——————, *Pigs Everywhere*. Storytellers' Press.
Scott-Mitchell, Clare, *When a Goose Meets a Moose*. Methuen.
Sendak, Maurice, *Alligators All Around*. Harper & Row.
——————, *One Was Johnny*. Harper & Row.
——————, *Where the Wild Things Are*. Puffin.
Spier, Peter, *Gobble, Growl, Grunt*. Doubleday.
Taylor, Dorothy and John, *Finger Rhymes*. Ladybird.
Ungerer, Tomi, illustrator, editor, Timothy John, *The Great Song Book*. Benn.
Wagner, Jenny, *John Brown, Rose and the Midnight Cat*. Puffin.
Webb, Kaye, *I Like this Poem*. Puffin.
Wildsmith, Brian, *ABC*. Oxford.
Williams, Sarah, *Round and Round the Garden*. Oxford.
Yeoman, John, *Sixes and Sevens*. Puffin.

FURTHER READING

Argent, Kerry, *At the Beach. Friends, Hiding, Surprise!* Puffin.
Brown, Marc, *Party Rhymes*. Collins.
Covernton, Jane, *Four and Twenty Lamingtons: A Collection of Australian Nursery Rhymes*. Omnibus.
Lester, Alison, *Books for Babies, Bumping and Bouncing, Crushing and Splashing, Bibs and Boots, Happy and Sad*. Viking Kestrel.
Machin, Sue and Vivas, Julie, *I Went Walking*. Omnibus.
⁀ke, Charlotte, *First Things First: A Baby's Companion*. Walker.

5 FURTHER FLIGHT: THE PICTURE BOOK

CLARE SCOTT-MITCHELL

> Fine picture books exert a far more subtle influence in the formation of reading habits than it is possible to estimate, for their integrity is unshakeable.
>
> Ann Carroll Moore
>
> A picture book really only exists when a child and a book come together, when the stream that formed in the artist's mind and heart flows through the book into the mind and heart of the child.
>
> Marcia Brown

It is hard to imagine a world in which children do not have easy access to picture books. They have become so much a normal part of the Western child's experience that it is possible to take them for granted, but a picture book that stands the test of time is a complex art form and despite the great number published each year, few survive this sifting process. Picture book, in this chapter, means a work of fiction in which text and pictures are at least of equal importance, the pictures being an integral part of each page opening or 'double spread', or a book in which pictures alone tell a story, in which case they are called, more specifically, wordless books.

THE EMERGENCE OF PICTURE BOOKS

The picture book as we know it emerged with the work of three artists who lived in England in the late nineteenth century — Walter Crane, Randolph Caldecott and Kate Greenaway. Up to this time, children's books were rare and those that were available were sheets of folded paper called 'chapbooks' because they were sold by pedlars or 'chapmen'. These were usually classic fairy tales, ballads or nursery rhymes illustrated with flat black and white woodcuts. Crude as they were by today's standards, they heralded a changing attitude towards children; it was becoming permissible for them to be entertained, not only taught exemplary ways of behaving and thinking.

Crane illustrated fairy tales such as 'Bluebeard' and 'Beauty and the Beast', using strongly-coloured wood blocks. His style was sophisticated and his interpretation of the stories was ironic and conveyed strong emotions. The texts were often adapted as verse and the illustrations provided settings and contexts for the stories which made them more accessible to young children than the verses on their own would have been.

Caldecott had a more direct influence on the future of the picture book. He took traditional nursery rhymes and treated them line by line, extending them pictorially into self-contained books. His wry sense of humour, his perception and his drawing skill have never been surpassed, and it is appropriate that the American award for the outstanding picture book of the year is called the Caldecott Medal.

Greenaway's pictures of old-fashioned children accompanied her own verses as well as traditional nursery rhymes. Her books are beautifully designed: small masterpieces. They contain gentle, idyllic representations of children in a less complicated century and still appeal, especially to those with a sense of nostalgia for a bygone era. The British picture book award is named after her.

WORDS AND PICTURES

One of the reasons for the survival of the works of the early picture book artists is the interaction of text and pictures to form a whole — the bringing together of two symbolic systems, language and pictographs, to tell a story. This implies that one medium is inadequate without the other and to some extent this is true. Oral literature (stories told by word of mouth) has existed since prehistoric times: pictures, too, told stories (as ancient tapestries, cave paintings and hieroglyphs bear witness), but the way in which the two art forms combine and overlap is a fascinating study.

Schwarcz (1982: 10) suggests that language unfolds its meaning in *time* like music. It moves in a linear progression and when written down, goes in a fixed direction; but the picture is presented all at once as a surface, an expanse. Now, although it might seem that on the one hand story is processed in a linear progression and pictures globally all at once, it is not quite as straightforward as that because when children, or adults for that matter, listen to a story being read, or read it themselves, the meanings have to be stored up and fitted together to make sense of the whole. The better we know a story, the greater is our sense of it as a whole indivisible object or unit of meaning. Paradoxically, when we have looked at a picture to gain a first impression, we focus on it section by section or piece by piece, consecutively. Although these processes are very complex, children learn to handle them very early, especially when they are given the opportunity to do so from infancy. They characteristically hear the text read by an adult and at the same time process the pictures so that the two are synchronised; the opportunity to return to the picture book many times helps them to make the story their own. They rehearse what they remember of the language, expanding or contracting the text as they reinterpret the pictures to match their own experiences of life. Every good picture book contains more than any one person can detect, because it comes from the imagination of the writer or artist and works on many levels — words and pictures independently but also together, what is written and what is illustrated, and, just as importantly, what is left unsaid (the spaces in between) activate the imagination of the individual and can contribute to the growth of the person emotionally, spiritually and intellectually.

PICTURE STORIES

From their early beginnings and for at least the next sixty years, picture books reflected a protective and gentle attitude to children. A secure childhood was regarded as imperative, if not always achieved. Beatrix Potter's small books could be held comfortably in children's hands, which made them initially approachable as physical objects. Her genius as a storyteller allowed her to retain the natural characteristics of the animals she used as her characters and at the same time make them believable as people — anthropomorphism at its best. Like her picture book predecessors, Beatrix Potter was English. Her hallmark is *style* whether in her use of language or in her finely-drawn water colours. Her prose is elegant, cadenced and rhythmical; her vocabulary is wide; she does not 'write down' to children but facilitates understanding of unfamilar words by the context of the sentences (which is after all the way language is learned). The illustrations reinforce and extend the texts — detail is provided, settings are defined, and these reflect the English countryside in which she lived for the latter part of her life. But above all, Potter wrote good stories. Her plots are interesting, full of suspense and action, and children stay with the stories to find out what happens. Her best-known character, Peter Rabbit, is at the same time rabbit and boy. Like many children, he is impatient to throw off the restrictions of parental control, so he disregards his mother's warnings, is foolhardy, but also fearful and despairing, and finally returns, chastened, to the warmth of home. In the *Tale of Peter Rabbit* (1905), Mr McGregor, the antagonist, is threatening enough for the child reader to experience relief when Peter eventually escapes from his garden. It is nevertheless a safe and secure tale, and children demand many rereadings to experience the thrill of suspense, but at the same time are assured that Peter will be home safely with his mother and sisters again.

The imperative for security in early picture books is reflected in the works of many fine author/illustrators who worked in the first half of the twentieth century, such as Wanda Gag, Marjorie Flack and Virginia Lee Burton (all American artists). Flack's Angus books are still enjoyed by children. The texts are simple yet very good to read aloud: page turning always seems to occur at the right moment. Like Peter Rabbit, Angus is irritated with being kept at home. He is curious about the outside world where he gains wisdom, and in the process, has a series of adventures and misadventures, always returning to home and safety. Flack's uncluttered artwork is designed to incorporate the type which becomes a part of the design of the double spread. In this respect, she resembles Burton, whose books such as *The Little House* (1945) have become a model of good design. Burton, however, turned from the personification of animals to the use of inanimate objects (machines and houses) as her protagonists or coprotagonists. *Mike Mulligan and his Steam Shovel* (1938) work together to overcome prejudice and the redundancy caused by technological progress. In *The Little House* Burton turns to questions of conservation and the urban sprawl and uses the house itself as the chief character. Gag's *Millions of Cats* (1928) combines mid-European-styled woodcuts printed in black and white with a rhythmical text. The recurring refrain helps to give a shape not only to the text itself but contributes to the visual shape of the book. The serious theme is softened by the humour and absurdity of the plot, all elements combining to form a masterpiece of children's literature.

COSY COMPANIONS

On the whole, realistic plots were not as common as gentle fantasies using animals or inanimate objects as characters and Lois Lenski's books are an exception to this rule. She believed that children are preoccupied with themselves and the 'real' world and need to learn about the world through realistic 'true' stories. Her large number of books, such as *Davy's Day* (1947), *Papa Small* (1957), and *The Little Fire Engine* (1947), told stories of everyday events in the lives of her characters. However, literature is always shaped experience — events are selected from an infinite number of possibilities — and Lenski chooses the benign, avoids tension and thereby eliminates any possibility of real plot development. So Davy never comes to life. We do not know how he reacts to frustration: he is always the ideal child, never a flesh and blood person, and the diagrammatic drawings tend to reinforce this impression. By comparison, Ezra Jack Keats' Peter is a child who *feels* — whether it be the joy of walking in new snow or the disappointment of discovering that his snowball had melted whilst he was in the bath, or feeling ambivalent towards a baby sister. The child or adult enjoying Keats' stories becomes involved with the lives of others, experiences empathy and discovers something about what it is to be a human being. Keats uses the illustrations to extend the emotional power of his spare texts. In *Peter's Chair* (1960), the strong colours of the collage paper convey either emotional warmth or the cold of distance — psychological distance from the mother and baby, who are bathed in warm pinks and purples; Peter, peeping from behind the door, is clad in cold blue and green. Space too — separation on the page, reinforces the emotional intensity of the story through visual symbolism.

ARDIZZONE

Edward Ardizzone was an English artist of enormous talent who had the sea in his blood and the sound of waves in his ears. The memory of his own childhood seemed to remain with him throughout his long life and resulted in an exceptional rapport with children. Ardizzone was a prolific illustrator of anthologies but he also made a significant contribution to the picture book.

His superb washed drawings of ships and sailors, storms and gales accompanied wildly ironic fantasies of child protagonists running away to sea and returning as heroic figures who rescue puppies or against difficult odds manage to bring the ship home to port. Little Tim is 'every child' who ever wished for an adventure. Ardizzone's prose is fluid, the nautical terms give an authentic flavour to the sea stories and the tone is intimate and well-cadenced. The format of these books is really a half-way house between the traditional picture book (large pictures and brief text) and the illustrated book. The texts are longer, but in addition to the more dominant illustrations numerous smaller drawings punctuate the texts so that children gaining independence in reading can have the experience of a more demanding text with the relief of stopping frequently to linger over the pictures.

WILD THINGS AND MONSTERS

By the early sixties, picture books had become firmly established as the cosy companions of children. When Maurice Sendak's *Where the Wild Things Are* was published in 1963, early childhood educators raised their voices loudly, some in praise, but many in disapproval, predicting nightmares and disturbance to children's minds and emotions. There is no doubt that *Wild Things* was a watershed: stories of mild adventure, going out from home and returning back like Angus or Ping, or exemplary striving for personal achievement like *Mike Mulligan* or *Choo Choo*, had given way to the inner conflicts of a child battling against adults, and feelings of personal frustration and powerlessness. Sendak's monsters became symbolic of 'the beast within' which some thought should not even be acknowledged (children were innocents not monsters!) and because they assumed visual shape it was thought that children would be terrified. To add to the supposed fear, the controlled and symmetrical text is overtaken by a visual fantasy which fills the page with colour and action — Max rides high in total control of his own fantastic creations, the king of all wild things who 'looks into their eyes without blinking once' and says, emphatically, 'No'. Perhaps it would not have been such a problem if Sendak had been a lesser artist. The text is like a myth (he treats serious human problems by using symbolic stories and paintings) and because of its power, it could not be ignored. Not all are convinced, even today, of the validity of Sendak's argument that such works as his are cathartic and help children cope with their own strong emotions, but whatever one's viewpoint, the genius of his work and its importance to children's literature is unquestionable. Sendak brings to his work strong memories from his own childhood. He remembers childhood as a time of conflict, doubt and struggle — a long way from Kate Greenaway's idyllic definition or Joan Walsh Anglund's sentimentality. Micky, in *In the Night Kitchen* (1970), is outraged by night noises emanating from the bakery, a residue of Sendak's own childhood responses to the idea of bakers working whilst he and his family were asleep. The inspiration for the illustrations comes from Laurel and Hardy, the comic strips of Winsor McKay as well as Disney. This is a combination bound to stir a public used to conservative and improving picture books — for improving they had been in the sense that 'right' behaviour was rewarded, wrong behaviour punished (*Ping*); effort was its own reward (*Choo Choo* and *Little Toot*); gentleness brought desired results (*Play With Me*); and conceit ended in disaster (*Millions of Cats*). Previous assumptions were now questioned, stories aimed at influencing social behaviour and conformity were set aside and in their place came the urgency of psychological equilibrium — coming to terms with the self. It was not always seen as an issue in these terms. In *Wild Things*, people worried about the monsters themselves, but in the long run, it is surely the portrayal of internal struggle by the symbolic use of monsters on the page and the unbridled dancing of child and monsters together that caused the stir.

Peter Rabbit's struggle for autonomy has much in common with Max's struggle for autonomy in *Wild Things*. Peter also resists parental constraint — he even ventured into the very garden where his father met his end and 'was put in a pie by Mrs McGregor'. His problem too was hubris and whilst Max's supper was waiting for him on his return and was still hot, Peter had only a dose of camomile tea, because he felt rather sick. So what is the difference and why should Peter Rabbit cause no stir, whilst *Wild Things* does? Is the psychological distancing of protagonist the key — rabbit, rather than human child? Is it the size and vigour of the illustrations? Or is it the monsters themselves coming from Max's fantasy instead of the human gardener as antagonist? Whatever the answer, one thing is certain — the picture book will never be the same again.

THE ART OF BURNINGHAM AND THE DIVIDED STORY

John Burningham is a contemporary of Sendak who has made a significant contribution to the genre. Bold use of colour and form give his books an easily recognisable character. While his whimsical figures are strangely anonymous, with pin-pointed eyes and much cross hatching, his literary style is deceptively simple. Read aloud, even the beginner books such as *The Baby* (1974) have a true rhythmic quality. The choice of verbs in *Mr Gumpy's Outing* (1970) contributes much interest and energy to the text but it is the irony of his writing which creates the resonances in his books — those areas of doubt and ambiguity in the spaces between text and picture. Taken at face value, *Mr Gumpy's Outing* seems to be a book about the need to conform to rules set by adults. If you don't conform then disaster follows. Perhaps Burningham is really having a quiet prod at adults and the futility of unreasonable demands which defy natural laws. (Can we expect pigs not to muck about?) Seen in conjunction with the two 'Shirley' books (*Come Away from the Water, Shirley* (1975) and *Time to Get Out of the Bath, Shirley* (1979)), Burningham's comments on adults and children are very astute. Like Sendak's, these latter books deal with children's fantasies. The picture book format serves his purpose well, the central gutter of the book dividing the picture into two halves. On the left-hand pages, text and pictures depict the literal action and interaction of child and adults, whilst on the right-hand pages, the child's thoughts take off and the narrative of her fantasies is shown without words. So the narrative is divided. There is, as Aidan Chambers remarked, (*Signal Approach to Children's Books* No. 40: 37) now a new element in children's stories, one of relativity and the question can be posed 'Which is more real; what seems to be happening on the beach or in the bath, or what is happening inside Shirley's head?'

Burningham's latest picture book *Granpa* (1984) is perhaps his most complex to date. In it he explores the poignant relationship between a small girl and her grandfather. The pair are shown in a variety of situations 'playing' together, through which Burningham is able to expose the complexities of adult-child interactions: divided texts reveal their relative fantasies, and the pictures, which alternate between sepia drawings and full colour washed drawings remind us that shared physical space is not the same thing as shared consciousness. In this book Burningham is also exploring aspects of loss and death and the everlasting circle of life.

Pat Hutchins uses a divided story in *Rosie's Walk* (1968). This very sophisticated book also seems deceptively simple. It introduces children to irony — you can't take everything you hear in a text at face value. Two stories happen simultaneously — one is told in words, the other, superimposed as it were onto the text, is told by the pictures. On one level, *Rosie's Walk* introduces to children a nice collection of prepositions. On another level, it reveals a fox in pursuit of a meal. Does the hen know she is being followed? — if not, is it by chance that she leads him into one disaster after another? And what of the goat who observes it all? This book is a fine example of design — patterns, colour co-ordination, stylised movement — but it is one in which the questions are open-ended. It never finishes: there is always something more to ask, and this characteristic applies equally to contemporary adult literature.

AUSTRALIAN PICTURE BOOKS

In Australian picture books, a comparable shift in emphasis and complexity can be seen by comparing two examples from the 1940s with two published in the 70s. Two of our early picture books are *Quippy* by Olive Mason and *Katherine* by Elisabeth MacIntyre. *Quippy* is a small book (now out of print) with uncluttered flat illustrations. It is the story of a lost duckling who goes in search of a meal, is repeatedly thwarted, goes to sleep, eventually finds his mother but, strangely, remains hungry. MacIntyre's *Katherine* tells what it is like to be an Australian country child living on a station:

> This is young Katherine
> Who lives in Australia,
> With her toys, and her pets,
> And her paraphernalia.

The illustrations, black outlines and strong primary colours, treat the text literally. It reads like a rhymed letter to cousins in England to let them into the secrets of Australian life. Katherine has her pony, her dog and lives in a 'homestead'. When she goes on the long journey to Sydney, she goes to the zoo, rides on trains and discovers that she really prefers to be back in the country. There is no high point in the story and no real plot is developed, but its mild didacticism was successful within these limits.

By contrast with the preceding writers, Jenny Wagner and illustrator Ron Brooks have collaborated to produce picture books of great significance. The text of *The Bunyip of Berkeley's Creek* (1973) is structurally simple. The patterned repetition of the question 'Who am I?' belies the profundity of the theme — 'to be is to be perceived' a proposition put by the eighteenth century philosopher Bishop Berkeley — and endorsed again, it appears, by contemporary quantum physicists! Wagner wanted to handle the question in such a way as to make it understandable to her own children. Her idea to use an Aboriginal dreamtime creature, the bunyip, as protagonist, a creature believed by whites to be nonexistent, is ironic and brilliant, for it is surely the story of all individuals everywhere who search for self-knowledge. The brooding colours and static forms of the creatures are an excellent foil for the laconic language. Brooks' bald scientist is particularly powerful. He is depicted with his back to the bunyip, whom he does not see because he is unwilling to look to verify its existence, preferring to trust his own experiments rather than the evidence behind him.

The collaboration of Wagner and Brooks culminated in the publication of *John Brown, Rose and the Midnight Cat* (1977), widely acclaimed and appearing in many languages. The text resonates with layers of meaning and like many fine stories the plot revolves around three characters. Rose, an ageing widow, lives with her Old English sheepdog, John Brown (possibly a reference to the Scottish companion of the widowed Queen Victoria!) He keeps her safe from harm but his love is possessive. When the enigmatic Midnight Cat appears amongst the shadows, Rose wants to let him in, but John Brown is disturbed and threatened, and draws a magic circle around the house to protect himself and Rose from the intruder. The book's tension comes from John Brown's struggle with himself — his feelings of jealousy and fear, the unresolved significance of the mysterious intruder, and the need to let Rose have her wish. The depth and significance of this book in no way reduce its accessibility on the literal level. Children and adults return to it again and again and, as with any great book, gain increasing insight into its meaning for their own lives. This book is equally successful visually. Brooks sets the story in an old Australian timber house in the country. The attention to architectural detail, old wooden fences, gnarled old trees, almost makes us smell the surrounding bush. The pictures splendidly reflect the conflict of Rose, and the painful battle going on within John Brown is conveyed by the set of his head and the position of his paws. Like Burningham, Brooks uses cross-hatching extensively, but his use of subdued colours not only serves the purposes of the text, but reflects the sombre colours of the Australian landscape. Burningham's, by contrast, are as clear and bright as an ideal English summer.

Details such as background landscape contribute significantly to the potent effect of the picture book as an art form. A diet of northern hemisphere picture books in early life has probably conditioned generations of Australian children to a painful nostalgia for the woods and meadows, moles and badgers, elves and fairies of Europe and North America. Another team of artists, Dick Roughsey and Percy Trezise, have produced many fine picture books which reflect the landscape of Northern Australia so vividly that Southern Australians could think that they are exaggerations. Roughsey (Goobalathan) was a tribal Aborigine from Mornington Island, off the Queensland coast. For many years, he worked with Trezise creating picture books based on Aboriginal traditional tales. Roughsey had a store of Aboriginal lore in his head: he remembered the coming of the white missionaries to his island. And when he sang in the lonely northern night, his melodies ranged from the haunting tribal songs of his people to snatches of gospel songs learnt on the missions. Traditional Aboriginal stories have a complex structure. Unlike the typically symmetrical shape and repetition of the European folk tale which is easy for children to follow, Aboriginal stories reflect the meanderings of the spirits of the Dreamtime who moved across the continent creating as they went. When children learned these stories, they did so over time, one section after another, not in one sitting. The early books are true to the traditional form and *The Rainbow Serpent* (1975) and *The Giant Devil Dingo* (1973), for example, are not easy stories for young children to follow. Since *The Quinkins* (1978) was published, however, the stories have centred on child protagonists and the material has been shaped to resemble European tales: home-adventure out-home. Whilst this makes the stories more accessible, they have inevitably lost some of their Aboriginality, yet they offer children (and adults) a view of this country through the eyes of a people who have known it for thousands of years, and instead of elves and fairies and European animals, the land is inhabited by quinkins, imjin, kangaroos and Aborigines.

Pamela Allen is another Australian author/illustrator to have captured the imagination of children. Like Wagner, she has posed serious questions in her books, but treats them in a far more light-hearted manner. In *Mr Archimedes' Bath* (1980), animals and man together create wild splashing and noise in an effort to discover Archimedes' principle of water displacement. Whether or not the lesson is learnt makes little difference to the enjoyment of the story and very funny pictures. Allen's *Who Sank the Boat* (1982) is a simpler story — a 'Tale of the Turnip' in reverse. It too is a riotous quest for the answer to a question, 'Who Sank the Boat?'. When one animal after another crowds into a small dinghy and at last it is sunk by — the mouse? we discover the answer. Or do we? Perhaps the ending is open.

THE OPEN END

There is a growing tendency for picture book endings to *be* left open, and more often than not, they pose questions to which there is easy answer. Often the themes are what Egoff (1981: 251) calls 'the darker side of human experience', as if authors wish to insist that the security of childhood be shattered as soon as possible, or maybe inferring that it is a fiction anyhow. Subjects such as loneliness and death are occurring more and more frequently. One of the earlier books in this category was Charles Keeping's *Through the Window* (1970). It is a sombre book and very powerful — disturbing to many. The text is a stream-of-consciousness account of an incident told by a boy who looks down on his London street from behind a veil of curtains. An old woman's dog is trampled to death by a runaway team of horses. Nothing in the text is explicit, the paintings withhold as much as they tell, inferences must be made, and Keeping's message of hope at the end of the book — the smiling woman holding her dog drawn on the steamed-up window — contains only a hint of immortality.

Anthony Browne brings a sophistication to the picture book which suggests that the genre is no longer the sole province of very young children. *A Walk in the Park* (1977) is not only open-ended but surrealistic: nothing is quite what it seems. In this ironic book Browne makes inferences about social class, gender and the potentially egalitarian nature of childhood. It is a book to be enjoyed for its hard-edged visual delights and puzzles, yet the tense text suggests dissonance and ambiguity which take maturity to comprehend.

Chris van Allsburg uses the picture book as a vehicle for exploring problems of space and form. In *Jumanji* (1981) and *The Garden of Abdul Gasazi* (1979) he has used carbon pencil to produce black and white pictures whose statuesque quality evoke a strange stillness. Sombre landscapes and architectural mass become the setting for lone child protagonists. The element of illusion is matched by the surrealistic narratives which, although simple enough at the linguistic level evaporate like dreams and linger unresolved in the mind.

Also for older children are the handsome books of Fiona French. Hers are moral tales often derived from parables or fables. *City of Gold* (1974) comes from the parable of the two roads, the broad leading to destruction, the narrow to life. French has produced a gothic book of vibrant colour reminiscent of stained glass windows. *The Princess and the Musician* (1981) is a Persian fairy tale which evokes the colours and designs of the Middle East, whilst *King Tree* (1973) is another moral tale set in the formal gardens of Versailles.

In his latest picture book Sendak has once again produced a profoundly significant work. *Outside Over There* (1981) springs from childhood memories and impressions developed and sifted through the creative processes of a genius. The result is so complex and multi-layered that its place in children's literature is ambiguous. By far the least approachable of Sendak's work, it is a book which can never be fully fathomed. A host of emotions and memories is generated in the adult reader, ranging from fear to joy, which, for Freudians at least, could be explained by attributing them to the workings of the unconscious. Time will tell if children or adults will be its chief admirers, but for Sendak-watchers it is a treasure. The illustrations are reminiscent of the style of Botticelli — romantic landscapes, lowering skies and Mozart composing.

WORDLESS BOOKS

We have come a long way from the traditional tales and verses illustrated by Crane, Caldecott and Greenaway, in which illustration 'fleshed out' literature which had previously been transmitted by word alone. We have reached a point at which the visual elements have not only become equally important but at which in some cases words have been omitted entirely. We have noted that since the sixties, picture books like *Where the Wild Things Are* and *Rosie's Walk* relied on the pictures to tell parts of the story left out by the text and pictures were becoming more and more important in moving the narrative along. There is now a growing fashion for wordless books in which pictures alone tell the story.

Raymond Briggs' *The Snowman*, first published in 1978, is an outstanding example of this wordless genre. Each episode is shown inside a frame which proceeds across the page from left to right and from top to bottom as in English print. They are meant to be 'read' sequentially: there can be as many as twenty-four frames to a double spread or one frame can span a whole double spread. The narrative is 'told' from a child's viewpoint and is a sensitive account of a child making a snowman. As the snowman becomes larger and larger, the child is repeatedly shown going inside the house for warmth and security. When the larger-than-life snowman is finished, the child loses control as the snowman becomes animated, and eventually in the night when the parents are asleep, invites the snowman inside. Together they explore the mysteries of the household appliances. This intensely emotive story works like a series of dream images but although no words are used, there are strong conceptual elements like the classification of hot and cold things in the house. And adult humour is aroused when the snowman wilts at the sight of a Van Gogh print of *Sunflowers*. The use of consecutive frames to tell a story seems to suggest the influence of television on children's books, plus of course comics, and reminds us that we are undoubtedly becoming more and more conditioned to the visual mode, whether it be in order to convey the news of the day, or to dramatise a story on film.

The Australian artist Jan Ormerod, has produced two very fine wordless books, *Sunshine* (1981) (which won the Australian Picture Book of the Year award in 1982) and *Moonlight*. These too are child-centred narratives and the view is very much a commentary on the child in contemporary society. The father is a student, the mother the breadwinner, and the child is, in some ways, an island in between, needing to be autonomous and responsible but at the same time intensely vulnerable. Once again, the episodes are contained in consecutive frames, and epitomise the art of story-telling without words. But is this literature? Not in its traditional sense as 'writing'. Some authorities argue that, in fact, wordless books generate the production of language as children or adults 'interpret' the pictures by using words; others that the left to right progression is good practice for learning to read. It would seem that the genre has come to stay whether we endorse it as a desirable development or not. It is being used increasingly in stories for older children and indeed adults. Briggs' *Fungus the Bogeyman* (1977) and *When the Wind Blows* (1982), although not dispensing with words, use the comic format. The latter is a comment on nuclear war and has been adapted as a radio play for adults, as well as having been translated into several other languages — more examples of the fact that picture books are not only for young children.

ANNO

Mitsumasa Anno is a Japanese artist who has made a major contribution to the picture book genre. Many of his works are wordless books and depict a lone traveller riding his horse across a wide landscape in Britain, Europe, or the United States and one day, expectantly, in Australia. The books are significant because of their visual impact, fine detail and for the distillation of the historical and cultural aspects of each country visited. Anno is the outsider looking in with keen eyes, with humour and above all creating a perspective which those involved in their lives do not see — a synthesis as well as an analysis of the whole. But there is also the fact that this is a Japanese artist interpreting Western culture and landscape, and so the traditions of Japanese art become a window through which all is viewed. The pictures abound with references to literary characters — Winnie-the-Pooh, Alice, Shakespeare. Many will be unknown to children and maybe even adults, but the offerings are rich and the potential for discovery great. But it is not only for wordless books that Anno is renowned. *Anno's Medieval World* (1980) is a picture book for older children of a very special kind. In this masterpiece (which holds its own with the French *Jeanne d'Arc* (1980) by Boutet de Monvel), Anno traces the history of ideas in physics, astronomy and philosophy from the Middle Ages to the present. His subtle use of perspective reflects concepts of the universe pictorially, from flat earth to concepts of space. *Anno's Counting Book* (1975) offers young children the opportunity to count from 0–12 and a lot more besides. There are a host of problems and situations to explore. A landscape is empty at 0, and over twelve months develops into a thriving town: seasonal changes are shown, and fine details give young children many opportunities for discovery.

FOLK AND FAIRY TALES

Finally, we need to mention the vigorous return to the illustration of traditional folk and fairy tales which is occupying many fine artists both in Europe, the United States and Japan. Every illustrator of traditional tales is a reinterpreter, and is doing so within a contemporary context. Jane Doonan has said that 'The artist is faced with the necessity of creating her own visual once upon a time ... she has to work within the spirit of the text, whether she describes, illuminates, extends or decorates it' (Signal *Approach to Children's Books* No. 40: 93). We are restricting comment to the folk/fairy tale as picture book, although finely-illustrated collections abound from Rackham to Sendak.

Two contrasting approaches are those used by Anthony Browne and Lisbeth Zwerger. Browne's *Hansel and Gretel* (1981) is treated as a 'split' story. On the one hand, there is the traditional text translated from the Brothers Grimm, and on the other is a contemporary spelling-out of the psychological meanings behind the story by way of symbolic pictures. This is a treatment which evokes exaggerated responses from many adults, who recoil from the implications of 'shocking revelations'. Shadows are used to cast the step-mother as the witch herself. Bars on chairs and vertical lines in general create the illusion that the children are already in cages at home, while the modern brick house sits on the edge of a primaeval forest. Strong stuff, this, and a long way from the delicate treatment of artists like Susan Jeffers. Perhaps there are many adults who do not care to look under the surface of these stories and are certainly not going to encourage children to do so, in which case Anthony Browne is not for them.

On the face of it, Lisbeth Zwerger has produced an innocuous enough book in *Little Red Cap* (1983). Delicate and beautiful as her treatment is, this picture book artist also uses shapes and space symbolically to convey emotion, cruelty and greed. But she manages to contain these emotions within the 'once upon a time' frame and we do not feel the story to be threatening to our lives now; therefore the shock element is missing.

Nancy Burkert's *Snow White* (1974) whilst not a fully-integrated picture book (text and pictures are on separate double spreads), is an example of a superbly-realised work — symbolic and distanced, yet of great significance and appeal to children. Literal detail of peasant designs and the use of space and form convey emotional intensity and contribute to the book's enormous appeal.

The picture book, then, is a diverse and complex art form. Every year many more come onto the market. Some will go into many editions, while others will join the 'remainder' shelves for those which will not survive even the first edition. Adults have the power to bring these books to children or to withhold them from them. It is a challenge and a responsibility but also a great privilege.

REFERENCES

Chambers, Aidan and Doonan, Jane, in *Signal Approach to Children's Books* No. 40, January 1983. Lockwood, Gloucester: Thimble Press, 1983.
Egoff, Sheila A., *Thursday's Child: Trends and Patterns in Contemporary Children's Literature*. Chicago: ALA, 1981.
Schwarcz, Joseph, *Ways of the Illustrator*. Chicago: American Library Association, 1982.

BOOKS REFERRED TO IN THE CHAPTER

Allen, Pamela, *Mr Archimedes' Bath*. Collins.
——————, *Who Sank the Boat?* Collins.
Anno, Mitsumasa, *Anno's Counting Book*. Bodley Head.
——————, *Anno's Medieval World*. Bodley Head.
Ardizzone, Edward, *Little Tim and the Brave Sea Captain*. Oxford.
Boutet de Monvel, Maurice, *Jeanne d'Arc*. Plon Nourrit/Viking.
Briggs, Raymond, *Fungus the Bogeyman*. Hamish Hamilton.
——————, *The Snowman*. Hamish Hamilton.
——————, *When the Wind Blows*. Hamish Hamilton.
Browne, Anthony, *Hansel and Gretel*. Julia MacRae.
——————, *A Walk in the Park*. Hamish Hamilton.

Burkert, N., illustrator, *Snow White*. Puffin.
Burningham, John, *The Baby*. Cape.
——————, *Come Away from the Water, Shirley*. Cape.
——————, *Granpa*. Cape.
——————, *Mr Gumpy's Outing*. Cape/Puffin.
——————, *Time to Get Out of the Bath, Shirley*. Cape.
Burton, Virginia Lee, *Choo Choo*. Faber.
——————, *The Little House*. Faber.
——————, *Mike Mulligan and His Steam Shovel*. Faber.
Caldecott, Randolph, *Hey Diddle Diddle*. Routledge.
Crane, Walter, *The Bluebeard Picture Book*. Warne.
Ets, M.Hall, *Play With Me*. Viking.
Flack, M.,illustrator, writer, Kurt Wiese, *The Story About Ping*. Bodley Head/Puffin.
French, Fiona, *City of Gold*. Oxford.
——————, *King Tree*. Oxford.
——————, *The Princess and the Musician*. Evans.
Gag, Wanda, *Millions of Cats*. Faber/Puffin.
Gramatky, H., *Little Toot*. World's Work.
Greenaway, Kate, *Under the Window*. Warne.
Hutchins, Pat, *Rosie's Walk*. Bodley Head/Puffin.
Keats, Ezra Jack, *Peter's Chair*. Bodley Head.
Keeping, Charles, *Through the Window*. Oxford.
Lenski, Lois, *Davy's Day*. Oxford.
——————, *The Little Fire Engine*. Oxford.
——————, *Papa Small*. Oxford.
MacIntyre, Elisabeth, *Katherine*. Angus & Robertson.
Mason, Olive, Walter Cunningham, illustrator, *Quippy*. Sands.
Ormerod, Jan *Moonlight*. Kestrel.
——————, *Sunshine*. Kestrel.
Potter, Beatrix, *The Tale of Peter Rabbit*. Warne.
Roughsey, D. and Trezise, P., *The Giant Devil Dingo*. Collins.
——————, *The Quinkins*. Collins.
——————, *The Rainbow Serpent*. Collins.
Sendak, Maurice, *In the Night Kitchen*. Harper & Row.
——————, *Outside Over There*. Bodley Head/Puffin.
——————, *Where the Wild Things Are*. Bodley Head/Puffin.
Van Allsburg, Chris, *The Garden of Abdul Gasazi*. Houghton Mifflin.
——————, *Jumanji*. Houghton Mifflin.
Wagner, Jenny, illustrator, Ron Brooks, *The Bunyip of Berkeley's Creek*. Puffin.
——————, *John Brown, Rose and the Midnight Cat*. Puffin.
Zwerger, Lisbeth, illustrator, *Little Red Cap*. Hutchinson/Neugebauer.

A SELECT LIST OF AUSTRALIAN PICTURE BOOKS

Allen, Pamela, *Bertie and the Bear*. Nelson.
——————, *Mr Archimedes' Bath*. Collins.
——————, *Who Sank the Boat?* Nelson.
Armitage, R. and D., *The Lighthouse Keeper's Lunch*. Hutchinson.
Cox, D., *Tin Lizzie and Little Nell*. Aurora Press.
Fox, Mem and Vivas, Julie, *Wilfred Gordon McDonald Partridge*. Omnibus.
Greenwood, Ted, *Everlasting Circle*. Hutchinson.

Hunt, Nan and Smith, Craig, *Whistle Up the Chimney*. Collins.
Ormerod, Jan, *Sunshine*. Kestrel.
Pavey, Peter, *One Dragon's Dream*. Nelson.
Pender, Lydia and Cowell, Judy, *Barnaby and the Rocket*. Collins.
Roughsey, Dick and Trezise, Percy, *The Giant Devil Dingo*. Collins.
——————, *The Magic Firesticks*. Collins.
——————, *The Quinkins*. Collins.
Treloar, Bruce, *Bumble's Dream*. Bodley Head.
Wagner, Jenny and Brooks, Ron, *Aranea*. Kestrel.
——————, *John Brown, Rose and the Midnight Cat*. Kestrel.
——————, *The Bunyip of Berkeley's Creek*. Longmans.

MORE AUSTRALIAN PICTURE BOOKS

Baillie, Allan and Tanner, Jane, *Drac and the Gremlin*. Viking Kestrel.
Baker, Jeannie, *Where the Forest Meets the Sea*. Julia MacRae.
Ball, Duncan and Smith, Craig, *My Dog's a Scaredy-Cat*. Collins.
Base, Graeme, *Animalia*. Viking Kestrel.
Bedson, Jack and Gouldthorpe, Peter, *Don't Get Burnt! or The Great Australian Day at the Beach*. Collins.
Blackwood, Mary and Argent, Kerry, *Derek the Dinosaur*. Omnibus.
Cox, David, *Bossyboots*. Bodley Head.
——————, *Rightway Jack*. Bodley Head.
Denton, Terry. *Felix and Alexander*. Oxford.
——————, *The School For Laughter*. Oxford.
Edwards, Hazel and Niland, Deborah, *There's a Hippopotamus on Our Roof Eating Cake*. Hodder & Stoughton.
Fox, Mem and Smith, Craig, *Sophie*. Drakeford/Watts.
—————— and Mullins, Patricia, *Shoes From Grandpa*. Ashton Scholastic.
Graham, Bob, *Crusher is Coming*. Lothian.
——————, *Grandad's Magic*. Viking Kestrel.
Hilton, Nette and Wilcox, Cathy, *A Proper Little Lady*. Collins.
Jorgensen, Gail and Mullins, Patricia, *Crocodile Beat*. Omnibus.
Lester, Alison, *Imagine*. Allen & Unwin.
——————, *The Journey Home*. Oxford.
Odgers, Sally Farrell and Smith, Craig, *Dreadful David*. Puffin.
Rawlins, Donna, *Digging to China*. Ashton Scholastic.
Roennfeldt, Robert and Mary, *What's That Noise?* Puffin.
Vivas, Julie, *The Nativity*. Omnibus.
Wheatley, Nadia and Rawlins, Donna, *My Place*. Collins Dove.
Winch, Madeleine, *Come By Chance*. Angus & Robertson.

FURTHER REFERENCES

Alderman, Belle, *Breaking the Barriers: Picture Books for Older Readers*. Canberra: C.C.A.E., 1989.
Martin, Douglas, *The Telling Line: Essays on Fifteen Contemporary Book Illustrators*. Perth: Magpies, 1989.
O'Sullivan, Colleen, *The Challenge of Picture Books: A Teacher's Guide to the Use of Picture Books with Older Students*. Sydney: Methuen/Nelson, 1987.
Prentice, Jeffrey and Bird, Bettina, *Dromkeen: A Journey Into Children's Literature*. Melbourne: Dent, 1987.
Whalley, Joyce Irene and Chester, Tessa Rose, *A History of Children's Book Illustration*. London: John Murray, 1988.

6 ARCHETYPAL LITERATURE: FOLK AND FAIRY STORIES

MAURICE SAXBY

> So might I, standing on this pleasant lea,
> Have glimpses that would make me less forlorn;
> Have sight of Proteus rising from the sea;
> Or hear old Triton blow his wreathed horn.
> Wordsworth

THE LINEAGE OF LITERATURE

Before writing there was story. In the beginning was language and from language proceeded story — far back in the reaches of time. As early man, in whatever habitat, developed the art of speech, he began to explore his environment, and to penetrate beyond the immediately observable in an attempt to give meaning to life. Through dance, art and story great events were celebrated and heroes remembered.

But even as man began to recognise his humanity through the supremacy of a developed language, the suspicion of human fallibility grew into the certainty that there were invisible forces shaping his destiny: forces from without and within.

Outside were great forces — gods and unseen spirit hosts, some benevolent, some malevolent, controlling the environment and impinging on the lives of all creatures, for good or for ill. So there had to be appeasement, and for the great forces, reverence, even worship.

Within were opposing drives and desires needing definition: a groping toward the concepts of goodness and evil. From the beginning was the need to know.

Not that man was necessarily a puppet. There were always to be those who annexed power — heroes — those who outshone their fellows and did battle with invisible and often unknown monsters. Because life is harsh, apparently unyielding and fearful there had to be monsters: giants, dragons, creatures of the forest and the night who personify fear. And because some men are obviously wiser or more astute than their fellows there had to be magicians, wizards and tricksters along with the supermen and heroes.

And in that man is a creature of his landscape, his spiritual and emotional environment is shaped by his physical surroundings. So household gods and local spirits were created in the image of the place and the folk. As tribes banded together and kinship merged into nationhood, bigger gods and mightier heroes came into being.

But local lore was not subsumed. It remained side by side with the larger life forces: a local expression of the Law of Life.

So speculation and belief, the observable and the guessable, immediately remembered events and personalities, along with those whose shadows lingered, were all given substance in oral story.

Around the ancient world, in hidden valleys, in plain settlements, down the coast and along fertile riverways a network of story developed. It sometimes blended one tradition with another, meshing and overlapping and separating as cultures spread. The exodus of Israel from Egypt is representative of one way that story travelled and in the travelling was cross-fertilised. Later, caravans, sailing ships, explorations and crusades transplanted story: a two-way trade of story told and story heard.

Gradually there emerged a storytelling caste — the bard, the minstrel, the poet, the rhymer. Such were given pride of place in the Long Ships as the Vikings bowed to their oars across icy seas and were welcomed to the fire of the Mead Hall, and for such the portcullis of the Castle was gladly raised. The power of story:

> With a tale, forsooth, he cometh unto you;
> With a tale which holdeth children from play,
> And old men from the chimney corner.

So developed the tales of and for the people, the folk. Sometimes they were just that, household tales to comfort or frighten; sometimes they were stirring tales of heroes, celebrations and idealisations; sometimes they were remnants of belief, of the big stories, no longer sacred but part of the common bread of humanity. The big stories, religion, became the preserve of a priestly caste until they, too, were taken hold of by the folk.

AN ORAL TRADITION AND A WRITTEN TEXT

Because the stories were oral — passed on by word of mouth — they were both traditional and personal. Traditional in that they were derived from the soil of the folk, personal in that each teller shaped the language of the story with his own idiom, his perspective, his own peculiar way of knowing. Only when the stories were transmitted to paper could their shape and contours become relatively fixed. Even so, in most cases both teller and scribe were anonymous, and we have no way of knowing to what extent the voice of the teller has been distorted or refined by the writer, except that when the tale was sung in verse its form was more likely to be fixed and faithfully transcribed.

But it is obvious that at first, in the days of the chapbooks and broadsheets, that the folk flavour and idiom of the tales was retained. In the eighteenth century collection became an art and the versions more literary. And then it was that the stories of the folk became part of 'children's literature'. Perrault wrote down his

Contes with one eye on a fashionable court audience and the other on the children. His tales and those of the Brothers Grimm were speedily requisitioned as 'suitable for children', although children were always party to the oral story — for how else could they discover their roots? Story, like play, is a child's way of exploring, discovering and learning. But early in the nineteenth century as education became more formalised, a formidable band who saw themselves as guardians of the education of the young sought to ban the old tales because they lacked specific moral instruction, or they rewrote and falsified them. So the battle against the folk tale began. But despite repeated attempts to adulterate, bowdlerise and trivialise, and despite recent attempts of latter-day psychologists to gut them, traditional tales are resilient, indestructible.

Today the literary-educational pendulum has stopped swinging. Traditional literature has been recognised as fit food for the developing imagination and as a cultural medium. There is at present a return to the prototype, a general integrity among retellers, translators and publishers, in an attempt to remain faithful to the intent of the early recorded versions. After generations of distortion and exploitation of the pseudo-folk tale there is now a genuine desire to make the old tales once again accessible to children in a form which remains faithful to the earliest recordings, a gentle handling of children's literary birthright which in less scrupulous years was traded for a mess of potage. So, too, artists are returning to the tradition of the great book illustrators like Rackham, Dulac and Nielsen, and publishers are vying with one another to produce more sumptuous and more lavish editions of traditional stories.

Primers and school reading material which until the era of Dick and Dora drew heavily on traditional literature are being replaced with anthologies of literature in which traditional tales once again take precedence, because it is now being recognised that each child has to grow and develop, has to seek and explore as did the race before him. Each individual has to pass through his own rites of passage. In so doing those stories which have endured from when the world was young can provide comfort, guidance and a means of intuitive understanding. For they have endured because they embody ongoing truths of human experience and are thus universal symbols.

MOTIFS AND ARCHETYPES: THE MIRACULOUS PITCHER

In 1 Kings 17 in the *Bible* is recorded the story of the prophet Elijah who passed on the promise of his God to the widow who was prepared to share with him her last handful of meal and the last remaining oil in her cruse: 'The jar of meal shall not be spent, and the cruse shall not fail, until the days that the Lord sends rain upon the earth'. So, too, Baucis and Philemon were rewarded in their humble home in Phrygia with wine that renewed itself in the pitcher when unawares they gave of their hospitality to the gods Jupiter and Mercury. And from Ireland comes the tale of Deirdre and Eamonn who survived the Great Famine of 1846–7. When visited by the corpse-like Fear Ghorta, the Man of Hunger, they shared their last potato with the stranger:

> The Fear Ghorta put the half-eaten potato on the table beside him and his long finger passed over it, and immediately it was whole again. 'No matter how often you cut this', he said to Deirdre, 'keep back a little, and in a little while it will be whole again'. He pointed across, at the empty pitcher. 'And that will never be empty'.
>
> (Scott 1984: 138)

In these and related stories there are truths of human experience. In times of famine, particularly, generosity will be rewarded and meanness punished; again, any stranger may be a god in humble guise; or life will be sustained no matter what. And there are deeper truths, — such as the miracle of renewal and regeneration that we can all witness daily if we look on the world with unblinkered eyes.

Like the miraculous pitcher, folk literature is itself regenerative, renewing itself from within (as succeeding generations glimpse inherent truth) and from without (as the same tale appears in a new or updated version). Here are the roots of literature and the wellsprings of human behaviour.

In traditional literature is embedded those motifs and archetypes which are not only re-expressed in modern picture stories and novels but which will often be present in the child's inner imaginative, even dream, life.

Whilst in the study of folklore and the classification of folk stories, the *motif* is defined as the smallest element in a tale having power to persist in tradition, in the psychological sense (especially in Jungian psychology) it is a recurring shape, pattern or image — the gods in disguise, the miraculous pitcher itself, the changing of Baucis and Philemon into trees — having an underlying, often unconscious significance.

In Jung's terminology the *archetype* is the persistent tendency to give representation to *motifs*, or representations, which 'can vary a great deal in detail without losing their basic pattern' (Jung 1964: 58) and which are repositories of the collective unconscious. Hence the archetypal story of Jonah's task, his flight, his appeasement in the time of tempest, his metaphorical death and rebirth, symbolising perhaps a re-entry to the womb or the death of the old, inadequate self and a rebirth at a higher level of existence. Certainly Jonah attains full humanity only when he is no longer blindly subservient to either the life-force or the super-ego, but is able to recognise a divine wisdom in judging the people of Nineveh according to their human frailty.

So Bettelheim has given us *The Uses of Enchantment: The Im-*

portance and Meaning of Fairy Tales and Luthi *Once Upon a Time: On the Nature of Fairy Tales*. Cooper calls Fairy Tales 'allegories of the inner life' and embraces the spectrum of traditional literature.

> These themes [motifs], having come down to popular fairy tales, from the ancient myths, sagas and legends of the races, contain the familiar and common characteristics of them all and enshrine the archetypal nature of this heritage. The archetypal patterns embody primordial images and symbols, occurring the world over and constituting man's potential to understand himself and the world around him. There is a cosmic significance running through these patterns of myth, saga, legend and fairy tale, rooted deeply in human nature, continually striking chords and evoking responses. Solzhenitsyn, in his Nobel speech, said: 'Some things lead into the realm beyond words ... it is like that small mirror in fairy tales — you glance in it and what you see is not yourself; for an instant you glimpse the Inaccessible ... and the soul cries out for it.'
>
> (Cooper 1983: 16)

It would sometimes seem that for today's children Cyclops and Excalibur are but brand names, Maid Marian belongs only to TV commercials and the only fairy that has relevance is the Tooth Fairy.

Yet as the steamers gliding down the Rhine come abreast of the Lorelei the strains of the Lorelei song are heard anew. Rapunzel can still let down her hair, and Mirror, Mirror on the wall still reveals who is fairest of us all. Bettelheim only verbalised (perhaps overstated) what most of us suspected. The very spate of reissues of traditional stories attest a faith not only in the literary heritage of the folk but in the wisdom, insight, poetry, magic and wonder which is the life-blood of that literature and of those far-off, forgotten folk from whom it had its being.

THE FORMS OF TRADITIONAL LITERATURE

Each ritual, fragment or tale that springs from the folk has its own shape and dimension, determined by the occasion, time and place of its conception. Gradually over a long period of time it assumes a linguistic form. And particularly after it has been recorded, it conforms to a pattern of story — a literary form. Although labels are often used indiscriminately — folk or fairy tales, myths or legends — in collections of traditional literature, broad categories of story do emerge, and each has its own psychological relevance to the human condition. Those in verse form are the least variable. Both the ballad and the folk song tend to endure intact because of their rhyme and metric composition, and to retain a conventional pattern.

THE BALLAD

Ballads are essentially dramatic stories, which were sung. They often included passages of dialogue, a chorus or a refrain, and formalised phrases recur from ballad to ballad giving them a liturgical quality. These ancient songs tell of natural and supernatural events, of love and betrayal, of guilt, retribution and unhappy deaths. They are often archetypal and contain recognisable motifs within the archetype.

The sojourn of True Thomas with the Queen of fair Elfland is the archetypal submission of common man to a lady of high estate (the Queen of Heaven), but the ballad itself is a blend of motifs and resonant images: 'milk-white steed', 'marvels three', 'the apple from on high', 'till seven years were gone and past'. *Pilgrim's Progress, Rip Van Winkle, La Belle Dame Sans Merci* and countless journeyings in modern children's books, especially in the genre of fantasy, have literary links with *True Thomas*.

> O see ye not yon narrow road,
>   So thick beset with thorns and briars?
> That is the path of righteousness,
>   Though after it but few enquires.
>
> And see ye not yon broad, broad road,
>   That stretches o'er the lily leven?
> That is the path of wickedness,
>   Though some call it the road to heaven.

One of the most potent and evocative stanzas in folk literature follows:

> It was mirk, mirk night; there was no star-light;
>   They waded through red blood to the knee;
> For all the blood that's shed on earth
>   Runs through the springs of that countree.
>
> (Untermeyer 1963: 32–3)

These traditional ballads not only introduce the young to the themes of great literature, but attune the ear to the rhythms of poetry and the inner ear to fundamental imagery. Literary ballads like Cowper's *John Gilpin* and the Australian bush ballads not only have the same external appeal to the ear and eye but they, too, deal with elemental human predicaments from which children can glean understanding of themselves and society. The pathos and the humour of the most resilient of our Australian ballads is compounded by the illustrations of artists such as Desmond Digby, Quentin Hole and Deborah and Kilmeny Niland in the Collins picture books of *Waltzing Matilda, Bush Christening, The Man From Iron Bark* and *Mulga Bill's Bicycle*: poems and pictures in an Australian bush tradition, and in their way a part of folk literature.

THE FOLK SONG

So, too, the folk song, from the haunting words and melody of *Greensleeves*, the rollicking sea shanties like *We're Bound for the Rio*

Grande or the nostalgia of *Shenendoah*, to the lament of *Danny Boy*, is part of literature as well as music. John Anthony King's *Farewell to Old England Forever* and his *The Wild Colonial Boy* and Robert Ingpen's *Click Go the Shears* are triumphant unifications of word, painting and music — and fundamentally Australian.

The ballad and the folk song are, in a sense, the heralds of traditional literature.

NURSERY RHYMES; PLAYGROUND CHANTS: AUTOGRAPH PIECES, WISDOM IN RHYME

Chants, spells, curses, games, nursery rhymes, cradle songs and pithy sayings: these, too, belong to the folk — and especially to the young folk — and are precursors to a more sedate, if not more profound literature. Often they provide a child's introduction to metaphorical language and imagery. It matters little that 'Mary Mary Quite Contrary' was in reality Mary, Queen of Scots or whether Banbury Cross is actually a memorial to Lady Godiva or Queen Eleanor. The old rhymes imply that language can move at more than one level. The reverberations are inherent in the images and references. They are essentially open-ended.

Nonsense, superstition, belief, experimentation (with sound, particularly), speculation about adult roles and relationships ('Curly Locks, Curly Locks; Wilt thou be mine?'), the inconsequential yet often lyrical aspects of human experience abound in rhymes for the nursery. There is no better introduction to life or literature than a wide collection of Mother Goose rhymes: *The Mother Goose Treasury* of Raymond Briggs or *The Puffin Book of Nursery Rhymes* by Iona and Peter Opie, to begin with.

In the street and playground and in autograph books and that world fenced in from adults, children continue to indulge their love of rhyme (especially if it is audacious), their need for incantation (primitive chant, war-cry, provoking insult), their scatological humour (Captain Cook and the dunny door) and their irreverent need to 'send up' whatever is suspect:

> Half a pound of Mandy Rice
> Half of Christine Keeler
> Mix it up, what do you get?
> A very sexy sheila.

Like their elders they are quick to incorporate rhymed sayings and metaphorical observations into their verbal lore. The homespun wisdom of 'Red Sky in the morning, shepherd's warning', is processed linguistically at an early age. Ian Turner's *Cinderella Dressed in Yella* and June Factor's *Far Out, Brussel Sprout! Australian Children's Chants and Rhymes* are convincing proof of the enduring folk element of puns, parodies, riddles, rhymes and jokes that form a literature chosen by children, and therefore to be taken seriously.

IN PROSE: THE PROVERB, FABLE AND PARABLE

Literal folk sayings 'An Apple a Day Keeps the Doctor Away'; metaphorical advice 'Don't Count Your Chickens Before They are Hatched'; prediction or warning 'Hasten Slowly'; and homely philosophical observations 'Birds of a Feather Flock Together'; 'All that Glitters is Not Gold' like rhymed observations, chants and spells are first grasped in childhood and frequently linger as a mental shorthand and conversational tags.

The Fable

Such economical, pithy sayings are often associated with the literary form of the fable. Like the ballad, the fable is dramatic, based on a single incident, and usually embodies one, central conflict. Although the telling is brief to the point of terseness, prose is usually used. These aphoristic narratives seek to make abstract ideas of good and evil, wise and foolish behaviour, concrete and comprehensible and striking enough to be remembered. They also reflect the culture from which they have sprung, even to the animal characters which feature more frequently than humans. The fable is more overt than most folk narratives in that a universal truth is being expressed in a concentrated form, and often the moral or lesson is spelt out and appended in proverb or maxim form.

The most ancient 'children's book' in the Pierpoint Morgan Library of Early Children's Books in New York is composed of fragments of Greek papyrus dating from the third or fourth century, unearthed in Egypt, containing portions of three Fables of Babrius, a Greek poet: the earliest known collection of Aesopian fables in Greek verse. Gerald Gottlieb, curator of the Morgan collection says: 'Perhaps no book has been more read by children than Aesop's fables. Certainly no book for children has been illustrated more frequently' (Gottlieb 1975: 3). Gottlieb subscribes to the belief that Aesop was 'born in Thrace in the early sixth century BC and later was a slave on the island of Samos. There he won renown for telling clever stories in the form of pointed fables, chiefly about foxes and geese and lions and other animals' (Gottlieb 1975). Aesop's was an oral tradition and it wasn't until the fourth century BC that Demetrius of Phalerum collected and transcribed the fables of Aesop in Greek prose. Today, the fables of 'The Fox and the Grapes', 'The Dog in the Manger', 'The Lion and the Mouse' and 'The Hare and the Tortoise' are household stories and are still being used to alert children to the vagaries of human conduct. Besides, they are entertaining and models of the economical use of language.

From India in the fifth century AD came the *Jatakas*, beast tales which teach a moral lesson. *The Panchantantra* (sixth century AD) in which a wise brahmin uses animal stories to teach three somewhat naïve and ignorant princes worldly wisdom, contains stories like

'The Mice and the Elephant' (a 'Lion and the Mouse', a one-good-turn-deserves-another variant), 'The Mother Crow and the Serpent' and 'The Geese and the Tortoise' which are mildly satirical, yet comment shrewdly on the ways of the world. These stories came into English in the sixteenth century and are often referred to as *The Fables of Bidpai*. Leonard Clark has retold some of the Indian fables for children as *Tales From the Panchantantra* with illustrations by an Indian artist, Jeroo Roy.

Centuries later, the French poet Jean de la Fontaine included fables from the *Panchantantra* along with ones from Aesop and Phaedrus as well as those of his own invention in his witty, elegant collections of *Fables* in verse form, published in 1668 and 1678 and translated into English in 1734. They were later to be illustrated by such renowned artists as Gustave Doré.

How fables have travelled has been the concern of students for well over a century, scholars like Jeanette Beer who in 1980 published her *Medieval Fables*, a translation of thirty Fables from Marie de France superbly illustrated and decorated in the glowing colours and tradition of the illuminated manuscript by Jason Carter. 'Even the literary sources of Marie's fables remain obscure', writes Beer. 'She says she made her French verse translations from a collection that a certain 'Alvrez' — whom she thought was King Alfred — had translated into English. Alvrez must therefore have used a Latin version of Aesop's Fables for his English translation' (Beer 1980: 9).

Thus it is that fables, like all folk literature are self-perpetuating.

> Regardless of any transformations in their form and substance, fables continue down through the ages. They are the repository of men's wisdom about himself, for THESE ANIMALS ARE MEN.
>
> (Beer 1980)

Such a belief motivated Joel Chandler Harris who in 1880 published in America *Uncle Remus: His Songs and Sayings* which was, in essence, a collection of Negro fables gathered when Harris was a journalist in the Deep South. The popular story of 'Brer Fox, Brer Rabbit and the Tar Baby' is a variant of 'The Tar Dolly', an Anansi story, Anansi being a trickster spider from African and West Indian folklore. Like the classic fables it is a commentary on human gullibility, an acknowledgement of the supremacy of brains over brawn and the necessity for practical wisdom.

The timelessness and universality of the fable concept has created the literary fable — wry, modern commentaries on the human condition which subtly point up contemporary foolishness. They include 'The Crocodile in the Bedroom', the first of Arnold Lobel's near-cynical *Fables*, probably more for adults than children, but enjoyed by many children for their sly imagery.

The Parable

Akin to the fable in intent but usually making its point through human rather than animal characters is the parable, 'an earthly story with a heavenly meaning'. Certainly the story of the Good Samaritan as told in Luke 10 is one of the most economical yet highly-charged narratives in literature. The parables of Jesus will always be relevant for their literary as well as their spiritual inspiration.

Many brief folk stories are somewhere between fables and parables. Those Persian tales, for example, translated from *The Orchard* and *The Rose Garden* by the royal poet and storyteller Sa'di and retold by Arthur Scholey in *The Discontented Dervishes and Other Persian Tales* contain snippets of inherent wisdom and understanding.

> The Good Deed
> A village chief saw a man take a thorn out of the foot of an orphan. That night he dreamed of the man, sauntering with pleasure in the garden of Paradise and saying: 'Look how many roses blossomed from that thorn!'
>
> (Scholey 1977: 94)

THE FOLK TALE

So it is with the folk tale, a generic term used to include a vast multitude of stories, yarns, narratives, drolls and snippets which had their origin in an oral tradition, were handed down and ultimately transferred to stone or clay, parchment, papyrus or paper. They came from every settled spot on earth at the dawn of man's imagination. Such tales are truly timeless and universal and therefore a fit heritage for children.

> Taken all together, they offer, in their oft-repeated and constantly varying examination of human vicissitudes, a general explanation of life preserved in the slow ripening of rustic consciences; those folk stories are the catalog of the potential destinies of men and women, especially for that stage in life when destiny is formed, i.e., youth, beginning with birth, which itself often foreshadows the future; then the departure from home, and, finally, through the trials of growing up, the attainment of maturity and the proof of one's humanity.
>
> (Calvino 1980: XVIII)

Although these are tales of the hearth, *Kinder-und-Haus-Märchen* (as the brothers Grimm define them) they recognise that the equality of man finds expression through kings and commoners, rich and poor, the foolish and the wise, the handsome and the mean of visage, the innocent and the persecutors, the lovely and the unlovely. They recognise, too, the existence of spells (today called variously catatonic trances, psychoses, fixations, phobias, deep-rooted anxieties); of malignant forces; the need of every individual to search for freedom and selfhood; for wholeness. Above all they recognise that the trials, the tasks, even the struggle itself are nothing, if there is not love. For these reasons alone folk tales in some guise are essential to mental and emotional health in the young and maturing person:

> There must be fidelity to a god and purity of heart, values fundamental to salvation and triumph. There must also be beauty, a sign of grace that can be masked by the humble, ugly guise of a frog; and above all, there must be present the infinite possibilities of mutation, the unifying element in everything: men, beasts, plants, things.
>
> (Calvino 1980: XIX)

THE CHARACTERISTICS OF THE FOLK TALE

In spite of the tremendous diversity of folk tales there are general characteristics which make up the pattern which is present in any true art form, and which give the tales true universality, yet often unique individuality.

1. Traces of their origin can often be detected in setting, dialogue, detail or characterisation: a national, regional or local characteristic. Aladdin and Sinbad have the sumptuousness, the glitter, the colour, even the aroma of the East; Robin Hood smells of an English greenwood; The Three Billy Goats Gruff cross a Scandinavian bridge to climb a northern hillside. The troll epitomises a Scandinavian way of seeing. Whuppity Stourie is undeniably Scottish, and Tyll Ulenspiegel a Germanic trickster, just as Dick Whittington's bells are English pealing. Sometimes the locality is even pinpointed: Baghdad, Cairo or Sherwood Forest. Roger Duvoisin in a collection of Swiss tales, *The Three Sneezes* reminds us that there is hardly a mountain peak, a rock, a cave, a river, a lake or a castle in Switzerland which does not have its own story. So he commences the tale 'A Stubborn Man':

> Long ago, as everyone knows, the earth was full of fairies, and there were as many fairies in Switzerland as anywhere else. There were bad ones and good ones, but those that lived around the village of Clebes in Valais were exceptionally good. They did all manner of charitable acts. They helped the poor; they cured the sick; they guided the herdsmen as the cows were led to the high alpine pastures; they cleaned the chalets. In short they were the best of fairies.
>
> (Duvoisin 1957: 94)

2. While the stories may have a local flavour, the time setting is usually (although not always) indeterminate: 'Once upon a time at Benares ...'; 'As summers and winters passed, Tyll's mind grew in wit and mischievousness ...'; 'After he was married, Clag the Third no longer wanted to go to work ...'; 'A country man was one day selling his peas in the market ...'; 'It was long ago in the days of the ancients'. Many a tale has a ritualistic opening: 'Once there was and once there wasn't'; or, 'Once upon a time, and a very good time it was though it was never in my time nor in any one else's

time . . .' Thus are the stories really timeless, and the events, however fearful, are distanced from the hearer.

3. Similarly, although names may be given, they tend to be generic, typical of a time or a region rather than sharply delineating ones: Klaus; Old Tom, Molly, Lippo, Jack, Roland or Grace. Thus the characters become types of Everyman.

4. And in this time that was and wasn't, man interacts positively with his environment so that the boundaries between man and beasts disappear — Puss in Boots, Mr Fox, The Three Bears, Snow White and Rose Red, Beauty and the Beast. In their way the tales hold out the promise of a return to the Golden Age of man's innocency.

5. The language, even in translation (if the translation is a good one) is often strongly rhythmical, reflecting the speech pattern of the originating locality and the idiom of the early tellers. As with the ballads there are catch phrases and set descriptions that are derived from the oral tradition. The language is frequently repetitive, rhyming or cumulative, and chants and refrains can recur; from the ominous 'Oh! Falada, 'tis you hang there', in *The Goose Girl*, to the terrible threat of *Jack and the Beanstalk*:

> Fee-fi-fo-fum,
> I smell the blood of an Englishman,
> Be he alive, or be he dead
> I'll have his bones to grind my bread.

Children, who naturally experiment with sound and who savour play on words respond almost primordially to the verbal tonality of Henny-Penny, Turkey-Lurkey, and Cocky-Locky. And cumulative tales like *The Old Woman and Her Pig*, *The House that Jack Built* and *Millions of Cats* develop children's powers of prediction whilst satisfying their mastery of language patterns. Because folk tales are structurally predictable they provide the basis for all future literary appreciation.

6. Not only do phrases and descriptions recur in tales from the one region, but world-wide there is recurrent imagery and the repetition of events: the universal motifs of life and literature. These are repeated and elaborated in story just as they are in art or music: three bears, pigs, goats; the seventh son of the seventh son; the numbskull whose generosity gains him the hand of the princess; the golden goose, the magic harp; Aladdin's lamp or ring; seven league boots; the cloak of invisibility. As in life there are prohibitions and taboos to be observed: spells imposed and ultimately broken; wishes to be granted to the worthy and to rebound on the unworthy; tasks to be accomplished; journeys to be undertaken; rivers to be crossed; mountains to be climbed; enchanted gardens; golden apples; and long sleeps when time stands still. All obstacles, if met with courage and integrity, lead to reward and happy-ever-aftering. For in life, we each have our own hillside to climb, our

bridge to cross and our trolls to defeat before we can grow fat.

Such recurring themes and images and the many variants worldwide of the one story have caused linguistic and literary debate as to the origin of folk tales: the monogenesis versus the polygenesis theory as outlined by Arbuthnot and others (Arbuthnot 1961: 3). Research into the 345 or more variants of the Cinderella story would indicate that the same basic story pattern is to be found in India, the Philippines and Indonesia, among the North African Arabs, in Madagascar and on the island of Mauritius. Whilst in Europe both the Perrault and Grimm variants are widespread, versions which contain elements of each exist in both North and South America, and among the Zuni. Chinese and Vietnamese Cinderella stories have been published in illustrated form. In the nineteenth century Joseph Jacobs claimed with some irony that one version of the story which he printed was 'an English version of an Italian adaption of a Spanish translation of an Arabic translation of an Indian original' (Saxby 1979: 80).

Certain it is that any folk tale is related to the rites and beliefs of the pagan and animistic society which gave it birth, but that its life thereafter will have been shaped by its cultural journey and the literary environment in which it comes to rest. Calvino believes that the original tale (the prototype of the story as we have it) often absorbed a 'medieval stamp by osmosis which was followed by a wave of images and transfigurations of oriental origin'; that, 'the folk tale clothes its motifs in the habits of diverse societies' (Calvino 1980: XXVIII).

But whatever its origin and history the ritualistic quality of any given tale is pervasive and gives it a predictability which children need in their literary growth. Not only can psychological and spiritual truths be 'felt' behind the story (as Bettelheim, Luthi and Cooper, for example, reiterate) but through folk tales children learn the narrative pattern of story and the mechanism of discourse vitally necessary to a mature and able reader of the complex and sophisticated poetic forms of contemporary literature as found in writers like Philippa Pearce, William Mayne, Cynthia Voigt, Ivan Southall and Patricia Wrightson. From folk literature, too, children begin to develop a comprehensive view of life. Those stories frequently selected by compilers of books of nursery tales usually contain a rough poetic justice (*The Little Red Hen and the Grain of Wheat*), the villain getting his deserts and the hero his heart's desire (*The Golden Goose*). But as with *The Little Red Hen* they are — once the central image is apprehended — realistic comments on human endeavour. *The Three Little Pigs* can well be interpreted as a shrewd allegory of technological progress.

Collections more suited to older children and to adults have stories of hidden depths and psychological complexities such as *Beauty and the Beast*, horrific detail as in *The Juniper Tree* and more than a hint of cynicism in stories like *The Frog Prince*.

TYPES AND CLASSIFICATION OF FOLK TALES

Attempts to classify the world's vast array of folk tales go back to 1864 when Von Hahn derived an order based on narrative elements. In 1910 the Finnish folklorist Antti Aarne developed a more elaborate type-index but it was Stith Thompson who in 1928 produced his *Types of the Folk Tale* and in the 1930s developed an elaborate Index of Motifs.

However, for work with children it is better to avoid any rigid classification and to consider general story patterns or types which will be found later in more elaborated form in the longer stories and novels they read.

The Beast Tale

Examples are *The Wolf and the Seven Little Kids* and *The Adventures of Reynard* in which animals reflect human foibles, weaknesses, vices, virtues, strengths and insights — precursors of the modern animal story for children.

Droll Stories of Simpletons, Numbskulls and Dunderheads

These, however, frequently inherit the earth and have the basic humour that pervades latter-day writers for children — Roald Dahl without his black edge.

Trickster Stories

Brer Rabbit, Anansi, Coyote, Tyll Ulenspiegel, the Spanish Pedro and the Australian Crow are forerunners of today's confidence men.

Pour-quoi, or How and Why Stories

These are explanatory tales, telling Why the Sea is Salt, How the Southern Cross Was Formed or Why Kangaroo Hops. Explanations are psychological — why the narcissus bows its head to the pool — or metaphysical — How Rabaul Harbour was Formed (Beier 1972: 17–20); they foreshadow the modern psychological novel.

Tall Yarns and Exaggerations

Finn McCool, Lucky Owen, *The Jack Tales* from the Southern Appalachians and those Australian outback yarns collected by Bill Wannan and local folklorists are precursors of the larger-than-life modern novel.

Domestic Commentaries

In these the domestic routines and habits of common people are reflected in tales that include details of daily life and work: *Gone is Gone, The Elves and the Shoemaker, Hansel and Gretel, The Babes in the*

Wood. Like the realistic novels of today these tales reflect aspects of the society which gave them birth.

Commentaries on Human Traits and Characteristics

These are shrewd commentaries on human nature. Like the modern novel countless folk tales dramatise the human condition: *Diamonds and Toads.* Nemesis always follows hubris: Midas, Icarus and Daedalus. Pride always comes before a fall.

Moral Stories or Warnings

All societies depend for their survival and order on 'the Law'. The law of the jungle or the wild becomes more codified and refined as a society assumes the trappings of civilisation. But however primitive or complex, each society has its 'Law', written or unwritten. Breaking the law, the code, the taboo, brings retribution. The stories of Pandora's box or the Garden of Eden are prototypes of countless stories, novels, plays and scripts of our own era. In this country today writers like Joan Phipson, Patricia Wrightson and Bill Scott are giving expression to that basic primeval law of the land which must be heard and obeyed if modern man and society are to survive.

THE FAIRY TALE

In common usage, and also in the literature of the subject the terms folk tale and fairy story are used synonymously. Collections are labelled variously Fairy Tales, Folk Stories, or Folk and Fairy Tales. The Opies in their introduction to *The Classic Fairy Tales* (1974) date the use of the term 'fairy tale' in English to the 1699 translation of Madame d'Aulnoy's *Contes des fées* (*Tales of the Fairies*), but it should be remembered that the first three books of Spenser's *The Faerie Queene* were published in 1589 and that *A Midsummer Night's Dream* with Shakespeare's thistledown fairy song 'Over hill, over dale' was written in 1595 or 1596.

The term 'fairy' is a useful pointer to what we mean by fairy tales. It comes directly from the fourteenth century Old French 'faerie' (fairyland), from feie (later fée) (fairy), derived originally from the Latin 'fata' — the Fates. The Latin 'fatum' (oracular utterance) itself comes from 'fari' (to speak). Thus were derived the Greek Fates, the three goddesses who control the lives and destinies of man, and the Italian 'fatae', 'the fairy ladies who visited the household at births and pronounced on the future of the baby', (Briggs 1976: XV).

It was probably Spenser and Shakespeare who put wings on the fairy folk and so created a stereotype: 'Ill met by moonlight, proud Titania'. The character of Puck is, however, straight fairy — a creature who affects the fate of mortals, who can be benevolent or malevolent according to mood and whim or whether or not he has been satisfactorily pleased or appeased:

> Either I mistake your shape and making quite,
> Or else you are the shrewd and knavish sprite
> Call'd Robin Goodfellow: are you not he
> That frights the maidens of the villagery;
> Skim milk, and sometimes labour in the quern,
> And bootless make the breathless housewife churn;
> And sometimes make the drink to bear no barm;
> Mislead night-wanderers, laughing at their harm?
> Those that Hobgoblin call you, and sweet Puck,
> You do their work, and they shall have good luck:
> Are you not he?
>
> (*A Midsummer Night's Dream*, Act 11, Scene 1)

The Opies widen the definition of a fairy tale in the terms of common usage:

> A characteristic of the fairy tale, as told today is that it is unbelievable. Although a fairy tale is seldom a tale about fairy-folk, and does not necessarily even feature a fairy, it does contain an enchantment or other supernatural element that is clearly imaginary.
>
> (Opie 1974: 15)

Katharine Briggs, however, in her *A Dictionary of Fairies: Hobgoblins, Brownies, Bogies and Other Supernatural Creatures* differentiates between the specific use of the word fairy to 'express one species of those supernatural creatures ... varying in size, in powers, in span of life and in moral attributes but sharply differing from other species such as hobgoblins, monsters, hags, mer people and so on', and the wider use (which she favours and adopts) to cover 'that whole area of the supernatural which is not claimed by angels, devils or ghosts' (Briggs 1976: XV).

To accept this usage is helpful. For then all cultures have their fairies or spirit creatures who display local characteristics: leprechauns or cluricauns from Ireland; trolls from Scandinavia; kelpies from Scotland; servans (a 'borrower') from Switzerland and Northern Italy; the tomtra from Sweden — along with the hundreds listed in Briggs' directory of fairies of the British Isles, and as many again in Nancy Arrowsmith's *A Field Guide to the Little People* which moves across and around Europe.

We now know, thanks to Patricia Wrightson, that Australia has its own Aboriginal fairies: the rock-like Narguns, the Potkoorock tricksters who live in ponds, the Puk-wudgies of the desert: regional creatures or inhabitants of stone, sand, rivers, the spirits of the landscape.

In every part of the world their stories may be heard and whenever humans come upon them or their tracks they inspire awe or wonder. For they silently and invisibly impinge upon human life, rewarding or punishing, helping or hindering. Superstition, imagination, fantasy (man wondering); watered-down remnants of ancient deities; spacemen from the past; personified fears; poetic images: any or all of these elements make up the fairy folk of any culture. So who would deprive children of their folk images, or even of those creatures of a literary lineage, Peter Pan, Wendy, or the creations of Oz?

So if we accept Briggs' wider use of the word fairy we can concur with the Opies' view that:

> Usually the [fairy] tale is about one person, or one family, having to cope with a supernatural occurrence or supernatural protagonist during a period of stress. The hero is almost invariably a young person, usually the younger member of a family, and if not deformed or already an orphan, is probably in the process of being disowned or abandoned. The characters in the stories are, nevertheless, stock figures. They are either altogether good or altogether bad, and there is no evolution of character ... Fairy tales are more concerned with situation than with character ... They describe events that took place when a different range of possibilities operated in the unidentified long ago; and that is part of their attraction.
>
> (Opie 1974: 15)

They are clearly a species of folk tale and have obvious appeal and value to children.

1. They always tell a good story and provide an ideal introduction to narrative structure, mode and operation.

2. The language is conversational, anecdotal but polished in the telling when the words and style of the original teller are faithfully transcribed. Thus they provide the best possible introduction to the economic but fluid literary language of books:

> Once upon a time there were three goats who were to go up the hillside to make themselves fat — and the name of all three was Gruff.

3. The stories contain recurring imagery and the repetition of events and stock situations (younger children being treated badly by older siblings) which children recognise. Thus they can predict, yet, because most stories end happily, can be secure in the outcome.

4. Many are humorous, containing wild exaggeration and grotesque imagery (like a chain of characters stuck to a goose) which appeal to a juvenile stage in the development of humour.

5. Because so many of the old stories are part of man's early attempts to explain the inexplicable, to provide a rationale for the human and environmental phenomena they become part of, they are a stage in the development of more scientific and rational understandings.

6. Above all, they are awesome — an element integral to the development of imagination.

7. We can now see that folk and fairy tales contribute to the mental health of children: for too little fantasy in their lives is worse than too much. It is impossible to rid childhood of the dragons of dread, but it is worse to kill St George and to deprive children of a hero figure to serve as a model of behaviour.

8. The observant parent, teacher or librarian can see children coming to terms with the real world and their emerging understanding of self through fairy tales. *Cinderella* is essentially concerned with sibling rivalry, the displacement and restoration that every child at some time experiences. As with creative play, children can roleplay and work through their insecurities. The youngest Billy Goat Gruff outsmarts the lurking troll of fear, but the biggest brother pragmatically adds force to wit to send the troll back to the dark place from whence he came.

Preschool and early primary age children find in the old tales the enchantment and security they need to strengthen a developing sense of self. In middle childhood they can turn to the hero tales, myths and legends for models to reinforce a growing physical strength, social awareness and spiritual idealism.

Bettelheim entertainingly spells out his case for fairy tales in *The Uses of Enchantment: The Meaning and Importance of Fairy Tales*, summing it up thus:

> Fairy tales, unlike any other form of literature, direct the child to discover his identity and calling, and they also suggest what experiences are needed to develop his character further. Fairy tales intimate that a rewarding, good life is within one's reach despite adversity — but only if one does not shy away from hazardous struggles without which one can never achieve true identity. These stories promise that if a child dares to engage in this fearsome and taxing search, benevolent powers will come to his aid, and he will succeed. The stories also warn that those who are too timorous and narrow-minded to risk themselves in finding themselves must settle down to a humdrum existence — if an even worse fate does not befall them.
>
> (Bettelheim 1976: 24)

THE LITERARY HISTORY OF FOLK AND FAIRY TALES

Not only has man always had an urge to share his story-making orally but from the dawn of literacy has recorded and preserved narrative along with history. The *Old Testament* belonged to the folk as well as to the priestly caste. Indian collections date back a thousand years; there is a Hindu version of *The Princess and the Pea* from the third century AD; and Persian tales from the ninth century include Sinbad.

Throughout the Middle Ages there was a great migration of story. Travellers, merchants and crusaders carried and exchanged tales, and some of these were transmitted to manuscript.

It was in Italy that printed collections of folk literature: tales, crude jokes and snippets of story, first appeared. *Straparola's Nights* were published between 1550–3, in the Venetian dialect, and included a telling of *Puss in Boots*. In the Neapolitan dialect came the five volumes of Basile's *Il Pentamerone* (1634–5) with his versions of *Cinderella*, *Sleeping Beauty* and *Beauty and the Beast*. Translations into German and French soon followed.

But from France came the recorded fairy tale as we understand it. In 1697 Charles Perrault's *Histoires, ou contes du temps passé avec des Moralitez*, appeared. It was slanted largely towards the ladies of the Court of the Sun King, Louis XIV, but was quickly seen as having great appeal to children. The eight *Contes* were 'The Sleeping Beauty', 'Little Red Riding Hood', 'Bluebeard', 'Puss-in-Boots', 'Diamonds and Toads'; 'Cinderella', 'Rickety Topknot' and 'Hop-O'My-Thumb'. It is believed that Perrault's source was possibly a governess of his household:

> She, or her prototype, appears in the first edition frontispiece as a stout, middle-aged servant, spinning beside the fire, her lips parted in speech, while three slim and elegantly attired children sit listening. Incorporated into this picture is the legend *Contes de Ma Mère L'Oye* (Tales of Mother Goose), which seems to serve as an alternate title for Perrault's book.
>
> (Bierhorst 1981: 99)

Bierhorst claims that Perrault preserved much of the original storyteller's language but that he added witty embellishments of his own. Bluebeard's lavish hospitality, for instance, soon so impressed his young house-guest that she 'began to think that the host's beard was not so blue after all and that he was really quite decent'. (Bierhorst 1981: 26).

Perrault's *Contes* were translated into English in 1729 by Robert Samber. Bierhorst's translation (1980) claims to rectify some of Samber's minor inaccuracies. Certainly the Samber collection has formed the basis for multitudes of subsequent English retellings and adaptations of Perrault.

English collections of French fairy tales soon included tales like *The White Cat* and *The Yellow Dwarf* taken from Countess D'Aulnoy's *Contes des fée* (1699) along with *The Three Wishes* and *Beauty and the Beast* written down especially for children by a governess who emigrated from France to England about 1745, Madame de Beaumont.

These elegant tales from France were soon joined by the more sombre *German Popular Stories* (1823), a translation by Edgar Taylor of *Kinder-und Haus-Märchen* of Jacob and Wilhelm Grimm, published in Berlin from 1812–22.

The Brothers Grimm began the European nineteenth century vogue for collecting and preserving folk tales for the sake of literature and culture. They transcribed the tales as they were told by the folk, including Old Marie, the nurse and housekeeper of their neighbour, the apothecary Rudolph Wild, who was the most important source of their first volume. Their aim was expressed by Jacob: 'It is high time that these old traditions were collected — rescued before they perished like dew in the hot sun or fire in the stream, and fall silent forever in the unrest of our days' (Hammond 1968: 100).

Wilhelm was a poet and overrode Jacob's desire to publish the tales in their original local dialect. In later editions he tended to expand and polish, bringing out the latent poetry inherent in the tales, without destroying the basic simplicity of their style. His dictum (p. 100) can still be applied to folk and fairy tales generally:

> These fairy tales deserve a closer attention than they have received until now, not only for their content, which has its own charm, so that all who heard them in childhood bear with them on life's journey a golden rule and happy memory; but also because they belong to our national poetry, have lived on among the people for centuries.

In the same spirit, traditional tales from Norway were first rescued by P.C. Asbjörnsen and Jorgen E. Moe and published 1841—4. These *Norwegian Fairy Tales* were translated into English by Sir George Dasent from the English consulate. The selection best known today is *East of the Sun and West of the Moon*, which, along with the title story contains *The Three Billy Goats Gruff, The Husband Who Was to Mind the House, The Lad Who Went to the North Wind, The Princess on the Glass Hill*, and other stories.

Consistent with his belief that 'the taste of the world, which has veered so often, is constant enough to fairy tales', Andrew Lang (Alderson 1975: 349) included some of these Norse tales along with stories from Perrault, D'Aulnoy, Madame de Beaumont, the Brothers Grimm, the Arabian Nights and British sources in *The Blue Fairy Book* (1899), the first of a long series of Colour Fairy Books bequeathed to English readers.

Lang was a collector from afar. It was he who encouraged Kate Langloh Parker and wrote in an introduction to *Australian Legendary Tales*: 'Australia makes an appeal to fancy which is all its own ... But till Mrs Langloh Parker wrote this book, we had but few of the stories which Australian natives tell by the camp-fire or in the gum-tree shade'. He was a folklorist and one of the first to emphasise the universality of folk tales, 'that the same adventures and something like the same plots meet [the reader] in stories translated from different languages' (Alderson 1975: 349).

The great collector of British fairy tales was Joseph Jacobs who garnered his collections freely from English and Celtic fairy tales (1890—1894). He took stories that he 'found among English immigrants in America; a couple of others I tell as I heard them myself in my youth in Australia' (Jacobs 1890: vii).

Because his books were specifically for children he rewrote when he felt the dialect too demanding and reduced the 'flatulent phraseology of the eighteenth century chapbooks' and 're-wrote in simpler style the stories extant in "Literary English"'. But he wrote for telling, and his 'many unknown Little Friends' to whom he dedicated his books should always be grateful.

The work of collecting still goes on. Italo Calvino's *Italian Folktales* (1956), translated into English in 1980, is a careful assembling and retelling of tales from all over Italy that in their wholeness provide 'a general explanation of life ... the catalogue of the potential destinies of men and women' (Calvino 1980: xviii). Ulli Beier's *When the Moon Was Big* (1972) is a careful gathering of tales from children all over New Guinea told in their own words. Catherine H. Berndt's *Land of the Rainbow Snake* (1979) is a collection of tales told to her on Oenpelli mission station in Western Arnhem Land.

Recent collections of British tales reflect the scholarship and literary heritage of the editors. Kevin Crossley-Holland's *The Dead Moon: Tales From East Anglia and the Fen Country* (1982) has a nightmarish quality that comes from the authenticity of its sources. For his recent *Book of British Fairy Tales* (1984) Alan Garner has 'tried to get back, through the written word, to a sense of the spoken'. His are stories to be 'heard as well as seen', so that for the reader, 'the printed text may sing' (Garner 1984: 7). Both the collections of Crossley-Holland and Garner are atmospherically illustrated in styles that reinforce the emotional impact of the stories.

In spite of the argument that children should first hear the old tales, or read them in unillustrated versions, so that their imagination will be untrammelled, collections of fairy stories and sumptuously illustrated single stories are providing young readers with the best in art and literature. Established artists, from Marcia Brown and Barbara Cooney to more recent outstanding illustrators such as Svend Otto S (Denmark), Nancy Ekholm Burkert, Errol Le Cain, Moira Kemp, Joseph Palaček, Lilo Fromm, Laslo Gal and Lisbeth Zwerger, to name a few, have all added an artistic dimension to the folk and fairy tale. Whilst today there is a conscious effort to recapture the essential quality of the told tale and to hold fast to the verbal image of the preliterate tellers, there is a growing realisation that pure story also has a pictorial quality, that text and illustration can be two sides of the same coin.

THE LITERARY FAIRY TALE

There are, also, fairy tales whose language and form is fixed for they were written as literature, and did not evolve orally. Hans Christian Andersen was a creator of the literary fairy tale. Even when he used an idea from traditional literature like *The Princess on the Pea* he recrafted the material in his own fashion, but always in a style he would use when talking to children. Ten of Andersen's tales were published in England in 1846, having been translated by Mary Howitt as *Wonderful Stories For Children*. A 1978 publication using the splendid black and white illustrations of Rex Whistler today provides a definitive edition in English of the *Fairy Tales and Legends* by Hans Andersen.

John Ruskin's *The King of the Golden River* (1851) first illustrated with engravings by Richard Doyle was reissued in 1978 with coloured pictures by Krystyna Turska. Oscar Wilde's *The Happy Prince* and *The Selfish Giant* (1878) have frequently been reissued and reillustrated.

Modern fairy tales proliferate. Joan Aiken's collections, especially the title story, in *A Necklace of Raindrops*, is directly in the fairy tale tradition, but sits happily with her more contemporary stories. Terry Jones' *Fairy Tales* (1981) illustrated characteristically by Michael Foreman combines the author's passion for medieval history and Monty Python; they were written originally for his young daughter. *The Faber Book of Modern Fairy Tales* (1981) edited by Sara and Stephen Corrin brings together stories from the pens of writers as diverse as Alison Uttley, Eleanor Farjeon, Walter de la Mare, Edith Nesbit, Joan Aiken and Ted Hughes. *The Squirrel Wife* by Philippa Pearce included in the collection is in the best linguistic and psychological tradition of oral literature and one of the best modern English fairy stories.

Mercer Mayer has freely retold the traditional *Frog Prince* tale as *East of the Sun and West of the Moon* (1980) and illustrated it with the glowing colours and sweeping lines of his *Beauty and the Beast* (1978).

The diversity of mood and message of the modern fairy tale is nowhere better illustrated than in the worldly and witty *The Princess on the Nut, or, the Curious Courtship of the Son of the Princess on the Pea* (1981) by Michelle Nikly (translated from the German by Lucy Meredith), with operatic illustrations by Jean Claverie. And Roald Dahl's *Revolting Rhymes* (1982) is an irreverent tribute to the indestructibility of the fairy tale.

No only in the modern fairy story but also in the novel do the motifs and archetypes of the old tales renew themselves. In Australia, the realistic novels of writers such as Thiele, Southall and Norman re-employ the archetypal journey in contemporary terms: the testing of the protagonist by trial and ordeal. Fantasy, too, draws on structures from traditional literature. Not only has Patricia Wrightson recreated Aboriginal fairies in her own literary image, but the Wirrun trilogy particularly is reinforced with recurring images and motifs from the collective subconscious of folk literature. The cave, for example (that multilayered Aladdin's symbol) recurs in each of the books (and in many other Australian novels as well). And Wirrun himself is Hero, that larger than life figure that is the stuff of legend and the purveyor of myth.

REFERENCES

Alderson, Brian, editor, collector, Andrew Lang, *Blue Fairy Book*. London: Kestrel, 1975.

Arbuthnot, May Hill, *Time For Fairy Tales*. Glenview, Illinois: Scott, Foresman, 1961.

Arrowsmith, Nancy, *A Field Guide to the Little People*. London: Macmillan, 1977.

Beer, Jeanette, translator, illustrator, Jason Carter, *Medieval Fables*. Marie de France. Wellington, NZ: Reed, 1980.

Beier, Ulli, *When the Moon Was Big and Other Legends From New Guinea*. Sydney: Collins, 1972.

Berndt, Catherine H., *Land of the Rainbow Snake: Aboriginal Children's Stories and Songs from Western Arnhem Land*. Sydney: Collins, 1979.

Bettelheim, Bruno, *The Uses of Enchantment: The Meaning and Importance of Fairy Tales*. London: Thames & Hudson, 1976.

Bierhorst, John, translator, *The Glass Slipper: Charles Perrault's Tales of Times Past*. New York: Four Winds Press, 1981.

Briggs, Katherine, *A Dictionary of Fairies, Hobgoblins, Brownies, Bogies and Other Supernatural Creatures*. London: Penguin, 1977.

──────────, *The Fairies in Tradition and Literature*. London: Routledge & Kegan Paul, 1967.

Calvino, Italo, *Italian Folktales*. New York: Harcourt Brace, 1980.

Cooper, J.C., *Fairy Tales: Allegories of the Inner Life*. Wellingborough, Northamptonshire: The Aquarian Press, 1983.

Crossey-Holland, Kevin, *The Dead Moon and Other Tales from East Anglia and the Fen Country*. London: Deutsch, 1982.

Duvoisin, Roger, *The Three Sneezes and Other Swiss Tales*. New York: Knopf, 1947.

Garner, Alan, *Alan Garner's Book of British Fairy Tales*. London: Collins, 1984.

Gottleib, Gerald, editor, *Early Children's Books and their Illustration*. New York: Pierpoint Morgan Library, 1975.

Hammond, Muriel E., *Jacob and Wilhelm Grimm: the Fairy Tale Brothers*. London: Dennis Dobson, 1968.

Jacobs, Joseph, *English Fairy Tales*. New York: Putnam, nd.

Lang, Andrew, Brian Alderson, editor, *Blue Fairy Book*. London: Kestrel, 1975.

Luthi, Max, *Once Upon a Time: On the Nature of Fairy Tales*. Bloomington, Indiana: Indiana UP, 1976.

Opie, Iona and Peter, *The Classic Fairy Tales*. London: Oxford, 1974.

Saxby, Maurice, editor, *Through Folklore to Literature*. Sydney: IBBY, 1979.

Scholey, Arthur, *The Discontented Dervishes and Other Persian Tales retold from Sa'di*. London: Deutsch, 1977.

Scott, Michael, *Irish Folk and Fairy Tales Vol. 3*. London: Sphere, 1984.

Thompson, Stith, *The Folktale*. New York: Holt, Rinehart & Winston, 1946.

Untermeyer, Louis, editor, *Collins Albatross Book of Verse*. London: Collins, 1963.

BOOKS REFERRED TO IN THE CHAPTER

Aiken, Joan, *A Necklace of Raindrops*. Puffin.
Briggs, Raymond, *The Mother Goose Treasury*. Puffin.
Clark, Leonard, illustrated by Jeroo Roy, *Tales From the Panchantantra*. Evans.
Corrin, Sara and Stephen, *The Faber Book of Modern Fairy Tales*. Faber/Puffin.
Cowper, William, illustrator, Randolph Caldecott, *The Diverting History of John Gilpin*. Warne.
Dahl, Roald, *Revolting Rhymes*. Cape/Puffin.
Factor, June, *Far Out, Brussel Sprout*! Oxford.
Gag, Wanda, *Millions of Cats*. Puffin.
Harris, Joel Chandler, *Uncle Remus*. Routledge & Kegan Paul.
Ingpen, Robert, illustrator, *Click Go the Shears*. Collins.
King, John Anthony, illustrator, *Farewell to Old England Forever*. Collins.
─────────, *The Wild Colonial Boy*. Collins.
Lang, Andrew, *Blue Fairy Book*. Kestrel.
Lobel, Arnold, *Fables*. Cape.
Mayer, Mercer, *Beauty and the Beast*. Four Winds Press.
─────────, *East of the Sun and West of the Moon*. Four Winds Press.
Nikly, Michelle, *The Princess on the Nut*. Faber.
Opie, Iona and Peter, *The Puffin Book of Nursery Rhymes*. Puffin.
Paterson, A.B., illustrator, Quentin Hole, *A Bush Christening*. Collins.
─────────, illustrator, Quentin Hole, *The Man From Ironbark*. Collins.
─────────, illustrators, Kilmeny and Deborah Niland, *Mulga Bill's Bicycle*. Collins.
─────────, illustrator, Desmond Digby, *Waltzing Matilda*. Collins.
Ruskin, John, *The King of the Golden River*. Hamish Hamilton.
Turner, Ian, *Cinderella Dressed in Yella*. Heinemann.
Wilde, Oscar, *The Happy Prince and Other Stories*. Puffin.

COLLECTIONS OF FOLK AND FAIRY TALES

Andersen, Hans Christian, *Fairy Tales*. Selected by Naomi Lewis. Puffin.
Corrin, Sara and Stephen, *The Faber Book of Modern Fairy Tales*. Faber.
Grimm, Jacob and Wilhelm, *Grimms' Tales For Young and Old*. Penguin.
Haviland, Virginia and Briggs, Raymond, *The Fairy Tale Treasury*. Puffin.
Hayes, Barbara and Ingpen, Robert, *Folk Tales and Fables of the World*. Bateman.
Jones, Terry and Foreman, Michael, *Fairy Tales*. Puffin.
Martin, Eva and Gal, Laszlo, *Tales of the Far North*. Methuen.
O'Brien, Edna and Foreman, Michael, *Tales For The Telling*. Pavilion.
Oxenbury, Helen, *The Nursery Story Book*. Heinemann.
Riordan, James, *The Woman in the Moon and Other Forgotten Heroines*. Hutchinson.
Rockwell, Anne, *The Three Bears and Fifteen Other Stories*. Puffin.
Yolan, Jane, *Favourite Folktales From Around the World*. Pantheon.

7 THE WONDER OF MYTH AND LEGEND

MAURICE SAXBY

> Plato — who may have understand better what forms the mind of man than do some of our contemporaries who want their children exposed only to 'real' people and everyday events — knew what intellectual experiences make for true humanity. He suggested that the future citizens of his ideal republic begin their literary education with the telling of myths, rather than with mere facts or so-called rational teachings. Even Aristotle, master of pure reason, said: 'The friend of wisdom is also a friend of myth'.
>
> Bruno Bettelheim

LEGENDS AND HERO TALES

As with folk tale every culture has its store of legend. Indeed, most families treasure their private and local legend. 'Tell me about ...' demand the youth of the clan, the tribe, the nation. So exploits are passed down, gaining accretions of incident and heroic detail with each new generation. In the fullness of time the actual historic event(s) become clouded, and, sometimes, as in the case of the Arthurian legends, become tinged with the supernatural. For even before the birth of Arthur, Merlin the prophet and messenger had foretold the coming of one that was greater than he.

Originally transmitted orally, in mime or dance legends provide a sense of cultural identity, but unlike the Märchen or fairy tale they can be specific of place and person. Time is seldom exact but an historic era can be specified or implied. Cuchulain, the Hound of Ulster, who is reputed to have killed a guard dog with his bare hands when still a boy is said to have ruled Ireland in the first century AD. He was a man of great strength, an ancient playboy of the Western World.

The story of Samson the Israelite is almost a prototype of the hero tale. Born whilst his people were in a forty-year thralldom to the Philistines, his parents had long been childless yet longed for offspring. When an angel appeared to the woman a conditional promise was made: 'Take no wine or strong drink, and eat nothing unclean. For you will conceive and bear a son. No razor is to touch his head, for the boy shall be God's nazirite from his mother's womb. It is he who will begin to rescue Israel from the power of the Philistines' (Judges 13: 2-5 *Jerusalem Bible*).

The strength of the youthful Samson was such that he tore a lion apart with his bare hands (almost mandatory for heroes), and when bound by the Philistines burst his bonds asunder, snatched up the jawbone of an ass and slaughtered a thousand men.

Unlike the anonymous fairy tale heroes who live happily ever after, despite a miraculous birth, the hero of legend is not only mortal but fallible. And he is known by name. His choices are difficult and they are his alone. Samson, like David and countless heroes of literature, was dogged by misfortune, constantly tried and tested, and ultimately brought down by his own weakness of character. Like so many heroes, Samson's pride in his own strength, his hubris, was his undoing, but the legend testifies to his courage in the end. The ultimate personal triumph of the hero is never as important as the relentless pursuit of his quest, or the successful completion of each successive task.

These figures are a source of national pride and inspiration and for the young, not only an heroic example but a potent source of identification for their own emerging selfhood. Hence their endurance in literature, on the stage and screen, and their passionate appeal to the latent idealism and the need for worship of primary age children. All races and cultures have their national heroes, and it would seem certain that those from the heroic past will continue to outlive if not outshine the modern stars of rock and roll.

From Ancient Greece there are the tales of Heracles with labours to perform; feats that have been retold countless times down the centuries. Leon Garfield and Edward Blishen's *The Golden Shadow*, with sensuous and symbolic black and white images by Charles Keeping, places the hero both in the world of human frailty and in the eternal one of on-going conflict.

How Theseus, that early King of Athens and one of the mightiest of the Greek heroes, volunteered to sail to Crete as one of seven youths and seven maidens destined to be incarcerated in the Minotaur's labyrinth, and how he was aided by Ariadne, the daughter of the Cretan King, to thread his way to the heart of the maze and there to slay the monster, is but the culmination of a series of tasks and journeys of that archetypal hero. Far less frequently told are the tales of how Theseus overcame the monster Periphetes who battered travellers to death with a mighty club; paid in his own kind Sinis who ripped apart wayfarers by strapping their legs to separate saplings and then using the trees as a catapault; pushed Sciron over the cliff from which he had sent passers-by hurtling to their destruction; and how he stretched out Procrustes on his own bed of torment, and then beheaded him. The horrific but victorious journey of Theseus from his mother's home in Troizen to Athens typifies the painful path that youth must inevitably traverse before attaining maturity.

But tragically, even in his prime, Theseus, after slaying the Minotaur paid the price of his own neglect when he failed to hoist the white sail that would signal his presence on board to his father Aegeus, who then threw himself from a cliff to a despairing death. And although Theseus became a wise and just king he still had battles to fight and personal tragedy to face. Like all Hero figures, Theseus is Everyman enlarged and made into the image of what we would all like to be. He is the forerunner of countless heroes of children's books — the superman who is not infallible.

Writers today tell of ordinary, or less than ordinary children overcoming the buffetings of nature and a deep sense of personal inadequacy to blossom into whole people. The Greeks knew that undue self-confidence can lead to hubris, a trait never to be tolerated by the gods; that beyond pride looms Nemesis, retribution. So Icarus tries to fly to the sun and Bellerophon is tossed to his death by the winged Pegasus. For today's readers the confident optimism of contemporary writers is balanced by the insight of the ancients.

Jason's quest for the Golden Fleece and the inspiring symbol of the Argonauts; the noble figure of Perseus the Gorgon-slayer holding at his sword's end the gruesome head of Medusa, and, above all, the danger-strewn but purposeful wanderings of Odysseus, are pointers to constants that are part of being young and human. The lotus eaters, the Cyclops, the Circes and Sirens of today's society take on contemporary and alluring guises — and the dangers must be recognised if the young are to steer a safe course between the Scyllas of society and the Charybdis of peer pressure.

That each period of history and each society has previous insights and achievements on which to build, allowing us to be warned by the mistakes of the past, operates through literature. The Romans learned from the Greeks. Ulysses is a cross-cultured Odysseus. So the heroic line will be perpetuated through nations and across time.

From Britain comes the courtly and chivalric tradition epitomised by the Arthurian legends, and the psychological and spiritual warfare of St George. The fight against oppression and belief in the common man is expressed in the Robin Hood cycle. In the British tradition, too, Arthur has his fallible Guinevere and Robin his faithful Maid Marian.

The ballads of Robin Hood, transmitted orally, go back at least to the fifteenth century. His exploits featured in early chapbooks, and he was the champion of folk plays, May festivities and Morris dances from the sixteenth century. Children's retellings of Robin Hood have proliferated from the nineteenth century onwards. Robin's wit and humanity, his rustic practicality and, above all, his espousal of the ordinary man against oppressive authority along with the fact that his Merrie Men are representative figures of English society yet are deeply and recognisably human, have made him perhaps the most popular of all folk heroes — at least in England. In Australia, Ned Kelly is obviously a cultural and literary descendant, and America has produced Johnny Appleseed, Pecos Bill, Paul Bunyan and Davy Crockett.

The popularity of both Robin Hood and King Arthur is testified to by many place names in Britain. Arthur certainly figured in Celtic lore and was passed on to the Anglo-Normans and the French. As an English literary figure he was established by Geoffrey of Monmouth in the twelfth century, and accretions to the cycle were added until Caxton printed Mallory's *Morte d'Arthur* in 1485.

The Arthurian romances have attracted many scholarly retellings by children's writers such as Roger Lancelyn Green. In 1938 T.H. White wrote the novel *The Sword in the Stone*, and in 1958 *The Once and Future King*. Rosemary Sutcliff's trilogy remains one of the most accessible and poetic yet scholarly versions for children and adults. *The Sword and the Circle: King Arthur and the Knights of the Round Table* (1981); *The Light Beyond the Forest: The Quest for the Holy Grail* (1979); and *The Road to Camlann: The Death of King Arthur* (1981). Susan Cooper's sequence *The Dark is Rising* (1984) is linked by the figure of Merlin and the never-ending struggle between darkness and light. It would seem that as technology and materialism join forces, the quest for the Holy Grail becomes ever more urgent.

From Rosemary Sutcliff, again, has come *Tristan and Iseult* (1971), the tragic love story of one of King Arthur's knights, and also the story of *Beowulf: Dragon Slayer* (1966), the hero of the Old English saga who slew the monster Grendel, then Grendel's mother, but later forfeited his life for his victory over an evil fire dragon. Beowulf's story has also been told in verse for children by Ian Serraillier in *Beowulf the Warrior* (1954). This author has also given children a version of *The Song of Roland*, the French epic of Roland's friendship with Oliver, in *The Ivory Horn* (1960).

OTHER HERO TALES

Each culture produces its heroes: Attila from Hungary; Cuchulain and Finn from Ireland; Ogier the Dane; Roland and St Joan from France; Sigurd from the Norse and Icelandic sagas who becomes Siegfried in German stories; Antar of Arabia; Rustem of Iran; Rama the Indian hero; and Scarface of the Blackfoot Indians — to select only a few. Children's versions continue to appear. Perhaps because of the use of Welsh sources by Alan Garner and Lloyd Alexander or because of yet another Celtic revival, there has been a rediscovery of the Welsh heroes including Manawyddan and his son Pryderi. Whilst William Mayne's *A Book of Heroes* (1967) and Barbara Leonie Picard's *Hero Tales From the British Isles* (1963) included tales from the Mabinogion and *Welsh Legends and Folk Tales* (1955) by Gwyn Jones contained versions of all four branches of the Mabinogion, the more recent *Tales From the Mabinogion* (1984) by Gwyn Thomas and Kevin Crossley-Holland retells the four branches (or parts) in measured prose which is gloriously matched by the strong, stylised illustrations of Margaret Jones. In the introduction Gwyn Thomas writes:

The magic and wonder of these stories would have held rough warriors and their ladies spellbound in the Courts of Welsh kings and princes many centuries ago. Trained storytellers would have told of the Throne of Arbeth and of the enchantment of Dyfed, in the firelit darkness of medieval halls. And some of the stories would have been told by the ordinary people in their simple houses or on a hill on a summer day. In this way some of the old stories became folklore. In the twentieth century we can become our own storytellers and make the printed words bring back to life Rhiannon and Branwen and Gwydion and their strange world.

(Thomas 1984: 1)

EPIC AND SAGA

In ancient days tales of heroes were often sung by minstrels and gathered by poets in the form of an epic: a long narrative verse cycle clustered around the exploits of a named hero and embodying cultural symbols of those qualities which the society held dear. Such are the *Iliad* and the *Odyssey* of Homer (c 850 BC), the former telling of the Trojan war and the latter detailing the wanderings of Odysseus. Retellings for children are frequent, and incidents from both appear in numerous anthologies of traditional literature.

But the first known and recorded epic would appear to be the legend of Gilgamesh sung to the harp by Sumerians and recorded in clay some three thousand years before Christ. This exults in the wondrous exploits of Gilgamesh, King of Uruk, and celebrates his friendship with Enkidu. It probes the mysteries of life and whatever is beyond it.

THE RAMAYANA

In another tradition, travellers to Bali will almost certainly have been introduced through mime, dance and puppetry to the pervasive Indian epic, the *Ramayana* of the wise Valmiki, going back some 3,000 years. Although the *Ramayana* was originally written in rhymed couplets, it has been recited and orally passed on from generation to generation in the East, where it is still an integral part of culture and religion. Brian Thompson's *The Story of Prince Rama* (1980) makes this powerful struggle between good and evil readily accessible to young readers. This telling glows with the colour, mystery and fantasy of the East using reproductions of illuminations from ancient manuscripts. The journeyings, the tasks, the trials, the combats, the set-backs and the final triumph of Rama and his faithful brother, Lakshmana, provide not only a splendid introduction to the Indian epic, but link East with West as the patterns of universal story emerge.

THE KALEVALA

Early in the nineteenth century a Finnish folklorist and poet, Elias Lönnrot, began collecting the heroic songs of his people. They formed what he believed to be a lost epic and he called it the *Kalevala* — the Land of Heroes. They are songs (whose metre Longfellow adopted for *Hiawatha*) telling of Vainamoinen the Wise, Ilmarinen the Smith and Lemminkainen the scapegrace, and of their feud with Mistress Louhi, the sorceress of the bitter North. Ursula Synge has retold the stories in lyric prose for young readers in *Kalevala: Heroic Tales from Finland* (1977).

As it frequently is with heroes, the birth of Vainamoinen is both miraculous and supernatural:

> It is said of Vainamoinen the Wise that he was carried for thirty years in the womb of his mother Ilmatar; that he was born a man, full-grown in wisdom. It was he who sang the world into being.
>
> (Synge 1977: 9)

Synge's closing paragraphs catch the grandeur, the fulfilment, the sadness of the passing of a hero.

> [Vainamoinen] stood on the shore of the great lake and began to sing. It was the last of his songs and had all his remaining magic in it. He sang all the songs of the heroes so that their exploits would live forever. And then he sang for himself a boat. He had created many boats with song but this was his finest of all. It was made of burnished copper and it shone with all the glory of the sun and the splendour of the moon.
>
> Still singing, Vainamoinen stepped into the copper boat and it rose into the sky and disappeared among the clouds. No man has seen the Wise Singer since that day — but he left behind him the *kantele* and the songs of heroes.
>
> (Synge 1977: 222)

THE SAGA

In Scandinavia, heroic stories, especially of important families and dynasties were recorded in prose sagas. The many adventures of Sigurd (Siegfried) who slew the terrible dragon, Fafnir, are recorded in the Volsunga Saga. The awakening by Sigurd of Brynhild, whose pride had caused her to be pierced by the thorn of sleep, is an echo of tales told long ago and still heard in the nursery today. And it is the age-old story of love fulfilled.

> Then Sigurd set the ring on Brynhild's finger and their arms were about each other and their hearts were full and glad. The day grew old about them and eve and the sunset came. The twilight changed and died and the stars shone forth on the world, ere they turned and went the roads that go green to the dwellings of men.
>
> (Hosford 1949: 168)

Through the hero tale preserved in scripture, legend, epic and saga and perpetuated in the 'high' fantasies of Tolkien, Alexander, Le Guin, Wrightson and others, today's children are not only given an opportunity to identify with heroic men and women, but are confronted with the great human dilemmas and face complex moral choices and the sweep of human passion — love and hate, loyalty and betrayal. Here are the heights and depths of tragedy, the enduring themes of sin and suffering yet the possibility of reconciliation and redemption. These are the great themes of literature and in the broad strokes of epic and saga they are presented in universal terms.

The heroes of old lived in the shadow of the gods — gods who demanded respect, supplication and appeasement, who could be angered and who could wreak terrible vengeance on those who broke the law. Today these ancient ones have taken on new and terrible forms; youth lives with the fear of nuclear catastrophe and so searches for certainty. The Aristotelian principle that the friend of wisdom must also be the friend of myth is as true today as it was then. Mankind has always had his gods and needs a faith by which to live. Each generation must learn anew the lesson of acceptance that cost Oedipus the very gift of sight. But man's questioning never ceases. The supreme quest of every age is to look beyond the edge of present vision.

MYTH

So myth is basically religious and springs from the nature of man as a seeking, curious, speculative creature, providing him if not with the answers to the imponderables of life, at least with a faith to steady him and give him direction.

Down the ages ring questions as to the nature of humankind; where on the spectrum of might, power and understanding do men and women belong? Are they masters of their own destiny or playthings of the gods? How will the battle of good and evil end? Is death an end or a beginning?

In what we like to think of as more primitive times man speculated, and symbolised his answers in story: what we call myth. What causes night and day? Why do the seasons come and go? How? What's the origin of fire? Flood? Disaster?

Every culture, it would seem, has its mythology, needs answers to the unknown that satisfy an inner need, needs religion to govern life. Mythology, then, is sacred (at least at first); although non-sacred myth in time separates itself, and may even, in time, become fairy tale. But the myths themselves remain as models of human behaviour that help give meaning and value to life. As science provides answers, new questions and new dilemmas arise. Some still refute science, or remain unconvinced; and there are those who see these 'tales from eternity' (Haughton 1973) as images of man's ongoing spiritual search for a way to Truth and Life.

It has been argued, too, that society's ongoing preoccupation with the occult (obsessively so in some subcultures), the proliferation of pseudo-myth and religious splinter groups; children's fascination with wizards, witches and even with fighting fantasies, attest to an ineradicable need to push back the edges of vision.

But apart from the argument that myth can still help satisfy deep psychological needs, is the fact that a society's culture is embodied in its mythology. Not only is a close encounter with traditional literature a cross-cultural experience, it also provides an historical, cultural, aesthetic and spiritual perspective. It has been argued that to read the Greek myths is to experience the wonder of the morning of the world. Perhaps to apprehend something of the Aboriginal Dreamtime is, for Australian children at least, to experience not only the wonder of this most ancient of continents but also to grasp a little of its mighty power, and its demands, along with its rewards and healing gifts — if we but listen to its rhythm and its law. Some knowledge of the rituals of the Aborigines: 'As it was done in the Dreamtime, so must it be done today' is at least as relevant to an understanding of our environment as an understanding of Northern, Eastern or Western mythologies.

> One only has to consider the incalculable influence of the myths of ancient Greece or the literature, drama and art of the civilized world for over two thousand years, and that of the Nordic myths on music, dance and literature of Northern Europe, to realize how the living myths of the Aborigines, which belong so fully to Australia, could contribute to the cultural life of this country.
>
> (Mountford 1979: 15)

For decades Australian children have been well served with collections from mythology. Publications by Roger Lancelyn Green — such as *A Book of Myths* (1965) and *Heroes of Greece and Troy* (1975), and Kevin Crossley-Holland's *The Faber Book of Northern Legends* (1977), together with many standard collections, have recently been augmented by series such as the colourful and comprehensive World Mythologies of Hodder and Stoughton: *Gods, Men and Monsters From the Greek Myths* (1977) to *Warriors, Gods and Spirits From Central American Mythology* (1983). Penelope Farmer's *Beginnings: Creation Myths of the World* (1978) and John Bailey's *Gods and Men: Myths and Legends from the World's Religions* (1981) provide an excellent background for the exploration of myth.

And now Australia has the eight Collins picture books of Dick Roughsey, a tribal Aboriginal writer and painter, and Percy Trezise: *The Rainbow Serpent* (1975) to their latest (1985). These glow with the colours of tribal lands and tell something of their origins and inhabitants. From the Australian National University Press comes *Djugurba: Tales From the Spirit Time* (1974) and *Kwork-Kwork: The Green Frog and Other Tales From the Spirit Time* (1977), collections of stories told by young Aborigines themselves. The

Dreamtime (1965) and three other similar publications contain paintings by Ainslie Roberts and text by Charles Mountford.

Because mythology is as old as humanity and its line of descent complex, and because retellings can be less than faithful to the spirit of the culture of origin, the librarian or teacher who hasn't a personal store of traditional literature would do well to consult guides to versions such as *The Ordinary and the Fabulous: An Introduction to Myths, Legends and Fairy Tales* (Cook: 1976) and background studies like *Through Folklore to Literature* (Saxby: 1979). But also because myth and legend, folk and fairy tales are eloquent and arresting stories and prototypes for modern literature as we know it, they are a source of linguistic, psychological and emotional satisfaction and points of cultural contact, yet points of departure for a lifetime's study of story.

If the blue of the Aegean deepens and intensifies as Icarus and Daedalus fly overhead, and if at Delphi the Oracle still speaks to men of imagination, then the bora ring or a fish carved into rock can point to an ordering of life's chaos, the possibility of reconciling the present with the past and of personal harmony in a world threatened with disintegration.

REFERENCES

Bettelheim, Bruno, *The Uses of Enchantment: The Meaning and Importance of Fairy Tales*. London: Thames & Hudson, 1976.

Hosford, Dorothy, *Sons of the Volsungs*. New York: Holt, 1949.

Synge, Ursula, *Kalevala: Heroic Tales From Finland*. London: Bodley Head, 1977.

Thomas, Gwyn and Crossley-Holland, Kevin *Tales From the Mabinogion*. London: Gollancz, 1984.

BOOKS REFERRED TO IN THE CHAPTER

Bailey, John *Gods and Men: Myths and Legends From the World's Religions*. Oxford.

Blishen, Edward, *The Golden Shadow*. Longman Young Books.

Cook, Elizabeth, *The Ordinary and the Fabulous: An Introduction to Myths, Legends and Fairy Tales*. Cambridge University Press.

Cooper, Susan, *The Dark is Rising*. Puffin.

Crossley-Holland, Kevin, *The Faber Book of Northern Legends*. Faber.

Djurgurba: Tales From the Spirit Time. Australian National University Press.

Farmer, Penelope, *Beginnings: Creation Myths of the World*. Chatto & Windus.

Homer, *The Iliad*. Penguin.

——————, *The Odyssey*. Penguin.

Jones, Gwyn, *Welsh Legends and Folk Tales*. Oxford.

Kwork-Kwork: The Green Frog and Other Tales From the Spirit Time. Australian National University Press.

Mallory, Thomas *Morte D'Arthur*. Everyman.

Mayne, William, *A Book of Heroes*. Hamish Hamilton.

Mountford, Charles, illustrator, Ainslie Roberts, *The Dreamtime*. Rigby.
Picard, Barbara Leonie, *Hero Tales From the British Isles*. Puffin.
Roughsey, Dick, *The Giant Devil Dingo*. Collins.
——————, *The Rainbow Serpent*. Collins.
Roughsey, Dick and Tresize, Persy, *Banana, Bird and the Snake Law*. Collins.
——————, *The Flying Fox Warriors*. Collins.
——————, *The Magic Firesticks*. Collins.
——————, *The Quinkins*. Collins.
——————, *Turramulli the Giant Quinkin*. Collins.
Saxby, Maurice, *Through Folklore to Literature*. IBBY Australia.
Serraillier, Ian, *Beowulf the Warrior*. Oxford.
——————, *The Ivory Horn: Retold from the Song of Roland*. Oxford.
Sutcliff, Rosemary, illustrator, Charles Keeping, *Beowulf: Dragon Slayer* Bodley Head/Puffin.
——————, *The Light Beyond the Forest: The Quest for the Holy Grail*. Bodley Head.
——————, *The Sword and the Circle: King Arthur and the Knights of the Round Table*. Bodley Head.
——————, *The Road to Camlann: The Death of King Arthur*. Bodley Head.
——————, *Tristan and Iseult*. Bodley Head.
Thompson, Brian, *The Story of Prince Rama*. Kestrel.
White, T.H., *The Once and Future King*. Collins.
——————, *The Sword in the Stone*. Collins.
World Mythology Series: Hodder & Stoughton:
Al-Saleh, Khairat, *Fabled Cities, Princes and Jinn from Arab Myths and Legends*.
Branston, Brian, *Gods and Heroes From Viking Mythology*.
Gibson, Michael, *Gods, Men and Monsters from Greek Myths*.
Gifford, Douglas, *Warriors, Gods and Spirits from Central and South American Mythology*.
Liu Sanders, Tao Tao, *Dragons, Gods and Spirits from Chinese Mythology*.
Usher, Kerry, *Heroes, Gods — Emperors from Roman Mythology*.
Warner, Elizabeth, *Heroes, Monsters and Other Worlds From Russian Mythology*.
Wood, Marion, *Spirits, Heroes and Hunters from North American Mythology*.

MYTHS AND LEGENDS RETOLD

Anderson, Rachel and Brodby, David, *Renard the Fox*. Oxford.
Green, Roger Lancelyn, *King Arthur and His Knights of the Round Table*. Puffin.
Harrison, Michael, *The Curse of the Ring*. Oxford.
Lines, Kathleen, *The Faber Book of Great Legends*. Faber.
Saxby, Maurice and Ingpen, Robert, *The Gread Deeds of Superheroes*. Millennium.
——————, *The Great Deeds of Heroic Women*. Millennium.
Sutcliff, Rosemary and Keeping, Charles, *Dragon Slayer*. Puffin.

8 THE SUPREME FICTION: ON POETRY AND CHILDREN

GORDON WINCH

> Poetry is the supreme fiction, madame.
> Wallace Stevens, 'A High-Toned Old Christian Woman'
>
> ... I am the necessary angel of earth,
> Since, in my sight, you see the earth again.
> Wallace Stevens, 'Angel Surrounded By Paysans'

This chapter concerns itself with poetry: what it is and how it works. It concerns itself, too, with children and their 'connection' with poetry: why it is important to them, why they enjoy it and how we can help them to share it. As a result, the chapter is divided up into sections which will allow a reader more easily to consider the matter of poetry, and put those considerations into practice.

ON POETRY AND POETS FIRST

Poetry is an ancient and universal verbal art form which has stood the test of time in multiple manifestations. It is a private and public phenomenon, and always has been from the classical poets to the heroes of the modern electronic media. It is found in high and low culture, in the short runs of books from exclusive publishing houses, on gravestones, on the walls of public toilets and in children's games. Response to its magic is spread across humanity: in the mind of the intellectual, in the heart of the lover and in the rhythmical movements of dancers who respond to the lyrics of the songs which pound out in crowded rooms.

From this point of view 'Sticky beak, treacle nose, /Lolly legs and ice cream toes' is as much poetry as 'Shall I compare thee to a summer's day?/ Thou art more lovely and more temperate'. Comic verse is as much poetry as the ode; the limerick as worthwhile as the sonnet. Fortunately, as Charles Causley (1985: 12) points out, 'the world of poetry, like the Kingdom of Heaven, has many mansions'. Or as Fatchen (1985: 19) says: '... funny rhymes can help you keep your reason, just as serious poetry can probe your soul'.

There is as much of the poetic in Milligan's

> A Lion is fierce:
> His teeth can pierce
> The skin of a postman's knee.
> It serves him right,
> That, because of his bite,
> He gets no letters you see.

as there is in Lawrence's

> The tiny fish enjoy themselves
> in the sea.
> Quick little splinters of life,
> their little lives are fun to them in the sea.

or Keats'

> Fair youth, beneath the trees, thou canst not leave
> Thy song, nor ever can those trees be bare;
> Bold Lover, never, never canst thou kiss,
> Though winning near the goal — yet, do not grieve;
> She cannot fade, though thou hast not thy bliss,
> Forever wilt thou love, and she be fair!
>
> (from 'Ode to A Grecian Urn', Verse 11)

In each case the poet has done it well; he has effectively used the many subtle skills that are needed to make a poem from the stuff of language; he has shown a craftsman's skill with words.

A.D. Hope in his book, *The New Cratylus: Notes on the Craft of Poetry* (1979: 164) says:

> There is nothing mysterious about poetry. The whole endeavour of this book is to show that it is composed of ordinary materials familiar to us in other contexts and that it works by similarly familiar processes. Poets are not magicians, but a rather odd kind of craftsmen, working in a living material which is part of themselves.

The meaning of Hope's statement is made very clear when one looks at a line or verse which lacks the craftman's touch of excellence. Consider the terrible result if Coleridge's beautiful description of the sudden arrival of night in the tropics in his poem 'The Rime of The Ancient Mariner': 'The Sun's rim dips; the stars rush out:/ At one stride comes the dark', were to read '... the stars leap forth:/ In one jump night arrives'. Or, earlier in the poem, where Coleridge describes the bride at the wedding feast: 'The bride hath paced into the hall,/ Red as a rose is she': what if the simile had been 'Red as a nose is she'!

The reason a successful poem works is not easy to sum up. There is a perfection in the selection of words and word order, an effective matching of the mood to the metre; a certain balance; a reaching out with language; a wholeness. To achieve this success the poet-craftsman works hard with language before saying: 'That's it; it's right'.

In 1949, the Welsh poet Dylan Thomas, wrote a poem called 'Over Sir John's Hill'. It is about a hawk who is hunting in the estuary of the Taf and the Towy at Laugharne in South Wales where Thomas lived. Thomas was often criticised for his loose use of language: Llareggub language it was called. But the critics were wrong. Thomas, like other great poets, took pains with language. A testament to his careful craftsmanship in the writing of 'Over Sir John's Hill' is found in the forty pages of work sheets now held in the library at Harvard University. This sobering and majestic poem begins:

> Over Sir John's hill,
> The hawk on fire hangs still;
> In a hoisted cloud, at drop of dusk, he pulls to his claws
> And gallows, up the rays of his eyes the small birds of the bay ...

No Llareggub language here!

This is not to say that *all* poetry is good poetry. Sheila Egoff (1981: 223) warns us to beware of the second rate when considering children's poetry.

> There exists the questionable quality of children's verse, that poor cousin of children's poetry which through sheer quantity and numbing mediocrity has always threatened to drown out the music and delight in authentic children's poetry. Children all too often are given verse that is flawed in language, awkward in rhythm, laboured in rhyme, and infused with condescension and sentimentality.

It is interesting to note, however, that she endorses the point made earlier in this chapter: poetry comes in a variety of forms and each has its own intrinsic value:

> This is not to say that children's poetry should contain only lofty, so called 'high poetry' as distinct from popular or light verse. One does not expect the insight and transformation of lyric poetry in a light-hearted jingle, which has its own, quite different, values of humour, drama, and musical fun.

The idea of a poet as craftsman and poem as artefact does not seem to go far enough; there must be more to a form so celebrated that it spreads its appeal across the whole gamut of humanity. Clifton Fadiman (1982: 13) talks about this something more, this extra dimension, in his introduction to *A Swinger of Birches*, a collection of Robert Frost's poems for young people. When a poem is finished, Fadiman says:

> the poem should have said something about human beings or the natural world which adds to our sense of what living is all about.

This extra dimension is a large part of the appeal of poetry to young and old alike. Thomas' poem about the hawk reminds us that nature is red in tooth and claw and that life, no matter how we live it, is very short. Robert Frost's poem, 'The Pasture' is, on the surface, simply about an invitation to a child to clean a spring and fetch a calf. But it is also about something else which is found in the simple words, 'You come, too'. As Fadiman points out, the poem is about a loving and sharing relationship between an adult and a child. This is what gives it its extra dimension and adds to our sense of what life means.

The Pasture

I'm going out to clean the pasture spring;
I'll only stop to rake the leaves away
(And wait to watch the water clear, I may):
I shan't be gone long. — You come too.

I'm going out to fetch the little calf
That's standing by the mother: It's so young
It totters when she licks it with her tongue.
I shan't be gone long. — You come too.

Poets and poetry have even greater significance to Wallace Stevens. In his essay 'The Noble Rider and the Sound of Words' (1942) he puts the view that the poet, while saying something about human beings or the natural world, creates another world in the mind of the reader. This recreated world has to do with whatever the imagination and the senses have made of external reality and elevates the poet's role to one which will 'help people to live their lives' (Stevens 1949: 29).

> ... since what makes the poet the potent figure he is or was, or ought to be, is that he creates the world to which we turn incessantly and without knowing it and that he gives to life the supreme fictions without which we are unable to conceive of it. (p. 31)

Wordsworth, says Stevens, has done this in his sonnet 'Composed Upon Westminster Bridge, September 3, 1802'. No-one could stand on that bridge on a bright morning and think of Wordsworth's lines without being transported to a new plane of being created by the scene, the senses, the imagination and the poetry alike:

> This city now doth, like a garment, wear
> The beauty of the morning; silent, bare,
> Ships, towers, domes, theatres, and temples lie
> Open unto the fields, and to the sky;
> All bright and glittering in the smokeless air.

Wordsworth could well be speaking Stevens' lines:

> I am the necessary angel of earth
> Since, in my sight, you see the earth again.

In another poem, 'The Idea of Order at Key West', Stevens writes about a woman walking by the sea and singing. Through her song, which is in a sense a poem, she transmutes the world around her for 'she sang beyond the genius of the sea':

> It was her voice that made
> The sky acutest at its vanishing.
> She measured to the hour its solitude.
> She was the single artificer of the world
> In which she sang. And when she sang, the sea,
> Whatever self it had, became the self
> That was her song, for she was the maker.

The world she makes is the world that poets and poetry make; it is the world created by the senses and the imagination and provides that elevated experience, those supreme fictions which we all need to live our lives.

Aidan Chambers (1979: 24) in a more recent statement about poetry applies Stevens' idea to that for children. It is interesting that, like Stevens, he uses the word 'fiction'. More likely than not Stevens and Chambers are correct and poetry, the supreme fiction, is the greatest fact of all.

> 'A shared adventure' — that's the key. What bedevils poetry for the young is that so many adults insist on reading verse and teaching it as though it were just photographs-in-words: a representational medium for telling us about what they would call reality — the 'out there' externals of our lives. Sometimes verse is, of course, such a medium. But poetry is more than that. It is a Fiction. A world made by the writer in words.

Several important things have emerged from the discussion so far: the first is that poetry is a universal art form and spreads its appeal across the whole spectrum of humanity; secondly, it comes in many forms, each having prominence in its own right; thirdly, poetry has an important place in our lives. It recreates the world and gives us a new vision of reality which in turn enriches and guides us in our living. Aidan Chambers has pointed the way to children. The next task is explore the connection between them and poetry.

POETRY IN THE LIFE OF THE CHILD

For children, poetry is at the very heart of things; it is the centre of all they feel, imagine, say and do. As Dorothy Butler (1983) pointed out in the introduction to her anthology of poetry for children, *For Me, Me, Me*:

> Poetry and children go together. Babies are born loving rhythm and the sound of the human voice. Parents instinctively rock and croon to them from birth; surely, the first song in the world must have been a lullaby.

The universal and all-pervading quality of poetry is worth noting here. Just as Chinese, English, Russian, French and Vietnamese babies respond to and acquire language at the same time and at the same rate (babblers are the same the world over), so too do children respond to poetry. Paul Hazard (1944: 146) makes this point about the international quality of children's books generally; his comments apply even more to poetry:

> Yes, children's books keep alive a sense of nationality; but they also keep alive a sense of humanity. They describe their native land

lovingly, but they also describe faraway lands where unknown brothers live. They understand the essential quality of their own race; but each of them is a messenger that goes beyond mountains and rivers, beyond the seas, to the very ends of the world in search of new friendships. Every country gives and every country receives — innumerable are the exchanges — and so it comes about that in our first impressionable years the universal republic of childhood is born.

As children grow, their love of poetry develops as a natural part of the experience of language and the experience of living. They use rhymes for their play; for skipping, ball-bouncing, hand-clapping and chasing games. They delight in tickle rhymes, chants, tongue-twisters and nursery rhymes enjoyed in home, playground and classroom. The importance of a rich poetic experience is vital to effective language development, particularly at the early stages when the rate of language growth is at its highest. If we see reading and learning to read as fused with other aspects of using language, poetry with its rich concentration of the right words in the right order can be effectively used to make the important link with listening, speaking and writing. Children listen to the rhythms of poetry from an early age; they listen across a wide spectrum, including song and they *use* poetry in their speaking and singing in home and school. As children grow older they write and read poetry if they are given the opportunity to do so. It is important not to underestimate the child's interest in verse — Leave a good anthology or sprightly collection in the 'new books' section of your library or in a prominent place in your home or classroom — and see. Don't underestimate either the child's ability or pleasure in writing it. The following is an example of a poem written by Fenja, aged eight, who was away from school because of a cold.

My Illness

> I can't sleep;
> I'm feeling weak.
> I'm not allowed to run around,
> Not even on the smallest ground.
> I coughed all night;
> I wheezed and sniffed.
> I didn't go to school today.
> There's nothing to do;
> There's nothing to say.
> It's such a pity I stayed away.

A great deal can be said about this poem: its subtle exploration of a mood, an eloquent melancholy; its recreation of the actual physical pain caused by her illness, the frustrating inconvenience of it all; her sense of impotence in the hands of the malady, and the constraints set by her nurse (dad in this case); the sense of regret about what she is missing. And the actual skill in the use of the poetic form she has chosen should be noted: the use of rhyme, of assonance and the excellent control of rhythm. Not every child will reach this standard, but it is surprising what they can do. Her sister, aged nine, wrote the following in an examination at another time.

Lucinda
Creative Writing   Year 4. Half Yearly Exams, 19..

Rain

...ers, showers
...ywhere!
...ve days or more,
...uldn't care!

...ng down
...ime to say:
..."rain, Oh rain,
...go away!"

...rather hail,
...maybe snow,
...sick of rain.
...ess you know.

... is nice;
...warm each day,
...t's raining too much,
...uch for May!

...sick of the whispering tune of drops,
...irds, No songs, I hope it STOPS!

Poetry stimulates the imagination and enriches the emotions. Children feel, through the vicarious experience that poetry provides, the full array of humanity's pleasure and pain, hope and despair. Without poetry, children would live in a severely limited world; they would not really know themselves.

> People and places; feather, fur and shell; emotions lived, recollected and dwelt upon; stories told in rhyme; the past, the present and the future reflected in words — that's the stuff of poetry vital to every child and is, to be sure, at the very heart of things.
>
> (Winch 1984: 5)

If every reader of poetry took Eve Merriam's advice in her 'How to Eat a Poem', we would not be polite, but as she says, 'bite in':

> Pick it up with your fingers and lick the juice that may run down your chin.
> It is ready and ripe now, whenever you are.

Children have taken this advice. They do bite into poetry. It is natural for them to do so, with their 'tongues curling around the palpable words, plump as plums in the mouth' (Wilner: 1979: 87). They bite and savour with a sense of joy in what they are doing and with a genuine love of poetry that comes effortlessly and naturally to them as part of language, part of life. These 'supreme fictions' are easily accessible to children; they seem to know instinctively that the poet helps them to live their lives. Also, they have such catholic tastes: they love the gritty, earthy flavour of Mother Goose; they savour the emotions of lyrical poetry; they gulp down the comic and the witty; they chew slowly a narrative well told.

Watch children enjoy the image of the little cat in Carl Sandburg's 'Fog':

> The fog comes
> on little cat feet.
> It sets looking
> over harbour and city
> on silent haunches
> and then moves on.

or Eleanor Farjeon's personification of the tide in 'The Tide in the River':

> The tide in the river,
> The tide in the river,
> The tide in the river runs deep.
>   I saw a shiver
>   Pass over the river
> As the tide turned in its sleep.

What a choice poetic morsel! The tide runs and runs and then it sleeps — and then it stirs and shivers and turns, as a sleeper does just before waking: the shiver, a subtle movement of apprehension, maybe, of indecision, of something intangible and mysterious. Ever been fishing at night with the tide your only companion? You can almost feel its movements, hear it breathe.

Watch children welcome with undisguised appetite such poetry as Roald Dahl's irreverent, rollicking and rambunctious *Revolting Rhymes*. This piece is from his *Jack and the Beanstalk*:

> Jack's mother said. 'We're stony broke!
> Go out and find some wealthy bloke
> Who'll buy our cow. Just say she's sound
> And worth at least a hundred pound.
> But don't you dare to let him know
> That she's as old as billy-o'.

For evidence of relish in a heart-rending narrative poem, take these responses to Alfred Noyes' romantic historical poem 'The Highwayman' republished in 1982 by Oxford University Press with exquisite black and white illustrations by Charles Keeping. They are from nine-year-old boys in Year 4 at The King's School, Parramatta, New South Wales, in their reviews of this and other books for Michele Field and *The Sydney Morning Herald*.

The poem, we remember, is about two lovers whose mutual devotion and sacrifice win them a ghostly place in eternity. It's about treachery, too, and brutality, and red-lipped maidens and long black hair, and casements, and nasty soldiers ... but let's hear what the boys had to say: '"The Highwayman" is about a good woman loving a bad man', said one; 'The Highwayman was brave because he came back for revenge', said another; 'at the end of the story it's the same as the beginning except the Highwayman and Bess are ghosts', said a third; 'It's a good book because it tells me what it means', said another. And these two gems: 'I would recommend this story to anyone who has the nerve to read it' and ... 'I was pleased the horse was spared'.

But, what the nine-year-olds liked most about the book was the language. The Highwayman didn't race in on his horse — he comes 'riding, riding, riding'; he wasn't just determined — even hell couldn't 'bar the way'. The highwayman's breeches weren't just tight like the boys' big sisters' jeans, 'they fitted with never a wrinkle'; he did not wave his rapier, he 'brandished' it; the ostler was not only somewhat kinked, 'his eyes were hollows of madness', and the moon which lit the scene was not any old moon but 'a ghostly galleon tossed upon cloudy seas'.

It should be noted that of the twenty titles, mainly fiction, which the boys reviewed that month they loved 'The Highwayman' so overwhelmingly that the reviews they wrote of others were limp in comparison — no better evidence could be needed of biting in!

Finally, poetry is an indispensable part of our literary heritage and should be readily available to the child. The novel is a relatively recent literary form dating back no further than the eighteenth century. Poetry can be traced back to the earliest times, even before writing became a readily accessible form of communication.

WHAT POETRY, THEN? SELECTING POEMS TO SHARE

It is a common, and completely erroneous, belief that children do not like poetry. This distorted view usually comes from teachers who do not enjoy poetry themselves or from disillusioned children who have been subjected to poor selections of verse which have been terribly taught. The 'poetry-yuk' syndrome would not appear if poems and collections of them were well selected. The 'poetry-wow!' syndrome will take its place. Poetry selected for the young should be filled with vitality; it should, above all, be concerned with life as it is or could be imagined, and be written with ever-recurring echoes of the real language of modern children.

I believe that the age of a poem is not significant, but the sweet and nostalgic, the flabby and the sentimental should be avoided like the plague. Beware of sickly, sentimental Georgian verse that has no relevance to life — or death for that matter. The golden rule is to select poems that ring true. As John Rowe Townsend (1974: 194–5) says of the poetry of Walter de la Mare, it is 'never self-conscious, saccharine, coy or condescending — all of which are ways of being out of true'.

Cecil Day-Lewis (1944) has made this point very well in his juxtaposition of the following poems about death. Which one do you like better? Do you feel strongly about your choice? Read and see.

   1. As I was going down Treak Street
      For half a pound of treacle,
      Who should I meet but my old friend Micky Thumps.
      He said to me, 'Wilt thou come to our wake?'
      I thought a bit,
      I thought a bit,
      I said I didn't mind:
      So I went.
      As I was sitting on our doorstep
      Who should come by but my old friend Micky Thump's brother.
      He said to me, 'Wilt thou come to our house?
      Micky is ill'.
      I thought a bit,
      I thought a bit,
      I said I didn't mind:
      So I went.
      And he were ill;
      He were gradely ill.

He said to me,
'Wilt thou come to my funeral, mon if I die?'
I thought a bit,
I thought a bit,
I said I didn't mind:
So I went.
And it *were* a funeral.
Some stamped on his grave:
Some spat on his grave:
But I scraped my eyes out for my old friend Micky Thumps.

2. Man proposes, God in His time disposes,
   And so I wandered up to where you lay,
   A little rose among the little roses,
   And no more dead than they.
   It seemed your childish feet were tired of straying,
   You did not greet me from your flower-strewn bed,
   Yet still I knew that you were only playing —
   Playing at being dead.
   I might have thought that you were really sleeping,
   So quiet lay your eyelids to the sky.
   So still your hair, but surely you were peeping,
   And so I did not cry.
   God knows, and in His proper time disposes,
   And so I smiled and gently called your name,
   Added my rose to your sweet heap of roses,
   And left you to your game.

It is not hard to detect the sincerity in the first poem, the passionate feeling, the brilliance of the recreation of the scene of the funeral and the unembellished statement of grief. There is mounting tension, too, and an underlying sense of the rightness of the emotion and its portrayal in the bare language of suffering.

The second poem looks good on the surface: it does rhyme, has a clear metre and contains poetical language — 'roses', 'childish feet', 'peeping', 'gently', 'God disposes' ... and so on. A deeper look, however, shows that the poem is essentially false. Death is no game; one does not play with death; the sentiment is feeling gone wrong; it cloys and is insincere.

Consider, if you are still doubtful, the two endings: 'I scraped my eyes out for my old friend Micky Thumps' and 'Added my rose to your sweet heap of roses,/ And left you to your game'.

Basically, we should select a mixed bag of poetry for children. As well as poems that stir the emotions there should be plenty of sprightly comic verse laced with irreverence; there should be good gutsy lyrics and life that is wild, not tamed; there should be gripping narratives and gristly riddles and rhymes that need plenty of chewing. Social comment, when it is made, should be apt and satirical, like Eve Merriam's 'Teevee':

Teevee

In the house
of Mr and Mrs Spouse
he and she
would watch teevee
and never a word
between them spoken
until the day
the set was broken.
Then 'How do you do?'
said he to she.
'I don't believe
that we've met yet.
Spouse is my name.
What's yours?' he asked.
'Why, mine's the same!'
said she to he.
'Do you suppose that we could be — !'
But the set came suddenly right about,
and so they never did find out.

We often underestimate the ability of children to see the joke, understand the meaning, feel the emotion and enjoy the poem. Often they can do this with little or no involvement on our part.

Some poems are written to stress novelty in the use of language. Think of Alistair Morrison's use of 'Strine' in his delightful 'Hagger Nigh Tell?. It looks difficult, but try having your fifth or sixth-graders read it out. They will see the point and appreciate the fun:

Hagger Nigh Tell?

Hagger nigh telephime reely reel?
Hadder Y. Noah Fimere?
Car sigh ony nowered I thing ky feel,
An maybe I'm knotty veneer.

I mipey no lesson I mipey no more
Than a shadder we idle fancy.
Prabzyme the moon! Can I Telfer Shaw
That I'm nodgers a nant named Nancy?

I coobie jar sreely a loafer bread,
Or a horse, or a bird called Gloria.
I mipey alive — but I coobie dead,
Or a phantasmabloodygoria.

Hagger nigh tellime notonia dream,
Cook tarpner mare chick's pell?
Car sigh my pig zackly what I seem,
Bar towg nigh *reely* tell?

Wunker nawlwye stell; yegger nawlwye snow
If you're reelor yerony dreaming;
Yellopoff the topoff your nirra stow,
A new wafer the sander the screaming.

A rich array of poetry for the young comes first through the oral tradition. Nursery or Mother Goose rhymes are recited and sung to and by children who delight in the range of experience the rhymes provide. Lullabies, jingles, riddles, jokes, robust and life-like characters and good stories abound in Mother Goose: Humpty Dumpty; Georgie Porgie; Tom, Tom, the piper's son; Mary, Mary quite contrary; Little Boy Blue, Old King Cole and Solomon Grundy are the indispensable companions of every child. Collections of nursery rhymes are varied and abundant and their popularity never wanes. Brian Wildsmith's *Mother Goose*, illustrated with his unique and memorable art, was first published by Oxford University Press in 1964; it has been reprinted eight times since that date. Other collections, such as Raymond Briggs' *Mother Goose Treasury* have been equally popular. Because of their music, drama and humour, nursery rhymes are, as Egoff (1981: 224) points out, 'the miniature poetry of childhood'.

The play rhymes of children are another rich resource from the oral tradition. These are rhymes which children teach to other children and are different from nursery rhymes which, in the main, are passed on by adults. Play rhymes are used in street games and in the playground, are often made up *by* children themselves, are part of the folklore of the young and their forms and uses are varied: rhymes used for skipping, ball-bouncing and hand-clapping; rhymes full of puns, parodies and alliteration; rhymes that deal with or allude to race, religion, sex, politics, sport, parents, teachers; rhymes full of jokes, riddles, tall stories and autograph album entries: they are all part of this tradition.

Interest in the folklore of children and their play rhymes, in particular, have resulted in a number of studies and collections of these resources. The most famous is Iona and Peter Opie's *The Lore and Language of School Children* (1959). This monumental work is based on information collected from five thousand children in England, Scotland and Wales and includes selections from children's nonsense verse, chants, jokes, riddles, catcalls, tongue twisters and some eight hundred rhymes in full. In Australia, Ian Turner has made a selection of children's rhymes in his book, *Cinderella Dressed in Yella* (1969), and, more recently, June Factor (1983) in her collection of children's rhymes, *Far Out, Brussel Sprout!* has produced another. She makes the point that her book is *for* children because they have made it up — all she has done is write it down. She argues in an addendum for adults that, in a sense, her work is an intrusion into the world of children since we are not sure what long-term effects may result from our movement into the rightful domains of childhood. Her justification for the collection is that after nursery ones, play rhymes provide 'the major source of poetry for children' (Factor 1983: 108). Turner, on the other hand, does not recommend his collection for children, possibly because of the inclusion of what he terms 'vulgar' rhymes. But again, there are many rather delightful 'off colour' rhymes in June Factor's collection which children and adults find very funny. Maybe such 'vulgarity' is very much part of growing up.

> Of all the birds I'd like to be
> I'd like to be a sparra,
> So I could sit on Princes Bridge
> And help to fill the Yarra.

or

> The night was dark and stormy,
> The dunny light was dim,
> I heard a crash and then a splash —
> By gosh! He's fallen in!

Whatever the case, children's rhymes have a freshness and vitality which is instantly appealing. The variety and originality in the use of language is very much the stuff of poetry and the increasing popularity and spread of children's rhymes indicates that over time they will moult no feather.

Next we come to poetry that has been written for children. Many collections of such verse err on the side of Georgian sweetness: they are often mawkish in sentiment, adult and aloof. It is very refreshing to find anthologies of verse for young children which contain a wide range of poetry. A good example of such a collection is *When A Goose Meets A Moose* compiled by Clare Scott-Mitchell in (1980). This anthology contains many traditional poems by established children's poets such as Walter de la Mare, Rose Fyleman and Eleanor Farjeon, with more modern writers such as Lilian More and Patricia Hubbell. I like Jack Hall who's so small 'a mouse could eat him, hat and all' and the limerick (Anon.) about the old man of Peru who

> ... dreamt he was eating his shoe.
> He woke in the night
> In a terrible fright,
> And found it was perfectly true.

When selecting poetry for young children there are certain guidelines which are useful. First, look around. Consider the books that are available on the market and consider them objectively. Do not accept poems which you feel are not right, even if they are between glossy covers, sit beside the most lavish illustrations, are repeatedly anthologised and bear the stamp of respectable approval. Test the poems with 'real live' children and consider their judgement carefully.

Browse in the bookshops and peep into the pages of paperbacks. Know how to spot value for money. My copy of Lilian Moore's *Spooky Rhymes and Riddles* (1972) cost me seventy cents when I bought it and was the best value I have met in any book. While browsing, look for monographs, not just anthologies. Sometimes you can find a group of excellent poems in one book. Take, for instance, C.J. Dennis' *A Book for Kids* (with creaky but very apt illustrations by the author). This was first published by Angus and Robertson in 1921 and has been republished and republished and republished. Remember 'Hist', 'The Barber', 'The Sailor' ... and this one:

> The Looking-Glass
>
> When I look in the looking-glass
> I'm always sure to see —
> No matter how I dodge about —
> Me, looking out at me.
> I often wonder as I look,
> And those strange features spy,
> If I, in there, think I'm as plain
> As I, out here, think I.

Some poems have a universal charm and would be popular the world over. It is important to select those that are place-specific as well, poems that have an indigenous flavour: Australian children like to hear the sounds of their own bushland and echoes of the voices of the people they know.

Anyone working with children and poetry should develop a private collection of poems and books of poems. This can be done over a period of time so that old and new favourites can be shared. One's 'private poetry library' should always be augmented by the local library or school library holdings, but one's own collection is more near and dear.

When selecting poetry for the older child, the basic principles remain the same. The field is much wider, of course; the intellectual, social, emotional and language growth of the child make the range of subjects and their treatment much more varied and complex.

One fault which one should avoid is the over-reliance on poetry which has little appeal to modern children. If we hope to hold the attention of older readers it is necessary to make the poetry you select and they read relevant to their lives. And as we have stated earlier, it must ring true. Animals often fare badly in poetry. There are cats whose predatory instincts are ignored, dogs who have never marked a lamp post, rabbits who have never given a thought to reproduction. Children like to read about flesh-and-blood animals such as James Reeves' 'Mick':

Mick

Mick my mongrel-O
Lives in a bungalow,
Painted green with a round doorway.
  With an eye for cats
  And a nose for rats
He lies on his threshold half the day.
  He buries his bones
  By the rockery stones,
And never, oh never, forgets the place.
  Ragged and thin
  From his tail to his chin,
He looks at you with a sideways face.
  Dusty and brownish,
  Wicked and clownish,
He'll win no prize at the County Show.
  But throw him a stick,
  And up jumps Mick,
And right through the flower-beds see him go!

A growing number of contemporary poets speak directly to modern children. They include Michael Rosen, Ted Hughes and Max Fatchen. There are many poets, also, who have written poetry which is suitable for children while their main corpus is written for the young adult or adult. Their poems are found readily in anthologies such as Penguin's (1970) *Junior Voices* edited by Geoffrey Summerfield or the *Australian Voices* (1974) edited by Edward Kynaston. The names of the poets are far too numerous to mention here, but to give a flavour of the features of poetry which hold the modern young it is worthwhile dwelling for a moment on some aspects of two poets and several poems.

The English poet Michael Rosen appeals at the level of the child. In his poem 'I've had this shirt' Rosen captures aspects of the child's attitude to clothing which are very common among modern children. As we know, they have their favourite items and they wear them and wear them, clean or encrusted with dirt, until they become faded antiques or begin to disintegrate. This simple poem speaks intimately about the experience, in language which might well be the actual words of a child. It captures the mood, it relives the experience and it makes it memorable:

I've Had This Shirt

I've had this shirt
that's covered in dirt
for years and years and years.

It used to be red
but I wore it in bed
and it went grey
cos I wore it all day
for years and years and years.

> The arms fell off
> in the Monday wash
> and you can see my vest
> through the holes in the chest
> for years and years and years.
>
> As my shirt falls apart
> I'll keep the bits
> in a biscuit tin
> on the mantlepiece
> for years and years and years.

Rosen also experiments successfully with blank verse, coming even nearer to the language and experiences of children, and in the following case recreating the child's-eye view of the parent-dad, larger than lifesize; or in this case not dad, but dad's thumb:

> My dad's thumb
> can stick pins in wood
> without flinching —
> it can crush family-size matchboxes
> in one stroke
> and lever off jam-jar lids without piercing
> at the pierce here sign.
>
> If it wanted
> it could be a bath-plug
> or a paint-scraper
> a keyhole cover or a tap-tightener.
>
> It's already a great nutcracker
> and if it dressed up
> it could easily pass
> as a broad bean or a big toe.
>
> In actual fact, it's quite simply
> the world's fastest envelope burster.

Max Fatchen's poems cover a wide range but I have always shared children's pleasure in the comic ones. His limericks are delightful and his parodies of nursery rhymes equally so:

> Mary, Mary, quite contrary,
> How does your garden grow?
> With snails and frogs and neighbours' dogs
> And terribly, terribly slow.
>
> When Old Mother Hubbard
> Went to the cupboard
> Her dog for a morsel would beg.
> 'Not a scrap can be found',
> She explained to her hound
> So he bit the poor dear on the leg.

Like Rosen, Fatchen seems to be able to climb easily into the child's mind and to talk of children as they really are. The nimble quality of his verse is very reminiscent of Ogden Nash.

Not in Bed Yet

Getting Albert off to bed
  Is such an anxious task,
He never seems to want to go
  Although you ask
And ask.

'Just five more minutes', Albert says.
  Another five, and then
Before you know it, cunning boy,
  He stretches it
To ten.

He brushes teeth with lazy strokes
  He lingers and he plays.
'Please HURRY, Albert', people shout
  But Albert stays
And stays.

Getting Albert into bed
  Would seem a losing fight.
I think I'll go to bed
Instead.
So, everyone,
  Goodnight!

Children are, by and large, joyful creatures and delight in comedy, particularly when it relies on the incongruous for effect. I am reminded again of Roald Dahl, of Shel Silverstein, of Spike Milligan and then again of Hilaire Belloc, of Edward Lear, of Ogden Nash and ... (Have a good look at *The Puffin Book of Funny Verse* (1979), compiled by Julia Watson or *Oh, How Silly!* (1971) compiled by William Cole).

Finally, with reference to the other side of the coin, serious verse, it is often surprising how children respond when confronted with issues in poetry that may appear on the surface beyond their intellectual or emotional experience. Their fresh minds can often add a dimension to the reading which our sophisticated responses can't. Because the language of poetry has its own way of getting across, it is often not necessary to over-analyse. Just wait to hear what the children have to say. Likewise, a beautiful image may become implanted in a child's mind after one sensitive sharing of a poem, to bloom at another time.

When selecting poetry to share with children of this age the same basic principles apply as those outlined above. Naturally, the range of poetry will increase. The serious, reflective lyric will be more prevalent and a wider range of narrative poems should be included. The Australian bush ballad is very popular with children. Some of these have recently been published in picture book form and have instant appeal.

Poetry appears in many forms: the anthology which often groups a number of poems about a specific topic (animals, people); collections of poems by one author; collections of poems with one theme (humorous verse, spooky poems, poems written by children); poems for a particular age group; poems in theme books; poems in reading schemes. It is important to have available every possible source.

SOME FEATURES AND FORMS OF POETRY

Children need to know about the basic features and forms of poetry to help them with their appreciation and writing of verse. It is just as serious to ignore this side of poetry when sharing it with children as it is to over-stress it.

To begin, a poem has a meaning or meanings: these may be clear and literal; they may be subtle and suggestive or they may be both. It is important to consider that poetry has a plain sense meaning like any other verbal form. As I.A. Richards (1979: 184) points out, 'In most poetry, the sense is as important as anything else; it is quite as subtle, and as dependent on the syntax, as in prose; ... we miss nearly everything of value if we misread his [the poet's] sense'. A rich and most rewarding response to poetry is gained if we build on to the plain sense with our own thinking, feeling and imagining so that the final reading is a kind of three-way interchange among writer, poem and reader/listener.

Next, the language of poetry is significant in that words are used in a special way. Simile, metaphor and personification provide a heightened form of language use; children respond as readily to beautiful images in poetry as they do to other aspects of verse. This is not to say that a poem should be dissected like a biological speciman. Some are better left unexplained so that their magic can work in its own mysterious way. As Moira Robinson (1985: 47) points out, a great deal of art 'Thrives on ambiguity, on things half understood, half apprehended, on a degree of mystery rather than straight answers. It doesn't matter whether children know exactly what a "quinquireme" is when we read John Masefield's "Cargoes" — what does matter is the magic sound of the words themselves'. It could be argued, on the other hand, that the mystery is even deeper and the effect more pervasive if the reader sees in the mind's eye the *five* oars on the towering vessel dipping simultaneously into the water as they bring the romantic cargo home.

Rhythm and metre are important aspects, also. Much modern poetry is written in free verse which is less regular than more traditional poetic forms. Coupled with this is the use, or lack of use, of rhyme. Children should become familiar with poetry which does not rhyme and practise it in their writing.

One of the best ways to introduce children to various poetic features is to do so through the use of many types. Narrative verse and the ballad in particular show children how regular verse forms are written:

a He was hard and tough and wiry — just the sort that won't say die —
b There was courage in his quick impatient tread:
a And he bore the badge of gameness in his bright and fiery eye
b And the proud and lofty carriage of his head.
        (variations to this pattern are, of course, appropriate)

Limericks illustrate the discipline needed to write this form of humorous verse. The 'studied carelessness' of a good limerick is as difficult to reproduce as the classical tautness of the haiku. While this is not the place to carry out a detailed and penetrating analysis of the technical aspects of poetry, it is very important to see the issue in perspective. A valuable point to make is that poetry's various features are there for a reason and it is often important to highlight them. Sometimes a particular feature towers above another in a poem: the arresting visual image in Tennyson's 'The Eagle'; the swinging rhythm and the rhymes of Belloc's 'Tarantella'; the sheer enchantment of the sound of the words in Turner's 'Romance'.

> When I was but thirteen or so
>   I went into a golden land,
> Chimborazo, Cotopaxi,
>   Took me by the hand.
>
> My father died, my brother too,
>   They passed like fleeting dreams,
> I stood where Popocatapetyl
>   In the sunlight gleams.

Sometimes a poem appears to have no outstanding feature. Think of D.H. Lawrence's poem 'The White Horse': it does not rhyme; it has no arresting image; its rhythms are the rhythms of speech. Yet it supplies another dimension — some subtle truth, some *supreme fiction* which adds to our understanding of life and what it is:

> The youth walks up to the white horse, to put its halter on
> and the horse looks at him in silence.
> They are so silent, they are in another world.

SHARING POETRY WITH CHILDREN

Because children enjoy poetry it is important to find as many ways as possible to enhance this. Below are twenty helpful hints to make the most of every poetry experience (see Drummond 1984, McVitty 1985).

1. Share some poetry *every* day in *some* way. Poetry should be said, read (silently or aloud), performed, written or just thought about.
2. To build up children's taste use poems that are brief and clearly patterned at first; tasty morsels to whet the appetite. Cater for their preferences; trust their judgement.
3. Use different forms of poetry: concrete poetry, for instance:

Brother Jim

Jim
just
would
not
eat
his
dinner
so
he
kept
on
getting
thinner.
Now
he
has
become
so
slim,
when
he
stands
side
on
you
can't
see
him.

Or narrative poems, reflective lyrics, haiku, limericks ...
with different focus: serious, humorous (witty nonsensical) poems about people, about the sea, about animals ...
4. Involve children in sharing a poem with you: you read it, they read it, illustrate it, perform it — to you, themselves, to others. That is, make it an *active* sharing.

5. Use music with poetry. Much poetry is meant to be sung or can be set to music, but there is also music in words:

> Jeremiah Obadiah
> puff, puff, puff
> Montague Michael
> You're much too fat.

Background music is also effective (slow and spooky music for slow and spooky poems).

6. Drama and poetry go together: mime, reader's theatre, simple props are all valuable. Have the children dress up, act out parts of a poem, perform for an audience (see Winch and Monahan in McVitty 1985).

7. Explore various ways of getting to a satisfying response to a poem. Try: pre-discussion as well as post-discussion and analysis; group discussion *without* an adult (teacher, librarian, parent); encourage lateral as well as literal thinking; praise daring attempts at finding a meaning to a difficult poem.

8. Make poetry visual: Capitalise on the artist's response in a well-illustrated book (How does it enrich — or not enrich! — the poem?). Have children do their own illustrations, encouraging originality.

9. Be a good reader of a poem and use other presentations as well. Collect tapes of poets and professional actors reading poetry. Invite a poet or actor to read, or perform poetry.

10. Have children write their own verse of various kinds: pattern pieces, personal responses, experiments; use word-making games to sharpen their skills with words — rhyming words, word puzzles, word associations, synonyms and antonyms, slogans, advertisements, jokes and riddles (see Walshe in McVitty 1985). Remember Kornei Chukovsky's comment: 'In the beginning of our childhood we are all versifiers — it is only later that we begin to speak in prose' (1963: 64).

Other useful articles are Pat Edwards' 'Large Swans Fall off Cliffs: Large Strawberries Don't'; Moira Robinson's 'How Not to Teach Poetry' and Libby Hathorn's 'A Poetry Workshop', all in McVitty. Other very useful basic texts are Powell's *English Through Poetry Writing* (1969); the excellent PEN No. 9, 'Shapes and Forms of Writing' of PETA, Sydney; and the writing sections in Gordon Winch's and Paul March's *Language Skill Builders* (1978–81).

11. Display the efforts of poetry writers and the results of visible response such as art, music or drama. Do not *insist* on the display of children's efforts; some poetry is very private and should be respected as such.

12. Relive poems that are enjoyed by memorisation, rereading, further discussion, choral speaking and alternate forms of response.

13. Allow time for reflection on a poem that makes an emotional impact. It may be wise to leave the poem for a rereading.

14. To increase interest in poetry in a classroom or library allow time for browsing and borrowing. Have poetry books available for reading at home. In school time include the reading of poetry in sustained silent reading sessions.
15. Vary first encounters with:
    taped reading
    silent reading
    your oral reading
    the child's oral reading
    a prepared group reading
    a display of art
    mime or other dramatic work
    if suitable, use music or song
16. Enrich the experience of the poem with:
    group discussion
    group taping
    slide presentation or sound effects
    artwork (for example, a frieze for a period piece like 'The Highwayman' or 'The Ballad of John Gilpin' or bush ballads like 'The Man From Ironbark', 'The Man From Snowy River' or 'The Bush Christening'. Each child in a class could illustrate one part).
17. Use cloze procedures to focus on meaning, rhyme and rhythm.

>   Scratch, Scratch
>
>   I've got a dog as thin as a rail,
>   He's got fleas all over his —;
>   Every time his tail goes flop,
>   The fleas at the bottom all hop to the —.
>   Anon.

18. Have discussions about a poem, its meaning and technique, if the situation warrants it. (Some poems make children vocal; others make them as quiet as clams).
19. Use a variety of questions; some very specific; some open-ended, depending on the people involved. Many children prefer to chew over a poem rather than talk about it. (Please Sir, don't explain it!)
20. Prepare a class anthology of favourites, written or spoken. Include jokes, parodies, riddles, and rhyming games as well as a range of more formal poetry. Make children hunters for poems in anthologies, magazines, newspapers and other places. They will enjoy providing their own poems as well.

If you do half these things your poetry experiences with children are bound to be successful!

REFERENCES

Briggs, Raymond, *The Mother Goose Treasury*. London: Hamish Hamilton, 1966.
Butler, Dorothy, *For Me, Me, Me: Poems for the Very Young*. Sydney: Hodder & Stoughton, 1983.
Causley, Charles, 'Poetry and the Child', in McVitty, W., editor, *Word Magic: Poetry as a Shared Adventure*. Sydney: PETA, 1985.
Chambers, Aidan, 'Inside Poetry: A Shared Experience' in McVitty.
Chukovsky, Kornei, translator Miriam Morton, *From Two to Five*. Brisbane: Jacaranda, 1963.
Cole, William, editor, *Oh, How Silly*. London: Methuen/Magnet, 1980.
Dennis, C.J. *A Book For Kids*. Sydney: Angus & Robertson, 1979. First published 1921.
Drummond, Don, editor, *Primary Education*. Melbourne: January-February 1984.
Egoff, Sheila, *Thursday's Child: Trends and Patterns in Contemporary Literature*. Chicago: American Library Association, 1981.
Factor, June, *Far Out, Brussel Sprout!* Melbourne: OUP, 1983.
Fadiman, Clifton, introduction to *A Swinger of Birches, Poems of Robert Frost for Young People*. Sevenoaks, Kent: Hodder & Stoughton, 1983.
Fatchen, Max 'A Verse Along the Way' in McVitty.
Field, Michele, 'The Horse Was Spared' in *The Sydney Morning Herald*. Sydney: 5 June 1982.
Hazard, Paul *Books, Children and Men*. Boston: The Horn Book, 1972.
Hope, A.D. *The New Cratylus: Notes on the Craft of Poetry*. Melbourne: OUP, 1979.
Kynaston, Edward, *Australian Voices*. Harmondsworth: Penguin, 1974.
Lewis, Cecil Day, *Poetry For You*. Oxford: Basil Blackwell, 1944.
Moore, Lilian, *Spooky Rhymes and Riddles*. New York: Ashton Scholastic, 1972.
Opie, Iona and Peter, *The Lore and Language of Schoolchildren*. London: OUP, 1959.
Powell, Brian, *English Through Poetry Writing*. Sydney: Ian Novak, 1969.
Richards, I.A., *Practical Criticism: A Study of Literary Judgment*. London: New York: Harcourt Brace/Harvest. First published 1929.
Robinson, Moira, 'How Not to Teach Poetry' in McVitty.
Scott-Mitchell, Clare, editor, *When a Goose Meets a Moose*. Sydney: Methuen, 1980.
Stevens, Wallace, 'The Noble Rider and the Sound of Words' in *The Necessary Angel: Essays on Reality and the Imagination*. New York: Vintage Books, 1951.
Stevens, Wallace, *Poems By Wallace Stevens*. New York: Random House, 1959.
Summerfield, Geoffrey, editor, *Junior Voices*, Books 1–4, Harmondsworth: Penguin, 1970.
Townsend, John Rowe, *Written for Children*. Harmondsworth: Penguin, 1974.
Turner, Ian, *Cinderella Dressed in Yella*. Melbourne: Heinemann Educational, 1969.
Watson, Julia, editor, *The Puffin Book of Funny Verse*. Harmondsworth: Puffin, 1981.

Wildsmith, Brian, *Mother Goose: A Collection of Nursery Rhymes*. Oxford: OUP, 1964.

Wilner, Isabel, 'Making Poetry Happen: Birth of a Poetry Troupe', *Children's Literature in Education* Vol. 10, No. 2, 1979.

Winch, Gordon, 'Poetry for Children', in *Primary Education*. Melbourne: January 1984.

——————, and March, Paul, *Language Skill Builders*. Jacaranda Wiley, 1978–81.

POEMS REFERRED TO IN THE CHAPTER

'As I was going down Treak Street' and 'Man Proposes', authors unknown, in Cecil Day-Lewis, *Poetry For You*. Oxford.

'Brother Jim', Gordon Winch in *Popcorn and Porcupines*. Hodder & Stoughton.

'Composed Upon Westminster Bridge, September 3, 1802', in William Wordsworth, *Wordsworth: Poetical Works*. OUP.

'Fog', Carl Sandburg, in, chosen by Clare Scott-Mitchell, *When A Goose Meets A Moose: Poems for Young Children*. Methuen.

'Hagger Nigh Tell?' Alistair Morrison, in E. Kynaston, editor, *Australian Voices*. Penguin.

'How to Eat a Poem', Eve Merriam in S. Dunning *et al.*, editors, *Reflections on a Gift of Watermelon Pickle*. Scott, Foresman.

'I've Had This Shirt' Michael Rosen, illustrator, Quentin Blake, *Mind Your Own Business*. William Collins/Andre Deutsch.

'Jack and the Beanstalk', Roald Dahl, *Revolting Rhymes*. Jonathan Cape.

'Jeremiah, Obadiah' and 'Mongague Michael', Anonymons, in Dorothy Butler, editor, *For Me, Me, Me*. Hodder & Stoughton.

'Little Fish', D.H. Lawrence, chosen by Alice and Martin Proversen, illustrators, *Birds, Beasts and the Third Thing*. Julia McCrae.

'Mary, Mary, Quite Contrary', Max Fatchen, illustrator Michael Atchison, *Wry Rhymes for Troublesome Times*. Kestrel.

'Mick', James Reeves, in *A Puffin Quartet of Pacts*. Penguin.

'My Dad's Thumb', Michael Rosen, illustrator, Quentin Blake, *Mind Your Own Business*. William Collins/Andre Deutsch.

'My Illness', Fenja Berglund, written for the author of this article in 1980.

'Not in Bed Yet!' Max Fatchen, illustrator, Michael Atchison, *Songs for My Dog and Other People*. Puffin.

'Ode to a Grecian Urn', John Keats, W.H. Garrod, editor, *Keats: Poetical Works*. OUP.

'Of all the birds I'd like to be', children's rhyme in June Factor, editor, *Far Out, Brussel Sprout!* OUP.

'Over Sir John's Hill', Dylan Thomas, *Dylan Thomas: Collected Poems*. New Directions.

'Rain', Lucinda Berglund, poem written in half-yearly examination, Creative Writing, Year 4, 1985.

'Romance', W.J. Turner, in Margaret J. O'Donnell, *Feet on the Ground*. Blackie.

'Scratch, Scratch', Anonymons, in Butlen.

'Stickybeak, Treacle Nose', children's rhyme in Factor.

'Teevee', Eve Merriam, in H.P. Schoenheimer and G.C. Winch, *My World is Everywhere*. Jacaranda.

'The Highwayman', Alfred Noyes in *The Highwayman*, illustrator, Charles Keeping. OUP.
'The Idea of Order at Key West', Wallace Stevens, *Poems*. Random House.
'The Lion', Spike Milligan, *A Book of Milliganimals*. Puffin.
'The Looking-glass', C.J. Dennis, illustrations by the author, *A Book for Kids*. Angus & Robertson.
'The Man From Snowy River', A.B. Paterson, illustrator, Annette Macarthur-Onslow, *The Man From Snowy River*. Collins.
'The Night was Dark and Stormy', children's rhyme in Factor.
'The Pasture', Robert Frost, *A Swinger of Birches: Poems of Robert Frost for Young People*. Hodder & Stoughton.
'There was an old man of Peru', Anonymous, in Scott-Mitchell.
'The Rime of the Ancient Mariner', Samuel Taylor Coleridge, *Coleridge: Poetical Works*. OUP.
'The Tide in the River'. Eleanor Farjeon, in Scott-Mitchell.
'The White Horse', D.H. Lawrence in Proversen.
'When Old Mother Hubbard', in Fatchen.

SOME USEFUL TEXTS

McVitty, Walter (ed.), *Word Magic: Poetry as a Shared Adventure*. Sydney: PETA, 1985.
Winch, Gordon, *Poetry For Children*. Melbourne: Collins Dove, 1988.

POETRY COLLECTIONS

Butler, Dorothy (compiler), *For Me, Me, Me*. Sydney: Hodder & Stoughton, 1984.
——————, *I Will Build You a House*. Sydney: Hodder & Stoughton, 1984.
Factor, June (compiler), *A First Australian Poetry Book; A Second Australian Poetry Book*. Melbourne: OUP, 1983.
——————, *All Right, Vegemite!* Melbourne: OUP, 1985.
——————, *Far Out, Brussel Sprout!* Melbourne: OUP, 1983.
Heylen, Jill and Jellett, Celia (compilers), *Rattling in the Wind*. Adelaide: Omnibus, 1983.
——————, *Someone is Flying Balloons*. Adelaide: Omnibus, 1983.
Koch, Kenneth and Farrell, Kate (compilers), *Talking to the Sun*. Harmondsworth: Viking/Kestrel, 1986.
McGough, Roger, *The Kingfisher Book of Comic Verse*. London: Kingfisher, 1986.
McNaughton, Colin, *There's an Awful Lot of Weirdos in Our Neighbourhood*. Walker, 1987.
——————, *Who's Been Sleeping in My Porridge*. Walker, 1990.
Rosen, Harold (compiler), *A Spider Bought a Bicycle and Other Poems*. London: Kingfisher, 1987.
——————, *The Kingfisher Book of Children's Poetry*. London: Kingfisher, 1985.
Royds, Caroline (compiler), *Read Me a Poem: A Collection of Poems for Young Children*. London: Kingfisher, 1986.
Schenk de Regniers, Beatrice *et al* (compilers), *Sing a Song of Popcorn: Every Child's Book of Poems*. (Illustrated by nine Caldecott Medal artists). New York: Scholastic Inc., 1988.
Schofield, Phillip (introducer), *Poems For Pleasure*. Hamlyn, 1989.
Silverstein, Shel, *A Light in the Attic*. London: Jonathan Cape, 1982.
Winch, Gordon (compiler), *Mulga Bill Rides Again: A Book of Australian Poems Kids Can't Put Down*. Melbourne: Macmillan, 1988.

9 TALES OF ADVENTURE

LOUIS LODGE

> And in his turn, royal Odysseus told Penelope of all the discomfiture he had inflicted on his foes and all the miseries which he had undergone. She listened spellbound, and her eyelids never closed in sleep till the whole tale was finished.
>
> Homer

Many adults, when asked about important childhood influences on their reading development, will single out the adventure novel for particular mention. Indeed they will often cite their adventure reading phase as the turning point, after which they went on to read avidly and widely. I can remember when I was eleven being absolutely enchanted by Gene Stratton Porter's *Freckles* (1905), a compelling depiction of the adventures of Freckles, a handicapped boy who rises from unpromising beginnings to become a hero, loved and respected by everyone, including his boss, McLean, and the beautiful Swamp Angel. The story is set in the forest area of the Limberlost in Indiana, where Freckles establishes a rare rapport with all living creatures. I find it difficult to recall why *Freckles* appealed to me so much; I do remember, however, that after *Freckles* I became an avid reader of all kinds of adventure stories. From it I moved on to *Fifty Enthralling Stories of the Mysterious East*, a massive volume of adventure stories of unimaginable variety and excitement, and then through an assortment of adventure novels, both classical and trivial, from which I emerged in late adolescence with a passion for reading, attributable in large part to the interest generated by these novels. Perhaps the widespread appeal of the adventure story might lie in the marked similarity between this literary form and that of the ancient saga. Both are characterised by a mixture of action, suspense, surprise, disappointment and final resolution. Both can generate in their readers tension, excitement and a mysterious involvement in the action.

Many types of children's book could be classed as adventure stories — fantasy, science fiction, historical, social realism and so on. The *Macquarie Dictionary* defines *adventure* as 'an undertaking of uncertain outcome, a hazardous enterprise or an exciting experience', a definition that conjures up a great variety of fictional possibilities. Adventure has always been an important ingredient in children's books, particularly since the early nineteenth century.

ADVENTURE STORY ARCHETYPES

The archetypes of this type of story go back a long way, in fact into ancient history. For example, the story of Odysseus (Ulysses) is one of the world's oldest adventure stories. When Homer recorded it as *The Odyssey*, about 800 BC, it was probably already a fairly ancient folk tale. It has provided a pattern for the adventure story ever since. The fortunes of Odysseus alternate between achievement and failure, until finally, after a series of adventures that take twenty years, Odysseus returns home to his faithful wife Penelope (see E.V. Rieu's translation, Penguin 1946).

Of more recent influence on the modern children's adventure novel have been Daniel Defoe's *Robinson Crusoe* (1719), Jonathan Swift's *Gulliver's Travels* (1726) and Johann David Wyss' *The Swiss Family Robinson* (1814), although none of these was written for children. They illustrate the two main categories that adventure stories have tended to fall into. First there is the static kind of adventure (*Robinson Crusoe, The Swiss Family Robinson*) where, after an initial voyage, the setting becomes one which provides the background for the series of events that make up the adventure. The French coined the term *Robinsonnade* to describe stories of this kind. Then there is the journey or quest kind of adventure (*Gulliver's Travels*) in which the main character embarks on a physical journey with some specific purpose in mind: to find someone, to discover something, to seek a fortune or to solve a mystery.

The static kind of adventure, the Robinsonnade, often involves an individual or a group of people being marooned in some isolated place (often an island), managing to survive in the new environment after overcoming a series of obstacles (privations, natural calamities, warlike adversaries or illness) and finally being rescued. Theodore Taylor's *The Cay* (1969) and Jean George's *My Side of the Mountain* (1959) are fairly recent novels that stay closely to the Robinsonnade pattern.

A variation of this is the kind pioneered by such writers as Mark Twain in *The Adventures of Tom Sawyer* (1876), in which a familiar place, in Twain's case his childhood home town of Hannibal, Missouri, and its environs, is made the setting for a series of events centred on the lives of a small group of characters. Referring to both *Tom Sawyer* and *The Adventures of Huckleberry Finn* (1844) John Rowe Townsend writes:

> These books showed that adventure did not have to be sought at the other side of the world; it was as near as your own backyard. Adventure did not happen only to stiff-upper-lipped heroes of superior social status; it could happen to ordinary people, even to inferiors like Huck and to mere chattels like Jim.
>
> (Townsend 1976: 69)

In the twentieth century the Twain variation has been immensely popular with a range of writers from Arthur Ransome to Enid Blyton. In Britain, particularly, the 'holiday adventure' became a popular form of children's story. In it a group of children released from the restrictions of school, and often on their summer holidays, become involved in adventures in which parents play little or no part. The important action is outside normal daily family life, and may involve the children in dealings with a variety of interesting adult characters, sometimes shady, near-criminal types. The school story, similar in many respects to the holiday adventure, in that the action takes place in a static setting, is an offshoot of the adventure story. In the twentieth century the tendency has been to draw less on the survival tradition and to explore the small-scale, domestic adventure. The most significant development has been the emergence of writers interested in enlarging the spectrum of adventure ingredients to cater more adequately for the interests of girls.

The journey kind of adventure in the Gulliver tradition has also been widely used in the twentieth century. Ian Serraillier's *The Silver Sword* (1956), Ann Holm's *I am David* (1965), J.R. Tolkien's *The Hobbit* (1938) and Jean George's *Julie of the Wolves* (1972), are outstanding examples. In this kind of adventure there are often two journeys, closely linked and mutually dependent, one physical and the other spiritual. The protagonist, by means of a physical journey, experiences a growth in self-knowledge or subtle character development. An observant reader will respond to both journeys and be aware of the spiritual growth that has taken place.

Conflict in one form or another is an important element in most adventure stories. The protagonist is pitted against a formidable adversary, either human or environmental. As in *The Odyssey* there is often a series of adversaries, each more challenging than the one preceding it. This is a familiar device in fairy stories and classical tales, where generally the last obstacle to be overcome provides the ultimate test of the protagonist's endurance and skill. A. Rutgers van der Loeff's *Children on the Oregon Trail* (1954) provides an excellent example of this. Although the book contains an array of obstacles throughout the narrative — death of parents, fording a river, meeting warlike Indians, a buffalo stampede, encounters with bears and wolves, privation caused in turn by heat, cold, rain and drought — it is in the last episode that the most taxing trials are met and overcome. In twenty-four action-packed pages the children contend with a daunting number of difficulties, ranging from loss of guides and horses to an avalanche. In all adventure stories it is the drama that comes from the conflict of protagonist versus adversary that fires the interest. Young readers can find the created tension so unendurable that they feel compelled to sneak a glance at the final pages to assure themselves that all will turn out satisfactorily in the end. It is the thrill of the conflict that makes adventure stories addictive reading for many children.

THE ADVENTURE STORY IN THE NINETEENTH CENTURY

The adventure novel reached the height of its popularity in the nineteenth century. It captured the spirit of an age when new lands were being conquered and frontiers were being extended into unknown territories. The idea of the quest appealed to writers as a means of showing how the enlightenment of a civilised nation could be used to benefit those less fortunate — those whose lands were being taken away from them. Sir Walter Scott, James Fenimore Cooper, Captain Marryat, W.H.G. Kingston, R.M. Ballantyne, G.A. Henty, and Robert Louis Stevenson were some of the most influential adventure writers of the century. The staggering thing about these men is the sheer volume of their writing. Together they produced about four hundred novels, mainly of the adventure kind. The most prolific, Kingston, wrote a total of one hundred and seventy-one books over a period of forty-two years! As well as giving an idea of the industry of the writers, these figures also show the popular demand for novels of this kind.

An important aspect of the nineteenth century adventure story is that it was written almost exclusively for boys, and depicted a world in which all significant events were dominated by male characters. Women and girls tended to be background characters who exerted an important and wholesome influence on their sons, husbands, lovers or brothers, but who were removed from the main action of the novel. The adventure itself was often presented as a conflict, or series of conflicts, in which physical strength played as important a part as spiritual. The list of adjectives used to describe the typical hero remained fairly constant — he was good-looking, popular, honourable, manly, daring, cheerful, generous, brave and reliable.

> Jack Martin was a tall, strapping, broad-shouldered youth of eighteen, with a handsome, good-humoured firm face.
>
> (*The Coral Island*, Ballantyne, 1858: 14)
>
> Charlie Marryat's muscles were as trim and hard as those of any boy in the school. In all sport requiring activity and endurance rather than weight and strength he was always conspicuous ... He had a reputation for being a leader in every mischievous prank; but he was honourable and manly, would scorn to shelter himself under the semblance of a lie and was a prime favourite with his masters as well as his schoolfellows.
>
> (*With Clive in India*, Henty, 1984
> from Townsend 1976:63)

In return for such an endowment of admirable qualities the hero had the responsibility of achieving great things. To Victorian minds much was expected of those to whom much had been given. Often the hero was entrusted with the twin tasks of accomplishing something important and of furthering the cause of Christianity.

> Having done all I could, with a heavy heart I quitted the station ... I persuaded my sister-in-law to accompany Mary and me to England, where I have devoted a certain portion of the fortune of which I so painfully became possessed to her support and the education of her children, and at Mary's urgent request, another, what the world would consider a no inconsiderable portion, to the support of missions.
>
> (*The Cruise of the Mary Rose*, W.H.G. Kingston. The Religious Tract Society, 1881)

Because of the nature of its white settlement Australia became a popular setting for adventure stories. Conditions here suited the *Robinsonnade*. Of the novels that were written from 1841 onwards, many by writers who never visited Australia, few are now remembered. Apart from events brought about by the natural world of deserts, forests, mountains, fire, flood, heat and drought, other popular themes were shipwrecks, attacks by Aborigines, bushrangers and escaped convicts, and getting lost in the bush. It was the strangeness of Australia that the writers stressed, those features that were different from life in Europe, where most of the readers lived. Of enduring interest is Ethel Turner's *Seven Little Australians* (1894) and Mary Grant Bruce's Billabong series (1910–46). Both writers knew Australia well, and wrote about it sensitively and convincingly:

> Life at 'Billabong' represents the world in microcosm. Secure though it may seem, threat comes occasionally in the form of feckless swagmen, cattle-thieves, gold-stealers, fire, drought and flood. These things bring adventure but little undue violence.
>
> (Saxby 1969: 95)

Of the hundreds of adventure titles published in the nineteenth century few have survived. The combination of high adventure and blatant didacticism became increasingly unpopular and is now unacceptable to readers. One of the few books not to have passed into oblivion is R.L. Stevenson's *Treasure Island* (1881). In many respects it set a pattern that greatly influenced other writers. Stevenson achieved remarkable things in *Treasure Island*: he wrote an exciting tale free from moralistic preaching, and he depicted characters realistically, with good and bad traits shared by both heroes and villains. Long John Silver, a likeable rogue, was a radical departure from the stereotyped villain. Although Stevenson acknowledged the influence of Ballantyne and Kingston, he outclassed both of them and set the adventure novel in a new direction. By lifting characterisation out of conventional patterns, Stevenson prepared the way for the realistic writers of the twentieth century.

STRUCTURE OF THE ADVENTURE STORY

The basic structure of these stories is very simple: it's the same as that used by storytellers from ancient times. It is made up of a series of episodes that lead to a climax of compelling interest and ending with a short denouement where all is resolved. John Burningham's *Mr Gumpy's Outing* (Cape, 1978) shows this clearly. The story begins with Mr Gumpy, his house, a river and a boat. He is persuaded to take on board, in turn, two children, a rabbit, a cat, a dog, a pig, a sheep, some chickens, a calf and a goat. The passengers misbehave, tip the boat, and fall into the river. Having dried out on the river bank they all walk home across the fields and have tea with Mr Gumpy, who later bids them goodbye and invites them 'for a ride another day'. For the young child there are the basic ingredients of action, suspense, surprise and setback. The story finishes satisfactorily with everything resolved and with the prospect of another adventure. For older readers the Gumpy pattern is repeated chapter by chapter and arranged in such a way that it leads to the point of greatest interest after which the story ends satisfactorily.

However convenient as an explanation of structure this linear concept might be, it is too simplistic when applied to the finest adventure stories because it exaggerates the importance of events and diminishes or ignores the importance of other features, such as character development. A good adventure story is always something more than the sum total of its episodes. This can be seen in *The Adventures of Tom Sawyer*. In the first few chapters incidents seem to predominate. Tom tricks Aunt Polly by turning the fence whitewashing punishment into something that benefits him; he wins a coveted Bible prize at Sunday school by trading goods for the necessary reward tickets; he tries to stay away from school by feigning illness. However, in these early chapters Twain is using incident to build up a rounded picture of Tom in the context of his local community. In doing this he allows the reader to see the other side of his triumphs. Tom's cheating to win the Bible prize ends with an embarrassing exposure of his ignorance of the scriptures; he has to go through the painful ordeal of having a tooth removed in order to miss school. Twain carefully constructs a believable Tom, so that in Chapter 23 (the novel contains 35 chapters), when Tom speaks up in Mutt Potter's defence in relation to Robinson's murder, the reader can accept this courageous act as consistent with what has been already learnt about Tom's character. He may be dishonest, foolhardy and impulsive, but he is also kind, courageous and loyal. At the point where the major climax occurs, in Chapter 32, when Tom and Becky emerge from the cave where they have been trapped, the effect is considerably heightened by the reader having detailed knowledge of Tom's character.

POPULAR SERIES ADVENTURE STORIES

Discussion of the adventure novel would be incomplete without some consideration of the popular series adventure story as written by W.E. Johns, Enid Blyton, Carolyn Keene, F.W. Dixon and others. In her article 'In Defence of Adventure Stories', Judith Armstrong offers reasons for the continuing popularity of a genre that for many years has been disparaged by educationists and literary critics. She contends that the stories in these series follow the pattern of traditional storytelling with its reliance on cause and effect, expectation and surprise. Children become addicted to the stories, she says, because they not only find a satisfying narrative structure but also because in a series they find the structure repeated twenty or thirty times, with the same core of characters. That many children read any one series several times over seems to show that surprise and originality may not be the most important things sought. Armstrong feels that the stories appeal because they fulfil some psychological need not necessarily met in other kinds of literature. The predictable characters 'are collectively marvellous counterparts of [the reader's] self ... He could be any one of them if only criminals frequented his doorstep' (Armstrong 1982: 12). Blyton and others do not try to develop the characters in any depth, she says, because to do so would distort the expected pattern, — if the characters were depicted too subtly, and if the polarities between the heroes and the villains were blurred, the adventure story convention would be lost, and presumably the child reader would look elsewhere (perhaps to television) for a substitute. Armstrong maintains that the readers know that life is not like an adventure story, but it is precisely because they believe this that they are attracted to them. To them each remains a story in all its predictability and unreality. Perhaps the folk stories of old were related and received in the same spirit and with the same awareness.

There are other reasons for, say, Enid Blyton's continuing appeal than those given by Armstrong: I can think of three. In both the Five and Seven series Blyton presents the material as a mystery to be solved. She stresses the importance of group membership and encourages children to act with independence and assurance. She supplies plenty of clues for the reader to piece together, she uses the child's inherent wish to become and to remain part of a group; she also allows the characters almost free rein to solve their problems without adult aid, although adults are sometimes brought in to complete the good work that the gang has efficiently begun. Blyton constructs a secure world, where children are watched over, even if at a distance, by caring parents, with wisdom supplied by father and material comforts by mother. Within this world the chosen Seven and Five (and the readers) are completely safe.

I will take one typical example. In *Puzzle for the Secret Seven* (1969) the gang of seven are completely at home in their semi-rural setting, enjoying an enviable amount of freedom to come and go and make decisions: the whole ethos of the gang implies unity and mutual respect. The various parents of the Seven have faith in their children; they respect their need for secrecy. There is the familiar championing of the weak, this time the Bolans, that 'tragic' family whose *hut* (not house) is mysteriously burnt down, rendering them the recipients of a great deal of charity. The Seven behave with absolute reliability and truthfulness, two characteristics that distinguish them from Binkie and Susie, who are not of the Seven. To an adult there appear to be so many things wrong with the books — wooden, unrealistic characters, blatantly patronising attitudes and a hopelessly contrived plot, to name only three — and so little to commend the books that all criticism that has been levelled at Blyton over the years seems to be justified. Aidan Chambers has succinctly summed up the nature of the Blyton influence:

> There is about her stories a sense of secrets being told in whispers just out of earshot of the grown-ups, a subversive charm made all the more potent for being couched in a narrative style that sounds no more disturbing than the voice of a polite maiden aunt telling a bedtime story over cocoa and biscuits. Ultimately Blyton so allies herself with her desired readers that she fails them because she never takes them further than they are.
>
> (Chambers 1985: 45)

Yet children continue to read Blyton's books with seemingly undiminished enthusiasm. Is it possible that adults have overreacted? Perhaps so. Nicoll and Collerson adopt a tolerant, open attitude to the influence of such writers as Blyton. They suggest that series books may fulfil important needs in a child's development as a reader. In their study of the reading habits of one child over a period of more than two years they conclude:

> Juliet read and re-read over 40 books by Enid Blyton during the years in which she was developing independence as a reader ... Juliet's reading pattern is unusual in that reading of Blyton was concurrent with her reading of other books generally regarded as 'quality' reading for children several years older than herself. We need perhaps to be looking more closely at the structures and ideology of popular series such as those of Blyton ... to see what are features which children find so satisfying. It could be that these types of books are fulfilling a particular need in the development of a child's reading fluency and in the internalising of certain linguistic patterns and story structures which are important to subsequent reading and writing.
>
> (In Unsworth 1984: 100)

Perhaps adults should adopt a positive approach. First they could show their gratitude that their children are reading something. By becoming interested in stories for their own sake children are more receptive to suggestions for reading other books of greater literary value.

THE ADVENTURE STORY IN THE TWENTIETH CENTURY

As a genre the adventure novel has changed since the beginning of the twentieth century, especially since about 1950. A significant change has been the increasing importance given to the portrayal of character and the consequent diminishing importance given to events. Betsy Byars' *The House of Wings* (1973) illustrates this point well. With different emphasis this novel could have been an adventure story of the conventional kind. The youngest of eight children is dumped by his parents to be looked after by his eccentric grandfather; the boy runs away and is pursued by the grandfather. They find an injured crane, which they bring back to the old man's home, and which they both look after. The boy becomes used to his grandfather, grows to love him, and decides to stay.

This bare statement of the plot gives little idea of the richness of the novel. Betsy Byars uses a simple plot as a vehicle for character portrayal, her chief concern. She shows both Sammy and his grandfather pushed to the limits of endurance. Byars is interested in how they will cope, how these two hitherto neglected (but potentially loving) individuals will recognise their need for each other. She uses the accidental finding of the injured crane as the means of bringing both characters together. *The House of Wings* is an adventure story, in that it contains the ingredients of action, suspense, surprise and setback, but it is also a perceptive psychological study that involves the reader with characters more than with events.

Further evidence of the change in the adventure novel can be seen in the work of individual writers whose careers began before 1960. In Australia alone, Joan Phipson, Ivan Southall, Eleanor Spence and Patricia Wrightson, who started out as writers of adventure novels, have exchanged the romanticism of adventure for a realism that is more acceptable as an expression of the times. Many of their later novels could be still classed as adventure ones, in that they contain 'undertakings of uncertain outcome' and 'hazardous experiences', but the adventure element seems to have become less important, one of many that go to make up the texture of the novels. The reasons for the changes are probably closely linked with those in patterns of Western twentieth century living. Popular air travel and years of television exposure have made accessible even the remotest parts of the earth and there is no longer the motivation for writers to find exotic settings for their novels. Also greater freedom of expression of hitherto forbidden subjects has resulted in writers being encouraged to find adventure in their own familiar, domestic scene. Books are increasingly reflecting the societies in which they are written, mirroring social patterns and social problems.

Ivan Southall, who with the Simon Black series (1950—62) was the Australian equivalent of W.E. Johns (of *Biggles* fame), has become a fine observer of ordinary, non-heroic people, having exchanged exotic foreign settings for familiar Australian ones. In *Ash Road* (1966) he shows a small community at risk. As in the best adventure novels, setting is important. Southall leaves us in no doubt of the potential danger — a tinder-dry part of rural Victoria in mid-summer, fanned by a dangerous north wind. Three adolescent boys on a camping trip, elated by their new-found freedom from parental restraints, enter this setting. The adventure begins with Graham's thoughtlessness in lighting a spirit stove out in the open in the middle of the night. The central action concerns the three boys and the involvement with the fire they have started. Soon, of course, all the inhabitants of the community become involved. The catalyst for action is the sudden collapse of an old man while picking berries. Southall uses the drama associated with this event to bring many of the characters together.

Ash Road is about two things: first, the fire itself and the devastation it causes. At this level it is a thrilling adventure story, with plenty of suspense, danger, uncertainty and action. There is a sense of a world no longer dependable. Children have to take over adult responsibilities; old people have to be guided by children. Second, the novel is about moral responsibility. The boys cannot be excused of guilt simply because the fire was begun accidentally. Graham and the other two have to accept the guilt, and live with it. Southall has used an adventure as a means of exploring character: he has put his characters through a series of tests and he has charted their responses and development.

Lilith Norman has shown how the journey adventure model can be adapted for modern readers. In *Climb a Lonely Hill* (1970) she depicts a physical journey that two ordinary country children make when their uncle's accidental death forces them to assume responsibility for their own survival. In the lonely outback of New South Wales Jack and Sue have to make decisions about everything related to their lives. For Jack, who has previously shirked all responsibilities, the test is almost too great. However, both children do survive, having coped with a number of unpleasant aspects of existence — injury, thirst, exhaustion and loneliness. This is a powerfully-written adventure story with skilful use being made of events to focus on the psychological journey of two believable characters. In the hands of writers as proficient as Southall and Norman the adventure novel is in no danger of dying out, and will continue to serve the interests of children.

REFERENCES

Armstrong, J., 'In Defence of Adventure Stories' in *Children's Literature in Education* Vol. 13, No. 3, 1982.

Chambers, A., *Booktalk*. London: Bodley Head, 1985.
Children's Book Council of Australia (Victorian Branch), *Books for Children*, eighth edition. Melbourne: Children's Book Council of Australia, 1982.
Saxby, H.M., *A History of Australian Children's Literature, 1841–1941*. Sydney: Wentworth, 1969.
Townsend, J.R., *Written for Children*. Harmondsworth: Kestrel, 1976.
Unsworth, L., editor, 'Stories Read and Stories Written' in *Reading, Writing and Spelling*. Sydney: Macarthur Institute of Higher Education, 1984.

RECOMMENDED ADVENTURE STORIES

The following list includes titles mentioned in the text as well as others that would interest young readers from eight to twelve plus. For many of the titles I am indebted to *Books for Children*, a regular publication of the Victorian Branch of the Children's Book Council of Australia. (An asterisk denotes that the story is Australian).

Aiken, Joan, *The Wolves of Willoughby Chase*. Cape/Puffin.
Babbitt, Natalie, *Tuck Everlasting*. Chatto/Lions.
* Baillie, Allan, *Little Brother*. Nelson.
Bawden, Nina, *Carrie's War*. Gollanz/Puffin.
Brown, Jeff, *Flat Stanley*. Methuen/Magnet.
Byars. Betsy, *The House of Wings*. Bodley Head
* Chauncy, Nan, *Tangara*. Oxford/Puffin.
* Clark, Mavis Thorpe, *A Stranger Came to the Mine*. Hutchinson.
* Couper, S., *Pelican Point*. Hodder & Stoughton.
Dickinson, Peter, *Annerton Pit*. Gollanz/Puffin.
* Fatchen, Max, *Chase Through the Night*. Methuen.
George, Jean, *Julie of the Wolves*. Bodley Head /Puffin.
─────────, *My Side of the Mountain*. Bodley Head/Puffin.
* Green, Cliff, *The Further Adventures of Riverboat Bill*. Hodder & Stoughton.
Hoban, Russell, *The Mouse and his Child*. Faber/Puffin.
Holm, Ann, *I Am David*. Puffin.
Jones, Diane Wynne, *The Ogre Downstairs*. Macmillan/Puffin.
King, Clive, *Me and my Million*. Kestrel/Puffin.
Konigsburg, E.L., *From the Mixed-up Files of Mrs B. Frankweiler*. Atheneum/Dell.
Line, David, *Run for your Life*. Cape/Puffin.
* Norman, Lilith, *Climb a Lonely Hill*. Collins.
Norton, Mary, *The Borrowers*. Dent/Puffin.
O'Dell, Scott, *Island of the Blue Dolphins*. Kestrel/Puffin.
* Phipson, Joan, *The Boundary Riders*. Kestrel.
─────────, *Hide Till Daytime*. Kestrel.
─────────, *Keep Calm*. Macmillan.
Serraillier, Ian, *The Silver Sword*. Cape/Puffin.
* Southall, Ivan, *Ash Road*. Angus & Robertson/Puffin.
─────────, *Let the Balloon Go*. Methuen/Puffin.
* Spence, Eleanor, *The Seventh Pebble*. Oxford.
Stevenson, R.L., *Treasure Island*. Nelson.
* Stow, Randolph, *Midnite*. Puffin.
Taylor, Theodore, *The Cay*. Puffin.

* Thiele, Colin, *The Valley Between*. Rigby.
——————, *Blue Fin*. Rigby/Seal.
——————, *Shadow on the Hills*. Rigby.
Twain, Mark, *The Adventures of Tom Sawyer*. Dent/Puffin.
Vander Loeff, A. Rutgers, *Children on the Oregon Trail*. Puffin.
Wilder, Laura Ingalls, *Little House in the Big Woods*. Methuen/Puffin.
* Wrightson, Patricia, *The Nargun and the Stars*. Hutchinson/Puffin.
——————, *The Rocks of Honey*. Angus & Robertson/Puffin.

MORE ADVENTURE STORIES

Adams, Richard, *Watership Down*. Puffin, 1973.
Baillie, Allan, *Hero*. Penguin, 1990.
Banks, Lynne Reid, *The Indian in the Cupboard*. Lions, 1988.
Fisk, Nicholas, *The Worm Charmers*. Walker, 1989.
Garfield, Leon, *Smith*. Puffin, 1968.
Kelleher, Victor, *The Red King*. Viking, 1989.
Lisson, Deborah, *The Devil's Own*. McVitty, 1990.
Rubinstein, Gillian, *Flashback: The Amazing Adventures of a Film Horse*. Puffin, 1990.
Saxby, Maurice and Ingpen, Robert, *The Great Deeds of Superheroes*. Millenium Books, 1989.

10 VERSIONS OF THE PAST: THE HISTORICAL NOVEL IN CHILDREN'S LITERATURE

MARGERY HOURIHAN

> Whatever makes the past, the distant or the future, predominate over the present, advances us in the dignity of thinking beings.
>
> Dr Johnson

The historical novel began with Scott[1] and quickly became an approved genre for children. Nineteenth century respect for historical scholarship ensured that stories designed to provide children with knowledge of the past would find favour with parents and educators; in addition the historical tale proved a suitable vehicle for Victorian didacticism. Just as selected figures from classical literature had long provided models of behaviour for the British governing class, so characters and incidents from past ages, suitably presented, furnished moral exemplars for English children.

The work of Charlotte M. Yonge (1823–1901) shows clearly both the concern for accurate research and the emphasis upon ethical example. She was the author of several volumes of historical and scriptural retellings as well as over a dozen highly-regarded novels for children set in various periods and places. Her stories contain many details of contemporary customs and are embellished with background notes; they also highlight suitably upright and pious behaviour. A typical volume is *The Little Duke* (1854), which recounts the boyhood of Richard the Fearless, great-grandfather of William the Conqueror. In Yonge's story he is innately spirited and valorous, and so inclined to be impatient of piety and the discipline necessary to achieve literacy. Yet, guided by the memory of his saintly father (who, Yonge tells us, wore a hair shirt beneath his robes) and by his own good instincts, Richard acquires both piety and literacy, despite dangerous circumstances and wily enemies. Yonge's final background note sums up her concerns in this story:

> Few names in history shine with so consistent a lustre as that of Richard; at first the little Duke, afterwards Richard *aux longues jambes*, but always Richard *sans peur*. This little sketch has only brought forward the perils of his childhood, but his early manhood was likewise full of adventures, in which he always proved himself brave, honourable, pious, and forbearing. But for these our readers must search for themselves into early French history, where all they will find concerning our hero will only tend to exalt his character.
>
> (Yonge 1872: 231)

The result of such didacticism is, inevitably, a failure to suggest the way the people of the time actually perceived and experienced their lives, despite the accuracy of surface detail. Richard's father sounds more like a virtuous Victorian papa than a tenth century Norman, as he urges his son to work at his lessons and forgive his enemies, while his friends and retainers remind us of a house party at an English stately home:

> Richard was rather tired of their grave talk, and thought the supper very long; but at last it was over, the Grace was said, the boards which had served for tables were removed, and as it was still light, some of the guests went to see how their steeds had been bestowed, others to look at Sir Eric's horses and hounds, and others collected together in groups.
> The Duke had time to attend to his little boy, and Richard sat upon his knee and talked ...
>
> (Yonge 1872: 11)

Neither the information about the trestle tables, nor the use of the archaic 'steeds', is sufficient to overcome the pervasive impression of a gathering of Victorian gentlefolk chatting politely about their horses and dogs. Even Richard himself, daring in the hunt, brave in battle, and concerned always to do the honourable thing, seems less like a Christianised Viking than a British schoolboy who, in the most desperate moments of either a cricket match or a war, can be relied upon to 'play up! play up! and play the game!'[2]

In our own time overt didacticism has not usually been the concern of the historical writer for children, but other literary fashions have led to different distortions of the past. Two of the most frequent are the innumerable costumed adventure stories in the tradition of Alexandre Dumas' *The Three Musketeers* (1844), and the continuing stream of costumed romances in which spirited young heroines are eventually united with dashing, though fundamentally worthy, heroes. However, more serious twentieth century writers of children's fiction have produced novels in which meticulous research is combined with sensitivity and imagination to provide convincing insights into the past that, in turn, deepen the reader's understanding of the present. It was Geoffrey Trease[3] who first clearly insisted on the need for the children's historical novel to be honest and realistic, and to avoid pointless and affected archaisms.

At the simplest level such stories enable children to apprehend historical events and processes which have moulded the present world, by showing their impact on individual human beings with whom we can identify or sympathise. Thus, for instance, the ramifications of the invention of printing are made vivid in Cynthia Harnett's *A Load of Unicorn* (1966), where we see how the new technology threatens the livelihood of a family of scribes, who react in much the same way as people do today when their jobs are made irrelevant by computerisation. We see, too, something of the significance of the new invention for literature and education when the young protagonist is befriended by the enthusiastic Caxton and is instrumental in delivering to him the manuscript of Malory's *Morte d'Arthur*.

NOVELS OF ORDINARY LIFE

As well as illuminating major events and changes in this way the historical novel can create a sense of what ordinary life in the past was like. Unlike historians historical novelists can select according to artistic criteria so that significant and interesting events are highlighted for the reader and not overlaid with a weight of research findings. Conversely the historical novelist can make use of very minor, even trivial, details which would hardly merit inclusion in a history text book, but which can make vivid the texture of daily existence so that the past is brought to life. It is largely Ruth Park's skill in selecting such details that makes the world of the Sydney Rocks area in 1873 so convincingly present to the mind and senses of the reader in *Playing Beatie Bow* (1983). Two examples amongst many will serve to show the resonances of her sensitively-selected detail. First, when the twentieth century heroine, Abigail, stumbles into the Victorian past and is taken in by one of the families of the respectable poor she is forced to use a chamber pot, because a sprained ankle prevents her making her way to the outside lavatory. She is profoundly embarrassed by this, but is fascinated when Dovey, one of her benefactors, enters the room with a little brass shovel with a few red hot coals upon it:

> Abigail watched with interest as Dovey put sprigs of dried lavender on the coals and waved the resultant thin blue smoke about the room.
> 'There now! You're all sweet again'.
> 'Can't I have the window open?' asked Abigail.
> Dovey was shocked. 'But the spring air brings so many fluxes and congestions in the chest', she said.
>
> (Park 1983: 55)

This incident makes us realise how much closer the Victorians were to the biological realities of life and death than we can be in the sanitised twentieth century. At the same time we experience their fastidiousness about such things, and see that it arises as much from a genuine concern for the comfort of others as from aspirations to gentility. Over and above this the incident reinforces our awareness of the gains we have made in hygiene and the understanding of health.

Later in the story, when Abigail is able to go downstairs, she explores the confectionery shop from which the Bow family derive their living. Through her eyes we see the polished grates, spits and hooks, and the four large cauldrons in which the sweets are made.

We see 'a solidified cascade of toffee that Dovey had been pulling to make it creamy and malleable', (p. 73) and we inspect the variety of confections which Mr Bow produces:

> Gundy, flavoured with cinnamon or aniseed; fig and almond cake, which was a lemon-flavoured toffee poured over pounded fruit or nuts and allowed to set; Peggy's leg; liquorice; and the favourite glessie, a kind of honeycomb.
>
> (Park 1983: 73)

The scene is not only picturesque; it makes us vividly aware of how extensively the processes of manufacture and distribution have changed in the last hundred years, of how much physical labour our forebears had to perform and, conversely, of what we have lost in the way of individuality and immediacy when all our sweets come to us with identical chemical flavourings in identical plastic packets, whether we live in the Rocks or in Rockhampton.

Much of the fascination of Laura Ingalls Wilder's true stories of American pioneering life in the late nineteenth century resides in their accurate account of how things were made and managed. In *Little House on the Prairie* (1935) we learn how Pa builds a log cabin and makes a rocking chair, how Ma makes bean porridge and how the children are shining-eyed with excitement at Christmas when they receive tin cups of their very own and sticks of red and white striped candy. Again we are able to understand better both what we have gained and what we have lost.

The strength of Esther Forbes' classic, *Johnny Tremain* (1943), is that it illuminates both major events and ordinary life. It combines a vivid account of the preparations for the Boston Tea Party, which sparked off the American Revolution, with a memorable picture of the life of the times seen through the eyes of Johnny who is, first, an orphan apprentice silversmith and, later, a newspaper dispatch rider and spy for Paul Revere. Johnny's thwarted talent as a silversmith, his eagerness to love and to learn, and his enthusiastic commitment to the political idealism of his friend, Rab, help the reader to feel the excitement, the energy and the sense of enormous future possibilities, which led to the birth of modern America. The details of daily life in Boston — from the description of the bare attic where Johnny and his fellow apprentices sleep to that of the gleaming brass knocker on the panelled front door of smug, conservative Merchant Lyte — reveal the matrix in which the embryonic nation grew.

At a somewhat deeper level the historical novel can reveal patterns of change and interaction in the past which have parallels in our own time, and which are perhaps also indicative of permanent human concerns and dilemmas. Thus, for instance, readers of Rosemary Sutcliff's *Song for a Dark Queen* (1982), which recounts the life of Boudicca (Boadicea) and describes the revolt that she led against the Roman occupation of Britain, will recognise many similarities between that tragic struggle and the efforts of indigenous peoples in the twentieth century to throw off colonial rule. In Sutcliff's sensitive novel we see the Celtic inhabitants of Britain fighting not only for their lost freedom, but for their culture and way of life which they realise will inevitably be destroyed by the more technologically advanced Romans who are efficient road-builders, townplanners, administrators and military strategists, but who have no understanding of the Celts whose lives are lived in harmony with the rhythms of nature, whose art expresses nature's subtle asymmetries, who worship the Earth Mother, the great nature goddess, and who find straight roads and neatly laid out cities entirely alien. Today the black peoples of South Africa, and the Melanesian people of New Caledonia, to point to but two examples, are engaged in a similar struggle for both political independence and the preservation of cultural traditions which are threatened by the more advanced civilisation of European colonists.

Sutcliff's novel is narrated by Cadwan, Queen Boudicca's harper, so that we see the events through the eyes of a Celt. The language of his narrative, which is highly poetic, shimmers with all the subtle shades of nature and with the richness of the gold and bronze worked by the Celtic craftsmen of the high La Tène culture:

> I would sing of the horse herds grazing in the broad pastures ... And the wide-winged sunsets over the marshes ... I would sing of the wild geese flighting down from the north ... and the swirling red-enamelled pattern on the bronze face of the King's warshield ...
>
> I would sing of all these things, for it seems to me that all these things gave something of themselves to the making of the Lady Boudicca.
>
> (Sutcliff 1982: 15−6)

However, this narrative is interrupted at a number of points by letters supposedly written by a young Roman officer, Agricola, in which he tells his mother about the progress of the campaign. The language of these letters is flat, unemotional and cerebral. It has none of the imaginative richness of Cadwan's, and it suggests, strongly, that the Romans have none of Cadwan's sensitivity to the rhythms and beauty of nature. Thus we feel the differences between the two cultures. But, although our sympathies are primarily with the Celts, Sutcliff does not allow us to interpret the conflict in simple black and white terms. Agricola's letters show his intelligence, his efficiency, his courage and sense of responsibility, and his fundamental decency and concern for the welfare of others. So we are made aware of the tragedy implicit in the situation. The poetic culture of the Celts cannot survive the impact of the Romans with their logic, literacy and technology; Roman civilisation, too, has much to offer.

The dilemma is a permanent and fundamental one: each stage of human 'progress' entails loss, and human beings seem to have great difficulty in achieving an effective balance between their emotional/ imaginative potential and their intellectual/rational capacity. In our age, when the dominance of scientific, rational thinking has brought us to the brink of the nuclear holocaust, we are particularly aware of the need to attend to our more instinctual selves and recover something of the ability to live in harmony with nature. *Song For a Dark Queen* is rich with meaning for us.

NOVELS OF INDIVIDUAL DEVELOPMENT

As well as broad cultural patterns of this kind, the processes and problems of individual human development can also be illuminated in the historical novel. The different time setting may make it easier for a reader to see that, for instance, the difficulties of adolescence are not merely a matter of current social conditions, or of personal inadequacies and errors, but are rather part of an inevitable process of change in which a measure of suffering is a precondition for the emergence of a truly adult personality. Conversely the exploration of an earlier society can make it clear that some problems are not inevitable in this way, but are in fact, the result of social conditions and psychological preconceptions that can be changed. Those stories which highlight the role assigned to girls and women in earlier societies fall into this category. Elizabeth Speare's *The Witch of Blackbird Pond* (1958) contrasts the very restricted code of behaviour expected of girls in early Puritan north America with the much greater freedom, both mental and physical, allowed in Jamaica to the heroine, Kit, who faces great difficulties when she is sent to live with her relatives in America. The same device of contrast is used in *Playing Beatie Bow* where, for instance, we see that the educational opportunities automatically available to twentieth century Abigail were denied to nineteenth century Beatie. She, despite her obvious intelligence and fierce desire to learn watched her brother, Judah, being *sent* to school, while the family could see no point in education for Beatie. The reader of these novels can see clearly that there is nothing essential about the restrictions imposed on girls in any society.

Leon Garfield's stories create a dramatic, Hogarthian picture of the squalor and colour of eighteenth century London:

> After dark. Blackfriar's. Coalman's Alley. The Sun in Splendour! What a conjugation from gloom to glory! What a piling up of shades and shadows, of shrinking streets, unseen corners, wrong turnings and alleys blind as bats ... until the Sun in Splendour!
> It hung over an open doorway, a little tarnished ball in spikes. There were a few steps leading down, and a smoky yellow glimmer coming up, as if the sun had had a misfortune and fallen downstairs, and was limping back up, one step at a time.
>
> (Garfield 1981: 90)

At his best Garfield manages to suggest both the contingency of the evils of poverty and crime and the permanence of the personal problems which confront his young protagonists. Thus Smith, in the novel of that name (1967), is a ragged, sooty orphan who lives by picking pockets; he is a victim of the social injustices of eighteenth century society. But, as he slowly comes to realise the arrogance of blind justice and the emptiness of his swaggering hero, Tom the highwayman, he is undergoing the painful processes of learning which all adolescents must endure.

An outstanding example of a book which deals with a problem that is inherent in human nature is Rosemary Sutcliff's *Warrior Scarlet* (1958). Its theme is the transition from childhood to adulthood, the difficulty of winning a place in adult society, and the self-doubts and fear of failure which inevitably afflict all adolescents, so that, although it deals with a society far removed from our own, its relevance is deeply felt. It is set in Bronze Age Britain in about 900 BC when the first true Celts are thought to have arrived there. Their culture is heroic — a warrior society in which courage and physical prowess are admired above all other qualities. It tells the story of a boy, Drem, who has been born with a withered right arm, but must overcome this physical disability if he is to pass the test which will admit him to the warrior caste and full membership of the tribe. The test is to slay a wolf single-handed. Drem has courage and has acquired great skill with a throwing spear. Nevertheless he knows that failure is horrifyingly possible, and, in fact, he does fail. As a consequence he spends a lonely and bitter year exiled from the tribe until, during the following famine-ridden winter, he redeems himself by killing two wolves (one of them his original antagonist). When he is finally admitted to the tribe he realises that his year in exile has taught him a degree of patience and compassion that he would probably not otherwise have acquired.

The story appeals strongly to young readers for it is a parable of the difficulties they all encounter, while Drem's withered arm functions as an objective correlative of the personal inadequacies with which most adolescents feel, privately, they are uniquely afflicted. Finally, of course, the story suggests that easy success is not necessarily the most fruitful, that the very experiences of self-doubt and preliminary failure can be enriching.

Relatively simple, heroic societies, like the one that Sutcliff recreates in *Warrior Scarlet*, seem particularly appropriate contexts for stories which dramatise the primary concern of adolescents — the development of the ego, the building of self-confidence and a sense of self-worth and the achievement of an integrated personality. In a sense such societies are themselves at an adolescent stage of development: they emphasise exploration, action, adventure and outward achievement rather than the contemplative virtues and the joy of inner enlightenment. Perhaps this accounts for the large number of children's books that take the Vikings as their subject matter: the journeys and battles of the Vikings are a ready-made symbol for the psychological journey and conflicts of growing up. Rosemary Sutcliff herself deals with a group of Vikings in *The Shield Ring* (1956). Other authors who have done so include Clyde Robert Bulla and Christopher Webb, but it is Henry Treece who has written most extensively about them. His work is uneven. Some of his stories — *The Road to Miklagard* (1957) for instance — are little more than lively adventure yarns with a colourful setting. But at his best Treece combines excitement and historical verisimilitude with real insights into human nature and cultural development. *Viking's Dawn* (1956) tells of the voyage of the *Nameless*, in the earliest years of Norse exploration. Young Harald Sigurdson is one of her crew and, ultimately, is the only survivor of the daring and tragic expedition. Thus the book is in the direct tradition of the *Odyssey*, and the various trials and adventures of the voyage provide an allegory for Harald's inner journey from boyhood to the threshold of maturity. At the same time it reveals the nature of the Vikings, and for much of the time the focus of attention is not on Harald, but on the older crew members, especially the leader, Thorkell Fairhair. We see their courage, their keen curiosity, their sense of humour and their strong sense of loyalty. We also become aware of the limitations of their way of life: As plunderers they are essentially destructive rather than creative (despite their superb ship-building skills). Because they are illiterate, their intellectual and philosophical development is circumscribed and their lively minds constantly encounter a kind of bafflement. Having given themselves to fighting as a way of life they are essentially tragic; like Achilles they know they will not live long.

In their leader there is something else: a dim sense of these limitations, and a visionary longing. The blindness which the cruel Orkney winds inflict upon him is the outward symbol of the Vikings' limited understanding. When they capture a robust Irish monk, Thorkell senses that he possesses insights which surpass his own, and feels that destiny has brought them together:

> 'Now I know the answer to one thing at least, that there is another world, another life, beyond that which we know waking'. . . . It was as though he had found direction, blind as he was.
>
> (Treece 1967: 139)

A lesser writer might have been tempted to have Thorkell converted to Christianity, but Treece is grimly realistic. Thorkell 'holds to other gods' (p. 138) and he is drowned before the beginnings of his deeper awareness can develop. The brave but limited Vikings, facing the unknown and struggling towards understanding, must stir a deep sense of recognition in young adolescent readers.

•

POINT OF VIEW

The value of historical novels lies in the way they illuminate the present through the past and provide insights into human nature; the best of them, like *Viking's Dawn* and *Warrior Scarlet*, function simultaneously in both these ways. The degree of authority and imaginative depth which they achieve is, however, largely a matter of language. A sensitive selection of detail, as in *Playing Beatie Bow*, can create an effective picture of the past, but total conviction depends upon the sense that we are entering into the mind and experiences of someone from an earlier time. This requires that the story be narrated by, or from the point of view of, one of the characters, or that the narrative voice adopted by the author be one appropriate to the period. Ruth Park does not attempt this in *Beatie Bow*. The story is told from the point of view of twentieth century Abigail who has stepped back through time, so it is as though the reader, too, is a time traveller observing the past, but not experiencing it as those who lived there did. Most historical novels, however, are narrated from the point of view of a protagonist who belongs to the period, and few modern writers are guilty of either obvious anachronisms or self-conscious archaisms. But such neutrality is not in itself sufficient to suggest the perceptions of a mind belonging to an earlier age. Cynthia Harnett's pleasant, limpid prose in *The Load of Unicorn*, for instance, never jars, yet never quite persuades us that we are actually entering into the thoughts of a medieval protagonist:

> The roll was a collection of stories of King Arthur and his Knights of the Round Table, and Bendy knew them almost by heart. True that many had no beginning and no ending and some were no more than an odd page or two. But he did not mind; he filled in the missing bits out of his head. He loved stories and devoured all the ones that were written in the Crowing Cock, particularly any about adventure and romance. But these of King Arthur were the best of all.
>
> (Harnett 1966: 21, 22)

There is nothing here that would be out of place if Bendy were a twentieth century English child with a passion for reading rather than a schoolboy of Caxton's time. Neither vocabulary, syntax nor imagery makes us feel that this is necessarily the thinking of a fifteenth century mind. On the other hand Rosemary Sutcliff involves her readers in a profoundly convincing experience of life in the periods she has made her own, especially Roman and Celtic Britain. It is this which makes her, in the judgement of most critics,[4] pre-eminent amongst writers of historical novels for children, and in the front rank of historical novelists generally. Her choice of words, their arrangement in phrases, sentences and larger units, and, especially her imagery, function to convince us of the authenticity of perception of the narrator and/or the character whose awareness we are experiencing.

It is, of course, impossible to construct even a simulacrum of a primitive language, or to write in the actual English of an earlier age. Rather, the writer must avoid terms which are marked as modern, and use the resources of contemporary English in such a way as to suggest the perceptions and the general world view which may reasonably be assumed to have belonged to the people of the time. It is this which Sutcliff achieves. Further, at her best, the imagery in her books embodies their underlying themes, so that there is a total artistic unity of ideas, characters, setting, action and language. The following passage from *Warrior Scarlet* gives an indication of this unity. (The boy, Drem, through whose eyes we are seeing is present at the feast following a king-making ceremony):

> He tore a last mouthful from the piece of rib he had been gnawing, and gave the bone to Whitethroat against his knee; and turned with a sigh of contentment to listen to the blind harper who sat at the King's feet, striking music like a shower of shining sparks from the slim, five-stringed harp of black bog oak in his hands.
>
> (Sutcliff 1976: 118)

There are no words here which carry connotations of the twentieth century, nor are there any which imply a level of abstract thought that would have been impossible in a preliterate era. The words 'tore' and 'gnawing' suggest a primitive method of eating without superfluous description, but it is the image of 'music like a shower of shining sparks' that gives the sense of an authentic Bronze Age perception. While the details of the blind harper at the king's feet and the harp of black bog oak might have been included by any competent researcher (Charlotte Yonge would certainly have put them in), this image is the product of a deep historical and poetic sensibility. It suggests the clarity and beauty of the harp notes each falling separate from the rest, and shows that Drem is responsive to this beauty. It reminds us that wood fires, from which shining sparks shower, were an ever-present part of Bronze Age life: the comparison is a natural one for Drem to make. It implies that this culture had no abstract or theoretical systems of musical description. Finally it forms part of a constellation of images of light and brightness which are integral to the light/dark opposition that is at the core of the novel, which is concerned with the contrast between sun worship and worship of the earth mother; between the 'golden' Celts and the small, dark aboriginal people; between the bright warmth of the people's firesides and the terror of the night and the forest; between the spark of human intelligence and the darkness of unconscious nature.

Language is used in this way throughout the novel. Often it is an apparently unimportant phrase which carries a significant resonance. For instance, the characters consistently say 'It is in my mind that' rather than 'I think', thus suggesting that the people of the Bronze Age have not arrived at our level of introspective self-consciousness, but rather conceive of thoughts as fragments of a wider energy of being which may happen to enter the mind at any time. Likewise the passage of time is not referred to in numbers of days or by terms such as 'summer' and 'winter', but by references to seasonal events and tasks, e.g. 'from one bee harvest to the next'. Thus we come to feel that the people do not count and measure as we do, but operate according to a constant awareness of natural cycles.

The extent of Rosemary Sutcliff's achievement may be better understood if it is compared briefly with the work of another children's writer who also deals with preliterate Celtic culture. Mollie Hunter's prize-winning novel, *The Stronghold* (1974), is set in Scotland in the first century AD. The hero is determind to save the life of the chief's daughter who has been nominated as a sacrificial victim by the tribe's Druid. When he enlists the help of a friend and of the girl's sister, we encounter the following passage:

> He did not stand completely alone now, Coll thought, and with three minds working on the problem, something would surely occur to one of them. Yet still the weight of the defeat Anu had inflicted was heavy on him, and for long hours he lay awake staring at a vision of the days that might have to be lived through before one of them had even the germ of an idea for saving Fand.
>
> (Hunter 1978: 116)

To begin with it, is questionable that anyone belonging to a culture which accepts human sacrifice would try to subvert it in this way. (In *Warrior Scarlet* Drem simply comments that 'it is the custom' for harpers who are not born blind to have their eyes put out so that their inner vision of the music might be more intense). Further, the language suggests a high degree of intellectual self-consciousness: Coll is thinking that he is thinking. The phrase 'three minds working on the problem' has a distinctively twentieth century ring, suggesting a world in which unhappy situations are seen, not as inevitable destiny or the will of the gods, but as 'problems' susceptible to solution by reasoning. The final phrase is equally inappropriate; even if we concede that 'germ' in its sense of seed embryo is not necessarily anachronistic, the words still imply an understanding of the logical development of ideas as a result of mental effort which is alien to a preliterate people who did not possess our concept of 'mind'. It is precisely the sense of a different mode of perception and understanding which is so impressive in *Warrior Scarlet*.

Profoundly evocative language of this kind is the medium of all Rosemary Sutcliff's novels from *The Eagle of the Ninth* (1954) onward. Those set in Roman Britain combine what she describes as 'the sensible workmanlike language which one feels the Latin of the ordinary Roman citizen would have translated into' (Sutcliff 1974: 307), with a range of imagery that makes real for us her Roman characters' sense of the countryside and the life of the towns and barracks. Frequently this is set against a more metaphoric language given to the Celtic characters whose relationship to nature is much closer than that of the literate, civilised Romans who build straight roads and walls across the land. This contrast is a major theme of *The Eagle of the Ninth*. The point of view is that of the Roman ex-cohort commander, Marcus, but the perception of the conquered Celts is conveyed in the language of his slave and friend Esca, who announces his willing submission to Marcus in the words: 'I am the Centurion's hound, to lie at the Centurion's feet' (p. 77). The concrete image is one which would come naturally to a literate hunter like Esca, and it expresses a complex of feelings which we, or Marcus, would convey by means of abstract nouns such as submission, bitterness, admiration and loyalty.

However, it is in her later novels, which are told from the Celtic point of view, that the language is most fully expressive of the culture, the time and the place as well as the major underlying themes. Perhaps the most remarkable of these later works is the deceptively short *Sun Horse, Moon Horse* (1977) which evokes a deeply animistic awareness that is convincingly presented as the matrix from which the magnificent achievements of Celtic La Tène art developed. She explores the nature of art and of the artist, so that the book is, at one level, an investigation of her own inner self and her most profound concerns, as an artist in words.

In a whole series of images she suggests the way the people feel the presence of life in every aspect of nature, and we see that this is, at the same time, an artist's perception of the very essence of the thing itself, something close to Hopkins' 'inscape'. Her people are worshippers of the Great Mother in the form of Epona, the horse goddess, and their images show us how they feel towards the land — as though it were the very body of Epona herself:

> Even the sudden lift where the land reared up above plunging combes and hollows, carrying the dun on its highest crest, did not break the line. It was as though the High Chalk arched its neck as it passed on westward, no more.
>
> (Sutcliff 1977: 82)

The story is concerned with the creation of the White Horse of Uffington, the ancient picture cut into the chalk of a hillside in southern England, where a few sweeping lines, not all even interconnected, catch the quality of a cantering horse's grace and power. The language enables us to see how this impressionist technique expresses the vision of the imagined artist, Lubrin Dhu, who is entranced by the movement and rhythm of living things:

> He drew the speed and the power, and the blurred flow of manes and tails, and the thunder of hooves, and the restlessness of spring time in their heels.
>
> (Sutcliff 1977: 69)

Sutcliff's own technique in this book has a similar quality. The conventional shape of the novel, with characters interacting to produce crises, climax and resolution, as in *The Eagle of the Ninth* and *Warrior Scarlet*, is hardly there. Rather the story consists of significant moments in the life of the tribe and of Lubrin Dhu, which are laid down in such a way as to produce a picture full of meaning and beauty, just as Lubrin lays down the lines on the hillside to produce the impression of the white horse.

The language and structure of the book also make us aware of the transience of human life and human societies in comparison with the continuity of the land, and, to some extent, of works of art. We learn how Lubrin's people had conquered the earlier inhabitants, the 'little dark people'; we see Lubrin's people conquered by a later wave of Celts, the Attribates; and we know that the Romans, the 'red crests' of whom the Celts have only heard stories, will in turn conquer the Attribates. Of course, as modern readers, we know that the Romans themselves were later displaced by the Saxons and the Saxons in their turn conquered by the Normans. The repetitive pattern of human history which is like the repeated cycle of the seasons is felt in the structure of the sentences which are predominantly simple and compound, rather than complex, with a large number of 'ands' linking principal clauses, and strings of nouns, adjectives and phrases, thus suggesting a cumulative process, a piling up of days and years in a preordained and customary way:

> The life of the clan went on; and the years turned full circle after each other. The mares dropped their foals in early summer, and in autumn the herds were rounded up for branding, and in winter the leggy two-year-olds began their breaking to rider or chariot.
>
> (Sutcliff 1977: 26)

Thus *Sun Horse, Moon Horse* is a profoundly organic work in which the form itself realises the major thematic concerns, which are further implicit in patterns of syntax and imagery.

In the hands of an artist of the order or Rosemary Sutcliff the historical novel becomes much more than a colourful story that brings the past to life. Through a profound imaginative penetration of the past she deepens her readers' understanding of the very nature of human life and human civilisation, of our essential relationship with the natural world, and of our inner needs and aspirations.

NOTES

1. Sir Walter Scott (1771–1832) was the author of a large number of historical novels beginning with *Waverley* in 1813 and including *The Heart of Midlothian* and *Ivanhoe*. Georg Lukacs says of him: 'Scott endeavours to portray the struggles and antagonisms of history by means of characters

who, in their psychology and destiny, always represent social trends and historical forces' (Lukacs 1962: 34).
2. Cf. Sir Henry Newbolt's well-known poem 'Vitai Lampada' which celebrates the character-building qualities of cricket.
3. Geoffrey Trease is the author of numerous historical novels for children. For his views on the writing of historical fiction see 'The Historical Novelist at Work' in G. Fox *et al.* editors, *Writers, Critics and Children*, New York: Agathon Press, 1976.
4. See, for example, John Rowe Townsend, *Written for Children*, London: Pelican Books 1976, p. 219, and Margaret Meek, *Rosemary Sutcliff*, London: Bodley Head, 1962, p. 307.

REFERENCES

Lukacs, Georg, translators, Hannah and Stanley Mitchell, *The Historical Novel*. London: Merlin, 1962.
Meek, Margaret, *Rosemary Sutcliff*. London: Bodley Head, 1962.
Sutcliff, Rosemary, 'History is People' in Virginia Haviland, editor, *Children and Literature*. Oxford: Bodley Head 1974.
Townsend, John Rowe, *Written for Children*. Harmondsworth: Pelican, 1976.
Trease, Geoffrey, 'The Historical Novelist at Work' in Fox, G. *et al.*, editors, *Writers, Critics and Children*. New York: Agathon Press, 1976.

BOOKS REFERRED TO IN THE CHAPTER

Forbes, Esther, *Johnny Tremain*. Constable/Peacock.
Garfield, Leon, *John Diamond*. Kestrel/Puffin.
——————, *Smith*. Constable/Puffin.
Harnett, Cynthia, *The Load of Unicorn*. Methuen/Puffin.
Hunter, Mollie, *The Stronghold*. Hamish Hamilton/Piccolo.
Park, Ruth, *Playing Beatie Bow*. Nelson/Puffin.
Speare, Elizabeth, *The Witch of Blackbird Pond*. Gollancz/Peacock/Puffin.
Sutcliff, Rosemary, *Song for a Dark Queen*. Bodley Head/Knight.
——————, *Sun Horse, Moon Horse*. Bodley Head/Knight.
——————, *The Eagle of the Ninth*. Oxford University Press/Puffin.
——————, *The Shield Ring*. Oxford University Press/Puffin.
——————, *Warrior Scarlet*. Oxford University Press/Puffin.
Treece, Henry, *The Road to Miklagard*. Bodley Head/Puffin.
——————, *Viking's Dawn*. Bodley Head/Puffin.
Wilder, Laura Ingalls, *Little House on the Prairie*. Methuen/Puffin.
Yonge, Charlotte M., *The Little Duke*. Macmillan.

MORE NOVELS IN HISTORICAL CONTEXT

(foreword by Storm Jameson), *The Diary of Anne Frank*. Pan Horizons, 1989. (First published 1947)
Garfield, Leon, *The Empty Sleeve*, Penguin, 1989.
Hautzig, Esther, *The Endless Steppe*. Penguin, 1988. (First published 1968)
Koehn, Isle, *Mischling, Second Degree: My Childhood in Nazi Germany*. Penguin, 1989. (First published 1977).
Margorian, Michelle, *Goodnight Mister Tom*. Kestrel, 1981.
Paton Walsh, Jill, *A Parcel of Patterns*. Penguin, 1983.
Reiss, Johanna, *The Upstairs Room*. Puffin, 1979. (First published 1972)
Wheatley, Nadia, *The House That Was Eureka*. Puffin, 1985.
——————, and Rawlins, Donna, *My Place*. Collins Dove, 1987.

11 THE FAMILY STORY: A CONTEXT FOR CARE

LES INGRAM

> The next time she awoke, the family was there. Sadako smiled at them. She was part of that warm, loving circle where she would always be. Nothing could ever change that.
>
> Eleanor Coerr

The family story has a rich tradition in children's literature, extending over a period of some one hundred and fifty years. Not surprisingly, children of all ages respond to the artistic shaping of experiences they recognise, or have shared. In the context of the story form, with its focus on adventure, suspense and conflict, there is usually a caring family environment, as well as a positive relationship between the narrator and the implied reader, and between the narrator and the protagonists in the story. Humour, too, contributes to the essential warmth of the family story for children.

In the last twenty-five years, especially, the nature of the family unit portrayed in family stories has changed, mirroring the changes of the family in Western society, and so, too, have the personal problems that are explored; for example, fear of the dark in Russell Hoban's *Bedtime for Frances* (1960); divorce in Beverly Cleary's *Dear Mr Henshaw* (1983); adjusting to school in her *Ramona the Pest* (1968). In Judith Viorst's *The Tenth Good Thing About Barney* (1972) death is dealt with, as it is in Katherine Paterson's *Bridge to Terabithia* (1978). In fact, there has been a marked movement from family adventures and episodic works to those that concentrate on such personal and social issues.

In this chapter the qualities and concerns of family stories for the young reader will be discussed in the context of selected titles considered appropriate for readers up to Year 6 in the primary school. Of course, appropriateness is dependent on the interests and readiness of the individual reader. So the family story should be considered as part of a continuum that includes but goes beyond the primary school, and also as part of an historical tradition involving such classics as Louisa May Alcott's *Little Women* (1868), Susan Coolidge's *What Katy Did* (1872), Ethel Turner's *Seven Little Australians* (1894) and Edith Nesbit's *The Story of the Treasure Seekers* (1899).

FAMILY STORIES FOR THE YOUNG

Jan Ormerod's wordless picture books, *Sunshine* (1981) and *Moonlight* (1982) demonstrate the appeal of stories that focus on the family. Young and old have undoubtedly shared the experience of a morning that unfolds as it does in *Sunshine* where the reader is brought, by a creative patterning of illustrations, into a close relationship with the young girl and her parents as they follow, in their different ways, the family ritual of getting up, having breakfast, and going to work or school. This particular story is given dramatic interest when the parents realise that time has slipped away. Contentment gives way to frantic activity, but fortunately the time deadline is met, and off they go, with the girl farewelling her father when he goes to study, and later her rag doll, as she leaves for school with her mother. It is a book of warmth and movement, and works at many levels in what it suggests of each member of the family and the family unit itself. Jan Ormerod's achievement lies in the quality of her drawings, the impact of each picture and the patterning and sequencing of all the pictures, and what she has revealed of the small but significant details of family life.

For the young reader there are many books that have a similar focus and appeal. They range from Russell Hoban's Frances stories and Janet and Allan Ahlberg's Happy Families to Beverly Cleary's Ramona series. Russell Hoban's *A Baby Sister for Frances* (1964) presents a situation that is, again, well known to children and adults alike, that of the adjustments that have to be made when a new member of the family arrives. As in all of the Frances books there are qualities of humour and wisdom that are part of a simply, beautifully-constructed story. Just as in stories for older children such as Betsy Byars' *The House of Wings* (1973) and *The Pinballs* (1977), and Katherine Paterson's *The Great Gilly Hopkins* (1978), so in *A Baby Sister for Frances* there is a child who feels neglected and wants to run away. Through the parents' sensitive handling of the problem the author makes the point that space and self-esteem are important if a child is to come to terms with his or her feelings:

> 'I can almost hear her now', said Father, humming the tune that Frances had just sung.
> 'She has a charming voice'.
> 'It is just not a *family* without Frances', said Mother.
> 'Babies are very nice. Goodness knows I *like* babies, but a baby is not a family'.
> 'Isn't that a fact!' said Father.
> 'A family is *everybody all together*'.
>
> (Hoban 1964: 23)

This theme of 'everybody all together' is a significant one in many family stories, but especially those written for young readers. Certainly the cooperative spirit is highlighted in Janet and Allan

Ahlberg's series *Happy Families*. In *Mrs Wobble the Waitress* (1980), for example, Mrs Wobble loses her job because her wobbling leads to a series of disasters in her job as a waitress, and culminates in her dropping a plate of jelly on the manager's head. The rest of the family try to comfort her, and Mr Wobble hits upon the idea of turning their house into a cafe. It becomes famous for its juggling waiters who are in reality the children, who spend most of their time saving the meals that fall from their mother's tray. The pictures add a special dimension to the book's appeal, because they not only capture the spirit and experiences of the text, but also create a social context for the story itself. Together, the language and pictures convey a sense of fun and optimism.

Beverly Cleary's Ramona stories not only have buoyancy, but also a more serious side. They explore Ramona's relationships with the rest of her family, and with the children and adults who are close to her at home and at school, in ways that are appropriate to her stages of development. This can be demonstrated by an examination of *Ramona the Pest* (1968) when we meet her at the beginning of her school days, and *Ramona Forever* (1984) when she has entered third grade.

In kindergarten Ramona experiences those vicissitudes that befall many young people trying to come to terms with their first experience of school: misinterpreting, being misinterpreted; wanting affection, feeling rejected; seeking independence, needing protection; seeking recognition, needing acceptance. For Ramona and her friend Howie sharing is particularly difficult, and leads to a few stormy conflicts between them, and with their parents. She is acutely aware of injustice:

> Having been the youngest member of her family and of the neighbourhood, however, she had learned to watch for unfair situations.
>
> (Cleary 1968: 54)

In Tove Jansson's *Finn Family Moomintroll* (1961), Moomintroll becomes frustrated and feels rejected when he realises that his friends do not recognise him because of the physical changes caused by the Hobgoblin's hat. Ramona, too, experiences such fear at the school's Hallowe'en party, suddenly sensing that no-one can recognise her in her mask:

> ... and the thought that her own mother might not know her frightened Ramona even more. What if her mother forgot her?
>
> (Cleary 1968: 116)

Happily Ramona finds a solution to her problems, just as she overcomes her later feelings of inadequacy and stupidity. Her solutions are found in the context of a warm family setting with adults who behave fairly and firmly. But it should be stressed that the author does not avoid the more painful aspects of growing up and, in particular, of starting school.

In *Ramona Forever* Ramona's world has become more complex. Her father is retraining as a teacher; her mother is expecting another child; and she discovers that there are adults who do not like her. This story focuses more sharply on Ramona and her family, and reveals the ways in which the members of the family have to adjust to one another's emotional needs. In this sensitive, personal context, the narrator's position shifts more closely to the perceptions and feelings of Ramona herself:

> 'Really, I don't know what got into you children this afternoon'. Mrs Kemp was thoroughly provoked.
> Ramona could have told her in one word: *grown-ups*. Instead, she stated at her book and thought, I am never going to come back here again. Never, never, never. She did not care what anyone said. She did not care what happened. She was not going to be looked after by someone who did not like her.
>
> (Cleary 1984: 26)

Here, at the beginning of the story when she feels rejected and frustrated as a result of her conflicts with Howie's family, and later when she feels isolated and threatened by the arrival of the new baby, Ramona is able to cope because of the cooperation of the rest of the family. They help to create that sense of 'everybody all together'. She and her sister Beezus are given the responsibility of looking after themselves and the house while their parents are at work; they handle the crisis of the death of their pet cat; they learn to be sensitive to one another's feelings; and they think through such problems as the possibility of their having to move if their father is to get a teaching appointment. In spite of these serious concerns, the story still retains a quality of humour that is part of a young child's attitude and response to the adult world.

TRADITIONAL FAMILY STORIES

The family stories discussed in the preceding section reveal a concern for the security and warmth of the family unit; a young protagonist who experiences and resolves conflicts and problems similar to those experienced by most of the intended readers; humour of situation and dialogue; and usually some moral or lesson implicit in the interaction of the members of the family. In differing degrees these qualities can be found in the early classics.

Not the first but certainly the best known of these is Louisa May Alcott's *Little Women* (1868) which John Rowe Townsend includes in that section of his book *Written for Children* (1974) called 'Domestic Dramas'. This nomenclature reflects the focus in these early works on the family unit, even though one or two characters often emerged as protagonists, or as being of more interest than other members of the family.

To put Alcott's work in historical context one should refer to the influence of such writers as Elizabeth Wetherall (Susan Warner, 1819–85), Maria Cummings, and the best known British writer of the time, Charlotte M. Yonge (1822–1901). Maurice Saxby also draws attention to the influence of Catherine Sinclair's *Holiday House* (1839), 'a story with humour, and even gaiety' (Saxby 1969). This is important in terms of the thread of humour that was to lighten the didacticism and often sorrow of the early family stories, something that persists in different but significant forms in contemporary works.

Charlotte Yonge's *The Daisy Chain* (1856) is considered to be the best of her family stories (Townsend 1974: 78) and 'the most representative of the strong religious element that is found in Victorian family life' (Saxby 1969: 28). The religious element is particularly noticeable in Alcott's *Little Women*, where great stress is laid on such themes as Christian charity, hard work, good behaviour, repentance, and God as a father-authority figure. The girls' mother and the narrator draw the reader's attention to these concerns and to the desirability of a Christian code of living. However, the book's vitality lies in the activities of naturally mischievous children falling short of the idealistic exhortations of adults; in the author's handling of their relationships and adventures; as well as in the spirited behaviour of the *real* heroine, Jo March.

> *Little Women* marks not only an increased truth-to-life in domestic stories, with children seen as people rather than examples of good and bad; it also marks a relaxation of the stiff and authoritarian stereotype of family life, persisting from the still recent times when the Fifth Commandment came first and the earthly father was seen quite literally as the representative of the heavenly one . . . This mellowing was necessary before the family story, of which *Little Women* is the first great example, could come into its own. A relationship between rulers and subjects had to be replaced by one of mutual affection. The family story could not work in an atmosphere of repression or of chilly grandeur. The key characteristic is always warmth.
>
> (Townsend 1974: 79–80)

Commenting on the Australian classic *Seven Little Australians* Townsend makes the point that 'the shadow of the stern father still lies over this story' which is 'probably still the best known story of family life to have come from this country'. (Saxby 1969: 60). As in *Little Women* the narrative shifts from one character to another while foregrounding the sense of family by way of shared adventures. Although Captain Woolcot is a stern father, the novel evinces a feeling of warmth, especially in terms of the children's relationship with their young 'mother', Esther.

As in the case of other family stories, such as *Little Women*, Eve Garnett's *The Family From One End Street* (1937), and Elizabeth Stuckey's *Magnolia Buildings* (1960), which shift in focus from one character to another, problems arise with the emergence of one or more potential protagonists. Thirteen-year-old Judy, in particular, poses problems because she is a vital character whose conflict with her father is dramatically interesting. But she is sent away to boarding school, and the focus shifts to Meg who, again, is dramatically interesting in terms of her self-inflicted, but understandable, physical suffering, and her romantic interests. There is, however, no opportunity to follow her development, for Judy re-enters the story, having run away from boarding school. Judy's death has obvious connections with sacrifice and atonement, in spite of Ethel Turner's, disclaimer that the story is about 'model children, with perhaps a naughtily-inclined one to point a moral' (1894: 9). Judy's being sent away is comparable with the suppression of the rebelliousness and vitality that we recognise in the treatment of Jo March (*Little Women*) and Katy Carr (*What Katy Did*). Critical problems related to *Seven Little Australians*, and, in particular, questions about the focusing of the work, are raised and discussed in some detail by Felicity Hughes in 'Literary Criticism of Two Australian Novels' (1980).

Another significant nineteenth century family story is Edith Nesbit's *The Story of the Treasure Seekers* (1899). It concerns the adventures of the six Bastable children, who devise all sorts of schemes to restore their family fortunes which have shrunk because of the decline of their father's business. The reader is kept aware of the economic ills of the family, as is the case in *Little Women* and, to a lesser extent, in *Seven Little Australians*. There is no doubting the pressure of large families on parents trying to maintain a relatively well-to-do existence in times of economic difficulty. From an artistic viewpoint, though, the emphasis on the need for money and other resources in, say, *Little Women* or *The Story of the Treasure Seekers* has a somewhat embarrassing effect on the reader. To some extent Nesbit brings this problem out into the open in another of her family stories, *The Railway Children* (1906). The mother of the children becomes very angry when she learns how they have contrived to get her the medicine she needs, not to mention a delightful hamper:

> 'Now, listen', said Mother; 'It's quite true that we're poor, but we have enough to live on. You mustn't go telling everyone about our affairs — it's not right. And you must never, never, never ask strangers to give you things. Now always remember that — won't you?'
> They all hugged her and rubbed their damp cheeks against hers and promised that they would.
>
> (Nesbit 1906: 64)

In spite of their promise the children still have to learn, as they eventually do, that other people feel as their mother does. The lesson is brought home to them that gifts given in friendship can be misinterpreted as charity. The fact that these issues are developed in a dramatic context means that the work has a more positive tone than the pleading or protesting of the earlier texts.

As well as the portrayal of girls who are pressured to restrain their natural ambitions and spirit, there is also an interesting and, at times, disturbing portrayal of male attitudes and roles in the writings mentioned in this section. Undoubtedly the authors concerned reflected prevailing social attitudes, but the presence of characters such as Jo, Katy and Judy, at least at some point in their development, challenges such notions. Again, Nesbit confronts this issue in an interesting way. The narrator of *The Story of the Treasure Seekers* is Oswald, but the reader has to work this out because at the beginning he or she is simply told that it is one of the family who is telling the story. J.R. Townsend makes the point that 'even to a child it is obvious that it is Oswald who is telling the story from the number of puffs and the amount of self-congratulation that he manages to get in' (Townsend 1974: 104). Oswald makes a number of comments that reflect stereotypical male attitudes:

> Then after dinner we let the girls have a dolls' tea-party, on condition they didn't expect us boys to wash up ... (p. 140)
> ... We put tea-leaves in it for the pipe of peace, but the girls are not allowed to have any. It is not right to let girls smoke. They get to think too much of themselves if you let them do everything the same as men. (p. 141)
> ... We sat up till past twelve o'clock, and I never felt so pleased to think I was not born a girl. It was hard on the others; they would have done just the same if they'd thought of it. But it does make you feel jolly when your pater says you're a young buck! (p. 172)

There is a provocative edge to such comments which undoubtedly reflect the boy's point of view. Perhaps this needs to be put in the context of the irony of the work as a whole. The narrator, for example, demonstrates his concern for the art of storytelling, and often throughout the book, as indeed a number of writers of family stories do, tries to distance his account from the world of fiction. Ironically he fails because there is a consistent undercutting of his attempts to create a story of real life, culminating in a conventional romantic ending. As Townsend suggests, the discovery of a rich uncle is 'a device which was used by a great many Victorian writers, and which may generally be taken as an indication that no real solution was possible' (Townsend 1974: 104).

The deepest irony of the book can be attributed to the fact that the reader has a less limited view than the narrator. For example, the reader understands the effect on the family of the father's prolonged absences in a way that the children do not:

... Then Alice spoke.
Girls seem not to mind saying things that we don't say. She put her arms round Albert-next-door's uncle's neck and said —

'We're very, very sorry. We didn't think about his [Albert's] mother. You see we try very hard not to think about other people's mothers because —'

Just then we heard Father's key in the door and Albert-next-door's uncle kissed Alice and put her down, and we all went down to meet Father. As we went I thought I heard Albert-next-door's uncle say something that sounded like 'Poor little beggars!'

He couldn't have meant us, when we'd been having such a jolly time, and chestnuts, and fireworks to look forward to after dinner and everything!

(p. 83)

This absence of the parent is also a feature of Frances Hodgson Burnett's *The Secret Garden* (1910) which makes a number of significant points about the nature and role of family in the development of the individual and his or her relationships with other people. In this context of personal and social development it is the Sowerby family which provides a positive model for Mary Lennox whose parents died in India, and for her cousin Colin whose mother was killed in the garden and whose distracted father shunned him after his mother's death. Mary, Colin, and Susan Sowerby's son, Dickon, became close friends. They have a special relationship with nature, and with the gardener Ben Weatherstaff. The story gradually shifts in focus from Mary to Colin and, finally, to Colin's father who is overseas when he dreams of the garden and hears the voice of his dead wife. At this point he receives a letter from Susan Sowerby calling him home to Misslethwaite. He remembers his reaction to his wife's death and his refusal to see the weak child.

> He had not meant to be a bad father, but he had not felt like a father at all. He had supplied doctors and nurses and luxuries, but he had shrunk from the mere thought of the boy and had busied himself in his own misery.

(p. 24)

The magic of the garden reaches out to Mr Craven, and even before meeting his son again he begins to believe that he can take on the role of a caring parent. It is significant that he has this change of attitude before he meets Colin. In other words, the reader knows that he is willing to accept his parental responsibility towards Colin as he believed him to be rather than being swayed by the remarkable changes Colin has undergone. *The Secret Garden* is not a traditional family story with a series of episodes or adventures involving a family unit or some of the individual members in sequence, but one that reveals the development of each child's potentiality for love and growth in a special kind of family and a special setting. It is a complex story that has at its outcome the reconciliation of father and son.

DIFFERENT FAMILY CONTEXTS

A family story that broke new ground in terms of social setting is Eve Garnett's *The Family from One End Street* (1937) which focuses on dustman Joe Ruggles, his wife Rosie, a washerwoman, and their family. In its focus and concerns it provides a marked contrast to the historical and period stories of the best American fiction between the wars (Townsend 1974: 178), the Australian stories of 'homestead life and family fun' (Saxby 1969: 192), and those stories of the 1930s 'about families and their real-life activities' (Townsend 1974: 187).

Separate chapters of *The Family from One End Street* are devoted to each member of the family until they all go to London to see the Carthorse Parade. This structure presents artistic problems, particularly in regard to the children Katie and John, who are both interesting characters and certainly potential protagonists: their development as characters is restricted by the episodic structure. However, Eve Garnett is a skilful storyteller and, in spite of the predictable happy outcomes, she provides moments of action and suspense.

But there are less successful moments. Although the parents are proud, they are also embarrassingly grateful for cast-offs from the well-to-do. Furthermore, the narrator's occasionally mannered description contributes to a patronising tone that goes beyond even that of some of the supercilious characters such as those John Ruggles meets at the rich boy's party:

> And taking the bottle of ink off the dresser, and a sheet of her best professional Woolworth-printed notepaper from under the cushion in the wicker arm-chair, she sat down and wrote a letter to Mrs Beasely saying she would be very grateful for her niece's old clothes any time they could be spared.
>
> (p. 35)

Beneath the surface optimism, the Ruggles' acceptance of their lot, and the various adventures that turn out happily for them, there are disturbing issues that come to the surface with Kate's ambition to leave the Council school and go to college; the snubbing of the Ruggles at church by the grocer's wife; the Ruggles at the 'posh' restaurant; and even the suggestion that Mrs Ruggles is tired and harassed by having to cope with the demands of a large family. Yet, by and large, there is a feeling of optimism about this work:

> There is a warm sense of family solidarity which is the most attractive characteristic of the book and may account for its continuing popularity with children. Nevertheless it seems to me to be too condescending to be altogether commendable. Mr and Mrs Ruggles are seen from above and outside. Even their names, and the choice of their occupations as dustman and washerwoman, make them seem slightly comic. People from higher up the social scale are terribly nice to the Ruggleses; and the Ruggleses know their place.
>
> (Townsend 1974: 187)

Elizabeth Stuckey's *Magnolia Buildings* (1960) treats similar problems and situations — family frustrations; the pressures of a large family on its individuals; the need for privacy, adult-child relationships; and gang and peer pressures — in a much less romantic way. The story focuses on the Berners family who live in a block of flats, Magnolia Buildings. The children have different aspirations and different problems. The eldest child, fourteen-year-old Ally, dreams of a successful stage career while facing the reality of a lack of privacy, as well as the demands of assuming the role of mother in a family that has come to take that role for granted. One of the boys, Val, is unable to get work because of his reputation for fighting and unreliability. He belongs to the Black Hand gang that is markedly different from that portrayed in *The Family from One End Street*, and he lives in fear of another particularly vicious gang who operate in the same area. He resorts to stealing, but fortunately the problem is met head-on by his mother.

Within the framework of a traditionally-structured family story, conflicts and pressures of a less pleasant nature are raised and to some extent explored. It is made clear, for example, that for children like Doreen, competitive examinations such as the 11+ cause emotional and physical distress. There are also personal hardships related to the crowded family setting, and the oppressive life in a block of flats, particularly when the tenants find it difficult to make ends meet. Parents, too, have problems in adjusting when they have to share limited accommodation with a relative. The fact that Aunt Glad is fortunate enough to win a lottery prize and so take the pressure off the Berners family does not negate the fact that *Magnolia Buildings* raises significant personal and social problems.

THE INDIVIDUAL AND THE FAMILY

Nearly ten years later, Ivan Southall's *Let the Balloon Go* (1968) brought some of the personal conflicts noted in earlier family stories into sharper focus. Although this is not a family story in the wider sense of domestic drama, as described by Townsend and applied to such classics as those already discussed, there is no doubt that John Sumner's struggle to achieve victory over his physical disability is firmly rooted in family attitudes, rules and conflicts. As with Ally in *Magnolia Buildings* there is a gulf between his dreams of peer recognition and acceptance and the reality of what for John is a hostile social environment.

Through his words, thoughts and actions we are made aware of his mother's frustrations and suffering. She has to cope with being responsible for supervising John, while meeting the demands of part-time work. At a still deeper level we can appreciate the effect on her of the responsibilities she has to assume for John's welfare, and of the way in which she is compelled to stifle her emotions. Because the narrative shifts to John's point of view, the overall effect is that of a child's perception and understanding of his parent's conflicts and tensions:

> Sometimes Dad would say to her, 'Easy, old dear'. Other times Dad would lose patience and there would be a rip-roaring row. Then Mum would rush to another room and sob and John would hear his name mentioned and Dad would try to keep her quiet. 'Be quiet, be quiet', he'd say; 'if anyone comes to the door we'll never live it down'.
> There hadn't been a row or sobbing this time because Dad wasn't at home to start it off, but Mum's voice had become more and more breathless.
>
> (p. 29)

An understanding of the mother-son relationship is crucial not only to the tension of the early part of this book, but also to that of the concluding section in which each member of the family has to adjust to a new set of responsibilities and a new freedom for John. *Let the Balloon Go* is John's story, his search for identity within the family, but it points decisively to important developments in the family story in regard to the protagonist's point of view and parent-child conflicts.

These qualities are all realised in Ruth Park's *Callie's Castle* (1974), which is concerned with a young girl's desire for privacy, her coming to terms with the loss of her father when she was a baby, and the acceptance of her relationship with Laurens Beck, her stepfather.

As in *Let the Balloon Go*, so in *Callie's Castle* the reader is given access to the protagonist's perceptions. For example, even before the reconstruction commences, Callie senses a potential threat to her ownership of the cupola with its promise of privacy:

> The alarmed feeling had returned. Grandpa had climbed down the ladder to fetch some tools, and she had not even his understanding look to encourage her. Somehow, in some unexpected adult way, the cupola would be snatched away — if not now, then next month or next year — and it would all seem reasonable and proper. And she'd have no place of her own again . . .

There is a shift here to Callie's thought processes, and, more particularly, to her feeling of alarm. The opening sentence of this passage is a metaphor that says someone experienced alarm. The shift is, in effect, from the point of view of the omniscient narrator to that of Callie — the 'Someone' who is represented as *she*. The kinship term of address 'Grandpa' and the temporal adjunct 'now' contribute to the shift from the omniscient narrator towards Callie's point of view. This is reinforced by the use of commas and dashes, the contracted form 'she'd' and the repetition of the coordinating conjunction *and*. Examples can be found from the writers mentioned earlier of language being used in this and other ways to create a shift towards a character's consciousness, but these would be comparatively rare. Southall, Park and other contemporary writers are often concerned with a particular character and his or her thoughts and feelings about family events and relationships, and so use those resources that enable the sort of narrative shift alluded to far more than their predecessors. This shift of focus in family stories is directly related to a movement from a basically episodic structure to that which concentrates on one or two protagonists involved with a particular problem or conflict.

Another important aspect of Park's family story is the way in which the concept of family embraces the notion of life as a continuum. Callie experiences the thrill of adding her name to the list in the cupola of previous occupants of the house. She is demonstrably part of the history of that place. This theme is developed in both an historical and a family context in Ruth Park's later work *Playing Beatie Bow* (1980) in which the protagonist Abigail comes to the realisation that time is not a vortex but a river, and that a family is part of life's continuity. Alan Garner's complex work *The Stone Book Quartet* (1976) is also such a celebration of family, linking the young and the old, the dead and the living, the past, present and future.

Callie's Castle focuses on family relationships, with her grandfather playing a significant role in cementing the relationships between this eldest girl and her brother and sister, and between Callie and her parents. He, like Callie, has come to a time in life when privacy and acceptance are important. He finds time to listen to what she has to say. He appreciates that Callie and Laurens are, in fact, daughter and father, and, in time, Callie, too, comes to realise the love that Laurens has for her. It is the grandfather who makes the cupola livable so that Callie can enjoy a room of her own. As this suggests, not only the grandfather but the parents, too, play a significant role in *Callie's Castle*: their problems and attitudes are explored in the context of her conflicts. Although Callie's mother realises that her daughter's problem lies deeper than a need for privacy, she cannot always understand Callie's outbursts because as a wife and mother she is also attentive to the needs and responses of others. Her view is naturally a limited one, and it is only through the interaction of the members of the family that mother and daughter come to terms with their relationship.

Similarly, in Katherine Paterson's modern classic *Bridge to Terabithia* the young boy Jess and his parents achieve an understanding through the boy's traumatic loss of Leslie, his friend and mentor — the one who opened up and shared with him a world of the imagination and the spirit. The children's families provide a dramatic contrast to each other, and to some extent they are complementary. Jess gradually responds to Leslie's family and what it offers in terms of intellectual and artistic freedom and respect for the individual's talents and ideas. His own family provides a down-to-earth environment, but one in which economic hardship and family squabbles stifle his individuality. Here, love, like religion, has been taken for granted. Leslie's death breaks down a number of barriers, not only for Jess but for the rest of the family, especially his father.

> His father pulled Jess over on his lap as though he were Joyce Ann. 'There. There', he said, patting his head. *'Shhh. Shhh'.*
> 'I hate her', Jess said through his sobs. 'I hate her. I wish I'd never seen her in my whole life'.
> His father stroked his hair without speaking. Jess grew quiet. They both watched the water.
> Finally his father said, 'Hell, ain't it?' It was the kind of thing Jess could hear his father saying to another man. He found it strangely comforting, and it made him bold.
> 'Do you believe people go to hell, really go to hell, I mean?'
> 'You ain't worrying about Leslie Burke?'
> It did seem peculiar, but still — 'Well, May Belle said . . .'
>
> (p. 130)

The relationship between the young and old that is so significant in *Callie's Castle* is skilfully and movingly explored in Betsy Byars' *The House of Wings* (1973):

> 'Where's my mom and dad?' Sammy asked again. His voice rose because he suddenly knew that they had not merely gone into town or to the gas station. He reached out and grabbed the front of the railroad jacket and shook his grandfather. 'Where's my mom and dad?' His grandfather rocked slowly back forth like a buoy in the water.
> Then his grandfather said one word. 'Gone'. It was like the sound of an old sad church bell in the hot empty air. 'Gone'.
>
> (p. 20)

Ten-year-old Sammy the youngest of eight children, cannot believe that his parents would leave him, nor does he listen to his grandfather's assurance that Sammy will rejoin his parents in Detroit at a later date. For Sammy who has led an uncontrolled existence until this time, and for his grandfather who has lived on his own for ten years since his wife's death, this confrontation is the beginning of a learning process for both of them. In the course of their catching and tending a blind crane a close bond develops between them.

The House of Wings is a story told with humour and sensitivity within a relatively brief timespan, and it is one that raises important concerns. On one hand, the boy learns what it is to be wanted and acknowledged and what it is to care for a helpless creature such as the crane. On the other hand, the old man opens up about his feelings and experiences, and comes to make the sort of relationship with another person that he has lacked for so long.

Another novel that focuses on the child-adult relationship is Katherine Paterson's *The Great Gilly Hopkins* (1978). Gilly Hopkins is a foster child who dreams of rejoining her mother whom she idolises. But sadly her dream is based on a false image. Part of the book's irony is that only Gilly is ignorant of the fact that her mother does not really believe in the words of love and encouragement that she sends to her daughter. The reader meets Gilly when she is being taken to Mrs Trotter's home, Thompson Park, her third foster home in three years. From the outset we are given not only the dialogue of the characters but also the words of Gilly's inner voice. Here, for example, Gilly has just helped Mrs Trotter's blind neighbour get from his place to Thompson Park:

> Trotter appeared in the hallway with her hands on her hips. 'How you doing in this cold weather?'
> 'Not my best, I'm afraid. This sweet little girl had to keep me from falling right down on my face'.
> 'Did she now?'
> 'See there, Trotter?' I managed.
>
> (p. 21)

In this way the reader has access to Gilly's private world, not in the conventional sense of being *told directly* what a character thinks about a person or situation, but in the sense of their being 'silent' contributors to the discourse. At other times the narrative shifts to Gilly's perceptions and self-questioning. The following scene conveys the ways in which the narration shows Gilly's inner turmoil; her voice speaking silently to Mrs Trotter; the interchange between the two characters; and the description of Mrs Trotter in terms of Gilly's perception. Gilly has received a postcard from her mother and is most upset, as she thinks of other children who can be with their mothers while she, who has not seen her parent since she was three years old, has to bear her painful separation:

> Gilly sat up straight. Couldn't anyone have any privacy around this dump? She stuffed the postcard under her pillow and then smoothed the covers that she'd refused to straighten before school. She stood up at the end of the bed like a soldier on inspection. But the door didn't open.
> 'Anything I can do for you, honey?'
> Yeah. Fry yourself, lard face.
> 'Can I come in?'
> 'No!' shrieked Gilly, then snatched open the door. 'Can't you leave me alone for one stupid minute?'
> Trotter's eyelids flapped on her face like shutters on a vacant house. 'You OK, honey?' she repeated.
>
> (p. 35)

Although Gilly comes to understand what it is to be loved by others and to love them in return, she wants to throw off the tag 'foster child'. Underlying this dilemma is her belief in the idealised picture she has formed of her mother. It is only when she meets her that her dream is shattered, and she realises where her home really is.

But it is too late to return to Mrs Trotter. She has to adjust to a new life with her maternal grandmother.

The Great Gilly Hopkins shares with such significant works as Bersy Byars' *The Pinballs* (1977) and Eleanor Spence's *The Left-Overs* (1982), a concern for children who are torn between their lives as foster children and their desire to be reunited with their parents. Each story portrays patient, sensitive foster parents who help their children work through their problems, to overcome their prejudices, and to accept responsibility. Although they share with other family stories qualities of humour appropriate to the children's perceptions and predicaments, these stories do not ignore more painful conflicts and experiences. Just as Douglas Mariner in Eleanor Spence's *The October Child* (1976) is finally overwhelmed by the responsibility of looking after his autistic brother, so in *The Left-Overs*, Drew comes to the end of his emotional tether. He has taken on the task of arranging new homes for the other children because their foster home is threatened by closure. When one of the children, James, disappears in the crowd at the Festival of Sydney Drew decides he has had enough:

> He was hot and breathless and angry. Why *should* he wear himself out hunting James, anyway? It simply wasn't true that James was his brother. He, Andrew Appleby, had no real brothers and sisters. He was an only child. So what was he doing in this crazy place, chasing a kid called James?
> Let someone else find him.

For a number of the protagonists in these stories of foster children, letters and telephone calls assume a poignant significance as the young people try to contact others who may help them to restore broken relationships. This certainly applies to Leigh Botts in Beverly Cleary's *Dear Mr Henshaw* (1983). Leigh, who lives with his mother, is trying to come to terms with his parents' divorce. His letters to his favourite author, and his diary, which is an extension of these letters, help him to disclose his deeper concerns about his family, particularly his mixed feelings towards his father and his desire for the family to be reunited.

This theme of a child's longing to be united with a missing parent is at the heart of Philippa Pearce's gripping family mystery *The Way to Sattin Shore* (1983). Quickly and surely this strange adventure shifts from an omniscient narrator's view to that of the young protagonist Kate Tranter:

> Here is Kate Tranter coming home from school in the January dusk — the first to come, because she is the youngest of her family. Past the churchyard. Past the shops. Along the fronts of the tall, narrow terrace houses she goes. Not this one, nor this one, nor this ...
> Stop at the house with no lit window.
> This is home.

> Up three steps to the front door, and feel for the key on the string in her pocket. Unlock, and then in. Stand just inside the door with the door now closed, at her back.
>
> Stand so, in the hall. Ahead, to the right, the stairs. Ahead, to the left, the passage to the kitchen in the wider part, by the back door, a round, red, friendly eye has seen her — the reflector of her bicycle.
>
> To the left of the hall, Granny's room.
>
> (p. 7)

So begins this compelling mystery, with the reader seeing with Kate what she sees. But *The Way to Sattin Shore* is more than a mystery adventure story. It embraces family secrets, complex family relationships and personal conflicts that are resolved with different repercussions for the members of the two families involved. There is no sense of the adults being pushed to the background so that the children can get on with their adventures.

All these family stories based on the dislocation or severing of relationships foreground the give-and-take of adult-child discourse. In Byars' *The Pinballs*, for example, Mr Mason takes the eight-year-old Thomas J. to hospital to see the surviving Benson twin, one of the old ladies who had looked after the boy for six years before he was taken to a foster home at the Mason's. Mr Mason tells Thomas J. how by his just being at the hospital he can be a comfort to Miss Benson. He confesses to the young boy that he had found it impossible to tell his dying mother that he loved her, and that a nurse had covered up for him by telling his mother that her son had said it. He then tells Thomas J. about his marriage to Mrs Mason:

> 'You know, I think that was one of the reasons I wanted to marry Ramona'.
>
> 'Mrs Mason?'
>
> 'Yes. Because she was always touching people and hugging them and telling them how she felt about them. It seemed to come so natural to her. It appealed to me'.
>
> 'It should come natural'.
>
> 'Would you believe it took me five years of marriage — *five years* — before I could tell my own wife that I loved her?' Mr Mason said.
>
> 'Yes', Thomas J. replied earnestly. 'I can believe it'.
>
> (p. 79)

In this way the author conveys a sense of open, frank discussion between adult and child. Certainly there is a suggestion of didacticism but it is presented in the healthy context of shared thought and discussion. Just as with the old man and the boy in *The House of Wings*, both these characters are enriched by the exchange.

In *The Pinballs* the reticent boy Harvey works on lists such as 'Books that I Have Enjoyed', and the list that causes him distress is entitled 'Promises My Mother Broke'. Like Ben in Philippa Pearce's *A Dog So Small* (1962), Harvey had been promised a dog for his birthday but had been disappointed. Both Pearce and Byars pinpoint an important theme in the contemporary family story: that it is important to honour promises made to children. Related to this theme is the attempt of characters such as Ben and Harvey to escape reality by turning to romance or dreams, and, by so doing, to compensate for what is lacking in their lives.

CONCLUSION

There have been significant changes in the family story from the time of the early classics. The role of the narrator has obviously shifted from that of the traditional omniscient narrator recounting and commenting on the characters' behaviour and relationships, and on their moral development as well, to that of a less obvious or at least less obtrusive narrator whose plane of narration moves towards that of a protagonist. The effect of this shift is that the reader feels as the character feels, and perceives as the character perceives. Of course, one can find examples in earlier works of a narrator's closing the distance between him or herself and a particular character, and conversely one finds contemporary works in which such a shift does not occur. However, in terms of degree, the movement to the central character's view in books written in the third person has been much more pronounced in the last twenty years.

Another important change is that concerning the role of the parent or person who cares. In many of the nineteenth and early twentieth century family stories one of the parents is missing for reasons such as death, war, internment, or even business. Yet in these stories this absence contributes to a sense of family solidarity as the children try to support the remaining parent, or as they eagerly await the coming reconciliation. *Seven Little Australians* is a notable exception, for here one senses the conflicting loyalties and frustrations faced by the young wife Esther trying to cope with a much older husband and a large family. But in terms of the stories which focus mainly on families where one parent is responsible for the children, there is a sense of solidarity and security. On the other hand, since the 1960s the absence of one or both parents signals a lack of solidarity and great personal conflict for the protagonists. And sometimes warmth and security are found in a context outside a child's own family.

In the contemporary family story there is a freer exchange of ideas between parents and children, and a more sustained interaction of both in plot development. In other words, adults, particularly parents, are no longer just in the background serving as dispensers of moral judgements. However, as with the observations concerning the role of the narrator, this is more a matter of degree than absolute contrast.

From a structural viewpoint there has developed in the last twenty years a more intense focusing on personal problems or social issues affecting at least one member of a family. Since the nature of the family group itself has changed in these stories, a particular one may present a group of foster children with sensitive, caring foster parents. Or a single parent family may be trying to come to terms with a recent divorce. Or worn-out parents may leave a child with his grandfather on an isolated and run-down property. Within such contexts writers explore concerns such as individuals seeking identity in the family; an artistic child trying to communicate with others who are too busy or even too different to understand; a child torn between his love for his mother and his father; or children overcoming sex role stereotyping.

In spite of the differences between the past and present forms of the family stories, it should be acknowledged that the family story has always portrayed personal relationships, individual aspirations and, above all, a recognition of the security and warmth that a child may find in the family unit, even though its nature has changed. The last concern is expressed succinctly by Drew in *The Left-Overs*:

> But you had to have *some* kind of family to come home to after the fun and games were over. Otherwise, there was nobody to talk to about what you'd been doing.
>
> (Spence 1976: 80)

REFERENCES

Hughes, F., 'Literary Criticism of Two Australian Novels' in *Children's Literature: The Whole Story*. Victoria: Deakin University, 1980.
Saxby, H., Maurice *A History of Australian Children's Literature (1841–1941)*. Sydney: Wentworth Books, 1969.
—————, *A History of Australian Children's Literature (1941–1970)*. Sydney: Wentworth Books, 1971.
Townsend, J.R., *Written for Children*. Harmondsworth: Penguin, 1980.

BOOKS REFERRED TO IN THE CHAPTER

Ahlberg, Allan, *Mrs Wobble the Waitress*. Viking/Kestrel Puffin.
Alcott, Louisa May, *Little Women*. Roberts Bros/Puffin.
Ardizzone, Edward, *Little Tim and the Brave Sea Captain*. OUP/Scholastic.
Berg, Leila, *Little Pete Stories*. Puffin.
Burnett, Frances Hodgson, *The Secret Garden*. Heinemann/Puffin.
Byars, Betsy, *The Pinballs*. Bodley Head/Puffin.
—————, *The House of Wings*. Bodley Head/Puffin.
Cleary, Beverly, *Ramona the Pest*. Hamish Hamilton/Puffin.
—————, *Ramona Forever*. Julia MacRae/Puffin.
—————, *Dear Mr Henshaw*. Julia MacRae/Puffin.
Coolidge, Susan, *What Katy Did*. Collins.
Garner, Alan, *The Stone Book Quartet*. Collins.
Garnett, Eve, *The Family from One End Street*. Frederick Muller/Puffin.

Hoban, Russell, *A Baby Sister for Frances*. Harper & Row/Scholastic.
———, *Bedtime for Frances*. Harper & Row/Scholastic.
Jansson, Tove, *Finn Family Moomintroll*. Ernest Benn/Puffin.
Nesbit, Edith, *The Story of the Treasure Seekers*. Wells Garder, Darton/Puffin.
Ormerod, Jan, *Sunshine*. Kestrel/Puffin.
———, *Moonlight*. Kestrel/Puffin.
Park, Ruth, *Callie's Castle*. Angus & Robertson.
———, *Playing Beatie Bow*. Nelson/Puffin.
Paterson, Katherine, *Bridge to Terabithia*. Gollancz/Puffin.
———, *The Great Gilly Hopkins*. Crowell/Puffin.
Pearce, Philippa, *A Dog So Small*. Longman.
———, *The Way to Sattin Shore*. Kestrel/Puffin.
Southall, Ivan, *Let the Balloon Go*. Methuen/Puffin.
Spence, Eleanor, *The October Child*. OUP.
———, *The Left-Overs*. Methuen/Ashton Scholastic.
Stuckey, Elizabeth, *Magnolia Buildings*. Bodley Head/Puffin.
Tomlinson, J., *The Owl Who Was Afraid of the Dark*. Methuen/Puffin.
Turner, Ethel, *Seven Little Australians*. Ward, Lock/Lansdowne.
Viorst, Judith, *The Tenth Good Thing About Barney*. Collins.

MORE FAMILY STORIES

NOVELS

Duder, Tessa, *Alex*, Penguin, 1987.
Gleitzman, Morris, *Two Weeks With the Queen*. Pan, 1990.
Hathorn, Libby, *Thunderwith*. Heinemann, 1989.
Little, Jean, *Mama's Going to Buy You a Mockingbird*. Puffin, 1985.
Lowry, Lois, *A Summer to Die*. Lions, 1990.
———, *Number the Stars*. Collins, 1989.

PICTURE BOOKS

Browne, Anthony, *Gorilla*. Julia McCrae, 1983.
———, *Piggybook*. Julia McCrae, 1986.
Fox, Mem and Smith, Craig, *Sophie*. Drakeford, 1989.
Hunt, Nan and Niland, Deborah, *Families Are Funny*. Collins/Anne Ingram, 1990.
McKee, David, *Snowman*. Beaver, 1987.
Murphy, Jill, *Five Minutes Peace*. Walker, 1986.
Waddell, Martin and Dale, Penny, *Once There Were Giants*. Walker, 1989.
Wells, Rosemary, *Hazel's Amazing Mother*. Collins, 1986.

12   1: THE RISE, FALL AND REMARKABLE REVIVAL OF THE SCHOOL STORY

KEN WATSON

> ... a new kind of English in which words like cads and rotters and expressions like bally bounders and beastly fellows played a large part.
>
> H.E. Bates

When Thomas Hughes published *Tom Brown's Schooldays* in 1857 he did not realise that he had created a new and powerful genre. Over the next ninety years hundreds of men, most of them writers of surpassing mediocrity, peppered the fictional map of England with boys' boarding schools, within whose ivy-covered walls Olympian headmasters strode, caddish Flashmans plotted, and upright members of the Lower Fourth were unjustly suspected of cheating or thievery. The female counterparts of these writers (or sometimes, indeed, the same men hiding behind suitably feminine pseudonyms) created schools where the corridors echoed with the clash of hockey sticks and cries of 'You're a brick, Felicity!'

There are, of course, only a limited number of variations that can be played out on the theme of cads, bullies and those unjustly accused of breaking the code of the school. As anyone who has attended or taught in such a school knows, the main characteristic of boarding school life is its monotony. The number of possible plots is very small if one wishes to preserve some semblance of reality. A few, more skilful writers, such as P.G. Wodehouse, took the path of parody: 'Are you', Psmith asks Mike, 'the bully, the Pride of the School, or the Boy who is Led Astray and takes to Drink in Chapter Sixteen?' (*Mike* 1909). Most authors, desperate to inject something exciting or unusual into the basic plot, resorted to secret passages discovered behind the oak panelling of the school hall, buried treasure, adventures with smugglers (suddenly Cornwall became the favoured setting for such schools) or plots against young potentates from overseas who had been sent to England to be educated. When all else failed, a complete change of scene was tried, as when the whole of the Fourth Form of St Jim's was transported in Lord Eastwood's yacht to the South Seas, there to be shipwrecked on an island inhabited by fearsome savages who fell on their knees in awe at the sight of Arthur Augustus D'Arcy, the swell of the Fourth, who, despite having had to struggle through the surf after the sinking of the yacht, was still wearing top hat, monocle and flowered waistcoat. By the time the Second World War came along, the genre had, apparently, been exhausted.

There were, of course, some peaks relieving the monotony of this literary landscape. Film and television adaptations of *Tom Brown's Schooldays* testify to its enduring qualities; Talbot Baines Reed's *The Fifth Form at St Dominic's* remains for many the quintessential school story; Kipling's *Stalky & Co.* still has its admirers (and detractors!), and H.A. Vachell's *The Hill* is often recalled with affection; even the absurdly moralistic *Eric, or, Little by Little* has its strengths. And it cannot be denied that several generations of boys and girls derived great pleasure from the stories of Greyfriars, St Jim's and Rookwood, most of them highly improbable, flowing from the pen of that most prolific of writers of school stories, Charles Hamilton (alias Frank Richards, alias Martin Clifford, alias Owen Conquest, alias Hilda Richards). Hamilton, as Frank Richards, created Billy Bunter, who, after Tom Brown, must be the best known of all fictional schoolboys. No less a person than George Orwell, while castigating the values of Greyfriars and St Jim's, praised the weekly paper, *The Magnet*, for its 'really first-rate character in the fat boy, Billy Bunter' (Orwell 1957: 177).

In *Tom Brown's Schooldays*, Thomas Hughes drew on his own experiences at Rugby shortly after Dr Thomas Arnold, father of Matthew Arnold, became its headmaster. Arnold is generally credited with having moulded the Victorian public school,[1] but it is probably truer to say that Thomas Hughes created it. Hughes wrote his book with two aims in mind: to prepare his son, and other young boys, for the experience of a public school, and to extol the virtues and teachings of Dr Arnold. He wrote it as a moral tale: 'My sole object in writing was to preach to boys: if I ever write again, it will be to preach to some other age' (Quigly 1982: 42). But Hughes' version of what Arnold stood for is generally conceded to have been an unwitting distortion, and it was this version, rather than Arnold's views, that won the day. Arnold himself would have been horrified by Hughes' 'muscular Christianity', his adulation of athletic prowess, his ignoring of the intellectual side of school life. As Hughes' biographers note:

> The middle class public, indifferent or hostile to Arnold's intense spirituality, his almost heretical religious and social views and his deep respect for learning, responded readily to the more mundane idea of a group of self-reliant, manly boys tamed into submission to Christian principles ... The better discipline and *esprit de corps* that Arnold helped to establish in order to effect liberal moral aims became fetters binding the average public-school boy to that worst of idols, 'good form': a reverence for things established.
>
> (Quigly 1982: 50)

It is easy to see why *Tom Brown's Schooldays* proved so influential. If the preaching seems excessive to the modern reader (as it did, indeed, to some of Hughes' contemporaries) this is more than counterbalanced by the infectious enthusiasm with which the author describes school life. In the context of the story, it is hard not to respond positively to Tom's simple ambitions:

> I want to be A1 at cricket and football, and all the other games, and to make my hands keep my head against any fellow, lout or gentleman. I want to get into the Sixth before I leave, and to please the Doctor, and I want to carry away just as much Latin and Greek as will take me through Oxford respectably ... I want to leave behind me the name of a fellow who never bullied a little boy or turned his back on a big one.

(Hughes 1857)

Eric, or, Little by Little by Frederic Farrar (1858) has been the butt of so many derogatory comments in other school stories from *Stalky & Co.* onwards that it comes as something of a surprise to discover how readable it is. The religiosity and moralising are, of course, excessive, and Farrar himself admitted that the book had 'too much lacrimosity'. The schoolboy characters are absurdly priggish — the saintly Edwin Russell is horrified when Eric describes a master as 'a surly devil' — and the author's exhortations to Eric to stop his downward slide are hard for the modern reader to take:

> The first time that Eric heard indecent words in dormitory No. 7, he was shocked beyond bound or measure ...
> Now Eric, now or never! Life and death, ruin and salvation, corruption and purity, are perhaps in the balance together, and the scale of your destiny may hang on a single word of yours. Speak out, boy! Tell these fellows that unseemly words wound your conscience; tell them that they are ruinous, sinful, damnable; speak out and save yourself and the rest. Virtue is strong and beautiful, Eric, and vice is downcast in her awful presence. Lose your purity of heart, Eric, and you have lost a jewel which the whole world ... cannot replace.

(Farrar 1858)

Nevertheless, the narrative moves along at a surprisingly brisk pace for a Victorian novel, generating a good deal of tension; it is clear that Farrar, who followed *Eric* with another school story, *St Winifred's, or, The World of School*, was a writer of some ability.

Most young readers of school stories in the late nineteenth and early twentieth centuries encountered them not in book form but as serials running in *The Boy's Own Paper* (founded in 1879), *The Girl's Own Paper* (1880) and *Chums* (1892), or in the bound volumes of these magazines issued every Christmas. *The Boy's Own Paper*, or *BOP* as it soon came to be called, was established by the Religious Tract Society as a means of combating the excessively violent 'penny dreadfuls' of the time. The *BOP* proved so successful that in the following year the Society launched a similar magazine for girls. In the next few years a number of imitations of these magazines were launched, of which the most enduring was *Chums*, published by Cassell. Amazingly, the *BOP* lasted until 1967; the *GOP* (under a different name, *The Heiress*) expired in 1956; *Chums* was killed off by the paper shortage early in the Second World War. The importance of these magazines and annuals, in an era when school and children's libraries were almost nonexistent, can hardly be overestimated. The Christmas annual was a gift eagerly anticipated for months and read and reread throughout the year; as time went on it often developed an identity separate from the magazines. The *Holiday Annual*, for example, contained fresh stories about the characters readers had already met in the pages of *The Magnet, The Gem* and *Boy's Friend*.

The Fifth Form at St Dominic's, which appeared in the *BOP* in 1881, set the pattern for the school stories of the next sixty years. The point of view remains that of an adult, but a much more indulgent one than in *Eric, or, Little by Little*: the moralising is relatively restrained. The cad, in this case appropriately called Loman, is never denounced in the ringing tones adopted by Farrar when writing of Brigson, the 'ulcer' in Eric's school ('Never did some of the Roslyn boys, to their dying day, forget the deep, intolerable, unfathomable flood of moral turpitude and iniquity which he bore with him ...'), and instead of suffering a retributive death, as happens to Eric and countless of his imitations, Loman is simply packed off to Australia, there to be made a man of. More significantly, the implied reader is established, not as one about to experience, or already experiencing, the life of an English public school, but as the outsider looking longingly in through the school gates and wishing he could join the privileged few. (Like many of his followers, Talbot Baines Reed did not himself attend a public school). This explains why, when the school story later became more and more unrealistic, it did not immediately lose popularity; for most of its readers, it was describing an alien world where anything could happen.

After Reed, the main change that occurred in the school story was the gradual shift in point of view from that of indulgent adult to that of schoolboy or schoolgirl. This change can be seen most clearly in the writings of Angela Brazil, who produced an enormous number of girls' school stories between 1904 and 1946, and the amazing Charles Hamilton. Before considering the work of these and of some Australian writers of school stories, however, we must look at the one attempt to subvert the genre — Rudyard Kipling's *Stalky & Co.*[2]

Stalky & Co. (1899) must have come as a shock to readers brought up on Reed's *St Dominic's, The Willoughby Captains* and *The Master of the Shell*. In the first few pages Stalky, M'Turk and Beetle, the heroes of the tale, are seen smoking, an occupation hitherto reserved for cads and those slipping down the road to ruin. Shortly after, Stalky admits to having once got drunk ('... that was in the holidays, and it made me horrid sick'). Masters are misled by subtle distortions of the truth, house spirit is derided, and organised games are condemned.

John Rowe Townsend writes that 'After the knowingness of Stalky it was difficult ever again to assert the innocent values of the classical school story' (Townsend 1975: 118). If so, a large number of writers remained unaware of it. Angela Brazil, while proclaiming the importance of the honour of the school and the value of house spirit, even borrowed some of the slang of *Stalky & Co*: 'Twiggezvous?' asks Beetle, and gets the reply 'Nous twiggons'. Fifteen years later the same phrases occur in Brazil school stories. If *Stalky & Co.* did indeed have far-reaching effects, as Townsend asserts, it was less in undermining the genre than in freeing succeeding writers from their inhibitions regarding the use of slang in their stories.

While Australian boys and girls read school stories as avidly as their English counterparts, relatively few Australian writers explored the genre. One of the first, and perhaps the best, of these stories was Louise Mack's *Teens* (1897). Unlike its English counterparts, *Teens* is set in a girls' day school (Sydney Girls' High); in it can be detected the influence of the American Susan Coolidge's *What Katy Did at School* (1873). It is an episodic book that is both lively and realistic. Louise Mack was an exact contemporary of Ethel Turner at Sydney Girls' High, and one incident where the heroine, Lennie, and her rival both start school magazines, is apparently based on a similar rivalry between the two future novelists.

Between 1916 and 1921 Lillian Pyke wrote four novels set in a Melbourne boarding school, St Virgil's (clearly based on Wesley College): *Max the Sport, Jack of St Virgil's, A Prince at School* and *The Best School of All*. They are pallid versions of the English public school story, and her novels set in girls' schools, such as *Sheila the Prefect* (1923), are even less inspiring. As Brenda Niall has noted, 'It is almost enough to say of Lillian Pyke that her girls' schools were created for the sisters of her St Virgil's boys' (Niall 1984: 176). Another writer of the period, Constance Mackness, produced similarly undistinguished novels. Rather livelier are two stories, *Blue Brander* (1927) and *The Gang on Wheels* (1930), by Ethel Turner's nephew, D. Lindsay Thompson, again based on a real school, Sydney Grammar. But, with the exception of *Teens*, no Australian school story of real merit appeared until 1977, when Eleanor Spence's *A Candle for St Antony* was published.

In an age when adolescent readers discern homosexual overtones in something as innocent as Jim and Huck's voyage on the raft in *Huckleberry Finn*, it is startling to look back and find how often passionate friendships between boy and boy, and girl and girl, appear in Victorian and Edwardian times, and even as late as the 1930s. It is quite clear, however, that the vast majority of readers, and even the authors themselves, were unaware of the implications of some of the incidents they described. This becomes easier to understand if one remembers that even as late as the 1950s many well-educated women had never heard of lesbianism, and that a writer like Ernest Raymond, whose enormously popular *Tell*

England, part school story, part war story, was published in 1922, could, when rereading it fifty years later, be astounded at 'the indubitable but wholly unconscious homosexuality in it':

> The earlier part [i.e. that dealing with school] was written when I was eighteen or nineteen, and in those days 'homosexuality' was a word which — absurd as it may seem now — I had never heard ...
>
> (Avery 1975: 185)

The most famous story of such a love is Horace Annesley Vachell's *The Hill*, published in 1905 and set at Harrow some years earlier. It deals with John Verney's affection for Harry Desmond, and his rivalry with the caddish Reginald Scaife, known as the Demon, who is also drawn to Harry. To the modern reader, the book not only has homosexual overtones but is also insufferably snobbish; it was, however, possible, as late as the 1940s, to read it without being conscious of either aspect — to read it, in other words, as an uplifting story of an ideal friendship.

Similar themes can be found in dozens of stories for girls. The novels of Angela Brazil, such as *The Fortunes of Philippa* (1906), *Bosom Friends* (1909), *A Fourth Form Friendship* (1911) and *A Patriotic Schoolgirl* (1918), are full of such attachments. Brazil's biographer, Gillian Freeman, writes:

> Throughout her written accounts of friendships, whether her own or fictional, Angela used terms which generally relate to the romantic love of adults. Take Irene, 'love-lorn' for Peachy in *The School in the South*, for instance. 'She's just sweet to me, but I don't count first', she told herself. 'Well, it's no use being jealous. If you can't have the moon you must be content with a star'. The star was Lorna, and Lorna 'adored' Irene. Then there was Dona Anderson's 'immensely hot' friendship with Ailsa in *A Patriotic Schoolgirl*; 'they spent every available moment of the day together'. In *The Fortunes of Philippa* the heroine announced, 'I've simply fallen in love with Catherine Winstanley', and as for Aldred and Mabel [in *A Fourth Form Friendship*], whose friendship was complicated from the outset, their final scene after the traumatic drama of the fire reads like the closing pages of a novelette.
>   'I'd have given my life for you gladly!' gulped Aldred.
>   'I know, and I feel almost unworthy of such love'.
>   'Will you kiss me, to show you can forget what's past?'
>   Mabel bent her head. It was a kiss of complete reconciliation and forgiveness, and Aldred, with a glad leap of her heart, felt that the friendship she had striven to build upon the shifting sand of a false reputation was founded at last upon the rock of self-sacrifice and human endeavour.
>
> (Freeman 1976: 48)

The friendships in the stories of Charles Hamilton, whose enormous output over seventy years won him a place in the *Guinness Book of Records*, are much less intense. Like Kipling, Hamilton held in contempt the 'fervours and fevers' (Blishen 1981: 105) of *Eric, or, Little by Little* and similar books, and his boys are simply good chums, always willing to help one another out of scrapes but scorning more ardent expressions of attachment. Religion is also taboo. Noel Coward, who, like most of his generation, read *The Magnet* and *The Gem*, commented in his autobiography:

> They were awfully manly decent fellows, Harry Wharton and Co., and no suggestion of sex, even in its lighter forms, ever sullied their conversation. Considering their ages, their healthy-mindedness was almost frightening.
>
> (Coward 1937: 16)

As Frank Richards, Hamilton produced stories of Greyfriars School for *The Magnet*; as Martin Clifford he wrote of Tom Merry & Co. of St Jim's for *Pluck* and *The Gem*; as Owen Conquest he created Rookwood School for *Boys' Friend*. In addition to writing for these weekly papers, he wrote novelettes about the schools each month for the *Schoolboys' Own Library*. When the Second World War brought to an end the weeklies and monthlies, Hamilton began writing full-length novels, and between 1946 and 1961 produced some fifty or so, such as *Billy Bunter of Greyfriars School* (1947), *Tom Merry & Co. of St Jim's* (1949), *Billy Bunter Among the Cannibals* (1950) and *Billy Bunter's Treasure Hunt* (1961). He even contributed some school stories to an Australian boys' paper, *The Silver Jacket*, in the 1950s. (His other link with Australia lay in his writing of a Latin version of 'Waltzing Matilda'!) His total output, some 72 million words, was equivalent to about 2,000 full-length novels.

For Hamilton to have had such a devoted following over so long a period, he must have had qualities over and above his enormous capacity for work. Yet if one returns to the stories and begins reading, it is at first difficult to see where the appeal lay:

> 'Who's paying my fare?'
> Billy Bunter asked the question.
> He paused, like Brutus of old, for a reply.
> Like Brutus, he paused in vain.
> 'Don't all speak at once!' went on Bunter.
> Harry Wharton & Co. did not all speak at once. They did not speak at all.
> Billy Bunter blinked at them through his spectacles. He seemed perplexed.
> 'Deaf?' he asked.
> No answer.
> 'Dumb?' snorted Bunter.
> The five juniors in No. 1 Study, in the Greyfriars Remove, really seemed to be either deaf or dumb. If they heard Bunter, they heeded not.
> 'I say, you fellows! I asked you a question!' hooted Bunter. 'You're going over to St Jim's this afternoon for the football match. I'm coming'.

Silence.

'I'm coming along with you', explained Bunter.

'I knew you fellows would like me to come, so I've fixed it. See?'

A burst of enthusiam on the part of the Famous Five would have been appropriate at this point. The prospective pleasure of Bunter's company on a long train journey was sufficient to evoke enthusiasm — from Bunter's point of view, at least.

Still Harry Wharton & Co. did not play up. Enthusiasm would have been appropriate, but — As Fisher T. Fish, of the Remove, would have expressed it in the American language — they did not enthuse worth a cent! There was not a general brightening of faces, as Bunter seemed to expect. On the other hand, a sort of glumness became visible on five youthful countenances.

('What Happened to Bunter!' in *Holiday Annual*, 1927)

Push a little further into these tales of St Jim's and Greyfriars, however, and the reasons for their amazing popularity become clearer. The range of characters is such as to allow each reader the chance of imagining himself one of the select band. There is even at Greyfriars a boy from New South Wales — Sampson Quincy Iffley Field, known as 'Squiff'. These characters are not, however, described in much detail; the reader, in effect, is invited to build up each for himself, to become, as it were, co-creator of the stories. Then there are the eccentrics, whose one or two characteristics are magnified and played on throughout the stories: Billy Bunter, 'the Fat Owl of Greyfriars', whose 'I say, you fellows' heralds a request for food or for a loan against the postal order he is always expecting; Arthur Augustus D'Arcy, 'the Swell of St Jim's', with his lisp, his monocle, and his obsession with fashion; Hurree Jamset Ram Singh, the Nawob of Bhanipur, whose ambition it is to 'induce my esteemed and ludicrous chums ceasefully to stop talking slangfully and to use speakfully only the pureful and honoured English language as taught by my learned and preposterous native tutors in Bhanipur'. There is the highly individual style: exclamatory, slangy, often allusive in an oddly erudite way, and hypnotically repetitive. Finally, there are the plots which, if too often wildly improbable, are usually inventive and often very amusing in a fairly obvious way.

Of course, the stories have not been without their critics. George Orwell, in his famous essay, 'Boys' Weeklies', complained that they were 'sodden in the worst illusions of 1910' (Orwell 1957: 203); more recently, Arthur Marshall has condemned them as 'ludicrously false and feeble':

To their gullible juvenile readers they gave a markedly unreal picture of public schools and did a hearty disservice both to fact and to fiction. The wearisome repetitions, the implausibility, the tastelessness . . .

(Quigly 1982: 258)

Undoubtedly Hamilton's stories played their part in bringing about the demise of the public school story by raising it to such heights of unreality that serious writers felt unable to venture into its territory. But another, even stronger factor in the decline of stories set in public schools was the changing nature of society itself. The values inherent in the school story from *Tom Brown's Schooldays* onwards were no longer unquestioningly accepted. As Isabel Quigly has written:

> In the genre of school story, what counted was certainty and self-confidence, insularity, cheerfulness, and acceptance of the accepted; and in a world grown so much more self-conscious and uncertain, so much more international, gloomy and self-questioning, with schools that were changing almost out of recognition, it was impossible to keep it going.
>
> (Quigly 1982: 276)

Thus for a generation or more few school stories were written. Only writers impervious to fashion, like William Mayne in *A Swarm in May* (1955), dared to enter the field. Yet school is so central a part of the experience of the young that it cannot be ignored; moreover, it is a topic of intense interest to such a reader. After it had been left alone for a number of years a few writers began, rather tentatively, to explore the genre anew. It was evident, however, that a clean break had to be made with the public school: henceforth school stories, if they were to be successful, should not invite comparison either with the Rugby of Tom Brown or the Greyfriars of Billy Bunter. The theme of the individual adjusting to the world of school could still, of course, be explored, but in the context of the experience of the overwhelming majority of child readers. Hence the comprehensive day school has displaced the boarding school as the setting for most school stories, and a new realism, a new sophistication, are the hallmark of recent novels set in schools. The writers of such tales have realised, too, that stories of day schools allow a much greater interplay between the worlds of school and home, and have been quick to capitalise on the new freedom accorded to them to tackle themes once regarded as taboo. Of course, the move from boarding school to a home and school setting makes the genre less clearcut, and a problem of classification sometimes arises. Can Aidan Chambers' *Breaktime* (1978), for example, be regarded as a school story when so much of the action takes place outside school?

This revival of the school story began, a little shakily, with novels like Reginald Maddock's *The Dragon in the Garden* (1968), with its rather predictable plot, and K.M. Peyton's *Pennington's Seventeenth Summer* (1970), with its vividly-portrayed though rather unlikely semi-delinquent hero. It gradually gained strength in Britain with Bernard Ashley's *Terry on the Fence* (1974) and *The Trouble with Donovan Croft* (1974); Jan Mark's *Thunder and Lightnings* (1976) and *Under the Autumn Garden* (1977); Gene Kemp's *The Turbulent Term of*

Tyke Tiler (1977); Jan Needle's *My Mate Shofiq* (1978) and Aidan Chambers' *The Present Takers* (1983). In Robert Leeson's novels and on television, the *Grange Hill* series celebrated life in a large comprehensive school.

In the United States, where, with the early exception of *What Katy Did at School*, the school story had never had much of a following, there was a similar sudden flowering, with such books as Betsy Byars' *The Eighteenth Emergency* (1973) and *The Cybil War* (1981); Rosa Guy's *The Friends* (1973); Robert Cormier's *The Chocolate War* (1975); Nat Hentoff's *This School Is Driving Me Crazy* (1976). In Australia, Eleanor Spence wrote *A Candle for St Antony* (1977), and Simon French, having written *Hey, Phantom Singlet* (1975) at the age of fourteen, produced an outstanding school story in *Cannily, Cannily* (1981); while Lowell Tarling entertained in *Taylor's Troubles* (1982); and Robin Klein wrote *Hating Alison Ashley* (1984).

While an over-reliance on slapstick and stereotype is still occasionally to be found, this new wave of school stories is distinguished by a subtlety far beyond the capabilities of an Angela Brazil or a Talbot Baines Reed. Stories of bullying, for example, are much more concerned with the psychology of the bully than was ever the case before. In *Terry on the Fence*, Bernard Ashley helps the reader to understand and even to pity the violent Les Hicks. Betsy Byars, in the superbly witty *The Eighteenth Emergency*, lets her hero, Mouse, be beaten by the bully, Marv Hammerman; in the process he comes to realise that physical violence is the only means by which Hammerman, a much older boy 'kept back' in a lower grade, can retain some self-esteem. By his skilful use of vignettes from Melanie Prosser's home life, Aidan Chambers, in *The Present Takers*, illuminates her actions at school. (Melanie Prosser is such a vivid creation that she may well become for the twentieth century school story what Flashman is for the nineteenth).

Another area which the new school story explores with much greater sensitivity is the clash of cultures and races. The old public school story tended to use the foreigner simply for humorous purposes — witness Hurree Jamset Ram Singh and Wun Lung, the Chinese junior, in the Greyfriars stories. But in Jan Needle's *My Mate Shofiq*, for example, 'the nettle of race relationships [is] firmly and unsentimentally grasped' (Moss 1979: 69) when Bernard is rejected by his gang after siding with the Pakistani Shofiq and his sisters against the school bully. Simplistic notions of racial prejudice are overturned in Rosa Guy's *The Friends*, which deals with the persecution of a West Indian child by Negro children in a New York school, and in Petronella Breinburg's *Us Boys of Westcroft* (1975), which portrays the antagonism of a London-born black boy to the appearance of a black woman teacher in a school with a hitherto all-white staff. Eleanor Spence's *A Candle for St Antony* not only deals with the way in which the superficial knowingness of the modern adolescent can misinterpret and destroy a friendship, but also with the difficulties confronting the European migrant in adapting to an Australian school.

The most controversial of all modern school stories is Robert Cormier's *The Chocolate War*, in which a corrupt school gradually becomes a microcosm of society as a whole. Jerry Renault, the lone dissenter, stands out against the manipulation of the boys of Trinity High by Brother Leon, the school's deputy principal, and Archie Costello, leader of the school's secret society, the Vigils. Almost all school stories, whether of the nineteenth or twentieth centuries, would show the hero triumphant at the end, but Cormier, in the final scene, has Jerry being rushed to hospital, too battered to be able to tell his friend Goober that dissent is futile, that one must conform.

> The American Adam is brought low; Huck Finn turns Jim over to the slave-catchers; Gary Cooper lies in his own blood in the street at high noon — no wonder the critics gasped. In one brief, bitter paragraph, Cormier has abandoned an enduring American myth to confront his teenaged readers with life as it more often is — with the dangers of dissent, the ferocity of systems as they protect themselves, the power of the pressure to conform.
>
> (MacLeod 1981: 76)

With the possible exception of *A Candle for St Antony*, the best of recent Australian school stories is Simon French's *Cannily, Cannily*. It tells of the struggles of Trevor Huon, only son of parents whose idea of happiness is to be always on the move, as he tries to settle into a new school in a rigidly conservative country town whose values contrast sharply with those of his parents. Not only Trevor and his schoolfellows, but also the adults who enter the story are convincingly portrayed, and if the resolution of Trevor's difficulties comes a little too easily, then it must be remembered that French, who wrote the novel when he was nineteen or twenty, is still a very young writer indeed.

Young readers today can, if they wish, explore the tastes of past generations through reprints of *Tom Brown's Schooldays*, *Stalky & Co.*, and P.G. Wodehouse's *Tales of St Austin's* (originally published in 1903). But they also have a rapidly expanding range of modern school stories to draw on. They and their parents will delight in Jan Mark's two hilariously funny stories of a comprehensive school, paired in the volume *Hairs in the Palm of Your Hand* (1981): (What's the second sign of madness? Hairs in the palm of your hand. What's the first sign? Looking for them!). They will follow the adventures of Tyke Tiler in Gene Kemp's *The Turbulent Term of Tyke Tiler* with enthusiam, and, if they are males, will probably find the ending infuriating. They will share the indignation of the teenagers engaged on a school project on factory life when they discover the appalling working conditions at Ratcliffe's Clothing Factory in Gillian Cross's *Revolt at Ratcliffe's Rags* (1980). They will be both challenged and entertained by Bernard Ashley's *All My Men* (1977), Gene Kemp's *Gowie Corby Plays Chicken* (1979), Jane Gardam's *Bilgewater* (1976), Jean MacGibbon's *Hal* (1974) and John Branfield's *Brown Cow* (1983). The rich vein of school life, though it has been mined by writers for nearly one hundred and thirty years, is by no means exhausted.

NOTES

1. The term 'public school' originally applied to certain long-established, richly-endowed boarding schools like Eton, Harrow, Winchester, Rugby, Charterhouse and Shrewsbury, and to two equally ancient day schools, Merchant Taylors' and St Paul's. The word 'public' seems to have been used to distinguish them both from fee-paying schools which drew their pupils only from the local area and from schools privately owned and run for profit. As time went on, the term was loosely applied to most fee-paying boarding schools not run for private profit.
2. Another book published a few years earlier had also portrayed school life warts and all — F. Anstey's *Vice Versa* (1882). Since, however, it was cast in the form of a fantasy (the magical Garuda Stone causes father and son to inhabit each other's bodies) it did not have the impact of *Stalky & Co.*

REFERENCES

Avery, Gillian, *Childhood's Pattern*. London: Hodder & Stoughton, 1975.
Blishen, Edward, 'The Fifth Form at St Dominic's: a Re-reading', in *Children's Literature in Education* Vol. 12, No. 2, 1981.
Coward, Noel, *Present Indicative*. London: Heinemann, 1934.
Freeman, Gillian, *The Schoolgirl Ethic*. London: Allen Lane, 1976.
MacLeod, Anne Scott, 'Robert Cormier and The Adolescent Novel' in *Children's Literature in Education* Vol. 12, No. 2, 1981.
Moss Elaine, *Children's Books of the Year: 1978*. London: Hamish Hamilton, 1984.
Orwell, George, 'Boy's Weeklies' in *Inside the Whale*. London: Penguin, 1957.
Quigly, Isabel, *The Heirs of Tom Brown*. London: Chatto & Windus, 1982.
Townsend, John Rowe, *Written For Children*. New York: Lippincott, 1975.

BOOKS REFERRED TO IN THE CHAPTER

Ashley, Bernard, *Terry on the Fence*. Puffin.
——————, *The Trouble With Donovan Croft*. Puffin.
Branfield, John, *Brown Cow*. Gollancz.
Brazil, Angela, *Bosom Friends*. Nelson.
——————, *The Fortunes of Philippa*. Blackie.
——————, *The Fourth Form Friendship*. Blackie.
——————, *A Patriotic Schoolgirl*. Blackie.
Breinburg, Petronella, *Us Boys of Westcroft*. Macmillan/Topliner.
Byars, Betsy, *The Cybil War*. Puffin.
——————, *The Eighteenth Emergency*. Puffin.

Chambers, Aidan, *The Present Takers*. Bodley Head.
Coolidge, Susan, *What Katy Did at School*. Puffin.
Cormier, Robert, *The Chocolate War*. Gollancz/Lions.
Cross, Gillian, *Revolt at Ratcliffe's Rags*. Oxford.
Farrar, Frederic, *Eric, or, Little By Little*. A. & C. Black.
——————, *St Winifred's, or, The World of School*. A. & C. Black.
French, Simon, *Cannily, Cannily*. Puffin.
——————, *Hey Phantom Singlet!* Angus & Robertson.
Gardam, Jane, *Bilgewater*. Hamish Hamilton.
Guy, Rosa, *The Friends*. Puffin.
Hentoff, Nat, *This School's Driving Me Crazy*. Piccolo.
Hughes, Thomas, *Tom Brown's Schooldays*. Puffin.
Kipling, Rudyard, *Stalky & Co*. Macmillan.
Kemp, Gene, *Gowie Corby Plays Chicken*. Puffin.
——————, *The Turbulent Term of Tyke Tiler*. Puffin.
Klein, Robin, *Hating Alison Ashley*. Puffin.
Leeson, Robert, *Grange Hill Home and Away*. Lions.
MacGibbon, Jean, *Hal*. Heinemann/Puffin.
Mack, Louise, *Teens*. Angus & Robertson.
Maddocks, Reginald, *The Dragon in the Garden*. Macmillan/Topliner.
Mark, Jan, *Hairs in the Palm of Your Hand*. Puffin.
——————, *Thunder and Lightnings*. Kestrel/Puffin.
——————, *Under the Autumn Garden*. Kestrel/Puffin.
Mayne, William, *A Swarm in May*. Oxford.
Needle, Jan, *My Mate Shofiq*. Collins.
Peyton, K.M., *Pennington's Seventeenth Summer*. Magnet.
Pyke, Lillian, *The Best School of All*. Ward Lock
——————, *Jack of St Virgil's*. Ward Lock.
——————, *Max the Sport*. Ward Lock.
——————, *A Prince at School*. Ward Lock.
——————, *Sheila the Prefect*. Ward Lock.
Raymond, Ernest, *Tell England*. Cassell.
Reed, Talbot Baines, *The Fifth Form at St Dominic's*. Latimer House/Religious Tract Society.
——————, *The Master of the Shell*. BOP.
——————, *The Willoughby Captains*. Latimer House.
Richards, Frank, *Billy Bunter Among the Cannibals*. Charles Skilton.
——————, *Billy Bunter of Greyfriar's School*. Charles Skilton.
——————, *Billy Bunter's Treasure Hunt*. Charles Skilton.
——————, *Tom Merry & Co. of St Jim's*. Mandeville Publications.
Spence, Eleanor, *A Candle for St Antony*. Oxford.
Tarling, Lowell, *Taylor's Troubles*. Puffin.
Thompson, D. Lindsay, *Blue Brander*. Ward Lock.
——————, *The Gang on Wheels*. Ward Lock.
Twain, Mark, *The Adventures of Huckleberry Finn*. Puffin.
Vachell, H.A., *The Hill*. John Murray.
Wodehouse, P.G., *Mike*. Out of print.
——————, *Tales of St Austin's*. Penguin.

2: WILL FIVE RUN AWAY WITH BIGGLES? — A SERIES QUESTION

What do Nancy Drew, the Secret Seven, Dimsie, Biggles, the Famous Five, Jennings, William, the Bobbsey Twins and the Hardy Boys have in common? The answer, as we all know, is that they are heroes of series fiction. Few of us passed through childhood and early adolescence without a period of addiction to one or more of them. My own allegiance was to Biggles, and in this brief discussion of series fiction I shall take him as one of my two examples. The other, of course, has to be one of Enid Blyton's creations, for she is still the world's best-selling children's author and, after Shakespeare, Lenin and possibly Agatha Christie, the writer whose work has been most often translated into other languages.

The general line about Enid Blyton — I took it myself until recently — is that her plots are hackneyed, her characters stereotyped, her language impoverished, her attitudes outdated, and that her popularity is to be deplored in an age when so many excellent children's books are available. For me, this conventional view was challenged when an undergraduate majoring in English said to me: 'If it weren't for Enid Blyton I wouldn't be here!' What she meant was that it was Enid Blyton who transformed her attitude to reading, who first who made her aware of the enormous pleasure to be had from reading fiction. I have since discovered that her experience was by no means unique: several other university students have told me that the world of books was opened to them by Blyton or W.E. Johns or Anthony Buckeridge. It may be, of course, that they are giving these writers the credit for something that was really done for them much earlier when they encountered A.A. Milne or Michael Bond or Dr Seuss; nevertheless, such testimony to the importance of series writers is not to be ignored.

With the possible exception of the Noddy stories, the Famous Five was Enid Blyton's most successful series. Between 1942 and 1963 she produced twenty-one Famous Five books, and by the time the last one, *Five Are Together Again*, made its appearance, the series had sold six million copies. It seems appropriate therefore, to take this series as my example.

The name Famous Five had already been used by Charles Hamilton in his Greyfriars stories to refer to Harry Wharton & Co. — the five were Harry himself, Bob Cherry, Frank Nugent, Johnny Bull and Hurree Jamset Ram Singh — and it seems likely that Enid Blyton borrowed the name from him.[1] In her series, the five are four cousins, Julian, Dick, Anne and George (Georgina) and George's dog, Timmy. Bob Dixon (1974) says of them that they are

> scarcely distinguished as separate beings, certainly as far as their social views are concerned. Timmy is usually recognisable as a dog but he is just as narrow and prejudiced as the others. Amongst the

other four, the only distinguishing feature is one of culturally conditioned male and female roles but here, as we shall see, there is a certain amount of confusion in the case of George. The boys, Dick and Julian, are scarcely nonentities — it is a single nonentity split into two. They have a prep school background and are jolly plucky. They know right from wrong and their literary destiny is, clearly, to figure in the stories of *Woman's Own*. Anne is quite insignificant but George is, perhaps ... Enid Blyton's most fortunate invention. She is a very bad case of that castration complex, or penis-envy, first described by Freud, and her success with readers rests almost entirely upon the fact that, in our society, and for what seem very obvious reasons, small girls wish they were boys.

(Dixon 1974: 52–3)

Even if one rejects the Freudian interpretation and feels that Julian can be distinguished from Dick by his rudeness if nothing else, the rest of what Dixon says is true enough. But, as I have argued in this first part of this chapter — and I am, of course, not the first to make the point — an important factor in the appeal of such stories for children lies in the very fact that the characters are not rounded, that they have only one or two distinguishing characteristics. This leaves the reader free to impose whatever characteristics he or she likes — to mould them, if so desired, into the reader's own image.

The plots of the Famous Five novels are full of the clichés of a thousand adventure stories. If a piece of parchment is found, it turns out to have a map on it showing the whereabouts of buried treasure. If there is a castle, it will have a dungeon where someone is imprisoned. If there is a panelled hall, there will be a secret passage behind it. If a wall has to be climbed, it will be conveniently covered with vines. No wonder Enid Blyton in her autobiography confessed that in writing her stories 'I do not have to stop and think for a moment'! Her plots are the stuff of every child's daydreams and this is one means by which she ensures their appeal.

What particularly distresses the adult reader of Blyton's books is their snobbery. The lower classes are usually portrayed as not very bright, often dirty and sometimes sinister. They are approved of only when they show a proper deference: police constables and fishermen get good marks when they say 'Master Julian, sir' or 'Miss Anne' (or 'Master George'!). Any policeman below the rank of chief inspector is considered a social inferior whose stupidity is emphasised by his being given a name like 'Goon' or 'Plod'. Being rude to one's social inferiors is permissible. Here is Julian, in *Five Run Away Together*, talking to the Sticks (admittedly the villains of the story, though Julian does not yet know this):

'Now, now, look 'ere!' began Mr Stick, from his corner.
'I don't want to look at you', said Julian at once.
'Now, look *'ere'*, said Mr Stick angrily, standing up.

'I've told you I don't want to', said Julian. 'You're not a pleasant sight'.
And again:
'Now, look 'ere!' began Mr Stick, angrily, furious at seeing his lovely supper walking away.
'You surely don't want me to look at you *again*', said Julian, in a tone of amazement. 'What for? Have you shaved yet — or washed? I'm afraid not. So, if you don't mind I think I'd rather *not* look at you'.

But do child readers necessarily view such scenes as these as invitations to look down on those of 'lower' social status? We have had enough evidence in the last few years of the variety of ways in which adults can interpret a particular book — C.S. Lewis' *The Lion, the Witch and the Wardrobe* being denounced as anti-Christian, for example, and Harper Lee's *To Kill a Mockingbird* condemned as immoral and racist — to be wary of making judgements about the values that children take from their reading. Charles Sarland (1983) has asserted that the children who read Enid Blyton see her characters as classless. Certainly when I read sections of *Five Run Away Together* to a group of trainee teachers a few years ago, those who remember enjoying the book as children were amazed that they could have been so unaware of the writer's snobbery. They did remember, however, being delighted at Julian's victory over the Sticks, who were clearly going to be the villains anyway because of the way they were described: Mrs Stick 'a sour-faced woman', her son Edgar 'a stupid, yet sly-looking youth' with a spotty face and 'over-long nose'. Enid Blyton may give her young readers plenty of room to build up their own pictures of the Famous Five, but she leaves them in no doubt about how to view those she has cast as the Five's adversaries. Even Tinker, the Sticks' dog and therefore Timmy's opponent, is described in unflattering terms (and also desexed):

> Suddenly a mangy-looking dog appeared out of the kitchen door. It had a dirty white coat, out of which patches seemed to have been bitten, and its tail was well between its legs.

It is also true enough that the Famous Five books place few linguistic demands on their readers, but, as Sarland has pointed out, 'virtually every technique that is available to adult authors may be found in embryo' in her books (Sarland 1983: 170). It is likely that the very ease with which they can be read instils in young readers a confidence in their own abilities and gives them courage to tackle more demanding works.

After Enid Blyton, W.E. Johns must rank as the twentieth century's most successful writer for children. As well as the Biggles books, he wrote a much shorter series about a commando called Gimlet and another about a WAAF called Worrals. All three were brought together in *Comrades in Arms* (1947) but, sadly, romance did not blossom between the RAF and the WAAF. As A.E. Day has remarked, it would have been intriguing if Colonel Raymond had given the bride away in the last chapter

> with Gimlet acting first as best man and then as godfather when, after a decorous interval, a little Biggle or Worral came taxi-ing out of the hangar.
>
> (Day 1974: 22)

The Biggles books probably have more in common with the Greyfriars and St Jim's stories already dealt with than with the Famous Five. Like Charles Hamilton, W.E. Johns provides his readers with a large range of characters, presumably in the belief that each reader will find someone to identify with. As well as Biggles's offsiders Algy and Ginger, there are the monocled Lord Bertie Lissie (Lord Arthur Augustus D'Arcy grown up?), Angus Mackail, the brawny Scot, Taffy Hughes, a Welshman, Tex O'Hara, an American, and many more. Even the style occasionally recalls the Greyfriars stories: at Greyfriars, the boys rarely *say* anything; instead they 'stutter', 'snort', 'breathe', 'groan', 'hoot' or 'ejaculate'. Similarly, Biggles and his friends 'gasp', 'breathe', 'groan' and 'snap'. Occasionally Johns, sensing the need for variety, brings adverbs into play: Biggles 'smiles faintly', 'nods slowly', 'mutters hoarsely', 'grates harshly'.

According to Geoffrey Trease (1978), Biggles is the hero of about sixty books; according to my count there are over ninety titles, beginning with *The Camels are Coming* (1932) and ending with the posthumous *Biggles Sees Too Much* (1970). *Biggles in Australia* (1955) was the fifty-third to appear and by that time Johns's enthusiasm was flagging. The characterisation is perfunctory in the extreme: it is almost impossible to distinguish Algy, Ginger and Bertie from one another, and when the pilot of the plane of Biggles's archenemy von Stalhein is described as 'a young, good-looking fellow', we know that he is going to prove the 'right' type.

Johns did his homework on the Australian scene — though he slipped up on the spelling of QANTAS (QUANTAS throughout), and one doubts whether sombreros were really as much in evidence in the streets of Darwin in the 1950s — but the writing is tired and cliché-ridden. Oddly, the clichés are underlined for fear the reader might miss them:

> In an instant the air was full of flying spears, thrown by blacks who had appeared from nowhere, as the saying is . . .

The highly improbable plot has von Stalhein masterminding a Mau Mau-style uprising in 'Arnhemland'. Biggles, an instant authority on Aborigines, lectures Bill, the Australian policeman, on the subject after they find the body of a murdered prospector:

> Bill tipped his hat on the back of his head. 'I still can't believe it. This sort of thing was common enough years ago but it doesn't often happen now — not in these parts anyway. Poor old Joe. And to think

how many times he's shared his water and tucker with the devils'.
  Biggles shook his head. 'That cuts no ice with blacks when the savage inside 'em bursts through the thin skin of the apparent friendliness they pick up from contact with whites. More than one doctor has been murdered by the man he's just cured ...'

A couple of pages later, he observes:
  'If I know anything about natives, that bunch is all keyed up to jump. They themselves, with their animal brains, don't know yet which way they'll go. They may run. If they don't, anything can happen'.

Biggles in Australia is typical of the later books in the series and enough has been said about it for anyone unfamiliar with Johns to guess the sorts of complaints made about them. The style is pedestrian, the plots are improbable, the attitudes racist. Anyone who has delved into the series will know that Johns has an obsession with mixed race — sinister half-breeds abound — and sure enough, two 'mixed breeds of questionable ancestry' pop up in *Biggles in Australia*. While I have suggested in discussing Enid Blyton's snobbishness that the values evident to the adult reader may not be those which young ones take from her books, the racist attitudes in some of the Biggles books are so marked that few young readers could fail to be aware of them. I recall that as an eleven-year-old I was made uncomfortable by the constant equating of half-breeds with villainy, but since my value-system had been built up from many other influences besides my reading, I no more thought of carrying such attitudes over into my life than of linking the sinister Chinamen that abounded in my other reading (in the novels of P.C. Westerman, for instance) with the two Chinese boys in my class.

  If one turns to the earlier Biggles books, a somewhat different picture emerges. *The Camels Are Coming* and other stories of the First World War, reprinted in the 1950s under different titles, such as *Biggles, Pioneer Air Fighter*, are written with more verve and give an accurate picture of what it must have been like to be a pilot in that conflict. Johns was, of course, able to draw on his own experience as a member of the Royal Flying Corps in these stories. And books like *Biggles Flies South* (1938), which begins with an impressively vivid account of the loss of Cambyses' army in the Egyptian desert in 525 BC, show that his prose was not always flat and his plots were not always hackneyed. Further, the racial slurs are not quite as evident in the earlier books.

  It was in one of these early stories, as A.E. Day's 1974 article on Biggles reminds us, that Biggles had his only romantic encounter. In a short story entitled 'Affaire de Coeur', Biggles, forced by engine failure to land in a field in France, walks to a nearby house.

>   An old iron gate opened into the orchard; entering, he paused for a moment, uncertain of the path.
>   'Are you looking for me, monsieur?' said a musical voice.
>   Turning, he beheld a vision of blonde loveliness, wrapped up in

> blue silk, smiling at him. For a moment he stared as if he had never seen a woman before. He closed his eyes, shook his head, and opened them again. The vision was still there, dimpling.
> 'You were looking for me, perhaps?' said the girl again.
> Biggles saluted like a man sleep-walking.
> 'Mademoiselle', he said earnestly, 'I've been looking for you all my life' ...

From the start, Johns's feel for the cliché was unerring.

But if the prose was always clichéd, the hero was not. Biggles may have become the archetype of the stiff-upper-lipped, unflappable Englishman in the later stories, but, as Day (1974: 20) points out, the early ones give a different picture:

> His careless attitude suggested complete indifference, but the irritating little falsetto laugh which continually punctuated his tale betrayed the frayed condition of his nerves.

While I have tried to suggest that at least some of the books of Enid Blyton and W.E. Johns have more merit than their detractors will admit, I have to agree that, when compared with the work of Leon Garfield or Alan Garner or Jan Mark or Patricia Wrightson, their output is mediocre. But I do find it curious that the very adults who admit to relaxing with a thriller will call for the removal of the Famous Five and Biggles from school and municipal libraries. In an interesting article. 'A Defence of Rubbish', Peter Dickinson, himself a children's writer of the highest calibre, suggests that there are very good reasons why most of us need to read rubbish occasionally:

> ... I am fairly sure in my own mind that a diet of plums is bad for you, and that any rational reading system needs to include a considerable amount of pap or roughage — call it what you will.
>
> (Dickinson 1976: 74)

The phenomenon of the child who reads Susan Cooper's *The Dark Is Rising* and Ivan Southall's *Ash Road* with evident enjoyment, and who then rereads *Five Fall into Adventure* with gusto, is not so puzzling if one reflects on adult reading patterns. After all, professors of English have been known to read, and even to write, detective stories.

As for the propensity of series fiction to become addictive, this need not be a subject of concern. As Kenneth Sterck (1974: 61) has argued in a dissenting note to the Bob Dixon article already quoted, it may well be that addiction is one of the conditions for development — 'voracious reading refines itself'. If the addiction appears all-consuming, then the sensitive teacher, who will be unobtrusively observing reading tastes during wide reading periods (Hildick 1970: 192) can tactfully suggest other books that might be of interest.[2] In his *Children and Fiction*, Hildick argues that lively-minded children can use series fiction as vehicles for imaginative explorations of their own:

A close analogy would be the sort of educational toys — highly regarded by many adults who would be among the first to banish a Blyton book from playroom or library — which can, because of this same simplicity of design and freedom from too closely identifying detail, be made to serve all manner of purposes in the games of an imaginative child. In fact with this analogy and its own attendant paradox, we come close to resolving the original perplexity: by regarding a book of this kind as 'game-material' rather than an intended work of literature. The *universal* popularity of Enid Blyton's books now becomes easier to understand. A child of limited intelligence, who has nevertheless learned to read with reasonable fluency, will derive great pleasure from a Blyton book's mechanical easiness alone; while a child of higher intelligence — to whom that form of easiness is irrelevant — will derive great pleasure from using it as an efficient screen on which to project fantasies of his own.

(Hildick 1970: 192)

As for the values in these books, I have tried to suggest the dangers of a too-ready assumption that those of a particular writer will automatically be absorbed by the child reader, or even that the child reader sees them in the same terms as the adult. Agreed, the Biggles books are racist, the Blyton books snobbish, sexist and racist. It is, however, probably unreasonable to expect a man brought up in pre-First World War Britain not to have felt that one Englishman was worth half-a-dozen foreigners, and that the tasks of Empire were noble ones. Equally, it is perhaps unrealistic to expect a woman who grew up in middle-class suburbia in the same era to be able to rise above the prejudices of her class. Again, the teacher can help to counteract any dangers by cultivating in pupils an historical perspective, by helping them become aware that the view of the 'proper' role of women that one finds in *What Katy Did* is inevitable, given the social conditions of the time, and that one can hardly expect E. Nesbit's *The Railway Children*, published in 1906, to be free of class divisions (though Bob Dixon (1977: 58) seems to do so). Even if the Famous Five are holidaying in post-Second World War England, and Biggles is involved in adventures with Russians during the Cold War, the values of their authors were shaped by the fact that they grew up in Edwardian England. It is the teacher's task to ensure a sense of balance by introducing modern writers attuned to the dangers of class and race prejudice — writers of the calibre of Bernard Ashley, Jan Needle, Robert Leeson.

And, let us face it, is the prose of Enid Blyton and W.E. Johns any more pedestrian than that of, say, Judy Blume (always excepting *Tales of a Fourth Grade Nothing* and *Tiger Eyes*)? Are the characters flatter, or the values really so much more distasteful, than in the typical Blume novel? After reading *Forever* ... or *Are You There, God? It's Me, Margaret* one feels like crying 'Don't run away, Famous Five! Come back, Biggles! All is forgiven'.

NOTES

1. An article on Enid Blyton which discusses at length the same story that I have taken as an example, is Peter Wright, 'Five Run Away Together — Should We Let Them Back?' *English in Education* Vol. 14, No. 1, Spring 1980.
2. In upper primary and secondary schools, the practice of setting aside at least forty minutes a week for wide reading is growing. Typically, the pupils either choose from a range of books brought in by the teacher or bring in their own books. Often the last ten minutes is given over to sharing reading experiences.

REFERENCES

Day, A.E. 'Biggles; Anatomy of a Hero', in *Children's Literature in Education* No. 15, 1974.
Dickinson, Peter, 'A Defence of Rubbish' in Geoff Fox *et al.*, *Writers, Critics and Children*. London: Heinemann, 1976.
Dixon, Bob, *Catching Them Young Vol. 1: Sex, Race and Class in Children's Fiction*. London: Pluto Press, 1977.
────── 'The Nice, the Naughty and the Nasty: the Tiny World of Enid Blyton' *Children's Literature in Education* No. 15, 1974.
Hildick, Wallace, *Children and Fiction*. London: Evans, 1970.
Sarland, Charles, 'The Secret Seven Versus the Twits: Cultural Clash or Cosy Combination?' *Signal* No. 42, September, 1983.
Sterck, Kenneth, 'Editorial Note' in *Children's Literature in Education* No. 15, 1974.
Trease, Geoffrey, entry on W.E. Johns in D.L. Kirkpatrick, editor, *Twentieth Century Children's Writers*. London: Macmillan, 1978.

BOOKS REFERRED TO IN THE CHAPTER

Blume, Judy, *Are You There, God? It's Me, Margaret*. Piccolo.
────── , *Forever . . .* Pan.
────── , *Tales of a Fourth Grade Nothing*. Piccolo.
Blyton, Enid, Famous Five series.
Coolidge, Susan, *What Katy Did*. Puffin.
Cooper, Susan, *The Dark is Rising*. Puffin.
Johns, Captain W.E., Biggles and Worrals series.
Lee, Harper, *To Kill a Mockingbird*. Penguin.
Lewis, C.S., *The Lion, the Witch and the Wardrobe*. Bles.
Nesbit, Edith *The Railway Children*. Puffin.
Southall, Ivan, *Ash Road*. Angus & Robertson.

13 FEET ON THE GROUND: THE PROBLEM NOVEL

STELLA LEES

> The rich man in his castle,
> The poor man at his gate,
> God made them, high and lowly,
> And ordered their estate.

So wrote the nineteenth century hymn writer, Mrs Alexander. And this was the philosophy motivating much early writing for children. Hesba Stretton's waif in *Jessica's First Prayer* (1866) may well have had spiritual aspirations but her earthly estate and status had been ordered for her and she was content to accept without complaint her role in life. That she had problems, and that life's path was thorny was to be expected. But that such problems were socially imposed or unjust was not admissable.

Even earlier writers such as John Newbery, Mrs Trimmer and Maria Edgeworth, in the previous century, had been aware of the 'moulding' aspect of books, but their concern, like that of Hesba Stretton, had been with the saving of the immortal soul of their young readers. Whilst Carroll's *Alice in Wonderland* (1865) was seen as a spiritual volcano in that it rejected much of the moralising in children's literature, didacticism continued to be part of such literature and even today is apparent, albeit in new guises.

But the 1950s saw a change in the direction of children's books. The study of sociology and the popularisation of psychology had a major impact on how literature was presented to children. The new writers of the second half of the twentieth century began to express a concern as to how children were to survive in a complex industrialised society where the structure of family and marriage was undergoing profound changes, where television brought the world into everyone's living room but made experience private by reducing conversation; where the contraceptive pill enabled greater freedom from pregnancy, while rock and roll music openly pleaded a case for sexuality. Post-war capitalism moved into a stage where consumerism became a fetish.

New issues needed to be raised if children were to explore specific problems thoughtfully so that their childhood and adolescence could be as free of trauma as possible and if children's books were accurately to explore the real life experiences of their readers (Peck 1983).

SECURE AND LOVING FAMILIES

In the early twentieth century most books for children and young people turned on the security of a loving family, where the world was ordered and children protected from the harsh realities of society. That is not to say that the Woolcots in *Seven Little Australians* (Turner 1894) had no problems, but these, while true to their time, were not portrayed in a social context which highlighted them. Meg Woolcot makes innocent overtures to Andrew Courtney but her humiliation is complete when she is brought to her senses by his brother Alan. When Bunty lies he is caught and beaten for it. Both scenes ensure that the young reader will learn the consequences of stepping out of line with the demands of the morality of the time: women were to be innocent and uncalculating, children should not tell lies.

Turner's message is subtly conveyed, without the didactic tone of earlier writers such as Charlotte Barton (1841) but every novel of course does reflect the values of the writer. These may be expressed in such a way that they are not immediately identifiable, but they will be clear if the reader considers the resolution of a problem in the light of those outcomes which could have been selected. Inevitably, as the structure of society changes, the issues to be explored through literature also change.

The all-embracing acceptance of an elderly migrant grandmother, now living in inner-city Sydney in *Five Times Dizzy* (Wheatley 1983) suggests that it may be up to the minority culture to solve the problem of cultural tensions, or even that the problem has simple solutions. In the post-war children's novel the theme often becomes an exploration of a particular issue: alienation from parents; sibling rivalry; broken homes; sexual development; drugs; poverty; coping with handicap or disability; being part of a minority culture; social injustice; personal alienation or isolation; and the ultimate problem: death. Some critics have been concerned that authors may take up an issue at the expense of characterisation and style, so that one-dimensional figures are merely sounding boards for the author's preoccupations or even prejudices (Eagle 1979: 183–90). In Mavis Thorpe Clark's *Solomon's Child* (1981) the difficulty which Jude faces when her father leaves the family is shown through her alienation from school and friends, and the reader's concern for her grows naturally as the world is seen through her eyes. The concluding scene, where her problem is discussed in the Children's Court is staged and unconvincing and mars this otherwise strong novel. Australian writers seem too often to require a straightforward resolution to a problem, something particularly evident in novels about migrant children or family conflicts.

There are indications, however, that around the world children's writers are increasingly recognising the complexities of contemporary Western society. The Austrian writer Christine

Nostlinger, for example, takes a hard look at marital relationships as seen through the eyes of her young protagonists. She is their voice, crying out their concerns, particularly for a muddled family life where economic and social pressures often leave parents bewildered as to the state of their own relationships and emotions and therefore too busy, preoccupied and unaware to be able to give their children the time, love and support they need. Often it is the older generation — the grandparents — who do have the time, who understand and care most. Nostlinger also brings out the funny side as well as the pain of young people's interpersonal relationships. In *Luki-live* (published in English as *Luke and Angela* 1979), a wonderfully comic book, Luke returns from a visit to England as a punk with a fit of identity crisis. Luke and Angela consequently have to learn lessons in friendship, loyalty and consistent behaviour. In *Das Austauschkind* (*But Jasper Came Instead*, 1983) a rude and frightful English boy, Jasper, comes to stay with an Austrian family who gradually come to understand the problems of this mixed-up foreigner and reach out to him in true friendship.

From Britain, Philippa Pearce's *The Way to Sattin Shore* (1983) is a sensitive peeling away of the band-aids which adults apply for children to relationships that have gone wrong. The American writer Cynthia Voigt has the courage in her moving trilogy to confront head-on the problem of parents who abandon their children physically or emotionally: *Homecoming* (1981), *Dicey's Song* (1982) and the Newbery Award Winner, *A Solitary Blue* (1983).

Here in Australia children's writers are linking the problems of the past with those of the present. Both Deirdre Hill in *A Bridge of Dreams* (1982) and Nadia Wheatley in a strongly political, complex and award-winning novel *The House that Was Eureka* (1985) probe problems of unemployment and social injustice in times of economic depression. Wheatley adeptly connects conditions in Sydney in the Great Depression of the 1930s with today's economic crisis.

Because children's writers can now treat any aspect of human behaviour that is within the mental and emotional grasp of their readers it is inevitable that social realism should increasingly become a part of children's fiction. And if children's books are to reflect the realities of contemporary society they can no longer contain outmoded stereotypes of sexism, racism, sexuality, disability and references to minority groups. Hence the widespread popularity of Judy Blume, and the contribution of writers such as Betsy Byars in the United States and Eleanor Spence in Australia who explore them and suggest possible solutions.

SEXISM

Drawing on the experience of the women's liberation movement, female characters have became more assertive and capable than their predecessors. Assertive girls existed in literature long before the 1960s but these girls either defined themselves in terms of ultimate domestication, like Jo Marsh (Alcott 1868) or died in their struggle to maintain their initiative. Judy Woolcot's life of courage and defiance was vindicated in the ultimate sacrifice she made for the General. Through this brave (yet womanly) act, laying down her own life for the baby, the problem of how she was to grow up was resolved. How could one have made a lady from such a wayward girl? Captain Woolcot had forseen the difficulties.

> ... he was wishing almost prayerfully she had not been cast in so different a mould from the others, wishing he could stamp out that strange flame in her that made him so uneasy at times.
>
> (Turner 1894: 29)

The girl of the 1970s was no longer a mere supporter, but an initiator of action, and behaviour which was once benignly tolerated as tomboyish was embraced by those writers who wanted to provide role models for girls which eschewed sex-role stereotyping. The strongest body of work in this area can be found in novels from the United States: the work of Rosa Guy, Virginia Hamilton, Norma Klein and other feminists has provided an impetus for writers around the world.

In Britain, Gene Kemp's *The Turbulent Term of Tike Tyler* (1977) abandoned forever the concept of rigidly-defined sex roles and proved enormously popular with readers — not just because of the writer's non-sexist attitudes, but because she knows the world of today's young. In it, secondary modern children enthusiastically recognise themselves and their peers.

In Australia much of the initiative for non-sexist literature for children can be credited to the Women's Movement Children's Literature Cooperative, founded in 1973. A group of Melbourne women involved in 'consciousness raising', one of the early techniques used by women to develop confidence in themselves, was concerned about sex-role stereotyping in picture books. They set out to write books which portrayed girls with initiative and courage, and boys who were nurturing and sensitive. While much of their work is now directed to the non-fiction area the legacy of this dedicated group has been very significant. Penny Pollard's forthright opinions sit comfortably in their modern context in Robin Klein's *Penny Pollard's Diary* (1983), and can be seen as a rejection of the feminine docility which she believes her mother wishes to impose on her. The reader is on the side of Penny, and while she has much to learn about social relationships, we appreciate her struggle against convention. 'I feel sick every time I look at that pink dress from Aunty Janie (Aunty Traitor). She knew very well I wanted a stock-whip for my birthday (Klein 1983: 6). A comparison can be made between the mothers and grandmothers of the 1950s and such women as Josh's aunt (Southall 1971), or the domesticated mothers in *The Summer in Between* (Spence 1959) or *It Happened One Summer* (Phipson 1951); and Mark's mother in *Breaking Up* (Willmott 1983). We know this latter mother by her first name, she has a career, and in the end provides stability for the two brothers.

Sex-role stereotyping still exists. Very few nurturing boys have been portrayed, although writers such as Wrightson and Phipson have provided models of sensitivity in the boys who protect Andy (Wrightson 1968) and Mark's relationship with the handicapped Connie Peterson (*A Tide Flowing*, Phipson 1981). A nurturing boy can, however, be found, in Crabtree's novel *Nicking Off* (1975) and in Spence's *The Left-Overs* (1983). In the latter, Drew's concern for his foster brothers and sisters shows an engaging departure from the majority of fictional heroes.

The situation is by no means satisfactory. Boys still take pivotal roles in books for children. A survey of Australian prize winners concludes that 'some androgynous characters are developed in the award-winning books, and some sex roles are shared or swapped, but examples of these are the exception rather than the rule' (Reeder 1981: 10–16). Qualities such as independence, strength of character, care for others, unselfishness and sincerity should not be seen as 'masculine' or 'feminine' characteristics, but virtues in both sexes.

SEXUALITY

One aspect of nineteenth and early twentieth century novels was a reluctance on the part of the author to explore sexuality in books for young people. Even as late as 1965 Josephine Kamm's *Young Mother* avoids dealing with the circumstances of the conception of the illegitimate child. While Paul Zindel does reveal some of these circumstances in *My Darling, My Hamburger* (1969) and discusses the consequences of an unwanted pregnancy, the details of sexual love remain shrouded in mystery. Liz's abortion is the horrifying result of what is seen as a transgression, and there is no discussion of alternatives open to a girl in such a situation. It took some years before the new realism was able to shake off conventional attitudes. Judy Blume's *Forever* ... (1975) is much more sexually explicit. Michael and Katherine's love-making is described in detail, as is Katherine's successful attempt to obtain contraceptives. While Blume's characters may remain one-dimensional, and the sex may lack sensual power, *Forever* ... was a landmark in novels with sexual themes written for young people.

Later writers such as Gabrielle Carey and Kathy Lette could explore the lifestyle and sexuality of Cronulla surfies in an Australian best-seller *Puberty Blues* (1979), and Liz Berry could capitalise on the alcohol, drug and sex-dominated rock music area in *Easy Connections* (1983), where the story stops just short of rape.

Homosexual love has also been introduced and described without condemnation, particularly in novels such as *In The Tent* by David Rees (1979) and Sandra Scoppetone's *Trying to Hear You* (1974) and *Happy Endings Are All Alike* (1978). Characters who find sexual fulfilment with their own sex are less likely to meet a catastrophic death than they were in books of a decade ago when society was less tolerant of homosexuality and the gay movement unorganised.

Eleanor Spence develops the theme of a loving friendship in a sometimes misunderstood novel, *A Candle for St Antony* (1977). The strain which the two boys suffer can be seen as the result of a clash of cultures rather than a sexual imperative. A franker account of sexual development was made possible through novels such as *I'll Get There, It Better be Worth the Trip* by John Donovan (1969) where the young hero masturbates and where there is a sexual interlude with his school friend. It was 1984 before any explicit sexuality was described in an Australian novel for young people, although there is an illegitimate child born in Elisabeth McIntyre's *It's Different When You Get There* (1978). Willmott's *Breaking Up*, however, opens with a reference to Mark having masturbated, and during the course of the novel he describes witnessing his mother and father making love. There are a number of American novels which deal with menarche, Louise Fitzhugh's *The Long Secret* (1965) being the most sensitive treatment, although Blume's *Are You There, God? It's Me, Margaret* (1970) is more popular.

Perhaps more than in any other area overt sexuality in material for young people is likely to offend adults, who have strong views about children's sex education. Those who promote books and reading need to be conscious of that sensibility and to take account of cultural and religious prescriptions. On the other hand, the prejudice and narrow prudery of parents should not be automatically visited upon their children. Open discussion of the issues involved, including the heightened awareness of ourselves as sexual beings, which is a feature of modern Western thought, is necessary if there is to be any resolution of this question.

THE DISABLED

In this area Australia has provided some of the finest work. The treatment of the physically and mentally disabled child in literature has moved a long way from the mad Mrs Rochester of Charlotte Brontë or the fearsome cripples who grope through the pages of nineteenth century literature. Those who are disabled increasingly desire a fictional treatment which honestly accords them dignity. The first part of Alan Marshall's autobiographical trilogy *I Can Jump Puddles* (1955) has established itself as a fine description of a boy who overcame crippling poliomyelitis to take on a vocation which made enormous demands on him, and the book became a worldwide inspiration for the physically disabled. Southall's *Let The*

Balloon Go (1968) examines one of the difficulties faced by a child with cerebral palsy: the reluctance on the part of his mother to allow him to experiment with his own capabilities. Andy in *I Own the Racecourse!* (Wrightson 1968) sees life through a darkened window, but despite his naïve belief that he has actually bought the racecourse his actions are depicted with gentle humour and sympathy. We are always on Andy's side and like his caring friends, want him to come through this impossible situation retaining his engaging good humour.

Life for Douglas in *The October Child* (Spence 1976) is not so cushioned, and Carl's autism is not easy to live with. Spence's courageous novel reveals the effect on a family of such a child: the despair of the parents, the alienation of one brother, the retreat of a sister, the growth in maturity of Carl's brother Douglas. Eleanor Spence's talents again turn to the disabled in her subtle and sensitive account of Straw in *The Left-Overs*.

MINORITY GROUPS

Societies are rarely homogeneous, although often one particular group assumes power. In Australia, Britain and the United States, because of historical circumstances, this has been the Anglo-Celtic group. Increasingly, less powerful groups have demanded a larger share of a place in the sun and part of this demand has been a more sympathetic treatment in literature. During the 1960s black Americans in the United States took action to obtain recognition of the discrimination against them throughout American society. Books which examined the movement for integration in education such as *Mary Jane* (Stirling 1959), their historic origins, such as *The Slave Dancer* (Fox 1973), their economic disadvantage, such as *Sounder* (Armstrong 1969), and which portrayed black people as the saviours of whites, such as *The Cay* (Taylor 1969), were produced. Some of these books, written in the main by white authors, have been criticised as patronising or worse, racist (*Racism and Sexism in Children's Books* 1979). Voices have appeared in the 1970s such as Virginia Hamilton's and Mildred Taylor's. They describe black lives from a personal perspective. In Britain, too, writers like Farrukh Dhondy and Rukshana Smith passionately reveal Asian and West Indian experience. Australian Aborigines have not yet written any major novels for young people, but writers such as Kath Walker and aritists like Dick Roughsey have produced significant material. In Australia, too, attempts by white writers have been made to write about Aborigines, Wrightson's being the most notable (*The Wirrun* trilogy). A survey of books with Aboriginal characters was published in 1982 (Dunkle 1982: 55–7).

Australia is second only to Israel in the number of countries from which we have drawn our population. Over the past decade many Australian authors have attempted to write about the multi-cultural nature of our society, including writers who were migrants themselves, such as David Martin. His most successful books in this area are *The Chinese Boy* (1973) and *The Man in The Red Turban* (1978). Recently novels have been published which either continue his theme of exploring characters who are migrants themselves or incorporating them into the action of the novel. Klein's *Junk Castle* (1983), Willmott's *Breaking Up* and Mayne's *Salt River Times* (1980) are examples of the latter. Until the mid-1980s brave attempts to identify the tensions inherent in a multi-cultural society have usually foundered because the authors presented solutions which were too facile. The strength of *Moving Out* (1983) by Helen Garner and Jennifer Giles lies in its recognition of the complexities faced by the protagonist, torn between two cultures.

These four areas which have occupied the attention of many children's writers are only examples of the many issues which have to be faced in contemporary society along with the inevitable problems of being human and therefore finite.

DEATH

Previously, this subject was either taboo in children's fiction or tended to be used as a vehicle for sentiment. Pain, death and dying have been faced unsentimentally in more recent children's books like Isabelle Holland's *Of Love and Death and Other Journeys* (1975) where the divorced mother of a fifteen-year-old dies of cancer. Jeremy in Jean Little's *Mama'a Going to Buy You a Mockingbird* (1984) is even younger when he faces his father's battle against cancer. Death, grief and rage have to be met head-on by young people in Katherine Paterson's *Bridge to Terabithia* (1978); in Joan Phipson's *A Tide Flowing* (1981) and David Day's *Are You Listening, Karen?* (1983), in which Jay reaches out from the inner core of his loneliness to his elder sister who is killed in a motor accident before he has had time to confide in her. In *Charlotte's Web* (1952) by E.B. White, Wilbur the Pig lives in constant fear of death, but it is Charlotte, the heroic spider, who demonstrates that death is part of ongoing life. And it is the cruel death of his beloved Mr Percival that causes Storm Boy, in Colin Thiele's novel, to reach beyond grief to acceptance.

SOCIAL ISSUES IN AUSTRALIA

Many other problems have provided themes for novels in the last twenty years and Australian writers, like their counterparts in Britain and the United States have taken them up.

The theme of the conservation and the preservation of the Australian environment was voiced as early as 1880 by Louisa Anne Meredith in her 'Family Chronicle of Country Life', *Tasmanian Friends and Foes; Feathered, Furred and Finned*. More recently, it's been explored by Mavis Thorpe Clark (*Blue Above the Trees* 1967), Hesba Brinsmead (*Longtime Passing* 1971) and by Colin Thiele (*The Fire in the Stone* 1973). A reverence as well as a deep concern for the ancient land of Australia is inherent in the writings of Patricia Wrightson; and in *Papio* (1984) Victor Kelleher confronts the issue of animal experimentation.

J.M. Couper faced the issue of war and peace as early as 1970 in his *Thundering Good Today*, while more recently Christobel Mattingley has written the text of two picture books that probe painful questions of peace after war — *The Angel With the Mouthorgan* (1984) out of the war in Europe, and *The Miracle Tree* (1985) from the terror and horror of Hiroshima. And out of the internecine conflict in Kampuchea has come Allan Baillie's *Little Brother* (1985), a moving story of two brothers caught in the crossfire of the Khmer Rouge.

Robin Klein in *People Might Hear You* (1983), Ted Greenwood in *The Boy Who Saw God* (1980) and Eleanor Spence in *The Seventh Pebble* (1981) have all explored the corrosive effects of fanaticism, bigotry and hypocrisy in religion.

Klein, too, has raised the problem of the elderly in their relationship with society in *Penny Pollard's Diary* (1983). Indeed, a sensitive handling of ageing has been part of Australian children's literature since *Timothy and Gramps* by Ron Brooks (1978). There is the splendid collaboration between Mem Fox and Julie Vivas in *Wilfrid Gordon McDonald Partridge* (1984) which tenderly tells how the small Wilfrid Gordon helps his friend Miss Nancy in the old people's home next door find her lost memory, Patricia Wrightson's portrait of that redoubtable lady, Mrs Tucker, in *A Little Fear* (1984), a book which deals with ageing and shows that a successful and popular children's story need not contain youthful characters. Increasingly, the Australian novel for young people has explored family tension and instability. Diane Bates in both *Terri* (1981) and *Piggy Moss* (1982) shows the effects on adolescent girls, whilst Willmott's *Breaking Up* (1983) and *Suffer Dogs* (1985) explore the same issues with adolescent boys.

Australian writers, so far, have avoided the seeming pessimism of Cormier's *The Chocolate War*. Rather they seem committed to the belief that the young do need reassurance, that resolution is usually to be found in our own hands, and that life is ultimately optimistic: security has not and will not disappear. Ruth Park's Abigail in *Playing Beatie Bow* (1980) discovers through her slip into times past not only that the present is redeemable but that time itself is not a 'great black vortex down which everything disappeared', but 'that it was a great river, always moving, always changing, but with the same water flowing between its banks from source to sea' (Park 1980: 195). And Joan Phipson's *Dinko* (1985) which considers the possibility of a nuclear attack on Australia, also suggests the continuing survival of humanity. Dinko's vision is prophetic, ultimately reassuring and life-affirming:

> The people around him were looking at him and they were smiling. He felt both his hands taken and held fast. The joy was still there, and he knew that at last he had found the thing he had been looking for. If it was a road, he and those with him would reach the end of it in time, and he was content.
>
> (Phipson 1985: 190)

The reader who meets Abigail and Dinko or the many displaced persons like Lee Harding's Graeme (1979) may well be better able to reconsider some of the painful experiences of childhood and adolescence with greater insight, and be better equipped to grapple with the problems and issues which bedevil their society. Perhaps as they ask: 'How would I behave in this situation?' they will come to know themselves more closely. Writers often suggest solutions: whether that path is possible or even desirable for the individual could well engender discussion and personal attention.

A good novel requires more than a strong theme centred on a contemporary issue to be successful, but where rounded characters, a believable setting and an assured style are present, books about a specific issue can be very attractive to young readers.

REFERENCES

Dunkle, Margaret, 'The Changing Scene: A Look at Aboriginality in Contemporary Children's Literature' in Herr, Twila A.J., editor, *The Aboriginal Motif in Children's Literature*. Hobart: University of Tasmania Library, 1982.

Eagle, Audrey B., 'Writing the Teen-age Soap Opera' in *School Library Journal*, April 1979.

Peck, Richard, 'The Invention of Adolescence and Other Thoughts on Youth' in *Top of the News* Vol. 39, No. 2, Winter 1983.

Racism and Sexism in Children's Books. London: Writers and Readers Publishing Cooperative, 1979.

Reeder, Stephanie Owen, 'Sex-role Stereotyping in Australian Children's Book of the Year Award Winners 1950–1980' in *Reading Time* October 1981.

BOOKS REFERRED TO IN THE CHAPTER

Alcott, Louisa M., *Little Woman*. Roberts Brothers.
Armstrong, William, *Sounder*. Puffin.
Baillie, Allan, *Little Brother*. Nelson.
Barton, Charlotte, *A Mother's Offering to Her Children*. Sydney Gazette.
Bates, Dianne, *Piggy Moss*. Penguin.
———, *Terri*. Penguin.
Berry, Liz, *Easy Connections*. Puffin Plus.
Blume, Judy, *Are You There, God? It's Me, Margaret*. Gollancz/Piccolo.
———, *Forever* ... Pan.

Brinsmead, Hesba, *Longtime Passing*. Angus & Robertson.
Brooks, Ron, *Timothy and Gramps*. Collins.
Carroll, Lewis, *Alice in Wonderland*. Puffin.
Carey, Gabrielle and Lette, Kathy, *Puberty Blues*. McPhee Gribble.
Clark, Mavis Thorpe, *Blue Above the Trees*. Hodder & Stoughton.
——————, *Solomon's Child*. Hutchinson/Puffin.
Cormier, Robert, *The Chocolate War*. Gollancz/Lions.
Couper, J.M., *The Thundering Good Today*. Bodley Head.
Crabtree, Judith, *Nicking Off*. Brown Wren Books.
Day, David, *Are You Listening Karen?* Puffin Plus.
Donovan, John, *I'll Get There, It Better be Worth the Trip*. Macdonald.
Fitzhugh, Louise, *The Long Secret*. Lions.
Fox, Mem, illustrator, Julie Vivas, *Wilfred Gordon McDonald Partridge*. Omnibus.
Fox, Paula, *The Slave Dancer*. Macmillan.
Garner, Helen and Giles, Jennifer, *Moving Out*. Nelson.
Greenwood, Ted, *The Boy Who Saw God*. Puffin Plus.
Harding, Lee, *Displaced Person*. Puffin Plus.
Hill, Deidre, *A Bridge of Dreams*. Hodder & Stoughton.
Holland, Esabelle, *Of Love and Death and Other Journeys*. Lippincott.
Kamm, Josephine, *Young Mother*. Brockhampton Press.
Kelleher, Victor, *Papio*. Kestrel.
Kemp, Gene, *The Turbulent Term of Tyke Tiler*. Puffin.
Klein, Robin, *Junk Castle*. Oxford.
——————, *Penny Pollard's Diary*. Oxford.
Little, Jean, *Mama's Going to Buy You a Mockingbird*. Kestrel.
MacIntyre, Elisabeth, *It Looks Different When You Get There*. Hodder & Stoughton.
Marshall, Alan, *I Can Jump Puddles*. Longman.
Martin, David, *The Chinese Boy*. Hodder & Stoughton.
——————, *The Man in the Red Turban*. Hutchinson.
Mattingley, Christobel, *The Angel With the Mouth-organ*. Hodder & Stoughton.
——————, *The Miracle Tree*. Hodder & Stoughton.
Mayne, William, *Salt River Times*. Hamish Hamilton.
Meredith, Louisa Ann, *Tasmanian Friends and Foes; Feathered, Furred and Finned*. Marcus Ward.
Nöstlinger, Christine, *But Jasper Came Instead*. Andersen Press.
——————, *Luke and Angela*. Andersen Press.
Park, Ruth, *Playing Beatie Bow*. Nelson/Puffin.
Paterson, Katherine, *Bridge to Terabithia*. Puffin.
Pearce, Philippa, *The Way to Sattin Shore*. Kestrel/Puffin.
Phipson, Joan, *Dinko*. Methuen.
——————, *It Happened One Summer*. Angus & Robertson.
——————, *A Tide Flowing*. Methuen.
Rees, David, *In the Tent*. Dobson.
Scoppetone, Sandra, *Happy Endings Are All Alike*. Harper & Row.
——————, *Trying Hard to Hear You*. Harper & Row.
Southall, Ivan, *Josh*. Angus & Robertson.
——————, *Let the Balloon Go*. Methuen.
Spence, Eleanor, *A Candle For Saint Antony*. Oxford.
——————, *The Left-Overs*. Methuen.
——————, *The October Child*. Oxford.

———, *The Seventh Pebble*. Oxford.
———, *The Summer in Between*. Oxford.
Stirling, *Mary Jane*. Kestrel.
Stretton, Hesba, *Jessica's First Prayer*. Religious Tract Society.
Taylor, Theodore, *The Cay*. Puffin.
Thiele, Colin, *The Fire in the Stone*. Puffin.
Turner, Ethel, *Seven Little Australians*. Ward Lock.
Voigt, Cynthia, *Dicey's Song*. Collins.
———, *Homecoming*. Collins.
———, *A Solitary Blue*. Atheneum.
Wheatley, Nadia, *Five Times Dizzy*. Oxford.
———, *The House that Was Eureka*. Kestrel.
Willmott, Frank, *Breaking Up*. Collins.
———, *Suffer Dogs*. Collins.
Wrightson, Patricia, *I Own the Racecourse!* Puffin.
———, *A Little Fear*. Hutchinson/Puffin.
Zindel, Paul, *My Darling, My Hamburger*. Bodley Head.

FURTHER READING

Chambers, Aidan, *Dance on My Grave*. Bodley Head.
Collins, Alan, *The Boys From Bondi*. U.Q.P.
Crew, Gary, *The Inner Circle*. Heinemann.
———, *The House of Tomorrow*. Heinemann.
Duder, Tessa, *Alex*. Puffin.
Greene, Bette, *The Summer of My German Soldier*. Puffin.
Hall, Penny, *The Paperchaser*. Walter McVitty/Collins.
Hathorn, Libby, *Thunderwith*. Heinemann.
Hinton, Nigel, *Buddy*. Puffin.
Howker, Janni, *The Nature of the Beast*. Julia MacRae.
———, *Isaac Campion*. Julia MacRae.
Klein, Robin, *Came Back to Show You I Could Fly*. Viking Kestrel.
Lowry, Lois, *Find a Stranger, Say Goodbye*. Collins.
McCuaig, Sandra, *Blindfold*. Collins.
Noonan, Michael, *McKenzie's Boots*. U.Q.P.
Peek, Robert Newton, *A Day No Pigs Would Die*. Dell.
Pershall, Mary, K., *You Take the High Road*. Puffin.
Phipson, Joan, *Bianca*. Viking Kestrel.
Pople, Maureen, *The Other Side of the Family*. U.Q.P.
Rubinstein, Gillian, *Beyond the Labyrinth*. Hyland House.
Sharp, Donna, *Blue Days*. U.Q.P.
Talbert, Marc, *Dead Birds Singing*. Hamish Hamilton.
Wheatley, Nadia, *The Blooding*. Viking Kestrel.
Winton, Tim, *Lockie Leonard, Human Torpedo*. McPhee Gribble.

14 SHARED SPACES: THE HUMAN AND ANIMAL WORLDS

JOYCE KIRK

> One touch of nature makes the whole world kin.
> Shakespeare

As with most literature, the genesis of the modern animal tale can be found in the folklore of the past, in the folktales, myths, epics and fables which were created during the dawning of most cultures. In this folklore of past times the animal characters generally have one of two main functions: either as the antagonists of human heroes in tales of survival against the elements of nature, or as a guide to human nature and behaviour in fable and folk tale. The depiction of animals in the traditional tales is very often almost human, and it is the similarities between the animal and human dwellers of the earth that occupied the earliest storytellers, who affirmed in their tales a spiritual unity in the natural world. In some instances animals were elevated to a position equal to humans, but rarely above them.

The more realistic characterisation of animals as animals dates from the latter part of the nineteenth century according to Magee (1980: 233) and Anna Sewell's *Black Beauty* (1877) is credited by Blount (1974: 18) as being the first genuine animal novel. The emphasis here is on the differences between the animals and their keepers rather than on their similarities, with the result that the horses are not the disguised human beings of folklore.

It is generally accepted that there are three basic kinds of animal story in modern children's literature, although the distinctions among them are not always clear-cut and it is possible for a story to have some features of all three kinds in it. First of all, there is the story which focuses on animals living in their natural habitats with the narrator sometimes adopting the viewpoint of an animal or, at other times, that of a human character. In the nature stories, animals are the protagonists, are fully developed and have an existence generally outside human society and independent of it. Moving closer into human society and having some of the characteristics of the nature stories are those where the focus is shared between an animal and a human. A pattern common to these is the maturing of the human character through his or her association with animals.

The second kind of story is fantasy, where the animals inhabit a secondary reality, most often an Eden in which animals communicate freely with each other and behave very much as human beings. This created place in which humans and beasts are equal, transcends the world as we know it, but the vision of it nevertheless has relevance for us.

The third kind of animal story is the 'talking beast' or fanciful tale in which the animals retain a large measure of their own natures. Some of these have a moral or didactic purpose, whereas others express a sheer joy of living and the wonder of the world around us.

Although the discussion of animal stories in this chapter concentrates on these kinds of stories in novels, it should be pointed out that the three kinds of animal stories are found also in picture books. Two examples of nature stories are Ted Greenwood's *Everlasting Circle* (1981) which describes the life cycle of a shearwater bird in gentle, poetic pose and delicately-coloured illustrations, and Jenny Wagner's *Aranea: The Story of a Spider* (1975) which details the spider's struggle for survival against the forces of nature and the whims of humans both in the text and in Ron Brooks' black and white line drawings.

The more usual nature story in picture books however, deals with the relationship between humans, usually children, and one or more animals. *The Useless Donkeys* (1979) written by Lydia Pender and illustrated by Judith Cowell is a warm story about the Quigley family and the special bond between the children and their pet donkeys. A similarly close relationship is explored in Jenny Wagner's *John Brown, Rose and the Midnight Cat* (1977), illustrated by Ron Brooks, and a winner of the Picture Book of the Year award. This haunting tale has several layers of meaning, but on one level is a story of a dog's acceptance of his widowed mistress' desire for a black cat. Jenny Wagner and Ron Brooks have also produced an award-winning animal fantasy, the *Bunyip of Berkeley's Creek* (1973) in which the bunyip behaves as a human in its search for identity and finds joy in recognising its individuality. *Possum Magic* (1983) written by Mem Fox and illustrated by Julie Vivas, explores a similar theme as the invisible Hush gradually become increasingly visible after eating lamingtons, pumpkin scones, minties and pavlova.

There are many talking beast tales in picture books. Arnold Lobel's Caldecott Medal winner *Fables* (1980) bears a close stylistic similarity to Aesop's *Fables*, but each tale has a characteristic twist to it, so that the moral is not quite what is expected. *Hetty and Harriet* (1981) by Graham Oakley has a strong didactic element and the two hens return to their farmyard wiser and more contented, having risked their lives in a false bid for freedom. This brief and by no means exhaustive listing indicates what is available in the three main categories which will be examined in further detail with reference to novels.

CHILDREN AND ANIMAL STORIES

Anyone who has observed children's responses to animals will be aware of the interest that they have in them and the curiosity that they have about their ways: it is not surprising that animal stories are popular with children.

The characteristics of children's thinking to a large extent underlies the appeal of these stories. Bruno Bettelheim (1978: 45) asserts that the child's thought processes are animistic, at least until the age of puberty. Because this mode of thinking is reflected in most animal stories, they are credible and convincing to the young reader who does not clearly delineate living things from objects, and who expects that all life is lived in a way similar to his or her own. The child assumes that animals, toys and other objects will talk about things which are significant to him or her and that they understand and feel for the child, even though they may not express their feelings openly. Children have no difficulty accepting the anthropomorphised animals they meet in stories. In fact, children's animals and toys behave this way in their own play.

Children's development can be enhanced by the literature they choose to read or hear and animal stories are no exception. Schlager's (1978) research suggests that children read those books which reflect aspects of cognitive, moral and psycho-social growth appropriate to their particular developmental stages. Huck (1979: 31—6) has developed a schema which relates the growth characteristics of children aged from three to twelve to aspects of story, and has suggested titles, many of which are animal stories. Donelson and Nilsen (1980) have taken a similar but less detailed developmental approach to literature for young adults and there are animal stories on their recommended reading lists.

Reading interest surveys, although open to criticism, confirm the importance of animal stories to children. Studies by Elley and Tolley (1972) in New Zealand, and Norvell (1950) in the United States found that these stories were consistently read in primary and secondary schools. Whitehead *et al.* (1977) in a national British study identified several animal story titles as being widely read by ten to fifteen-year-olds. Recent Australian research reported by Bunbury, Finnis and Williams (1983) includes several animal stories on a list of fiction named by teachers as being highly successful for classroom discussion in Years 5, 7, 9, and 11.

One of the advantages of the animal story is that emotionally-charged experiences and challenging concepts can be explored by young readers with less threat than might be the case with others. This does not mean that it is a dilution of reality or that it avoids the darker side of life, for the honestly-conceived and well-written story presents a rounded view of the world. What it does mean is that the

> problems of human relationships and the enigma of life can be examined without allowing the reader to realise he's being so involved. If fiction is vicarious living, animal fiction puts two filters between the individual and the harshness of reality.
>
> (Saxby 1971: 180)

THE ANIMAL WORLD

The animal world has been described and used in fiction in various ways and in recent years the nature story has taken new directions. For some writers the world of an animal has a beauty and unity all its own. Stories of survival show them with people, at the mercy of the forces of nature; some stories of animals living in the wild raise questions about the meaning of freedom. Other stories raise the issue of conservation.

Perhaps the worlds of animals and people merge most closely in stories of tamed or domesticated animals. Here the focus is not exclusively on the animal but also on a person with whom there is an affinity. It follows that the degree of human presence in stories about the animal world varies from an absence of humans altogether to their having a significant place in terms of the development of a story, as either a destructive or healing force.

Nature stories are based firmly in the real world and they pose special challenges for writers, particularly in relation to the nature of the animals portrayed and the means used to reveal that nature. For instance, in Patricia Wrightson's *A Little Fear* (1983), an Australian Book of the Year Award winner, old Mrs Tucker and her dog are clearly shown to be intruders into the valley near the sea. Some of the most vivid scenes in the book show midges crawling over everything in sight, and hens being disturbed in the fowl house. The power of these scenes lies in the cleverly-realised detail. The ancient spirit of the land, the Njimbin, has won the battle against these intruders, and guarantees that harmony will be restored. This carefully-balanced book is essentially a poetic statement about letting things live in their own way: something that applies equally to the land, its creatures and its people.

Sutherland (1977: 341) suggests that in realistic fiction about animals the main requirement is that they be objectively portrayed and that speculation about their motives should be based on scientifically-recorded observations of animal behaviour. That this has in fact occurred in some stories is the basis of the claim by Stodart (1982) that fiction which portrays animals faithfully can be used in teaching biology.

Given factually-based background information there is still the challenge of presenting the animals in terms which will arouse the reader's empathy. One writer of animal stories claims that

> even in the most accurate, the most objective of wildlife fiction writing there has to be a certain amount of falsification, of humanization in order to engage the reader's interest and make him identify with the protagonists. This is true even if the animals are endowed with only a few basic qualities such as courage or physical endurance. You cannot actually be said to have courage unless you have a concept of death, or at least of pain ...
>
> (Rayner 1980: 47)

One of the finest, perhaps the finest, nature story ever written *Tarka, the Otter: His Joyful Water-Life and Death in the Two Rivers* (1927) by Henry Williamson, is certainly based on accurate observation. In a Preface to the 1963 revised edition (p. 7) the reader is told that Williamson's aim was to write a truthful story, and that for a time the world of otters was more real to him than the world of people. The reader's perspective on Tarka's habitat is in fact the otter's and although Williamson writes from within the animal character he has created he has such a profound respect for the animal's dignity that sentiment and melodrama have no place. Tarka is very much an otter, and lives on the edge of human society in a setting which is a world in itself. The presence of humans is strongly felt, but they are seen by Tarka as fellow inhabitants of it. The cycle of the seasons mirrors Tarka's life giving this elegant novel an artistic cohesion. By way of contrast, a less convincing otter story is *Samaki: The Story of an Otter in Africa* (1979) by J.A. Davis in which the setting is an imaginary river and the author's knowledge of otters comes from his experience of them in captivity.

Contributions by North American writers to the realistic animal story have been quite significant, and one of the earliest novels is *Red Fox* (1905) by Charles G.D. Roberts. Both Tarka and Red Fox are humanised, if at all, to the least degree, and both are equally memorable.

A more recent wild fox story is Glyn Frewer's *Fox* (1984). Frewer seems to be making a plea for fairer treatment of foxes by humans rather than recreating their life cycle. While a reader may be awed by the beauty of Red Fox or Tarka, Flik does not inspire that same wonder. The factual information about foxes is not completely integrated into the narrative but, nevertheless, the fear that Flik inspires in the South Midland village is keenly felt.

The theme of freedom in the wild has been explored by several writers. Buck, a St Bernard and Scotch shepherd dog crossbreed, gradually reverts to his untamed state in Jack London's *Call of the Wild* (1903). His instincts are rekindled and the veneer of domestication falls from him as he suffers abuse from human beings together with the ravages of conditions in the Klondike during the gold rushes. London writes from first-hand experience but lacks the objectivity required of the animal story and attributes thoughts and morality to Buck. Like Flik, Buck is elevated to legendary status in his life time and the implication is that he is larger than life.

The red heifer in Frank Dalby Davison's *Man-Shy* (1931) escapes to the scrub rather than join the grazing herd. The harsh, hot and relentless inland Australian climate is the background of the novel's action. Unlike London, Davison treats the characters in a consistently objective manner and neither stockman nor animal is transformed into hero nor villain.

The challenges to animals living in the wilderness are central to Elyne Mitchell's series of stories about a wild stallion, the best known of which is probably *Silver Brumby* (1958). Unlike the animals discussed so far, Mitchell's horses are able to communicate with each other and with other bush animals in the Australian Alps. These stories take account of the intrusion of humans through the annual brumby runs: hunters are perhaps more of a threat to the horses than are the forces of nature. Helen Griffiths in *Black Face Stallion* (1980) also considers similar threats to wild horses in the desert of northern Mexico, where the routes to their grazing lands are blocked by the building of a dam and the herd's stallion is shot by a trapper, the first man he has ever seen.

A moving but unsentimental story of the endurance of an animal is Colin Thiele's *Magpie Island* (1974). Magpie is swept off course to a desolate, cold and windswept island off the coast of South Australia. A mate eventually arrives on the island but she is killed by a plane spotting fish for trawlers. Magpie's strength and resilience are admired by Ben, a boy whose father occasionally travels near the island and it is for these qualities that he remembers the solitary bird.

In stories where wild animals threaten the lives and safety of humans the emphasis is usually on the people and their behaviour and reactions. In Ruskin Bond's *Night of the Leopard* (1979), the Indian villagers fear the leopard which has taken Raki's dog and the postman but still have a grudging admiration and respect for him. Bond's view of the leopard is a detached one and it effectively reinforces the villagers' acceptance of the danger posed by the wild animal.

Implicit in these realistic stories of animal life is the writers' respect for the natural world and a recognition of the respective places of animals and humans in it. The theme of conservation has become more explicit in recent years. The hare, Kee, in Joyce Stranger's *Hare at Dark Hollow* (1973) faces threats from her natural enemies, as well as from humans in the forms of the poacher and the destruction of the forest to make way for an airport. Although the airport finally provides a sanctuary for Kee, Dark Hollow is converted to a rubbish tip and she loses the territory of her birthplace. The theme is kept within the bounds of the narrative and Kee remains very much a hare.

In Vincent Smith's *Musco — Blue Whale* (1978) the message is so strongly presented that the story's impact is weakened. The zealous depiction of the whales exaggerates their sense of the past beyond the probable level of scientifically recorded fact, but it does manage to engage the reader's sympathy for their plight. Similarly, the theme disturbs the balance of *Cat Tracks* (1981) by Gordon Aalborg, a story about feral cats around Canberra. The effect here is that the cats never fully achieve the status of characters and there is little tension in the plot as the focus moves more to the human characters.

Christobel Mattingley is another Australian writer whose strong feeling for the natural world is evident in her books. Writing of *The Battle of the Galah Trees* (1973) in which Matt saves a young galah and then a stand of eucalypts in which the birds nest, she says

> The story evolved in part as a result of sixteen years of observing and loving the beautiful gum trees in the district where we now live.
>
> (Dugan 1979: 44)

The strategies of Matt's fight against the council take over from the interest in the birds themselves but nevertheless the book is an example of the different directions which a nature story can take. Another is an examination of animals in captivity. *Uhu* (1969), an Australian Book of the Year Award winner by Annette Macarthur-Onslow is the tale of a tawny owl raised in a country cottage in England. The observations of his behaviour are detailed but humanised and this is also the case in the accompanying illustrations which are impressionistic rather than naturalistic. The viewpoint presented is very much a human's rather than an animal's, as in, say, *Tarka the Otter*.

Victor Kelleher's recent novel *Papio: a Novel of Adventure* (1984) extends the captive animal theme to considering animal rights and the cause becoming an obsession. David and Jem release some baboons from an experimental research station and join them in the wild, in effect becoming part of the troop. In the shattering climax, they are forced to concede that they as well as the hunter have been responsible for the eventual slaying of most of the baboons. In concentrating on an issue in this way this novel has much in common with the 'problem' novel. Characterisation is complex, but the baboons remain animals. An author's note at the conclusion of the book confirms Kelleher's concern about these apes being hunted on the Zambezi escarpment and outlines the extent to which the story is based on actual fact.

Related to these realistic stories of animals are those which follow the development of a caring relationship between a young person and an animal. Margery Fisher (1964: 59) notes that in these stories, factual pieces and adventures occur side by side as the stories follow a double pattern. The adventures have their roots in the conflicts presented in the plot, which may be built on the playing out of a human dilemma. Although the human element is stronger than in the stories of animals in nature and the focus is often on the maturing of a hero, the animal or pets must be credible as animals. Whether the animals are humanised to any degree depends largely on the author's purposes and themes.

Typical of the animal-human relationship story is Mary Elyne Patchett's *The Brumby* (1958). As the hero, Joey, learns more about the ways of horses in the bush and of the men who pursue them, he draws closer to his father and finally releases to the herd a mare he had planned to keep. Another Australian story and one which is more cohesive is *Storm Boy* (1963) by Colin Thiele, set in the Coorong in South Australia. When Mr Percival, the pelican who has been raised by Storm Boy, is shot by hunters, he is ready to move beyond his beloved country to the wider world and to go to boarding school in the city.

Similarly based on accurately observed details of animal life is Jean George's *Julie of the Wolves* (1972), a Newbery Medal winner. Julie, too, grows through the course of her journey in the Alaskan wilderness with a wolf pack, and finally accepts that life for both Eskimoes and the wolves is changing. Like Joey and Storm Boy, she respects the forces of nature and has a profound sense of her place in the scheme of things.

Another journey story is *When Jays Fly to Barbmo* (1968) by Margaret Balderson, an Australian Book of the Year Award winner. In this war story, the journey which Ingeborg undertakes is also a journey to a new self-awareness through a psychological, emotional and physiological ordeal. Even her dog Benne is infected with her disquiet as she comes to terms with her feelings and her confusions. The sparseness of the writing evokes very clearly the cold, harsh Norwegian winter.

Margaret Balderson's other book *A Dog Called George* (1975) also features a dog, this time a domesticated one. Through his association with the old English sheepdog George, Tony begins to make friends and even to see his father in a new light. As a mark of his new-found maturity, at the end of the novel he is able to share George with a friend.

Similarly, in James Aldridge's *The Broken Saddle* (1982), Eric gains a measure of self confidence and self-awareness as a result of his taming a wild pony, given to him by his long-absent father, a drover. In developing a capacity for true friendship Eric draws away from the pony, and at the same time finds his place in the world, rejecting his father's way of life based on rapport with the land rather than with people. The relationships between people are finely crafted and the setting of the small town is strongly recreated through Aldridge's graceful prose.

A boy and his cat reflect the dynamics of a family in Emily Neville's *It's Like This Cat* (1963), a Newbery Medal winner. The stray cat which he befriends fills a void in Dave's life and assists him in sorting out his feelings and attitudes towards his father. The story is narrated by the fourteen-year-old Dave, so it is through his eyes that Cat is made real to the reader. Consequently the depiction of Cat is not as objective as it usually is in nature stories, although Cat is very much a street-wise stray, and not humanised to any great extent.

Clarence the cat and Sebastian the Labrador act as foils to the main child characters in Joan Dalgleish's *Cats Don't Bark* (1978) and *The Latchkey Dog* (1980). The pets are seen from the viewpoint of the narrator in each story and remain distanced from the human characters, although they are at times the instigators of some hilarious incidents. Both books highlight the links between animal and family stories.

Children's yearnings for animals are also the basis for some stories and although not animal stories in the naturalistic sense in that they are more studies of the human protagonists, they are an extension of human-animal relationship stories bordering on being animal fantasies. Philippa Pearce's *A Dog So Small* (1962) is perhaps one of the most widely known. She explains the origins of the story this way:

> ... the story began with a boy who longed to have a dog ... I started knowing him from the inside ... I knew that at the very centre of that boy — at the heart of him — was his longing for a dog. That was my idea for the story, and from that the boy grew, and the story grew round him, because what he wanted and what he was caused the story.
>
> (Pearce 1975: 141)

Ben Blewitt is alone in his family and his parents cannot really communicate with him. This in part explains his obsession with having a dog. When he is finally given a real one, he is disappointed that it is not the tiny dog of his imaginings. But he accepts it and in so doing recognises that he has to live in the real world and that compromise is part of life.

In *A Dream of Seas* (1978), Lilith Norman explains a boy's obsessive wish to join the seals he sees off Bondi Beach in Sydney. The tensions in Seasie's life — his father's death, the move from the country with his mother, the uncertainties that crowd him at his new school, his mother's relationship with Frank — are eased as boy and seal metaphorically become one, and Seasie finds his true self. Norman has based part of the story on her research into seals, and factual sections on the seal's life are interspersed in Seasie's story. Whether boy and seal are convincingly metamorphosed in the novel itself is open to question but Norman presents an interesting interpretation of the relationship between the animal and human worlds.

Another unusual story which deals with an almost mystical bond between an animal and a young person is L.M. Boston's Carnegie Medal winner, *A Stranger at Green Knowe* (1961). In the carefully-structured narrative, Ping's life as a displaced person is echoed in Hanno's early life in the African jungle and his years in captivity in the gorilla compound at the London zoo. When Hanno escapes, Ping helps him enjoy his final days of freedom. Hanno is shot by the man who first captured him, but for Ping, Hanno's freedom has been secured. Ping's freedom is guaranteed not by death but by the offer of a place in the world at Green Knowe.

ANIMAL FANTASY

In contrast with the stories of the animal world which are rooted deeply in reality and are mainly concerned with those in their natural habitats whether they be wild or domestic, are the animal fantasies which have the characteristics of stories in the broader fantasy genre. Not that fantasy and reality are mutually exclusive in children's books: indeed many journeys to a fantasy world, or a secondary reality, are undertaken

> ... not to escape reality but to illuminate it, to transport us to worlds different from the real world, while demonstrating certain immutable truths that persist in any and every possible world, real and imaginary.
>
> (Egoff 1981: 26)

This illumination is very often expressed poetically through images, in a style quite unlike the more straightforward naturalistic one of most stories of the animal world. The animals in some of the animal-child relationship stories such as *A Stranger at Green Knowe* (1960) or *A Dream of Seas* (1978) represent something other than themselves, and in fact link the two kinds of stories: they share the factual detail of the naturalistic ones and at the same time give the reader a glimpse of another world in which animals and people live in a unique unity.

In fantasies, the animals generally function as people and it is the reader's willing suspension of disbelief which ensures that they are accepted as the equal of humans. They are anthropomorphised to a greater degree than those in the more realistic tales but this is an appropriate technique for presenting an holistic view of the world. While the similarities between the animal and human kingdoms is stressed, fantasies very often concentrate on the brighter side of human nature — on the promise and potential of humanity.

Rudyard Kipling's *The Jungle Book* (1894) explores the tension that exists between the animal and human worlds. Mowgli, the boy raised by wolves, vacillates between the jungle and civilisation, learning to comply with, but never wholly accepting, the rules of society. As a wolf cub following the Jungle Law he embodies the spirit of humanity, but as a youth among people he is misplaced, having lost touch with his origins.

The invented myths of the *Just So Stories: for Little Children* by Rudyard Kipling (1902), reflect the kinship between animals and people and look back to a time when these two groups of the world's inhabitants were in fact one. The prose is masterly in its lyricism, particularly in the story of the Elephant's child who acquires his trunk while satisfying his 'satiable curtiosity' in the 'great grey-green greasy Limpopo River'.

Kenneth Grahame's *Wind in the Willows* (1908) also looks to a golden age and recreates a pastoral idyll, a sort of Eden, the almost pantheistic ethos of which is presented through the chapter 'The Piper at the Gates of Dawn'. Underpinning the adventures of the four friends, Mole, Ratty, Toad and Badger is Grahame's keen appreciation of the beauty and bounty of nature. The story of Toad's foray into the wide world of cars and trains provides a salutory lesson. As one commentator puts it, it serves as

> ... a small mirror on the stability of society which wild behaviour puts at risk and which is restored only by loyalty and constancy in the face of danger.
>
> (Sterck 1973: 24)

The friendship, warmth and security embodied in the world of the River Bank, albeit a male one, are enormously appealing to children. Here there are no human characters, but there are some in the wide world, where Toad also encounters machines as forces of destruction and disintegration.

A few humans, in this case children whose innocence is the quality shared with animals, inhabit Narnia, the created world of C.S. Lewis' series of seven books. In the opening of the first book of this rich religious allegory, *The Lion, the Witch and the Wardrobe* (1950), Narnia is suspended in the chill of winter by the White Queen. With the end of her rule the rhythms of nature are restored. Aslan, King of the Beasts and new ruler of Narnia is the superior being but as an affirmation of the new order, a new Eden, humans emerge as another kind of Talking Beast with, as Blount (1973: 305) describes it, a mandate to rule under Aslan.

Charlotte's Web by E.B. White (1952) is a fantasy which endorses the idea that the most fully-realised lives are those that move in accord with nature's patterns and cycles. Through the selflessness of Charlotte the spider, the life of Wilbur the runt pig is saved, and further, he is transformed in character through his friendship with Charlotte. The cycle of birth and death in Charlotte's life is reinforced by the cycle of the seasons in the rural settings of the barnyard and the fairground. Although Wilbur, Charlotte and Templeton, the rat, talk to each other, Charlotte is the only animal with special powers: she can spin words in her web, but more importantly she carries the wisdom of nature and in passing it on to Wilbur, she alerts him to the joy of living.

William Steig's *Amos and Boris* (1971) and *Abel's Island* (1976) are also celebrations of life. Amos, a mouse, rolls overboard from his boat when overwhelmed by the mystery and beauty of the 'vast living universe' (Steig, 1971: np.) but is saved by Boris, a whale. The two become friends but finally separate, Amos to live on land and Boris to live in the sea. Years later, Boris is beached, facing death, and Amos, with the help of two elephants, restores him to the sea. The two friends are aware that though they may never meet again, they will never forget each other. The depth of their friendship characterises the humanisation of these two mammals and the telling of their tale, and links them with the world of human affairs in a way quite unlike Fontaine's fable of two unlikely friends, 'The Lion and the Rat'. In *Abel's Island* (1976), essentially a survival story in a vein similar to some of the naturalistic stories, Abel, an Edwardian mouse, is stranded on an island uninhabited by humans. As in *Amos and Boris* it is the almost complete humanisation of Abel and the animals he meets which underlies the fantasy. Abel develops new skills and artistic talents as well as a renewed sense of self and purpose. A continual thread through the story is his love and yearning for Amanda, his wife. Steig himself presents an interesting comment on the role of animals in his stories.

> I think using animals emphasizes the fact that the story is symbolical about human behaviour. And kids get the idea that this is not just a story, but that it's saying something about life on earth.
>
> (in Higgins 1978: 6)

An animal with special powers is Chester the singing cricket, the hero of George Selden's *Cricket in Times Square* (1960). This is no pastoral idyll or Eden; the River Bank, Narnia and the barnyard are replaced by the New York subway and Chester's friends are an alley cat, Harry and Tucker Mouse. What Chester does have in common with Charlotte, Abel and their ilk is that he responds to the yearnings of his kind and returns to his native fields in Connecticut. Significantly, the boy Mario who finds Chester and for whose family's benefit the cricket sings opera, knows intuitively that Chester has left the city and is pleased that he has done so. Throughout the story the animals observe the life of the Bellini family, although the two groups of characters do not communicate directly with each other.

By contrast, Paddington Bear who makes his début in *A Bear Called Paddington* by Michael Bond (1958) is very much an equal with the other members of the Brown household and is able to converse with humans. His daily life and his behaviour is very child-like, although he himself is in no doubt that he is a bear from darkest Peru. More humanised than most of the animals in fantasy, he is an astute observer of the world around him.

Miss Bianca, a mouse poet, is also a shrewd observer of human affairs, so much so that she uses many familiar customs in her role as President of the Mouse Prisoner's Aid Society, which ironically assists human prisoners. The world outside her mouse environs is an unusual place, with barren wastes, salt mines and the Black Castle. The mouse society functions much like human society, and in *Miss Bianca in the Salt Mines*, Margery Sharp (1966) describes in detail some of its traditions such as the investiture of the order of Tybalt Stars. Like the characters of the *Wind in the Willows*, those in the Miss Bianca stories are recognisably human and cause us to reflect on our world and those truths which are evident in all worlds where humans find themselves.

TALKING ANIMAL STORIES

In addition to the nature stories which focus on the animal world and the fantasies which create other worlds occupied by animal-humans, there is a large group of stories in which the animal characters are neither themselves nor images, but disguises for a particular human foible or even a moral stance. Although these animals are to some degree anthropomorphised, they are not the disguised humans of most of the fantasies. They are recognisable as animals to the extent that, according to Wrightson (1977: 236), anthropormorphism starts with the reality of an animal and then moves beyond to the nature of the subject being explored by the writer. Usually these animals behave as animals except for the fact that they can talk. Some of these stories have their antecedents in the fables of folklore, while others can be traced back to tales of romance. Consequently there are two strains in the modern talking animal stories, the didactic and the fanciful, both of which comment on some aspect of human behaviour but for different purposes. Blount (1974: 58) claims that the animal characters are an acceptable guise for 'plain speaking', and the reader has the choice of accepting what he or she reads at face value or letting it work at a deeper level.

It was with a crusading purpose in mind that Anna Sewell wrote *Black Beauty* (1877). Her diary tells us she wrote it

> ... to induce kindness, sympathy and an understanding treatment of horses
>
> (Thwaites 1963: 192)

Although Black Beauty herself uses the first person narrative in the story, it is set firmly in the human world, one in which animals are in fact servants to people. Sewell assumes that the horses' perspectives on their world are the same as her own and so the reality of the novel is distorted.

In contrast with the English setting of *Black Beauty*, that of *Dot and the Kangaroo* (1899) is the Australian bush. Ethel Pedley, like Anna Sewell, had a clear purpose in her writing: it lay in her concern for the preservation of bush creatures. In this story, Dot is lost while picking bush flowers and is rescued by animals, particularly the Kangaroo whose pouch Dot uses for shelter and transport. It is through Kangaroo that Dot learns of the animals' fear of humans and of the ways of nature. Although she finds security in the bush, and can understand the animals' language, after eating the berries of understanding, Dot remains a girl, and confronts none of the ambiquity which haunts Mowgli. Pedley's novel highlights the noble qualities of the animals and suggests, as does Sewell's, that people have much to learn about themselves and their behaviour from sharing their world with all creatures.

Hugh Lofting, whose Dr Dolittle has the ability to talk to animals, is also concerned with human affairs in his stories. They originated while Lofting was fighting in the trenches of the First World War, observing the role played by horses. Explaining the creation of Dr Dolittle, Lofting is cited as writing:

If we made the animals take the same chances as we did ourselves, why did we not give them similar attention when wounded? ... [It] would necessitate a knowledge of horse language.

(Blishen 1968: 12)

The Story of Doctor Dolittle (1920) is the first in the series of exotic adventures shared by the doctor, Chee-chee the monkey, Polynesia the parrot, Dab-Dab the duck and Pushmi-Pullyu, a creature with a head at each end. In the later books, the Doctor's, or Lofting's, concerns for the future of the world dominate and the tone is overly didactic. The books are criticised today for the moral and racial values expressed but they nevertheless serve as an illustration of the purpose of the modern talking animal tale.

The Mousewife (1951) by Rumer Godden is a carefully-structured parable which comments on the nature of freedom and oppression. Although it has a theme similar to some of the animal world stories, the mouse is humanised, although expressing her feelings in her own mouse terms. She is downtrodden by her life and by her family, especially her husband who asks, 'What more do you want?' She finds the answer through her friendship with a caged dove who tells her about the hills, the corn and the clouds. She eventually frees him and he flies away. Because he has kindled her imagination she develops a new outlook even though her circumstances do not alter. This is also a survival story, not of animals, but of people, and the view of humanity which is presented is a bleaker one than that shown in the animal fantasies.

The rats in Robert O'Brien's *Mrs Frisby and the Rats of NIMH* (1971) a Newbery Medal winner, also echo some aspects of the darker side of human beings. The rats' intelligence can be explained by the injections they were given at NIMH, an experimental laboratory, so they are convincing as animals. Mrs Frisby, the mouse whose home and family are threatened by humans, befriends the rats who help her move house because of the part her late husband played in their escape from the laboratory. The story demonstrates the destructiveness and corruption of human beings and suggests that people are not yet able to live in harmony with animals. The rats reject technology in their desire to adopt a natural way of life, yet their very existence is challenged by the elaborate technology of the unthinking and unfeeling human world.

Watership Down (1972) by Richard Adams, a Carnegie Medal winner, creates an elaborate myth to comment on social and political organisation. Hazel and his flock of rabbits visit two warrens, one decadent, the other ruled by a warlord, and take the best features of each before setting up their own participatory democracy. Firmly steeped in rabbit lore and natural history, the story keeps the rabbits fixed in the animal world. The book is imbued with Adams' love of the countryside and like so many other animal stories, has a strong sense of place, suggesting a pastoral idyll. This novel attempts to merge many elements, some more successfully than others. Hammond (1973: 57) finds the didactism disturbing and argues that much of the information in the story about rabbits is not synthesised in a way that evokes the reader's intuitive response.

The theme of *Song of Pentecost* by W.J. Corbett (1982) is concerned with an allegorical quest for truth rather than with forms of social organisation, although it does deal in part with leadership. The mouse colony, whose leader traditionally bears the title of Pentecost makes its epic journey from a tip near a housing estate to the more rural Lickey Top. The mice are guided by Snake and later by Fox and on their way they meet other animals, each of which reveals particular human follies. The characters, however, maintain their essentially human natures. The song of Pentecost reflects the rebirth and hope of the Spring festival:

> The family sleep
> And though tomorrow they may laugh or weep
> Still life goes on ...
>
> (Corbett 1982: 234)

The pastoral elements are strong and as in *Watership Down*, comment is made on the attitudes and behaviour of humans toward the environment.

Much less serious in tone is Randolph Stow's *Midnite: The Story of a Wild Colonial Boy* (1967) which is an hilarious debunking of the Australian bushranger myth. It is Midnite's gang of animals which entices him into bushranging, and in a reversal of the so-called natural order, Midnite is dependent upon the animals.

Institutions, traditions and customs of Australian society are also satirised in Norman Lindsay's adventure, *The Magic Pudding: Being the Adventures of Bunyip Bluegum and his Friends Bill Barnacle and Sam Sawnoff* (1918). The court scenes, where the pudding thieves are brought to justice, are unforgettably bizarre. Another parody, and again an Australian one, is Tony Edward's *Ralph the Rhino* (1982) which is a spoof on the Victorian adventure tale. The cat TiTi is more clever than the two explorers Ralph and Captain Seaweed and he serves as a foil for the humans' conceit.

Less concerned with human affairs and the differences between the animal and human worlds are those stories which are more romantic in tone. Animal life is zestful and happy, and magic is sometimes a strong possibility in these tales, many of which appear as picture books.

An animal with the power of speech who finds a human he can talk to when holding a certain broomstick is Carbonel, a royal cat (*Carbonel* 1955). Through her adventures with Carbonel, Rosemary learns to ride a broomstick and finds a new friend, John, in what turns out to be an eventful holiday. At the end of Barbara Sleigh's book, the cat is installed as ruler of his kingdom after being released from the power of the disagreeable Mrs Cantrip.

In another fanciful story, the scourge of Keith's mother is Ralph the mouse, the main character in Beverly Cleary's *The Mouse and the Motorcycle* (1965). Ralph enjoys riding Keith's toy motorcycle through the hotel where he is staying with his family. The mouse is more life-like than the boy, and the character development is not so much in Keith, but in him. Ralph is fêted as a hero by his family when he takes risks in getting an aspirin to the ailing Keith. The story highlights the satisfactions as well as the tensions of family life for Ralph, and in this respect is akin to a family story.

The world of animal stories is a richly-textured one. Animals of the earth, the air and the sea have all found their way into children's literature. The focus in some is on the uniqueness of the animal world; in others it is on the unity in the world shared by humans and animals. The characterisation of the animals varies from the least degree of humanisation, as they are observed by writers in their natural habitats, to marked humanisation as they luxuriate in very human surroundings. The functions served by the animals range from protagonist, to symbol, to chronicler of human behaviour. The common link in all this diversity, the one which will confirm the strength of animal stories in children's literature in the future is that

> the good animal story is not only about an animal. It is about a whole environment, the heritage of all young people.
>
> (Fisher 1964: 58)

REFERENCES

Bettelheim, Bruno, *The Uses of Enchantment: the Meaning and Importance of Fairy Tales*. Harmondsworth: Penguin, 1978.

Blishen, Edward, *Hugh Lofting*. London: Bodley Head, 1968.

Blount, Margaret, *Animal Land: the Creatures of Children's Fiction*. London: Hutchinson, 1974.

Bunbury, R.M., Finnis, E.J. and Williams, G., 'Teachers Talk about their Teaching of Fiction: A Preliminary Report of the National Reading Project, Children's Choice' in *English in Australia* No. 64, June 1983, 3–15.

Donelson, Kenneth L. and Nilsen, Alleen Pace, *Literature for Today's Young Adults*. Glenview, Illinois: Scott Foresman, 1980.

Dugan, Michael, compiler, *The Early Dreaming: Australian Children's Authors on Childhood*. Milton, Queensland: Jacaranda Wiley, 1980.

Egoff, Sheila A., *Thursday's Child: Trends and Patterns in Contemporary Children's Literature*. Chicago: American Library Association, 1981.

Elley, W.B. and Tolley, C.W., *Children's Reading Interests: a Wellington Survey*. Wellington: NZCER, 1972.

Fisher, Margery, *Intent upon Reading: A Critical Appraisal of Modern Fiction for Children*. London: Brockhampton Press, 1964.

Hammond, Graham, 'Trouble with Rabbits' in *Children's Literature in Education*, No. 12, September 1973.

Higgins, James E, 'William Steig: Champion for Romance, *Children's Literature in Education* Vol. 9, No. 1, 1978.

Huck, Charlotte S., *Children's Literature in the Elementary School*. New York: Holt, Rinehart and Winston, 1979.
Magee, William H., 'The Animal Story: A Challenge in Technique' in Egoff, Sheila, Stubbs, G.T. and Ashley, L.F., editors, *Only Connect: Readings on Children's Literature*. Toronto: Oxford University Press, 1980.
Moss, Anita, 'The Spear and the Piccolo: Heroic and Pastoral Dimensions of William Steig's *Dominic* and *Abel's Island*' in *Children's Literature*, Vol. 10, 1982.
Norvell, George W., *The Reading Interests of Young People*. Boston: D.C. Heath, 1950.
Pearce, Philippa, 'Writing a Book: *A Dog so Small*' in Blishen, Edward, editor, *The Thorny Paradise: Writers on Writing for Children*. Harmondsworth: Kestrel Books, 1975.
Rayner, Mary, 'Some Thoughts on Animals in Children's Books' in Chambers, Nancy, editor, *The Signal Approach to Children's Books*. Harmondsworth: Kestrel Books, 1980.
Saxby, H.M., *A History of Australian Children's Literature: 1941–1970*. Sydney: Wentworth Books, 1971.
Schlager, Norma, 'Predicting Children's Choices in Literature: A Development Approach' in *Children's Literature in Education* Vol. 9, No. 3, Autumn 1978.
Sterck, Kenneth, 'Rereading *The Wind in the Willows*' in *Children's Literature in Education* No. 12, September 1973.
Stodart, Eleanor, 'Works of Fiction that are of Value in Teaching Biology' in *Reading Time*, No. 83, April 1982.
Sutherland, Zena and Arbuthnot, May Hill, *Children and Books*. Glenview, Illinois: Scott Foresman, 1977.
Thwaite, M.F., *From Primer to Pleasure: An Introduction to the History of Children's Books in England, from the Invention of Printing to 1900*. London: Library Association, 1963.
Whitehead, F., Capey, A.C., Maddren, W. and Wellings, A., *Children and their Books: Schools Council Research Studies*. London: Macmillan, 1977.
Wrightson, Patricia, 'The Nature of Fantasy' in *Readings in Children's Literature: Proceedings of the First National Seminar on Children's Literature*. Frankston, Victoria: Frankston State College, 1977.

BOOK REFERRED TO IN THE CHAPTER

Aalborg, Gordon, *Cat Tracks*. Hyland House.
Aldridge, James, *The Broken Saddle*. Julia MacRae.
Adams, Richard, *Watership Down*. Penguin.
Balderson, Margaret, *A Dog Called George*. Oxford University Press.
───────, *When Jays Fly to Barbmo*. Oxford University Press.
Bond, Michael, *A Bear Called Paddington*. Collins.
Bond, Ruskin, *The Night of the Leopard*. Hamish Hamilton.
Boston, L.M., *Stranger at Green Knowe*. Faber & Faber.
Corbett, W.J., *The Song of Pentecost*. Penguin.
Dalgleish, Joan, *Cats Don't Bark*. Hodder & Stoughton.
───────, *The Latchkey Dog*. Hodder & Stoughton.
Davis, J.A., *Samaki: The Story of an Otter in Africa: A True-to-Life Novel*. Sphere Books.

Davison, Frank Dalby, *Man-shy*. Angus & Robertson.
Edwards, Tony, *Ralph the Rhino*. Wellington Lane.
Fox, Mem, *Possum Magic*. Omnibus Books.
Frewer, Glyn, *Fox*. London: Patrick Hardy Books.
George, Jean Craighead, *Julie of the Wolves*. Hamish Hamilton.
Godden, Rumer, *The Mousewife*. Macmillan.
Grahame, Kenneth, *The Wind in the Willows*. Methuen.
Greenwood, Ted, *Everlasting Circle*. Hutchinson.
Griffiths, Helen, *Blackface Stallion*. Hutchinson.
Kelleher, Victor, *Papio: a Novel of Adventure*. Kestrel Books.
Kipling, Rudyard, *The Jungle Book*. Macmillan.
——————, *Just So Stories: For Little Children*. Macmillan.
La Fontaine, Jean, translated by Kitty Munggeridge, *Fables from La Fontaine, including his Life of Aesop*. Collins.
Lewis, C.S., *The Lion, the Witch and the Wardrobe: a Story for Children*. Bles.
Lindsay, Norman, *The Magic Pudding: Being the Adventures of Bunyip Bluegum and his Friends Bill Barnacle and Sam Sawnoff*. Penguin.
Lobel, Arnold, *Fables*. Jonathan Cape.
Lofting, Hugh, *The Story of Doctor Dolittle*. Jonathan Cape.
London, Jack, *Call of the Wild*. Penguin.
Macarthur-Onslow, Annette, *Uhu*. Ure Smith.
Mattingley, Christobel, *The Battle of the Galah Trees*. Brockhampton.
Mitchell, Elyne, *The Silver Brumby*. Hutchinson.
Neville, Emily, *It's Like This, Cat*. Penguin.
Norman, Lilith, *A Dream of Seas*. Collins.
Oakley, Graham, *Hetty and Harriet*. Macmillan.
O'Brien, Robert C., *Mrs Frisby and the Rats of NIMH*. Penguin.
Patchett, Mary Elwyn, *The Brumby*. Penguin.
Pedley, Ethel, *Dot and the Kangaroo*. Angus & Roberton.
Pearce, Philippa, *A Dog So Small*. Penguin.
Pender, Lydia, *The Useless Donkeys*. Methuen.
Roberts, Charles G.D., *Red Fox*. Penguin.
Selden, George, *The Cricket in Times Square*. Penguin.
Sewell, Anna, *Black Beauty*. Brockhampton.
Sharp, Margery, *Miss Bianca in the Salt Mines*. Heinemann.
Sleigh, Barbara, *Carbonel*. Penguin.
Smith, Vincent, *Musco — Blue Whale*. Harper & Row.
Steig, William, *Abel's Island*. Farrar, Strauss Giroux.
——————, *Amos and Boris*. Hamish Hamilton.
Stow, Randolph, *Midnite: the Story of a Wild Colonial Boy*. Penguin.
Stranger, Joyce, *The Hare at Dark Hollow*. Dent.
Thiele, Colin, *Storm-Boy*. Rigby.
Wagner, Jenny. *Aranea: The Story of a Spider*. Kestrel.
——————, *The Bunyip of Berkeley's Creek*. Longman.
White, E.B., *Charlotte's Web*. Penguin.
Williamson, Henry, *Tarka the Otter: His Joyful Water-life and Death in the Two Rivers*. Penguin.
Wrightson, Patricia, *A Little Fear*. Hutchinson.

15 WINGS OF FACT: NON-FICTION FOR CHILDREN

ELEANOR STODART

> Now, what I want is Facts ... Facts alone are wanted in life.
>
> Charles Dickens

I can still remember the excitement *The Kon-tiki Expedition* (Heyerdahl 1950) gave me when I first read it as a child bordering on my teens, and my sense of involvement in Rachel Henning's letters. I am sure other people can quote similar examples. Yet so great has been the development of children's fiction over the past two decades, and so thorough has been its acceptance as one of the ideal requisites for a child's full development, at least among proponents of children's literature, that the place of non-fiction is often neglected.

There is no substitute in fiction for such mind-expanding adventures as *The Kon-tiki Expedition* or Joshua Slocum's *Sailing Alone Around the World*; or for the artistry in the logical deduction of Isaac Asimov's *Extraterrestrial Civilizations* in which he examines whether there could be other intelligent life in the universe. And yet, as Jo Carr states in *Beyond Fact* (1982: ix) 'we find consistent, if unconscious, denigration of non-fiction for children': most (almost all!) prizes go to fiction; children's literature courses give non-fiction very little attention; teachers and parents rarely read it aloud; and librarians do not check it out by reading it in the way they do fiction.

THE NEED TO KNOW

Young children *want* to 'know'. They incessantly ask 'What is it?' and 'Why?'. I remember my son as a toddler insistently wanting to know how long things were. Educational theorists said that he could have no understanding of measurement at that age and implied that there was no point in telling him, but measurements were 'names' he wanted to know. Later he would build these into his understanding of measurement.

As children get older and reach school age the questions become more 'Why?' than 'What is it?' as they seek to know more than what lies on the surface. This need to know is a great stimulus to reading in the lower primary school, although by the upper primary frustration with the difficulties in obtaining answers to their questions will have caused a few to assume a lack of interest. One difficulty with information books for children who are still mastering the skills of reading is that the child's language ability is less than his or her concept ability, particularly in written language. Books for this age need to put ordinary experience into comprehensible language as well as to introduce further knowledge, and they need to do it in a sufficiently interesting way to grasp a child's attention.

The openings of three nature study books for beginning readers, and those still being read to, show how language can be used to set the scene and to excite the same interest as in a story. Of the very familiar:

> Out in the garden,
> under leaves and in damp corners,
> that is where the snails live,
> waiting,
> curled up in their shells,
> for the dampness after rain,
> or the cool damp night.
>
> (Stodart 1971)

Of the less familiar:
> No enemy found this egg.
> Safely
> in the dark of the burrow it lay
> warmed
> through fifty-three days
> fifty-four nights
> before its shell cracked
> and a chick emerged,
> all in the dark of a burrow.
>
> (Greenwood 1981)

And of the less familiar still:
> Millions and millions of years ago,
> at the time of the dinosaurs,
> strange-looking animals lived in the sea.
>
> (Selsam 1977)

As reading skills develop further some children take off into the realms of fiction. For these there are few non-fiction books that are constructed like a well-told story and so offer the same satisfactions as a work of fiction, so teachers, librarians and parents need to make the most of any they find. It is probably worth presenting these mixed in with fiction before children get into the habit of thinking 'fiction is fun; non-fiction is work'. For other children non-fiction offers the only reading they are prepared to do, perhaps because they have not grown up with the reading of stories at home. Often these are less skilled readers who will not cope well with slabs of text. For them it is most important that non-fiction develops language skills. Unfortunately most of the factual books they open will not. One example of a well-written book to suit this category of reader, with one or two paragraphs of text per page opposite a colour photograph, is *Bonneville Cars* by E. and S.R. Radlauer (1973) about the Bonneville Speedway on Utah's Great Salt Desert.

The books quoted in the opening paragraphs are 'adult' books in that they were written for the general reader rather than for a specifically limited young audience, and as such are of interest in the primary school only for the best of older readers. Their use by good readers must not be forgotten, but the main purpose of this chapter is to look at information books suitable for the whole range of primary school children, that is, books which have been written with this specific audience in mind.

QUALITIES NEEDED IN THE WRITER OF NON-FICTION

Before we turn to the books themselves, let us look at the qualities we can expect in writers of ideal non-fiction:

1. These writers will know their subject well and will present it accurately.
2. They will also know the age group for which they are writing so well that they can select their information and present the essence of the subject in terms understood by the age group addressed. That is, they will be able to see the world with the innocence of childhood while still retaining their wider adult view.
3. They will write simply and clearly, but they will use correct terms as required in such a way as to explain them in context, as for example, by the qualifying phrase that does not interrupt the flow of the text.
4. They will present information as part of ideas and concepts, and they will leave those that they cannot explain simply enough for the required level of thinking to an older age group.
5. They will respect their audience and not 'talk down' or use any misleading manner, such as anthropomorphism.
6. They will sort and select information according to an underlying theme that will give the book shape, and
7. Through it all will shine their involvement and care for the subject.

REALITIES IN THE PUBLISHING OF NON-FICTION

Ideally, publishers and buyers will support such writers of quality but because of preconceived ideas of what form an information book should take, this does not necessarily happen. In practice, publishers often opt for a name that is known professionally for expertise on a subject, whether this person knows children and can write well or not. Such a person often looks at his or her knowledge and puts it down without thinking through which parts are most relevant to a child's point of view. This danger is particularly great where a publisher commissions a series of books on similar subjects by different authors. The standard and approach can vary enormously: the fact that one book may be good does not mean the others are. Each much be evaluated on its own merits.

THE EFFECT OF A RESEARCH BIAS ON NON-FICTION

In recent years emphasis in schools has been on non-fiction for research only, so that much of publishers' best efforts have gone into producing books from which it is relatively easy for all primary school children to dig out facts rather than for them to find inspiring reading and develop the ability to think independently. This emphasis has reinforced the belief that non-fiction is not really for 'reading': these books may not be but others are. Books which fit into this category, those based on an encyclopaedic style of presentation of facts, perhaps expanded with many clear diagrams, have been produced very well by Macdonald Educational. One rather lavish example, *The Book of Music*, edited by Gill Rowley, has over thirty people listed as contributing in some way. The work put into the research and illustrations for such a book means that the subject must have a fairly universal appeal so that it can be sold on a world market.

Other books have exploited the crowded fascination of Richard Scarry's *What People Do All Day* in a more formal educational way. The See Inside series, edited by R.J. Unstead, provides good examples. One can see that such books, although satisfying the child's curiosity when browsing for information, will not have the inspiring effect of a great teacher, as can some outstanding non-fiction writing.

The availability of these encyclopaedic books in some areas has perhaps helped make children shy of (or lazy about) wading through slabs of text for research. They are often supported in this by adult expectations. It is difficult to get some children to read, as distinct from browse through, non-fiction for research, or even just for interest, so we cease to expect them to do so. As a result, good competent writing as found in Rigby's Pageant of Australia series, which includes books with a wide variety of subjects, is underutilised. For all these reasons, recently in Australia we have not seen the same flowering of non-fiction that we have of fiction, although some excellent reference books are being produced. When they do appear they are not often given recognition for their outstanding qualities. This of course makes it hard for the newcomer to the field to find them.

A book with the main aim of enabling a child to reproduce material for a project, with some exceptions will have a different style of writing from one in which that aim has been secondary to allowing the child to absorb material as part of his or her own knowledge.

Books which have this second aim will also have at least one of the following:

1. Storytelling skill
2. Descriptive power
3. Graphic excellence
4. Sharply-defined focus
5. Eloquent style
6. Emotional appeal
7. Grace of language

That is, the best of them will be literature just as much as the best fiction is. Just as most fiction produced is not 'literature' if that word is used to connote quality of writing, neither is most non-fiction, but the best of both are equal in this sense.

APPROACHING THE USE OF NON-FICTION

If children are to use their knowledge as a base on which to build further understanding they must grasp ideas which link the facts, and learn these ideas as their own intuitive discoveries or insights, and not just as more facts. (By intuitive I mean not consciously worked out — that will come later when, and if, their ability to think is fully developed).

However, when facts are presented as part of an idea it is often not easy for a child consciously to sift them out. A primary school child's ability in comprehension exercises is not great, although it will develop with training. Hence the popularity and need for the encyclopaedic types of book that provide nothing but facts and do not attempt to fully educate. In planning and evaluating projects in the primary school the teacher should bear in mind the need for gradual training in the skill of sifting out facts from a block of material. Comprehension exercises can be aimed at helping a child extract separate pieces of information from a work of non-fiction as well as at appreciating the content of a work of fiction.

If we look for example at Don Goodsir's *The Gould League Book of Australian Birds* we find a reference book for young children in which each description is written with a degree of language skill that is not often found in books where pictures of animals are the main feature. Let us look more closely at one sentence — for example, this one about the emu: 'When chased, this well-camouflaged, flightless bird can run as fast as fifty kilometres per hour'. We find that it contains three quite separate pieces of information. As well as the obvious main point of the sentence, the emu's speed, we are told that it is flightless and camouflaged well. Children need practice in picking out points like this. It is partly because they are not picked out neatly that the text is interesting to read.

A book for older children, of ten and above, that is also written with literary skill is *Running Wild* by Eric Rolls (1973). It is both history and nature study. It has an index, but its value lies more in its ideas and feeling for the country, with understanding of the reasons for people's actions than for a gathering of facts, even though the ideas are presented on the solid foundation of the author's knowledge. It tells how and why people introduced a number of animals into Australia, and shows how the result was not exactly what was intended.

Books where human interest is high can have some of the appeal of fiction with the added fascination that 'this really happened'. But biography is a very weakly-developed field of writing for young children. Sometimes an author may take striking events and write about the people involved in them, as Eve Pownall has done in *Elements of Danger* (1976).

It appears, then, that ideally there should be at least two types of non-fiction book for the primary school child — the encyclopaedic type in which facts are presented in an easily recognisable way, and the more subtle kind from which the child can absorb facts and ideas together, ready for later use.

The first kind will include both encyclopaedias and shorter books dealing with one subject in some detail.

It should also be recognised that although educationists may aim to get as many children to read as much quality literature as possible, there will be those whose reading does not get past the exploration of facts, so that the encyclopaedic type of book may be their *only* reading matter. Their eagerness to learn will allow them to read facts, but they will not readily progress to the greyer and more exciting areas of idea (particularly where there may be several possible conflicting ideas) and story. That is their loss, unfortunately: we can lead them only where they will go.

CRITERIA FOR EVALUATING NON-FICTION

Having followed those lines of thought on the uses on non-fiction we come now to look at ways in which we need to evaluate it. As we do so we must not forget those children who will only browse through the encyclopaedic type of presentation.

1. Accuracy

The first and apparently most obvious point is accuracy of information. In an encyclopaedic type of book this is paramount, as it is all that it has to offer; but in some books the ideas expressed, the enthusiasm for the subject, or the thought aroused are far more important than a few small errors of fact. After all, 'fact' is what we believe to be true now and our ideas of the truth of many things change as our knowledge of ourselves and of the universe does. An important part of a broad education is to understand this nature of the flexibility of knowledge, and so some errors of fact can be used to introduce this understanding. They can help a child develop a healthy scepticism towards the written word so that he or she will seek confirmation of information where possible.

How can we determine how accurate a book is? We cannot have broad enough knowledge of all subjects ourselves. We must depend on the reputation of the author or of the publisher, and on reviewers. Unfortunately, even in this most obvious requirement of an information book reviewers are often not as explicit as they might be, perhaps because they are too limited by space or do not have the right background. They, too, depend on the reputations of author and publisher. Also, reviews take time to come out and many books are bought before they appear. What happens when a library already has a book that is in reviews criticised for inaccuracy? Pasting a copy of the review into the front of the book may have the benefit of helping the older child see that not everyone felt they could rely on that book.

2. Style

The style of presentation of the information is one of the most important factors in evaluating information, for that is what makes the book readable or not. There are several inter-related facets to style — clarity; suitability for the age group; grace and fluency of language; and appropriateness of order used: chronological, or by topic in a history or biography.

a. Clarity

Clarity is closely related to suitability for age group, as what may be a clear logical presentation for an eleven-year-old can be confusion to a five-year-old. However, there is a style of clear writing that, because of its simple direct clarity with no 'talking down', can reach a broad age range.

b. Suitability

For the younger child language needs to be simple, but oversimplification of a subject can falsify and mislead. This happens just as readily in history as in science. It is not possible to present any subject in its full complexity, but when selection is made, it must be true to the spirit of the whole subject. Two books that may be compared to illustrate this point are *Watch Out! These Creatures Bite and Sting* by Anne Ferns and *Take Care! Poisonous Australian Animals* by Dr Struan Sutherland, both published in 1983. Both cover the subject of poisonous animals in Australia, the former for upper primary level and above, and the latter for lower primary level and above. *Take Care!* has one of those simple direct presentations that rise above age levels, being simple enough for younger children, but suitable for a quick reference for any age. Both make good reference books but *Take Care!* is a good example of the essence of a subject being distilled to produce a clear book for younger children: in achieving this, the design of the layout is at least as important as what is said and not said in the text. *Watch Out!* can be used as a follow-up book for a child who wants more information.

Two books about the history of Australia also make interesting comparison. Eve Pownall's *Australia From the Beginning* is written in simple language which a child in mid to upper primary school should understand easily. Although it is very readable the large amount of uninterrupted text and the generally bland appearance of the book, which is amply illustrated with black and white line drawings, will not attract a child as readily as the more broken appearance of Don Watson's *The Story of Australia* with its mixture of photographs of actual equipment, and original scenes and drawings. The latter is unfortunately marred, when taken as a whole, by the fragmentary choice of typefaces used in the headings, and the text is more difficult: suitable for upper primary and above. It contains much information, skilfully presented and with concision. A quotation from each about the Depression will serve to show the differences in style of writing:

> But in 1929 Australia, like many other countries, found itself in trouble. Once again Australia was unable to sell its wool and wheat and metals overseas. There was no money to pay for the building works which had employed so many people in the previous years. The Australian government was heavily in debt to Britain.
>
> With no money people stopped buying goods. The factories that made the goods stopped producing so many, or closed down altogether. So more people lost their jobs.
>
> (Watson 1984: 148)
>
> The hard times began for Australia when other countries stopped buying wool, and the other goods we sold brought much lower prices. Countries which had lent money to Australia now wanted it back. That meant less money to carry on business or hire people for Government work on schools, hospitals, roads and bridges. The years of the Great Depression had begun.
>
> (Pownall 1980: 95)

As well as oversimplification we must beware of the use of incorrect terms in an attempt to make a subject understood by younger children. If correct terms are introduced with a formal explanation or a qualifying phrase that does not interrupt the flow of the text they can be readily understood by the reader, who will then benefit by an expanding vocabulary, as long as not too many difficult terms are introduced at once. A glossary is valuable for checking. If a subject does require too many specialist terms it is probably better left to an older age group with a wider vocabulary.

However, anyone who has encountered a young dinosaur enthusiast will know that children can learn a sequence of long words if sufficiently interested. As Jerome Bruner has indicated, our ability to teach a subject to a given age is more limited by our skill at translating ideas for that age level than by the maturity of the children (Bruner 1963: 108). One of the great skills of the non-fiction writer for young children is the ability to present the subject in a form understandable to the child, but so that the psychology, the ways of thinking in that subject, and the facts, are still true to the fullest understanding of it.

c. Language

A skilled use of language is essential for this correct presentation. The use of some terms in a metaphorical sense, such as saying a bee or even a grass plant is 'born', may be permissable for very young children especially if it avoids a long-winded alternative, but the use of 'teacher' for computer programmer, for example, is a retrograde use of language. Evaluation of what is permissable and what is not of course is subjective. One may here use the same criteria that are used in appreciating the use of words in poetry: some help us find a truer understanding and some obscure it.

Even though a good use of language is an essential part of a good non-fiction book, it is one aspect that is often underrated, often not even considered, in reviews. Just as with fiction, part of the function of a non-fiction book is to expand a child's knowledge of language. The broader a person's linguistic understanding, the greater can become their ability to think clearly, for we cannot clearly conceive things we have no language for. We can feel about them, and we must not discount the value of our feelings, but an ability to think can help us know ourselves, our feelings, and the world around us, in a way that is essential in today's crowded world. Particularly since poorer readers often rely on non-fiction for their reading we cannot afford to neglect its role in language development.

We need also to be aware of one major difference in the use of language between fiction and non-fiction. In non-fiction words are often deliberately limited to a single precise meaning, but in fiction an author can play on a double meaning to give greater depth to the phrasing. Primary school children will probably not be conscious of this, but a broad exposure to both types of writing will widen their understanding of the possible scope.

Use of language is but one aspect of style: another is the author's attitude, which of course will affect his or her language use.

d. Approach

The approach to the subject and the order of presentation, also need to be evaluated for effectiveness. In history the most common approach is chronological. In science books it is most commonly one of straightforward explanation based on the author's knowledge of the subject. This may be a mere recitation of facts, a logical development of them, as, for example, along the paths by which people discovered them (see Isaac Asimov's How We Found Out About series), or by the process of logical deduction (see Asimov's *Extraterrestrial Civilizations*). More rarely the approach may be a method of thinking about a subject, as in Millicent Selsam's *A First Look at Monkeys and Apes* (1979). As small children are egocentric, starting from what is familiar to them and expanding to the less familiar is an obvious course, and one that I follow in my own books.

A straightforward exposition may be expanded with explanatory or extensionary discussion. This may be didactic, as happens too often with fashionable topics such as nature conservation at present, or it may allow a reader to reason the conclusion out for him or herself.

One area where it is difficult to avoid an overtly didactic approach is in religion, and Peggy Heeks in *Ways of Knowing* notes that she found in England a lack of books about religions other than Christianity and about religion as a living force today; there was a need, too, for books about personal values and moral issues. The five books that make up the God's Hand in History series by Mary Wilson go part of the way towards filling this gap. Following a chronological order, they introduce religions which have a belief in one god. They retell stories from Old and New Testaments, and about Buddha, Zoroaster, Confucius; they discuss the growth of Christianity and the foundations of Islam; they illustrate the effect on events today of the strong sense of personal and moral values of people such as the Biblical prophets, Socrates, Mohammed, and the Syrian, Alopen, in China. The stories are told with scholarly insight and yet in the simple direct language that children understand and appreciate. While the belief in God and 'God's plan' runs through the books they are not particularly didactic and could even be acceptable to atheists as well-told history.

3. Illustrations and Graphics

As illustrations are usually important in non-fiction their quality as art and as interpretation or illumination of the subject, as well as their accuracy, all need to be evaluated. Graphs, diagrams, maps and charts can all be subjected to these criteria; in looking at their quality as art we are looking more for a sense of design and that kind of simplicity which makes a point obvious, rather than for skill with pen or brush.

Illustrations may be as important as the text, especially for the young child. In fact, when well done they are what sell the books, so that buyers, and consequently publishers, often do not give the text the attention it should have. In books with short texts and generous illustrations, there is a need to guard against words that do not match up to illustrations; in books with a great deal of text, against illustrations that do nothing to enhance the words.

Illustrations have a range of qualities to be evaluated, many similar to those of the text — accuracy, clarity, success in the interpretation of text or extension of it, and then artistic skill. When each is done well the result is illumination — extension — of the text. Ideally the illustrator will have some background to the subject and so will be able to avoid the small errors that can creep in due to ignorance. They will not depict gum trees in Spain in the seventeenth century or a bandicoot with a forward opening pouch, and so on. Clarity can often be obtained more readily with drawings rather than photographs, especially where economy of printing is important. The Practical Puffin series has good examples of the clarity produced by good clear outlines and colour wash. Photographs can add a sense of direct reporting to a science book, and original photographs can be very important in documenting a history or biography. Photographs need to be selected to illustrate what the text actually says rather than something similar. If, for example, it describes the formation of a coral atoll an atoll should be depicted and not a cay, which is a single island and not several around a lagoon. (On the production side an alternative would be to alter the text to fit the available illustration).

The placing of illustrations next to the appropriate text may seem an obviously desirable quality, but surprisingly often it is not achieved. My books, *Alive and Aware* (1978) and *Alive and Active* (1980) show what can be achieved without much difficulty, provided there is sufficient interest in production.

Interpretation can be literal or it can take the subject matter a stage further, as done by Craig Smith in *Rain, Hail and Shine* by Nan Hunt (1984), a picture book that is not strictly non-fiction but is informational. In *Anno's Medieval World* (1980) people's changing idea of their world is illuminated by the illustrations.

Colour is often considered desirable in illustrations, yet black and white drawings can be more informative and decorative particularly where cheap printing is required, for otherwise incorrect colours may be produced.

In many ways non-fiction books require more skills to produce than does fiction. They also require a wider range of skill in evaluation. Not only must we look at the ability to select material, language use and creativity of both author and illustrator, but unfortunate choices of headings, of captions to illustrations, of inadequate time or care taken in indexing or checking proofs, can all ruin a good text. It is important that these aspects are all considered when we evaluate non-fiction for children so that we may steadily work towards an ideal situation where all the non-fiction available to them ranks high for each quality, and where we have books with readily accessible facts, and others to stimulate thought, so that our children may truly fly on the wings of their knowledge and creative ideas.

REFERENCES

Arbuthnot, May Hill and Sutherland, Zena, *Children and Books* Glenview, Illinois: Scott, Foresman, 1972.

Bruner, Jerome, 'On Learning Mathematics' in *On Knowing*. Cambridge, Mass.: Harvard University Press, 1963.

Carr, Jo, compiler, *Beyond Fact: Nonfiction for Children and Young People*. Chicago: American Library Association, 1982.

Fisher, Margery. *Matters of Fact*. Leicester, England: Brockhampton Press, 1972.

Heeks, Peggy, *Ways of Knowing: Information Books for 7—9 Year Olds*. A Signal Book Guide; Lockwood, Gloucestershire: Thimble Press, 1982.

Huck, Charlotte S. and Young Kuhn, Doris, *Children's Literature in the Elementary School*. New York: Holt, Rinehart & Winston. 1968.

BOOKS REFERRED TO IN THE CHAPTER

Anno, Misumasa, *Anno's Medieval World*. Bodley Head.

Asimov, Isaac, How We Found Out About Series. Harlow, Essex: Longman first published as How Did We Find Out About, New York: Walker, 1970—80s (e.g. *Electricity, Black Holes, The Beginning of Life*).

—————, *Extraterrestrial Civilizations*. Crown, Pan.

Ferns, Ann, *Watch Out! These Creatures Bite and Sting*. Lansdowne.

Goodsir, Don, illustrator, Tony Oliver, *The Gould League Book of Australian Birds*. Golden Press.

Greenwood, Ted, *Everlasting Circle*. Hutchinson.

Henning, Rachel. *Letters*. Bulletin Newspaper Co.

Heyerdahl, Thor. *The Kon-tiki Expedition*. George Allen & Unwin.

Hunt, Nan, illustrator, Craig Smith, *Rain, Hail and Shine*. Collins.

Pownall, Eve. *Elements of Danger*. Collins.

—————, illustrator, Walter Cunningham, *Australia from the Beginning*. Collins.

Radlauer, E. and S.R., *Bonneville Cars*. Franklin Watts.

Rolls, Eric., *Running Wild*. Angus & Robertson.

Rowley, Gill, editor, *The Book of Music: A Visual Guide to Musical Appreciation*. Macdonald Educational.

Scarry, Richard, *What Do People Do All Day*. Collins.

Selsam, Millicent. illustrator, John Hamburger, *Sea Monsters of Long Ago*. Four Winds Press.

—————, *A First Look at Monkeys and Apes*. Walker.

Slocum, Joshua. *Sailing Alone Around the World*. Reprint Society.

Stodart, Eleanor, photographer, Ederic Slater, *Snails*. Angus & Robertson.

—————, illustrator, Frank Knight, *Alive and Aware. Alive and Active*. Hodder & Stoughton.

Sutherland, Struhan. *Take Care! Poisonous Australian Animals*. Hyland House.

Wilson, Mary, God's Hand in History Series: Book One: *Pioneers* Blandford; *The Son of God*. Blandford/Grosvenor, *A Mighty Rushing Wind*. Blandford; *Builders and Destroyers*. Blandford; *The Word and the Sword*. Grosvenor.

Watson, Don. *The Story of Australia*. Nelson/McPhee Gribble.

16 INNER REALITY: THE NATURE OF FANTASY

GLENYS SMITH

> Hold fast to dreams
> For if dreams die
> Life is a broken-winged bird
> That cannot fly.
>   Langston Hughes

Fantasy, of all the genres of writing for young readers, offers the greatest challenge and, I would argue, the greatest rewards to its authors and its readers: to authors because it is the most difficult form of literature to create and sustain convincingly; to readers because in its most demanding form it asks for the most complete involvement, the most personal response.

DEFINING FANTASY

Any discussion of fantasy must first wrestle with the task of definition. *The Macquarie Dictionary* offers as its first meaning 'imagination, especially when unrestrained', and continues to include the connotations of 'grotesque', 'caprice or whim', 'hallucination', 'daydream', and the qualities of 'visionary' and 'ingenious'. On its path into the English language through Old French and Latin from the original Greek it carried the meanings of 'idea', 'fancy', 'impression' and 'image'. In a specific psychological sense it is defined as 'an imaginative sequence fulfilling a psychological need'. All of these meanings make it clear that in fantasy we encounter the mind at work in a particularly inventive way; at work with ideas and at work with images. Further, this function of the mind relates directly to psychological needs.

THE PLACE OF FANTASY

What place, then, does fantasy have in the development of the child as a person and as a reader? Children's earliest behaviour is 'adaptive', a direct response to, and practical interaction with, the immediate environment. Later they add to this 'reflective' behaviour, when their curiosity leads them to seek knowledge, not just to adapt, or adapt to, their environment, but for its own sake. These two forms of activity, the 'adaptive' and 'reflective', together form their 'cognitive' behaviour, their way of understanding and making sense of their experience. It requires an act of the imagination for children to construct a coherent picture of their immediate world from the wealth of images which they receive. Commonly children use language as a way of organising their perceptions and building a world of ideas. But words are only one medium children and adults use to order their experience. They continue to see both the real and the imagined world in visual images. Describing his approach to fantasy writing, C.S. Lewis (1969: 218) states that 'images always come first'.

The impulse to imagine, to fantasise, is evident in children from an early age. James Britton (1977: 42) defines children's fantasy as 'the handling of images as play' and sees it as a developmental activity in children which goes beyond the purely cognitive. Play is a voluntary activity which frees children from the need to equate their 'play' images with their experience of reality and by so doing enables them to be in some sense 'more themselves'. Britton sees daydreams, make-believe play and a child's storytelling as play activities, occupying in the child's life a space between the verifiable external world which is shared with others and the inner psychic world which is individual to each child.

In that 'third world' which children's play inhabits, the literature of fantasy with its strong sense of play keeps alive children's sense of wonder and reinforces for them the inner truth of the seemingly irrational but compelling and keenly-sensed world of their imagining. Before the age of about seven, children have difficulty in internalising literary fantasy. Red Riding Hood, for example, couldn't be visited 'because I don't know where she lives'. Before five, too, children have difficulty in identifying the shifts from reality to fantasy in stories. By age seven most children can do this as well as respond to such causal questions as 'Why did Max in *Where the Wild Things Are* return home in his dream?'

Conscious attempts to anchor children in reality by depriving them of the literature of fantasy have been singularly unsuccessful. Chukovsky (1963: 118–20) gives evidence that the impulse to fantasise or 'story' is an integral part of the child's development. Children use their imagination not only to escape from, but to escape to, often finding a greater reality when the *Bridge to Terebithia* (Paterson 1978) has been crossed than is to be found on the everyday side of the stream.

'Escapism' is a charge that has been levelled against fairytales and fantasy with the intention of discrediting both as literary experiences for children. It is an accusation which C.S. Lewis (1969: 214–5) refutes most positively from his own experience.

> It [fantasy] is accused of giving a false impression of the world they live in. But I think no literature that children could read gives them less of a false impression ... I never expected the world to be like the fairy tales. I think that I did expect school to be like the school stories. The fantasies did not deceive me: the school stories did. ... Fairyland arouses a longing for he knows not what. It stirs and troubles him (to

his lifelong enrichment) with the dim sense of something beyond his reach and, far from dulling or emptying the actual world, gives it a new dimension of depth. He does not despise real woods because he has read of enchanted woods: the reading makes all real woods a little enchanted.

THE BOUNDARIES OF FANTASY

There has been much debate in the field of children's literature about what fantasy does and does not include. The boundaries can be drawn to encompass only 'high' fantasy of serious purpose, or widened to embrace science fiction and the lighthearted animal and adventure tales which have fantastic elements. I propose to include in the books discussed both the serious and lighthearted forms of fantasy. The line between fantasy and science fiction is a debatable one, difficult to draw. In those books which I have included, the literary emphasis has been placed on character and ideas rather than on technology. This is not to deny either the popularity or imaginative value of other science fiction but rather to recognise it as a genre with a history, attributes and laws which make it worthy of a separate study.

THE IMPULSE TO FANTASY

1. Early British Fantasies

In the history of children's literature in English the impulse to write fantasy appears to have come in waves. The first cluster of books appeared in the mid-nineteenth century, then successively at the turn of the century, the 1920s and 1930s, and the 1950s and 1960s. The impulse to fantasy came from traditional literature: from myth, legend, folk and fairy tales, epics and medieval romance. After a period of disfavour and neglect, there was a revival of interest in these traditional forms of literature in the mid-nineteenth century.

Hans Christian Andersen, whose original fairy tales were first translated into English in 1846, paved the way for a renewed interest in such tales in Britain where Ruskin had published *The King of the Golden River* in 1841, and Thackeray's *The Rose and the Ring*, the first 'funny' fairytale, appeared in 1855. Quite different in nature were Lewis Carroll's 'dream' fantasy *Alice in Wonderland* (1865) and Kingsley's *The Water Babies* (1863), a tale of redemption.

Significantly, as a testimony to the durability of good fantasy, all these early British fantasies remain in print but, of them all, *Alice in Wonderland* has been the most successful. The framework of its fantasy, the device which allowed characters to move between the real and the unreal world by passing through a hole, or in the case of *Alice Through the Looking Glass*, through a mirror, has fascinated fantasy writers ever since, reappearing as entry through pictures, doors, wardrobes, burial mounds and numerous other apertures.

Thackeray's idea of the Fairy Court clearly influenced George MacDonald's *The Light Princess* (1864). But this is not one of the three books which are remembered as his main contribution to fantasy. The first was the highly original *At the Back of the North Wind* (1871). As a child reader I recall that exhilarating first experience of imaginatively riding the wind, an experience which Australian children may locally encounter when reading of Wirrun's journey with the Mimi over a very different landscape in Patricia Wrightson's *The Ice is Coming*. MacDonald's imaginative power was demonstrated even more successfully in *The Princess and the Goblin* (1871) and *The Princess and Curdie* (1877). The Italian classic *Pinocchio*, translated into English in 1892, provided a model for later fantasies about animated toys.

2. Twentieth Century Fantasy

Rudyard Kipling, with the *Jungle Books* and the *Just So Stories* (1894–5), Kenneth Grahame with *The Reluctant Dragon* (1899) and Edith Nesbit with *Five Children and It* (1902) carried fantasy into the twentieth century in England, while across the Atlantic L. Frank Baum wrote the first great American fantasy in *The Wizard of Oz* (1899). At the same time two durable imaginative books for young children appeared in *The Tale of Peter Rabbit* (Potter 1901) and Helen Bannerman's *Little Black Sambo* (1898), now out of favour because it is felt to be racist, but long beloved by children for its humour and all those pancakes!

All of these turn-of-the-century books were more robust contributions to the development of children's fantasy than the next landmark, J.M. Barrie's play *Peter Pan* (1904) and its novel form *Peter Pan and Wendy*. Most memorable were its villains, Captain Hook and the crocodile. Immensely popular for several decades, it spawned numerous less inventive imitations which copied its whimsical, self-conscious and condescending tone. Even C.S. Lewis is not entirely free from it in his asides to the reader, though his heroes and heroines are made of much sterner stuff and their fantasy world has a demanding reality unlike the Never-Never Land in which Peter escapes the demands of growing up. As Hugh Crago (1972: 49) explains:

> Literary history is as much about bad books as about good ones: the good books create the fashions, the conventions, the trends — but the indifferent books embody those conventions and, as often as not, transmit them to a much wider public.

By contrast, Kenneth Grahame's *Wind in the Willows* (1908) with its humour, its evocation of the countryside with its beauty and its terror made its animal characters much more real than Barrie's Tinkerbell and nursery dwellers.

3. Early Australian Fantasy

In Australia the first fantasies in the 1870s were anaemic fairy stories or pallid imitations of *Alice in Wonderland*. *Dot and the Kangaroo* (1899) by Ethel Pedley was the earliest successful attempt to incorporate native Australian animals into a logical fantasy framework. In 1918 Angus & Robertson published Norman Lindsay's *The Magic Pudding*. This joyous, earthy, hearty and highly original book is as outstanding in Australian children's literature as was *Alice in Wonderland* in that of England. The illustrations of this artist/author form an integral part of the story and with its humour, its inventiveness, its rollicking verse and lively characterisation it is the most widely known and best loved of Australia's fantasies. It is significant, too, that *The Magic Pudding*, like *Alice in Wonderland*, the *Just So Stories*, *The Rose and the Ring* and *The Tale of Peter Rabbit*, is an example of a person skilled and known in a different field of endeavour, writing a distinguished children's book which is, by their choice, a fantasy. Also published in 1918, May Gibbs' *Snugglepot and Cuddlepie* is a battle for good and evil in which the flora and fauna of Australia are accurately observed. It remains a survivor in Australian children's literature with Dorothy Wall's *Blinky Bill* (1933) and the strikingly-illustrated *Way of the Whirlwind* (1941), an Aboriginal fantasy by Mary and Elizabeth Durack.

4. Post-First-World-War Fantasy

Between 1920 and 1930 in a new wave of fantasy writing in England, most outstanding were Hugh Lofting's twelve tales, beginning with *The Story of Doctor Dolittle* (1920), A.A. Milne's *Winnie-the-Pooh* (1926) and its sequel *The House at Pooh Corner* (1928). Doctor Dolittle has suffered in popularity from the fact that it reflected the insensitive attitude of its day to races of a different colour, but the endearingly simple, animated nursery toys of A.A. Milne continue to be enjoyed, not least because of the superior craftsmanship of their author.

The imagination of John Masefield took a much more virile turn in *The Midnight Folk* (1927) and *The Box of Delights*. Created Poet Laureate in 1930, Masefield wrote in these two works for children stories which are richly adventurous and ingenious in their invention of incident and character as well as their manipulation of the fantasy framework. I find in them a strong parallel with Joan Aiken's work from *Nightbirds on Nantucket* onwards.

Undoubtedly the most remarkable fantasy of this wave of writing was J.R.R. Tolkien's *The Hobbit* (1930). An authority on Anglo-Saxon and Norse sagas, Tolkien later completed his own saga, *The Lord of the Rings*, an extension of *The Hobbit* and a quest for the Rings of Power. These books remain the most widely read and known fantasies of the twentieth century. Further, they seem to have gathered adherents as they have grown older. In comparison with this totally conceived 'other' world, Mary Poppins (Travers 1934), *My Friend Mr Leakey* (Haldane 1937) and *The Ship that Flew* (Hilda Lewis 1939) now seem rather dated by their domestic detail.

Tolkien's books appeal to a very wide age range. Their only challenge in popularity with children has come from the American farmyard tale *Charlotte's Web* (1952) by E.H. White, and C.S. Lewis' allegorical Narnia series, beginning with *The Lion, the Witch and the Wardrobe* (1950). These two writers lead us into the realm of contemporary children's fantasy which has continued to attract outstanding children's writers in the last three decades. Their creations range in subject and scope from the purely domestic to the intergalactical, but few would deny the shaping influence in the genre of their nineteenth and early twentieth century forerunners.

In this increasingly sceptical age, in which the relevance of even the old magic of myth and fairy tale is challenged, what place is there for the conscious literary creation which draws on the wellsprings of culture to present a personal vision? Has modern technology made fantasy irrelevant? I think not. I believe as passionately as does Patricia Wrightson (1977: 222):

> Fantasy *isn't* a dead study — *can't* be outgrown and discarded: not by the individual nor by the race. How should it be, when fantasy is an ongoing part of our common human experience? We all dream.

'Dream' is at the heart of one of the most satisfying and endurable of fantasies, *Tom's Midnight Garden* by the English writer, Philippa Pearce. Tom visits his aunt and uncle in what was once a 'grand' old English house and finds himself living in both the past and the present. His experience is unusual in that only the young girl, Hatty, can see and communicate with him in the past. His contacts with her start in the midnight garden which Tom enters when the old hall clock strikes thirteen. On the clock's face is the motto 'Time No More', and indeed the natural laws of time *are* defied. For while Tom stays the same age, Hatty grows up and marries in the space of a few weeks in Tom's present. It is only as he is leaving to return home, that Tom and the reader meet and recognise in the strange old lady upstairs the Hatty of his midnight adventures. She has been weaving the young Tom into her dreams of her youth in the house's heyday.

It is not only the permeating sense of mystery which captures and holds the reader's interest in this fantasy. Careful craftsmanship makes each step of the fantastic adventure believable; the characters of the two lonely children, Tom and Hatty, are appealing and memorable and their meetings have a freshness and charm made all the more poignant as they grow apart in age. The late-Victorian garden with its paths, trees and flowerbeds is fragrantly and visually recreated. The transition from present to past and the reverse is convincingly handled. Outwardly different, the two worlds Tom inhabits share the same fundamental heartbreaks, joys and anxieties. As a piece of writing it satisfies the imagination, the mind and the senses. It has an inner reality.

John Rowe Townsend names this book not just as an example of the best of fantasy writing, but as his chosen 'masterpiece' of English children's literature written in the thirty years between 1945 and 1975. Again, it is a work of fantasy which demonstrates the durability of children's literature, and prompts us to ask what it is about fantasy that attracts outstanding children's writers.

THE FUNCTION OF FANTASY

What is the special function of fantasy, and how is the reader's belief in it created and sustained? Fantasy's main function, like that of fairytales, is to express imaginative experiences or insights into the human condition by images or ideas or possibilities which remain essentially true to what we know about life and good and evil; observations about the human condition without preaching. Fantasy takes for granted the existence not only of the physical world you can see and touch, the world of reality, but also the supernatural — the imaginative possibility of travelling to *Where the Wild Things Are* (Sendak) or sharing your attic bedroom with *The Ghost of Thomas Kempe* (Lively) or making contact with beings from other worlds who have fallen through some *Forgotten Door* (Key); or even of waking up some *Freaky Friday* (Rodgers) as your own mother, or finding you are only *Charlotte Sometimes* (Farmer).

REALISM AND FANTASY

There are endless possible combinations of realism and fantasy, but most fall into one of two basic groups: either real people in fantastic situations or fantastic characters in real situations. Either way books of fantasy all contain imaginary elements that are contrary to life as we know it. How clear is the boundary between the real and the fantastic? The boundaries keep crumbling. Everyday things happen which would have seemed purely imaginary the day before: recorded signals of animals' communication with man, exploration of the ocean depths, moon visits, interplanetary trips — all these have crossed the boundaries from the fantastic to the real. But where does the real stop and the fantastic begin? Even that very real alarm clock inside the crocodile in *Peter Pan* (Barrie), ticking audibly inside and continuing to tick *unwound* until almost the end of the book may now in this electronic age have crossed the boundary from the fantastic to the real. Some new imaginative leaps will have to be taken to make time stand still. This surely, has always been one of the functions of fantasy — its creative power. By keeping alive a sense of wonder, by adumbrating the impossible, it has often pointed the way for Reason and Science to follow. As Tolkien (1964: 50) says:

> Fantasy is a natural human activity. It certainly does not destroy or
> even insult Reason; and it does not either blunt the appetite for,
> nor obscure the perception of, scientific verity. On the contrary, the
> keener and the clearer is the reason, the better fantasy will make it.
> ... For creative fantasy is founded upon the hard recognition that
> things are so in the world as it appears under the sun; on a recognition
> of fact, but not a slavery to it.

The mid-air tea party in *Mary Poppins* (Travers) is surely no less credible than television's pictures of the weightlessness of astronauts in space, nor is the evident fun and enjoyment of the situation by the characters involved very different. Where the boundary between the real and the fantastic is drawn depends on the vision of the observer and on the reader who is travelling progressively further away from the centre of real experience. It is not so much a question of the reader's credulity as of what Coleridge defined as 'a willing suspension of disbelief which constitutes poetic faith'. Some readers are reluctant to cross the boundary at all. Yet the real world is full of fantastic events and combinations. If you can cross the Atlantic Ocean in a rowboat, why not go to sea in a bowl, as did the three wise men of Gotham? Would that be more fantastic? The real world is full of possibilities — of giant pies (Cresswell's *The Piemakers*) — or giant pizzas, of perils such as underground caves and tunnels (Gee's *Under the Mountain*) — and not all of them are published every day. Some no less and no more fantastic happenings have not yet been reported — so far they have happened only in fantasy.

Lillian Smith in *The Unreluctant Years* suggests that a child's imagination *is* at times his real world. There is for the child no abyss between the real and the unreal. He or she moves from one to the other as from one window to another. The adventures of a beloved toy such as Winnie-the-Pooh or the imagined pet as in *A Dog So Small* (Pearce) and *Lion in the Meadow* (Mahy) are as real for some children as their own siblings.

Patricia Wrightson (1977: 229) writes of fantasy as 'man thinking: thinking about reality but beyond the known facts'. The writer of fantasy extends reality in a variety of ways, sometimes in several different ways within one book.

THE FORM OF FANTASY

1. Fantasy Worlds

One extension is the creation of new worlds beyond the known; and this is the province of the science fiction writer as well as the writer of fantasy. But in fantasy the universality of the characters is more important than the strangeness of new technology.

In some books, such as *The Lion, the Witch and the Wardrobe* (Lewis), *Elidor* (Garner), *A Game of Dark* (Mayne) and *The Midnight Folk* (Masefield), the fantasy world is entered and returned from. In others, visitors from the fantasy world intrude into the real one, coming *Down to Earth* (Wrightson) or suddenly appearing from nowhere like *The Iron Man* (Hughes). In *A Wrinkle in Time* (L'Engle) the traffic is two-way. The real world is visited by strangers and a new world journeyed to as well. Less commonly the metaphysical world is imposed on the everyday world — side by side as it were — but only the chosen or special (usually children) can apprehend it, as in *Grinny* (Fisk), *The Night Watchmen* (Cresswell), *The Flame Takers* (Norman) or the 1980 Australian Children's Book of the Year *Displaced Person* (Harding). For the writer the central problem is often how to effect with credibility the transference from one world to the other; from the real or primary world to the fantastic or secondary world when both overlap.

When a complete new world is created without reference to the real world the problem becomes not one of transfer but of mapping the new territory in such a way that it becomes a believable country of the mind, as in *The Hobbit* and *The Lord of the Rings* (Tolkien), *A Wizard of Earthsea* (Le Guin), *Finn Family Moomintroll* (Jansson), *Fungus the Bogeyman* (Briggs), *The Luck of Brin's Five* (Wilder) or *The Ennead* (Mark).

Some fantasies which impress most by the wholeness of their imaginings belong here. New landscapes, new beings, new social frameworks, new codes of ethics, new powers — all ask the reader to look and compare what he sees with the real world in which he lives. To follow the story, often through a sequence, as in the Prydain novels (Alexander) or McKillip's *Riddlemaster of Hed* or Ursula Le Guin's Earthsea trilogies, the reader needs to grow with the protagonist in understanding; but when the writing is distinguished the rewards are commensurate with the effort involved.

2. Beings of Other Dimensions

Less all-embracing are fantasies which introduce beings of other dimensions like *The Borrowers* (Norton), *Flat Stanley* (Brown), or *Mistress Masham's Repose* (T.H. White); or which animate or personify toys, statues or the landscape. Magic is often used for humorous effect in such stories for younger children; but this way of extending reality can also be the vehicle for the exploration of human strengths and weaknesses as in *Pinocchio* (Collodi), *The Mouse and His Child* (Hoban), *The Stonewalkers* (Alcock) and *The Dark Bright Water* (Wrightson).

3. Breaking the Tyranny of Time

Fantasy can also break the tyranny of time, defy physical laws and manipulate time and space patterns. The 'intimations of immortality' most humans experience at some time in their lives can find an echo in *The Owl Service* or *Red Shift* (Garner); or in *Charlotte Sometimes* (Farmer). The past may project a character into the present as in *Earthfasts* (Mayne), *Stig of the Dump* (King) or *The Devil on the Road* (Westall); and the reverse can also be true for *A Traveller in Time* (Uttley). When the time-shift vehicle is whimsical, as in *A Castle of Bone* (Farmer) and *The Phoenix and the Carpet* (Nesbit), the unpredictable results can range from the humorous to the near-tragic.

4. Bounds Between Humans and Animals Disappear

When the bounds between humans and animals disappear a window is opened into the animal world. For many children *Charlotte's Web* (E.B. White) has been this window, while *Wind in the Willows* (Grahame) and *Watership Down* (Adams) prove that adults as well as children are susceptible to its charm. Even for the young it can carry an Orwellian message as in *The Voyage of QV 66* (Lively) or an intimation of where scientific experiments on animals may lead, as in *Mrs Frisby and the Rats of NIMH* (O'Brien).

5. Characters are Accorded Unusual Powers

Often in fantasy characters are accorded unusual powers which enable them to exercise a more-than-realistic control over their environment and so shape events. These can be powers of perception or understanding as in *The Gift* (Dickinson); powers derived from virtue or innocence as in *The Grass Rope* (Mayne) or *Greenwitch* (Cooper); special or inherited powers as in *The Weathermonger* (Dickinson) or *The Penny Tin Whistler* (Fair); or powers which derive from some magic token as in *The Story of the Amulet* (Nesbit), *The Hobbit* (Tolkien), *The Ice is Coming* (Wrightson), *The Apple Stone* (Gray). In the lighthearted fantasies for younger readers the magic often resides in the extravagant characters of such denizens of the nursery as *Nurse Matilda* (Brand) and *Mary Poppins* (Travers), or in such indefatigable and irreducible comestibles as *The Magic Pudding* (Lindsay), or the irrepressible *Pipi Longstocking* (Lindgren).

But irrespective of what form fantasy takes or what devices are used, the quality of a book of fantasy lies in the creative imagination of the writer and the personal expression of this. Both Lewis Carroll in *Alice in Wonderland* and George MacDonald in *At the Back of the North Wind* use the device of a dream within which the fantasy takes place, but the result is different because each imagined the fantasy world very differently.

THE SCOPE OF FANTASY

The subject matter of fantasy is as diverse as the forms chosen for achieving the shift from reality. Keeping close to fantasy's roots in traditional literature some writers have rewritten or extended the old fairy tales and legends. Tony Scott has humorously and controversially updated such classics as *Little Red Riding Hood*. Wildsmith updates the Noah story in *Professor Noah's Space Ship*. Delia Huddy and Victor Kelleher give a completely new twist to an old tale in *The Time Piper* and *The Green Piper*. Recently Robin McKinley, an American author, has written a powerful retelling of *Beauty and the Beast*. In *The Land of Green Ginger* Noel Langley hilariously continues the adventures of Aladdin with the addition of an assortment of improbable characters. In *The Sword in the Stone*, T.H. White relives the Arthurian legend delineating the magic powers of Merlin. One of the most delightful collections for young children is Joan Aiken's *A Necklace or Raindrops*, while *The Golden Bird* by Edith Brill is an extended modern fairy tale. Oscar Wilde's *The Happy Prince* has demonstrated its appeal to several generations of children. Michael Foreman, in his picture book *All the King's Horses*, and Jay Williams in *The Practical Princess* have lightheartedly sought to rescue fairy tale maidens from their subservient roles.

1. The Quest

One of the most persistent subjects in children's fantasy writing, and one which has attracted some of the most distinguished writers in this genre, has been the quest or epic journey, to either find the protagonist's true identity or to control some source of power which will allow the forces of Good to triumph over Evil. Tolkien, Susan Cooper in the sequence beginning with *The Dark is Rising*, Ursula Le Guin in the Earthsea trilogy, Lloyd Alexander in the Prydain novels beginning with *The Book of Three*, Kelleher in *The Master of the Grove*, McKillip in *The Riddlemaster of Hed* trilogy and Corbett in the refreshingly original *The Song of Pentecost* have all contributed in this subject area.

2. Word Play

A good deal of the enduring charm of *Alice in Wonderland* comes from Lewis Carroll's delight in word play, a feature also of Milne's *Winnie-the-Pooh* books. In *The Phantom Tollbooth* Norton Juster creates the city of Dictionopolis, and a land of words. Just one word's meaning prompts *The Search for Delicious* (Babbitt). Both Joan Aiken and Margaret Mahy bring a bubbling delight in word play to their fantasies such as *The Wolves of Willoughby Chase* (Aiken), and *The Great Piratical Rumbustification* and *Raging Robots and Unruly Uncles* (Mahy). Lilith Norman's very Australian *My Simple Little Brother* has the same kind of problems as *Amelia Bedelia* (Parish), because he interprets words literally. All of these and many other fantasy writers have successfully recognised what Beatrix Potter's 'soporific' rabbit demonstrated in 1902 — children's delight in the magic of words, both in their sound and in the many ways in which their flexible meanings can be juggled. Their response to Roald Dahl's *The BFG* confirms this.

3. The Supernatural

The world of the occult with its witches and wizards, ghosts and hauntings, has been a fertile source for fantasy writers and a controversial one. The results of their efforts range from lighthearted entertainments for young children such as *Half Magic* (Eager) and *Which Witch?* (Ibbotson) to the malevolent and terrifying intrusions of powerful forces into the real world. Should young readers be spared what Patricia Wrightson (1977: 223) describes as 'the dark edge of vision'? It is an area which certainly seems to have a continuing fascination and attraction for young readers.

It is worth recalling in this context Tolkien's comments on Fantasy, by which he meant fantasy in its serious and most creative form:

> Fantasy, of course, starts out with an advantage: arresting strangeness. But that advantage has been turned against it, and has contributed to its disrepute. Many people dislike being 'arrested'. They dislike any meddling with the Primary World or such small glimpses of it as are familiar to them.
>
> (1964: 44–5)

Tolkien is careful to distinguish between 'true' fantasy, which is difficult to achieve, and the frivolous, half-serious, 'fanciful' writing for children, a category into which many 'magic' tales fall. C.S. Lewis distinguishes between 'phobias' or pathological fears the child may have and 'the knowledge that he is born into a world of death, violence, wounds, adventure, heroism and cowardice, good and evil . . . and the atomic bomb' a world which he needs to know about. In his experience the child wants 'to be a little frightened'. It is not surprising to find English writers of fantasy in their land of old houses and haunted castles showing an interest in ghosts, from Dickens' *A Christmas Carol* onwards. *The Ghost of Thomas Kempe* (Lively) is a disruptive nuisance, capable of spite but not real malevolence, but the spirits of *The Ghost Downstairs* (Garfield) and *The Scarecrows* (Westall) are more disturbing apparitions. Few modern fantasies are more powerful than *The Haunting* by New Zealand author, Margaret Mahy.

RECENT AUSTRALIAN FANTASY

Since *The Magic Pudding* the realistic novel has been the province of most Australian writers for children. But there have been some notable exceptions, though success in this genre has been comparatively late in coming and difficult to achieve for Australian authors. S.A. Wakefield's *Bottersnikes and Gumbles* peoples the Australian bush with ridiculously amusing creatures. Ted Greenwood realistically captured childhood fears in pictures in Southall's *Sly Old Wardrobe*. Striking illustrations accompany Thomas Keneally's

Ned Kelly and the City of the Bees. Cherry Wilder presents a fascinating new world in *The Luck of Brin's Five*. Magic powers are a female inheritance in Susan Stanton's *The Rise of the Morpeths*. Joan Phipson writes convincingly in *The Way Home* and in *The Watcher in the Garden*, a skilful exploration of relationships between two adolescents and an old man, involving thought transference. *Mindwave* by Mary White also explores telepathic communication. Victor Kelleher writes 'high' fantasy in the quest tradition in *The Master of the Grove* and *Forbidden Paths of Thual*. Old Japan is the setting for Ruth Manley's *Plum-Rain Scroll* and its sequel. Lee Harding's *Displaced Person* inhabits an awful world of alienation and withdrawal. Both Lilith Norman's very different fantasies are set in Sydney, *The Flame Takers* in the parks and tunnels of the centre of the city and *A Dream of Seas*, with its echoes of the Scots seal legends, in Bondi, full of the light and water of the seaside. In Sydney, too, Patricia Wrightson sets her early fantasies, *Down to Earth* and *An Older Kind of Magic*. For *The Nargun and the Stars* and the Wirrun trilogy, beginning with *The Ice is Coming* the setting moves to the Australian countryside in which the spirits of Aboriginal folklore and the hero contend in distinctive and distinguished Australian fantasy. The picturebook *The Bunyip of Berkeley's Creek* by Jenny Wagner is just as uniquely Australian as *Midnite* by Randolph Stow. Early Sydney is vividly recreated in Ruth Park's time-slip fantasy *Playing Beatie Bow*.

FANTASY AND SCIENCE FICTION

On the borders of fantasy and science fiction are those books which concern themselves with visions of society; past or future glimpses of what may be in store for the inhabitants of Earth or new extra-terrestrial worlds. Their concerns are personal freedom or its absence, the structures of government and society and the future effects of such human follies as nuclear war. These can be as simply devastating as Raymond Briggs' picturebook *When the Wind Blows*, as personal a dilemma as that which the girl survivor faces in *Z for Zaccharia* (O'Brien) or the chilling prospect in *The Wrinkle in Time* (l'Engle) of a totally controlled world whose icy grasp only love can melt. Whole societies come under scrutiny in Jan Mark's *The Ennead*, Wilder's *The Luck of Brin's Five* and Engdahl's *Heritage of the Star*. In Peter Dickinson's Changes triology, beginning with *The Weathermongers*, England's inhabitants have turned their backs on modern technology and reverted to a feudal world not unlike that in which Jan Mark's Viner travels between the extremes of flood and drought in *Aquarius*. Escape to *The White Mountains* in Europe is the only recourse for those seeking to avoid being programmed for life, in John Christopher's new England. In these and other challenging books fantasy writers are thinking about reality but beyond the present; asking readers to stretch their imaginations to contemplate where the world is going and what their role in it may be.

ASSESSING FANTASY

Whatever the subject of fantasy — and only some of its many subjects have been suggested here — its quality lies in the consistent integration of the original idea with the events that take place in it. Whether it be the simple magic of a talking cat like *Carbonel* (Sleigh) or the complex world of Middle Earth, the elements must obey the unwritten laws of consistency if they are to be believed. The world must be all of a piece, and 'what appears gossamer is, underneath, solid as prestressed concrete' (Alexander). This may be achieved by convincing detail, as in Mary Norton's *The Borrowers*, or by the naturalness with which the characters accept their new surroundings, or by the completeness of the imagined new world, unattractive as it may be, in *Fungus the Bogeyman* (Briggs). Once the fantasy has been established, its characters and events must observe the rules of that fantasy environment whether of language, behaviour or science.

THE DEMANDS OF FANTASY

What special demands does fantasy make upon its young readers? Only that they be willing to encounter the supernatural and receive the book as a whole. For the younger child this is often made easy by humour. In fantasy a child sees his dreams come true: of flying in *Fly by Night* (Jarrell); of moving through water as though belonging to that element in *A Dream of Seas* (Norman) and *The Sword in the Stone* (T.H. White); of growing larger and smaller with Alice or *The Shrinking of Treehorn* (Heide); of becoming invisible like *The Hobbit*; or having power over others like Max in *Where the Wild Things Are* or Ged in *A Wizard of Earthsea*, with the responsibility for using it wisely.

THE GIFTS OF FANTASY

What gifts does fantasy offer the believer? With its origins in mythology and folklore it explains the inexplicable. It takes objects and scenes and reshapes them, bringing magic and the irrational into our world. It also asks readers to look at their own world with fresh vision, clearing away the cobwebs of familiarity. What lies behind the familiar domestic scene can be sinister or benign. Terror belongs to fantasy as much as wonder and beauty. 'Whatever moves at the dark edges of vision' (Wrightson 1977: 223) — that too is fantasy. Even the simplest fantasy may have a liberating effect because as in *The Owl Who Was Afraid of the Dark* (Tomlinson), *The Sea-Thing Child* (Hoban), *Clever Polly and the Stupid Wolf* (Storr) or

The Wolves of Willoughby Chase (Aiken) it brings into the open some deep-seated childhood fear.

HIGH FANTASY

When fantasy becomes the battleground of Good and Evil, as it does in the novels of such writers as Lloyd Alexander, Susan Cooper, Alan Garner, Ursula Le Guin, C.S. Lewis, J.R.R. Tolkien and Robert Westall; we call it high fantasy — a developed poetic art form which gives meaning to life, enhancing the primary or real world, leading to the solution of problems and the development of characters to maturity. Lillian Smith describes the Narnia books as:

> carrying the reader exuberantly through strange and wild adventures that, half-consciously they come to recognise are those of a spiritual journey toward the heart of reality ... Above and beyond the events of the story itself there is something to which the young can lay hold; belief in the essential truth of their own imaginings.
>
> (1969: 174-5)

What is it that has made *The Hobbit* and *The Lord of the Rings* the best-selling paperbacks that they are? In our troubled times, it has been suggested, children and adults need Tolkien's gutsy fictional dragons more than ever they did to harden the heart 'though the body be soft'. This vital function of fantasy Bruno Bettelheim elaborates on in *The Uses of Enchantment*, while at the same time documenting fantasy's power to nurture the faculty of the imagination, encourage an expansion of the mind and nourish and keep alive a sense of wonder — all essential ingredients in any worthwhile education.

Of all the forms of writing fantasy is the most difficult to achieve, but when it is successful it offers its readers special felicity in the development and interplay of characters and in the use of language, originality of ideas and penetrating comments on human behaviour. In Lloyd Alexander's words:

> Fantasy presents the world as it should be ... sometimes heartbreaking but never hopeless ... If we listen carefully it may tell us what someday we may be capable of achieving.
>
> (1973: 245)

REFERENCES

Alexander, Lloyd, 'The Flat-Heeled Muse' in *Children and Literature: Views and Reviews* editor, Virginia Haviland. Scott, Foresman, 1973.

Britton, James, 'The Role of Fantasy' in *The Cool Web: the Pattern of Children's Reading*, editor Margaret Meek *et al.* Bodley Head, 1977.

Chukovsky, Kornei, *From Two to Five*. University of California Press, 1963.
Crago, Hugh, 'Terra Incognita, Cognita' in *Fantasy Science Fiction, Science Materials*, papers, editor Margaret Trask. University of New South Wales, 1972.
Lewis, C.S., 'On Three Ways of Writing for Children' in *Only Connect: Readings in Children's Literature*, editor Sheila Egoff et al. OUP, 1969.
Smith, Lillian, 'News from Narnia' in Egoff *et al.* OUP, 1969, pp. 170–75.
Tolkien, J.R.R., 'On Fairy-Stories' in *Tree and Leaf*. Allen & Unwin, 1964.
Wrightson, Patricia, 'The Nature of Fantasy' in *Readings in Children's Literature*, proceedings, editor, Moira Robinson. Frankston State College, 1977.

BOOKS REFERRED TO IN THE CHAPTER

Adams, Richard, *Watership Down*. Penguin.
Aiken, Joan, *A Necklace of Raindrops*. Puffin.
————, *Nightbirds on Nantucket*. Puffin.
————, *The Wolves of Willoughby Chase*. Puffin.
Alcock, Vivien, *The Stonewalkers*. Lions.
Alexander, Lloyd, *The Book of Three*. Heinemann.
Babbitt, Natalie, *The Search for Delicious*. Chatto & Windus.
Bannerman, Helen, *Little Black Sambo*. Grant Richards/Stokes.
Barrie, J.M., *Peter Pan*. Hodder & Stoughton/Puffin.
Baum, L. Frank, *The Wizard of Oz*. Puffin.
Brand, Christianna, *Nurse Matilda*. Brockhampton/Dutton.
Briggs, Raymond, *Fungus the Bogeyman*. Hamish Hamilton.
————, *When the Wind Blows*. Hamish Hamilton.
Brill, Edith, *The Golden Bird*. Puffin.
Brown, Jeff, *Flat Stanley*. Methuen/Magnet.
Carroll, Lewis, *Alice in Wonderland*. Puffin.
————, *Through the Looking Glass*. Macmillan.
Christopher, John, *The White Mountains*. Hamish Hamilton/Puffin.
Collodi, Carlo, *Pinocchio*. Puffin.
Cooper, Susan, *The Dark is Rising* Sequence. Puffin.
————, *Greenwitch*. Puffin.
Corbett, W.J., *The Song of Pentecost*. Puffin.
Cresswell, Helen, *The Night-Watchmen*. Puffin.
————, *The Pie Makers*. Puffin.
Dahl, Roald, *The BFG*. Cape/Puffin.
Dickens, Charles, *A Christmas Carol*. Puffin Classics.
Dickinson, Peter, *The Gift*. Puffin.
————, *The Weathermonger*. Puffin.
Durack, Mary and Elizabeth, *The Way of the Whirlwind*. Consolidated Press.
Eager, Edward, *Half Magic*. Macmillan.
Engdahl, Sylvia, *Heritage of the Star*. Gollancz/Puffin.
Fair, Sylvia, *The Penny Tin Whistler*. Gollancz.
Farmer, Penelope, *A Castle of Bone*. Puffin.
————, *Charlotte Sometimes*. Puffin.
Fisk, Nicholas, *Grinny*. Puffin.
Foreman, Michael, *All the King's Horses*. Hamish Hamilton.
Garfield, Leon, *The Ghost Downstairs*. Puffin.
Garner, Alan, *Elidor*. Collins/Lions.
————, *The Owl Service*. Collins/Lions.

————, *Red Shift*. Collins/Lions.
Gee, Maurice, *Under the Mountain*. Puffin.
Gibbs, May, *Snugglepot and Cuddlepie*. Angus & Robertson.
Grahame, Kenneth, *The Reluctant Dragon*. Bodley Head.
————, *The Wind in The Willows*. Methuen/Puffin.
Haldane, J.B.S., *My Friend Mr Leakey*. Puffin.
Harding, Lee, *Displaced Person*. Puffin Plus.
Heide, Florence, *The Shrinking of Treehorn*. Kestrel/Young Puffin.
Hoban, Russell, *The Mouse and His Child*. Faber/Puffin.
————, *The Sea-Thing Child*. Gollancz.
Huddy, Delia, *The Time Piper*. Hamish Hamilton/Greenwillow.
Hughes, Ted, *The Iron Man*. Faber.
Ibbotson, Eva, *Which Witch?* Piccolo.
Jansson, Tove, *Finn Family Moomintroll*. Puffin.
Jarrell, Randell, *Fly By Night*. Bodley Head.
Juster, Norton, *The Phantom Tollbooth*. Collins.
Kelleher, Victor, *The Forbidden Paths of Thual*. Puffin.
————, *The Green Piper*. Kestrel.
————, *The Master of the Grove*. Puffin.
Keneally, Thomas, *Ned Kelly and the City of the Bees*. Methuen/Puffin.
Key, Alexander, *The Forgotten Door*. Westminster.
King, Clive, *Stig of the Dump*. Puffin.
Kingsley, Charles, *The Water Babies*. Puffin Classics.
Kipling, Rudyard, *The Jungle Book*. Macmillan.
————, *The Second Jungle Book*. Macmillan.
————, *Just So Stories*. Macmillan.
Langley, Noel, *The Land of Green Ginger*. Puffin.
Le Guin, Ursula, *A Wizard of Earthsea*. Puffin.
L'Engle, Madeleine, *A Wrinkle in Time*. Puffin.
Lewis, C.S., *The Lion, the Witch and the Wardrobe*. Bles.
Lewis, Hilda, *The Ship that Flew*. Oxford.
Lindgren, Astrid, *Pippi Longstocking*. Oxford/Puffin.
Lindsay, Norman, *The Magic Pudding*. Angus & Robertson.
Lively, Penelope, *The Ghost of Thomas Kempe*. Puffin.
————, *The Voyage of the QV66*. Piccolo.
Lofting, Hugh, *The Story of Doctor Dolittle*. Puffin.
MacDonald, George, *At the Back of the North Wind*. Puffin Classics.
————, *The Light Princess*. Gollancz.
————, *The Princess and Curdie*. Puffin.
————, *The Princess and the Goblin*. Puffin Classics.
McKillip, Patricia, *The Riddlemaster of Hed*. Futura.
McKinley, Robin, *Beauty*. Julia MacRae.
Mahy, Margaret, *The Great Piratical Rumbustification*. Young Puffin.
————, *The Haunting*. Dent.
————, *A Lion in the Meadow*. Dent.
————, *Raging Robots and Unruly Uncles*. Puffin.
Manley, Ruth, *The Dragon Stone*. Hodder & Stoughton.
————, *The Plum-Rain Scroll*. Hodder & Stoughton.
Mark, Jan, *Aquarius*. Kestrel.
————, *The Ennead*. Kestrel/Puffin Plus.
Masefield, John, *A Box of Delights*. Heinemann.
————, *The Midnight Folk*. Heinemann.
Mayne, William, *A Game of Dark*. Dutton/Hamish Hamilton.

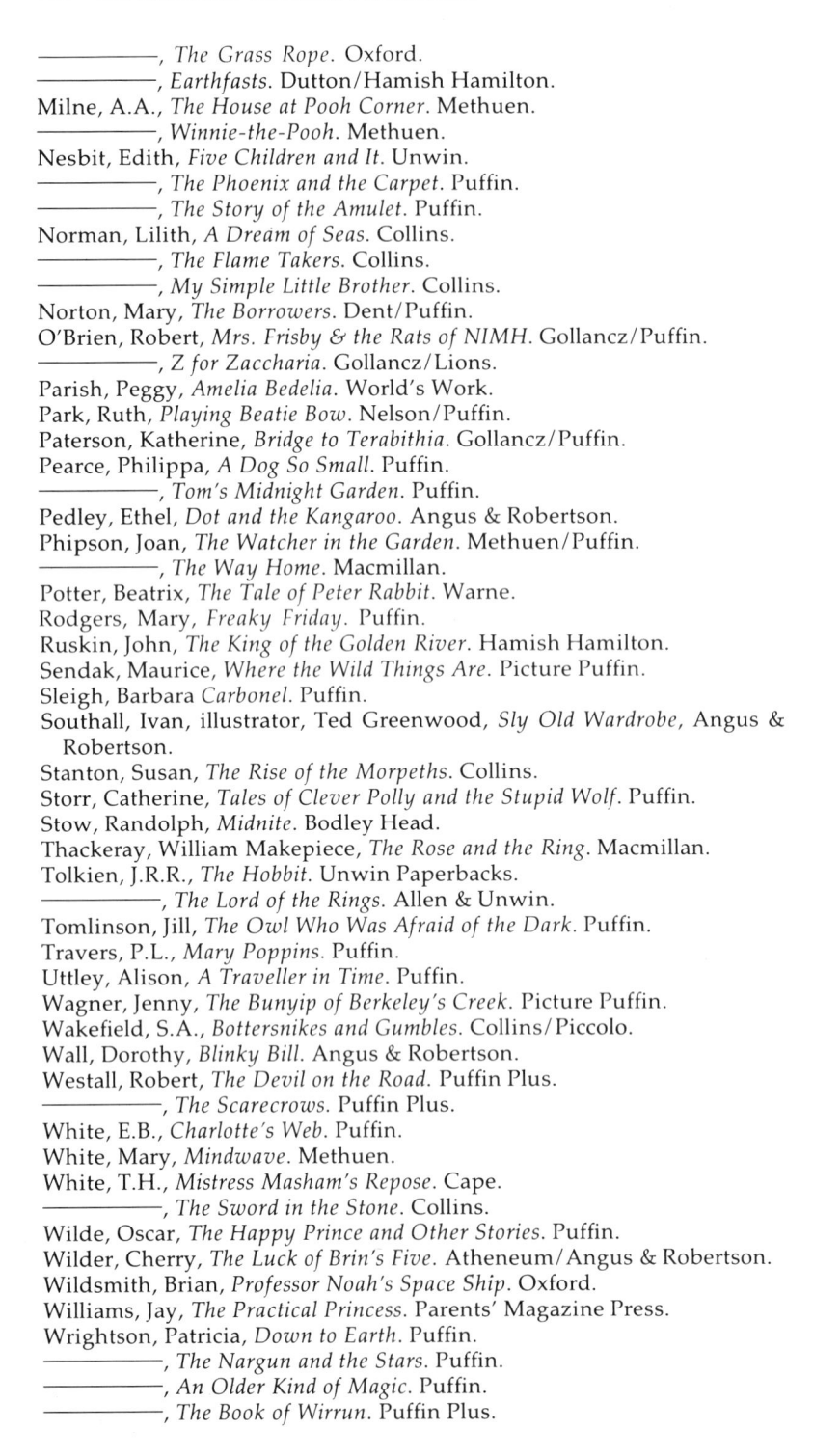

———, *The Grass Rope*. Oxford.
———, *Earthfasts*. Dutton/Hamish Hamilton.
Milne, A.A., *The House at Pooh Corner*. Methuen.
———, *Winnie-the-Pooh*. Methuen.
Nesbit, Edith, *Five Children and It*. Unwin.
———, *The Phoenix and the Carpet*. Puffin.
———, *The Story of the Amulet*. Puffin.
Norman, Lilith, *A Dream of Seas*. Collins.
———, *The Flame Takers*. Collins.
———, *My Simple Little Brother*. Collins.
Norton, Mary, *The Borrowers*. Dent/Puffin.
O'Brien, Robert, *Mrs. Frisby & the Rats of NIMH*. Gollancz/Puffin.
———, *Z for Zaccharia*. Gollancz/Lions.
Parish, Peggy, *Amelia Bedelia*. World's Work.
Park, Ruth, *Playing Beatie Bow*. Nelson/Puffin.
Paterson, Katherine, *Bridge to Terabithia*. Gollancz/Puffin.
Pearce, Philippa, *A Dog So Small*. Puffin.
———, *Tom's Midnight Garden*. Puffin.
Pedley, Ethel, *Dot and the Kangaroo*. Angus & Robertson.
Phipson, Joan, *The Watcher in the Garden*. Methuen/Puffin.
———, *The Way Home*. Macmillan.
Potter, Beatrix, *The Tale of Peter Rabbit*. Warne.
Rodgers, Mary, *Freaky Friday*. Puffin.
Ruskin, John, *The King of the Golden River*. Hamish Hamilton.
Sendak, Maurice, *Where the Wild Things Are*. Picture Puffin.
Sleigh, Barbara *Carbonel*. Puffin.
Southall, Ivan, illustrator, Ted Greenwood, *Sly Old Wardrobe*, Angus & Robertson.
Stanton, Susan, *The Rise of the Morpeths*. Collins.
Storr, Catherine, *Tales of Clever Polly and the Stupid Wolf*. Puffin.
Stow, Randolph, *Midnite*. Bodley Head.
Thackeray, William Makepiece, *The Rose and the Ring*. Macmillan.
Tolkien, J.R.R., *The Hobbit*. Unwin Paperbacks.
———, *The Lord of the Rings*. Allen & Unwin.
Tomlinson, Jill, *The Owl Who Was Afraid of the Dark*. Puffin.
Travers, P.L., *Mary Poppins*. Puffin.
Uttley, Alison, *A Traveller in Time*. Puffin.
Wagner, Jenny, *The Bunyip of Berkeley's Creek*. Picture Puffin.
Wakefield, S.A., *Bottersnikes and Gumbles*. Collins/Piccolo.
Wall, Dorothy, *Blinky Bill*. Angus & Robertson.
Westall, Robert, *The Devil on the Road*. Puffin Plus.
———, *The Scarecrows*. Puffin Plus.
White, E.B., *Charlotte's Web*. Puffin.
White, Mary, *Mindwave*. Methuen.
White, T.H., *Mistress Masham's Repose*. Cape.
———, *The Sword in the Stone*. Collins.
Wilde, Oscar, *The Happy Prince and Other Stories*. Puffin.
Wilder, Cherry, *The Luck of Brin's Five*. Atheneum/Angus & Robertson.
Wildsmith, Brian, *Professor Noah's Space Ship*. Oxford.
Williams, Jay, *The Practical Princess*. Parents' Magazine Press.
Wrightson, Patricia, *Down to Earth*. Puffin.
———, *The Nargun and the Stars*. Puffin.
———, *An Older Kind of Magic*. Puffin.
———, *The Book of Wirrun*. Puffin Plus.

17 HUMOUR IN CHILDREN'S LITERATURE

MOIRA ROBINSON

> ... he gave me a book to read.
> It is called *The Ragged Trousered Philanthropist*.
> I haven't looked through it yet, but I'm quite interested in stamp-collecting.
> Adrian Mole (Sue Townsend)

Humour is the Cinderella in the world of children's literature. Volumes are devoted to fantasy, to folklore and myth, even — belatedly — to poetry, but humour is lucky to rate even an occasional chapter or article, despite the fact that for every twenty children who have enjoyed Susan Cooper's *The Dark is Rising* (1973) there are probably two hundred who have enjoyed Roald Dahl's *The BFG* (1982). It is partly that we always underestimate humour, whether for children or adults, because we think that it, being humorous, is not to be taken seriously and therefore must be lightweight and of no importance. But we also dismiss it because it presents us with all sorts of problems.

Tragedy is fairly easy to define, and we will all respond in much the same way to King Lear's plight, but humour is much harder to pin down and far more subjective, so that what appears uproariously funny to one adult may seem silly or objectionable or totally unfunny to another. Little wonder then that we are sometimes perplexed or downright irritated by children's response to humour when individual differences are aggravated by factors like age or emotional or intellectual development. The more we examine humour, in fact, the more it turns out to be slippery, elusive, darksided and, at close quarters, not even very attractive or funny. And yet we make a great mistake if we underestimate it, for though we may be exalted by our experience of tragedy, we survive and develop as individuals because of our experience of humour.

WHAT MAKES US LAUGH?

Laughter is a reflex. Tickle children under their feet and they will start to laugh. Shine a light on their eyes and they will automatically blink. The difference between the two responses is that laughter, as Koestler points out in *The Act of Creation* (1969), is a 'luxury reflex', one that appears to have no function except to get rid of 'excitations which have become redundant, which can not be consummated in any purposeful manner'. That is why people will occasionally break into totally inappropriate laughter during a film or play — it is a way of releasing and dispersing tension. Similarly, if we read aloud: 'In the dark dark wood there was a dark dark house ...' tension builds up and up until we reach the climax: 'and in that dark dark box there was a ... GHOST!', and pent-up apprehension and shock escape in laughter.

We are invariably surprised into laughter, surprised because we have been logically led to expect one conclusion and receive instead another, that belongs to a different train of logic. 'Coat of Arms' proudly proclaims *Milligan's Book of Bits* (1967) then one turns the page and instead of a heraldic device there is a coat festooned with severed arms of different lengths. In Roald Dahl's *Charlie and the Chocolate Factory* (1967) Mr Wonka enthusiastically describes how, with a dose of Vitamin Wonka Mike Teavee's toes will 'grow out until they're as long as his fingers ... It's most useful. He'll be able to play the piano with his feet'. It's a logical assumption, but not quite the reassuring remark that we are expecting, and our surprise spills over into laughter. Anthony Browne in his delightful picture book describes how *Willy the Wimp* (1984) 'wouldn't hurt a fly' and is always apologising 'even when it wasn't his fault'. Spurred on by an advertisement Willy goes on a vigorous course of exercise and diet until one day he 'looked in the mirror. He liked what he saw'. So when Willy 'saw the suburban gorillas attacking Millie ... They ran. Willy was proud. "I'm not a wimp, I'm a hero". Bang! (He collides with a lamp-post). "Oh, I'm sorry", said Willy'. We are expecting a heroic ending, and when we are deprived of it, we laugh, as Willy, reverting to type, apologises to the inanimate lamp-post.

Hobbes, the English moral philosopher, would say that we also laugh at Willy because he is humiliated, and this gives rise to 'a sudden conception of some eminency in ourselves'. In fact, the minute one starts to analyse stock pantomime situations — the dame slipping on a banana-skin, custard-pies being inverted over the head, etc. — one has reluctantly to admit that the degradation of others, aggression and the resulting self-affirmation, all have a major part to play in humour. It would be 'nice' if humour were 'nice', but it is not. Much of it belongs to the part of our psyche we would like to pretend doesn't exist — a frightened, resentful, potentially violent part, intent on clawing its way to security over the misfortunes of people like the hapless captain in Margaret Mahy's *The Pirates' Mixed-up Voyage* (1983):

> The pirate captain charged forward and slashed at Mrs Hatchett, but she, with tremendous skill and a sword of razor sharpness, parried his lunge and cut through his thick leather belt, so that his trousers fell down. He dropped his sword and seized at them desperately, then slipped on one half of the banana and slid across the room.

The captain's troubles with his trousers and backside reaffirm that 'we're all right, Jack': this time round it's someone else who has made a fool of himself. Think of Aunt Sponge and Aunt Spiker in

Roald Dahl's *James and the Giant Peach* (1967), ironed out upon the grass 'as flat and thin and lifeless as a couple of paper dolls cut out of a picture-book', or of the Magic Pudding in Norman Lindsay's work of that name (1918) telling the Mayor that he's 'a sausage-shaped porous plaster', or Roger Thesaurus' constant humiliations at the hands of his 'Worst Best Friend' in Max Dann's *Adventures with my Worst Best Friend* (1982) and one quickly realises that degradation, defiance and aggression form the bedrock of humour in children's books — indeed of all humour — although aggression may be veiled by urbanity and wit.

Although it is easy to pick out the common denominators — such as incompatibility of ideas and aggression, we are still left with the unpredictability of response. One person reads a Thurber short story and is helpless with laughter, while someone else reads it without even a twitch of the mouth. Laughter may be a reflex, but unlike an involuntary knee jerk, it can be produced by stimuli that involve mind and emotion, so that what we laugh at is influenced by the sort of people we are and by our mood at a given moment. In fact, the more we think about the factors that influence our response to humour, the more surprising it is that we ever laugh at all, and certainly that we ever laugh *with* anyone else.

FACTORS AFFECTING OUR RESPONSE TO HUMOUR

The setting and our own expectations, for instance, govern our response. If we go to Flinders Street Station and hurriedly read down the list of stations to make sure we are on the right platform, it does not usually strike us as amusing; but if we listen to Barry Humphries' Sandy Stone, hot water bottle clasped to dressing-gowned stomach, slowly listing all the stations on a suburban line, it can seem excruciatingly funny; and similarly, if Grade 1 think they are going to hear a story that will make them laugh, they are prepared to laugh even before the first page is turned. We are not going to laugh so readily if we are emotionally involved in a situation. It is easy to laugh at the pirate captain's trousers falling down, but the same thing happening to our nearest and dearest or, even worse, to ourselves, would fill us with embarrassment or anger. Gender, too, affects our response. Girls, for instance, are generally less amused by slapstick and crash-bang-wallop humour, although whether that is a matter of conditioning or genes I wouldn't like to hazard a guess.

Different races laugh at different things. The English complain that the French have no sense of humour. They have, of course, but it is different from the English one. Humour is bound to be shaped to some extent by cultural values and mores, by the structure of society and its ethical beliefs. Saki's short stories, for instance, or novels like Evelyn Waugh's *Scoop* are funnier the more we know about England, its snobberies and its modes of etiquette. We need some frame of reference for all but slapstick humour. Jokes about the Stock Exchange or the Vatican are not going to strike us as funny unless we know enough about the background and can see the joke, and even a book about a hippopotamus eating cake on the roof will not be amusing unless a child has enough concept of the size of a hippopotamus to appreciate the unlikelihood of such an event. A book like Norman Juster's *The Phantom Tollbooth* (1974) is only going to appeal strongly to children with enough language experience to appreciate remarks like 'The duke here can make mountains out of molehills. The minister splits hairs ... and the under-secretary hangs by a thread'. Intelligence and a degree of imagination are both going to affect our response to humour, for in something like *Handles* by Jan Mark (1983) the reader is required to make mental leaps:

> Some juvenile marrows were already loitering with intent, not at all like piglets, unless they should be the farrow of a wild boar. She could see their pale rounded backs swelling ... swelling ... and she hurried on before one of them could raise its bloated body from the damp earth and come after her, snarling and grunting.

Even religious beliefs and ethical mores have a part to play. Barbara Robinson's *The Worst Kids in the World* (1974), for instance, seems to go down particularly well in church schools, partly because the children know the Christmas story and so can appreciate the terrible Herdmans' offbeat interpretation of it, but partly also because they feel sufficiently at ease with Biblical characters like Mary and Joseph to feel happy joking about them.

Our personality, our mood, our particular hang-ups, all influence our response to humour, and the older we become and the more hung about with quirky beliefs or inhibitions or prejudices, the more individual our response. As Katherine Kappas has pointed out, prep grade children 'will evidence a much greater degree of homogeneity in their perception of humour than a comparable group of high school children; particularly at primary school, one can see distinct stages in children's responses to humour.

DEVELOPMENTAL STAGES OF HUMOUR

Children in lower grades don't generally have the mental equipment to make puns or enjoy knock-knock jokes, and so visual humour predominates. They enjoy picture books in which the incongruity is blatant, books in which tigers come to tea, hippos take their ease in the bathtub or on the roof, giraffes stand in the fireplace with necks protruding up the chimney. They enjoy the obvious absurdity of Horton the elephant crouched in his spindly tree trying to hatch Mayzie's egg, or the predicament of Margaret

Mahy's *The Boy Who Was Followed Home* (1977) by more and more hippopotami. Everything is exaggerated — the mountains in Dr Seuss' books unbelievably steep and pointed, the trestle bridges in *Green Eggs and Ham* supported on tottering poles tied together with string. Richard Scarry's books are often popular, and though adults may criticise them, particularly on sexist grounds, they sometimes give children their first intimation of the comic possibilities of life, the possibility of a 'five-seater crayon car' for instance, or a 'bananamobile'. They are also rich in slapstick humour — cars bumping into each other, people falling into the water, clothes flying off the washing-line — and slapstick humour, although it figures largely in children's play at this stage, is none too common in the rarefied world of children's literature. Children like books in which children or animals are naughty, those like Gene Zion's *Harry, the Dirty Dog* (1960) or Russell Hoban's *Bread and Jam for Frances* (1976) because they can enjoy a glow of smug virtue and the thrill of vicarious wickedness simultaneously, and as children reach Grade 2 and enter middle primary school, they relish defiance humour more and more.

Seven to nine-year-olds are beginning to think of themselves as people in their own right, and they emphasise their independence by cocking a snook at adult authority figures. Outside in the playground they chant rhymes like 'Glory, glory, hallelujah/ Teacher hit me with a ruler/ I hit her on the chin/ With a rotten mandarin/ And her teeth came marching out'. Inside the classroom they delight in the grisly humour of Roald Dahl's *The Twits* (1980) or in the nonchalant dismissal of Grandma when she has shrunk away to nothing at the end of his *George's Marvellous Medicine* (1981): 'Ah well, I suppose it's all for the best, really. She was a bit of a nuisance about the house, wasn't she?' 'Rude' words like 'bum' and 'burp' in Dahl's *Charlie and the Chocolate Factory* (1967) excite more attention than the subtleties of 'square sweets that look round', and the most pored-over picture in Raymond Briggs's *Father Christmas* (1973) is the one showing that venerable gentleman sitting in the dunny, muttering to himself, 'I hate winter'. Their favourite jokes and rhymes are those designed to shock adults to their very core — the most popular rhyme in June Factor's *Far Out, Brussel Sprout*! (1983), for instance, is 'Ooey gooey custard,/ Green maggot pie/ Four dogs' gizzards/ And one cat's eye,/ Four blood sandwiches/ Coated on thick,/ All washed down/ With a cup of cold sick'. So far as adults are concerned, it doesn't seem a very edifying stage of humour, but eight and nine-year-olds are testing out where they stand in relation to the world around them through their attempts to shock themselves and other people by their use of forbidden words or forbidden subjects.

When the silly season is at its height, children go on laughing jags for no particular reason. They play silly bumping games (known as 'bodging' in our family); they exchange moronic jokes like 'Have you heard the one about the bed? It hasn't been made yet!' It is perhaps the hardest stage for adults to recall, and only a few writers like Norman Hunter and Spike Milligan can recapture the glory of pure silliness:

> To-day I saw a little worm
> Wriggling on his belly.
> Perhaps he'd like to come inside
> And see what's on the telly.
>
> (Milligan 1968)

Slapstick continues to be popular the whole way up primary school, but children can move from this purely visual form to something like *Bernice Knows Best* (1983), Max Dann's very funny story about an accident-prone boy, or to the robust humour of Roald Dahl's *Revolting Rhymes* (1982). Obvious visual incongruity gives way in upper primary to the bizarre detail found in some of Anthony Browne's picture books or in *Patatrac* by Jean-Jacques Loup (1975), or to humour that hinges on deviations from the norm, whether they be of situation or language. By Grade 5 to 6, for instance, most children have enough familiarity with the English language to know that the BFG's doesn't sound quite right:

> Here is the repulsant snozzcumber! I dispunge it! I squoggle it! I mispise it! But because I is refusing to gobble human beans, like the other giants, I must spend my life guzzling up icky-poo snozzcumbers instead. If I don't I will be nothing but skin and groans.

Generally speaking, however, the joys of irony, wit and satire still lie well ahead in the teen years, and one sees plenty of adults whose appreciation of humour has, alas, never really progressed beyond the lavatory door.

THE ACQUISITION OF HUMOUR

In her study on the developmental stages of children's humour, Katherine Kappas goes on to argue that we should study its form, the level of its intellectual and emotional content and its frame of reference before using a humorous book with children, otherwise they may not laugh in the right places. This seems like arguing that we should give a seven-year-old only the words he knows already. It ignores the idea that new concepts of humour, like new vocabulary, have to be acquired. We laugh when tickled, and that is an innate reaction, but I would cautiously suggest that all other responses to humour are learned.

A toddler shuts his eyes, and thinks he has disappeared because he can no longer see anyone. He opens his eyes and he's back again. If we laugh at his cleverness, what may have started as an accidental trick becomes part of a performance designed to arouse our laughter, and if there were no audience and no reciprocity in the play, I doubt very much whether he or she would go on to develop more sophisticated games of, say, 'boo' or find them funny. A preschooler listening to a story watches the reactions of the adult reading it, and learns that the book is funny before he knows for himself that it is. I asked a friend which book his five-year-old found funniest, and he promptly said, *How Tom Beat Captain Najork and His Hired Sportsmen* (Russell Hoban 1974). 'Does she really find it funny or do you?' I asked. There was silence for a moment and then he said, slightly defensively, 'Well, I enjoy reading it, and she enjoys listening to it'. This, of course, is what matters. Bridget at three, when she first heard the book, probably didn't laugh uproariously at sentences like 'When it was his turn to rake, he did not let Captain Najork and the hired sportsmen score a single rung, and at the end of the snetch he won by six ladders', but she quickly learned that adults laughed at it, and that it was a fun book to enjoy together. When we gave her another book illustrated by Quentin Blake, her eyes lit up and she said, 'A Captain Najork book': the expectation of enjoyment, if not of understanding, was already there.

This expectation almost always precedes understanding of the content. In lower primary school, for instance, children quickly learn that knock-knock jokes are considered funny. They are valuable currency in the playground, and so they make up their own ones, like 'Knock, knock. Who's there? Shane', and then double up with laughter, because that is what everyone does after a joke. A Grade 2 child wrote in the class joke book, 'Why does an elephant sit on a fence? Because it's time to get a new fence', having again understood the form of the joke, but quite failed to understand the point of it. Becoming familiar with the rituals of joking, however, or at least recognising the presence of comedy, is a necessary part of acquiring a sense of humour, and rather than waiting for the right experiences in a child's life to match with a book, the read experiences may later add comic piquancy to life.

Literature is a two-way process: the writer gives the reader a new way of perceiving a place, a person, a situation, and the reader brings back to literature his own perceptions and experiences. Children listening to A.A. Milne's *The House at Pooh Corner* (1928) for the first time, may not find the Pooh-sticks episode particularly funny; they may be intrigued by Eeyore's predicament as he turns round and round in the current rather than amused by it. But if they subsequently play Pooh-sticks, dropping sticks into a creek from one side of a bridge and then hurrying to the other side to see whose stick emerges first — the humour of the incident becomes plain. Just suppose a stiff, ungainly Eeyore were to come floating out with four legs pointing up into the air like ram-rods. Similarly, a boy reading Betsy Byars' *Cybil War* (1981) may not yet have dated a girl, so Simon's misery at the cinema with Harriet will not be particularly funny, but when experience catches up with literature, it will be like a double reflection:

> She looked so big in her skirt and blouse that she seemed to block the whole front of the theatre ... Simon's eyes misted over, either from the nearness of the screen or the fact that his whole adult life was stretching ahead of him as a series of dates, one Harriet Haywood after another.

A joke which is too explicit quickly ceases to be a joke, for humour largely depends on the shock of the unexpected, and if this has to be explained, the humour trickles away in the telling. So most humour, apart from basic slapstick or the obvious and immediate shock of a 'rude' word, demands from the reader a certain mental agility, an ability to jump the gap between one line of logic and another or to appreciate the contradictions in a pseudo-serious statement like, 'On Monday, which is Good Friday, there will be a Mothers' Meeting for men only'. It's easy to give children too little exercise in this sort of thinking; we know that defiance humour will always be successful, so we start the Grade 2s off with Roald Dahl's *Fantastic Mr Fox* (1970), and progress by way of *The Twits* (1980) to *The Witches* (1983) in Grade 6, with a few of Jane Covernton's *Putrid Poems* (1985) and Dahl's *Revolting Rhymes* (1982) thrown in along the way, and then are surprised that secondary school schildren fail to appreciate Jane Austen's wit. The way to Jane Austen is via writers who revel in irony, writers like Margaret Mahy or Jan Mark, via comments like: 'Victor's writing was a sort of code to deceive the enemy, with punctuation marks in unlikely places to confuse anyone who came too close to cracking the code'.

Maybe some childen won't laugh at this — but what does it matter? We scarcely ever all find the same things funny anyway, and every narrative has more to offer the reader than simply its humour. In Jan Mark's *Thunder and Lightning* (1978), for instance, there are the wonderful descriptions of aeroplanes, as well as the story of Andrew and Victor's somewhat unlikely friendship and the delights of the prose. What is important is that children are becoming familiar with the terseness of language being used in a particular way, with the conventions of irony, with sorts of demands placed on readers, even if they are not yet ready to accept all the challenges offered.

THE VALUE OF HUMOUR

The reason, perhaps, that we often fail to explore all the possibilites of humour with children is that we underestimate it; we have the sneaking conviction that humour generally is not only a bit lightweight, but that it's second-class literature. Yet, if tragedy in classical terms is about the collapse of a noble person marred by a fatal flaw, comedy is about the fierce survival of the ordinary person, warts and all. Humour is our safety valve, our way of coping with life and its stresses. Think of Judy Blume's *Are You There, God? It's Me, Margaret* (1978). She took the subject of menstruation and puberty — a topic many girls didn't know about and didn't like to ask — and has made out of it a funny, realistic story in which the four PTS's (Pre-Teen Sensations) chant 'I must, I must, I must increase my bust' and wait excitedly for their first period. The matter-of-fact humour and general good cheer blow away the cloudy fears and anxieties draped around the subject for years. Similarly in something like *There's a Nightmare in My Cupboard* (1976) Mercer Mayer gives night fears a tangible and somewhat ludicrous shape, and helps children to smile at what has seemed alarming.

'You've got to laugh', people sometimes say, usually somewhat sourly, but the phrase contains a truism — we laugh to maintain some sense of equilibrium, and if our sense of humour is sometimes aggressive, it has to be, for it champions the puny individual against 'the slings and arrows of outrageous fortune'. We joke with Marvell about death in the irony of, 'The grave's a fine and private place/ But none, I think, do there embrace' or the macabre *Ruthless Rhymes* of Harry Graham (1984): 'Billy, in one of his nice new sashes,/ Fell in the fire and was burnt to ashes./ Now, although the room grows chilly,/ I haven't the heart to poke poor Billy'. We must laugh at death, for we cannot avoid it, nor can we entirely deny our fear of its unknowableness, and so we belittle it in Belloc's *Cautionary Tales* (1980) or in Dahl's story of the woman who kills her husband with a leg of lamb and then invites the baffled police to partake of roast blunt instrument. Famine and other disasters that seem beyond the control of humankind usher in a wave of hideous jokes that seem the ultimate in bad taste, but are basically our shout of defiance: 'Do your damnedest; we're still here'. There is an element of superstition in it too; we deliberately set out to shock others as well as ourselves, and if no thunderbolt immediately strikes us down, we feel triumphantly safe, just as we do when we have dared to walk under a ladder. Exactly the same process is at work when children chant rhymes like 'Oh, dear, what can the matter be?/ Three old ladies got locked in the lavatory'. They have deliberately taken an adult song and put their own outrageous words to it as an assertion of independence, a refusal to be put down by adults; again, it is a slightly superstitious testing out of the perimeters of safety, part of growth to maturity.

While tragedy is concerned with universal themes like death or friendship, comedy is industriously engaged in looking after Number One. We reaffirm our own security through laughter at the misfortunes of others, and though it is a reaction that hasn't the nobility of catharsis, it is, like so much of humour, a survival skill. We need characters like Robin Klein's Penny Pollard who are brash and fearless and who assert themselves on our behalf, saying the things we might think but be afraid to say — things like 'No way was I going to stand up on stage like a galah and look at creepy old wrinklies all afternoon'. Comedy, whether it be in the guise of Penny Pollard on Sir Toby Belch, speaks for our alter ego, the part of us that, because of convention or inhibition, we often hide. When we laugh at a joke, there is invariably an element of self-assertion, with a degree also of self-satisfaction; in Sue Townsend's *The Secret Diary of Adrian Mole* (1982) the obnoxious Adrian writes: '... he gave me a book to read. It is called *The Ragged Trousered Philanthropist*. I haven't looked through it yet, but I'm quite interested in stamp-collecting ...' and our laughter is a congratulatory pat on the back, because we know the difference between 'philanthropist' and 'philatelist', while Adrian does not. In fact all the humour in Sue Townsend's novel hinges on the fact that Adrian thinks he's exceptional in every way, while readers know that he is an ignorant, conceited hypochondriac; they are in the god-like position of seeing the gap between fantasy and reality just as they are in Thurber's story of Walter Mitty, the eternal henpecked little man, lost in his dreams of glory.

Perhaps all this makes humour sound despicable. But few people's self-esteem is so high that it doesn't benefit from being bolstered by comedy, and most of us need the reasurance that it offers, providing us with a much less complex world in which characters behave according to type and are therefore comfortably predictable. Augustus Gloop is simply walking greed; Toad in *The Wind in the Willows* remains gloriously, unrepentantly conceited; Fudge in Judy Blume's *Tales of a Fourth Grade Nothing* (1979) and *Super Fudge* (1980) is the archetype of a pestiferous younger sibling. It's a world that frequently relies on exaggeration, on deviation from the norm, and we become more confident about what actually constitutes the norm. Tommy's fantasies in Betsy Byars' *The Midnight Fox* (1970), for instance, about being 'the only kid in the world to be stampeded by a bunch of baby lambs' only emphasises the unlikelihood of such a catastrophe.

So humour is part of our human survival kit, but also, as much as tragedy, it is a part of literature, and shares many of the same functions. It provides us with a means of articulating our responses to people or places, or to situations like buttering fresh brown bread:

> My brother is making a protest about bread.
> Why do we always have wholemeal bread?
> You put the butter on
> And it all rolls up.
> You put the butter on
> And it all rolls up.

It gives us a fresh way of looking at the world around us, perceptions that are frequently unforgettable because unexpected, like Mouse's instructions in Betsy Byars' *The Eighteenth Emergency*

(1974): written above a crack in the wall, 'TO OPEN BUILDING TEAR ALONG THE LINE'. Then again, the Prime Minister in Randolph Stow's *Midnite* (1967) with his laugh like a 'waterfall of brilliantine'. We are made constantly aware of 'life's infinite possibilities', because so much of humour depends upon the bringing together of seemingly incompatible or incongruous ideas or images or concepts. Think of the mind-dazzling shifts of logic and meaning in Lewis Carroll's *Alice's Adventures in Wonderland* (1865) or Anthony Browne's delight in bizarre or surreal detail in picture books like his *A Walk in the Park* (1979) or *The Visitors Who Came to Stay* by Annalene McAfee and Anthony Browne (1979), with the picture of the woman basking on the beach with fried eggs in place of breasts. We are presented with a whole new vision of a world far less restricting than our own, one with its own logic and consistency, and yet, at its best, one described with the precision of poetry, as in the wonderful description of Mrs Fangboner in Margaret Mahy's *The Changeover* (1984):

> Laura had never seen her without lipstick, had never seen her naked smile.
> 'I've been married ten years and I've never let myself go', Laura had once heard her tell a friend, and had thought that even if Mrs Fangboner did let herself go, she probably would not go far ... On this particular day she was punishing the grass edges with instruments of gardening torture.

Words and phrases like 'naked', 'let myself go' or 'punishing' all contain within them differing, conflicting thought processes that result in wit. Humour is, in fact, a way of thinking creatively, just as fantasy is, and of course the whole point of Koestler's fascinating book is that the creative act is basically the same for the jester, the sage and the poet, only the emotional context being different.

Children who are deprived of humour in their literary diet or are not given an opportunity to become familiar with all the forms that comedy can take are being deprived both of a means of coping with existence and a different stimulating way of thinking. In *Handles*, Erica has already discovered the delights of punning, of allusions, of fantasising about marrows or her aunt's ancient bicycle, delights she shares with Elsie, the unorthodox young man who runs a garage. Robert, her cousin, moving in his stolid way, simply thinks she's daft:

> She [Erica] had been considering for a moment, inviting him to share a joke, but she knew it would be useless. Robert's jokes came out of comics and joke-books, ready pre-packaged. He would never believe that anything you *said* could be a joke ... 'Why don't you talk straight?' was all he said, and Erica knew that he would never have a 'password' and never follow her into Elsie's Kingdom.

Children need humorous books of every type to become familiar with the 'passwords' and to gain access to another kingdom of the mind where untold pleasures lie waiting to be discovered and enjoyed.

REFERENCES

Chapman, Anthony J., and Foot, Hugh C., editors, *Humour and Laughter: Theory, Research and Applications.* New York: John Wiley, 1976.
Gessell, A. and Ilg, F.C., *The Child from Five to Ten.* London: Hamish Hamilton, 1946.
Kappas, Katherine H., 'Children's Responses to Humour' in Fenwich, Sara Innes, editor, *Critical Approaches to Children's Literature.* Chicago: University of Chicago Press, 1967.
Koestler, Arthur, *The Act of Creation.* London: Hutchinson, 1969.

BOOKS REFERRRED TO IN THE CHAPTER

Belloc, Hilaire, *Selected Cautionary Verses.* Penguin.
Blume, Judy, *Are You There, God? It's Me, Margaret.* Gollancz/Pan.
——————, *Super Fudge.* Bodley Head/Pan
——————, *Tales of a Fourth Grade Nothing.* Bodley Head/Pan.
Briggs, Raymond, *Father Christmas.* Hamish Hamilton/Picture Puffin.
Browne, Anthony, *A Walk in the Park.* Hamish Hamilton.
——————, *Willy the Wimp.* Julie MacRae.
Byars, Betsy, *Cybil War.* Bodley Head/Puffin.
——————, *The Eighteenth Emergency.* Bodley Head/Puffin.
——————, *The Midnight Fox.* Faber and Faber/Puffin.
Carroll, Lewis, *Alice's Adventures in Wonderland.* Puffin.
Cooper, Susan, *The Dark is Rising.* Chatto & Windus/Puffin.
Covernton, Jane, *Putrid Poems.* Omnibus.
Dann, Max, *Adventures with My Worst Best Friend.* OUP.
——————, *Bernice Knows Best.* OUP.
Dahl, Roald, *The BFG.* Jonathan Cape/Puffin.
——————, *Charlie and the Chocolate Factory.* Allen & Unwin/Puffin.
——————, *Fantastic Mr Fox.* Allen & Unwin.
——————, *George's Marvellous Medicine.* Jonathan Cape/Puffin.
——————, *James and the Giant Peach.* Allen & Unwin/Puffin.
——————, *Revolting Rhymes.* Jonathan Cape/Puffin.
——————, *The Twits.* Jonathan Cape/Puffin.
——————, *The Witches.* Jonathan Cape.
Factor, June, *Far Out, Brussel Sprout!* OUP.
Graham, Harry, *Ruthless Rhymes.* Edward Arnold.
Grahame, Kenneth, *The Wind in the Willows.* Methuen.
Hoban, Russell, *Bread and Jam for Frances.* Faber & Faber/Picture Puffin.
——————, *How Tom Beat Captain Najork and his Hired Sportsmen.* Jonathan Cape.
Juster, Norton, *The Phantom Tollbooth.* Collins.
Klein, Robin, *Penny Pollard's Diary.* OUP.
Lindsay, Norman, *The Magic Pudding.* Angus & Robertson.
Loup, Jean-Jacques, *Patatrac.* Jonathan Cape.
McAfee, Annalene and Browne, Anthony, *The Visitors Who Came to Stay.* Hamish Hamilton.

Mahy, Margaret, *The Boy Who Was Followed Home*. Dent/Methuen.
——————, *The Changeover*. Dent/Methuen.
——————, *The Pirates' Mixed-up Voyage*. Dent/Methuen.
Mark, Jan, *Handles*. Kestrel/Puffin.
——————, *Thunder and Lightning*. Kestrel/Puffin.
Mayer, Mercer, *There's a Nightmare in my Cupboard*. Dent/Pocket Bears.
Milligan, Spike, *A Book of Bits*. Tandem.
——————, *Silly Verse for Kids*. Puffin.
Milne, A.A., *The House at Pooh Corner*. Methuen.
Robinson, Barbara, *The Worst Kids in the World*. Faber & Faber/Hamlyn.
Rosen, Michael, *Mind Your Own Business*. Deutsch/Collins.
Seuss, Dr., *Horton Hatches the Egg*. Collins.
——————, *Green Eggs and Ham*. Collins.
Stow, Randolph, *Midnite*. MacDonald/Puffin.
Thurber, J., *The Secret Life of Walter Mitty* in *Thurber Carnival*. Penguin.
Townsend, Sue, *The Secret Diary of Adrian Mole Aged 13¾*. Methuen.
Zion, G., *Harry, the Dirty Dog*. Bodley Head/Puffin.

HUMOROUS BOOKS

NOVELS

Fleischman, Sid, *The Whipping Boy*. Magnet, 1988.
Jennings, Paul, *Unreal! Unbelievable! The Cabbage Patch Fib. Uncanny: The Paw Thing*. Puffin, 1985–1989.
King-Smith, Dick, *The Fox Busters*. Penguin, 1978.
——————, *George Speaks*. Penguin, 1988.
Klein, Robin, *Hating Alison Ashley*. Penguin, 1984.

PICTURE BOOKS

Ahlberg, Janet and Allan, *The Jolly Postman or Other People's Letters*. Heinemann, 1986.
Dodd, Lynley, *Hairy Maclary's Rumpus at the Vet*. Keystone, 1989.
Graham, Bob, *Crusher is Coming!* Viking, 1988.
Mahy, Margaret, *The Great White Man-Eating Shark*. Dent, 1989.
——————, and McRae, Rodney, *The Spider in the Shower*. Shortland, 1984.
Nobile, Trinka Hakes and Ross, Tony, *Meanwhile Back at the Ranch*. Andersen/Beaver, 1987.
Samuels, Barbara, *Duncan and Dolores*. Dent, 1987.
Steig, William, *Doctor De Soto*. Andersen, 1983.

18 RITES OF PASSAGE: ADOLESCENT LITERATURE

BELLE ALDERMAN

> What really knocks me out is a book that, when you're all done reading it, you wish the author that wrote it was a terrific friend of yours and you could call him up on the phone whenever you felt like it. That doesn't happen much though.
>
> J.D. Salinger

Adolescent literature: two words which suggest a readily identifiable body of works. Opinions differ, however, on the inclusions. Should the novels be those adults' and children's books widely read by this audience or simply those in which adolescents feature as protagonists? Or perhaps it is only that literature which is so labelled, packaged, marketed and promoted. While all of these are likely candidates for adolescent literature, sufficient novels with common characteristics have emerged in recent years to form a loose category from them.

EMERGENCE OF ADOLESCENT LITERATURE

Several sources maintain adolescent literature, as a recognisable body of work, appeared in the mid-twentieth century (Carpenter and Prichard 1984: 518; Donelson and Nilsen 1980). Burton (Bator 1983: 310–18) concurs and provides an overview of the rise of the adolescent novel in the 1940s and 1950s. The main theme at that time was the personal problems of an adolescent protagonist; its general characteristics were clear:

Unwritten taboos

These prevented treatment of explicit sex, drug abuse, alcoholism and the dark side of human nature.

Didacticism

This reigned, as novels provided guides to proper behaviour, protrayed adults as always right and punished rebellious or unconventional adolescents.

Characters

These were white and middle-class.

Style

This featured an omniscient point of view with few flashbacks.

Plots

These were built to a climax near the end, quickly resolved and featured few subplots.

The standard American text, *Literature for Today's Young Adults* (Donelson and Nilsen 1980: 55–140) surveys the range of adolescent reading matter prior to this time: religious, domestic and dime novels, annuals and popular weeklies, adventure stories, comics and the classics. Niall (1984) surveys Australian reading matter, and Townsend (1983) British.

By the 1960s, editors and publishers, writers and promoters of books recognised the genre though opinions differed as to the need and value of such literature. According to one editor of adolescent literature (Briley in Rogers 1979: 17, 19) the Young Adult (or YA) novel as it is termed in the American book trade, was invented by publishers in the 1960s 'to make it more convenient to market books to those who bring books and adolescent-age children together'. American publishers then and now actively seek writers for their young adult lines but generally do not publish under a series title, with the exception of those specifically designed for reluctant adolescent readers. British publishers recognised the need to produce 'teenage literature' (in their jargon) and so emerged the Peacock series from Penguin in 1962 (revamped and renamed Puffin Plus in 1981), and A Book for New Adults series from Bodley Head in 1970. Australian publishers are wary of targeting their books to a narrow market and avoid any such categories.

Some writers of adolescent literature question the desirability of categorising literature for specific age groups. Duncan (1981) maintains the best of adolescent literature is better understood by the adult and that the YA label is 'stigmatising'. Townsend (1983: 291), a writer of adolescent literature, argues, however, for a separate category, stressing that such novels treat youthful concerns from a 'young' point of view.

Offering a completely different view on the emergence of adolescent literature, Ray (1972: 22) maintains it is an artificial category devised by public libraries wishing to bring together books from the children's and adults' sections, thus smoothing the transition from one collection to the other. Each of these views poses valid points and there is an element of truth in each. At the very least, the diversity of views demonstrates some of the difficulties of reaching a precise definition of adolescent literature.

Added to these difficulties is the term adolescence itself. Biologically, it begins with the onset of puberty when sexual maturation and accelerated height and weight start and concludes with the completion of physical maturation. So adolescence begins somewhere between the years of nine and ten and concludes in the early twenties. However, to describe adolescence solely in such terms belies complex cultural factors which affect not only physical maturation but also mental, emotional and social development. Various experts suggest a range of factors which typify adolescence (Conger and Petersen 1984: 11–22) placing different emphasis on the most important factor but agreeing that as a stage of human development, adolescence has certain characteristics.

To narrow the focus of this chapter, a number of these characteristics will be highlighted and drawn upon to examine a range of fiction central to these concerns. Such an approach is only one of several which could be taken, but it allows a discreet sampling of literature and is one which invites comparison with Burton's overview of adolescent literature in its early development.

THE ADOLESCENT STAGE OF DEVELOPMENT

One aspect of adolescent development considers cognitive maturation. According to psychologists Bärbel Inhelder and Jean Piaget (1958), the adolescent around the ages of eleven or twelve years reaches the stage of formal operations characterised by an ability to think abstractly; he or she can consider possible or alternative futures, build theories and construct ideals (Inhelder and Piaget 1958: 335–50).

Another perspective on the adolescent stage of development is that of psychologist Erik Erikson (1968) who studied the evolution of personality and emotions within a cultural framework. While Inhelder and Piaget (1958: 335) consider the fundamental concern of adolescence to be that of taking up adult roles, Erikson's theory suggests the most pressing concern to be the establishment of an identity which entails the uncertainty of adult roles ahead, the search for people and ideals worthy of their faith and the search for avenues of duty and service. As well, such personal concerns as sexual maturation and a self-image are part of achieving an identity.

The adolescent stage of development then is both an introspective one, preoccupied with self, and extroverted, devoted to examining individuals and society. Our focus on adolescent literature will draw on these concerns and concentrate on various subdivisions within two broad themes: firstly, developing a self identity and secondly, developing a world view. Featured will be a representative sampling of British, American and Australian novels, with an emphasis on the latter. The bias will be towards those authors who have made a significant contribution to the genre in one way or another. As discussion proceeds, literary elements and issues germane to the genre will be considered.

DEVELOPING A SELF IDENTITY
Acquiring Sexual Maturity

Few themes within adolescent fiction cause more concern amongst adults than those which explore either physical or emotional aspects of sexuality. Those concerned argue along these lines: the novels' explicit nature encourages experimentation; 'educates' youth before they are 'ready', or promotes the author's own set values. Increasingly such novels have come under attack as documented in a recent survey of protests against books over the last thirteen years (Donelson 1985).

The author most frequently protested against is Judy Blume, whose themes are often concerned with aspects of sexuality. Her candid first person narratives feature a colloquial style which establishes a comfortable rapport with her reader, and she is by far the most popular author in the field. Her first novel, *Are you There, God? It's Me, Margaret* (1970) concerns a self-conscious eleven-year-old who confides in God and prays that He will 'fill her bra' and see to it that she is not the 'last to get it' (menstruation). Usually, Judy Blume's novels reflect female preoccupations with sexuality but *Then Again, Maybe I Won't* (1971) is an exception. Tony Miglione worries about his developing sexuality, too, noting untimely erections in school and succumbing to voyeurism when the next door neighbour fails to lower the shades.

Forever . . . (1975) differs from these tentative explorations of sexuality. Originally published as the first of her two adult novels, *Forever . . .* is acclaimed by adolescents for its informative exploration of the development and demise of a sexual relationship between two seventeen-year-olds. Despite its sensitive treatment of the emotional as well as the physical side of first love, it is a novel overcrowded with concerns: differing attitudes towards morals, intercourse, impotence, contraception, homosexuality and the inner workings of a family planning clinic.

Like Blume's book, Aidan Chambers' *Breaktime* (1978) also concerns the *angst* of the first sexual experience. Again, the first person narrative is employed, but thereafter the two novels differ. Chambers experiments with a range of narrative techniques, establishing a rapport between reader and seventeen-year-old Ditto. For example, there is Ditto's stream of consciousness, then a recorded diary of emotions and finally three simultaneous narratives in one episode. Other, somewhat contrived, visual techniques litter the text: graffiti, footnotes, handwritten and typewritten letters, balloon dialogue and computer-generated illustrations.

Stylistically and thematically more traditional but still expressing Chambers' male point of view of the first sexual experience is *Goodnight, Prof, Love* (Townsend 1970). At its time of publication it was a breakthrough in British literature for no novel for adolescents had examined sexual passion and experience in such depth and detail. Like Chambers, Townsend uses a stream of consciousness narrative to establish rapport with the reader and the protagonist, Graham Hollis, who is approaching his seventeenth year. Usually absorbed in his own personal daydreams of beautiful, responsive Barbara, Graham has an opportunity to experience reality when over-solicitous parents leave town and he falls in love with Lynn, a worldly waitress. A swiftly-paced narrative is created by the lively dialogue between brittle, hardened Lynn and the softer, sensitive Graham. Eventually a wiser Lynn plots the return of a sadder but wiser Graham to parental expectations.

The first sexual experience again is the central focus of *A Very Long Way From Anywhere Else* (Le Guin 1976). Seventeen-year-old Owen Griffiths mourns his own self-image, that of a 'bright little jerk', and confesses his inability to satisfy either peer or parental expectations. Natalie Field has no such identity problems; her life is singularly dedicated to becoming a composer. The two share a unique friendship until Owen decides a sexual relationship must inevitably follow. Le Guin differs from many adolescent writers who either consummate or painfully break the physical relationship for she sensitively and realistically allows these two adolescents to consider their own thoughts and feelings and make a reasoned joint decision.

Sexual experiences were limited to the heterosexual variety until the unwritten taboo against homosexuality was broken with the first brief hint of sexual feelings between two boys in *I'll Get There: It Better be Worth the Trip* (Donovan 1969) and further explored in *The Man Without a Face* (Holland 1972). In these early years of the 1970s, when novels were tackling hitherto untried themes of sexuality, reviewers and other adults were inclined to consider the 'message', the 'models' or the values rather than the novel as a whole.

Writers, too, responded to untried themes, often centring their novels around a 'problem' or issue. Scoppetone (1979: 108) relates that the 'ambiguous message' of *The Man Without a Face* inspired her to explore a homosexual relationship in *Trying Hard to Hear You* (1978) and produce a novel about a lesbian relationship, *Happy Endings Are All Alike* (1979) from personal experience (Scoppettone 1979: 108). The danger of starting a novel with a problem is that the result may become propaganda rather than art.

Australia writers have yet to produce the equivalent detailed and explicit sexuality common to these novels, some British, but mostly American. Such topics are more likely, on the Australian scene, to be implied, or the surrounding issues explored. Such is the case with *A Candle for St Antony* (Spence 1977), inspired, the author revèals (Spence 1984), by an overheard taunt about homosexuality. Rather than explore a homosexual relationship *per se*, Spence concentrates on the small-minded prejudice that so frequently misinterprets male friendships.

Australia has also produced its own token exploration of the effects of the first sexual experience ending in pregnancy. *It Looks Different When You Get There* (MacIntyre 1978) is a pseudo-trendy novel espousing a number of well-meaning messages. Jenny, a university student, becomes pregnant in a contrived one-night fling with her best friend's boyfriend, and further unlikely events follow. Following a trend of the 1970s in presenting less than perfect parents, *It Looks Different* ... suggests hypocritical and uncaring ones and thus Jenny is left on her own to discover various voguish groups: feminists with extended families and communes with 'uncorrupted' lifestyles. She learns very little about the realities of life until she embraces the traditional values of education and hard work once again.

Similarly unrealistic is Paul Zindel's treatment of pregnancy, abortion and inept parents in *My Darling, My Hamburger* (1969). Zindel's novel also demonstrates one of the inherent problems facing adolescent literature, that of rapidly dating social concerns and social attitudes. Were the novel to be published today, Liz's lack of alternatives to her pregnant condition, the hack abortion and the unsympathetic parents would all be treated differently.

The Lure of Romance

The theme of sexuality in adolescent novels ranges widely: from the tortuous decision as to whether to indulge in intercourse; the trial of discovering sexual inclinations; the task of coping with pregnancy; the difficulties of sole parenthood, to stigmatising abortion. Such treatments make it all seem rather more woeful than pleasureable. Do adolescents wish to read of such trials or do they desire far simpler treatments of sexual behaviour? The recent publishing phenomenon of the 1980s, the adolescent romance, suggests many youth indeed seek the latter.

The flood of series romance novels for adolescents began in 1979 when the American publishers, Scholastic, marketing directly to adolescents through schools, noted that their teenage romance sold extremely well through the Teenage Book Club, TAB (Ramsdell 1983: 175). Scholastic then introduced the Wildfire Romances series in 1980; it proved very successful. By 1982, Scholastic had added Wishing Star and Windswept Romances, and several other publishers had followed suit. While the majority of the romance series are American, they are widely availably in Australian book stores, and Wildfire titles are also available through Australia's Ashton Scholastic book club in secondary schools. Their British equivalents, Mills and Boon and Harlequin romances, are aimed largely at adults but widely read by adolescents.

The best literature dealing with love and sexuality follows no formula. Not so these romance novels, which purposely follow set guidelines. Indeed, publishers produce their own guidelines for their writing (Altus 1984) and numerous books advise would-be writers (Falk 1983; MacManus 1983). From format to characterisation, plot and style, each is a slight variation on the one before. And their theme? — the age-old story of girl gets boy.

The initial appearance of these novels was greeted by some adults as just another popular series — useful bait for non-readers. Even in their early days, however, the romance novels did not please everyone. A joint meeting in 1981 of several American organisations condemned the teenage romances and issued a joint statement that these books

> teach girls that their primary value is their attractiveness to boys; devalue relationships and encourage competition between girls; discount the possibility of nonromantic friendships between boys and girls; depict middle class, white, small-town families as the norm; and portray adults in stereotypical sex roles.

(Smith in Ramsdell 1983: 177)

Others, like Marilyn Kaye (1981), dismissed such attacks, countering objections with her own reading of a sample of such novels. Simplistically, Kaye concludes that their sheer popularity suggests that demand should be met. The question of quality, she contends, is irrelevant. More important is the basic freedom of the publisher to publish and the reader to read material of their own choice. The difficulty in assessing the 'messages' and literary quality of the romance series is the volume of output, for several titles are produced monthly in each series (Ramsdell 1983: 175). Obviously a large sampling of romance novels must be undertaken before a clear picture emerges, enabling selector and reader to make choices with full knowledge of the genre. Marilyn Altus (1984) has completed such an extensive study of the romance genre based on close readings of the Mills and Boons and Bantam texts with some reference to the Scholastic and Dell series. She concludes that using these books as 'bait' is 'absolutely unthinkable', and admonishes:

> Teacher/librarians are duty bound to present balance in the world views to which students are exposed. We must not present them with an unreal, romanticised world where women completely abdicate responsibility for themselves, where 'love' is accompanied either by ringing bells or male aggression, where the sexual attraction between male and female is the only thing that matters. Such a world does not exist.

(Altus 1984: 129)

Adolescents who choose to read of such a world are not denied the opportunity, for book shops stock a wide range at affordable prices, while the adolescent exchange of titles between peers multiplies access. Adult promoters of adolescent literature will most likely embrace the argument for providing 'quality' rather than satisfying popular demand. Whatever the stand taken, it is important to recognise the romance novel as one choice made by adolescents themselves, highlighting the sometimes divergent taste of adult and youth.

Acquiring sexual maturity has in this section been seen as a time of discovering emotions and physical sensations and occasionally intellectualising their meaning. Characters are preoccupied with their self-image, revealing feelings of inferiority, insecurity and ineptness in confessional narratives. Some authors have concentrated on issues and problems rather than integrating these into the novel as a whole. Where such is the case, the message, not the art, is what strikes the reader.

Breaking Away from Family and Asserting Independence

As the adolescent characters move toward sexual maturity, there is often a concomitant break from the family. The adolescent novels of the 1970s generally included one dimensional adults who were either solely in nurturing roles or, more likely, acting in bumbling and insensitive ways. Prior to the 1970s, parents and other adults were more likely to appear in idealised form. *The Feather Star* (Wrightson 1962) exemplies the idealised approach. Fifteen-year-old Lindy and her family are close and supportive and within such an environment and amidst much blushing and stammering, she discovers the opposite sex and discusses the uncertain life ahead.

Planning for this life, discovering self and the opposite sex are themes present too in the work of Hesba Brinsmead, widely acknowledged as a writer for adolescents. The writer, Brinsmead (Stodart 1985: 91) felt, can provide guidance for the adolescent, and hence her novels suggest the value of hard work, education, strong family support and such qualities as tolerance and honesty. Ryl Merewether in *Pastures of the Blue Crane* (Brinsmead 1964) matures amidst an unfamiliar lush coastal farming property, forming new relationships with family and peers, discovering tolerance and building self-esteem through the development of talents suggesting a future career. Ryl's maturation is romanticised by convenient plot coincidences and over-propitious circumstances, but empathetic characters, a poetic style and impish humour have appeal.

Beat of the City (Brinsmead 1966) reveals the author at her most didactic. Using a variety of obvious symbols, she uses a Melbourne city setting to illustrate the many 'side streets' which lure the unwary adolescent in the 'wrong' direction. The right path is epitomised by Mary Laurel, stable, hard-working, ambitious and devoted to family and traditional values. In contrast, Raylene Slater cares little for family, home and education, and her values clash with the law. Not surprisingly, Raylene is lured down the wrong street by the personification of evil, Blade O'Reilley, clothed in black leather jacket emblazoned with a death's head and claw, and mounted astride a bike, 'black and silver like the Devil himself' (Brinsmead 1966: 18). Raylene, the reader realises, is on the right path when she takes a job at the 'New Way Car Park'.

Like these earlier works, Brinsmead's latest novel, *The Sandforest* (1985) again portrays adolescents in propitious and unfamiliar surroundings, searching for an identity. Sky Herriot has finished school and has half-heartedly enrolled in university. Clippie Nancarrow, like Sky, is restless, flying light aircraft for a living. Both travel to Western Australia, and again through a series of coincidences, meet under a crisis situation which resolves Sky to settle down and work towards a future career and Clippie to realise that he too 'knows where he is going'.

Novels which feature breaking family ties and asserting independence, prior to the 1970s characteristically featured groups of adolescents. Ivan Southall's *What About Tomorrow* (1977) illustrates the increasing emphasis on the individual. The depression of the 1930s sets the scene for fourteen-year-old Sam's decision to leave home, when a wrecked bicycle ends both his paper route and his ability to contribute to the family income. His life reels backward and forward in an episodic narrative revealing scenes of childhood and adulthood and exploring the fears, hopes and dreams of a boy who becomes a pilot, a husband and a father.

A flashback technique again reveals the adolescent breaking from family and asserting independence in *Playing Beatie Bow* (Park 1980). Fourteen-year-old Abigail Kirk, living in the Rocks area of contemporary Sydney, strenuously objects to the reunion of her mother and father. From her limited experience, she is unable to understand the depth of physical and emotional love until she is transported back to Victorian Sydney where she experiences these emotions herself.

Twelve-year-old Eleanor compares her emotions with those of an earlier time, too, in *Eleanor, Elizabeth* (Gleeson 1984). She discovers, like Abigail, that adolescent emotions are similar from one generation to the next. The reader shares, through Eleanor's stream of consciousness, her insecurities when the family moves to new surroundings and she must face conflicting desires for childhood security and adult independence, with all the trials accompanying each. To sort these out, she seeks the privacy of a derelict schoolhouse and there finds similar emotions recorded in her grandmother's diary.

In *The True Story of Lilli Stubeck* (Aldridge 1984) a diary once again reveals a young woman. But interestingly the diary itself is not presented; rather it becomes the means of glimpsing secondhand the perplexing relationship between two strong women, and the efforts of the elder to subdue and ultimately subjugate the younger. Miss Dalgleish, the wealthiest woman in town, offers poverty-stricken Lilli an escape from her circumstances and accordingly Lilli undergoes external changes but retains the integrity of her principles. Appropriately, the reader is left to ponder and admire those whose principles cannot be bought.

Conforming and Rebelling

The transition from childhood to adulthood is a stage of development marked by the adolescent's ability to consider a range of possibilities, construct ideals and examine the values of self, family and society. The adolescent period also includes times of conformity and rebellion as both old and new are tested and evaluated. The classic novel of rebellion is *The Catcher in the Rye* (Salinger 1951), originally written for an adult audience, but widely viewed as adolescent reading. If any novel loosely termed adolescent literature emerges as a classic, Salinger's novel is the likely contender, for reasons of literary quality and prototypical features which many later adolescent novels emulated. Seventeen-year-old Holden Caulfield tells his story in a first person narrative, using the frank and colloquial language of youth. Like many adolescent characters to follow, Holden blunders his way towards adulthood through a range of often bizarre episodes: an abortive one-night stand with a prostitute; a violent brush with a pimp; a feverish romance with an old girlfriend and a frightening sexual confrontation with a revered schoolteacher. Holden faces all these traumatic moments amidst constant guilt because he fails to conform to family and peer expectations. With such a host of worries, an unrelieved pessimism and downbeat ending is inevitable. Few writers of adolescent novels follow these final two features of Salinger's, most preferring an optimistic tone and a positive resolution.

But some characteristics of Salinger's work are replicated in that of S.E. Hinton: colloquial language, first person narrative and a rather pessimistic tone. The extraordinary feature of *The Outsiders* (1967), however, is its author's youthful sixteen years at its time of publication. Her closeness to the age of her readers and their concerns has gained her work an enormous following. In this novel conformity reigns, when two gangs, the middle-class Socs and the lower-class Greasers, engage in a vicious circle of violent acts and reprisals. The need to rebel and also that to conform is the underlying theme.

Australia's strident example on the theme of conformity and rebellion appeared in 1979. Gabrielle Carey and Kathy Lette were eighteen when they wrote *Puberty Blues* (1979), an insiders' view of the highly-conformist youth subculture of the Cronulla surfies. Crowded with sensationalised accounts of sex, drugs, rape and the rejection of family, school and society in general, *Puberty Blues* examines girls or 'chicks' whose sole purpose is to serve the narcissistic pursuits of their boyfriends and boys whose sole concerns are the next big wave and an endless supply of ready sex.

Another youthful Australian writer examines conformity and rebellion, too, but with far greater literary skill and sensitivity. *Cannily, Cannily* (French 1981) protrays Trevor Huon as different, an 'outsider' like many of the characters observed thus far. His parents are seasonal workers, causing the family to move from town to town. In one Trevor discovers the entire community, including his peers, their parents and his teachers, obsessed with football. The rejection of Trevor and his inept attempt to conform are told with feeling, for the author remains close to the character's emotions. Revealing his own personal understanding of conformity from secondary school days, French (Alderman and Harman 1983: 151) reels off a list of conformist 'rules' and concludes, 'If you did none of these things at my high school, you didn't belong. You could bluff, but that didn't always work. If you were not swimming with the tide, you were vaguely subhuman ...'

Fourteen-year-old Josh Plowman, unlike Trevor who attempts to 'swim with the tide', refuses to alter his position of outsider (Southall 1971). When Josh, the city Plowman, who writes poetry, visits his Aunt Clara in a small country town, he meets, like Trevor, a different breed. After physical scuffles, a stalemate occurs when Aunt Clara insists Josh conform and play with the cricket team or return to Melbourne. Asserting his right to remain true to his own nature, Josh starts the long trek home. The trying scenes of bullying and teasing are all the more intensely felt since the reader experiences Josh's emotions through a stream of consciousness narrative.

Changing Family Structures

One of the major developments characteristic of the adolescent novel is the much expanded view of the family. Prior to the late 1960s few novels portrayed other than a nuclear family, model parents and agreeable relationships. Youth rarely saw reason to question or rebel, and generally adolescence seemed a smooth period, though the opposite sex and the future were objects of interest. Novels since the 1960s have admitted different family structures exist and the previously smooth life revealed ripples of discontent.

Two novels which sensitively and candidly explore adolescents within one-parent families are *Mom the Wolf Man and Me* (Klein 1972) and *Dominic* (White 1977). Brett and Dominic both have mothers who are strong individualists: Brett's is a professional photographer and Dominic's a sculptor. Both youths enjoy close relationships with their mothers, sharing personal thoughts, interests and ambitions; but adult males become a threat to the status quo until adjustments are made. Minor themes, part of the new realism in family structures, are the life styles of unmarried mothers, live-in relationships and open ones between parents and children.

Only recently have Australian writers attempted to treat family relationships as a crucial impetus to crisis situations. Dianne Bates in *Terri* (1981) examines her heroine's traumas in adjusting to her mother's remarriage, living in a blended family and coping with her father's girlfriend. Emotional scenes are somewhat overplayed, though the novel is an important recognition of different family structures. *Piggy Moss* (Bates 1982) again treats a blended family and the tension between parents and youth as the family income disappears. Piggy's problems both at home and school consume the novel, allowing 'problems' to become the main concern, and weighing down a writer with talent.

Similarly, *Solomon's Child* (Clark 1981) overplays the adolescent trauma of family breakdown, again resulting in a novel largely about 'problems'. A low socio-economic urban setting provides an all-too-convenient one for an overlong list of woes: shoplifting, drugs, alcohol, violent behaviour, children's rights and the Children's Court.

While these novels of family woes generally conclude on a positive and optimistic note, some writers reflect the disillusionment earlier portrayed in *The Catcher in the Rye*, leaving characters coping but not resolving problems. These open-ended resolutions can nevertheless suggest that inner resilience tempers difficulties. An occasional sense of humour alleviates what could otherwise be a depressing tone. These points are borne out in a publishing sensation of the 1980s, *The Secret Diary of Adrian Mole Aged 13 ¾* (Townsend 1982) and *The Growing Pains of Adrian Mole* (Townsend 1984). Together, these novels concern two-and-a-half years in the life of Adrian, self-professed intellectual, poet and in his own words an 'existentialist nihilist'. Through his daily diary entries, the reader shares Adrian's personal problems: a constant eruption of 'spots'; the length of his penis; unfulfilled sexual desires and passing his 'O' levels. But Adrian's troubles concern, too, the complex love affairs of his parents. Obsessed by daily trials and feelings of superiority, Adrian views his family, peers, school and British society with disdain and growing disappointment until he eventually leaves home, returning to wallow in a nervous breakdown, theatrically staged and emotionally self-indulgent, like his amusing adolescent experience of life.

Just as Adrian is disillusioned by family, school and society, so too is fifteen-year-old Mark who shares, again through a diary, the disintegration of his family in *Breaking Up* (Willmott 1983). While Adrian Mole's woes are an indulgent self-portrait, Mark tells both of his own and those of his parents. Mark's father, an overly-dedicated teacher, defends a sexually-abused female student and suffers a beating as a result; a complication is the possibility of a sexual relationship between the two. The father becomes depressed, leaves teaching and withdraws from his family, each stage observed and commented upon by Mark, who guiltily ponders his own contribution. Adding to the throes of breakup are his own maturing sexuality and confusing relationships within school and society.

DEVELOPING A WORLD VIEW

Examining the System

According to theories of the adolescent stage of development, the period is one of examining both self and society. While the adolescent may be preoccupied with self-image, conforming and rebelling to models and ideals and testing and evaluating family relationships, he or she is also examining the wider community, its various systems and institutions.

Only a few authors writing for adolescents are political, that is, examine the effects of society's institutions and organisations on the individual. Cormier's work for adolescents is totally concerned with the manipulation of individuals by powerful organisations and institutions. His personal view of the world (Silvey 1985: 155), as reflected in his novels, is one of nervous fear: 'I am frightened by today's world, terrified by it ... I'm afraid of big things ... Big government frightens me; so does big defense'. While *The Chocolate War* (Cormier 1974) examines power and manipulation within a school, the parallel with any large political system is clear. Jerry Renault is beaten into submission both physically and emotionally by a Mafia-like gang and by the school administration. Pessimism prevails as a heavy weight of guilt rests upon individuals who by acquiescence condone the misuse of power.

Again the individual is defeated or, in the language of *I Am the Cheese* (Cormier 1977) 'terminated'. In this instance, the power is an institution acting, presumably, as a government agency. Young Adam faces a similar fate to his parents murdered under ominous circumstances after acting as government witnesses. The conclusion suggests that the individual is powerless against the insidious powers of government.

Individuals are manipulated not just by institutions and organisations, but by abstract ideals in *After the First Death* (Cormier 1979). The youthful terrorist whose blind loyalty to a cause leads to innocents' deaths, and the general whose blind loyalty to the state leads to the sacrifice of his son, both demonstrate the power of patriotism as a potential evil.

Cormier's portrayals of the defenselessness and ultimate defeat of individuals arouse both dismay and anger. Could such manipulations take place unheeded? While many would argue that they can and do, readers are provoked to question Cormier's inevitable annihilation of the individual. Perhaps because the general tone of adolescent novels is optimistic and resolved endings the norm, his departure is difficult to accept. Defending his pessimism, Cormier (Chambers 1979: 129) suggests his novels as antidotes to those with happy endings which 'seduce people into thinking things are easier out there in the world than they actually are'.

It is the world which appears manipulated by an even more insidious power than organisations and insititutions in *Displaced Person* (Harding 1979). Seventeen-year-old Graeme Drury increasingly finds his world fading to a dismal grey. Joining two other 'displaced persons', Graeme exists in a nether world separated from the outside one by the interface, an invisible membrane. Imagery is appropriately dismal and relentless pacing adds to the mood of powerlessness. Though Graeme is returned to the outside world, he questions whether the world itself is being manipulated by an unseen force, experimenting with humans and occasionally misplacing pieces until an accounting returns each to its proper place. It is a chilling story of alienated youth on the one hand, and manipulation of humanity on the other.

Finding the Ideal Society

If adolescents are presented in their literature with societies which can be manipulated at the whim of unseen, unknown forces or by calculating, corrupt powers, they are also given alternative societies to consider. Part of the adolescent's concern is searching for the ideal alternative. Two Australian novels present exclusive religious groups as alternative societies and examine their attractions and weaknesses.

In *People Might Hear You* (Klein 1983), the temple uses the comforting belief that its people are the 'chosen ones', and espouses a strong sense of propriety to control its members. The fate of unbelievers, the difficulties caused by insularity and the suffocation of the individual will are believably explored.

The Society for World under Divine Rule (SWORD) believes too, that they are the one hundred chosen to build a new world after the destruction of the old. Its believers isolate themselves from contamination like the temple believers and retreat to an island where the occupants keep, as its title suggests, *The Long Night Watch* (Southall 1983) for either a Japanese invasion or God. Flashbacks reveal the persuasive sermons of the SWORD leader, giving believers their identity and promise of deliverance. The unresolved fate of the colony arouses questions as to whether any closed society, blind to the outside world, can assure salvation for its members.

While *People Might Hear You* and *The Long Night Watch* view religious societies, *Is That You, Miss Blue*? (Kerr 1975) examines a single individual obsessed by religion. In public Miss Blue is an excellent science teacher in a religious boarding school for girls, but privately she converses daily with Jesus, a relationship the school administration rewards with dismissal. Questions raised here are how Miss Blue changed from the popular extrovert of her youth to an aged religious fanatic and how a religious institution can embrace Christianity on the one hand and hypocrisy on the other.

The institutions of school and society demonstrate one form of inhumanity for the adolescent reader's consideration. Inhumanity perpetrated by individuals can be even more provocative. In *The Pigman* (Zindel 1968), secondary school students John Conlan and Lorraine Jensen tell their story in alternating first person narratives. Feeling their lives unduly controlled by home and school, they concoct a scheme to amuse themselves, and find a kindred spirit in the elderly and lonely Mr Pignati. But ultimately they misuse the friendship and cause Mr Pignati's death; they are left pondering the consequences of their behaviour and realising their own sense of responsibility.

Townsend's novel, *Noah's Castle* (1975), is also concerned with the morality of human actions. Britain of the future is suffering economic disaster; food prices soar and families struggle to survive. But Norman Mortimer, an ex-army quartermaster, has prepared for the shortage, secretly stockpiling food and essentials for his family, and turning a newly-acquired country home into a fortress. Conflict arises when his children question the morality of such actions. The situation is a difficult one: the conflict between providing for family and caring for a wider society.

The needs of a community are at issue again in *Papio* (Kelleher 1984) which pits human and animal against one another. Experimental baboons on an African research station have outlived their scientific usefulness and are doomed to die. But two idealistic youth reject the morality both of animal experimentation and extermination, and brazenly free the animals. But freedom is meaningless to animals accustomed to captivity, so the children join them, eventually blending with a larger baboon community and rejecting their own kind. The solution seems appropriate, the runaways drawing hunters who eventually slaughter the baboons, not only to retrieve the children but to thin the numbers of animals which are ravaging the crops and spoiling the livelihood of villagers. The reader is left to ponder the complex issue of animal versus human rights and the difficult balance between the two.

CONCLUSION

The adolescent literature examined in this chapter has been linked with theories of adolescent development which characterises the period as one preoccupied with examining self, other individuals and society. Contemporary works reiterate the same major theme as adolescent literature emerging in the 1940s and 1950s: the adolescent's personal problems, but otherwise great changes have occurred, reflecting a more realistic reflection of adolescent life.

Style exhibits the most remarkable change. Moving away from the omniscient point of view, authors establish rapport with readers with more personal viewpoints: first person narratives, stream of consciousness, diaries and flashbacks linking child, adolescent and adult. These allow a realistic exploration of the private emotions, thought processes and physical reactions of such intense concern to adolescents. The frank and colloquial language of youth adds a further dimension of reality.

Characters, too, offer a more genuine reflection of a society with a full range of social classes and family structures. 'Out' are the exclusively happy nuclear families; 'in' are one-parent households, unmarried mothers and blended families where parents are not always right and may indeed be insensitive or preoccupied with their own problems. While there is a trend toward more well-rounded adults, by and large they are not the models worthy of emulation and faith which adolescents seek.

Plots and themes now embrace all aspects of life, tackling the early taboos of explicit sex, drug abuse, alcoholism, the dark side of human nature and much more. The majority of such treatments are American, and to a lesser extent British, but the Australian novel, too, has moved in the 1980s towards more candid treatments. Many novels, however, continue to be too narrowly focused on a single issue or problem, thus limiting their viability as art.

The most interesting change has occurred in the adolescent novel's mood and tone. Unresolved endings, pessimism and disillusionment with self and society all appear, and call upon the adolescent's ability to consider alternatives. Along with these changes is the move away from didacticism. Rebellious and unconventional adolescents are less often punished and non-judgemental portrayals of alternative life styles abound. Nevertheless, many authors conclude their novels with characters espousing the value of an education and embracing a career, despite plots which defy such conclusions.

While adolescent novels today reflect a more complex society including a greater range of characters and themes and provoking a closer examination of self, society and its institutions, few consider adult life ahead or offer sufficient, in-depth characters which would satisfy the older adolescent's concern for people, ideals and avenues worthy of their faith and service. For these adolescents, adult literature becomes more appropriate reading.

The major contribution of adolescent literature continues to be its exploration of self, peers and those individuals and aspects of society which immediately touch upon their world. With the last of the taboos which hindered portraying life in all its complexity gone, the adolescent novel should continue to offer a unique category of literature examining life from a youthful point of view.

REFERENCES

Altus, Marilyn. 'Sugar-Coated Pills: A Study of Formula Romance Fiction for Adults and Teenagers' in *Orana* Vol. 20, No. 2, May 1984.

―――――, 'Sugar-Coated Pills: A Study of Formula Romance Fiction for Adults and Teenagers' in *Orana* Vol. 20, No. 3, August 1984.

Briley, Dorothy 'Publishing for the Young Adult Market' in Rogers, JoAnn V., editor, in *Libraries and Young Adult Media, Services and Librarianship*. Littleton, Colorado: Libraries Unlimited, 1979.

Brinsmead, Hesba, 'Why Write for Teenagers or Something to Give' in Stodart, Eleanor, editor, *Writing and Illustrating for Children: Children's Book Council ACT Seminars 1975—80*. Canberra, ACT Branch of the Children's Book Council: 1985.

Burton, Dwight L. 'Pap to Protein? Two Generations of Adolescent Fiction' in Bator, Robert, editor, *Signposts To Criticism of Children's Literature.* Chicago: American Library Association, 1983.

Carpenter, Humphrey and Prichard, Mari *The Oxford Companion to Children's Literature* Oxford: Oxford University Press, 1984.

Chambers, Aidan. 'An Interview with Robert Cormier' in *Signal* No. 30, September 1969.

Conger, John Janeway and Petersen, Anne C., *Adolescence and Youth: Psychological Development in a Changing World.* New York: Harper & Row, 1984.

Donelson, Kenneth, 'Almost 13 Years of Book Protests ... Now What?' in *School Library Journal* Vol. 31, No. 7, March 1985.

——————, and Nilsen, Alleen Pace, *Literature for Today's Young Adults.* Glenview, Illinois: Scott, Foresman, 1980.

Duncan, Frances, 'The Young Adult Novel: One Writer's Perspective in *Horn Book Magazine* Vol. 57, No. 2, April 1981.

Erikson, Erik, *Identity: Youth and Crisis.* London: Faber & Faber, 1968.

Falk, K. *How to Write a Romance and Get It Published.* New York: Crown, 1983.

French, Simon, 'Reporting on Real Life' in Alderman, Belle and Harman, Lauren, editors, *The Imagineers: Writing and Illustrating Children's Books.* Canberra, Reading Time, 1983.

Inhelder, Bärbel and Piaget, Jean, *The Growth of Logical Thinking from Childhood to Adolescence: An Essay On The Construction of Formal Operational Structures.* London: Routledge & Kegan Paul, 1958.

Kaye, Marilyn, 'The Young Adult Romance: Revival and Reaction' in *Top of the News* Vol. 38, No. 1, Fall 1981.

Macmanus, Yvonne, *You Can Write a Romance! And Get it Published!* New York: Pocket Books, 1983.

Niall, Brenda, *Australia Through the Looking Glass: Children's Fiction 1830–1980.* Melbourne: Melbourne University Press, 1984.

Ramsdell, Kristin, 'Young Adult Publishing: A Blossoming Market' in *Top of the News* Vol. 39, No. 2, Winter 1983.

Ray, Sheila G., *Children's Fiction: A Handbook for Librarians.* Leicester, England: Brockhampton, 1972.

Scoppettone, Sandra, 'Trying Hard to Reach Them: an Interview with Sandra Scoppettone' in *Top of the News* Vol. 36, No. 1, Fall 1979.

Silvey, Anita, 'An Interview with Robert Cormier, Part I' in *Horn Book Magazine* Vol. 61, No. 2, March/April 1985.

Spence, Eleanor, 'Realism in Children's Fiction; A Writer's View,' a talk delivered to the Children's Book Council, ACT Branch, 30 September 1984, Canberra.

Townsend, John Rowe *Written for Children: An Outline of English Language Children's Literature.* New York: Lippincott, 1983.

BOOK REFERRED TO IN THE CHAPTER

Aldridge, James, *The True Story of Lilli Stubeck.* Hyland House/Puffin.
Bates, Dianne, *Piggy Moss.* Puffin.
——————, *Terri.* Puffin.
Blume, Judy, *Are You There God? It's Me, Margaret.* Gollancz/Piccolo.
——————, *Forever ...* Pan.

———, *Then Again, Maybe I Won't*. Piccolo.
Brinsmead, Hesba, *Beat of the City*. Oxford.
———, *Pastures of the Blue Crane*. Oxford.
———, *The Sandforest*. Angus & Robertson.
Carey, Gabrielle and Lette, Kathy, *Puberty Blues*. McPhee Gribble.
Chambers, Aidan, *Breaktime*. Bodley Head.
Clark, Mavis Thorpe, *Solomon's Child*. Hutchinson/Puffin.
Cormier, Robert, *After the First Death*. Pantheon.
———, *The Chocolate War*. Pantheon.
———, *I Am the Cheese*. Pantheon.
Donovan, John, *I'll Get There: It Better be Worth the Trip*. Macdonald.
French, Simon, *Cannily, Cannily*. Angus & Robertson/Puffin.
Gleeson, Libby, *Eleanor, Elizabeth*. Angus & Robertson.
Harding, Lee, *Displaced Person*. Hyland House/Puffin Plus.
Hinton, S.E., *The Outsiders*. Viking.
Holland, Isabelle, *The Man Without A Face*. Lippincott.
Kelleher, Victor, *Papio*. Kestrel.
Kerr, M.E., *Is That You, Miss Blue?* Harper.
Klein, Norma, *Mom, The Wolf Man and Me*. Pantheon.
Klein, Robin. *People Might Hear You*. Puffin.
Le Guin, Ursula, *A Very Long Way From Anywhere Else*. Gollancz/Puffin.
MacIntyre, Elisabeth, *It Looks Different When You Get There*. Hodder & Stoughton.
Park, Ruth, *Playing Beatie Bow*. Thomas Nelson/Puffin.
Salinger, J.D., *The Catcher in The Rye*. Penguin.
Scoppettone, Sandra, *Happy Endings Are All Alike*. Harper.
———, *Trying Hard to Hear You*. Harper.
Southall, Ivan, *Josh*. Angus & Robertson.
———, *The Long Night Watch*. Methuen
———, *What About Tomorrow*. Angus & Robertson.
Spence, Eleanor, *A Candle for St Antony*. Oxford.
Townsend, John Rowe, *Good-Night, Prof. Love*. Oxford.
———, *Noah's Castle*. Oxford.
Townsend, Sue, *The Growing Pains of Adrian Mole*. Methuen.
———, *The Secret Diary of Adrian Mole Aged 13 ¾*. Methuen.
White, Mary, *Dominic*. Methuen.
Willmott, Frank, *Breaking Up*. Collins.
Wrightson, Patricia *The Feather Star*. Hutchinson.
Zindel, Paul, *My Darling, My Hamburger*. Harper.
———, *The Pigman*. Harper.

FURTHER REFERENCES

Donelson, Kenneth L. and Nilsen, Alleen Pace, *Literature For Today's Young Adults*. Glenview, Illinois: Scott, Foresman, 1980.
Hoogstad, Valerie and Saxby, Maurice, *Teaching Literature to Adolescents*. Sydney: Nelson, 1989.
Kennerley, Peter (ed.), *Teenage Reading*. London: Ward Lock, 1979.
Thomson, Jack, *Understanding Teenagers' Reading: Reading Processes and the Teaching of Literature*. Sydney: Methuen/Croom Helm, 1987.

PART III
THE INTERNATIONAL WORLD OF CHILDREN'S BOOKS

19 THE INTERNATIONAL WORLD OF CHILDREN'S BOOKS

MARLENE NORST

> ... each of them is a messenger that goes beyond mountains and rivers, beyond the seas, to the very ends of the world in search of new friendships. Every country gives and every country receives.
>
> Paul Hazard

INTRODUCTION, OR A BRIEF GAME OF TAG IN THE TERMINOLOGICAL JUNGLE

There are three terms which sooner or later appear in any discussion of children's literature world-wide: *universal*, *international* and *multi-cultural*. My first instinct was to play the coward and avoid them altogether. Good sense rather than bravery convinced me that this would only lead to complicated separate dealings with their horde of tiresome relations, value-laden synonyms and antonyms like ethnic, ethno-centric, multi-national. Face it (I tried to encourage myself), if you follow Humpty Dumpty's advice in *Alice Through the Looking Glass* and use a firm hand with them, these terms may well prove helpful in tracing significant changes in children's literature. After all, terms are only human constructs which we have created, complete with synonyms and antonyms; the effort involved in unpacking and resorting *these* three major terms may well help to throw some light on the way human beings story their world.

So my starting point will be three terms together with three opposites chosen from a range of possibilities in the hope that they will reveal interesting patterns when juggled in the mind:

> universal: individual
> international: national
> multi-cultural: mono-cultural

And now 'let the wild rumpus start'!

UNIVERSAL: INDIVIDUAL

> So Ananse took the golden box of stories back to earth, to the people of his village. And when he opened the box all the stories scattered to the corners of the world, including this one. This is my story which I have related. If it be sweet, or if it be not sweet, take some elsewhere, and let some come back to me.
>
> (Haley 1970: 30)

So ends the African story of the origins of the Spider tales which have indeed travelled from Africa to the West Indies and America and have then been 'scattered to the corners of the world'. We hear of a triumphant Kwaku Ananse returning from his quest for stories, proudly bearing the divine seed all over the world but reaping in return a never-ending story harvest.

The Universals

A Story, A Story is about a universal triad: the story, the story-teller and the story-listener. It affirms the divine origin of story, establishes the need to share it with the whole world and promises an eternal cycle of exchange as a reward.

Signs of the universality of story, story-telling and story-sharing are everywhere. As Barbara Hardy has shown so clearly, narrative is a primary act of mind:

> For we dream in narrative, daydream in narrative, remember, anticipate, hope, despair, believe, doubt, plan, revise, criticize, construct, gossip, learn, hate and love by narrative. In order really to live, we make up stories about ourselves and others, about the personal as well as the social past and future.
>
> (Barton 1977: 13)

In short, *narrative is essential to our existence as human beings*. No people living anywhere on our planet can resist the urge to communicate in story or be immune to the lure of a tale well told. The sense of story, that sixth, most quintessentially human sense, marks us out from all other species.

In general, *human beings also seem to agree on the principal function of story*: to shape personal and communal experience in order to share and remember it. The transmission of story to those who were not actual witnesses of the event is intended to involve them in our existence. This would seem to explain why everywhere and always we are intent on using story to teach the next generation what we consider memorable whether it be our exploits and achievements or simply our way of doing things.

There is also *a universality about the kinds of stories we tell and the way we shape them* to attract the listener. Communities remote from each other in time and space all produce creation myths, ancestral myths and legends of heroes. Certain forms in both rhyme and prose such as proverbs, fables, pour-quoi stories, jocular and nonsense tales are found all over the world. There is also a recurrence of human types: the lucky and the luckless; the brave and the fearful; the small cunning ones and the large stupid ones; the generous and the mean-spirited. The main themes are small in number and recur everywhere. They include the Journey or Life Cycle with its Quest and Rites of Passage; the confrontation of Good and Evil; the relation of the Conscious to the Unconscious; Reversals of Fortune; Human Nature in conflict with 'the Other' whether that Other is part of the natural or supernatural world. Even the smallest elements of narrative, the motifs, the verbal images, are omnipresent and invested with similar meanings the whole world over: the significant number three; the power inherent in names; dream images; sexual images; images of death. Anyone who fears that there are no cultural universals left need only turn to Stith Thompson's great reference works, *The Types of the Folk-tale* and *The Motif-Index of Folk-Literature* to find instant reassurance.

Our response to other people's stories from all over the world is the best of living proofs that they do indeed work for us all. Idries Shah in his *World Tales*, one of the most exciting collections of recent times says:

> there is a certain basic fund of human fictions which recur, again and again, and never seem to lose their compelling attraction.
>
> (Shah 1977: vii)

Each tale represents a universal type and illustrates 'the extraordinary coincidence of stories told in all times in all places'. The fascinating scholarly introduction to each of the tales makes one aware of the many thousands of stories that these sixty-five, in fact, embody.

Individual Aspects of Story

In reading the Algonquin Indian version of *Cinderella* or the Norse version of *William Tell* we naturally compare them with the French and Swiss versions and become aware both of the universals which are operating and of the specific cultural differences. Such differences emerge over time not only because the stories reflect a different social reality but also because each community and each age makes different demands on its story-tellers. The need to attract and hold the attention of the audience is the one universal imperative for all story-tellers and Ananse, sidling creature, full of cunning tricks which he uses to ensnare the unsuspecting listener in his powerful web of story, is a classic example of the type. But *A Story, A Story* is told not by Ananse, but by another story-teller who is at pains to assert his/her achievement as an artist: 'This is *my* story ... which *I* have related', implying that this telling is unique. There is more than the artist's sensitive ego involved here. The *universal can only be translated by the local story-teller speaking to his own audience.*

Different cultural groups will in various periods indicate a preference for certain themes, narrative structures and narrative styles. They will make different choices from amongst the universal range of possibilities. The community also exercises other social controls. Depending on the status of men and women, adults and children, and the relationship between them, every community reserves for itself the right to determine who may tell which story to whom on which occasion and in which kind of language. The Japanese, for instance, show a marked distinction between the language considered suitable in telling stories for children and for adults. In English this distinction is increasingly blurred and 'baby-talk' in child-adult interaction has been outlawed. Usually there is also a cultural expectation that by a certain age or stage an individual claiming membership of the group will have become familiar with a basic stock of approved stories — whether or not this be a set of nursery rhymes, Bible stories, novels or TV sagas, as in our culture. Interestingly, an 'excess of stories' seems in most cultures to be accorded respect and to mark the individual as a wise, learned or 'cultured' person.

The individual story-teller works within these constraints, selecting what affords him or her the most satisfying performance in the particular context of time, place and audience.

The individual listeners also play a role in transforming story, and modern criticism is beginning to focus more attention on them. While the inter-cultural study of story reception is still to come, it may well prove the most rewarding area of research. Three incidents may illustrate this new area. Some years ago while visiting Perth I met a group of Aboriginal children aged between seven and ten who were attending a rural Aboriginal school. Their white teacher had recently taken them camping for a weekend, and on a suitably dark and stormy night had told them a story about a werewolf. The children were unanimous that this had been the highlight of the trip and were eager to draw me illustrations for the story. It was intriguing to find that the werewolf (whom the teacher had not described) appeared in a number of the drawings as a huge kangaroo.

On my return to Sydney I asked two non-Aboriginal children to illustrate the story. The five-year-old boy responded with a large bird with many feet and claws (he was very insistent on the large number) and then offered to draw me a 'real wolf'. The second picture consisted of a large black circle with a bright red centre. When asked for some explanation he remarked, rather impatiently, that it was, of course, the wolf *after* he had eaten Little Red Riding Hood. For a small Australian city child werewolves and 'real' wolves are clearly equally mythological creatures. The six-year-old girl, on the other hand, produced an abstract in very dark, murky colours.

While it is, of course, impossible to draw any valid conclusions from so minute a sample these responses do show that child listeners will interpret new information (here a new image) in one of two ways. They will refer to images with a similar function in a known story or story-cycle (kangaroo, the Red Riding Hood wolf) or they will respond directly, emotionally, with an image produced in the subconscious (the bird and the abstract). In each case, the given element — the werewolf — was transformed into three different images in the minds of these particular individuals.

Oral and Written Stories

The discussion so far has drawn its examples from oral telling and the traditional tale which is intended for adults and children combined as one single audience. Do the same observations about universality apply equally to written children's literature? One could argue that they do not.

In the time of oral transmission neither geographical nor language barriers seemed able to impede the movement of story but travel was slow. The gradual dominance of writing increased the speed with which stories were diffused, particularly in the form of collections like *The Arabian Nights*, but, paradoxically, it also limited the audience by turning the universal listener into the reluctant reader or illiterate. From the sixteenth century on, the written form, as print, accelerated the process of relegating the oral story to the lower classes and reserving the written tales, increasingly deemed to be the only ones of value, for the 'educated' classes. It also decisively separated children from adults. By contributing to the rise of nationalism it also further restricted the audience.

As long as the oral tradition prevailed and the universality of story as common property was accepted, language and dialect borders were crossed with relatively little effort. It was the establishing of national borders which radically altered this free flow. 'Standard' languages were promoted to 'unify' the nation and alternative forms of speech such as dialects or regional accents were downgraded as 'common/uneducated/vulgar'. The standard national language was then said to be imbued with innate qualities which made it both aesthetically and morally superior to all others and was thus an accepted token of national pride. Gradually it became unnecessary, impossible and unpatriotic to learn other languages. Stories written in these despised languages or dialects were thus increasingly rendered inaudible and invisible.

INTERNATIONAL: NATIONAL

Philippe Aries (1962), Lloyd de Mause (1974), Neil Postman (1983) and others have all traced the emergence of the concept of 'childhood' in Europe and shown convincingly that as a distinct period between infancy and adulthood it is an adult invention which can be dated. While agreeing in principle, these writers tend to differ on the details. Some see the beginnings in the Renaissance, others would push it into the eighteenth century and so adduce different causes for its appearance. Postman, who defends the earlier date, stresses the significance of the invention of printing in altering people's view of themselves and their life cycle. He sees printing and the change from the oral to the literary tradition as promoting both individualism and nationalism; restricting interpersonal communication and institutionalising education.

> Print made the vernacular into a mass medium for the first time. This fact had consequences not only for the individuals but for the nations. There can be little doubt that fixed and visualizable language played an enormous role in the development of nationalism. Indeed, linguistic chauvinism coincides exactly with the development of printing: the idea of a 'mother tongue' was a product of typography ... From print onward, adulthood had to be earned. It became a symbolic, not a biological achievement. From print onward, the young would have to *become* adults, and they would have to do it by learning to read, by entering the world of typography. And in order to accomplish that they would require education ... Therefore Eruopean civilization reinvented schools. And by so doing, it made childhood a necessity.
>
> (Postman 1983: 33–6)

There seems to be general agreement that children's literature, that is, books specifically written for children, existed by the seventeenth century. By then the category 'childhood' had been sufficiently accepted to warrant the creation of a separate world filled with its own rules of conduct; institutions, games, dress and printed reading matter. Depending on the nation compiling the literary history the title 'father of children's literature' (at least in Europe) is awarded either to the English printer Caxton (1422–91); to the Bohemian Bishop, Jan Amos Komensky (Latinised as Comenius) or to the French academician, Charles Perrault (1628–1730). All three used the vernacular and emphasised the importance of the child's own language even if it was as in the case of Comenius' *Orbis sensualium pictus* (1658) to serve as a bridge to Latin, the European language of scholarship.

Nationalism

The increasing importance of nationalism in Europe, particularly in the nineteenth century affected children's literature both positively and negatively. It fostered a feeling of group identity by promoting a sense of tradition but also by encouraging aggressive militarism in the name of patriotism. The new nationalism led to a cultural revival based on digging up the past. There was a positive mania for collecting everything that was felt to enhance the glory of the nation, and the story tradition, previously rejected as vulgar, was now saved from extinction as a national treasure. The work of Jacob and Wilhelm Grimm provides a good example. As linguists and historians they focused attention on their own region, particularly the village of Zwehr near Kassel, and were intent on using the rediscovered traditional material to inspire in the German people a feeling of national pride at a time when Germany was occupied by the French during the reign of Napoleon. The first volume of their *Kinder-and-Hausmärchen* appeared in 1812 and by the time it reached England eleven years later in its translated form, the *Stories for Children and the Home* appeared as *German Popular Stories* (1823). The new title clearly proclaimed the national origin rather than the function of the stories.

The dangerous impulses that came from nationalism, however, soon made themselves felt too in children's literature. Children's books were used to engender feelings of national superiority, to encourage aggressive rivalry and to promote xenophobia. A study of the full range of European books of the mid and late nineteenth century shows a terrifying emphasis on militaristic conquest parading as 'adventure' and the glorification of the young male hero who fights and, preferably, dies (gloriously) for his nation. Never mind the cause, the place of battle or the human cost: to question is not to reveal onself a coward, a traitor or a spy. There are many examples of ABC books in England, France and Germany from that period which dispense with A for Apple or Alligator in favour of A for Army, illustrated by pictures of children in paper hats marching along like 'real little soldiers'. The symbolic markers of nationalism — flag, anthem and uniform and heroic vocabulary keep in time with the small marchers. Aggressive nationalism when linked to colonialism produced various forms of racism and unfortunately the first book for children written in Australia, *A Mother's Offering To Her Children*, *'by a Lady Long Resident in New South Wales'* (1841) provides a classic example of the type. Clara, Emma, Julius and Lucy, the children in the story, are left in no doubt as to the superiority of white ways in everything from birth to death. They are encouraged to chorus 'bad, cruel, wicked, ungrateful savages' whenever their mother draws breath in her narrative. Julius' aggressive jingoism is treated with fond indulgence by Mrs S. This is illustrated by a piece of dialogue which interrupts her story of Malay boats approaching a Portuguese settlement — for entirely peaceful purposes, as is later revealed:

> Julius: We do not care if there were 500 of their frippery vessels: our roaring cannon will soon teach them to keep among their islands; and let the white people alone. I wish I had been there, I would have helped to fire away upon them; leaving only a few to go back; and tell the rest, how we will treat such bad people in future.
> Mrs S.: Stay Julius. You have brought your roaring cannon into use too soon: these Malays are only come to ask the English to let them be under their protection while they collect and cure the Trepang.
>
> (1976 facsimile: 148)

A book inspired by what Hürlimann terms 'creative patriotism' was Selma Lagerlöf's *Nils Holgerssons underbara resa genom Sverige (Nils Holgersson's Wonderful Travels Around Sweden)*, published in Stockholm, 1906-7 in two volumes. Intended originally as a geography book for Swedish children, it became a best-seller all over Europe, and a great influence on modern writers for children. The story of a rather unpleasant small boy who is swept up by wild geese and taken on a journey of self-discovery as he shares the life and traditions of every corner of his homeland made Sweden more familiar to many children than their own lands. It is a very Swedish book concerned with transmitting a sense of place and recounting traditional folk tales but it is in no sense a nationalistic book. Nils learns where he belongs because he shares in the life of the many communities that constitute his country. He acquires a sense of community, not one of nationalistic superiority.

Unfortunately the 'patriotic racist' books far outnumbered the 'creative patriotic' ones in the nineteenth and early twentieth centuries. The encouragement they gave the development of national prejudice, racism, militarism and jingoistic patriotism in their child readers certainly contributed to the naïve enthusiasm of those who rushed to fight in the national war of 1914–18.

Internationalism

The nationalistic fervour of the nineteenth century did, however, produce its own antidote — the spirit of internationalism. At the political level this became evident in the creation of international bodies designed to cooperate across national boundaries in the interest of a common goal. At the individual level it expressed itself in an interest in communicating with people in other countries and discovering how they lived, through institutions such as pen-friend clubs.

Children's writers, at least some of them, also felt this need to show children that they were members of the human family rather than national patriots, particularly in times of national conflict. The theme of peace based on international understanding marks the work of a number of writers in the time of the two World Wars. The Russian writer Maxim Gorky actually planned an international series in 1916 when war was still being waged. He invited writers such as H.G. Wells, Fridtjof Nansen and Romain Rolland to write the biographies of 'great men the world over', in each case choosing the hero of a nation other than his own. Rolland was asked to write about Beethoven, Wells about Edison, Nansen about Columbus, while he himself worked on the life of Garibaldi. The letter which launched the project shows the spirit which motivated it:

> This stupid war bears eloquent witness to our moral weakness and the collapse of our culture. Therefore we ought to remind our children, at least, that people were not always as wicked as alas! we are today ... there have been and still are great men and noble hearts in every nation!
>
> The one thing you must tell a child so that he understands it before everything else is this: Humanity must be looked upon as a single, world-wide family, which must always be drawing towards a closer unity in the struggle for improvement which is common to all its members.
>
> (Hürlimann 1967: 185)

The tragedy of the Second World War led to the first concerted effort to support 'creative internationalism' through children's literature. The credit for this must go primarily to one woman — Jella Lepman. She was a German journalist who sought refuge in England during the Nazi period and returned to Germany immediately after the War as an official adviser on the cultural and educational needs of women and children in the American zone. She chose to make the renewal of children's literature on an international basis her first priority. In a letter to officials in many countries she pleaded for gifts of books:

> We are searching for ways to acquaint the children of Germany with children's books from all nations ... These children carry no responsibility for this war, and that is why books for them should be the first messengers of peace.
>
> (Lepman 1969: 35)

By July, 1946 she had set up an International Book Exhibition in Munich which then travelled throughout Europe. This became the basic stock for the International Youth Library in Munich which was officially opened on 14 September 1949. Greatly expanded, this library, which houses many national collections, produces valuable book lists, organises exhibitions and seminars and conducts classes in art and languages. It has recently been relocated in Schloss Blutenburg, a castle on the outskirts of Munich.

Jella Lepman was also responsible for establishing the *International Board on Books for Young People,* more generally known as IBBY, in November 1951. This organisation, which has its headquarters in neutral Switzerland holds international conferences bi-annually; awards the Andersen Writer's Medal and Illustrator's Medal bi-annually for the best children's writer and illustrator world-wide; and since 1963 publishes an international journal *Bookbird,* which is produced in neutral Austria. Since 1967 an International Children's Book Day has been celebrated on 2 April, Hans Christian Andersen's birthday. The Mildred Batchelder Award has been given since 1968 for translations into English published in the United States. In recent years the African and Asian nations have been making important contributions to the work of these international bodies, and there has been a shift from a European-centred internationalism to something approximating a little more closely to the 'global village' concept.

But international organisations, while they achieve much and are essential mechanisms for information exchange — which may lead to understanding — also have inherent weaknesses. Beneath the rhetoric of international understanding the old national rivalries often operate as savagely as ever. Many people, and that includes many writers for children, simply cannot think internationally, so ingrained is the nationalism of their childhood.

An interesting example of the dilemma is provided in the Foreword to Jella Lepman's book *Kinderbrücke* (*Bridge of Children's Books*) in the English translation published in 1969. The author of the book was J.E. Morpurgo, the Director General of the National Book League in England and a willing supporter of Jella Lepman's work. Yet his reservations about 'one world' are firmly expressed:

> There is much in Jella's philosophy that is beyond me ... I cannot find it in me to wish to remove the hyphen from internationalism. I want a British child to be thrilled by the story of Oliver Cromwell or Nelson, an American child to be proud of George Washington or Robert E. Lee. Jella, I suspect, objects to such as these for children's idols because they were all military, all were nationalists.
>
> (Lepman 1969: 7)

Where Gorky in 1916 deliberately set out to show that great human achievements belong to us all by virtue of our membership of the human race, Morpurgo clings to his national heroes whom he cannot share, because their achievements consisted in killing 'the other side'. Their victories meant someone else's defeat and death.

Why Read Across Language and National Boundaries?

So many worthwhile books for children are written in English today that both the book trade and parents may be tempted to look no further. But to exclude the children of any nation from sharing in the best stories that the whole world has to offer is to impoverish them unnecessarily.

It would seem that only in childhood do we have the capacity to recognise and accept each other as members of the one human family. Adults confined in nationalistic, religious and class straitjackets, blinkered by prejudice, can no longer embrace so much life. If books, as has often been said, can serve as bridges, children's books can do even more. *They can provide a common literary heritage for all children.* If certain literary heroes and heroines, literary adventures, humour and illustrations form at least part of the basic cultural material that all children have in common — providing a shared children's culture — then as adults they cannot be total strangers to one another.

It has, furthermore, long been accepted that *recognising and appreciating cultural differences and other value systems* is an essential part of the cognitive and emotional development that we term intellectual growth. We begin life aware only of our own existence. Gradually other individuals impinge — parents, family, friends — and these form part of our world while remaining distinct, autonomous beings. The circle widens at school for some but not for all. Often the growth of understanding which should develop naturally through sharing everyday life with people from different backgrounds is impeded by adult fears. The curriculum still equates education with the acquiring of information about other lifestyles, but the 'hidden agenda' all too often preaches the absolute superiority of the particular lifestyle of a dominant group. Neither the curriculum nor children's literature can be a substitute for human interaction, but they can be powerful allies in promoting curiosity, tolerance and respect for other ways of living. A delightful book by Edith Battles, *What Does the Rooster Say, Yoshio?* shows how early one can begin. In this story for kindergarten, Yoshio from Japan and Lynn (from, presumably, the United States) cannot communicate in each other's language and insist that the animals all speak only their language. Gradually from stubborn ethnocentrism and angry confrontation they move as equals to a position of exchange: of learning from each other, of discovering what is the same and what is different. They feel extremely pleased with themselves and with their now extended world when they realise that the cow says 'moo' in both Japanese and English.

Literature by its very nature is a global business. Authors are influenced by the writers of other lands, just as the earlier storytellers greedily pounced on a good story wherever it ran wild.

It we want access to the best stories — oral and written — then we must jump national fences. Adult readers have been adept at this feat for centuries and child readers are not even aware of the fence until some more defensive adult tacks a 'Keep Out' to the spiky palings. For those who want to keep children penned in, there are any number of rationalisations available: children will be confused by the unfamiliar; the translation will be inadequate; comparisons may lead to questioning of values represented as absolute. But for those who want to equip their children to live peacefully with their neighbours in our global village, the question is not whether they should read across language and national boundaries, but only *how* it can best be accomplished. Internationalism in children's literature has reached a very exciting, experimental stage and nowhere is this more in evidence than in Australia, a country which is a continent and well on the way, in recent years, to being a world within a nation.

MULTI-CULTURAL: MONO-CULTURAL

The twentieth century will be remembered (if we do not succeed in erasing all memory by blowing ourselves up before the century is out) for being a period of migration. What we have experienced in Australia is part of a world-wide movement. By its position Australia, though an island, has succeeded in attracting people from every corner of the world, rather than one or two main groups, as is the case in Europe. Changing one's self image is not easy and can indeed be a rather painful process. Australian society for about one hundred and fifty years after European settlement ignored Aboriginal culture; disregarded the contributions of early sizeable communities of Chinese, Germans and, later, Italians; and saw itself as homogeneously, harmoniously mono-cultural: Anglo-Saxon. The Irish, Scots and Welsh could have told a different story but they, too, have only very recently put a voice to it. Mass migration after the end of the Second World War made such a view untenable. Demographically, Australia was clearly now at the other end of the spectrum from 'mono' in almost every respect. The acceptance of this fact as a feature of Australian society and beyond that the recognition that it can prove a source of great strength to the country will be a very gradual process, one for the twenty-first century to comment on.

Children's literature is part of the cultural baggage that migrants bring with them in the oral and written tradition. It is preserved in the home and, if conditions are favourable, exchanged in the playground in counting games, jokes and playground rhymes. Perhaps the next edition of *Cinderella Dressed in Yella* may already have a multi-cultural flavour to it. A diverse community can also introduce the classics of one culture to another and make each other aware that other childhoods mean other books, often spendidly-crafted ones. A recent example is the reception accorded the Chinese sixteenth-century epic *Monkey* in Australia.

Perhaps most significantly it can lead to experimentation in making new and old material available in other languages. Besides simple translation, there is the bilingual book where two or more languages share the same cover, graphically showing the conviction that languages must be equally visible to gain equal respect, and counteract fear and prejudice.

There are authors who are conscious of the very different society in which an Australian child is growing up today. Early examples were novels by David Martin, Deirdre Hill's *Mario Visits Australia* and *Marani in Australia* by Faith Bandler and Len Fox, which made cultural differences the central issue. The recent novels of Nadia Wheatley make an even bigger impact, because they actually allow the Greek characters to speak Greek. Rather than providing the translation in an academic footnote, the words are allowed to explain themselves through the context.

Publishers such as Ashton Scholastic, Puffin, Methuen, Thomas Nelson (City Kids), Childerset and The Bodley Head initially produced some of their popular books in other language versions or bilingually, but because the financial returns were below their expectations, they seem to have withdrawn from the field. This is unfortunate, since the reasons for the financial failure were probably never analysed. Most of the books were published in 1978 when 'multi-culturalism' had just appeared like a new brand name and meant very little to the average reader, nor to the publisher's representatives who had had no experience in dealing with books in community languages. There is now one established publisher, Hodja Press in Melbourne, which specialises in books of this kind and has done excellent work in encouraging new writers to present their work, but unless mainstream publishers rethink, writers and readers will be short-changed. Booksellers are tentative too, unless they happen to specialise in language books. They are, understandably, nervous of unchartered waters: of new publishers, strange titles, worries that contents may offend someone, fear that the mono-lingual customer will turn tail. It seems to be a vicious circle that only the reader can break, by asking for books by Australians about Australian society today, preferably with at least some of the text in the language that is part of the characters' life.

Interest in one's background has also meant a greater acceptance of the books written in non-English-speaking countries, and gradually some of these are appearing on Australian shop and library shelves. These are not like the bland products of certain multinational book publishers whose stories are not rooted in any real soil, whose plastic characters never speak a real language, let alone a dialect. They are books which have a strong appeal because they are natural homegrown products which deal with universal issues in a clearly identifiable setting complete with smell, taste and texture.

A story which 'works' precisely because it is firmly set in place and time and which is proving very popular with Australian readers, is Christine Nöstlinger's *But Jasper Came Instead* (1983) (in German: *Des Austauschkind*, Jugend und Volk, Wien, 1983). Its central concern is the relationship between an English child and an Austrian family. Cultural barriers abound not only between the two nations but between the generations within the nationals of one family. The resolution comes — with much humour — only when there is recognition of the basic human need for love which transcends any differences.

REFERENCES

This chapter has focused on books for children seen as significant tokens of cultural exchange. In one sense, therefore, the bibliography could include everything fished out of that vast ocean of story which comprises all languages and all cultures. How then can we establish a basis for selection and readership? As a poor compromise the following titles have been assembled under several headings, which may serve as signposts for those keen to venture beyond their own backyard.

Background Reading: Books

Hürlimann, B., *Three Centuries of Children's Books in Europe*. Cleveland, Ohio: The World Publishing Co., 1978.

Lippmann, Lorna, *The Aim is Understanding. Educational Techniques for a Multi-cultural Society*. Sydney: Australia and New Zealand Book Company, 1977.

Office of the Commissioner for Community Relations. *Let's End the Slander*, Canberra: CCR 1979.

Preiswerk, R., editor, *The Slant of the Pen. Racism in Children's Books*. Geneva: World Council of Churches, 1980.

Rasmussen, R. and Rasmussen, H. editor, *Prejudice in Print. The Treatment of Ethnic Minorities in Published Works*. Melbourne: Monash University, 1982.

Saxby, Maurice, editor, *Through Folklore to Literature*. Sydney: IBBY Australia, 1979.

Periodicals

Book Bird, Vienna: IBBY/IICLRR.

Book Promotion News, Paris: UNESCO.

Interracial Books for Children. Kalyani, West Bengal: Intertrade Publications.

Multicultural Children's Literature Bulletin. New York: Council on Interracial Books for Children.

Multicultural Library Services Newsletter Sydney: State Library of New South Wales.

Wertheimer, L., editor, *Library Trends* Vol. 29, No. 2, Fall 1980. Illinois: Graduate School of Library Science 1980.

Articles and Collections

Aitken, M., 'Multiculturalism and Australian Children's Books' in *Orana* Vol. 17, No. 1, 1981.

Carpenter, H. and Pritchard, M. in *The Oxford Companion to Children's Literature*. Oxford: OUP, 1984.

Carroll, Frances Laverne, 'An Internationalized Children's Literature'. Paris: UNESCO, 1979.

Crampton, Patricia, 'Will It Travel Well? International Understanding Through Children's Books' *Bookbird* No. 15: Vienna IBBY, 1977.

Factor, June, 'Drop Dead, Pizza Head! Racism in Children's Culture'. *Meanjin* 3. Melbourne: University of Melbourne, 1984.
Nist, Joan Stidham, 'Cultural Constellations in Translated Children's Literature' *Book Bird* No. 2. Vienna: IBBY, 1979.
Singh, M.J., 'Children's Literature for Our Multicultural Society' *Orana* Vol. 17, No. 3. Sydney: 1981.
Lumb, P. and Hazell, A., *Diversity and Diversion. An Annotated Bibliography of Australian Ethnic Minority Literature*. Richmond: Hodja Educational Resources Co-operative Ltd, 1983.
Mattingley, C., *Recent Translations of European Fiction for Older Children and Young Adults*, Sydney: Library Association of Australia, NSW Group, 1978.
O'Sullivan, C., *Literature for a Multicultural Australia. An Annotated Bibliography of Novels/Prose for Years 7–10*. Sydney: Catholic Multicultural Education Programme, Catholic Education Office, 1982.
Pellowski, Anne, *The World of Children's Literature*. New York: Bowker, 1968.
————, *The World of Children's Storytelling*. New York: Bowker, 1977.
Scherf, W., editor, *The Best of the Best*, Munich: Dokumentation, 1976.
Stanelis, N., *Resources for Schools, Multicultural Education*. Canberra: Schools Commission, 1978.
Audiovisual Materials Available in Language Versions Other Than English. Weston: Weston Woods Studios, 1984.

Bi-lingual Books

Busch, Wilhelm, *Max und Moritz Polyglott*. Munich: DTV, 1985.
Davey, Gwenda, *Multicultural Cassette Series*. Kew (Victoria): Institute of Early Childhood Development, 1980.
Hoffmann, Heinrich, *Der Struwwelpeter Polyglott*. Munich: DTV, 1984.
Serventy, V. and Carnegie, M., *Wildlife of the Australian Bushlands*. Sydney: David Ell Press, 1985 (English/Japanese).

Australian Books in Translation

Norman, Lilith, *Climb a Lonely Hill*. Tokyo: Tuttle, 1970 (Japanese).
Stow, Randolph, *Midnite Käpt'n Mitternacht*. Munich: DTV, 1975.
Thompson, Valerie, *Rough Road South/Gefährlicher Ritt nach*. Melbourne/Mödling (Austria): St Gabriel, 1977.
Multi-lingual Series: Ashton Scholastic (English, Italian, Greek and French); The Bodley Head Dual-Language Picture Books (English, Italian, Greek, Turkish, Gujerati); Thomas Nelson's City Kids; Penguin's Practical Puffins (English, Italian, Greek).

References (in Chapter)

Aarne, Antti and Thompson, Stith, 'The Types of the Folk-Tale' in *Folklore Fellows Communications* Vol. XXV, No. 74.
Aries, Philippe, *Centuries of Childhood*. London: Cape, 1962.
Barton, G., Meek, M., Warlow, A., editors, *The Cool Web*. London: Bodley Head, 1977.
Hazard, Paul, *Books, Children and Men*. Boston: The Horn Book, 1944.
Hürlimann, Bettina, *Three Centuries of Children's Books in Europe*. Cleveland, Ohio: The World Publishing Co., 1978.

Lepman, Jella, *A Bridge of Children's Books*. New York: American Library Association, 1969.
Mause, Lloyd de, editor, *The History of Childhood*. New York: Condor, 1974.
Postman, Neil, *The Disappearance of Childhood*. London: Allen & Unwin, 1983.
Shah, Idries, *World Tales: The Extraordinary Coincidence of Stories Told in All Times, In All Places*. Harmondsworth: Penguin, 1977.
Thompson, Stith, *The Motif-Index of Folk Literature*. Indiana University Studies, Vols. XIX—XXIII.
Turner, Ian and Factor, June, *Cinderella Dressed in Yella*, Melbourne: Heinemann, 1969.

Books Referred to in the Chapter

Bandler, Faith and Fox, Leonard, *Marani in Australia*. Rigby.
Barton, Charlotte C., *A Mother's Offering to her Children 'by a Lady Long Resident in New South Wales'*. Facsimile edition, Jacaranda.
Battles, Edith, *What Does the Rooster Say, Yoshio?* Whitman.
Carroll, Lewis, *Alice through the Looking Glass*. Macmillan.
Comenius (Komensky, Jan Amos) *Orbis sensualium Pictus/Die sichtbare Welt*. Nürnberg.
————, *Orbis sensualium pictus/Visible World*. Facsimile edition, the Osborne Collection of Early Children's Books.
Grimm, Jacob and Wilhelm, *Kinder-und-Hausmärchen*. Dieterichsche Buchhandlung, *German Popular Stories*. Translator, Edgar Taylor, C. Balwyn.
Haley, Gail, *A Story, A Story*. Methuen.
Hill, Deirdre, *Mario Visits Australia*. Methuen.
Lagerlöf, Selma, *Nils Holgerssons underbara resa genom Sverige*. London: Dent, 1950.
Nöstlinger, Christine, *And Jasper Came Instead*. London: Andersen Press, 1983; *Das Austauschkind*. Vienna: Jugend und Volk, 1983.
Wheatley, Nadia, *Five Times Dizzy*. Oxford University Press; *Dancing in the Anzac Deli*. Oxford University Press.
Wu Cheng En, translator Arthur Waley, *Dear Monkey*. Glasgow: Blackie, 1973.

20 THE KEY TO THE KINGDOM: ACCESS TO CHILDREN'S BOOKS IN AUSTRALIA

ROSEMARY MOON

> Literature is the news that stays news.
>
> Ezra Pound

The key to the world of books for children turns on the attitude of parents and professionals who take care of young people. What lies behind the door depends on whether they are care-takers or care-givers, whether they like children and story, and whether they are in a position to have books easily within reach or have a strong tradition of story in their background. Children's attitudes towards fiction are first formed in the home. Parents, teachers and librarians are in a unique position to open worlds of experience to the young and place these in a perspective which adds depth and quality to their lives. Since children model their behaviour on those closest to them and absorb information at an enormous rate in the preschool years, parental attitudes towards books and reading are critical in developing a love of literature. If books and printed materials are seen around the home, if parents are seen reading, if they converse with their children about new experiences and if they introduce children to books in a caring environment, children will demand books of all kinds at an early age.

If teachers are enthusiastic about their vocation and are educated and informed about children's literature, this will influence children to read fiction more than they do at present. In public and school libraries, it is the librarians' attitude towards their small clients and commitment to encouraging their literary enthusiasm which will make the library an indispensable place to visit and the literary experience it provides at once social and creative. Given a wider perspective, access to children's books relies on publishers, academics, reviewers and journalists all pursuing standards of literary excellence, while bearing in mind elements that appeal to children when they choose and promote books.

The location and scale of public libraries have advantages for children and encourage usage. Since they are community based, they are able to provide a non-threatening and personal service. Children become familiar with the librarian and support staff and with the location of the library, since in metropolitan areas it is often within a short distance of their homes. Also, many public libraries are located near parking facilities, making access for young children and parents easier. Most libraries are open on selected mornings and evenings allowing preschoolers to come before lunch and older children to study later in the afternoon.

Formal access to collections is often through a simplified catalogue, listing author, title or subject. While some libraries give user education classes, others, such as Sutherland in New South Wales, give this service to parents, so they can help their children find project material. All help children on an individual basis.

All media are shelved within reach and are not overwhelming. In many libraries children's furniture or beanbags are provided, and bright decoration gives a warm attractive atmosphere.

The collections are divided into picture books for preschool children, junior fiction and non-fiction and sometimes a separate youth collection. Junior non-fiction is occasionally integrated with adult. Ideally, space should be allocated for story times and for craft activities which develop prereading skills. Stock often includes audio-visual media including film strips of well-known stories, films are sometimes available and, increasingly, video is being introduced. Electronic story programmes are available for use in libraries which have microcomputers.

Usually a children's specialist is employed or a member of staff is given responsibility for collections and services. Staff should like children and have some knowledge of child development and should also be familiar with children's media and programming activities.

The budget for a children's library depends on the level of funding from the local authority and the state. In New South Wales and Victoria it is also affected by the decision of the chief librarian who considers local priorities and demography when allocating money for children's materials. An average estimate for the children's book vote is one third of the total budget for resources, but this varies. Western Australia and Tasmania have a central purchasing procedure for all public libraries, and Queensland and the Northern Territory only partially select media at local library level.

When children's specialists select, they use a variety of reviewing journals which cover the Australian, English and American markets. These may include *Reading Time, The Booklist* and *Junior Bookshelf*. They spend time in publishers' warehouses and, particularly in country areas, are visited by publishers' and distributors' representatives. Children's librarians will often tell you that it is better to look at the book itself rather than purchase from reviews which may reflect rarified adult tastes out of touch with children. This view has a great deal of validity.

Often, children's collections are described as conservative in the sense that they emphasise award-winning books and well-established authors. Very popular material is also purchased, but there is a bias towards 'literary' rather than widely-read material if this choice is necessary. It is apparent that large numbers of 'literary' novels are not often read in the junior library, while there is a high turnover of fiction by Blume, Dahl, Goscinny and Klein and other popular writers. Similarly, in the series areas, there are never enough Sweet Dreams and Chose Your Own Adventure books. The tension between what children *want* to read and what they *should* read is a widely-debated issue amongst children's librarians.

The Library Association of Australia designates a minimum of one to two books per capita, depending on the child demography of the population served. Policy on the number of books a child can borrow varies. Some allow access to the adult library at ages twelve to fourteen; others have an open policy and once children have joined they can use all library resources.

In city libraries and those in large regional centres, promotional activities such as storytelling, puppet shows and craft activities are widely advertised and extend public awareness of the fact that children's books are readily available.

Preschool children are probably the best catered for in terms of activities in public libraries. No other library service usually exists for this group and 'getting them young', in the Dorothy Butler tradition, is a prevailing philosophy. Prereading skills and introduction to literature loom large in the professional consciousness of children's librarians. Picture book collections are well developed, prenatal classes and the baby health centre clientele addressed. There is an enormous demand for talks on choosing books for children, especially from new parents, and this could be assisted by the cooperation of mass media, particularly television. Increasingly, children's librarians talk to the local press, appear on community radio and occasionally on television. Some parents, however, say that they prefer face-to-face advice appropriate to their child's needs and situation.

Primary age children have a variety of needs, not the least of which is homework assistance and resources. Book promotion activities for this group take place mainly in the school holidays and include puppet shows, reader's theatre, literature competitions, and innovative programmes such as creating cartoons.

Children's librarians meet informally with groups having similar interests, such as local school librarians, workers in homes for disabled children, family day care and youth workers. They establish themselves as part of a community network to improve access to their collections and services by maintaining a presence. The more closely integrated with the community the library is, the more visible it becomes to parents and children in terms of active service. As a visible part of the local cultural and social landscape, it is seen as an accepted part of daily community routines. Personal contact is most important. Librarians make visits to local schools, give book talks and arrange for school classes to visit the library, particularly during Children's Book Week in late July.

Travelling book and library promotions are an excellent way of reaching children. Victoria's Jolly Jumbuck Media Mobile brings book-related activities to children throughout the state, and a similar concept, the Bookburra at Lake Macquarie Municipal Library in New South Wales, provides a travelling puppet theatre/cinema and storytelling space in a converted bookmobile. Some libraries take requests for book purchases from children and often for inter-library loan services. If these procedures were universal they would broaden the scope of library services to children. The Children's Subject Specialisation Scheme and Junior Fiction Reserve in New South Wales was established in 1981 and does offer inter-library loans. Organised by the metropolitan public librarians in Sydney, its function is to collect children's books as comprehensively as possible. Discarded children's literature in reasonable condition is retained and distributed to specialist city libraries. It is available if children request it.

Young adult collections are not well developed in Australia. Promotion of material to this group is not often done and books are usually included either in the children's or adult collections. There is not a great deal of local fiction published for this age group, but where young adult services have been researched and established, their success makes it evident that access to what there is could be improved. There is certainly a demand for local fiction dealing with contemporary life and issues which affect adolescents, and a need to survey their literary preferences.

SCHOOL LIBRARY SERVICES

These vary from state to state, but schools throughout Australia have access to some library services and many have well-appointed libraries with professional staff.

Bookstock is primarily purchased to support the curriculum of the Departments of Education but recreational media are also available to children attending school. School library hours usually start half-an-hour before classes start, and finish half-an-hour after they finish. Some schools have library periods and user education classes, but, increasingly the trend is towards integrating the school librarian's activities with other aspects of the school curriculum. For example, fiction may be recommended to support a historical or scientific theme, and students will receive library instruction when their assignments are set.

School librarians are in a good position to promote children's literature since they have a 'captive' audience and can suggest material to teachers. Many tell stories, give book talks and provide in-service courses. They can encourage daily uninterrupted reading, the preparation of book reviews and book clubs.

State Education Departments also publish useful review journals for the guidance of school librarians. Among these are the *Tasmanian Resources Review, Lines* (South Australia), *Scan* (New South Wales), *Review Bulletin* (Victoria), *Review Point* (Queensland). School magazines also assist in the promotion of literature to students. The

Department in New South Wales publishes *School Magazine* which is exclusively of a literary nature. It is circulated free to all children from ages eight to eleven in state schools. Western Australia produces *Crest, Zip* and *Range* for particular age groups, and in Victoria *Explore, Pursuit* and *Challenge* run curriculum-based articles as well as puzzles and stories.

ASSOCIATIONS

There are a number of associations in the field of children's literature which indirectly foster access to children's books by providing conferences and seminars for workers with children and interested individuals, talks for the public and book promotions. These are known within the network of those professionally concerned with children's literature but not by the public at large. Occasionally some appear in the mass media, notably the Children's Book Council of Australia, and all are in close contact with their members by newsletters. It is usual that the executive of one group will share common members with another within each state. The network is highly communicative and the functions of one association are often attended by members of another. Though the group throughout Australia may appear small, on an international basis it figures well. In 1982, fifty delegates were sent to the IBBY (International Board on Books for Young People) Conference in Britain. There are limited formal contacts between states, particularly if an association does not have a national coordinating body. This fragmentation would be a greater disadvantage if the groups were more politically active but on the whole they do not concern themselves with political issues. Individuals, however, have excellent interstate contacts within their own specialisation. For example, storytellers know about others in the field and academics have the opportunity to meet at national conferences or on exchange visits.

The association which encourages the most international contact is the *International Board on Books for Young People*. Its role is to 'promote international understanding through children's books, to encourage high literary and artistic standards and the wide distribution of literature for children, the continuing education of those involved with ... children's literature, the publication of imaginative and challenging books and the use of children's literature in education (Huus 1985: 787). Its secretariat operates from Basel, Switzerland and its membership encompasses fifty nations. IBBY Biennial Congresses focus on a particular theme in children's literature. Recently, 'Children's Book Production and Distribution in Developing Countries' was the theme for a Cyprus congress, and 'Why Do You Write for Children? Children, Why Do You Read?' is the theme for Japan in 1986. Delegates attend from around the world.

IBBY consults with UNESCO and UNICEF, among a host of international bodies. It is represented at the Children's Book Fair,

Bologna, and at all important trade functions. It awards the prestigious Hans Christian Andersen Medals, 'the little Nobel prize for children's literature' to living authors and illustrators who have made an outstanding contribution to children's literature. Winners include Astrid Lindgren, Tove Jansson, Christine Nöstlinger and Mitsumasa Anno. Titles are selected for translation for worldwide distribution. *Bookbird*, the journal of IBBY, appears quarterly with news from the Board.

In Australia, IBBY is based in Sydney. Its small but intensely active executive mounts exhibitions of international children's books, runs a national conference which addresses topical fields of interest, from books for children with disabilities to electronic stories, and is widely attended. Two conferences 'Through Folklore to Literature' and 'The Art of Storytelling', in particular, were seen by participants as stimulating the growth of interest in storytelling in Australia in the late 1970s. IBBY's forums focus on relevant contemporary issues and create discussion. International speakers have included Caroline Fella Bauer, Aidan Chambers and Dorothy Butler.

The proceedings of the congresses are published. IBBY has compiled bibliographies, produced videotapes on storytelling and audio-tapes on cataloguing multi-cultural collections. It does not deal directly with children, although its awards, its exhibitions, poster material and presence at fairs all promote literature to the young. News about activities appear in the IBBY newsletter. Its work forms an extremely valuable contribution to the intellectual climate surrounding children's literature in Australia.

THE CHILDREN'S BOOK COUNCIL OF AUSTRALIA

In 1945, a group of authors, publishers, librarians, teachers and representatives from the Australian Broadcasting Corporation formed a committee to organise Children's Book Week in Sydney under the banner 'United through Books'. They had been asked to cooperate in an international celebration by the Children's Book Council of the United States. From this activity the Children's Book Council of Australia emerged (Pownall 1980). Since then the Council, a voluntary organisation with a branch in each state, has promoted children's literature through its book awards, and its judges have endeavoured to set a high standard of excellence in Australian publishing for children. These awards are the best known in Australia and are made in a number of categories: to a children's book published by an Australian author which has wide appeal to children, and is of outstanding literary merit. There is also a Junior Book of the year and a Picture Book of the year. The awards are often contentious, a healthy sign, and are eagerly awaited each year.

The Children's Book Council also organises talks, exhibitions and book fairs directed at parents and children. Each year, it encourages the book trade, teachers and librarians to promote Australian children's books during Children's Book Week, and decides on a national theme such as 'Blast Off with Books' or 'Book Banquet'. The awards are announced in Book Week late in July. The Council publishes a reviewing journal *Reading Time*, which is widely supported. As well as this Young Reader's Dinners are held, at which children meet favourite authors and have the opportunity to ask them about their work. Remote area visits by authors are organised to reach children in outlying country districts. The Council has also organised classes of children from country schools to visit the city during Book Week and has provided books for children's homes. The Lu Rees Archive was an initiative of the ACT Branch of the Council. The Children's Book Council of Australia has provided incentive and encouragement for writers and publishers and its presence has helped to provide a sense of continuity and perspective in the field.

THE STORYTELLING GUILDS

There are Storytelling Guilds in New South Wales, Tasmania, South Australia, Western Australia, the ACT and Queensland. Their aim is to share stories and various techniques amongst their members. Membership is open to anyone, but tends to be composed of children's librarians and school librarians. Storytelling weekends, evenings and conferences are arranged by the Guilds for participants to improve their technique, seek opinions from other storytellers, discover new material and overcome the difficulty of working on their own.

There is a huge demand for professional storytellers in schools and libraries. The medium is fun, has the capacity to dramatise literature, enhance language skills and introduce children to material which is otherwise unavailable, difficult to find or to read. Different storytelling techniques emphasise participation or listening skills and storytellers are usually versatile enough to perform in almost any location, to large or small audiences. Fees are reasonable when compared with theatrical troupes or puppeteers and are within the reach of librarians, community organisers or schools working on a small budget. Storytelling's popularity with children makes it one of the most effective means of increasing access to children's literature, and the Guilds are planning a National Storytelling Festival.

THE CHILDREN'S AND SCHOOL LIBRARIES SECTIONS OF THE LIBRARY ASSOCIATION OF AUSTRALIA

The Children's Libraries Section and the School Libraries Section of the Library Association have branches in most states, and operate largely in the area of professional education. They often work in cooperation with each other or with the Children's Book Council or Storytelling Guilds. Their concerns are with children's media of all types as well as library services. Broadly, children's librarians are less concerned with issues of the curriculum than school librarians but there are large areas of overlap on issues such as reading, provision of quality fiction and promoting Australian children's authors. Two recent gestures towards public education and entertainment which set an important precedent in the perceived role of the Children's Libraries Section were the Twilight Possum Magic Party held at Taronga Park Zoo in Sydney where performances of readers' theatre, storytelling and music in front of an audience of five hundred added to public awareness of library services as well as children's books. A public meeting with New Zealand author and children's reading authority Dorothy Butler held by the Western Australian Section in cooperation with several other associations also met with great success. The South Australian Children's Section of the Library Association is currently putting its holiday programmes for children onto microcomputer software for public access at all branch libraries in the state.

HISTORICAL LITERATURE

Historical children's literature is found in all state library collections where children's books are placed on legal deposit for the particular state served. There are several collections of special interest whose holdings are substantial. Access to historical material varies, depending on the priorities of the parent institution, its role and funding. These roles fall roughly into three categories: first, the libraries collections are seen to exist for the education of members of the public who know little about children's literature and would like to know more. Secondly, the collections are research-oriented at a postgraduate level, and third, they have a preservation function for the nation. There may be overlap in these roles, and policies about access will be determined by them.

The Children's Literature Research Collection at the State Library of South Australia is one of the largest national sources for researchers of children's literature. Its holdings include 40,000 children's books and magazines, a small collection of comics, children's greeting cards, toys and games and a reference collection of about 2,500 titles. There is a collection of children's books from England and another from the United States (Double 1985: 5), although priority is given to Australian material. All major movements in children's literature from 1599 to the present are represented in the collection.

A research service is also available for scholars, students and the public. Displays are mounted regularly and travel around the state. Promotional material is published for public information.

One of the many treasures held is a copy of *A Mother's Offering to her Children, 'by a Lady, Long Resident in New South Wales'* dated 1841 and believed to be the first children's book published in Australia.

Access to the collection has been improved by the preparation of a microfiche catalogue of Australian Children's Literature published prior to 1890. This includes books published internationally which make reference to Australia. There are many school visits to the collection, and bookings for talks can be made by contacting the librarian.

The Mitchell Library in Sydney is primarily a research one. It includes extensive holdings of published Australian children's literature, related manuscripts and pictorial records of historical to contemporary work. Its policy is to acquire comprehensive holdings of children's literature by Australian authors and which relate to Australia. Exceptions are educational texts which are collected for New South Wales only.

Access to the collection is through the catalogue. The library has an international responsibility to preserve rare and original materials and readers' tickets are not generally issued to children. However, if a child is working on a special research project unrelated to school, access will be granted. Similarly undergraduates in approved courses may also by given readers' tickets.

The Children's Literature Selection Committee at the State Library of New South Wales was established in 1983 with the dual objective of building a substantial reference collection for researchers of children's literature, and of supplementing the holdings of the *General Reference Library* with children's books published internationally, an objective not systematically pursued elsewhere in the state. Its emphasis is on award-winning and critically-acclaimed books and it includes samples of popular fiction. The General Reference Library is open without restriction to the public for reference enquiries and for private study.

The public library system in New South Wales plays a complementary role to the collection and services of the Mitchell Library. It provides for children's educational and leisure needs on a local basis and is designed to be highly accessible.

The Lu Rees Archives Collection of Children's Literature has been housed in the library of the Canberra College of Advanced Education since 1980. The library contains 7,000 titles in the student lending collection — a good representative collection of international children's publishing. The archives themselves contain about 2,500 volumes of Australian children's literature, dating from the turn of the century. They aim to collect all editions and translations, and maintain files on individual illustrators and authors, copies of reviews, photographs and biographical material. They are available to serious research within the library and are fully catalogued.

The Humanities and Social Sciences Library at the University of New South Wales contains a small collection of historical children's literature largely uncatalogued and accessible to researchers on application to the Social Sciences and Humanities Librarian.

In the New South Wales public library system, the Children's Subject Specialisation Scheme and Joint Fiction Reserve was established primarily to meet current demands for material from children. Since its formation, however, a certain amount of historical material has been deposited in local libraries, and public donations are also forthcoming. In the future it is likely that valuable holdings of children's material will be accumulated by the scheme to add strength to more formally-selected material in the state collections.

The concept of *Dromkeen* is described by its founders as one of a 'a living collection, not locked away for posterity but open for public enjoyment. The preservation of material was important yet it was seen as vital that children have access'. Close to Melbourne in a historic homestead at Riddell's Creek the collection was established in 1973 by the Oldmeadow family who originally planned to use the building as a warehouse for their bookshop. They decided that there was insufficient collection of manuscript and artwork material, even less provision for its display and felt that part of the literary heritage could be lost (Oldmeadow Booksellers 1982: 1).

Although their original focus was on Australian material, Dromkeen now includes work from Asian countries, the United States and Britain. There is a gallery on site and hundreds of children visit each year to enjoy activities which are held to promote children's books. These include talks by authors, storytelling, exhibitions of illustration and publishing processes. The original intention of displaying all materials is now impossible because of their expansion. Résumés exist of the artwork, and a catalogue of the collection is in preparation. Though much is contemporary, there is also a large core of historical work. A reference collection is available to research workers on appointment. An annual award, the Dromkeen Medal, is presented to an Australian citizen who has made a significant contribution to children's literature.

In 1976 the work of Joyce and Court Oldmeadow received world acclaim when they received the Eleanor Farjeon award in recognition of their services to children's literature — the first time that award has been made outside Britain.

The Children's Literature Research Collection at the State Library of Victoria of approximately 10,000 items was brought together and organised from 1976−80. Items date from the sixteenth century, though most were written during the nineteenth and twentieth. Little material has been added in the last few years and there are some gaps it is hoped will be filled in the future. Australian material, however, is well represented. Access is available during library operating hours and the collection is fully catalogued.

The James Hardie Library of Australian Fine Arts, established in 1980, is a small research one in Sydney which includes a collection of children's books. It contains, according to its 1984 promotions brochure, 'many rare and elusive works including the earliest nineteenth century English and Australian imprints for children, school text books, colour plate works, music and first edition works by Mary Gibbs and Ida Rentoul Outhwaite among others'. The Librarian has already helped in the development of exhibitions of historical art and literature, including the highly successful May Gibbs Exhibition at the Botanical Gardens, and has acted as consultant to groups of researchers into children's literature.

Collections of children's literature are also to be found in the libraries of tertiary institutions which offer courses in education and this kind of literature. The majority of books held, however, have been published from the 1960s to the present, depending on the date the library was established.

MAJOR AWARDS FOR CHILDREN'S LITERATURE

As well as the Children's Book Council of Australia awards, there is in New South Wales the Premier's Literary Award for Children's Literature. The Festival Awards for Literature in South Australia include a category for children's literature, and the Angus & Robertson Writers for the Young Fellowship awards prizes in the categories of fiction, non-fiction, picture book text, and illustration.

Children vote for the winners of the Western Australian Young Readers' Book Awards, inaugurated by the School Libraries Section of the LAA, albeit from a large, but preselected list. The Northern Territory Young Readers' Book Awards is organised by public and school librarians on similar principles. These awards provide a refreshing counterpoint to others for children's literature which are selected by adults. Adult judges are not only at a different psychological and social stage of development from the audience for whom they are selecting, but also may be out of touch with children's preferences. The shortlists make a valuable contribution by helping librarians select books they know children will like.

BOOKSHOPS

Some well-known bookshops which specialise only in children's literature are The Little Bookroom and Oldmeadows in Melbourne, Book Nook in Brisbane, The Singing Tree in Perth and Darwin, The Children's Bookshop in Adelaide, Nancy Shearer's Young People's Bookshop and the Children's Bookshop in Sydney, and Jacaranda Educational in Canberra. Usually these are in high-income areas or near the central business district. This has implications for the accessibility parents and children have to quality children's books if they live in other areas. Supermarkets and newsagents would be the best source in many places around the country as far as a more general public is concerned, although most general bookshops carry a children's literature section.

In general terms, then, access to literature written in English for children in Australia is reasonable in metropolitan areas, and adequate, though sometimes barely, in all but remote areas. Rising book prices, particularly those of imported books will mean that parents, public libraries and school libraries may be unable to keep pace, and future provision could diminish. Books in other languages are only moderately to poorly provided for in the community and bilingual books and books translated into English are similarly difficult to find.

Historical children's literature is collected systematically as far as Australian publications and books about Australia are concerned, but there is scope for greater comprehensiveness in the collection of international children's publishing by library services.

Within the forums provided by various associations concerned with children's literature, there is also room for more discussion of literature in a socio-political context. Although issues of class, sexism, and racism in children's books are raised and addressed to some extent by state education departments, they are not discussed on a continuing basis by independent professional forums.

Another problem is that children's book reviews do not appear often enough in the mass media to advise parents about books available to their children. Where criticism does appear, it is often ill-informed, parochial or trivial in approach.

In March 1986, the first issue of *Magpies: Talking About Books for Children*, a children's book journal based in Perth, appeared.

There is enormous scope for parent education as a means of improving access to children's books, and for those concerned about children's books to emphasise strongly the merits of education in literature, from preschool onwards. It is vital that student teachers and trainee children's librarians should have some formal education in children's literature within their courses. These are the places to make the push in order to assure improved access to children's books on a long-term basis.

REFERENCES

Double, Amanda, 'Children's Literature Research Collection, South Australia' in *Reading Time*, January 1985.

Huus, Helen, 'Meet IBBY — The International Board on Books for Young People' in *The Reading Teacher* Vol. 38, No. 8, April 1985.

The James Hardie Library of Australian Fine Arts, Publicity brochure, Sydney: 1984.

Dromkeen: A Home for Australian Children's Literature Oldmeadow Booksellers, Melbourne: 1982.

Pownall, Eve, compiler, 'The Children's Book Council in Australia, 1945–1980' in *Reading Time*, 1980.

21 FROM MANUSCRIPT TO MARKETPLACE

ANNE BOWER INGRAM

> A book, tight shut, is but a block of paper.
> Chinese Proverb

During Children's Book Week I was invited to speak to a group of ten-year-olds on 'How a Book is Made'. At the end of my talk one young lad got to his feet, looked me straight in the eye, and said: 'Are you sure that's right, Miss? I thought the author sat at the typewriter and the book came out the other end'.

No doubt many authors wish that that was the way it worked! However, every published book represents a team effort, with the author the central, vital person, providing the creative idea, while the publishing house offers the skills of editor, designer, typesetter, printer and sales force, to bring the creative idea into a reality and, finally, into the hands of the reading public.

To most people the functions of a publishing house are shrouded in mystery, while the editor remains an enigma.

THE AUTHOR AND HIS MANUSCRIPT

When an author has finished his manuscript he sends it to the publishing house whose list is closest to the type of book he has written.

Over the years publishing houses become identified with a particular style of publishing. An example of this was The Bodley Head children's list in Britain when Judy Taylor was the editor. The Bodley Head became known as the publishing house for picture books. When a publishing house appoints an editor they choose one who will continue the style of their list and maintain their standards and their place in the market. Sometimes an author will have a literary agent to look after his work. The agent reads the manuscript and decides which publisher to offer it to. If the author is a 'big name', then the agent calls several publishers together and an auction is held, with the manuscript going to the highest bidder. But this only happens for the top few. The agent's fee works out at about 10 per cent of the authors' earnings.

In Australia, there are very few literary agents, and the ones who are here do not take many children's authors on to their lists. In the United States and Britain it is the opposite, and almost every children's author has an agent to look after his interests and promote his work, not only to publishing houses but also to film and television companies.

There are times when authors are approached by a publishing house and commissioned to write a specific book. This usually happens in the areas of educational text books or when a publisher is developing a particular series of non-fiction books.

Commissioning seldom happens with fictional writing except in the case of popular, money-earning writers like Ruth Park, who will often receive offers to write a novel from several publishing houses.

STYLES AND AREAS OF CHILDREN'S PUBLISHING

Publishing houses not only have their particular style of publishing, they also publish for specific areas of the market. In the field of children's books there are four distinct areas that can be identified:

1. Educational

A specialised area of publishing, this caters entirely for the text book market. It requires editors who are well aware of all the trends and changes within the educational system.

2. Mass Market

This is the fast turnover, high print run and large return rate style of publishing. At present it is full of novelty books — the pop-up, pop-out type. Series are also popular in this area, with books like the Alfred Hitchcock Mysteries and the Hardy Boys Series.

3. Middle Market

This style of publishing is probably responsible for teaching more children to read than any other. It is also the area where the 'favourite' authors are to be found, writers like Judy Blume who have a tremendous, very personal following and whose books never sit on a library shelf.

4. Quality

This 'highbrow' area is aimed at the educated élite of our children. Sales figures are often lower in this area than in the middle market, but this is the group which wins the awards and the books are found on every library and school shelf.

Australian publishing houses which have children's lists, all follow one or several of these particular areas of publishing. So, if an author has an educational text he will send it to Jacaranda Wiley; if it is a quality or middle-market book it will be sent to William Collins or Angus & Robertson or Hodder and Stoughton; while the mass market is catered for by Lansdowne or Golden Press.

When an author's manuscript arrives in a publishing house it is immediately recorded and given a number. This helps to keep track of it if the manuscipt is given to several people to read. A postcard is sent to the author acknowledging receipt and advising that it will be several weeks (or months, depending on the particular editor), before a decision is made. Unsolicited manuscripts arrive at a publishing house at an incredible rate. In one year the number that would cross my desk is between 700 and 800. My colleagues in Britain receive about 1,200 while in the United States the number is closer to 2,000. It's a mammoth task to read and assess them all. In publishing houses overseas the junior or trainee editor in the children's department culls them first and returns the absolutely hopeless ones. In Australia the children's editorial department is usually one person only, the editor, so all the manuscripts end up on her desk.

CHILDREN'S EDITORS IN AUSTRALIA

Australian publishing houses have been very slow to establish children's book publishing as a specialised department, or to appoint specialist children's editors to their staff. In fact our first children's editor, Joyce Saxby, was appointed as recently as 1963, almost forty years behind the United States.

It was Angus and Robertson, that respected publisher of Australian literature, who appointed Joyce. They were aware that for many years Australian children's authors had been sending their manuscripts to British publishers. With the opening up of cheap printing in Hong Kong and Singapore, as well as the effects of the post-war baby boom, they realised they were missing out on a very profitable market.

During the 1890s and through to the 1930s, Australian authors, like Ethel Turner and Mary Grant Bruce, both bestsellers, had their work published with British publishers.

These were the days of 'juvenile' publishing, when children's books were treated as the poor relations and the trainee editor or the office junior was the person detailed to 'look after' the juvenile list — because they were closest in age to the reader!

Thanks to the pioneering work of the Children's Library Movement in the United States during the 1930s, this whole attitude to children's publishing began to change. Editors with the particular skills required for this genre were appointed and became senior members of the editorial departments in publishing houses in the United States and, later, in Britain.

Joyce Saxby's pioneering work at Angus and Robertson was carried on by Barbara Ker Wilson, who had been children's editor for William Collins in London before moving to Australia. She built an incredibly strong fiction list with authors like Ivan Southall, who reached the peak of his career under her careful and creative editing. For several years Barbara was the only children's editor working in this country.

Then, in September 1971, I was approached by the late Sir William (Billy) Collins, to start a Collins' children's list in Australia. The challenge was one I couldn't resist. The chance to create an entirely new list, with the freedom to develop it as I felt Australian children's literature deserved to be, was almost unbelievable. It took a truly great publisher like Billy Collins to see that Australia had creative talent, and he was prepared to give it the chance to grow.

During the mid-70s more children's editors were appointed. Barbara Ker Wilson moved from Angus and Robertson to Hodder and Stoughton (doing some freelance work in between for Cassells and several other publishers). David Harris filled her place at Angus and Robertson. Shortly after this Barbara left children's publishing, and this has been a great loss to the genre. Hodders then appointed Margaret Hamilton and she has taken their list to the forefront of Australian publishing. At this time Methuen also moved into the children's book market. They appointed Elizabeth Fulton, who had received her training in Britain under Judy Taylor at The Bodley Head. Unfortunately Elizabeth has also left publishing. There seems to be a growing trend not to replace editors.

In the second half of the 1980s there are still very few qualified children's editors working in this country. What is worrying for the future is the present trend of publishing houses to slow down on the number of books they publish, because of economic problems within the publishing industry. Coupled with this is the tendency to employ freelance 'specialist' editors. This means that there are no new, young editors receiving training within publishing houses. The future does not look bright.

THE ROLE OF THE EDITOR

The involvement of a creative editor in every book published is essential, and this involvement is both looked for and acknowledged by every creative author.

What does an editor do? One thing is certain, I do not sit quietly in an office, surrounded by hallowed silence, reading manuscripts all day. Would that I could!

Nowadays an editor is really a conglomerate. The best way I have found to describe myself is as a 'one-person, multi-faceted company'. This is because I work on a manuscript from the time it arrives on my desk, through until all copies are, hopefully, sold!

As a 'one-person, multi-faceted company' I have to:

1. Work closely with authors
2. Be aware of marketing
3. Plan a publishing list
4. Have a knowledge of type and printing
5. Understand finances
6. Check stock-holdings

7. Work on publicity
8. Arrange sales overseas
9. And, lastly, be patient!

AT THE EDITOR'S DESK

The relationship which is built up, over the years, between an editor and an author, is a very special, very precious, one. It comes about through trust, and this trust is a two-way affair — the author trusts that what the editor is suggesting must be changed, is right for the book; whilst the editor trusts the author to listen carefully to suggested changes and act on them, if they both agree.

So editing is the process by which an editor helps an author make his book the book he hoped it would be. Some manuscripts need little editing; some need a great deal. The essence of editing is knowing which is which, and giving what is needed — that much and no more.

When a manuscript from an established author arrives on my desk, everything else is put aside and my whole attention is given over to it. Manuscripts that have been recommended to me, or unsolicited manuscripts, often have to wait a week or two before they are read.

However, with every manuscript, the way I approach it is the same. Firstly, it is read straight through, preferably at one sitting with as few interruptions as possible (at these times the phone is taken off the hook and my door firmly shut — the only time my office is peaceful!). The purpose of this first reading is to get the 'feel' of the manuscript — that is, the characters, plot, ideas and style, all of which make a very sharp impression, which is essential for an editor to have because on all subsequent readings this sharpness is dulled. (This is normal because it is no longer a new and unknown thing you are dealing with). So the first reading must be a 'total one', and by that I mean you must have every one of your senses working and be alert to *everything* the author has written.

The next reading is the one for making notes. This comes a few days later when the impact of that first reading has been thoroughly digested and I have, maybe, re-read here and there to clarify something.

I always need to live with a manuscript for a few weeks before I am ready to work on a one-to-one basis with the author. This is because I need to *know* the manuscript as thoroughly as the author, if possible — I need to be a part of it yet remain apart from it so that I can offer the outsider's viewpoint.

Now the trust element really comes in. I am sitting with an author, manuscript between us, and I have to ask for a rewrite of a chapter. If that trust has already been established, then my task is so much easier.

I remember when Lilith Norman sent me her manuscript, *The Flame Takers*. The accompanying note read: 'You alter one b ... word and I'll cut your b ... throat!' It was a marvellous manuscript except ... everything depended on the time sequence and Lilith had missed out a whole day; this meant the plot wasn't working. I phoned her, she came into my office, my throat was *not* cut, — and she rewrote the section that needed to be adjusted. And the book is brilliant.

When I work with a 'first time' author, then my approach is different. Tact, patience and honesty are the things I use — especially honesty, because at no point should an author be encouraged, or offered false hope when it is not deserved, as this is both a waste of everyone's time and unfair to the would-be author. However, if I feel that the author really does have the ability to write, then I shall spend any amount of time with them, encouraging the rewriting process and helping the author to find the book that is there, somewhere, inside them.

This is how it was with N.L. Ray's (also known as Nan Hunt) first novel, *The Everywhere Dog*. When I had finished my first reading of that manuscript I knew there was a great story there — we just had to get rid of all the excess characters (thousands), unnecessary plots (hundreds) and stick to the main thread of the story. Nan now tells all sorts of horror stories about how much work I made her to do on that (and subsequent) manuscripts — now, ten years and twelve published books on, we are closer friends than ever.

Sometimes it only takes an author a week or two to do the rewriting, but for others it can take months. Nan reminded me that *The Everywhere Dog* took ten months of rewriting, the manuscript travelling back and forth between my office in Sydney and Nan's desk in Bathurst, at least once a month.

It is not just the major rewriting problems of a manuscript that I look for. Consistency is vitally important in all books and many authors are not consistent. They will suddenly change the colour of the eyes of one of their characters, or move the furniture around in a room. These may seem like stupid writing mistakes but it is amazing how frequently such discrepancies creep in.

Then there is the basic editorial role of correcting spelling errors and punctuation — the process called copy editing. Some authors have a tendency to use a particular word again and again, and this must be corrected because there is nothing more annoying to a reader than having every event described as 'magnificent' or every happening as 'way out'.

Neither do I encourage authors to use current 'slang' expressions, or refer to an 'in' pop group or person (unless the story is definitely set in that time), because this will immediately date the story and it can work against the sales of the book because some booksellers and librarians often feel it is already out of date and of no interest to the young reader.

With all the rewriting done and all the copy editing completed, I then take the manuscript to the designer and the next processes begin — design, typesetting and printing.

THE PICTURE BOOK

The editing of a full-colour picture book presents its own particular set of problems.

The text for a picture book will receive as much attention from the editor as the text for a novel. In fact, it is probably far more difficult to write a 700 word picture book text than a 40,000 word novel, because every one of those 700 words must be exactly right: there is no room for error and no padding to hide a sloppy writing style.

The picture book text can be written either by an author, who has no ability to illustrate, but who knows and understands this particular market, or by the artist who has the skill to write as well as to illustrate; or the text can be taken from a traditional source, such as a ballad, folk tale or legend.

What is essential though, is that the text must come first. It is almost impossible to take a set of beautiful illustrations and then write a text to fit them — it has been done, but it usually leads to disaster and a lot of heartache. As an example, in October 1981, a large parcel arrived on my desk, inside which were fourteen of the most incredible paintings I have ever come across. They were obviously painted by someone with a remarkable talent and a vivid, creative imagination. The text was absolutely hopeless.

Since then, on an average of once a year, that artwork has been returned to my desk, each time with an entirely new text and the order of the paintings changed around to fit the new words.

Not one of those new texts has been suitable. What will become of this artwork I do not know. What has happened is that one very talented artist is wasting years trying to make something work when she should have had the strength to put it aside and start on something new.

This is why my advice to all artists is *not* to illustrate a text written by a friend, or by themselves, or by anyone, before showing it to an editor. If the text is hopeless then no matter how stunning the artwork, it won't be published. The essential ingredient for every successful picture book is a well-written, imaginative text — and these are few and far between.

As an editor I love the challenge that this area of publishing offers. A picture book reaches so many age levels from the child of eighteen months, being read a story, to the eighteen-year-old student studying art. In between a picture book can touch many children: those learning to read, who need a large, clear typeface and the illustrations to encourage them; or the slightly older child having problems with words; or the reader of any age who wants to relive a cherished memory.

How does an artist find a text and have his work published? As an editor I give a lot of my time to seeing as many students as possible. I also make regular visits to art galleries in all cities and towns. While still others will be recommended to see me because I have a reputation for being interested in the publishing of picture books.

When I find a text that is suitable I work with the author until we have it right. Again, it is Nan Hunt who tells stories about how many times she has rewritten a picture book text for me. Nan rewrote *Whistle up the Chimney* three times before she sent it to me; then, after working on it together, she rewrote it a further three times. On the way it also changed titles from *Ghost Trains* to *Half a Door from a Bogey Louvre* and finally to *Whistle up the Chimney*.

Artists who write their own texts work in various ways. Pamela Allen works slowly and carefully with each word, saying it aloud over and over again until she has exactly the right 'sounds'. That she is extremely successful with this method is obvious when her books are read aloud, especially *Who Sank the Boat?*, *Bertie and the Bear* and *A Lion in the Night*.

Bruce Treloar sketches his books roughly right through, while scribbling the text all over it as he goes. This way the story and pictures come together and grow with each other.

The artwork for a picture book is different to any other art form. It is *not* a series of separate paintings faithfully reproducing the text. Neither is it a place for the artist to do his own thing with total disregard for the text. The closest analogy I can come up with is that an artist for a picture book needs to be like a stage designer — working with a proscenium arch (the size of the page); each scene must follow logically in colour and design mixtures; the extras, like the adjectives that are not in the text, should be added.

The economics of publishing a full-colour picture book state that it has to be a set number of pages — either 24, 28, 32 or 36, with or without endpapers — and there is also a limit to the variety of possible shapes. This is because paper costs are high and a publisher does not want to cut and waste paper, because the printer still charges for what he doesn't use.

So publishing houses usually have a selection of three shapes that an artist can choose from, and that choice is governed by the content of the story. It would have been crazy for Craig Smith to illustrate *Whistle up the Chimney* in any other shape than the one he chose, which was landscape, giving him the width he needed for the trains. Just as it was logical for Judy Cowell to use a portrait shape for Lydia Pender's story *Barnaby and the Rocket*, because this shape gave her the height needed for the rocket. Percy Trezise and Dick Roughsey always used the square format for their Aboriginal legends because this shape gave them both the width and the height they required for the story.

When an artist shows both the interest and the ability for this particularly demanding area of art, I will give him an edited text and ask him to prepare a dummy rough of the book. This means that the artist has to carefully read the text, (if they don't like it then I insist that it is returned and I send another, because they will never come up with a good idea if they don't have a 'feel' for the story). The artist then works out the page breaks, that is, where the text goes on each page. This is very important because the climax can be ruined by the turning of a page at the wrong moment.

With the pages worked out, and the ideas flowing, the artist now puts his ideas onto paper. These are in rough form, showing where things will fall on each page, where the text will sit and how the page will be designed. When the whole book has been planned, I sit down with the artist and the editorial process begins again.

The more problems that can be solved at this dummy stage, the better, although most new, young artists are busting to begin painting the finished artwork, thinking that they will solve everything as they go along. However, it doesn't work this way and usually leads to lots of throwing away of hours of work, which is expensive both in time and money.

The experienced artist knows this and will work and work on the roughs to solve *all* the problems. Many make up very finished dummies which are a work of art in themselves. Gwenda Turner, an Australian living in New Zealand, sends me dummies that deserve to be published, they are so perfect.

The involvement of the designer right from the beginning is essential. The artist needs to know what size and style of typeface will be used, as well as being given advice on the printing process, which can have a bearing on the style of artwork used. An example of this is when cross-hatching, such as Craig Smith used in *Whistle up the Chimney*, becomes too excessive. The printing process will exaggerate this in reproduction, widening the lines and darkening the work overall. Other problems can arise with the excessive use of some colours, especially the purples, which can become very muddy when printed.

The choice of the typeface is also important. The designer will read the text and look at the artist's style before he decides. A poor choice can ruin the book. It is most unusual to use an italic typeface in a picture book. However, for Annette MacArthur-Onslow's version of the A.B. Paterson ballad, *The Man from Snowy River*, the only typeface to use was Times Italics, as it is absolutely right for both the poem and the artwork.

There are many points that the artist must be aware of as he prepares his finished artwork. Every piece of artwork must be the same size. It can be larger than the final size of the book — in fact most artists work half-up, or 50 per cent larger — but every piece *must* be the same because of the costs involved if each piece of artwork has to be reduced by a different percentage.

It is usually the designer within the publishing house who is responsible for the positioning of the text on the artwork, but it is always done in close consultation with the artist and the editor.

Sometimes artists will prefer to do all their own design and layout. Both Bob Graham and Gwenda Turner work this way, but they have experience and training in this area. Others will work with their own designers. Craig Smith shares his studio with a designer so his work is always done there, which means Craig keeps a tight control over the whole design.

Finally, all the artwork is finished and delivered to the editor. The next step along the road to the finished book begins.

DESIGN, TYPESETTING AND PRINTING

Looking again at the novel, the design is just as important for it as for a full-colour picture book. The typeface must be clear and attractive, and the margins should be wide so that the page does not look over-crowded — a factor that can turn many a reader off starting a book. The length of the line, and the number of lines on the page, also need to be planned. It is often the use of white space that can make a book look attractive.

The size of the typeface chosen is dependent on the age level of the reader. For a picture book the choice is naturally a large, clear type — usually between 18 and 22 point in size. For the next age level, the beginning-to-read-alone group, the size of the type is usually about 16 to 18 point. A novel for the older reader is set in the 12 to 14 point range.

The jacket for every book is the main selling tool, and finding the artist who can produce it is a big problem. Designing a jacket is one of the hardest jobs of all — it has to compete with all those other jackets in the bookshop, and give the potential buyer some indication of the contents, as well as being unique, attractive and different from every other book jacket ever designed! A tall order.

Good jacket artists are hard to find. It is interesting to record that picture book artists are not necessarily good jacket artists and often have tremendous problems when they come to design the jacket for their own book.

Often a painter is the best person to approach, or someone who works in the commerical art field, including advertising work.

Nowadays, the trend in jackets for paperbacks is to use either very realistic photographs or artwork that looks like a photograph, or sometimes a combination of both.

When a manuscript has been thoroughly edited, it is handed to the designer who chooses the typeface, and marks up the manuscript so that the typesetter will know when he is to use capitals, or italics or any other special effects that might be required.

Nowadays typesetting is done by computers so the whole process is quicker, and certainly easier when corrections have to be made. There are always corrections, because the typesetter is human and does make the occasional mistake.

From the typesetter the designer will receive several sets of galley proofs. This is the whole manuscript set in the type chosen. These galleys have to be carefully read and checked by the editor, the author and the designer. When all corrections are correlated the typesetter provides the corrected film of the text.

By this time the designer will have the jacket art ready, if it is a novel or, if it is a picture book, all the artwork. Everything is now ready to be sent to the printer.

The printing of a novel is fairly straightforward. It is with full-colour work that the printing process takes time. It is essential that the printer adjust the colours to be as near as possible to the original artwork. To check this the designer requires colour proofs to be run so that they can be corrected before the actual printing of the book commences.

The correction of the colour proofs is done by the designer, the editor and the artist. If necessary the designer may ask for a second, or even a third, set of proofs. Each time the colour is adjusted, or other corrections, such as removal of dirty spots on the film, made. Finally, it meets with everyone's approval and printing begins.

Several weeks later the first air mail copies arrive on the editor's desk. A copy is immediately sent to the author, and the rest are for the sales force and the publicity department who now take on the job of getting the book into the marketplace.

INTO THE MARKETPLACE

An entirely new team now swings into action as publicity is arranged, review copies are sent to the media, and interviews with the author arranged. All this must be coordinated with the actual publication date so that stocks of the book are available in bookshops, newsagents and department stores, as the promotion reaches the public.

Every publishing house has a publicity department which is responsible for making the general public aware that a book is now available. With so many new books arriving in the market each year, an active and effective publicity department is essential.

How it is promoted depends on the 'style' of the book. For an educational book the publicity department would produce a leaflet (or flyer) which explains the new educational ground being covered. This would be mailed to all the educational bodies, review journals that specialise in that field, and to specialist teachers and academics. In some instances sample copies are sent and comments requested.

In the area of the middle and quality children's market, promotional material and review copies are sent to the library journals and into the school library systems in all states. Also, specific journals such as *Reading Time* receive copies and anything extra in the way of 'notes on the author' that they might be able to use in an article or editorial.

While the publicity department is at work the sales people are out on the roads with their advance copies, taking orders and drumming up interest by talking about the book.

One of the biggest problems in Australia is the lack of review space given to children's books in the newspapers and popular magazines. Children's books are only brought to the notice of the general public about twice a year — once in July, during Children's Book Week, and again at Christmas.

The direct result of this is that most newsagents, department stores and general bookshops are reluctant to carry a range of children's books — they usually stick to the mass-market books that do not require staff with particular skills to sell them.

Because of this we have seen the growth in recent years of the specialist children's bookshop. Here the staff have the knowledge and interest to help parents, teachers and librarians choose their books. These shops usually offer extra services, such as setting up displays within a school to help a P and C function. They also arrange for children to meet with authors and illustrators in their shops, or organise competitions related to particular books. The best thing of all is that these shops encourage children to browse and to choose their own reading matter.

DISTRIBUTION

When stocks of the finished book arrive from the printer they go straight into the publisher's warehouse. Nowadays these are computer-operated which, in theory, means that the publisher offers a faster delivery service on all orders received.

Over the past decade there has been a tendency for the larger publishing houses to take on the selling and distribution of other, smaller publishers', lists. Unfortunately this can lead to the sales force being overloaded with new titles to sell each month and, sadly, it is usually the children's books that suffer in these situations. The representative will show his adult bestsellers first and, by the time he reaches the children's list, the bookseller has run out of time, or money, or both, so very few are ordered.

This is where the specialised children's bookseller and the library supplier have helped keep the market for children's books alive. The library supplier keeps a sales force on the roads visiting schools and libraries, in many instances selling directly out of a specially-equipped van or bookmobile.

The last few years have seen a rapid growth in the area of small publishers, and now many of them, who have become disappointed with the service offered by the large publishing houses, have combined their efforts and skills to set up their own co-operative warehousing and sales force. It will be interesting to watch how this develops over this next decade.

FOREIGN RIGHTS

One very special area that children's editors become involved in is the sale (and in some cases, purchase) of the rights of the books they have brought to publication.

Each April in Bologna, Italy, a Children's Book Fair is held. This is a trade fair devoted entirely to children's books, where editors from around the world meet to offer their books for translation rights, or co-editions, or purchase books for their own lists.

This fair has become more and more important as the cost of printing rises and publishing houses face various economic difficulties (caused by cutbacks in grants to school and public libraries, as well as the dumping of cheap books in the marketplace).

The sale of a co-edition of even one book can earn a reasonable return for both the author and the originating publisher. A co-edition means that the publisher is printing the quantity he requires for his own market, plus that required by the foreign publisher. The higher the print run the lower the unit cost, so everyone benefits.

Co-editions are possible with picture books only, because the colour work for all languages can be printed at the same time. With novels it is the rights that are sold. It is impossible to run an English, French and German edition of a novel off the same film!

Since the mid-1970s Australia's presence at Bologna has grown from a single editor representing the whole country — I manned the stand alone in 1974 — to a contingent of twenty, ten years on.

Australian children's books have made their mark on the international scene. I feel this is because we are far enough from the large markets of Europe and the United States to be able to develop in our own way, being aware of what they are doing but not influenced or dominated by their market demands or trends; Australia retains a special individuality.

CONCLUSION

It is a wise editor who remembers that, once a book is published and out in the marketplace, it has a long life ahead. It may be a thing of the past for author, illustrator and editor, but for the reader it is a thing of the present: its impact lasts. As an editor it is essential for me to know that what I agree is ready to be published is as near to being the best the author and illustrator is capable of producing, before releasing it to the reader who is both judge and executioner!

BOOK REFERRED TO IN THE CHAPTER

Allen, Pamela, *Bertie and the Bear*. Nelson.
————, *A Lion in the Night*. Nelson.
————, *Who Sank the Boat?* Nelson.

Hunt, Nan, illustrator, Craig Smith, *Whistle Up the Chimney*. Collins.
Norman, Lilith, *The Flame Takers*. Collins.
Paterson, A.B., illustrator, Annette MacArthur-Onslow, *The Man From Snowy River*. Collins.
Pender, Lydia, *Barnaby and the Rocket*. Collins.
Ray, N.L., *The Everywhere Dog*. Collins.

REFERENCES

Alderman, Belle and Harman, Lauren, *The Imagineers: Writing and Illustrating Children's Books*. Canberra: Reading Time Publication No. 5, 1983.

Alderman, Belle and Reeder, Stephanie Owen, *The Inside Story: Creating Children's Books*. Canberra: Children's Book Council of Australia, A.C.T. Branch, 1987.

Brandenberg, Aliki, *How a Book is Made*. London: Bodley Head, 1986.

Dunkle, Margaret, *The Story Makers: A Collection of Interviews with Australian and New Zealand Authors and Illustrators for Young People*. Melbourne: Oxford, 1987.

—————, *The Story Makers II*. Melbourne: Oxford, 1989.

Ingram, Anne Bower and Graham, Bob, *Making a Picture Book*. Sydney: Collins, 1987.

Lloyd, Pamela, *How Writers Write*. Sydney: Methuen/Nelson, 1987.

McVitty, Walter, *Authors and Illustrators of Australian Children's Books*. Sydney: Hodder & Stoughton, 1989.

Stodart, Eleanor, *Writing and Illustrating for Children*. Canberra: Children's Book Council of Australia, A.C.T. Branch, 1985.

PART IV
LITERATURE AND RESPONSE

22 SPACE TO PLAY: THE USE OF ANALYSES OF NARRATIVE STRUCTURE IN CLASSROOM WORK WITH CHILDREN'S LITERATURE

GEOFF WILLIAMS

> The work can be held in the hand, the text is held in language.
>
> Roland Barthes

Jason, in his third year of school, is having some difficulty in learning to read. His teacher thinks it would be as well for him to practise his reading scheme book at home. This he does for half-an-hour each night by reading to his mother. He enjoys his time with her but has to spend a lengthy period with one book, reading 'I am a dog. My name is Spot'. After a week with one book he throws it across the room and screams to his family 'Who cares what the bloody dog's name is anyway?' Who indeed?

Here is Jason again, at school and working with a young teacher who has just tentatively introduced him to Anthony Browne's *Bear Hunt*. She reads:

> One day Bear went for a walk.
> Two hunters were hunting.
> They saw Bear.
> Look out! Look out, Bear!

Jason looks up and asks 'Who said that?'

What is the teacher to conclude from his question? That the book is 'too hard' for him? That he lacks the 'comprehension skills' to be able to understand it? Neither of these judgements is very educationally fruitful, though they are still made often enough.

An alternative construction is to analyse what Jason needs to do in order to be able to find an answer for himself: what, in the text, has caused him to raise this query, and what he can find in the text, with the teacher's help, to answer his question for himself?

At the opening of *Bear Hunt* the voice is that of a third person narrator who is in a position to see (or at least know about) Bear beginning his walk and, also, to see what Bear can't see. We would normally expect, especially in a children's book, that a narrator of this kind would tell the reader who was authorised to say 'Look out! Look out Bear!'. Part of the intrigue of the text lies in the frustration of this expectation; there is no right answer to Jason's question, just plausible alternatives suggested by the illustrations.

Jason's need is not for a direct answer to the specific question but to become more resourceful in relating to the teller, and the form of the telling, in order to be able to enjoy the tale.

What he hasn't yet learned, perhaps because of the sort of reading material to which he previously had access, is that an author doesn't always tell readers directly all that they need to know. Jason is invited to play with the story by a disconfirmation of his expectations about the way that stories work but, being such an 'inexperienced' reader (Meek 1983), he needs some help in accepting the invitation. If he does play, the text offers him an invaluable reading lesson: not to be subservient and expect to be told the whole story but to use whatever in his previous experience, the language and the illustrations, helps him to make some guesses about who warned Bear. He might also learn from his initial frustration that this book, if he wishes to keep playing with it, requires him to let go of some of his familiar reading footholds and make a new game around new forms. Neither he nor the author makes all the rules, but they both need to contribute if the game is going to be much fun. Certainly it will not be a classroom exercise of the traditional comprehension passage and questions which will help him forward: the experience of reading this particular text with a more experienced reader whom he is free to ask for help will be one small step, and the nature of the help given will be crucial.

In this chapter I should like to argue for the potential contribution of analyses of narrative structure to classroom work in reading. Through considering the form, as well as the theme, of stories in planning work around enjoyed books, teachers can help children into more perceptive reading and, indirectly, help them become aware of elements of narrative structure, an awareness which is a powerful resource for all narrative encounters, not just fictional narrative. The purpose is not to teach narrative structure theory to children; rather, it is to use structural analyses to plan reading experiences which assist children to enjoy texts more through finding new roles for themselves as readers. Analysis of narrative structure helps in reconceptualising what is involved in children's reading development, and therefore in rejecting limited, reductionist definitions of the 'skills' children need in order to read independently.

Recently in Australian primary schools there has been a wider understanding that literature, especially picture books, poetry and novels, makes an important contribution to children's reading development, from the earliest years. (Some teachers have held this view for years, of course, but it has not been the predominant one in Australia). The argument most often employed in favour of literature is that it is simply much more interesting to read than the artificially constructed language of much commonly-used reading material. A linked argument suggests that because authors concentrate on telling stories which will interest young readers, the language of their books is both richer and more natural, and therefore able to contribute more effectively to children's language development. The linguist Gunther Kress (1982) makes the point concerning children's writing that, 'The models provided by Readers are positively detrimental to the child learner as models of the written language'. These basic ideas have served well in deflating such reading skills training material of the overblown role attributed to it just a decade or less ago, but they are insufficient in themselves to take us very far in planning an intelligent, sensitive reading approach which will be of real assistance to children.

What young readers have to *do* to read a particular story is a very significant question for us to address as teachers. The answer always involves much more than interest, and access to vocabulary and syntax. Because of lack of understanding of what reading literature involves, people with children's interests very much at the centre of their concerns have sometimes subjected stories to the same 'treatment' as reading skills training material, as though the language of the two were the same. It is as if children could be taught to read using story with the same conceptualisation of basic skills and the associated behaviourism which underlies skills training material. There have, for example, been books published recently which take excerpts of stories originally published as novels and require children to complete matching exercises, to answer arbitrary questions, to identify synonyms and antonyms or even to find some of the more commonly-occurring parts of speech. Few experienced readers read novels to find parts of speech.

Reading process theory and theory of narrative structure are both needed for forming ideas about what experienced readers do when they read. It is, of course, outside the scope of this book to attempt to advance a review of reading process theory: my point in suggesting the need for it is to stress that using literature in association with behaviourist methods which conceptualise written narrative as a stimulus requiring set responses to build dubious 'basic skills' is essentially to walk the same behaviourist treadmill with children, but with the added danger of making real stories unattractive to them.

Narrative theory is useful for analysing what children have to do in reading fiction because it is concerned with the structure of stories: how, for example, their form influences an understanding of the themes they explore; how old stories are transformed into fresh narratives for a contemporary setting; what relationships and distinctions there are between authors, narrators, characters and readers and how the nature of these relationships requires different forms of reading; and, very recently, how written narrative is made accessible to relatively inexperienced readers. These are all important educational as well as literary questions of which, in many ways, exploration has only just begun.

Concepts of narrative structure can be of direct practical use in reading lessons. They help to create lively environments in which all the group members, teachers included, can be involved in constructing ideas about the texts they are reading. Using narrative theory, it is easy to stop thinking about stories as a form of stimulus which must produce a certain kind of response before they can become a legitimate part of classroom reading.

Stories, from the perspective of narrative theory, are like an adventure playground in which the nature of the game played is strongly influenced but not wholly determined by, the structures available. We can't play just any game around the structures, but there is also not just one game we are allowed to play. Given the space the playground makes available, we can find many different positions for ourselves and go on playing until we decide to explore new spaces and new structures within them.

Narrative theorists make a crucial distinction between 'story' and 'narrative discourse' (Genette 1980; Chatman 1978). Economically expressed, it is the idea that the one story can be represented differently by language, and that the different linguistic forms will require varying degrees of activity by the reader in making meaning. Suppose we take the closing event of *The Emperor's New Clothes* as an example. We might read:

> A child began to laugh loudly and, pointing to the king, called to his mother that the king was not wearing any clothes. His mother tried to silence him but it was too late. His cry was taken up by people all along the road who pointed rudely at the king's ignorance and misfortune.

Alternatively, the same event might be portrayed in a rather different way:

> 'Look, Mum, he ain't wearing nothing'.
> 'Shush, child! Who do you think you are?'
> 'But, Mum, it's true! You can see his great fat belly'.
> 'The kid's right you know. The silly old sod ain't got nothing on.
> Hey, George, look at the king! He's starkers!'

In the first example the narrator *tells* the reader about the setting, the characters and the events. In the second, through *showing* dialogue between the characters and understating the directing role of the narrator, the writer requires the reader to build a sense of the characters without interpolated comment. There are no explicit evaluations such as those carried by 'rudely', 'ignorance' or 'misfortune', for example. The use of a dialect form, which is rare in written English, the untagged conversation, the heavy information load carried by the punctuation — all these require the reader to do much more of the work of making meaning than is the case in the first example where, we might say, the narrator is much more obviously present. The different forms of the discourse, though they narrate the same story event, require different relationships between narrator and reader.

Forms of relationships between narrators and readers have changed markedly in children's literature in the last ten years.

It used to be very common for writers for children to use an omniscient third person narrator who occupied a point somewhere above the story so that he or she could 'see' all the events and guide the reader to an understanding of them. Sometimes narrators of this kind could see into the heads of all the characters, but more often they would use the thinking of just one character. Here is the narrator in Roald Dahl's *James and the Giant Peach* (1973: 7) breathlessly guiding the reader through the need to dispose of James' parents and get on with the events:

> Until he was four years old, James Henry Trotter had a happy life. He lived peacefully with his mother and father in a beautiful house by the sea. There were always plenty of other children for him to play with, and there was the sandy beach for him to run about on, and the ocean to paddle in. It was the perfect life for a small boy.
>
> Then, one day, James's mother and father went to London to do some shopping, and there a terrible thing happened. Both of them suddenly got eaten up (in full daylight, mind you, and on a crowded street) by an enormous angry rhinoceros which had escaped from the London Zoo.
>
> Now this, as you can well imagine, was a rather nasty experience for two such gentle parents.

This was the usual way to tell stories in children's books and is still likely to be the form children most commonly experience, as a cursory reading of Enid Blyton will show.

Not all third person narrators in children's books guide the reader as directly and thoroughly as do Dahl and Blyton. Some require the reader to do much of the work, leaving the narrative open in a way which both invites the reader to participate in making the story and which signals what kind of a story this is. Picture books are a particularly fascinating area of change in narrator-reader relationships. Even where on a first reading it seems that the narrator guides the young reader very strongly, a close reading often reveals subtle shifts in the narrator's presence. In fact, one is forced towards the conclusion that young readers who have read many contemporary picture books become competent in handling narrative relationships which are far more complex than many of the novels they are invited to read at a later age.

Alfie Gets in First, Shirley Hughes' amusing story of a little boy's attempt to establish himself as first in the family, provides an illustration of a sensitive balance between ushering young readers towards meaning and telling them directly. Early in the story, as the pattern of interaction between Alfie, his mother and his sister is established, much is told directly: Alfie is drawn running ahead to the house, and the language informs directly: 'Alfie ran on ahead because he wanted to get home first'.

Similarly, he is depicted in language and picture, sitting on the top step in triumph, waiting for his mother and sister to arrive: 'I raced you!' called Alfie. 'I'm back first, so there!'

A subtle shift in narrator-reader relationship occurs at the point where Alfie, inside the house on his own with the shopping basket containing the key to the door, bangs the door closed. In advance of the language, the illustrations suggest the dimensions of the problem: Alfie is inside, his mother is still outside: he clearly can't reach the catch and the letter box is also too high. The simple formulations of how the problem might be solved are immediately but indirectly disconfirmed by the illustration, then directly disconfirmed by the language of the next page. Young readers are shown first, then told.

The shift towards indirect narration is extended at the point where the crowd of neighbours on the doorstep is joined by the milkman who promises to have his 'mate' out of trouble very soon. Only the illustrations show that Alfie is no longer waiting for outside help but has already started to solve the problem by getting a stool. It is only after two double page frames in which Alfie unlocks the door that the reader is told explicitly that outside help is unnecessary.

It is a simple story, but it is not simply told. The text is organised to offer a very rich experience to young readers, an experience through which their thinking and prediction is valued by the author in a way which takes account *both* of ability and inexperience. Many picture books do so: *Rosie's Walk, Where the Wild Things Are, John Brown, Rose and the Midnight Cat,* and in a quite exceptional way, John Burningham's *Granpa,* are all familiar examples to which many more could be added.

In more complex texts, shifts in narrator-reader relationships become very significant to readers' formulation of an initial position of interpretation which allows further reading, but which is in itself inadequate and requires reformulation as the narrative develops. Without *incomplete* formulation deriving from the narrator's withholding of information, a story is likely to fold in on itself very quickly, and become unreadable.

Notice, for example, how Ursula Le Guin in the opening paragraph of *A Wizard of Earthsea* marks the tenor of the narrator-reader relationship by 'some say' and 'the man called Sparrowhawk'; how she places the source of Sparrowhawk's fame outside this text by inventing a saga called *The Deed of Ged,* thus allowing the reader to decide within this discourse whether or not fame was justly attributed to him; and, by withholding the information that Sparrowhawk and Ged are in fact identical, opening a gap for the reader to fill in active construction of the text at a later point (Iser 1974):

> The island of Gont, a single mountain that lifts its peak a mile above the storm-wracked North East Sea, is a land famous for wizards. From the towns in its high valleys and the ports on its dark narrow bays many a Gontishman has gone forth to serve the Lords of the Archipelago in their cities as wizard or mage, or, looking for adventure, to wander working magic from isle to isle of all Earthsea. Of these, some say

> the greatest, and surely the greatest voyager, was the man called Sparrowhawk, who in his day became both Dragonlord and Archmage. His life is told in *The Deed of Ged* and in many songs, but this is a tale of a time before his fame, before the songs were made.

The narrator gives her explicit support to his being the greatest voyager, but not her support at this point to his being the greatest Gontishman, withholding from a view which later in the trilogy she is clearly prepared to endorse. Thus the author creates space for a reader to formulate views about the relative quality of Ged in relation to his teacher, also a considerable Gontishman, views which can shift as the narrative develops. No space, no reformulation and therefore a much less significant story.

Space for participation can be created in many different ways. In this chapter so far I have been concerned with one only, the nature of relationships between narrators and readers. In summary, the argument has been this: texts define roles for readers in different ways, especially in terms of what a reader has to do in order to construct a story; one immediate task for a reader is to determine (and subsequently modify as necessary) what relationship he or she is to have with the narrator; and only through reading a wide variety of texts which take account of both ability and inexperience can inexperienced readers become resourceful in learning how different narrative discourses 'work'.

Young readers must travel a long way from *Alfie Gets in First* to be able to read *A Wizard of Earthsea* with enjoyment. If the path of that journey lies through reading scheme material, or predominantly through texts which tell readers what to think explicitly, it will take young readers a long time to reach Gont, and very many will never reach it. If on the other hand, the path passes through the rather more spacious landscape of texts in which directions are helpfully marked but banal guidebooks are absent, Gont will be reached at least as soon and it will be the more enjoyable. This is *not* to suggest that children's reading only develops when they are reading 'uphill' as it were, reading complex texts with unfamiliar narrative structures: such a view is patently false. Rather, it is to suggest that without the benefit of texts which employ a variety of narrative forms, the confidence and autonomy of young reader-travellers will be seriously diminished.

On the journey forward to increased literary competence, reading with an experienced reader who acts as a resource rather than an arbiter of accuracy can help children become more resourceful in their reading and gain access to texts which would otherwise be denied to them. 'Reading with' implies both the experience of being read to, and of having opportunities to work around a text with a teacher who has done careful background analysis and constructed learning experiences designed to help young readers into making meaning with the author.

To develop these arguments, I want to take some practical examples of work which teacher colleagues and I have recently been engaged in with *The Present Takers* by Aidan Chambers. The point is not so much to suggest practical activities to 'use' with the book, but to show that familiar activities such as painting, puppetry, drama, writing, model construction: all activities which teachers have used for many years as means of encouraging 'response' to literature gain new significance when they are used in association with analysis of narrative structure to help young readers.

School bullying is the major theme of *The Present Takers*. The immediate aesthetic problem for the author is therefore how to tell a story which will not simply be a reiteration of plots which have been fashioned around this theme since long before the commencement of compulsory primary education. He also has to find a way of structuring the narrative so that it is not read as a didactic handbook on how to cope with bullying. Look then at the first words of the book:

> LUCY BEWARE MELANIE PROSSER
> SHE IS OUT TO GET YOU Angus X X X
>
> How do you know? And stop sending me notes.
>
> I HERD X X X Angus

Here are immediate indications to the reader that he or she will have to work actively with this text, even in forming an initial sense of the setting in which the exchanges take place. Put in a slightly different way, the suppression of the telling role of the narrator acts as a signal to readers that they are to supply much of the detail and therefore be located alongside the author in interpreting the events. Whose authority in interpretation will prevail in the long run is then established from the beginning: it is the reader who must decide.

Notice, though, that even in these first four lines of text there are ambiguities and uncertainties which will make it difficult for a reader to arrive at a simple judgement: Lucy's query and rejection, significantly arranged in that order, suggest her ambivalent relationship with Angus. Angus himself is at once intrusive, persistent and kindly. So readers join the 'story space' with the author as active contributors to, but not sole determiners of, the story.

How do readers with vast experience of skills training material but very little experience of such a pattern of narrative learn to make the first steps into the space without having their role as players destroyed by being told what to do? One simple way we found with a group of young primary school readers was to ask them, before their teacher began reading the book to them, secretly to make a list of all the things that were in their school bags. They, of course, thought this was great fun in itself, discovering lost objects of doubtful hygiene. We tried to identify the owners of a few of the lists using only the information the lists themselves contained — minimal information for building a sense of character. The children were, of course, intrigued by the frequency with which it was possible to predict an owner. When we came soon after to read *The Present Takers* the teacher simply listed the opening lines of text on an overhead transparency and, revealing each in turn, asked the children to talk about what they thought about each of the characters. We found that the children were able to discuss the implied setting, the ambiguity, the uncertainty, their sense of unease about what was to come and even at this early stage they commented on their intrigue with the form.

In some ways this activity may appear to be like an oral comprehension or even a close reading activity, the kind of work that has been a part of teaching for so long with such questionable effects. Two distinctions need to be emphasised. The activity was introduced to help the children find their own spaces in which to construct their readings. They were not asked to answer the teacher's questions and then told whether they were right or wrong according to the teacher's reading of the story. The children themselves were being invited to ask the questions, to 'interrogate the text' as is now often said. Further, there was no sense of 'skills' training, no sense in which the reading of this story was in some way justified because it might develop more facility with a skill. The reading of the story in itself is *both* the purpose and the means by which the children will learn over many readings of many books to adapt their reading to the space created for them by the narrative structure of the book.

We found that there was no shortage of activities to do once we had clearly established that this was a book with which the children wanted to play. However, rather than make up a list of activities which were thematically related in a loose way to the book, we tried to find ways in which what the children did worked with the text to build a sense of the intensity of the conflict the characters faced and the nature of the resolution they achieved. This is a particular contribution that analysis of a narrative can make to teaching: it can help to make the planning of work more sensitively and indirectly supportive of children's reading development so that the children learn to do what experienced readers do without being told what to do in a way which destroys a story they are enjoying.

The resolution of the intense conflict between the children in *The Present Takers* provides an illustration. Possible resolutions to Lucy's problem are carefully formulated and then undercut so that all the more obvious steps she and Angus might take are shown to be fruitless. Angus' first reaction is the simple, obvious one of threatening back:

> 'I'm warning you', Angus said, straining against his anger.
> 'Don't forget old Hunt', Melanie said.
> Angus hesitated; then, seething, slowly backed away round the shed corner.

(p. 12)

Later he proposes the same resolution that Mouse in Byars' *The Eighteenth Emergency* adopted — to restore a sense of lost honour by punching it out with the enemy. The text is self-consciously inter-textual at this point, hinting that *The Eighteenth Emergency* is the book that Angus is describing by focusing on equivalent symbols such as a garbage-snuffing dog and a hole in Angus' sandshoes. Lucy rejects the suggestion for the reason that the enemy's alliance is much stronger than hers. Subsequently, the children contemplate adult intervention and reject it; then it is tried unilaterally by Lucy's mother and found worse than futile.

Our experience in listening to children talk about what they believed to be possible resolutions showed that they matched the text very closely in the proposals they advanced and in the order in which these proposals are perceived by the characters: with Angus who says 'I should have kicked them to death', with Lucy who believes that the only option is to ignore her oppressors, and so on. The course of the narrative acts as a source of disconfirmaton (Iser 1974) for existing beliefs, but again, as in the examples of the books discussed earlier, in a way which takes account of children's breadth of experience and their need for assistance in understanding the nature of that experience.

It proved very fruitful for our particular young readers to write about what they believed might be a way of overcoming the, by then, very oppressive dilemma at the point in the plot where adult intervention failed. When the children wrote about what the characters could do in this situation, they had to think out exactly what they themselves *would* do, which option they would take up: which form of fight or flight. They had to explain, first to them-selves, then others, just why they arrived at their decision. Many chose a further form of adult intervention, an appeal to the school principal, and were surprised that it was not the inevitable course. Thus placed, writing became an important mode of analysis and commitment in which the formulation of each reader's own position became a resource for understanding the nature of the unpredicted, partial resolution of the plot.

The text suggests many avenues to take in collaborative work in the classroom. The difficulty is to choose which of these avenues is worth pursuing with which groups of children. The inter-textuality of *The Eighteenth Emergency* is an example: with one group which was rather more experienced in reading, we patterned our work so that *The Eighteenth Emergency* became a text with which the children could make links if they chose by simply reading it a few weeks before beginning *The Present Takers*. Some children in the group became very excited when they noticed the links for themselves, and showed their classmates how to make them. With the less experienced readers, *The Eighteenth Emergency* remained unmentioned, unnoticed and unmissed, though of course always open as a possibility for reading after *The Present Takers*.

SPACE TO PLAY: THE USE OF ANALYSES OF NARRATIVE STRUCTURE

The structure of the discourse in which the bully, Melanie's, brief telephone call is portrayed provides a further example:

> Melanie picked up the telephone and dialled.
> 'Hi' she said. 'Guess what! Want to come over?'
> She listened.
> 'A new viddy. You'd think she'd left the crown jewels. A rubbishy one as well. Bring one of yours'.
> More listening. She giggled.
> 'You aren't half rude!'
> She listened again.
> 'Not till late. After your bedtime anyway'.
> She laughed.
> 'See you', she said, and put the receiver down.
>
> (pp. 32–3)

What is the sex of the person to whom Melanie speaks? There is little point in raising the question with children who might appreciate the text primarily for its plot, but a good deal of point in talking with older children about their assumptions about sex (and gender) in the novel, and about the way the patterning of the text at this point is likely to affect a reader's sense of the later scene in which Melanie's parents arrive home unexpectedly: ambiguity placed at such an emotive point foregrounds form and becomes a reading 'lesson'. But all the roads open to us are not necessarily ones to which we must respond, either as readers or teachers.

An interesting feature of the structure of the *The Present Takers* is that oral reading is made much more appropriate by the use of multiple voices. (This is true, too, for many contemporary picture books, of which Burningham's *Granpa* is a powerful example). In a scene in *The Present Takers* in which Lucy and Angus struggle with Melanie in a crowded supermarket, the dialogue is presented in three vertical columns (p. 89). It is impossible for a single reader to give voice to the writing in the way that the form of the language suggests. We saw these limitations on a single oral reader as a cue to what children might enjoy dramatising. We were delighted to find that, as these particular children worked on dramatisation, they made insightful observations about the form of the written language, what it required a reader to do, and how significant the timing of the voice was for the effect the three characters' row had. The text required collaboration, which in turn worked back to help the children understand the form.

This is a rich text which rewards close critical attention. It opens out rather than closes down a reading at its conclusion, again by its *form* preventing any simple acceptance of a resolution. In one group we spent some time talking, for example, about the different tenor of the relationship between Lucy and Angus coded in:

> TODAY 1700 RAILWAY CROSSING
> GOT PLAN TO STOP PROSSER
> xxx Angus
>
> (p. 18)

and the final words of the book:

W8 4 U RLY XING 1630 A xxx

(p. 128)

The children were excited to be able to work out a first meaning for the codes, but even more excited when we told them that there were other possible readings of the letters which might suggest more than they'd been directly told about Angus' and Lucy's friendship. They constructed many ideas, commenting for example on the different tenor of the two notes and on the ambiguity of the 'x' in the second note. Such is the manner of good writing for children, that it creates spacious possibility for both collaborative and individual play with language.

A statement such as this may seem to imply that classroom work using analysis of narrative structure is only appropriate with bright, articulate children who can already read independently. I do not think this is so. In work with children in a Special Education class (Williams and Jack 1986), we have found that such analyses very much assist us and that the children make leaps in understanding about narrative form even when they have been struggling to learn to read through Distar or similar materials for many years. Within a single conversation about Anthony Browne's *Hansel and Gretel*, in which two of the children spent some time playing with contradictions between language and illustration, they were able to challenge the authority of the unreliable narrator (Booth 1983) and make their own relationships between the apparently disparate characters of the stepmother and the witch. Such moves by readers to assert their own authority over the written language are not optional extras, added on to some 'basic' reading. They are what all readers have to do to make a story with an author. Otherwise Jane Austen's novels are merely gossip and *Granpa* a nonsense.

I have concentrated in this argument on relationships between narrators and readers. Analysis of narrative discourse takes us, though, into many other concepts of narrative form which can be equally useful in assisting the development of young readers. Concepts such as order, duration and frequency of events (Meek 1984), focalisation of the discourse, and variation in functions of the narrator's voice which Genette (1980) has described so intriguingly, are likely to prove very useful in classroom work. These concepts also provide a way of thinking about texts, and classroom work around them, which is in sharp contrast with the highly reductionist, rather mechanistic accounts that the story grammarians have so far been able to provide. They are not concepts which deserve a place only in the esoteric discussions of the university guardians of literary value. They are concepts which, in describing narrative, describe a form of language use which is probably the most democratic of all.

In the end, our discussion is one about power: power to individual readers to be equal makers of stories with authors rather than servants who can only do a narrator's bidding; power to range across texts rather than only feel secure in a dependent relationship with a narrator who makes the way obvious; power to question narrative voice in any narrative, not only fictional narrative. Authors of children's literature have been at the forefront of educational change to give inexperienced readers ways into a resource of knowledge about narrative structure by providing texts which offer lessons about reading available from no other source. For teachers, such texts are invitations to share their reading experience with children in ways which will enhance the children's enjoyment, confidence and independence. The structures of the adventure playground are, after all, more attractive to most children than a workcard in a box.

ACKNOWLEDGEMENTS

I should like particularly to thank Lee Pledger, Alison Lockhardt and Fiona McKay for discussions about their work in the classroom in connection with the book on *The Present Takers* by Aidan Chambers.

REFERENCES

Booth, W., *The Rhetoric of Fiction*. Chicago: University of Chicago Press, 1983.
Chatman, S., *Story and Discourse: Narrative Structure in Fiction and Film*. Ithaca and London: Cornell University Press, 1978.
Genette, G., translator, J.E. Lewin, *Narrative Discourse*. Oxford: Basil Blackwell, 1980.
Goodman, K., editor, F.V. Gollasch, *Language and Literacy: The Selected Writings of Kenneth S. Goodman*. Boston: Routledge & Kegan Paul, 1982.
Iser, W., *The Implied Reader*. New York: Johns Hopkins, 1974.
Kress, G., *Learning to Write*. London: Routledge & Kegan Paul, 1982.
Meek, Margaret, *Learning to Read*. London: Bodley Head, 1982.
——————, 'Speaking of Shifters' in M. Meek and J. Miller, editors, *Changing English: Essays for Harold Rosen*. London: Heinemann, 1984.
——————, et al. *Achieving Literacy: Longitudinal Studies of Adolescents Learning to Read*. London: Routledge & Kegan Paul, 1983.
Smith, F., *Reading*. Cambridge: Cambridge University Press, 1978.
Williams, G., and Jack, D., 'The Role of Story: Learning to Read in a Special Education Class' in *Revaluing Troubled Readers*, occasional paper No. 15. Program in Language and Literacy, Arizona Centre for Research and Development, College of Education, University of Arizona, February 1986.

BOOKS REFERRED TO IN THE CHAPTER

Burningham, John, *Granpa*. Jonathan Cape.
Browne, Anthony, *Bear Hunt*. Scholastic.
────────, *Hansel and Gretel*. Julia MacRae.
Byars, Betsy, *The Eighteenth Emergency*. Puffin.
Chambers, Aidan, *The Present Takers*. Bodley Head.
Dahl, Roald, *James and the Giant Peach*. Puffin.
Hughes, Shirley, *Alfie Gets in First*.
Hutchins, Pat, *Rosie's Walk*. Puffin.
Le Guin, Ursula, *A Wizard of Earthsea*. Puffin.
Sendak, Maurice, *Where the Wild Things Are*. Puffin.
Wagner, Jenny, *John Brown, Rose and the Midnight Cat*. Puffin.

FOR FURTHER STUDY

Browne, Anthony, *The Tunnel*. Julia MacRae.
Burningham, John, *Oi! Get Off Our Train*. Cape.
Chambers, Aidan, *Now I Know*. Bodley Head.
Fleischman, Sid, *The Whipping Boy*. Methuen.
French, Simon, *All We Know*. Angus & Robertson.
Gleeson, Libby, *I am Susannah*. Angus & Robertson.
Ingpen, Robert, *The Idle Bear*. Lothian.
────────, *The Age of Acorns*. Lothian.
Kelleher, Victor, *The Red King*. Viking Kestrel.
Kidd, Diana, *Onion Tears*. Collins.
McAfee, Annalena and Browne, Anthony, *Kirsty Knows Best*. Julia MacRae.
MacLachlan, Patricia, *Sarah, Plain and Tall*. Julia MacRae.
Paterson, Katherine, *Park's Quest*. Gollancz.
Rosen, Michael and Oxenbury, Helen, *We're Going On a Bear Hunt*. Walker Books.
Wheatley, Nadia, *The House That Was Eureka*. Viking Kestrel.
Wrightson, Patricia, *Balyet*. Hutchinson.

23 LANGUAGE AND LITERATURE: THE CLASSROOM EXPERIENCE

VIVIENNE NICOLL

A LOVE OF READING

The main reason for using 'real' books in the classroom is to develop a love of reading. Unless children want to read, they won't and if this is the case, then they will not be able to experience the satisfaction that comes from entering into the world of a book.

LITERATURE AND PERSONAL DEVELOPMENT

Literature contributes to the personal growth of children by nourishing their souls and imaginations. It is therefore extremely important in the classroom, as many writers have pointed out.

Louise Rosenblatt (1970) makes the distinction between efferent and aesthetic learning. Most of the learning under the auspices of the school, she states, is efferent, i.e., concerned with rationality and with facts. Aesthetic learning, on the other hand, concerns itself with the heart and with human values. David Jackson, in contrasting the effects of television viewing and the reading of fiction, describes the latter as 'active confrontation' (1983: 10). He explains that a good children's story has the ability to make its readers confront habitual, conformist and unthinking values which have been conditioned and reinforced by other forces, including much of the popular, heavily-marketed literature of the mass media.

Betsy Byars' *The Eighteenth Emergency*, for example, may cause the child reader to consider the resolution of anger, the role of physical violence and the stereotype of bully and victim. The author achieves this questioning without detracting from the story as a most enjoyable reading experience. In *John Brown, Rose and the Midnight Cat*, author Jenny Wagner (1977) exposes the very young reader to the conflict between loving another individual and possessing him or her. Although teachers should not expect books to provide lessons in morality, they should be aware of the potential of children's fiction to develop in its readers a capacity to respond with sensitivity to the feelings of others.

LITERATURE AND LANGUAGE DEVELOPMENT

Research indicating the value of literature in the development of children's language is very convincing, if somewhat limited in scope. Researchers in the early childhood area, for instance, have shown that the development of children's oral language is much enhanced through hearing books read aloud (Cohen 1968). Studies of children who read early also show that they were read to regularly by their parents, who themselves were avid readers or had a deep respect for books (Durkin 1966, Clark 1976). There is much anecdotal evidence from parents and teachers as to the effects of reading literature upon the vocabulary development and linguistic competence of primary age children, as well as classroom research with very positive findings (e.g. Cullinan, Jaggar and Strickland 1974). Children are quick to pick up language structures from the many sources bombarding them daily: parents, peers, teachers, television and radio. However, the language of literature is very different from that of conversation or the media. In the best children's books, authors delight in their creative but precise use of words, words which appeal directly to the emotions and the imagination. Kindergarten children revel in the rich, vigorous language of John Burningham's *Mr Gumpy's Outing* (1970), or the simple, poetic beginning to Eric Carle's *The Very Hungry Caterpillar* (1970): 'In the light of the moon, a little egg lay on a leaf'.

Through their familiarity with the language of children's literature, children who are constant readers will grow as speakers and writers of the English language. They will encounter, time and again, a variety of sentence forms used for specific effect. They will encounter different methods of narrating a story and different ways of reporting dialogue. They will come across description of story settings in which the words evoke in their minds a very powerful mental image. The child who is able to experience a varied reading diet will bring to his or her reading and writing not only a sound sense of story, but an awareness of the different kinds of language patterns which authors have employed over the centuries.

THE TEACHER'S RESPONSIBILITY AND IMPORTANCE IN BRINGING CHILDREN AND BOOKS TOGETHER

Next to the parent, the classroom teacher is likely to be the person most influential in the development of children's attitudes towards reading. Primary school teachers are particularly fortunate in the opportunities they have to encourage a lasting love of reading while simultaneously developing children's reading strategies. As illustrated later in the chapter, all aspects of the primary curriculum can benefit from the teacher's knowledge and use of good children's books. Through their own reading teachers will be able to communicate tremendous enthusiasm to children, and this is probably the most important ingredient of a classroom literacy programme.

The Classroom Environment

First, there must be plenty of children's books. These will come from many sources and will be made up of a core of fifty to one hundred books especially purchased with the particular class in mind. These will be supplemented by collections of books borrowed in bulk from either the school or municipal library, or both. There will be books on temporary loan from home, books children have 'grown out of', and books from the teacher's own personal collection. The bulk loans will be changed monthly, carefully selected by rostered members of the class. Some teachers find it valuable to spend time at the beginning of the year drawing up with the class guidelines for book selection, recorded on a special card for children to consult while at the library. One fifth grader's card looked like this:

> IDEAS FOR THE CLASS LIBRARY BULK LOAN
>
> Five picture books
> Five anthologies of poetry
> Three joke or riddle collections
> Five books of legends or fairy tales
> Two 'how-to' books
> Five big non-fiction books
> Five novels or short story collections

The guidelines will of course be revised from time to time. The three or four children responsible each month for the bulk loan selection may additionally wish to canvass the ideas of their fellow class members. When they return to the classroom with their selection, there will be time for them to display, advertise, and, where necessary, explain their choices.

The collection of permanent and borrowed books will be chiefly used for children's leisure and wide reading, although some books, especially fiction titles, will be used as part of the instructional reading programme. Where teachers are engaged in thematic work, particularly in social science or science, they need to borrow additional books specifically related to the theme, including relevant fiction and poetry, as well as informational texts appropriate to the range of reading capabilities of their classes. Prime considerations in the selection of any books for classroom reading will be interest and reading difficulty. It is crucial that books span a wide range of reading difficulty, with no indication that one book or another is intended for a particular ability level. Interest will play a major role. Many parents and teachers are astounded to discover that, because of interest, children can read books which seem far too difficult for them.

It is hoped that the reader can now picture a classroom containing a rich store of attractive, interesting children's books. The next aspect of the classroom organisation that will require attention, therefore, is space. Not only do the books need to be readily accessible to their consumers, they need to be displayed with eye-catching effect. Many classroom teachers find wire display stands ideal for setting books out, their covers facing potential readers as they browse before making their choice. Consideration will need to be given to the height of shelving and to the ways in which the classroom collection will be subdivided. Some teachers prefer to keep all books in a classroom reading 'corner', others prefer to separate some out, with a separate Theme Corner, for instance. Thought should also be given to the location of the classroom library in relation to other classroom activities. Even if it is only a space for storing books, rather than actually reading them, it needs to be large enough to accommodate a number of children comfortably, and quiet enough for them to concentrate upon making their choice. A classroom reading corner close to a 'wet area', complete with children painting, experimenting, or cleaning up at a sink, is therefore totally inappropriate!

Some teachers 'furnish' the classroom library corner with bean bags, cushions or an old couch, so that readers can curl up comfortably for their leisure reading. Others create an exciting reading atmosphere by periodically turning the reading corner into an imaginative new world, perhaps a castle, a space capsule or an underwater paradise. One teacher, whose class was enjoying C.S. Lewis' *The Lion, the Witch and the Wardrobe* (1950), positioned an old wardrobe, minus its back, at the entrance to the reading corner. The children were encouraged to decorate the walls and noticeboards with their own art and craft representations of the land of Narnia. The scene as they walked through the wardrobe was most exciting.

Our picture now is of a classroom flooded with attractively-displayed books, with some welcoming nooks and crannies in which children can settle down and read. To complete it and bring it to life, the teacher must find time in his or her busy daily schedule to bring the children and books together. There needs to be a time for the teacher to read aloud to the whole class; a time for the class to read silently; time for reading books related to particular curriculum areas; and time for children to respond to their reading, through discussion, writing, drama, art and craft.

At first it may appear that the teacher may need to devote almost the whole school day to children's literature. This is not so. Apart from an additional fifteen to twenty minutes for reading aloud to children, and up to thirty minutes for their own silent reading, almost all the activities suggested in this chapter can be neatly integrated into the class instructional reading and writing workshop time, and into lessons in specific subject areas. There is no reason why the benefits associated with using children's books should in any way be at the expense of other teaching priorities.

The remainder of this chapter seeks to describe and explain practice in detail sufficient for other teachers to follow the example, to create a classroom programme with a sound literature base.

PROMOTING CHILDREN'S INTEREST IN BOOKS

Although there is little concrete evidence of children's reading habits today, that which does exist indicates that many children do not acquire a lasting love of books. Aidan Chambers has written about the submerged 60 per cent of teenagers in Britain who have literacy skills, but who have opted out of reading (Chambers 1974). There would appear to be a serious misjudging of priorities in an education system which concerns itself with developing the skills of reading without paying at least equal attention to the development of reading attitudes. Evidence of children's television viewing habits, from both Australia and abroad (e.g. Postman 1983) confirms the anecdotal evidence of many teachers about the way in which television and video compete for children's leisure time: for many children the experience of story comes prepackaged in formula television series which allow little room for exercising the powers of either language or imagination.

The classroom teacher and the teacher-librarian need to work in partnership with one another, for the teacher-librarian generally has the specialist knowledge of children's literature which most teachers have not had opportunities to acquire, while classroom teachers have the advantage of being in daily contact with their children, and of knowing their individual interests and needs. There is much that classroom teachers can do to promote literature on a daily basis. The ideas listed below were drawn up recently by a group of teachers in Sydney:

Share your own enthusiasm and knowledge of books.
Advertise the books in the reading corner.
Read a selection from the story, particularly an exciting extract, to whet children's appetites. A discussion of what the story may be about can occur through a careful perusal of the illustrations. Some teachers find that simply reading and discussing the published 'blurb' on the book's back cover is enough to promote curiosity.

Read one of a series, to lead into the others.
Some examples for younger readers are John Ryan's Pugwash, Beverley Cleary's Ramona, Edward Ardizonne's Little Tim, Alf Proysen's Mrs Pepperpot and Jill Murphy's Worst Witch. Older readers may enjoy Mary Norton's Borrower series, or C.S. Lewis' Narnian chronicles, or the humorous adventures of Helen Cresswell's Bagthorpe family or Norman Hunter's amazing Professor Branestawm.

Promote the range of works of individual authors.
Promote titles in one literary genre.
From time to time, in conjunction with the planned reading aloud programme, the teacher collects from various sources all sorts of books which have in common a humorous theme, or one of adventure, or stories featuring an animal as the central character. The teacher reads extracts, encourages predictions,and generally 'advertises' the

books before letting the children loose upon them. It is possible that wide reading of the books could later lead to more careful comparison of the various titles. For instance, children might be asked to consider the question 'What makes a good adventure story?'. After class members have each read a couple of titles, the question could be discussed in a whole-class situation. One teacher of seven-year-olds plans two or three special literature days each term, when the whole class celebrates Animal Story Day or Fairy Tale Day.

Provide teacher-written book reviews.
Short snappy 'book ads' could be displayed on the covers of a few classroom library titles. Philippa Pearce's *The Battle of Bubble and Squeak* (1978) might be accompanied by a card inscribed:

> When Sid and Peggy brought home some new pets, a family battle began.
> Why? Because Mum detested furry little creatures! Quite a different book by the author of *Tom's Midnight Garden*.

Encourage membership of the local library.
Book news or book show and tell.
Take a poll of children's favourites.
Display lists of these favourites.
Have children publish their written opinions.
Display children's creative responses to literature, through art and craft, dramatisation and interpretation through film, music, dance and writing.

LITERATURE STUDY

A good literature programme will assist in children's development as readers and writers, speakers and thinkers. Over the last decade there has been increasing interest in the systematic study of literature as an imaginative art as part of the primary curriculum. (see, for instance, the work of Glenna Davis Sloan 1978). Through discussion, art and craft, drama and writing, children can not only deepen their enjoyment and comprehension of individual stories and poems, but also build a basic understanding of the significance of literature and the magic possibilities of words.

READING ACROSS THE CURRICULUM

Literature may be readily accommodated into the existing primary curriculum, not only in the time devoted to the language arts, but also in the 'content' areas such as social studies and science. Creative responses to literature can be encouraged without burdening the weekly timetable: they can be easily integrated with regular art, craft, drama and music activities.

The Two Daily Constants

Teachers who have been successful in promoting the reading of literature in their classes usually engage in two daily rituals with the whole class: a reading aloud programme and a period of sustained silent reading. Both of these activities have a very specific function and format, and each deserves elaboration.

The Teacher's Reading Aloud Programme

There are many good reasons for developing a carefully-chosen programme of literature to be orally presented by the classroom teacher. First and foremost is the enjoyment derived from the sharing of story or poem. An interesting story, enthusiastically presented and read with expression and conviction will do much to demonstrate to children the satisfactions and delights to be experienced in the world of books. In addition, the teacher who reads aloud well is providing his or her class with a very powerful model of fluent, expressive reading. It should be stressed again that for many children the teacher is the only consistent and regular model of a positive attitude towards reading and a fluent reading style.

Mention has already been made of evidence which points to the effects of reading aloud to children upon their linguistic growth. Primary age children are at their peak for language learning and well-written books have an essential role to play in extending their awareness of the sounds and rhythms of good language. As Jim Trelease (1984) asserts:

> Literature's words, as opposed to those of the electronic media, offers a wealth of language for children to use. Because good literature is precise, intelligent, colourful, sensitive, and rich in meaning, it offers the child his best hope of expressing what he feels.

The reading aloud period needs to be timetabled, carefully planned and properly documented in the teacher's programme. While it is often a good spur-of-the-moment idea to read the class a book at the end of a hot, tiring day, such an *ad hoc* exercise to fill time cannot be compared with a systematic programme of experiences read aloud, and carefully chosen and rehearsed before presentation to the class. Many teachers find that children gain most from an early morning session of reading aloud, when children are fresh and eager to listen. Certainly children will benefit less when they are tired, overexcited, or when they are asked or allowed to split their attention between listening and other activities, such as completing unfinished work, or 'colouring in'. The length of the read aloud session will obviously vary from class to class and within the one class from day to day. Many teachers find fifteen minutes daily appropriate as a rule of thumb.

Selecting Literature for Reading Aloud

There are many considerations to be taken into account in selection of read-aloud material. If a prime aim is to introduce children to excellent examples of literary language, then certain 'formula books' which are already easily accessible to children in supermarkets and newsagents may be excluded from the teacher's programme, since children are likely to read them in any case, and because they really do not provide a good model of language use. Many teachers choose for reading aloud books which they believe a number of children may never choose to read for themselves, but which are regarded by them as too good to miss. Certainly some children's classics, such as Lewis Carroll's *Alice in Wonderland* (1865) or Kenneth Grahame's *The Wind in the Willows* (1908), deserve to be brought to life through a good oral presentation. In choosing books to be read aloud, the teacher should always look for stories with good plots and interesting characters.

Teachers of very young children begin the year with picture books which can be completed at one reading. As children develop both their attention span and their sense of story, they should be introduced to longer picture books and to short chaptered novels, the reading of which may extend over four or five days. The experience of listening to episodic stories, or of stories with subplots interwoven into the main story line, prepares children for their own move to the silent reading of these more complex texts. Sensitive teachers encourage prediction at the end of significant minor episodes, and commence each successive reading aloud session with opportunities for the class to refresh their memories through orally retelling the story so far. Upper primary children should be eager to listen to quite lengthy serialised stories, but will still enjoy picture story books, especially those with sophisticated humour, language and illustrations. Two recent examples are Ted Greenwood's *Everlasting Gircle* (1981) and Michael Foreman's *War and Peas* (1974).

At any grade level, the teacher should strive to introduce children to a variety of literary genres. As well as modern children's picture story books and novels, there is the world of folk and fairy tale, which, of course, has its origins in oral storytelling, and therefore is admirably suited to reading aloud. Longer narrative poems, such as Alfred Noyes' *The Highwayman* or the bush ballads of Banjo Paterson are most suitable for reading at a single sitting, and many primary age children enjoy single short stories, such as those found in the collections of Joan Aiken or Jan Mark. A short selection of poems may successfully be used to open or close the reading aloud session, although there will of course be other classroom time exclusively devoted to poetry. While literature with a humorous theme is often chosen for its obvious appeal to children, the reading aloud session should also encompass the more serious side of life:

many classes have silently shared their grief when listening to their teacher's sensitive reading of Katherine Paterson's *Bridge to Terabithia* (1978) or Theodore Taylor's *The Cay* (1969).

The reading aloud session is not the only opportunity which teachers have for orally presenting literature. Mention has been made earlier of the way in which teachers may promote reading through the sharing of brief excerpts from a number of books. The writing workshop period may occasionally begin with excerpts from books chosen specifically to exemplify an aspect of writing. For instance, there are descriptive passages in E.B. White's *Charlotte's Web* (1952) which could be read aloud to demonstrate the power of language in painting 'word pictures'. Another focus could be the building of tension towards the climax of a chapter, or a comparison of a number of different introductory paragraphs to illustrate how authors lead their readers into the world of the story.

Science, social science, craft, music and other curriculum areas also provide opportunities for reading aloud, particularly of non-fiction books. The language of expository text is quite different from that of narrative. Children of all ages should hear how factual information is presented, as a preparation for their own reading of non-fiction and text books. Obviously, teachers need to use only a few minutes of a lesson for this purpose.

Making the Most of Reading Aloud

Because the reading aloud session is planned, the teacher will never read aloud to his or her class any book or poem which he or she has not already read silently. In making the selection, the teacher will have noted whether there are lengthy descriptive passages which may need editing or omission, and whether the selection requires any preliminary introduction or discussion. A successful oral interpretation of literature deserves rehearsal. Most primary teachers are too busy to rehearse everything they read aloud, but a quick skimming of the story or chapter will enable teachers to give a more polished interpretation and to make more eye contact with the class. The reading should be clear, expressive and convincing, but this does not mean that teachers have to overact or distract the audience with excessive gestures: the aim should be to adopt the tone which the author seems to be conveying. Some terms or vocabulary may be unfamiliar to children, and it is best to let them work these out from context rather than interrupt the flow of the story to define them. If a term is crucial to the listeners' comprehension, it may be best to explain it before the reading. Children need to be seated comfortably around the teacher, preferably on carpet rather than at desks, so that the story or poem may be shared without undue distractions, and so that any illustrations may be visible to all. At the end of the session, the teacher should take the lead from the mood of the children. They may wish to discuss and share the highlights of Roald Dahl's *Revolting Rhymes* (1982), but, after a reading of E.B. Whites *Charlotte's Web*, premature discussion would destroy the private silence which the story's conclusion demands.

The Sustained Silent Reading Period

While there is much for children to gain in listening to good literature read aloud, they must also learn for themselves the joys of getting lost in a book, and this takes time. As indicated earlier, many homes provide neither the environment nor the opportunities for the sustained reading which literature requires. Teachers who devote classroom time daily to such sustained silent reading realise that this is only one of its benefits.

Known in America as USSR (Uninterrupted Sustained Silent Reading) and in Great Britain as DEAR (Drop Everything And Read), whichever one chooses, the name says it all. The aim of USSR is to provide daily time for children to practise their reading strategies in a natural, meaningful and enjoyable way. In a class where children engage in this practice for twenty minutes each day, every child will have spent in a week two hours in real reading, free from instructional constraints. Because books are selected *by* the readers and not *for* them, children are also being given frequent opportunities to read different authors, genres, and styles; to choose books which they feel comfortable with, and to ultimately refine their own selection strategies and begin to develop a personal taste in literature. This is of crucial importance in a class where the books used instructionally are chosen only by the teacher, or prescribed by the sequence of a school-wide commercial scheme.

Anecdotal accounts from Australian teachers indicate that the success of USSR/DEAR lies in the teacher's hands. Firstly, there must be sufficient variety of books for every child to find a book with which he or she can settle down. Secondly, the teacher must follow a number of simple guidelines, as recommended by Robert and Marlene McCracken (1971; 1978), who have familiarised American teachers with the technique and who have evaluated its effectiveness over many years. Briefly, these are their recommendations:

> 1. USSR/DEAR must happen daily. Teachers should show they value it as much as any other important classroom ritual, therefore it should never be cancelled to make way for other activities. (In one school, time was even found for USSR at the school sports carnival!)
> 2. USSR/DEAR should be given a regular time slot. Many teachers find the first twenty minutes after lunch an appropriate time.
> 3. The teacher should limit the USSR/DEAR period. It may be as brief as ten minutes with kindergarten children, and as long as forty with adolescents. Teachers will adjust the time according to the class, acting on the principle of stopping USSR/DEAR before children's concentration wanes.
> 4. Children should make their selections before USSR commences. Initially, this may take some time. Some teachers suggest at first that

class members take two different book choices to their desks. There should be no changing of books during the USSR/DEAR period.

5. The teacher, and any other adult in the room, should engage in USSR along with the class, both to indicate the importance of the activity and to provide a good model of the reading process.

6. As the name implies, there should be no talking. Once USSR has become an established ritual, the children will enforce this 'rule' themselves: they will not tolerate anything which interrupts their concentration!

7. The time should be seen as enjoyable and free from any instructional requirements. Children are promised that they will not be required to 'follow up' USSR/DEAR with oral or written reviews, nor to maintain records of their reading.

There is no pressure for children to read only fiction or poetry during the USSR/DEAR period. However, teachers should discourage children from the selection of texts such as magazines which promote only skimming or browsing. Teachers who are enthusiastic in the promotion of literature will find their efforts rewarded through USSR/DEAR, as children make a beeline for titles recommended by their peers or the teacher. Although there is no formal sharing time built into the technique, teachers will find that children are very eager to informally recommend favourites to their friends.

Classroom studies of the effects of USSR/DEAR are encouraging, showing great improvement in participants' attitudes to reading, and, in many cases, improvement in reading skill (e.g. Allington 1977). And, of course, the benefits which always accrue from the reading of literature, are also likely to flow. Anecdotal evidence from Australian schools suggests that the greatest benefit of USSR/DEAR is the way in which it turns many children into committed recreational readers. Twenty minutes per day is a small price to pay for such a return.

OTHER OPPORTUNITIES FOR WIDE READING

USSR is one time in the school day when teachers can directly encourage children to read widely. There are, however, numerous other opportunities during the week for children to read widely from books they have freely chosen. For instance, one teacher stocks her classroom library with plenty of paperback poetry anthologies, collections of short stories and folk tales, and more sophisticated picture story books, including the textless books of Mitsumasa Anno, Charles Keeping and the cartoon-format books of Raymond Briggs. Children are encouraged to go quietly to the classroom library and choose one to read when they finish work early, with five or ten minutes to spare. They are not only allowed, but encouraged, to have a poetry anthology under the desk to dip into at such times.

Many teachers find that wide reading of both fiction and non-fiction can be developed in conjunction with a theme. Teachers of younger children often group books together by subject matter: Pirate Stories, Witch Stories, or Stories about Bears, for instance. The collection of books is then utilised in the reading aloud time, the USSR time, and in various art, craft and dramatic activities. With older children the teacher might plan a social studies theme around both these and literature. One teacher of eleven and twelve-year-olds took as a focus question 'What was life like for children during the Second World War?' He found there were many novels which explored this question from quite varied perspectives: a Polish family's, in Ian Serraillier's *The Silver Sword* (1956); a Jewish-German family's, in Judith Kerr's *When Hitler Stole Pink Rabbit* (1971); British children in Michelle Margorian's *Goodnight Mister Tom* (1981); and Dutch-Jewish sisters in Johanna Reiss' *The Upstairs Room* (1975). The children were encouraged to borrow and read these and other titles, while the teacher read in serial form Robert Westall's *The Machine Gunners* (1975).

Every teacher hopes that the enthusiasm for reading developed in school hours will spill over into children's leisure activities. Teachers can assist children in this regard by sending class library books home overnight and by encouraging reading as an alternative to more formal homework. The school library will probably remain the main source for children's leisure reading choices. Often the teacher can aid the teacher-librarian in promoting reading by showing enthusiasm for children's library choices when they return to the classroom, or by actually being physically present at the class's library borrowing time to assist reluctant readers in their choice. There is value also in teachers taking time at special parent-teacher functions to suggest ways in which reading may be encouraged in the home. Membership of various commercial book clubs which provide monthly a selection of titles at discounted prices is another way in which wide reading may be influenced by the school.

THE INTENSIVE TREATMENT OF A BOOK

Wide reading of many different titles will go a long way towards fulfilling the aims of a classroom literature programme. Children will increase their enjoyment of literature, and also begin to develop a personal sense of taste in books. Wide reading will certainly contribute to children's language and literacy growth, and particularly to vocabulary growth and fluency in reading. In a recent study Hepler (1982) found that upper primary children, who were introduced to a wide reading programme in place of the school's usual basal readers, read on average forty-five books each a year.

There is growing recognition, however, that free choice wide reading programmes need to be complemented by some deeper treatment of individual titles. Glenna Davis Sloan (1978) and Charlotte

Huck (1982) stress the importance of such intensive reading in developing children's critical reading skills, their awareness of fine writing and their appreciation of literature for its own sake. Jill Bennett (1979), Don Holdaway (1979), Moira McKenzie (1977) and others have shown how picture books and rhymes, read over and over again, can become the major means of developing initial literacy in a natural, enjoyable way. The term 'shared book experience' has become so familiar amongst teachers of young children that it will not be further explored here. Interested readers wishing to extend their knowledge of the methodology are directed to the writings of Holdaway (1979) or Johnson and Louis (1985). Further, as Anthony Jones and June Buttrey (1970: 115) so aptly put it:

> Stories are not rest from work nor a body of knowledge to be taught. They should be a substantial and integral part of the life of the class, contributing to the framework of reference by which they learn to know themselves and see themselves in relation to the outside world; and stories should be a stimulus, direct and indirect, to the imaginative work by which the class as a whole and the children individually express themselves.

THEMATIC TREATMENT OF A NOVEL SERIALISED BY THE TEACHER

Many teachers eager to plan literature-based activities find the serialised story selected for reading aloud an excellent starting point. The illustrative example given here is of a fifth grade teacher who had chosen to read aloud Betsy Byars' *The Eighteenth Emergency* (1973). Before commencing his oral reading, he obtained for the classroom library at least six additional paperback copies of the story, so that children could refer to the text when necessary. The book he had chosen was sufficiently straightforward to require no introductory discussion, so he launched straight into the reading. The story's humour and robust portrayal of school life soon had the children caught up in its web. At the end of the first chapter, the teacher left off reading, and asked the children what they made of the story so far. Such an open-ended question is preferable to a series of questions which aim simply to test children's recall of the chapter. Through further skilful questioning he invited class members to explore Mouse's dilemma and feelings, and to relate these to their own experiences. Children were also asked to think about the problem from the point of view of his antagonist, Marv Hammerman. Why do some people become bullies? Do bullies have feelings too? They were next asked to anticipate some ways in which Mouse would resolve the emergency he had accidentally created for himself. The suggestions were recorded on butcher's paper, to be tested against the solution created by the author.

The serialisation of the story continued daily over about a fortnight. Whole class discussions were planned from time to time for children to reflect on the story and their perceptions of it. Some discussion was also aimed at examining the author's craft in composing the story. Suggestions for developing effective questioning skills are made later in this chapter. As the class proceeded further into the story, the teacher found there was scope for them to embark upon various creative activities as a means of interpreting the book. He suggested some to the class, who also contributed their own ideas. Eventually a brief contract sheet was negotiated and drawn up. Children were expected to choose activities they found stimulating, and to pursue these individually or in a group, as appropriate. For instance, they could reread key incidents such as Mouse's first hurtful encounter with Marv, and use these as the basis for group role-play. Some children extended the idea of fanciful emergencies by creating in writing their own crazy emergencies, and relevant solutions. Others chose to rewrite the two crucial Mouse and Marv encounters from Marv's point of view. Children were asked to contribute to a wall chart upon which they recorded reasons why Mouse found Ezzie a good friend. As an oral reading activity, children were asked in pairs to choose a scene from the book which exemplified Betsy Byars' use of realistic dialogue, and to rehearse a reading of it for taping like a radio play. Some children decided to illustrate major parts of the story for display, and every child was asked to design a different dust jacket for the story, complete with back cover blurb. A day after the final chapter had been read the teacher led a discussion in which children gave their opinions about the credibility of the ending in terms of their reading of the story. This led into a more serious discussion of the role of violence in the restitution of wrongs. As a closing activity, they were invited to write letters to Betsy Byars, expressing their opinions about this and others of her stories they had read. The teacher's own evaluation of the thematic treatment indicated that he felt children had explored more deeply the issues in the book, had learnt a little more about the ways in which narratives work, and had become more aware of particular aspects of Betsy Byars' style, such as her use of dialogue and humour. Obviously such an in-depth treatment need not occur with every book shared with the whole class, but it can be very fruitful if tried once or twice per term.

THE GROUP NOVEL APPROACH

Another approach which is becoming popular amongst teachers who have a good knowledge of children's fiction is the group novel approach. They use a picture story book, bridging novel, or novel with a group of about six readers. Once again, multiple copies are necessary; ideally each reader should have access to his or her own copy. The procedures followed are similar to those suggested for a thematic serialised treatment, with adaptations related to small group teaching. The teacher usually introduces the new story, links it to previous reading or to the children's range of experiences, and promotes it with enthusiasm. He or she then reads the first chapter or section aloud, and engages the group in discussion. The aim is to get children involved in both the story and its narration. The teacher tries to do very little talking: a well-phrased question thrown in from time to time should be all that is necessary to stimulate the group to share their perceptions of the characters, the sorts of people they are and their ideas about the directions the story might follow. The teacher may draw the children's attention to interesting vocabulary or particularly apt phrases, sentences or passages. The children finally are asked to share any questions they would like the author to answer in the subsequent pages or chapters. They are then encouraged to continue their reading silently in subsequent language workshops, coming together independently of the teacher from time to time to share their thoughts. Some teachers provide structure for these sharing sessions by giving the group a card of 'discussion starters', but the ultimate aim is for the group to engage in free-flowing, meaningful discussion about the story without teacher intrusion. Teachers who are initially worried that children will not 'stay on task' may ask the group to tape-record their first discussions. The recorder acts as a monitoring device, but does tend to lead the children into less spontaneous discussion.

In addition to engaging the children in small-group discussion, the teacher encourages them to extend and share their responses to the story through a selection of appropriate creative activities which are negotiated with the children. In the early stages of this approach, groups will benefit from teacher guidance, but as children become familiar with ways of working with books, they will become increasingly independent. It is generally a good idea for the teacher to introduce this kind of work with only one group of readers at a time: once the first is working effectively the teacher has an excellent model and motivation for subsequent ones. One of the advantages of using literature within the instructional reading and writing period is that it can break down the practice of fixed-ability grouping which occurs all too often when teachers follow a commercial reading scheme. Children's literature is not readily accommodated into 'reading age levels'. The only reason for not bringing a child and a book together is if the child finds the book uninteresting or frustrating. One book can be read and responded to at many levels, so a teacher could, for instance, give Ted Hughes' *The Iron Man* (1968) to a mixed-ability group of fifth grade readers. The less experienced readers in the group would benefit greatly from engaging in activities with their more experienced peers. The less experienced may need more time rereading the book, perhaps with an accompanying listening tape, while those needing extension could be encouraged to go from Ted Hughes' modern myth back to myth in the traditional literature of various countries.

THE INDIVIDUALISED LITERATURE PROGRAMME

The notion of an individualised reading programme employing children's fiction and non-fiction has been around for many years. In its original form (Veatch 1978) it involved the teacher assembling a selection of books across a variety of difficulty levels. Task cards were then written for each book, in order to develop and test readers' comprehension and to encourage creative follow-up activities. Readers worked through the selection as they chose, maintaining a personal reading record. A vital aspect of this approach was the conference between teacher and child, in which the teacher, through adroit questioning, could assess the child's comprehension. The child could be asked to read aloud a part of the book, and in this way the teacher could work on any problems the child was experiencing in applying reading strategies. The approach shares some of the features of a recreational or sustained silent reading programme, but whereas the latter is aimed primarily at developing enjoyment and fluency, the former actually has instructional intent.

The individualised approach remains popular, particularly since various commercial publishers have produced attractively-housed selections of literature at different levels, accompanied by teachers' and pupils' materials. These 'core libraries' save the teacher much work, but teachers who have read children's literature widely are sometimes dissatisfied with both the selection of books and the kinds of activities suggested. They prefer therefore to take the extra time to design their own individualised programme.

The approach has, however, come in for its fair share of criticism. Cairns (1985) draws attention to research literature which links teaching effectiveness to 'time-on-task', which in turn is related to the amount of instructional teacher-contact time children receive. He suggests that in an individualised approach the teacher must divide his or her time thirty ways, so that for most of the time children are working independently, and therefore have frequent opportunities to go 'off-task'. Johnson and Louis (1985: 16–17) are critical of the vague nature of the tasks suggested to children. They point out that such tasks are based on the unfounded assumption that children have already acquired the skills necessary for the tasks' successful completion, rendering the teacher's skill superfluous. They suggest that children are left floundering vaguely, and that they do not develop the understanding of text for which such programmes aim.

There is much validity in the above criticisms, but this author believes that any good teacher will see the need to provide models, instruction and guidance before expecting independence of children. Given this effective teaching, there is still much merit in the approach, especially if used flexibly. Some useful variations are suggested by Sloan and Latham (1981), who include a range of possible response activities. One caution needs to be sounded about this and other lists: they can be construed as requiring every child to 'follow up' every book he or she reads, a sure path to turning children off books, and teachers may assume that every activity is equally applicable to every book. This is clearly not the case: a book with lengthy description is not as suitable for readers' theatre as is one with plenty of action and dialogue. Many works of realistic fiction are not suitable for puppetry, but may give rise to some excellent use of role-play. To this end, teachers are recommended to avoid the practice of providing children with a list of activities to apply to any book: through guidance and negotiation teacher and child should together arrive at interesting and appropriate activities.

Any individualised reading programme will be enhanced if both teacher and child have read the same book. The conference is much more likely to become a meaningful discussion between two readers, rather than a ritual in which the teacher takes the question card and 'tests' the reader out. Conferences are a crucial element of any literature-based reading programme, whether between the teacher and one child, the teacher and a small group, a child and a peer, or a group of children independent of the teacher. The process approach to the teaching of writing has shown many teachers the value of the conference as a teaching skill. A reading conference needs to have purpose and direction: the aim is not to test the reader, but both to help him or her come to a deeper understanding of text and, where necessary, to work with the child in a meaningful context on reading strategy development.

GROUPING BOOKS IN THEMES

Another approach is to have a 'literature theme'. The teacher may assemble a collection of books suitable for the class, each having something in common. With young children, she may choose picture books which, although very different in style and theme, all deal with the same topic, for instance, Bears or Brothers and Sisters. Alternatively, books may be selected because they have in common some emotional theme, such as friendship, or jealousy or loneliness. Through a judicious mix of reading aloud, recreational and instructional reading and response activities, the children explore the theme in relation to the books and their own lives, in greater depth than might be expected otherwise.

Mention has been made showing how this approach can be employed with older children in a social studies unit. The approach could, however, be from a literary viewpoint. Children might explore a question such as 'What features do the folk literature of different cultures have in common?', or even 'How do people get on in families?' The first is almost entirely based on literature, whereas the second would involve children's own experience as well as the reading of many different stories of family life, from the non-nuclear family in Barbara Bolton's intense *Jandy Malone and the Nine O'Clock Tiger* (1980) to foster-families like those in Betsy Byars' *The Pinballs* (1977) and Katherine Paterson's *The Great Gilly Hopkins* (1978). An historical perspective could be approached through Ruth Park's *Playing Beatie Bow* (1980) or Eleanor Spence's *The Seventh Pebble* (1981).

As discussed earlier, literature ranges over many different genres, some with distinctive features and conventions worthy of study. Later in this chapter appears an example of how a literature genre study can be integrated with the classroom writing programme.

EXTENDING AND SHARING RESPONSE TO CHILDREN'S LITERATURE

Throughout this chapter the reader will have noted frequent references to 'response' and to 'literature activities'. There are eminent people in the field of children's literature who believe that there is no place in the classroom for 'doing things with books'. They believe that the teacher's role in relation to literature is to promote enjoyment. In so far as this is the primary aim of any literature programme, they are correct, but many other specialists in children's literature believe that enjoyment can be enhanced by the judicious implementation of activities which '... promote pupils' active, questioning engagement with the text' (Jackson 1983: 67). In an excellent article, Charlotte Huck reminds the literature purists that:

> ... one literature experience builds on the last one, provided children can see the connections and are helped to wind them into a ball.
>
> (Huck 1982: 315)

The reason the purists fear 'letting teachers loose with books' is that they suspect teachers will turn the reading of fiction and poetry into a meaningless stream of literal comprehension questions or busy-work stencilled sheets or cute art and craft activities only marginally related to the literature with which they have been linked by the teacher. There is a danger, certainly, of some teachers engaging in such activities, and therefore acting in a counter-productive manner. However, a skilful teacher with a growing knowledge of children's literature and a valid rationale for using books in the classroom programme is very unlikely to fall into such a trap. To this end, readers are referred back to the discussion above. A good programme promotes a love of reading and assists readers to grow in their awareness and appreciation of literature, even though it may at the same time be fulfilling other classroom goals such as assisting the development of children's reading strategies or encouraging their growth.

THE ROLE OF TALK

The kind of discussion that has already figured in this chapter is not a Socratic question and answer session in which the pupils learn from the teacher, but the kind of exploratory talk proposed by Douglas Barnes (1976). In a seminal article on literary response in children, D.W. Harding (1977) provides some clues as to the reasons for classroom discussion. On some occasions the teacher may follow the oral presentation of a story with a couple of open-ended questions. Through further questioning, but with children doing the lion's share of the talking, the teacher can help them refine their responses, to make connections between books read, and to relate stories to their own world of childhood experience, thereby making greater sense of both their own world and that of literature. There will be differences in perception, and, through confronting different opinions, a child will learn as his or her initial point is modified, reinforced or challenged.

Teacher-led discussion should also be planned predominantly for small group situations: the research literature abounds with instances of the inadequacy of large group discussion. In these children tend to address their comments to the teacher rather than to each other, with teachers tending to do more than their fair share of the talking (see Johnson and Louis 1985: 150–1, Sloan 1978: 49).

ASKING QUESTIONS

If children are to exchange ideas about the books they read, and articulate their perceptions with growing literary appreciation, they need a little help from the teacher. This should come in the form of carefully-framed questions. Questions which provoke reflection on a book read, which encourage a comparison of different author's approaches, or which help children make connections between the book and their own experience are very different from the bread-and-butter literal questions which all too frequently have been the main diet of classroom reading programmes. Although from time to time teachers may need to encourage literal recall, questions such as 'Who was Mouse's best friend?' or 'Where is *The Lion, the Witch and the Wardrobe* set?' have no role to play in developing response. Also, as Johnson and Louis (1985) point out, children are most likely to perceive such questions as a test, since it is obvious that the teacher already knows the one and only correct answer.

The kind of questions envisaged here are those which in Bloom's taxonomy tend to fall into the comprehension, analysis and evaluation categories. Such questions often start with 'What do you think ..?', 'How do you think ..?', 'How ..?' or 'Why ..?' and most often encourage diversity rather than conformity of response. They should not be abstract, but instead should focus on the characters and events in the story. For instance, one teacher (Watson 1980: 64) whose fifth grade class was enjoying their class exploration of Clive King's *Stig of the Dump* (1963), used these and other similar questions to promote discussion:

> How do you think Barney feels about not being able to talk to Stig?
> How do you think Stig feels about not being able to talk to Barney?
> If you discovered a Stig, do you think you would tell anyone about him?
> (Follow up with Who? and Why?)
> Do you think Barney might be dreaming in Chapters Eight and Nine?

Questions which require thought also require time, and therefore teachers should be careful not to hurry children's responses. Over time, a pattern of good questioning should lead to less reliance on the teacher's quesions, as the children begin to discuss, building on each other's ideas or challenging them. To this end, an informal, relaxed and non-judgemental environment is most desirable.

QUESTIONS WITH A LITERARY FOCUS

Questions which focus on the author's craft or on the way stories work will be different from those which are concerned with exploring the characters as people or the story as a fictional happening, Glenna Davis Sloan (1978: 77) asserts that the aim of literary questions is

> to guide them [children] to see relationships, patterns and analogies among many stories and literary experiences, not to transfix them in the detailed examination of a single story, even though that story is first considered as an entity.

The kinds of questions Sloan recommends tend to concentrate therefore more on form and structure than on content, and need not be either abstract or forbidding. The examples that follow apply to Philippa Pearce's *The Battle of Bubble and Squeak*:

> Did you expect that Mrs Sparrow would change her attitude towards the gerbils?
> What was the event which Philippa Pearce chose as the turning point in Mrs Sparrow's changed feelings?
> Did you find any clues to Mrs Sparrow's kindness before this incident?
> Earlier this year we read *A Dog So Small*. Apart from the fact that they were both written by the same author, can you think of any other ways in which they are alike?
> Do you think it was a good idea to bring Jimmy Dean's cousin back into the story in the final chapter?
> Do you think there could have been any other way of ending the story? What other changes would you then have to make to the story?

INCIDENTAL DISCUSSION

Children should be encouraged to pose their own questions and to share them with the group. However, not all discussion need occur as the result of specially-planned discussion sessions. Much worthwhile discussion will occur incidentally if children are working in small groups on creative but concrete tasks which require them to share their thoughts and opinions about a story or its characters, in order to complete the task effectively. For instance, a group of children might be given a sheet of cardboard upon which they are eventually to list in one column all the reasons why Peggy, Sid and Amy should be allowed to keep the gerbils; and in another, all the reasons why Mrs Sparrow is right in wanting to get rid of them.

CREATIVE ACTIVITIES AND THE EXPRESSION OF RESPONSE

Throughout this chapter there are numerous references to the notion of following up the reading of a book with some form of creative response or interpretation. As D.W. Harding (1977: 191) defines it,

> Response is a word that reminds the teacher that the experience of art is a thing of our making, an activity in which we are our own interpretative artist.

Creative activities, therefore, afford children the opportunity to express, extend and refine responses to the stories they read, responses which are otherwise felt inwardly, but nor articulated. Such activities allow children to rethink their comprehension of a story, or to represent it in a different medium, and to take the 'aesthetic' or emotional stance which allows readers to experience and live through it (Rosenblatt 1982). Of course, each reading or hearing of a story is a new experience in itself, and each experience involves a response. The role of activities after the reading of a chapter or story is to help young readers to return to the text, and to relive the literary experience in a different way.

RESHAPING THE EXPERIENCE THROUGH ART AND CRAFT

Literature will provide many opportunities for interpretation through drawing, painting, or making. For example, children may reshape their experience of a fantasy story by making concrete their mental images of the story's fantasy world. They could do this by creating a mural, or a long, narrow frieze cumulatively representing the story's events. A story like *The Iron Man* could be represented more abstractly in a collage: painting and drawing would interweave with the addition of different found objects and materials. At a very simple level, young children enjoy painting a character or scene from a story. The settings of these can be concretely realised by the construction of a diorama or 'peepshow' in a shoe box. Characters can be constructed life-size, using everything from old panty-hose and newspaper stuffing to cardboard cartons and all manner of reverse garbage.

Some stories provide very detailed descriptions of setting, and children may go back to the text, reading it closely in order to recreate that setting in a model. One teacher asked children to do this with Mary Norton's *The Borrowers* (1952). Very accurate reading was necessary in order to collect and assemble the household objects such as bottle tops, stamps, thimbles, pins and cotton reels used by the Borrowers to furnish their tiny rooms.

While some artistic interpretation will be pursued individually, much can be done cooperatively, in pairs or small groups. The activity may even involve the entire class, particularly if all are sharing the experience of a serialised book. One class recreated in the corner of their classroom both the barn and the fair from *Charlotte's Web*. From the ceiling they hung a giant web, and onto it they pinned all the words Templeton collected in the attempt to save Wilbur's life. Class members were encouraged to think of other 'fantastic' words which might have been accessible to Templeton as he scavenged through the dump. As time went by children attached to the mural some of the published writing which the reading had stimulated.

Recreation through art and craft depends, of course, on the teacher's providing the time, the space and the variety of materials necessary for such activity. The quality of children's reshaping of the literary experience will also depend on the skill of the teacher in helping them to think through the kind of details they might include, and their choices of media. Readers wishing to explore further in this regard are referred to Huck (1976).

INTERPRETATION THROUGH DRAMA AND PUPPETRY

Very young children quite naturally turn to dramatic play as a way of reliving a literary experience. This natural activity can easily be built on in the classroom. Very young children will love being one of the animals who contributed to the capsize of Mr Gumpy's boat, or the one in *Who Sank the Boat?* They will love joining on to the line of characters who have a turn at unearthing the 'great big enormous turnip' from Alexei Tolstoy's repetitive story. To the accompaniment of appropriate music, they love to engage in an eye-rolling, teeth-gnashing, and roaring wild rumpus, until Max (the teacher) commands that they be still.

Older children will enjoy some of this improvised activity, but may find role-play and puppetry more satisfying, particularly if they are becoming a little shy about 'looking silly'. Puppetry seems to be most appropriate to the retelling of humorous and fantasy stories. Puppets need not be elaborate and may be made from such things as paper plates, ping-pong balls, old socks, cardboard or paper. Shadow puppets can be made to work very effectively with small cutouts on an overhead projector, while tiny finger puppets allow one child to retell a story by him or herself. Role-play seems more appropriate to realistic or 'serious' fantasies, and is best done in pairs or small groups, as children try to step into the skin of characters and relive the story's main dilemmas. An example of role-play was cited earlier in this chapter. Again, the degree of satisfaction children gain from such activities is largely dependent on the way the teacher approaches the activity, helping children to think about how a character would speak or move. In role-plays the teacher needs to assist children to think their way into the characters they take on. Drama is a most effective means of developing and demonstrating comprehension of story.

READERS' THEATRE AND RADIO PLAYS

Sometimes children enjoy taking a short story or episode from a longer one, and scripting it as a play. If they don't wish to actually act it out, they may like to rehearse and tape-record their small play for later replaying to groups at the listening post. Much incidental discussion occurs as children work out the dialogue: how it should be read, the role of the narrator, and any necessary sound effects or atmospheric music. The formulation and rehearsal of the play is a very meaningful and effective oral reading activity.

Readers' Theatre is a simple dramatic activity which has grown in popularity in recent years. A small group of children find a short story, such as that found in folk and fairy tale, and then rework it into a script. This involves rewriting the story fairly simply, with a new line for each new event or piece of dialogue. Children then decide how to allocate these blocked parts within the group. Each child takes a number, and these are written down the script beside appropriate sections. Sometimes a line may be read by just one child, or by two or three, or, for dramatic effect, by all. They then privately rehearse their dramatic oral reading of the scripted story, using a minimum of props and costume. The emphasis is on facial and vocal expression, movement generally being restricted to that which can be done on the spot. In rehearsing, children need to consider how to 'get the story over', and might even pencil on the their scripts symbols or annotations which remind them about decisions they have made in regard to volume, tone, pausing or emphasis. Eventually the group, reading from their scripts, which are now very familiar, simply stand, usually in a semi-circle, in front of the class, and present their dramatised reading. From the middle years on, Readers' Theatre is an ideal technique for synthesising all language modes: listening, talking, reading and writing. As with all innovations, the first few experiences of Readers' Theatre need to involve the teacher's modelling, demonstrating and structuring.

However, children will very quickly assume responsibility themselves. This account of the technique is necessarily brief, and readers are referred to Anderson's Chapter 24, following, to her other writing (1983) and to the work of Sloyer (1982) and Coleman and O'Sullivan (1985).

Music and creative dance can be very effective ways of interpreting stories. Two examples from the author's experience of watching teachers at work are memorable. One involved kindergarten children interpreting the *Three Billy Goats Gruff* with percussion instruments. Every child was involved, and they thought about and selected, with teacher guidance, the instruments most appropriate to a character. The 'trip-trap, trip-trap' of the different-sized goats was represented by different-sized wooden tone blocks and castanets, the Troll by a small drum, voices by finger bells and triangles, and the Troll's demise as he splashed into the water was recreated with a clashing of cymbals. The activity greatly aided satisfaction and comprehension of the story.

The second example involves a haunting dance drama designed, rehearsed and performed by a group of inner-city Greek-Australian girls, assisted by the specialist ESL teacher. The girls wished to express the deep commitment they had to the hero tales of their country's folklore. Their dance drama was virtually a medley of the stories of Ulysses, Hercules, Theseus and assorted monsters, together with others they encountered during their travels. They selected appropriate music on record to accompany the dance, again from their own heritage. Their only prop was a long flowing royal blue cloth, which was variously waved to represent the ocean. The entire effect was deeply moving for all who viewed it.

The opportunities for creative interpretation of literature are virtually limitless. They require only teacher energy, commitment, and sensitivity to literature. Although initially teachers may find themselves suggesting and directing such activities, they will soon find the children equal partners in the negotiation or choice of ideas for refining response.

LITERATURE AND CHILDREN'S OWN WRITING

There was a time when teachers and researchers perceived of reading and writing as two quite separate processes. Reading was seen as 'receptive', a passive taking in of another's ideas, while writing was seen as 'productive', involving an active, creative and individually original construction of ideas. It is now well-accepted that reading is a very active process, one in which the reader is constantly engaged in making meaning by bringing to the text his or her own wealth of linguistic and real world knowledge (see Cambourne 1979). Louise Rosenblatt (1970) reinforces the notion of an active process when she writes of the 'live circuit' which is set up between the reader's expectations and perceptions and the text itself. Recent studies (e.g. Tierney and Pearson 1983) have focused upon the similarities between the processes of reading and writing, and it is generally agreed that the two are complementary aspects of one composing process. The implications of this for classroom practice are very exciting: the more children are helped to become aware of the author's craft in writing, the more skilled and perceptive readers they will be. Conversely, the more perceptive and sensitive children become as readers, the more adept they are likely to become in putting their own thoughts to paper.

The 'process/conference' approach to the teaching of writing, as explicated by Graves (1983), Walshe (1982a; 188) and Turbill (1982; 1983) has led to today's children developing a greater understanding of the author's craft than their predecessors. Whereas children may once have been involved in writing one-off texts for the teacher, on topics of the teacher's choosing, and with an emphasis on first-go correctness of surface features such as spelling and punctuation, the emphasis today is on writing as a purposeful, meaningful communication between author and reader. Children are required to give thought to what they wish to write, for what purpose and for whom. Since the emphasis is on making the message clear, they realise that a piece of writing may need editing and revision, and because the written text is intended for a real audience, rather than just the teacher's red pen, children are involved in 'publishing' their texts and in reading each other's 'published' works.

The one area that is most neglected in the teaching of writing is a consideration of how children develop the pool of ideas, vocabulary and language structures upon which to draw in their writing. Reference has been made earlier in this chapter to evidence for literature's contribution to linguistic growth in children. Furthermore, both linguists and cognitive psychologists agree that the reading of stories contributes to children's understanding of how stories are put together, and hence to their own use of narrative structure in writing.

Anecdotal evidence from teachers indicates that children often 'try out' in their own writing literary patterns, themes, story and character conventions which are derived as much from their narrative experiences in literature as from stories told orally or served up on television. In one study it was found that a young reader who was an avid reader and rereader of the works of Enid Blyton wrote stories which, quite unwittingly, reflected that author's ideas, story conventions and literary style (Collerson and Nicoll 1984).

LITERATURE AS AN INDIRECT MODEL FOR WRITING

In summary, a classroom programme in which a rich and varied reading diet of fiction, poetry and non-fiction is encouraged, should contribute positively to any classroom writing programme. The role of literature is mainly an indirect one: there is no suggestion that reading *The Great Gilly Hopkins* or *The Way to Sattin Shore* will turn an eleven-year-old child into an instant literary clone of Katherine Paterson or Phillipa Pearce. Nor is this desirable: what is achievable and desirable is a gradual growth in children's ability to write imaginatively, to use language which is clear and precise, but also evocative to the mind and delightful to the ear. The wide and intensive reading of fiction should contribute to the development of young writers who can capture their readers' interest with involving plots which invite mental participation, and with rounded characters which invite readers to exercise their capacity to empathise. Similarly the reading of non-fiction which features excellence in presentation and the logical organisation of facts, concepts and opinions should contribute to children's own competence in expository text writing.

The teacher can help this development along. In the reading aloud programme, there may be occasions when he or she may wish, after the day's reading, to draw attention to aspects of fine writing. Adroit questioning will help children to analyse the author's craft more carefully. How does Ted Hughes build an air of excitement and suspense into the first chapter of *The Iron Man*? How does Roald Dahl's use of 'new' words such as 'swizzfiggle' or 'whizzpoppers' add to the freshness of style and humour in *The BFG*? Why is the lead sentence of E.B. White's *Charlotte's Web* so effective in inviting readers to continue with the story? Donald Graves (1983) has provided case studies of classrooms in which this intertwining of reading and writing occur quite naturally. He demonstrates how children who have become experienced in discussing each other's writing, through peer conferences and author circles, can quickly learn to apply similar questioning skills to the writing of professional authors. One teacher role-plays the author in such discussions, in order to demonstrate to her class 'the options that authors, characters, and readers have for interpreting passages and events' (Graves 1983: 74). Graves also recommends the practice of inviting local professional authors to the classroom, providing children with a powerful model of how even a favourite author with many published titles to his or her name goes through the same processes of writing that the children themselves do. Children obviously will gain more from such a visit if both they and the author have first spent time preparing: they should be familiar with the author's works, and may even have spent time preparing relevant questions for the interview; while the author may be asked to bring along to the classroom material which illustrates his or her techniques for gathering information, drafting, revising and editing.

Some teachers go as far as encourage the class to collect on charts examples of various kinds of fine writing, by both professional and child authors. Others begin the writing session by 'modelling' an aspect of writing, or by reading aloud and commenting on passages of writing which exemplify a particular quality. For instance, a teacher may wish to show children how authors evoke mental imagery through painting pictures in words. She may read to her class White's description of the barn at dawn from *Charlotte's Web*, the description of a sudden storm in Lydia Pender's *The Useless Donkeys* (1979), and some excerpts from Patricia Wrightson's *A Little Fear* (1983), with its detailed description of the Australian bush. She may even choose to enlarge parts of these texts on the overhead projector so that children may see as well as hear the writing. Characterisation, dialogue and narrative devices such as the use of suspense are other features of writing which may be focused upon, as well as literary devices such as the use of simile and metaphor. One note of caution should be sounded here. There is a danger of engaging in too much analysis, so that children are turned off reading. Perhaps the secret lies in knowing children, knowing their books, and knowing too how to achieve a balance between simply presenting literature for enjoyment and exploring the ways in which the author invites such enjoyment. As Stewig (1975: 23) says, the purpose of using literature in conjunction with writing should be

> to draw out from children their reactions to what they read rather than consciously implant in their minds large amounts of cognitive information.

THE IMPORTANCE OF EXPOSURE TO MODELS

There has been a growing emphasis in the teaching of writing upon encouraging children to become adept at doing it for different purposes and in different forms (e.g. Kress 1982). They cannot be expected to manipulate genres and styles of writing if they have not experienced many different models of that genre. Too often teachers ask them to write poetry without having them concurrently read it extensively. How can children ever be expected to become effective users of figurative language, if they have no access to a store of favourite poems which use language to paint memorable word pictures? Every genre of writing has its own peculiar set of literary and linguistic conventions by which it is recognised, and children must gradually gain mastery over these, as part of the process of learning to write. The teacher's role is to provide many good examples of a particular genre, with the intention that children will to a large extent learn by osmosis. Additionally, there will be opportunities after much exposure to a genre for teacher and children to examine more carefully some models, in order to articulate some generalisations about the literary conventions of that genre. Teachers who have provided such opportunities to their classes should be rewarded by the differences they find in children's writing within those genres.

PLANNING A GENRE STUDY

Certain genres have such distinctive literary conventions that they lend themselves to special study. A classroom-based action research project in Sydney encouraged teachers to engage their classes in special studies of traditional literature (Colman and O'Sullivan 1985). One upper primary teacher chose to focus on fables as a genre. Many different ones were read aloud and also silently; these included those of Aesop, La Fontaine, Bidpai and the modern ones of Arnold Lobel. Discussion encompassed the stylistic and linguistic differences between tales, and the children were soon able to categorise them according to the type of characteristic portrayed in each, such as wisdom, stupidity, compassion or interdependence. As a reading activity, the class members were asked to read fables whose morals had been deleted. In pairs, they tried to word for themselves an apt moral for their self-selected fable, subsequently comparing this with the author's original. This extensive study of the genre resulted in various writing activities. The teacher at first structured the writing activity by providing the class with the title of a possible fable and the corresponding moral, and then challenged class members to write its text. Finally, children were encouraged to write, illustrate and publish their own 'original' fables during the normal classroom process/conference writing programme. The teacher reported that the children's writing was cohesive, creative and imaginative.

There are many other distinctive genres worthy of special study. Fairy tales, for example, provide examples for children of the narrative genre reduced to its bare essentials of orientation ('Once upon a time, in a far off place ...'), complication ('But the young prince had nothing to say to any of the young ladies, and told his father he did not wish to marry'), and resolution ('... and after the King's death Dullhead succeeded to the kingdom, and lived happily with his wife for many years after'). In addition, children will enjoy comparing the tales they read, and then discovering and charting some of the literary conventions or patterns which abound in folklore, such as the three sons, the youngest of whom achieves success against all odds; fairies who make wishes for a princess on her birth; talking beasts; or cruel step-parents. Writing activities may include retelling old tales as well as creating new ones. One teacher encouraged his class to read modern parodies of fairy tales, including Michael Foreman's *All the King's Horses* (1976), Roald Dahl's *Revolting Rhymes* (1982) and Raymond Briggs' *Jim and the Beanstalk* (1970). They then chose a traditional fairy tale to retell with a humorous ending, or attempted their own parodies.

Other possibilities for genre study are creation myths, pour-quoi stories, as exemplified by Rudyard Kipling's *Just So Stories* (1902) and Ted Hughes' *How the Whale Became and Other Stories* (1963), and tall tales. One genre which is ideal for study in the primary years is the picture story book. In one school it has become almost a tradition that primary children write picture story books for the incoming kindergarten children. To accomplish their task, they are encouraged by their teacher to read as many different published picture books as they can. Each child rehearses the oral reading of one self-selected story and then reads it to a small group of kindergarteners. Children then choose one young child each for whom they will write an original story. Much classroom discussion ensues about everything from story structure and vocabulary choice to the way in which illustration supports the text, and how the text and illustrations should best be laid out. After much drafting, conferencing, revising and polishing, the proud young authors once again visit their kindergarten friends, to present them with their published books, which, of course, the younger children demand should be read aloud again and again.

LITERATURE AS A DIRECT MODEL OF LANGUAGE PATTERNING

Whilst the emphasis in this chapter is upon the indirect modelling of literary genres and forms, there is a place for more direct imitation of literary patterns, particularly with beginning writers. Such writing will often occur with a whole class, part of a shared book experience programme. Children, with teacher guidance, may compose their own class story modelled on Anita Lobel's *The Pancake* (1978) but using different characters and a different ending. This story is characteristic of many picture story books which exhibit repetitive structures, either at the phrase, sentence or verse level, often with so much use of rhyme and rhythm that they beg to be chanted. One class of seven-year-olds often enjoyed the repetition and rhyme of Rosemary Wells' *Noisy Nora* (1976), and came up with their own *Messy Milly*.

A simple starting point for such structured innovation on a given text might be to add a new episode to the story. The creation of this, featuring a different animal, could easily be achieved with John Burningham's *Mr Gumpy's Outing* or Pamela Allen's *Who Sank the Boat*? both highly predictable stories with strong patterning of language. Cumulative tales such as 'I Know an Old Lady' or 'The Old Woman and Her Pig' can be similarly treated. Slightly older children could add an animal character, and therefore another episode, to Roald Dahl's *The Enormous Crocodile* (1977). This would necessitate the class initially, in a very close reading of the book, to work out the characteristic elements of each episode. Teachers wishing to read more extensively on the possibilities for such patterned writing are directed to the work of Johnson and Louis (1985) and Ryan (1984).

LITERATURE AS A SOURCE OF INSPIRATION FOR WRITING

Imaginative teachers will find a multitude of ways for promoting writing from a literature stimulus. Although some of the suggestions which follow are classified here as 'writing activities', readers will readily see that they also contribute to children's reading, understanding and appreciation of literature in its own right. The author has attempted to choose activities on this basis. It is also assumed that teachers will pursue such suggestions within the context of a writing programme which emphasises process over product, and which therefore encourages children to choose their own topics and audience. To this end, teachers need to give thought as to how they can feed ideas into the writing programme. Some have an 'ideas file' available as part of a Writing Centre, others suggest approaches to children as part of their prewriting activities. Stimulus ideas will remain gimmicks unless children see them as meaningful starting points from which their own ideas can develop. Once the children become familiar with some of the ways in which it is possible to respond in writing to literature, they are likely to write quite spontaneously, provided that the literary experience has been sufficiently inspiring. Kolczynski (1978: 57) makes the point that

> ... authentic writing comes about only when the child has something to say for real reasons and when writing is an outgrowth of meaningful experiences (direct or vicarious).

Extending the Story

Children enjoy creating a further adventure of a favourite character. Episodic stories are often appropriate for such treatment. Children could create a further adventure for flattened Flat Stanley, or Mrs Pepperpot. After reading Byars' *The Eighteenth Emergency*, they might join up like Mouse and Ezzie to draw up their own list of unlikely emergencies.

Try the Form Out

A growing number of stories feature letters, diaries or journals as part or all of their narrative structure. Children who are acquainted with Louise Fitzhugh's *Harriet the Spy* (1966), Libby Gleeson's *Eleanor, Elizabeth* (1984) or Robin Klein's *Penny Pollard's Diary* (1983) may wish to write diary selections for another character.

Finding Alternative Endings

Some stories could have quite different endings and still remain credible to readers; others, particularly those exploring serious human dilemmas, seem to have an inevitability about them. Children and teacher may discuss various possible alternative endings to stories in the former category, such as some of Margaret Mahy's fantastic short stories. Some teachers encourage children to 'think like an author', by stopping the reading aloud of a story at a crucial point and asking them to predict possible endings. They are asked to substantiate their predictions from their understanding and interpretation of the text. They may then choose to write their own alternative endings to the story for later comparison with the original.

Filling in the Gaps

One crucial aspect of the author's craft is the ability to leave sufficient space in the narration for the reader to exercise his or her powers of imagination and recreation. Occasionally the nature of the reader-author transaction can be demonstrated by the teacher suggesting that children write about the characters before the story's first page, or at some period of time after the story's resolution. Alternatively, children might take a particular incident and sketch in the details left to the reader's imagination. Sometimes the 'filling in' can take a different writing form: characters from the story might exchange letters, or those from different stories may write to each other.

Writing from a Different Point of View

Another aspect of literature worthy of study is the point of view taken by the narrator. Both discussion and writing can help children perceive how the story is shaped by the decision by the author to tell the story from one or another character's viewpoint. Taking a different viewpoint also allows children opportunities to 'step into the shoes' of a different character. For instance, how would Jenny Wagner's *John Brown, Rose and the Midnight Cat* (1977) be told if viewed through the eyes of each one of the story's three main characters?

Creating the Text for a Wordless Picture Book

There are many picture story books published in which the story is completely told through the sequence of illustrations, without any words. Obviously, the success of such books lies in the illustrator's ability to tell a story without text: and children will soon realise this. To suggest, therefore, that children might supply a written text seems contradictory. However, there are many children who experience difficulty in their own story writing with the logical sequencing of a story around some organising principle, such as time or causality. These children in particular can benefit from having the sequenced detail already provided. As they turn each page of the textless book, they decide what is happening and how best to tell it. Examples of suitable books are Mercer Mayer's *Frog, Where Are You?* (1969) or Shirley Hughes' comic-strip format *Up and Up* (1979).

Try Out the Theme

Discussion of a story read can open up areas of personal experience which children may explore on their own, often without any suggestion by the teacher. In one class where the teacher had serialised Ruth Park's *Callie's Castle* (1974), a number of children who identified with Callie's lack of personal privacy chose to write about their own situation. Some wrote about their own ideal 'place of my own'. Almost any good book can spark ideas for children's own writing: one nine-year-old girl told her teacher she wanted to write a book 'about a wombat'. In conference, her teacher discovered that the task which the young writer had set herself was to write a story which was true to wombats' characteristics (the class had been studying Australian mammals), which involved a bushfire (the teacher had shown the class Ivan Smith's *Death of a Wombat* (1972), and which was modelled on Ruth Park's *The Muddleheaded Wombat* (1962), 'only different'!

Writing a Personal Reaction to the Book

Many young children will choose to simply retell in their own writing a book which has been recently enjoyed. Older children may couple the retelling with thoughts about the personalities of characters, comments connecting the story to their own perceptions of life, or some rudimentary evaluation. This is quite a different proposition than the prescriptive, form-filling notion of a regular book review, and should be encouraged, if voluntarily chosen. The teacher's role might be in suggesting a real audience for such writing. For instance, there might be a Critics' Corner notice board close to the classroom library collection.

Communicating with the Author

Authors appreciate genuine expressions of appreciation of their work. Members of a class might round off their Author of the Month experience by writing to the author, giving their views or putting to him or her unresolved questions which arose in their writing. The communication is most usually reciprocated by the author, often at great length. As a courtesy, children should be requested to provide a self-addressed envelope or some contribution to the cost of replying — a very expensive enterprise for popular authors!

Writing as Part of an Expression of Response

Some of the suggestions previously mentioned as means of creatively interpreting stories read, involve writing in a variety of forms. Children who engage in the task of creating a new cover design for a book will need to encapsulate the story in the blurb, without spoiling it for other readers by giving away too much. Children who try Readers' Theatre for themselves will be involved in simple script-writing, as will those who try to retell a story through a scripted puppet play or radio drama. Artistic recreations such as models or dioramas may be enhanced by simple captions, another form of summarising. It should be noted once again that children will experience frustration with many writing tasks which involve a writing form unfamiliar to them. The teacher needs to provide many indirect models of a new form, as well as demonstrating the model directly in a small group situation before suggesting that children try the form for themselves. The criticisms of unstructured assignments made by Johnson and Louis (1985: 16–17) are very valid: the teacher's role should be to provide the means for children to absorb ways of thinking and responding.

Suggestions for writing could go on endlessly: those given above have been selected because they have been successfully tried, and because they focus on literature and response, rather than being motivational gimmicks. They can be incorporated into a process/conference writing programme without affecting young writers' freedom of topic choice.

PULLING THE THREADS TOGETHER

Many classroom possibilities have been explored in this chapter. Obviously they make demands on classroom time, but the beauty of a literature-based classroom is that it can effectively be integrated with almost any other area of the primary curriculum. There is every reason for it becoming a major part of the language arts component, reading, and indirectly, writing. The only additional classroom time necessary is one or two twenty-minute sessions each week for the community of readers to share, appreciate and enjoy each other's ideas and creative efforts. Teachers can move into literature as rapidly or tentatively as they like. Reports from teachers who have 'made the move' indicate that very often the decision is taken out of their hands: once the enthusiasm for literature catches fire amongst children and their parents, there is little the teacher can do to extinguish the flames!

REFERENCES

Allington, R., 'If They Don't Read Much, How They Gonna Get Good?' in *Journal of Reading*, October 1977.
Anderson, B.P., 'A Guide to Readers Theatre' in *Language Links* No. 6, 1983.
Barnes, D., *From Communication to Curriculum*. Harmondsworth, Middlesex: Penguin, 1976.
Bennett, J., *Learning to Read with Picture Books*, Stroud: Thimble Press, 1979.
Cairns, L., 'The Practicalities of Reading: What to Leave Out; What to Put in', unpublished paper presented at Third Conference of the Reading Association, 'Literacy and Change', Sydney: Milperra, 1985.
Cambourne, B., 'How Important is Theory to the Reading Teacher?' in *Australian Journal of Reading* Vol. 2, No. 2, 1979.

Chambers, A., *Introducing Books to Children*. London: Heinemann, 1974.
Clark, M., *Young Fluent Readers*. London: Heinemann, 1976.
Cohen, D., 'The Effect of Literature on Vocabulary and Reading Achievement' in *Elementary English* Vol. 45, February 1968.
Coleman, H.S. and O'Sullivan, C., *Traditional Literature: Teachers Engage in Classroom Research*. Sydney: Catholic Education Office, 1985.
Collerson, J. and Nicoll, V., 'Stories Read and Stories Written: A Case Study of One Child's Reading and Writing Experience', in L. Unsworth, editor, *Reading, Writing and Spelling, Proceedings of the Fifth Macarthur Reading/Language Symposium*. Sydney: 1984.
Cullinan, B., Jaggar, A., and Strickland, D., 'Language Expansion for Black Children in the Primary Grades: A Research Report' in *Young Children*. Vol. 29, January 1974.
Durkin, D., *Children Who Read Early*, New York: Teachers College, 1966.
Fader, D. and McNeil, E.B., *Hooked on Books: Program and Proof*. New York: Berkley, 1968.
Graves, D., *Writing: Teachers and Children at Work*. Exeter, New Hampshire: Heinemann, 1983.
Harding, D.W., 'Ways Forward for the Teacher: Making Way for the Child's own "Feeling Comprehension"' in Meek, M., Warlow, A. and Barton, G., *The Cool Web: The Pattern of Children's Reading*. London: Bodley Head 1977.
Hepler, S., 'Patterns of Response to Literature: A One-year Study of a Fifth and Sixth Grade Classroom', unpublished doctoral dissertation. The Ohio State University: 1982.
Holdaway, D., *The Foundations of Literacy*. New York: Scholastic, 1979.
Huck, C., *Children's Literature in the Elementary School*. New York: Holt, Rinehart & Winston, 1976.
———, 'I Give You the End of a Golden String' in *Theory Into Practice* Vol. 21, No. 4, Autumn 1982.
Jackson, D., *Encounters with Books: Teaching Fiction 11–16*. London: Methuen, 1983.
Johnson, T.D. and Louis, D.R., *Literacy Through Literature*. Sydney: Methuen, 1985.
Jones, A. and Buttrey, J., *Children and Stories*. Oxford: Blackwell, 1970.
Kolczynski, R., 'Reading Leads to Writing' in J.W. Stewig and S.L. Sebesta, editors, *Using Literature in the Elementary Classroom*. Urbana, Illinois: National Councils of Teachers of English, 1978.
Kress, G., *Learning to Write*. London: Routledge & Kegan Paul, 1982.
McCracken, R.A., 'Instituting Sustained Silent Reading' *Journal of Reading* May 1971.
——— and McCracken, M.J., 'Modelling is the Key to Sustained Silent Reading' in *Reading Teacher* January 1978.
McKenzie, M., *Becoming a Reader*. London: Centre for Language in Primary Education, ILEA Learning Materials Service, 1977.
Postman, N., *The Disappearance of Childhood*. London: Allen, 1983.
Rosenblatt, L., *Literature as Exploration*. London: Heinemann, 1970.
———, 'The Literary Transaction: Evocation and Response' in *Theory into Practice* Vol. 21, No. 4, Autumn 1982.
Ryan, D. and Snowball, D., *The Reading-Writing Connection*. Wagga Wagga: Australian Reading Association, 1984.
Sloan, G.D., *The Child as Critic: Teaching Literature in the Elementary School*. New York: Teachers College, 1978.

Sloan, P. and Latham, R., *Teaching Reading Is*. Melbourne: Nelson, 1981.
Sloyer, S., *Readers Theatre: Story Dramatisation in the Classroom*. Urbana, Illinois: National Council of Teachers of English, 1982.
Stewig, J.W., *Read to Write*. New York: Hawthorn Books, 1975.
Tierney, R. and Pearson, P.D., 'Toward a Composing Model of Reading' in *Language Arts* Vol. 60, No. 5, May 1983.
Trelease, J., *The Read-Aloud Handbook*. Harmondsworth, Middlesex: Penguin, 1984.
Turbill, J., editor, *No Better Way to Teach Writing*. Sydney: Primary English Teaching Association, 1982.
―――, *Now We Want to Write*. Sydney: Primary English Teaching Association, 1983.
Veatch, J., *Reading in the Elementary School*. New York: Wiley, 1978.
―――, *Donald Graves in Australia: 'Children want to write . . . '*. Sydney: Primary English Teaching Association, 1982.
―――, *Every Child Can Write!* Sydney: Primary English Teaching Association, 1982.
Watson, K., editor, *Reading is Response*. Sydney: St Clair Press, 1980.

BOOKS REFERRED TO IN THE CHAPTER

Allen, Pamela, *Who Sank the Boat?* Puffin.
Ardizonne, Edward, *Little Tim and the Brave Sea Captain*. Oxford.
Bolton, Barbara, *Jandy Malone and the Nine O'Clock Tiger*. Angus & Robertson.
Briggs, Raymond, *Jim and the Beanstalk*. Puffin.
Burningham, John, *Mr Gumpy's Outing*. Cape.
Byars, Betsy, *The Eighteenth Emergency*. Puffin.
―――, *The Pinballs*. Puffin.
Carle, Eric, *The Very Hungry Caterpillar*. Hamish Hamilton.
Carroll, Lewis, *Alice's Adventures in Wonderland*. Macmillan.
Cleary, Beverly, *Ramona the Pest*. Hamilton.
Cresswell, Helen, *Ordinary Jack*. Faber.
Dahl, Roald, *The BFG*. Puffin.
―――, *The Enormous Crocodile*. Puffin.
―――, *Revolting Rhymes*. Puffin.
Fitzhugh, Louise, *Harriet the Spy*. Lions.
Foreman, Michael, *All the King's Horses*. Hamish Hamilton.
―――, *War and Peas*. Hamish Hamilton.
Gleeson, Libby, *Eleanor, Elizabeth*. Angus & Robertson.
Grahame, Kenneth, *Wind in the Willows*. Methuen.
Greenwood, Ted, *Everlasting Circle*. Hutchinson.
Hughes, Shirley, *Up and Up*. Bodley Head.
Hughes, Ted, *How the Whale Became and Other Stories*. Puffin.
―――, *The Iron Man*. Faber.
Hunter, Norman, *The Incredible Adventures of Professor Branestawm*. Puffin.
Kerr, Judith, *When Hitler Stole Pink Rabbit*. Collins.
King, Clive, *Stig of the Dump*. Puffin.
Kipling, Rudyard, *Just So Stories*. Macmillan.
Klein, Robin, *Penny Pollard's Diary*. Oxford.
Lewis, C.S., *The Lion, the Witch and the Wardrobe*. Macmillan.
Lindgren, Astrid, *Pippi Longstocking*. Oxford.

Lobel, Arnold, *Fables*. Cape.
——————, *The Pancake*. World's Work.
Magorian, Michelle, *Goodnight Mister Tom*. Kestrel.
Mayer, Mercer, *Frog, Where Are You?* Dial Press.
Murphy, Jill, *The Worst Witch*. Puffin.
Norton, Mary, *The Borrowers*. Dent.
Noyes, Alfred, illustrator, Charles Keeping, *The Highwayman*. Oxford.
Park, Ruth, *Callie's Castle*. Angus & Robertson.
——————, *Playing Beatie Bow*. Nelson.
——————, *The Muddle-Headed Wombat*. Angus & Robertson.
Paterson, Katherine, *Bridge to Terabithia*. Puffin.
——————, *The Great Gilly Hopkins*. Puffin.
Pearce, Philippa, *The Battle of Bubble and Squeak*. Puffin.
——————, *Tom's Midnight Garden*. Oxford.
——————, *The Way to Sattin Shore*. Kestrel.
Pender, Lydia, *The Useless Donkeys*. Methuen.
Proysen, Alf, *Little Old Mrs Pepperpot*. Hutchinson.
Reiss, Joanna, *The Upstairs Room*. Puffin.
Ryan, John, *Captain Pugwash*. Puffin.
Sendak, Maurice, *Where the Wild Things Are*. Puffin.
Serraillier, Ian, *The Silver Sword*. Cape.
Smith, Ian, illustrator, Clifton Pugh, *Death of a Wombat*. Wren.
Spence, Eleanor, *The Seventh Pebble*. Oxford.
Taylor, Theodore, *The Cay*. Puffin.
Tolstoy, Alexei, illustrator, Helen Oxenbury, *The Great Big Enormous Turnip*, Pan.
Wagner, Jenny, illustrator, Ron Brooks, *John Brown, Rose and the Midnight Cat*. Kestrel/Puffin.
Wells, Rosemary, *Noisy Nora*. Puffin.
Westall, Robert, *The Machine Gunners*. Puffin.
White, E.B., *Charlotte's Web*. Hamish Hamilton.
Wrightson, Patricia, *A Little Fear*. Puffin.

FURTHER READING

Benton, Michael and Fox, Geoff, *Reaching Literature: Nine to Fourteen*. London: OUP, 1988.
Butler, Andrea and Turbill, Jan, *Towards a Reading-Writing Classroom*. Sydney: PETA, 1984.
Hancock, Joelie and Hill, Susan (eds). *Literature-based Reading Programs at Work*. Melbourne: ARA, 1987.
Hanzl, Anne (ed.), *Literature: A Focus For Language Learning*. Melbourne: ARA, 1988.
Johnson, Terry D. and Louis, Daphne R., *Bringing it all Together: A Program for Literacy*. Sydney: Methuen, 1987.
McVitty, Walter (ed.), *The PETA Guide to Children's Literature* (2nd ed.). Sydney: PETA, 1989.
Meek, Margaret, *How Texts Teach What Readers Learn*. Stroud: Thimble Press, 1988.
Michaels, Wendy and Walshe, Maureen, *Up and Away: Using Picture Books*. Melbourne: OUP, 1990.
O'Sullivan, Colleen, *Australian Literature in the Primary Classroom*. Canberra: Curriculum Development Centre, 1988.
——————, *The Challenge of Picture Books: A Teacher's Guide to the Use of Picture Books with Older Students*. Sydney: Methuen, 1987.
Walshe, Robert D., *Teaching Literature*. Sydney: PETA, 1983.

24 STORYTELLING: A SHARED EXPERIENCE

BARBARA POSTON-ANDERSON

> He talked, and as he talked
> Wall paper came alive;
> Suddenly ghosts walked,
> And four doors were five.
>
> Mark Van Doren in 'The Storyteller'

ORIGIN AND TRADITION

For thousands of years, storytelling has been a respected medium for sharing everything from the commonplace happenings of daily life to the more profound meanings of the universe. In early societies, the interpreter of such events, the storyteller, fulfilled a valued function. Wandering from cottage to court, this individual brought news of world events and transmitted a cultural heritage through stories which delighted, amazed, informed, and even persuaded. The power of these storytelling sessions was enhanced since the teller employed a full range of techniques from dramatics to song in captivating audiences.

Even though our world view today is vastly different from that of earlier times, storytelling is still a valuable means of communication. Through story, imaginations can be extended and lives enriched. This chapter examines storytelling for young people, focusing on practical approaches and techniques for sharing.

VALUES OF STORYTELLING

The values of sharing stories with young people are many. Perhaps most importantly, stories stimulate the imagination. Children fly with Pegasus, dig for buried treasure, or feel the joy of turning from a frog into a prince — all within the realm of their imaginations. They enter another world, where the temporal becomes the eternal. But instead of escaping from reality, their experiences with story give them added insight into life, fine-tuning their senses and developing their abilities to see issues from other points of view.

Some stories, especially folk tales, which have long been the staple diet of storytellers, abound in universal truths and values. Evil is punished; good is rewarded; hard work provides the basis for a meaningful life. Other traditional tales reveal the deeds of heroes and heroines — linking past to present, providing a perspective on time, and highlighting our common humanity. Above all, in most traditional stories there is hope — an optimism which cannot help but have a positive impact on children.

The medium of storytelling itself encourages participation through listening and involvement. As children willingly suspend their disbelief and immerse themselves in the world of story, they begin to relate to characters and events, both inwardly and outwardly. The storyteller notices smiles, sighs of relief, even cries of warning to alert an unsuspecting character of danger — all of them contributing to the children's enjoyment and understanding of the story.

APPROACHES TO STORYTELLING

Storytelling can be approached from a number of perspectives. Some storytellers, who regard the medium as an art form, appear to perform for their audiences, while others, who believe that nothing should detract from the words, keep dramatic involvement to a minimum. If these two orientations are regarded as opposite ends of a continuum, it is evident that there is room for much interpretation in between. The storyteller's personality, the story itself, and even, to a certain extent, the environment, may influence the approach that is chosen. It is reassuring to realise that there is no one right way to tell a story.

In this chapter the emphasis will be on storytelling as a shared experience in which both storyteller and listeners participate. The storyteller, through effective interpretation of the words of a story, helps the listener to visualise events, characters, feelings and actions. The listener uses imagination to fill in the details. No matter how old, the magic remains the same.

The traditional storyteller uses few props or aids. Focus is on interpretation of the words. These cues, with a minimum of dramatic embellishment, convey scenes, moods and characters, bringing tales to life.

However, some storytellers find it beneficial, especially when sharing with young people, to enhance the experience with props, puppets, musical instruments or dramatic action. In fact, when sharing with preschool and infant children, a higher degree of activity and direct involvement is probably advisable because, according to developmental psychologists, younger children respond more positively to concrete experiences.

With these approaches in mind, it is important to stress that each storyteller must develop his or her own style. There is no one correct method. The challenge is to discover and develop those means of sharing stories which bring the most enjoyment to both you — the storyteller — and to your listeners.

STORYTELLING BASICS

Locating an appropriate story to share amongst the wealth of stories available can be overwhelming. Folk tales provide an excellent starting point. Uncomplicated plots, straightforward characters, and universal truths make them appealing to a wide range of listeners. Also, repetition which is characteristic of most folk tales, serves as a valuable aid to memory for the storyteller. In addition, because such tales originated in oral tradition, the style of language usually lends itself well to retelling aloud.

Besides folk tales, consider poems, songs, finger games, or tales from picture books, short stories, and novels. The important criterion in selection is that you personally enjoy what you have chosen. Even if a tale is regarded by the critics as a 'classic', you should not select it unless it strikes a special chord with you. If you dislike a story, this will be apparent to your listeners.

As you prepare the story you have chosen, develop the attitude that the experience of storytelling will be a 'sharing' rather than a 'performance'. If you are able to do this, you will minimise the tension you may feel about sharing a story for the first time. Remember that the experience should be enjoyable for both you and your listeners.

Also, it helps you to feel at ease if you know the group with whom you will be sharing. Although some stories have a universal appeal for both children and adults, others may be more appropriate at certain developmental levels. For example, nursery rhymes and cumulative tales, such as John Burningham's *Mr Gumpy's Outing* (1970) or Pamela Allen's *Bertie And The Bear* (1983), are enthusiastically greeted by children in the preschool and infant years, both when shared in picture book form and as 'stories'. A large part of the reason for this is that their plots are easy to follow (i.e. cumulative, in that one event builds on the next) and that characters have personality traits which appeal to children in this stage of development. For example, in *Bertie and the Bear*, the bear's antics are both humorous and playful.

Increase your confidence by practising your story aloud several times before trying it with your group. Even try taping your story on an audio or video cassette. By listening to yourself, you will gain insight into how to prepare more effectively.

Unless your tale is written by an author with a distinctive literary style which demands it, avoid memorising word for word. Rather try to remember the order of the ideas and events. By developing a mental framework for the story in this way, you will become more flexible during your sharing. This freedom from a word-by-word approach will enable you to adapt your reactions to the responses of the children.

INTRODUCING A STORY

Introducing a story in an imaginative way is the key to gaining children's attention. Unlike sharing a picture book, in storytelling there will be no illustrations on which to focus. For this reason, you may find it helpful to introduce your story with an object. For example, in Hans Christian Andersen's *The Princess and The Pea*, an actual pea pod can create interest in the tale to follow, or, in Tomie de Paola's *The Magic Pasta Pot* (1979), a small cooking pot can foreshadow excitement to come. Other ways to introduce stories include: discussing the origin of a tale, which is appropriate when introducing tales such as Australian Aboriginal traditional narratives; or relating something about the author, if it is a literary story. For example, it is fun to learn that the picture book, *There's a Hippopotamus on Our Roof Eating Cake* (1980) by Hazel Edwards, was based on the imaginative ideas of her own children (Edwards 1980). You may enjoy sharing this book first as a 'story' and then sharing the picture book. Between the two sharings, children could create their own illustrations to compare with the humorous ones by Deborah Niland in the picture book version.

WHEN TELLING THE STORY

When storytelling, if possible, insist on an area which is away from the hustle and bustle of other activities. A distraction-free environment is essential. You may stand or sit as you prefer. Often this depends on the physical arrangements of the storytelling setting. If children are on the floor, you may choose to sit on a small stool. However, if children are sitting on chairs, you may find that standing is more appropriate. Standing also gives you more scope for movement. No matter what you decide, it is important that all children see you clearly.

Do not begin to share your story until the group is settled and quiet. You may find it useful, especially if you tell stories to the same groups as a regular activity, to initiate a certain ceremony which signals the beginning of story time. Ringing a bell, lighting a candle, or sitting in a special chair are all means which have been used.

Also remember that vocal variety in your sharing is necessary to interpret the story effectively and to maintain interest. Volume, vocal pitch, and the quality of your voice can be used to good effect. The soft pitter-patter of rain, the shriek of the cyclone, the hollow echo of footsteps in an abandoned mine — all seem real when effectively suggested by the voice. The rate of speech and the use of pause also positively influence the interpretation. Several key texts in oral interpretation are cited at the end of the chapter if you wish to pursue the basics further.

Be aware that movement also plays a significant role, both in interpretation, and in focusing the attention of the group. Even when movements are not extensive, they may serve to suggest many aspects of the story. For example, subtle turns of the head or shifting of the eyes may be enough to indicate that another character is speaking. A step or change in position may signal a transition in time or place.

You will find that movement can also be an excellent control device. Stepping toward a disruptive child may be all that is needed to regain attention. However, try to avoid any action which will interrupt the flow of the story and spoil it for others. Stop the story only as a last resort.

FOLLOW-UP

Follow-up can provide a meaningful extension to the story. Sometimes if a storyteller is sharing a number of tales in one session, the next story or song is a logical follow-up of the preceeding one. For example, if you share *The Three Billy Goats Gruff*, you might follow it with the song, 'My Highland Goat'.

However, there may be times when the storyteller prefers to focus on one story alone with follow-up activities. For example, after sharing Esphyr Slobodkina's *Caps for Sale* (1959) with young children, the storyteller could have a craft activity in which each child creates his/her own hat. A musical follow-up could occur with singing the song 'My Hat It Has Three Corners', or dramatically, the story could be re-enacted, with the children becoming the monkeys.

Role-playing, discussion and written expression may be appropriate follow-up activities as well. For example, in Jill Tomlinson's story, *The Owl who was Afraid of the Dark* (1973), children could discuss or write about their feelings toward darkness or role-play the part of Plop as this young barn owl learns to accept the merits of darkness.

In many cases what you decide to do will depend on the story and even on the group itself. It is not always necessary nor appropriate to follow a story with an activity. Some stories, such as Jenny Wagner's *John Brown, Rose, and the Midnight Cat* (1977), and Christobel Mattingley's *The Angel with a Mouth-organ* (1984), have just as much effect if children are allowed to ponder their significance on their own.

APPROACHES FOR SHARING AND FOLLOW-UP

The following sections provide a variety of approaches which could be useful during sharing or in follow-up sessions.

FLANNEL, FELT AND VELCRO BOARDS

Boards covered with flannel, felt or velcro may serve as visual aids when sharing a story. In particular, cumulative tales or songs lend themselves to board stories. As songs such as 'A Hole in the Bucket' or 'I Know an Old Lady who Swallowed a Fly' are sung, children add the bits and pieces to the board. Some storytellers prefer to use velcro as the backing material on their boards, because figures stick to it more readily, but flannel or felt are equally serviceable. Also, be sure to cover the backs of each of your figures with the chosen material.

When using flannel, felt or velcro boards, each piece of the story must be securely attached. If you are adding the pieces yourself, practise the story so that you are able to look at the listeners instead of concentrating on the board. It may help to pause while you attach the figures, and then look back at the group. If the group is small, you may prefer to sit on the floor with the children grouped around the board, which also is flat on the floor. In this way, there is no worry that pieces of the story will accidentally fall from the board.

The advantage of board stories is that they aid memory, especially when the plot is cumulative and repetitive. It helps children to remember what object comes next if they are assisting you to tell the story. If childen have access to the board and the story pieces, they may retell the story on their own, further increasing their enjoyment.

The following example shows a felt board which was designed for use with the Australian folk song, 'Click Go The Shears'. The fleece on the sheep is detachable so that it can be shorn at the point in the song when 'Click go the shears, boys, click, click, click' is sung. Appoint several children as shearers to participate at the appropriate moments.

OVERHEAD PROJECTOR STORIES

The overhead projector has potential for use in a storytelling setting. Projected cardboard or paper figures appear as silhouettes on the screen. This means that characters are only suggested and that listeners are still free to fill in the details from their imaginations. Striking shadow puppets can be made by cutting away portions of the cardboard figures and backing them with coloured acetate (i.e. overhead transparency film). Hinging the joints of the cardboard cutouts with thin wire gives the puppet a limited range of movement.

If you decide to try a story using the overhead projector, remember that when the figures are projected onto the screen, space is limited. For this reason, the number of characters must be few and the cardboard cutouts small. Also, because the nature of the shadow figures restricts their movement, choose shorter stories which do not demand vigorous action.

The following cardboard figures were created for an overhead projector story of the Aesop fable, *The Boy Who Cried Wolf*. The joint of the boy's arm has been hinged in order to enable him to raise his arm to call for help at the appropriate moments.

STRING STORIES

Anthropologists have found the equivalent of the string story in all parts of the world. This ancient form of storytelling still has a hypnotic effect on listeners. In short, as a storyteller tells a tale, a number of string figures are created to accompany it. The figures themselves may vary from the simple to the complex. Teacups, towers, bridges, diamonds, animals — all may take shape in the string.

Learning the techniques for creating these figures may take time, but it is certainly worth the effort. Perhaps the best way to begin is to learn several simple figures and create your own story for them. There are several excellent books on string figures, with clear instructions, which are included in the list at the end of the chapter.

The following story can be used with simple string figures:

The Adventures of Wiley Robin

Once there was a bushranger named Wiley Robin who wore a bright red cape wherever he went. He got his name because he was so wiley and also because he was always robbing someone. In fact, one day when the Governor's wife came to town, he had stolen the diamond earrings from her ears before she even knew they were missing. (*String figure: two diamonds*; see Elffers and Schuyt 1979).

When the Governor found out about the theft, he was furious and sent the troopers after Wiley Robin. But Wiley wasn't worried and stopped at Aunt Nancy's Boarding House as he always did for a cup of tea. (*String figure: Cup and Saucer*).

The troopers surrounded the Boarding House and called out, 'Surrender, Wiley Robin!'

But he replied, 'Never!'

'You'll be sorry! We've got you like a fly in a trap!' (*String figure: fly*).

A gun battle ensued. [Clap hands together furiously over knot], but when the smoke cleared, Wiley was nowhere to be seen. [Loose knot].

The troopers were furious and looked everywhere for Wiley. They never would have found him, except that a rival bushranger, Putrid Pete, gave him away. Pete directed them to a cave outside of town.

When Wiley heard the horses' hooves, he climbed a tall gum tree to discover who had tracked him to his hideout. When he saw it was the troopers, he gave a huge leap and spread his red cape out behind him. It served as a parachute and he sailed to the ground unharmed. (*String figure: parachute*).

But fortune was not with that wiley robber, for as he stood up, he tripped and broke his ankle. The troopers surrounded him and took him back to Sydney town for a trial.

The day of justice came and the verdict was 'Guilty'. It looked as though Wiley Robin had finished his bushranging days forever. They wrapped the rope around his neck once ... but knowing how wiley he was, they didn't stop there. They wrapped the rope around twice and again three times. (*String figure: string around your neck and pull*).

But Wiley Robin was so wiley that he escaped even his own death. [Pull rope from neck]. They say that he still rides in the dead of night through old Sydney town ... so if you're ever there, BEWARE of Wiley Robin. (See Elffers and Schuyt 1979, for all string figures used).

SOUND STORIES

Many stories lend themselves to the addition of sound or musical accompaniment. For example, the folktale, *The Tailypo*, can be enriched by having the children provide the sounds of the dogs barking, the wind in the chimney, and the swamp gurgling. Of course, if children are going to participate in the storytelling, they must know before the story starts what is expected of them. You may decide to use some sort of control device to signal when they should start and stop the sound. A tambourine or an arrow which indicates the level of sound expected may be advantageous. Have them practise several times before you begin.

Musical instruments such as drums, bells, cymbals, and wooden sticks may be used instead of vocal sounds. In a folk tale such as *The Three Billy Goats Gruff*, an instrument may symbolise each character. When that character's name is said by the storyteller, the child on the instrument must echo it with the musical sound. These musical effects add suspense and drama to the story as the troll is defeated by the big billy goat and falls into the water with a *splat*!

PUPPETS

Puppets have many advantages for the storyteller. First, they make friends easily. When a storyteller meets a group for the first time, a puppet can be used to gain immediate attention and to break the ice. Trying to coax a reluctant puppet to raise his head to say 'hello' or finding a name to suit his personality, are activities which children enjoy. Using time in the storytelling session to do this can provide valuable insight for the storyteller about the group and how to approach them.

Puppets also have other uses. They provide effective means for introducing stories; they lead songs well; and they are experts at telling jokes. In addition, within stories themselves, they can be used as characters to whom the storyteller speaks or they can tell the stories on their own.

When using puppets, it is not necessary to have them behind a stage. In fact, the use of a large stage has the effect of distancing the storyteller from the group because he or she will need to move behind the stage to work the puppets. A more versatile alternative is to place the puppets out of sight until they are needed — and then merely bring them out of their bag or box in full view of the children. Even if it is a story in which only the puppets talk, the storyteller's presence is soon forgotten as the puppets work their magic.

Puppets come in all shapes and sizes. However, if you have a certain story in mind, you may prefer to design your own. If you do, remember that the size and type of puppet you construct should fit the story, the group, and the setting. For instance, if you are telling stories in a large room, finger puppets would be too small to be easily seen. Hand puppets, however, are still easy to manipulate, and have the advantage of being much larger. On the other hand, marionettes, while easily seen, are usually more complex in design and demand more life-like movement. Reference to the books listed on puppets and puppet-making should provide much useful information on this topic.

DRAMATIC INVOLVEMENT

Dramatic involvement by the children may be appropriate before, during and after a story. Before a story, it may help establish the tone or setting. For example, in Ivan Southall's *The Sly Old Wardrobe* (1968), a young boy discovers a wardrobe at an opportunity shop. Through what hands has this item passed before arriving there? Have children enact the attempt of 'previous owners' to sell the wardrobe.

In Junko Morimoto's *The Inch Boy* (1984) have children consider what the life of an inch-high samurai warrior would be like. Explorations in movement could give children some insight into the challenges this character must face in the story.

Within some stories there is room for involvement of the listeners as the story is being told. In *The Little Red Hen* children could be divided into three sections to correspond to the cat, the dog, and the mouse. Every time the Little Red Hen asks each of these characters who will help with the work, the groups of children respond with, 'Not I!'

Another example of direct involvement during a story is sharing *The Pied Piper of Hamelin* as a news broadcast. You, the storyteller, are the news correspondent, while children become various citizens of the town of Hamelin who are interviewed about the severity of the rat plague. At other points in the story, children can consider what gift they would give the piper if he rid them of the rats, or whether they should bring the piper to trial for kidnapping their children.

Following a story, the entire tale can be re-enacted. For example, in *The Hare and the Tortoise* a race could be held, complete with spectators. Another idea is to create 'still photographs' from the fable. This involves having the children freeze in place as the storyteller suggests the different characters and situations.

'Still photographs' can be individually created, or the storyteller may involve several children in creating one scene, such as the thorny vines around the castle of Sleeping Beauty, the courtiers dancing at Cinderella's wedding, or the Seven Dwarfs weeping over the glass coffin. Once still photographs are 'created', they can be brought to life by the beat of a tambourine and then silenced again by a similar signal.

The possibilities for dramatic involvement are limitless. However, before launching into too much activity, establish a control device to signal the children. You may find it easier to begin with activities which are controlled and then gradually branch into more unstructured situations.

READERS' THEATRE

In one sense, readers theatre can be thought of as group storytelling. In this approach, a group of readers, usually three to seven, shares a story aloud using a script which has been divided into parts. Each reader reads one or more parts and also helps with any narration. Poems, stories, and sections from plays and novels can be successfully adapted to this medium.

Unlike a dramatic production, in readers' theatre there is no full-scale movement. In fact, action is kept to a minimum. A bowed head may be enough to suggest death, whereas walking in place may signify a long journey. In addition, elaborate costumes, sets or lighting are not utilised. Usually readers sit on stools or stand. The idea is to encourage the audience to participate by using their imaginations.

Another characteristic of this medium is that readers hold scripts and do not look at each other. Instead, they share their story directly with the audience. When one character speaks to another, the readers employ offstage focus, which means that they both look at a predetermined point in the audience as they speak. If another character joins the conversation, the point of focus will change.

Readers' theatre provides challenges for everyone involved — the adaptor, the readers and the listeners. The adaptor must choose materials which lend themselves to being shared aloud in this way; the readers must effectively suggest the story with a minimum of characterisation and action; while listeners must employ their imaginations to fill in the details. More detailed information on readers' theatre is available in the books listed.

The potential of storytelling with young people is confined only by the imagination. As you select, present, and share stories, you will find the effort personally rewarding and enriching. You and your listeners will enjoy participating together in the shared storytelling experience.

REFERENCES

Background to Storytelling

Alderman, Belle, editor, 'A Diet of Words' in *The Imagineers*. Canberra: Reading Time, 1983.
Baker, Augusta and Greene, Ellin, *Storytelling: Art and Technique*. New York: Bowker, 1977.
Bauer, Caroline Feller, *Handbook for Storytellers*. Chicago: American Library Association, 1977.
Colwell, Eileen, *Storytelling*. London: Bodley Head, 1980.
Pellowski, Anne, *The World of Storytelling*. New York: Bowker, 1977.
Ross, Ramon, *Storyteller*. Sydney: Charles E. Merrill, 1980.
Scott, Patricia, *Sharing Stories; Storytelling and Reading Aloud*. Oatlands, Tas.: Storytellers Press, 1979.
——————, 'Storytelling: A Guide to the Art', *Primary English Notes*, No. 29, 1985.
Sawyer, Ruth, *The Way of the Storyteller*. Ringwood, Victoria: Penguin, 1976.
Ziskind, Sylvia, *Telling Stories to Children*. New York: H.W. Wilson, 1976.

String Stories and Figures

Elffers, Joost and Schuyt, Michael, *Cat's Cradles and Other String Figures*. Ringwood, Victoria: Penguin, 1979.
Emory, Kenneth, *String Figures of the Tuamotus*. Canberra: Homa, 1979.
Gryski, Camilla, *Cat's Cradles and Other String Games*. North Ryde, New South Wales: Angus & Robertson, 1985.
Kalter, Joanmarie, *String Figures*. New York: Drake, 1978.
Leeming, Joseph, *Fun This String, A Collection of String Games, Useful Braiding and Weaving, Knot Work and Magic*. New York: Dover Publications, 1974.

Puppets and Puppet-making

Champlin, Connie and Renfro, Nancy, *Storytelling with Puppets*. Chicago: American Library Association, 1985.
Currell, David, *Learning with Puppets*. Boston: Plays, 1980.
Hodgson, Janie, *The Australian Puppet Book: A Resource for Teachers and Parents*. Real Books, 1984 (Distributed Horwitz Grahame Books).
Reiniger, Lotte, *Shadow Puppets, Shadow Theatres and Shadow Films*. Boston: Plays, 1970.
Ross, Laura, *Finger Puppets: Easy to Make, Fun to Use*. New York: Lothrop, Lee & Shepard, 1971.
——————, *Hand Puppets: How to Make and Use Them*. New York: Lothrop, Lee & Shepard, 1969.
——————, *Puppet Shows: Using Poems and Stories*. New York: Lothrop, Lee & Shepard, 1970.

Creative Drama and Movement

Complo, Jannita *Dramakinetics in the Classroom*. Boston: Plays, 1974.
Fox, Mem, *How to Teach Drama to Infants Without Really Crying*. Sydney: Ashton Scholastic, 1984.
Pereira, Nancy, *Creative Dramatics in the Library*. Rowayton: New Plays, 1976.
Sowden, Celeste, *Literacy Through Drama*. Elsternwick: Port Phillip Press, nd.
Way, Brian, *Development Through Drama*. London: Longmans, 1968.
Wiltshire, Gail, *Speech, Movement and Drama: Classroom Resources*. Brisbane: John Wiley, 1983.

Readers' Theatre

Coger, Leslie and White, Melvin, *Readers' Theatre Handbook*. Glenview, Illinois: Scott, Foresman, 1982.
Robertson, Marion and Poston-Anderson, Barbara, *Readers' Theatre: A Practical Guide*. Sydney: Hodder & Stoughton, 1986.

ORAL INTERPRETATION

Bacon, Wallace, *The Art of Interpretation*. 3rd edition. New York: Holt, Rinehart & Winston, 1979. Gottlieb, Marvin, *Oral Interpretation*. New York: McGraw-Hill, 1980.
Lee, Charlotte and Gura, Timothy, *Oral Interpretations*. 6th edition. Boston, Massachusetts: Houghton Mifflin, 1982.

BOOKS REFERRED TO IN THE CHAPTER

Allen, Pamela, *Bertie and the Bear*. Nelson.
Andersen, Hans Christian, illustrator, Dorothée Duntzie, *The Princess and the Pea*. Abelard-Schuman.
Asbjörnsen, Peter and Moe, Jorgen, illustrator, Marcia Brown, *The Three Billy Goats Gruff*. Harcourt Brace Jovanovich.
Burningham, John, *Mr Gumpy's Outing*. Cape.
de Paola, Tomie, *The Magic Pasta Pot*. Hutchinson.
Edwards, Hazel, *There's a Hippopotamus On Our Roof Eating Cake*. Hodder & Stoughton.
Galdone, Joanna, illustrator, Paul Galdone, *The Tailypo*. World's Work.
Galdone, Paul, *The Little Red Hen*. World's Work.
Ingpen, Robert, illustrator, *Click Go The Shears*. Collins.
La Fontaine, illustrator, Brian Wildsmith, *The Hare and the Tortoise*. Oxford University Press.
Littledale, Freya, illustrator James Marshall, *The Boy Who Cried Wolf*. Scholastic Book Services.
Mattingley, Christobel, *The Angel With A Mouth-organ*. Hodder & Stoughton.
Morimoto, Junko, *The Inch Boy*. Collins.
Rochut, Jean-Noel, *The Pied Piper of Hamelin*. Hamlyn.
Slobodkina, Esphyr, *Caps for Sale*. World's Work.

Southall, Ivan, *The Sly Old Wardrobe*. Angus & Robertson.
Tomlinson, Jill, *The Owl Who Was Afraid Of The Dark*. Puffin.
Wagner, Jenny, *John Brown, Rose and the Midnight Cat*. Kestrel.

SONGS REFERRED TO IN THE CHAPTER

'My Hat It Has Three Corners' in *Okki-tokki-unga: Action Songs for Children*. A. & C. Black.

'My Highland Goat' (as the variant 'Bill Grogan's Goat') in Winn, Marie, editor, *The Fireside Book of Children's Songs*. Simon & Schuster.

'A Hole in the Bucket' in *Appusskidu: Songs for Children*. A. & C. Black.

'I Know an Old Lady' in *Appusskidu*.

PUPPETRY SOURCES

Champlin, Connie, *Puppetry and Creative Dramatics in Storytelling*. Austin: Nancy Renfro Studios, 1980.

Flower, Cedric and Fortney, Alan, *Puppets: Methods and Materials*. Worcester, Mass.: Davis Publications, 1983.

Hunt, Tamara and Renfro, Nancy, *Puppetry in Early Childhood Education*. Austin: Nancy Renfro Studios, 1982.

—————, *A Pocketful of Puppets: Mother Goose*. Austin: Nancy Renfro Studios, 1982.

Renfro, Nancy, *Puppetry, Language and the Special Child: Discovering Alternate Languages*. Austin: Nancy Renfro Studios, 1984.

APPENDIX

AUSTRALIAN CHILDREN'S BOOKS OF THE YEAR

Year	Title	Publisher
1946	*Karrawingi the Emu* Leslie Rees	Sands
1947	Award withheld	—
1948	*Shackleton's Argonauts* Frank Hurley	Angus & Robertson
1949	Award withheld	—
1950	*Whalers of the Midnight Sun* Alan John Villiers	Angus & Robertson
1951	*Verity of Sydney Town* Ruth C. Williams	Angus & Robertson
1952	*The Australia Book* Eve Pownall	Sands
1953	*Good Luck to the Rider* Joan Phipson and	Angus & Robertson
	Aircraft of Today and Tomorrow J.W. and W.D. Martin	Angus & Robertson
1954	*Australian Legendary Tales* K. Langloh Parker, editor, Henrietta Drake-Brockman	Angus & Robertson
1955	*The First Walkabout* Norman B. Tindale and H.A. Lindsay	Longmans
1956	*The Crooked Snake* Patricia Wrightson	Angus & Robertson
1957	*The Boomerang Book of Legendary Tales* Enid Moodie-Heddle	Longmans
1958	*Tiger in the Bush* Nan Chauncy	Oxford University Press
1959	*Devil's Hill* Nan Chauncy and	Oxford University Press
	Sea Menace John Gunn	Constable
1960	*All the Proud Tribesmen* Kylie Tennant	Macmillan
1961	*Tangara* Nan Chauncy	Oxford University Press
1962	*The Racketty Street Gang* Leonard Herbert Evers and	Brockhampton Press
	Rafferty Rides a Winner Joan Woodberry	Parrish

1963	*The Family Conspiracy* Joan Phipson	Angus & Robertson
1964	*The Green Laurel* Eleanor Spence	Oxford University Press
1965	*Pastures of the Blue Crane* Hesba Brinsmead	Oxford University Press
1966	*Ash Road* Ivan Southall	Angus & Robertson
1967	*The Min-Min* Mavis Thorpe Clark	Lansdowne
1968	*To the Wild Sky* Ivan Southall	Angus & Robertson
1969	*When Jays Fly to Barbmo* Margaret Balderson	Oxford University Press
1970	*Uhu* Annette Macarthur-Onslow	Ure Smith
1971	*Bread and Honey* Ivan Southall	Angus & Robertson
1972	*Longtime Passing* Hesba Brinsmead	Angus & Robertson
1973	*Family at the Lookout* Noreen Shelley	Oxford University Press
1974	*The Nargun and the Stars* Patricia Wrightson	Hutchinson
1975	Award withheld	—
1976	*Fly West* Ivan Southall	Angus & Robertson
1977	*The October Child* Eleanor Spence	Oxford University Press
1978	*The Ice is Coming* Patricia Wrightson	Hutchinson
1979	*The Plum-Rain Scroll* Ruth Manley	Hodder & Stoughton
1980	*Displaced Person* Lee Harding	Hyland House
1981	*Playing Beatie Bow* Ruth Park	Nelson
1982	*The Valley Between* Colin Thiele	Rigby
1983	*Master of the Grove* Victor Kelleher	Penguin
1984	*A Little Fear* Patricia Wrightson	Hutchinson
1985	*The True Story of Lilli Stubeck* James Aldridge	Angus & Robertson

PICTURE BOOKS OF THE YEAR

1956	*Wish and the Magic Nut* Peggy Barnard, illustrator Sheila Hawkins	Sands
1957	Award withheld	
1958	*Piccaninny Walkabout* Axel Poignant, illustrator (photographs), the author	Angus & Robertson
1959 to 1964	Award withheld	
1965	*Hugh's Zoo* Elisabeth MacIntyre	Knopf/Constable
1966 to 1968	Award withheld	
1969	*Sly Old Wardrobe* Ivan Southall, illustrator, Ted Greenwood	Cheshire
1970	Award withheld	
1971	*Waltzing Matilda* Andrew Barton Paterson, illustrator, Desmond Digby	Collins
1972	Award withheld	
1973	Award withheld	
1974	*The Bunyip of Berkeley's Creek* Jenny Wagner, illustrator, Ron Brooks	Longman/Childerset
1975	*The Man from Ironback* Andrew Barton Paterson, illustrator, Quentin Hole	Collins
1976	*The Rainbow Serpent* Dick Roughsey	Collins
1977	Award withheld	
1978	*John Brown, Rose and the Midnight Cat* Jenny Wagner, illustrator, Ron Brooks	Kestrel
1979	*The Quinkins* Percy Trezise and Dick Roughsey	Collins
1980	*One Dragon's Dream* Peter Pavey	Nelson
1981	Award withheld	
1982	*Sunshine* Jan Ormerod	Penguin
1983	*Who Sank the Boat?* Pamela Allen	Nelson

| 1984 | *Bertie and the Bear*
Pamela Allen | Nelson |
| 1985 | Award withheld | |

JUNIOR BOOKS OF THE YEAR

1982	*Rummage* Christobel Mattingley, illustrator, Patricia Mullins	Angus & Robertson
1983	*Thing* Robin Klein	Oxford University Press
1984	*Bernice Knows Best* Max Dann	Oxford University Press
1985	*Something Special* Emily Rodda	Angus & Robertson

1986 AWARDS

Children's Book of the Year: *The Green Wind* by Thurley Fowler (Rigby)
Picture Book of the Year: *Felix and Alexander* by Terry Denton (Oxford University Press)
Junior Book of the Year: *Arkwright* by Mary Steele (Hyland House)

1987 AWARDS

Children's Book of the Year: *All We Know* by Simon French (Angus & Robertson)
Picture Book of the Year: *Kojuro and the Bears* by Junko Morimoto (Collins)
Junior Book of the Year: *Pigs Might Fly* by Emily Rodda (Angus & Robertson)

1988 AWARDS

Children's Book of the Year: *So Much to Tell You* by John Marsden (Walter McVitty)
Picture Book of the Year: *Crusher is Coming!* by Bob Graham (Lothian)
Junior Book of the Year: *My Place* by Nadia Wheatley and Donna Rawlins (Collins Dove)

1989 AWARDS

Children's Book of the Year: *Beyond the Labyrinth* by Gillian Rubinstein (Hyland House)
Picture Book of the Year (joint winners): *Drac and the Gremlin* by Allan Baillie, illustrated by Jane Tanner (Viking Kestrel)
The Eleventh Hour by Graeme Base (Viking Kestrel)
Junior Book of the Year: *The Best-Kept Secret* by Emily Rodda (Angus & Robertson)

1990 AWARDS

Children's Book of the Year: *Came Back to Show You I Could Fly* by Robin Klein (Viking Kestrel)
Picture Book of the Year: *The Very Best of Friends* by Margaret Wild and Julie Vivas (Margaret Hamilton Books)
Junior Book of the Year: *Pigs and Honey* by Jeanie Adams (Omnibus)

INDEX

Aborigines 83, 84, 212–13, 223, 314
   dreamtime 82, 83, 106, 112, 122, 263
Act of Creation, The 227, 287
adolescence 27, 33, 40, 43–5, 51, 140, 151, 168, 170, 205, 209, 217, 220, 226, 282, 373
   development 292–9, 301–4
   self-identity 293–9
   world view 301–4
   literature 290–305
Adrian Mole 301
adults 13, 16, 19, 26, 27, 35, 42, 44, 63, 64, 71, 76, 81, 97, 103, 127, 129, 137, 140, 151, 158, 168, 178, 179, 192, 201, 206, 209, 213, 219, 277, 281–5 *passim*, 290–7 *passim*, 305, 314, 321, 329
adventures 50, 51, 77, 79, 129, 151, 177, 181, 184, 185, 191, 196, 235, 243, 266, 270, 321
   stories 151–60, 191–2, 209, 261
   history and criticism 154–60
Adventures of Huckleberry Finn, The 152
Adventures of Tom Sawyer, The 152, 156
Ahlberg, Janet and Allan 62, 67, 178, 179
Aiken, Joan 112
Alcott, Louisa May 177, 180
Aldridge, James 51, 236, 298
Alfie Gets in First 259
Alice in Wonderland (1865) 217, 261, 263, 268, 269, 274, 287, 376
Allen, Pamela 23, 61, 63, 71, 84, 346
Allsburg, Chris Van 85
Andersen, Hans Christian 111–12, 261
animals, humanization 232–6 *passim*, 238–42 *passim*, 244
   world 229, 232–7, 238, 240, 242, 244
   see also stories
Anno, Mitsumasa 43, 70, 71, 86–7, 257, 379
Archetypes 93–4
Ardizonne, Edward 79
Are you there, God? It's me, Margaret 13, 215, 222, 285, 294
Armstrong, Judith 20, 157
Arthur, King 116, 118
artists 64, 66, 69, 71, 86, 87, 93, 146, 345–8
artwork 345–8 *passim*
associations 331–2, 337
   Library of Australia (L.A.A.) 329, 333–4, 337
attitudes 153, 183, 184, 186, 188, 191, 209, 220–1, 223, 327
authors 3–17 *passim*, 44, 46, 71–3 *passim*, 84, 92, 103, 129, 138, 152–60 *passim*, 163–75 *passim*, 177–94 *passim*, 196–215 *passim*, 217–26 *passim*, 247–57 *passim*, 259–73 *passim*, 278–88 *passim*, 291–304 *passim*, 321, 323, 333, 339–40, 342, 344, 357–62 *passim*, 373–88 *passim*, 394–8 *passim*, 400
   Australian 46, 82–4, 105, 200, 218–26 *passim*, 293, 300, 341
   non-fiction 249–50
   series 209–15

Babies Need Books 61, 64, 72
Baillie, Allan 50
Balderson, Margaret 236
ballads 61, 95–6, 117–18, 143, 144, 376
Ballantyne, R.M. 154
Barnaby and the Horses 7
Bear Hunt 355
Bedtime for Francis 177
behaviour 30, 31, 80, 121, 219, 220, 229, 241, 244, 272
   child 259–60, 290
Berg, Leila 64, 65, 72
Berndt, Catherine 111
Bertie and the Bear 23, 63
Bettelheim, Bruno 95, 108, 113, 115, 213, 244, 273
BFG, The 7, 22, 269, 282
Bible stories 93–4, 115–16, 314
Biggles 211–14, 215
Black Beauty 229, 241
Blake, Quentin 65
Blume, Judy 205, 215, 219, 221, 222, 285, 286, 329, 240
Blyton, Enid 153, 157, 158, 209–11, 213–16, 359
Books Before Five 72
books vii, ix, 3–17 *passim*, 19–20, 39–51, 61–73 *passim*, 75–88 *passim*, 96, 98, 129, 138, 151–60 *passim*, 209–15 *passim*, 217, 219, 229–40 *passim*, 247–57 *passim*, 259–73 *passim*, 278–88 *passim*, 311–24, 327–38, 370–401 *passim*
   awards ix, 19, 71, 76, 230, 235, 236, 320, 336
   enjoyment 19, 25, 41, 66–7, 283
   experiences 23–5, 39, 41, 45, 72, 73
   good vii, 10–11, 14, 19–37, 46, 47, 48, 133, 226
   medals and winners 76, 230, 236, 242, 320
   picture 4, 23–35, 46–7, 56, 61, 62, 64, 70, 73, 75–88, 220, 230, 243, 280,

282, 287, 339, 348-9, 356, 359, 376, 385
  story 45-8, 54-5, 62, 66, 67, 77-8, 376, 379, 382, 397, 399
  wordless 45-6 54, 70, 71, 85-6, 178, 399
  promotion 329-30, 349-50
  reference 250, 251-3
  right *vii*, 11, 26-37, 39-51
  selection 11, 39-41, 371, 385
  sharing *vii*, 61-75, 373, 397
  of the year 267, 419-22
Boy 7
Bridge to Terabithia 7, 9, 19, 25, 177, 188-9, 224, 260, 377
Briggs, Raymond 69, 71, 85-6, 97, 107, 137, 271, 272, 281, 379
Brinsmead, Hesba (H.F.) 225, 297-8
Brooks, Ron 82, 225, 230
Brown, Jeff 14, 43
Brown, Marcia 75, 111
Browne, Anthony 15, 44, 84, 87, 278, 355, 366
Bruna, Dick 64, 66, 71
bullying 49, 205, 300, 362-6, 381
Bunyip of Berkeley's Creek, The 6, 9, 16, 82, 271
Burkert, Nancy Ekholm 88, 111
Burnett, Frances Hodgson 184
Burningham, John 23, 64, 66, 70, 71, 80, 81, 83, 156, 360, 365
Burton, Virginia Lee 77, 78
Bush Ballads 96
Butler, Dorothy 64, 68, 72, 129
Byars, Betsy 49, 159, 178, 189, 192-3, 205, 215, 219, 221, 283-4, 286, 287, 293-5, 364, 369, 381, 382, 398

Caldecott, Randolph 75, 76
Call of the Wild 233
Callie's Castle 187-9 *passim*
Calvino, Italo 101, 103, 111
Candle For St Antony 8, 9, 200, 205, 206, 222
Cannily, Cannily 206, 299-300
Carle, Eric 39, 67
Carroll, Lewis 217, 261, 274, 287, 376
Catcher in the Rye 299
catharsis 79-80, 285
Cay, The 152
Chambers, Aidan 7, 81, 129, 148, 158, 204, 205, 293, 362-6
Changeover, The 287
Chapman, Jean 61
characters 12, 49, 51, 72, 77, 78, 87, 100, 101, 102, 108, 116, 137, 153-60, 163, 171-5 *passim*, 181, 182, 187, 188, 190, 193, 197, 209-12 *passim*, 215,

218, 221, 222, 236, 239, 244, 264-8 *passim*, 272, 280, 285, 286, 297, 299, 304, 305, 323, 343, 358, 359, 362, 366, 383, 390, 399
  animal 229, 230, 232-44 *passim*, 262
  school 197, 198, 199, 203, 205, 206
  types 12, 71, 87, 100, 153, 197, 198, 199, 203, 205, 206, 219-20, 224
Charlie and The Chocolate Factory 278, 281
Charlotte's Web 9, 11, 14, 15, 239, 264, 268, 276, 377, 378, 394, 395
child development 19, 26-37, 39, 93, 130, 139, 158, 231, 247, 259-61, 277, 292, 328, 369
  stages 26-37, 39, 40, 72, 139, 231, 277, 321
children 39-51, 61-73 *passim*, 75-88 *passim*, 97, 115-23 *passim*, 125-47 *passim*, 151-60, 163-75 *passim*, 177-94 *passim*, 249, 250, 253, 254, 270, 277, 280-8 *passim*, 314, 328, 329, 370-401 *passim*
  Australian 83, 139, 262, 327-37 *passim*
Children of the New Forest 8
Children on the Oregon Trail 153
children who read early 370
Children's Book
  Council of Australia *ix*, *x*, 331-4 *passim*, 336
  Fair 331, 351
  Week 329, 332-3, 339
children's books *vii*, 4, 10-17 *passim*, 19-20, 22, 23, 25, 39-51, 54-7, 61-73 *passim*, 75-87, 96, 98, 290, 311-24, 355, 370-2
  Australian 327-38, 351
children's literature *vii*, *ix-xiii passim*, 4, 11, 15, 19, 39-51, 61, 73, 75-87 *passim*, 217, 229, 244, 261, 311, 324, 327, 332, 334-8, 342, 355, 372, 383, 384
  collections 334-8
  historical 334-7
  humour in 277-88
  promotion 331-3
  universal 311-24
children's poetry 127, 130-47
Chocolate War, The 9, 206, 225, 302
Chomsky, N. 33-7
Cinderella 103, 108, 109
Clark, Margaret 370
Clark, Mavis Thorpe 218
classrooms 130, 369-402 *passim*
  collection (library) 371-2, 400
  experience 369-402
  organisation 371-2
  programmes 372, 380-1, 386-7, 393-4
  reading 370-2

Cleary, Beverly 178, 179, 180, 191, 244
comics 80, 86, 132, 135, 219, 291, 334
conflicts 153, 170, 177, 179, 180, 186, 187, 188, 191, 192, 193, 218, 225, 235
conformity-rebellion 48, 80, 81, 206, 299-300, 305
Coolidge, Susan 177
Cooper, J.C. 95
Cormier, Robert 206, 225, 302
Crane, Walter 75
Creber, J. 67
cultures 68, 69, 87, 92, 98, 106, 107, 115, 116, 118, 119, 121, 122, 123, 167, 169, 172, 173, 174, 205, 218, 222, 224, 229, 264, 314, 321, 322

Dahl, Roald 13, 14, 22, 104, 112, 133, 142, 269, 277-81 passim, 284, 285, 288, 329, 359, 378, 394, 396, 397
Dalgleish, Joan 236
Day-Lewis, Cecil 134-5
Dear Mr Henshaw 177, 191
death 11, 20-2, 25, 81, 94, 117, 121, 134-5, 153, 165, 177, 180, 182, 184, 188, 189, 193, 199, 218, 224, 239, 270, 285, 302
Defoe, Daniel 152
Dennis, C.J. 139
Dickinson, Emily 3
didacticism 82, 155, 163-4, 181, 191, 217, 218, 230, 241, 242, 243, 256, 290, 297
Dinko 225
disability 169, 218, 219, 222-3
Displaced Person 271, 302
Dog So Small, A 192
Donaldson, Margaret 27
Dot and the Kangaroo 241, 263
drama 46, 95-6, 127, 146, 153, 390-1
  radio 391-2, 401
Dream of Seas, A 12, 237, 271
Dromkeen *ix, x*, 336
Durkin, D. 370
Duvoisin, Roger 101

Each Peach Pear Plum 42
Eagle of the Ninth, The 174
experiences 10, 11, 16, 20, 23-5, 30, 33, 39, 41, 49, 50, 51, 61, 67, 72, 73, 75, 78, 84, 93, 94, 97, 108, 131-3, 141, 165, 169, 171, 177, 179, 180, 188, 189, 191, 197, 217, 226, 231, 248, 259, 260, 262, 265, 270, 277, 293, 295, 313, 360, 364, 389
editing 343, 344-8, 393
editors 291, 339, 341-4, 351
Edwards, Hazel 47

Eighteenth Emergency, The 23, 49, 205, 286-7, 364, 369, 381, 398
Eleanor, Elizabeth 298
epics 119-20, 121, 229, 261
Eric, or, Little by Little 198
Erikson, E., 32, 37, 49, 292
  theory 32-3, 35, 36, 49, 292
experimentation 97, 225, 235, 242, 303, 304

fables 85, 98-9, 229, 230, 313, 396
Factor, June 97, 137
Fair's Fair 22
fairy tales 6, 43, 49, 56, 61, 75, 87, 91, 93, 105-12, 115, 260, 261, 265, 269, 272, 277, 392, 396
family 48, 50, 67, 69, 107, 115, 177-94 passim, 217, 218, 225, 293, 297-302 passim, 204
Family From One End Street, The 185-6 passim
Famous Five 209-11, 214
fantasy *x*, 9, 14, 35, 44-5, 46, 50, 56-7, 65, 78, 79, 81, 96, 107, 112, 119, 121, 122, 151, 229-30, 237-40, 259-73, 277, 286, 287, 289
  history and criticism 259-73
Far Out, Brussel Sprout! 137, 138, 281
Farrar, Dean Frederick 198
Fatchen, Max 125, 141-2
fiction 45, 84, 125-47, 183, 224, 231, 247, 250, 327, 335, 341, 357, 369, 371, 379, 380, 384, 393
  science 151, 261, 266, 271
  series 209-15
Finn Family Moomintroll 179
Five Times Dizzy 218
Flack, Marjorie 77, 78
Flat Stanley 14, 15, 16, 43, 267
Folk Songs 96-7
folk-tales 6, 55, 83, 87, 91-9 passim, 100-5, 108-12, 229, 261, 272, 277, 379, 392, 405, 406-7
Forbes, Esther 166
Freeman, Gillian 201
French, Fiona 85
French, Simon 205, 206, 299
Frost, Robert 127

Gag, Wanda 77
Garfield, Leon 22, 168-9, 214
Garner, Alan 13, 15, 111, 118, 269
Garnett, Eve 185
genre study 396
George, Jean 152, 153
Giant Devil Dingo, The 83
Gibbs, May 263, 337
Gleeson, Libby 298
Goodnight Mr Tom 7

Goodnight Owl 63
Grahame, Kenneth 22, 238-9, 262, 376
Granpa 81, 360, 265
Great Gilly Hopkins, The 189-91 passim, 178, 386
Greenaway, Kate 19, 75, 76, 80, 85
Greenwood, Ted 230
Gretz, Susanne 66
Grimm, Jacob and Wilhelm 87, 93, 109-10
Gulliver's Travels 152

Haley, Gail E. 61, 62
Hansel and Gretel 87
Harding, D.W. 387, 389
Harding, Lee 226, 267, 271, 302-3
Harnett, Cynthia 164-5, 171
Harris, Joel Chandler 99
Harry, The Dirty Dog 281
Hazard, Paul 5, 10-11, 69, 129
heroes 79, 91, 107, 112, 115-19, 120, 121, 125, 154, 155, 164, 169, 199, 205, 220, 229, 233, 244, 313, 320, 321, 405
heroines 49, 164, 165, 200, 300, 321, 405
Hildick, Wallace 214-15
Hills End 12
Hoban, Russell 177, 178, 283
Hobbit, The 23, 153, 263, 267, 268, 273
Holdaway, Don 62
Holm, Anne 153
Homecoming 14, 16, 219
Hope, A.D. 126
House of Wings, The 189
House That Was Eureka, The 16, 219
How Tom Beat Captain Najork and His Hired Sportsmen 283
Huck, Charlotte 386, 390
Hughes, Thomas 196-8
humour 13, 14-15, 42, 43, 46, 48, 50, 68, 76, 86, 87, 96, 104, 127, 170, 177, 180, 181, 189, 191, 219, 223, 262, 263, 227-88, 297, 301, 321, 376, 381, 382
   developmental stages 280-4
   values 284-8
Hunt, Nan (N.L. Ray) 344, 346, 347
Hutchins, Pat 39, 63, 64, 81

I am David 9, 153
I Had a Little Hen 69
identity 25, 33, 37, 49, 50, 68, 108, 115, 121, 194, 219, 230, 295, 298, 317
   self- 292, 293-301
illustrations 15, 19, 42, 43, 44, 47, 65, 66-72 passim, 75-88 passim, 99, 112, 118, 133, 138, 146, 178, 230, 250, 256-7, 271, 314, 321, 335, 345, 355, 360, 366, 376, 397

illustrators 42, 44, 47, 68, 69, 71, 79, 82, 84, 133, 135, 379
imagery 14, 23-5, 97, 99, 102, 107, 171, 172, 173, 175
images 8, 9-10, 15, 64, 66, 67, 91, 94, 95, 96, 103, 112, 132, 142, 143, 144, 172, 174, 238, 259, 260, 265, 287, 295, 297, 302, 313, 315, 322
independence 35, 46, 48, 79, 80, 187, 232, 250, 297-8, 304
individualism 312-16 passim
infants 62-3, 64, 66, 67, 70, 72, 129
International Board on Books for Young People (IBBY) 320, 331-2
international-internationalism 311-13, 316, 318-22
irony 15, 81, 82, 84, 183, 190, 282, 284, 285
Island of the Blue Dolphins 33

Jackson, David 369
Jacobs, Joseph 103, 110
James and the Giant Peach 279
Jansson, Tove 179
Jeffers, Susan 88
John Brown, Rose and The Midnight Cat 6, 7, 9, 15, 42, 47-8, 65, 82-3, 230, 360, 396
Johnny Tremain 166
Johns, Captain W.E. 211-15
Johnson, T.D. and Louis, D.R. 387, 401
jokes 97, 109, 136, 146, 280, 281, 282, 283, 285, 286, 322
Josh 16, 221, 300
Joyce, James 9
Julie of the Wolves 153

Kalevala 120
Katherine 7, 82
Keats, Ezra Jack 78
Keeping, Charles 84
Kelleher, Victor 225, 235, 271, 304
Kemp, Gene 206, 207, 220
King, John Anthony 97
Kipling, Rudyard 197, 199, 200, 201, 238, 262, 275, 296
Klein, Robin 220, 224, 225, 285, 303, 329
Koestler, Arthur 227, 287
Kohlberg, L. 30-1

languages 3, 7-8, 14, 22-3, 27, 33-4, 39, 40, 43, 44, 46, 49, 51, 62, 64-5, 72, 76-7, 86, 98, 102, 107, 109, 126-30 passim, 132-6 passim, 138, 139, 142, 167, 172, 173, 203, 211, 248, 252, 254, 255, 256, 260, 272, 280, 284, 299, 304, 314, 316, 320, 321, 323, 338, 356-7, 359, 360, 365, 366, 369,

370, 375, 376, 377, 380, 383, 393, 394, 395
  development 7–8, 33–4, 91, 130, 255, 356–7, 369–402
  figurative 97, 98, 102, 137, 143, 146, 170, 174, 395
laughter 277–9, 283, 285, 286
Law and Language of School Children, The 137
Le Guin, Ursula 267, 272, 295, 360–1
Leftovers, The 191, 194, 220, 223
legends 56, 95, 108, 112, 115–21, 123, 261, 313
Lenski, Lois 78
Let the Balloon Go 186–7
Lewis, C.S. 10, 14, 211, 239, 240, 260, 262, 264, 270, 372
librarians 16–17, 41–2, 45, 108, 123, 247, 327, 329, 330, 333, 334, 344, 350
libraries 41, 42, 45, 66, 130, 139, 147, 214, 291, 327–31, 334, 338, 371, 381
life 11–12, 13, 68, 91, 92, 94, 100, 102, 103, 106, 121, 127, 129, 134, 135, 157, 165–6, 172, 175, 178, 181, 183, 186, 188, 219, 231, 265
  cycle 11–12, 81, 239, 242, 316
  styles 12–13, 170, 221, 293, 300, 305, 321
Lindgren, Astrid 49
Lindsay, Norman 243, 263, 279
Lion in the Meadow, A 64
Lion in the Night, A 346
Lion, the Witch and the Wardrobe, The 10, 264, 372
Lionni, Leo 65
literacy 161, 380–1
literary
  forms 95–113, 151
  history 108–11
  qualities 39–51
literature *vii, ix, x, xi,* 3–17, 44, 45, 76, 78, 91–113, 117, 157, 165, 217–26 *passim,* 260, 261, 283, 284, 321, 356, 357, 369–402
  adolescent 290–305
  appreciation 102, 387, 398–401
  archetype 91–112
  development 369–402
  experiences 4, 6–7, 39, 78, 389–90, 393, 398–401
  model 393–8
  programmes *x,* 374, 401
  promotion 329–30, 331, 370–95 *passim*
  response 19, 22, 374, 399–401
  selection 22–30 *passim,* 33, 34, 376–7
  traditional 8–9, 91–112, 119, 122, 383, 396,7
  value *vii,* 3–17, 369–402

see also children's literature, fantasy, fiction, novels, tales
Little Brother 50
Little Fear, A 12, 225, 232
Little House on the Prairie 166
Little House, The 78
Little Red Cap 88
Little Women 177, 180–2 *passim*
Little, Jean 13
Load of Unicorn, A 164, 171
Lobel, Arnold 99

Mabinogion, The 118–19
Macintyre, Elisabeth 7, 82, 222, 295
Magic Pudding, The 243, 263, 268, 275, 279
Magnolia Buildings 186
Mahy, Margaret 64, 270, 278, 281, 284, 287
Mama's Going to Buy You a Mocking Bird 7, 224
Man-Shy 233
manuscripts 119, 335, 336, 348, 349
  author's 339–50 *passim*
  marketplace 349–50
Martin, David 224
Mary Poppins 266, 268
Maslow, A.H. 31–2
Mason, Olive 82
Mattingley, Christobel 234
Meek, Margaret 43
Midnite: The Story of a Wild Colonial Boy 243
Mike Mulligan and His Steam Shovel 78, 79
Milligan's Book of Bits 278
Milligan, Spike 278, 282
Millions of Cats 78, 80
Milne, A.A. 209, 263, 269, 283, 289
minority groups 218, 223–4, 322
Mister Magnolia 42, 65
Mitchell, Elyne 233–4
monoculturalism 322–4
Moonlight 71, 86
Moonshine 182
Moore, Ann Carroll 75
morals 23, 48, 50, 98, 105, 160, 180, 182
Moss, Elaine 19
Mother Goose Treasury 68, 69, 97, 137
motifs 93–4
Mousewife, The 242
Mr Archimedes' Bath 84
Mr Gumpy's Motor Car 63, 68
Mr Gumpy's Outing 23, 64, 68, 81, 156
Mrs Frisby and the Rats of NIMH 242, 268
multiculturalism 311–13, 322–4
My Darling, My Hamburger 211, 295
My Side of the Mountain 152
mystery 9, 119, 152, 157, 191–2, 264

mythology 121, 122-3, 272
myths 13, 56, 95, 108, 112, 115, 121-3, 229, 261, 277, 313, 383, 396

Nargun and the Stars, The 9, 12, 13, 14, 23
narratives 39, 43, 45-6, 51, 67, 81, 85, 86, 100, 103, 108, 119, 132, 135, 143, 144, 145, 153, 167, 187, 198, 284, 312, 313, 364, 377
    pictorial 45-6
    shifts 186-8, 190, 193, 360
    structure 15, 16, 107, 157, 314, 355-67, 393
    techniques 3, 13-14, 34, 45-6, 81, 86, 171, 186-8, 291, 294-300 *passim*, 303, 304, 314, 355, 358-60
    theory 356, 357-8
narrator 177, 183, 193, 229, 236, 355, 357, 358, 359, 399
narrator-reader relationship 358-67
Nash, Ogden 7
nationalism 115, 116, 316, 317-18, 320
nature 121, 127, 168, 174, 175, 229, 230, 231
    cycle 20-2, 81, 175, 239
needs 31-2, 39, 51, 103, 121, 157, 175, 179, 180, 186, 188, 259, 372-4
Nesbit, Edith 177, 182-3 *passim*, 215, 262
Neverending Story, The 6
Niland, Deborah 7, 70
non-fiction 247-57, 377, 380, 384, 393, 394
    authors 247-57 *passim*
    books 247-57 *passim*
    history and criticism 247-57
Norman, Lilith 12, 13, 237, 269, 271, 344
Norton, Mary 390
Nostlinger, Christine 218-19, 323
novels 3-17, 44, 46-51, 56, 57, 61-73 *passim*, 104-5, 112, 133-4, 151-60 *passim*, 177-94 *passim*, 202, 217-26 *passim*, 260-76 *passim*, 278-88 *passim*, 294-7, 314, 348, 351, 356, 357, 372, 376, 380, 382, 388, 397, 398, 400, 407, 408
    adolescent 50, 57, 292-304 *passim*
    Australian 12, 222-3, 262, 263, 270-1, 305
    group 282-3
    historical 50, 163-75
    problem 217-26, 290, 293, 294
    serialisation 281-2, 283
    Victorian 196-201

O'Dell, Scott 33
Odysseus 117, 152
Odyssey, The 153
One Dragon's Dream 70

Opie, Iona and Peter 69, 97, 105-7, 137
Ormerod, Jan 45-6, 71, 86, 178
Outside Over There 15, 16, 85
Outsiders, The 299
Oxenbury, Helen 66, 71

parables 98, 100
parents 16-17, 39, 41, 46, 67, 71, 72, 108, 129, 157, 163, 178, 179, 182, 184, 185, 187, 188, 189, 191, 193, 194, 206, 219-20, 221, 222, 329, 337, 338, 350, 359, 370, 371
Park, Ruth 40, 44, 50, 165-6, 171, 187-8, 189, 225, 271, 386, 400
Parker, Kate Langloh 110
parodies 97, 137, 141, 196, 243, 396
Paterson, Katherine 22, 25, 177, 178, 188, 189-91, 224, 377, 386
Pavey, Peter 70
Pearce, Philippa 191-2, 219, 237, 264-5, 388
Peepo! 67
peers 36, 48-9, 117, 157, 186, 220, 297, 300, 370
Pender, Lydia 7, 230
Penny Pollard's Diary 220, 225
People Might Hear You 9
Perrault, Charles 93, 103, 109, 110, 316
Peter's Chair 78
Phipson, Joan 221, 224, 225-6, 271
Piaget, Jean 27-30, 35, 37, 40, 292, 306
    theory 27, 28-30, 35, 40
Pienkowski, Jan 71
Pigs Everywhere 69
Pinballs, The 191, 192 *passim*
Playing Beatie Bow 15, 40, 44, 50-1, 165-6, 168, 171, 188, 225, 271, 298, 307, 386
plays 39, 64, 66, 105, 108, 117, 291-2
plots 12, 77, 78, 82, 158, 159, 193, 196, 203, 209, 210, 212, 213, 235, 291, 292, 296, 305, 343, 344, 362
Plowdon Report 5
poetry 3, 6, 9, 42, 54, 64, 68, 69, 75, 85, 92, 95, 110, 125-47, 277, 287, 356, 376, 379, 393, 395
    enjoyment 42, 125-47
    experience 130, 134-43
    sharing 125-47
poets 100, 120, 125-47
Portrait of the Artist as a Young Man 9
Potter, Beatrix 63, 77
Pownall, Eve 252, 254
prejudice 205-6, 218, 222, 318, 321, 323
Present Takers, The 16, 362-3, 365
problems 44, 49, 87, 159, 177, 180, 182, 186, 188, 191, 193-4, 218, 219, 224, 226, 273, 277, 293, 294, 364, 365
    personal 290, 293, 304-5

promoting children's interest in books 372–4
prose 14, 19, 77, 98–100, 120, 143, 213, 313
protagonists 13, 78, 79, 80, 83–4, 107, 112, 153, 165, 171, 177, 180, 182, 185, 187, 188, 191, 193, 219, 224, 229, 232, 237, 244, 267, 290, 295
proverbs 98
puberty 285, 291–2, 297
Puberty Blues 221, 299
publishers 69, 93, 249, 250, 253, 256, 291, 294, 323, 327, 328, 333, 339–51 *passim*
puppetry 390–1, 401, 413–14

questions 81, 147, 387–9, 394
Quinkins, The 83
Quippy 82

racism 211, 213, 215, 219, 223, 242, 318
Rainbow Serpent, The 83
Ramayana 119
Ramona the Pest 177
readers 4–17 *passim*, 22–40, 44, 45, 48–51 *passim*, 71, 77, 103, 117, 132, 151–60 *passim*, 170, 177–94 *passim*, 209, 213, 215, 217, 248, 254, 255, 264, 266, 267, 271, 286, 321, 323, 355–67 *passim*, 369, 380, 384
  experienced 14, 45, 71, 356, 361, 383
  young 19, 119, 120, 169, 170, 177, 178, 198, 200, 201, 203, 206, 211, 215, 231, 259, 290, 344, 356, 358–67 *passim*
readers' theatre *ix*, 146, 329, 334, 391–2, 400, 415–16
reading *vii, x*, 4–5, 8, 9, 40, 42, 43–4, 65, 72, 86, 130, 142, 146, 147, 153, 158, 214, 231, 248–9, 250, 252, 255, 343, 355–8 *passim*, 369–402
  activities 355–67
  aloud 42, 43, 65 80–1, 145, 222, 372, 375–8, 383, 394, 396, 399
  development 54–7, 151, 356, 386
  enjoyment *vii*, 9, 10, 20, 209, 367, 384
  experiences 8, 10, 11, 16, 17, 19, 48, 77, 356, 367, 369–402
  interpretation 389, 390–1, 392
  programmes 370–401
  skills 12, 248–9, 357, 379
Reading Time 328
realism 151, 159, 170, 200, 204, 219, 265–6, 300
reality 35, 45, 47, 129, 164, 165, 230, 231, 238, 260, 265, 267, 286, 304
response 4ff
review (book) 253, 255, 335, 338, 350, 374

Revolting Rhymes 282, 284
rewards 80, 94, 102–3, 107, 108, 122, 312
rhymes 42, 61, 62, 63, 66–7, 70, 97, 125, 130, 135, 137–8, 144, 147, 285, 313, 314, 322
  nursery 6, 62, 63, 68–70, 76, 97, 130, 141
  play 68–9, 137–8
rhythms 14, 42, 62, 63, 68, 69, 96, 129, 143, 144, 147, 167, 375
Richards, Frank 202, 203
Robin Hood 117, 118
Robinson Crusoe 152
Robinsonnade 152, 155
roles *x*, 36, 77, 168, 183, 184, 188, 193, 210, 217, 219, 221, 240, 292, 297, 370
Roll of Thunder Hear My Cry 9
romance 120, 164, 193, 261, 294–7, 406, 408
Rosenblatt, Louise 16, 369, 389
Rosie's Walk 15, 39, 42, 64, 81, 85
Roughsey, Dick 83, 122, 124, 223, 346

sagas 95, 119, 120–1, 151, 314
Salinger, J.D. 11, 290, 299
Samson 155–6
Saxby, Maurice *ix*, 3, 73, 91, 103, 113, 115, 124, 181, 185, 231, 341
Schlager, Norma 26
schools 27, 43, 130, 139, 179, 182, 196–215 *passim*, 250, 280, 299, 369, 376
  primary 44, 45, 50, 177, 231, 247, 249, 254, 280, 281, 282, 329, 356, 370, 375, 380
Scott, Patricia 69
Scott-Mitchell, Claire 42
Secret Garden, The 9, 15, 23, 184
Sendak, Maurice 64, 65, 69–80, 85, 87
Serraillier, Ian 153
settings (story) 12–13, 27, 51, 75, 77, 87, 91, 101–2, 155, 159, 160, 165, 166, 168, 172, 177, 184, 185, 186, 204, 226, 233, 239, 240, 241, 301, 358
Seven Little Australians 155, 177–82 *passim*, 193, 218
sex stereotypes 220–1
sexism 219–21
sexuality 217, 219, 221–2, 293, 294–5
Shrinking of Treehorn, The 9, 15, 16, 272
Silver Brumby, The 234
Silver Sword, The 153
skills 3–4, 22–3, 248–9, 328, 329, 357, 382, 383
Sloan, Glenna Davis 388
Smith 168–9
Snow White 88
Snowman, The 85

Snugglepot and Cuddlepie 263
social issues 48, 51, 224–6
society 33, 48, 86, 96, 103, 105, 117, 119, 122, 169, 175, 177, 217, 218, 219, 222, 223, 224, 226, 233, 243, 271, 299, 322, 323
  ideal 303–4
  multicultural 223–4
Solomon's Child 218, 301
Song For a Dark Queen 166–8
Song of Pentecost 243
songs 68, 69, 96–7, 105, 120, 125, 130
Southall, Ivan 25, 103, 160, 186–7, 214, 221, 222–3, 298, 300, 303, 341, 414
Speare, Elizabeth 166
Spence, Eleanor 191, 205, 206, 219, 221, 222, 223, 386
Spier, Peter 63
Stalky & Co 197–200, 206, 207
Steig, William 239, 240
stereotypes 30, 105, 155, 205, 209, 219, 220–1, 286
Stevens, Wallace 125, 128
Stevenson, Robert Louis 155
Stone Book Quartet, The 188
stories 3, 12–13, 22–3, 34, 39, 42, 44, 46, 47, 48, 55, 61–73 *passim*, 75–88 *passim*, 92–5, 108, 119–23, 133, 137, 157, 162–75 *passim*, 201, 214, 263, 311, 312–16, *passim*, 321, 356–63 *passim*, 370, 376, 379, 388, 390, 397–9, 400, 405–16
  animal 229–31
  fantasy 229–30, 237–40
  nature 229, 237
  talking 230, 240–4
  dramatic involvement 414–15
  family 61, 177–94, 236, 244
  oral 315–16, 321
  personal 46, 47, 48, 64, 92
  response 71–2, 230–1, 313, 314, 315, 383, 387
  school 196–215
    history and criticism 196–215
  scripting 391–2
  sharing 64, 321, 373, 405–16
  string 411–13
  traditional 61, 92–5
  see also authors, books, fantasy, fiction, novels, tales
Storm Boy 6, 22
Story of Doctor Dolittle, The 242, 263
Story of the Treasure Seekers, The 177
storytellers 7, 14, 77, 92, 100, 109, 155, 185, 229, 312, 314, 321, 331, 405–16 *passim*
storytelling *ix*, 14, 76, 86, 92, 157, 183, 260, 312, 329–34 *passim*, 405–16
  follow-up 40–10

values 405–16
Stranger at Green Knowe, A 237
Stuckey, Elizabeth 186
Sun Horse, Moon Horse 174
Sunshine 45–6, 71, 86, 178
supernatural 91–2, 106, 108, 115, 122, 265, 268, 270, 313
suspense 9, 12, 51, 77, 151, 156, 159, 160, 177, 185
Sutcliff, Rosemary 166–75 *passim*
Swift, Jonathan 152
Swimmy 65
Swiss Family Robinson, The 152
symbols 28, 40, 62, 63, 93, 95, 117, 119, 170, 217
syntax 7, 143, 171, 175, 357

taboos 102, 105, 290, 305
Tales of Jemima Puddleduck, The 42
Tale of Peter Rabbit, The 65, 71, 77, 80, 262, 263, 276
tales 85, 102, 109, 115–20, 153, 313
Tarka the Otter 233
Taylor, Theodore 152
teachers 16–17, 41–2, 45, 108, 123, 247, 251, 300, 327, 333, 350, 355, 357, 362, 363, 369–401 *passim*
  role 370–401 *passim*
technology 118, 164–5, 242, 264, 266
Tell us Tales 61
Tenth Good Things About Barney, The 20–22, 177
texts 15, 16, 23, 43, 44, 65, 72–9 *passim*, 81, 82, 83, 87, 88, 92, 345, 346, 355
themes (book) 11–12, 50, 56, 57, 65, 82, 84, 85, 95, 96, 103, 117, 121, 134, 169, 170, 172, 174, 177, 178, 182, 191, 193, 201, 204, 218, 221, 224, 226, 230, 234, 290, 29?–305, 313, 314, 357, 380, 384
Theseus 116–17
Thiele, Colin 12, 22, 224, 225, 234, 235–6, 255
Thomas, Gwyn 118–19
Thompson, Stith 104
Three Musketeers, The 164
Through the Window 84
Tolkien, J.R.R. 25, 153, 213, 263–8 *passim*, 272, 273
Tom Brown's Schooldays 196–8, 204, 206
Tom's Midnight Garden 15, 264
Townsend, John Rowe 134, 152, 181, 183, 185, 186, 194, 265, 295, 304
tragedy 22, 117, 121, 167, 277, 284
Trease, Geoffrey 164
Treasure Island 6, 8, 12, 13, 155
Treese, Henry 170
Trezise, Percy 83, 12
True Story of Lilli Stubeck, The 51

Turbulent Term of Tike Tyler, The 220
Turner, Ethel 155, 177, 181, 200, 217, 218, 341
Turner, Ian 97, 137
Twain, Mark 152

Uncle Remus 99
Uninterrupted Sustained Silent Reading (U.S.S.R.) 378–80
Unleaving 15

Van der Loeff, A. Rutgers 153
Very Hungry Caterpillar, The 16, 39, 67
Viorst, Judith 20, 25, 177
vocabulary 7, 14, 23, 24, 39, 77, 171, 254, 257, 377, 380, 383, 393
Voigt, Cynthia 14, 103, 219

Wagner, Jenny 47, 65, 82, 230, 271, 369
Walk in the Park, A 84
Walsh, Jill Paton 13, 15
Warrior Scarlet 23, 169–75
Watanabe, Shigeo 46, 66
Watership Down 242–3, 268
Way of the Whirlwind, The 263
Way to Sattin Shore, The 16, 191–2, 219
What Katy Did 177
Wheatley, Nadia 218, 219, 323
When a Goose Meets a Mouse 42, 69
When the Wind Blows 7
Where the Wild Things Are 64, 65, 79–80, 85, 260, 360
White, E.B. 239, 377

Who Sank the Boat? 61, 68, 84
Wilde, Oscar 112
Wilder, Laura Ingalls 166
Wildsmith, Brian 63, 70
Wilfrid Gordon McDonald Partridge 12
Willmott, Frank 221, 224, 225, 301
Winch, Gordon 132, 146
Wind in the Willows, The 6, 12, 13, 14, 22, 238–9, 240, 262, 268, 286, 376
Witch of Blackbird Pond, The 168
Witches, The 7
Wizard of Earthsea, A 9, 15, 267, 272, 360
words 47, 61–8 *passim*
Wrightson, Patricia 12, 13, 14, 103, 107, 112, 214, 221, 223, 225, 232, 262, 264, 266, 267, 270, 271, 297, 395
Wrinkle in Time, A 9
writers, *see* authors
writing x, 3–4, 22–3, 65, 86, 130, 134, 345, 370, 377, 392–5
  children's 357, 392–401
  models 393–8
  promoting 398–401
Wyss, Johann David 152

Yonge, Charlotte M. (1823–1901) 163–4, 181
youth 11, 12, 100, 115, 116, 121, 151, 188

Zindel, Paul 221, 294, 295, 303
Zion, Gene 281
Zwerger, Lisbeth 87, 88, 111